Lecture Notes of the Institute for Computer Sciences, Social Informatics and Telecommunications Engineering 461

More information about this series at https://link.springer.com/bookseries/8197

Honghao Gao · Xinheng Wang · Wei Wei ·
Tasos Dagiuklas (Eds.)

Collaborative Computing: Networking, Applications and Worksharing

18th EAI International Conference, CollaborateCom 2022
Hangzhou, China, October 15–16, 2022
Proceedings, Part II

Springer

Editors
Honghao Gao
Shanghai University
Shanghai, China

Xinheng Wang
Xi'an Jiaotong-Liverpool University
Suzhou, China

Wei Wei
Zhejiang University City College
Hangzhou, China

Tasos Dagiuklas
London South Bank University
London, UK

ISSN 1867-8211   ISSN 1867-822X (electronic)
Lecture Notes of the Institute for Computer Sciences, Social Informatics
and Telecommunications Engineering
ISBN 978-3-031-24385-1   ISBN 978-3-031-24386-8 (eBook)
https://doi.org/10.1007/978-3-031-24386-8

This Springer imprint is published by the registered company Springer Nature Switzerland AG
The registered company address is: Gewerbestrasse 11, 6330 Cham, Switzerland

Preface

We are delighted to introduce the proceedings of the 18th European Alliance for Innovation (EAI) International Conference on Collaborative Computing: Networking, Applications and Worksharing (CollaborateCom 2022). This conference has brought together researchers, developers and practitioners from around the world who are interested in fully realizing the promises of electronic collaboration from the aspects of networking, technology and systems, user interfaces and interaction paradigms, and interoperation with application-specific components and tools.

This year's conference attracted 171 submissions. Each submission was reviewed by an average of 3 reviewers. After a rigorous review process, 57 papers were accepted. The conference sessions were: Session 1, Federated Learning and Applications; Sessions 2, 3 and 8, Edge Computing and Collaborative Working; Session 4, Recommendation Systems and Collaborative Working; Session 5, Blockchain Applications; Sessions 6 and 7, Security and Privacy Protection; Session 9, Deep Learning and Applications; Sessions 10 and 11, Collaborative Working; Session 12, Image Processing and Recognition. Apart from high quality technical paper presentations, the technical program also featured one keynote speech that was delivered by Prof. Kun Yang from the University of Essex, UK.

Coordination with the steering chair, Imrich Chlamtac, and steering committee members Song Guo, Bo Li, Xiaofei Liao, Xinheng Wang, Honghao Gao, was essential for the success of the conference. We sincerely appreciate the constant support and guidance. It was also a great pleasure to work with such an excellent organizing committee team, we thank them for their hard work in organizing and supporting the conference. In particular, we thank the Technical Program Committee, led by our General Chairs and TPC Co-Chairs, Xinheng Wang, Honghao Gao, Wei Wei, Tasos Dagiuklas, Yuyu Yin, Tun Lu, Minghui Wu, and Lqbal Muddesar, who completed the peer-review process on the technical papers and put together a high-quality technical program. We are also gratefulto the conference manager, Lucia Sedlárová, for her support and all the authors who submitted their papers to the CollaborateCom 2022 conference and workshops.

We strongly believe that the CollaborateCom conference provides a good forum for all researchers, developers and practitioners to discuss all science and technology aspects that are relevant to collaborative computing. We also expect that the future CollaborateCom conferences will be as successful and stimulating, as indicated by the contributions presented in this volume.

December 2022

Honghao Gao
Xinheng Wang
Wei Wei
Tasos Dagiuklas

Conference Organization

Steering Committee

Chair

Imrich Chlamtac — Bruno Kessler Professor, University of Trento, Italy

Members

Bo Li — The Hong Kong University of Science and Technology, China

Honghao Gao — Shanghai University, China

Ning Gu — Fudan University, China

Song Guo — University of Aizu, Japan

Xiaofei Liao — Huazhong University of Science and Technology, China

Xinheng Wang — Xi'an Jiaotong-Liverpool University, China

Organizing Committee

General Chairs

Honghao Gao — Shanghai University, China

Xinheng Wang — Xi'an Jiaotong-Liverpool University, China

Wei Wei — Zhejiang University City College, China

Tasos Dagiuklas — London South Bank University, UK

TPC Chair and Co-chairs

Yuyu Yin — Hangzhou Dianzi University, China

Tun Lu — Fudan University, China

Minghui Wu — Zhejiang University City College, China

Lqbal Muddesar — London South Bank University, UK

Web Chair

Hanghao Gao — Shanghai University, China

Publicity and Social Media Chairs

Rui Li	Xidian University, China
Yucong Duan	Hainan University, China

Workshops Chair

Yuyu Yin	Hangzhou Dianzi University, China

Sponsorship and Exhibit Chair

Hanghao Gao	Shanghai University, China

Publications Chair

Youhuizi Li	Hangzhou Dianzi University, China

Local Chairs

Shuoping Wang	Zhejiang University City College, China
Yuan-yi Chen	Zhejiang University City College, China
Jin Canghong	Zhejiang University City College, China

Technical Program Committee

Zhongqin Bi	Shanghai University of Electric Power, China
Shizhan Chen	Tianjing University, China
Lizhen Cui	Shandong University, China
Weilong Ding	North China University of Technology, China
Yucong Duan	Hainan University, China
Honghao Gao	Shanghai University, China
Fan Guisheng	East China University of Science and Technology, China
Haiping Huang	Nanjing University of Posts and Telecommunications, China
Li Kuang	Central South University, China
Youhuizi Li	Hangzhou Dianzi University, China
Rui Li	Xidian University, China
Xuan Liu	Yangzhou University, China
Tong Liu	Shanghai University, China
Xiaobing Sun	Yangzhou University, China
Haiyan Wang	Nanjing University of Posts & Telecommunications, China
Xinheng Wang	Xi'an Jiaotong-Liverpool University, China
Xiaoxian Yang	SSPU, China

Yuyu Yin	Hangzhou Dianzi University, China
Jun Zeng	Chongqing University, China
Zijian Zhang	University of Shanghai for Science and Technology, China
Li Yu	Hangzhou Dianzi University, China
Yueshen Xu	Xidian University, China
Yunni Xia	Chongqing University, China
Huang Jiwei	China University of Petroleum, China
Tong Liu	Shanghai University, China
Ding Xu	Hefei University of Technology, China
Ruihui Ma	Shanghai Jiao Tong University, China
Ying Chen	Beijing Information Science and Technology University, China
Kong Linghe	Shanghai Jiao Tong University, China
Bin Cao	Zhejiang University of Technology, China
Hongyue Wu	Tianjin University, China
Gangyong Jia	Hangzhou Dianzi University, China
Zigui Jiang	Sun Yat-Sen University, China
Xuan Liu	Yangzhou University, China

Contents – Part II

Deep Learning and Application

Collaborative Working

Images Processing and Recognition

Contents – Part I

Edge Computing and Collaborative Working

Blockchain Applications

Security and Privacy Protection

A Novel Risk Assessment Method Based on Hybrid Algorithm for SCADA

Chen Yenan[1], Lu Tinghui[2], Li Linsen[1(✉)], and Zhang Han[1]

[1] School of Cyber Science and Engineering, Shanghai Jiao Tong University, Shanghai, China
{chenyenan10,lsli}@sjtu.edu.cn
[2] Guangdong Power Grid Co., Ltd. Jiangmen Power Supply Bureau, Jiangmen, China

Abstract. With the frequent occurrence of cyber attacks in recent years, cyber attacks have become a major factor affecting the security and reliability of power SCADA. We urgently need an effective SCADA risk assessment algorithm to quantify the value at risk. However, traditional algorithms have the shortcomings of excessive parsing variables and inefficient sampling. Existing improved algorithms are far from the optimal distribution of the sampling density function. In this paper, we propose an optimal sampling algorithm and a selective parsing algorithm and combine them into an improved hybrid algorithm to solve the problems. The experimental results show that the improved hybrid algorithm not only improves the parsing and sampling efficiency, but also realizes the optimal distribution of the sampling density function and improves the accuracy of the assessment index. The assessment indexs accurately quantify the risk values of three widely used cyber attacks.

Keywords: SCADA · Cyber attack · Risk assessment · Improved hybrid algorithm

1 Introduction

With the continued growth of electricity demand, the security of the power system is becoming increasingly important. In a power system, the application of the SCADA (Supervisory Control And Data Acquisition) is the most mature [1], which reliability ensures the security of the entire system.

Cyber attacks against SCADA occurs frequently in recent years, which have become a major factor affecting the security and reliability of power SCADA. Therefore, how to conduct the risk assessment of the power system has gradually been an urgent issue. We need to study an efficient risk assessment algorithm to accurately quantify the impact of cyber attacks on system reliability and predict potential threats to SCADA. The power system risk assessment algorithms can be roughly classified into two categories: parsing algorithms and Monte Carlo simulation algorithms [2].

© ICST Institute for Computer Sciences, Social Informatics and Telecommunications Engineering 2022
Published by Springer Nature Switzerland AG 2022. All Rights Reserved
H. Gao et al. (Eds.): CollaborateCom 2022, LNICST 461, pp. 3–17, 2022.
https://doi.org/10.1007/978-3-031-24386-8_1

The parsing algorithm obtains the random state of the system by fault enumeration and the probability of the random state by parsing calculation. The mathematical model of the parsing algorithm is accurate and the reliability indexes are highly precise. However, the number of system states to be analyzed by the parsing algorithm grows exponentially with the number of system components, which is difficult to apply to large-scale power system risk assessment.

The Monte Carlo simulation algorithm uses random sampling to obtain the status of each component in the power system, thereby determining the overall status of the power system and assessing system risk. The sampling number is independent of the size of the system. Therefore, it is particularly suitable for the risk assessment of large-scale power systems. However, the algorithm has a contradiction of calculation accuracy and sampling number [3,4]. The more precise the assessment index, the greater number of samples and the longer the calculation time required. We need to optimize the existing sampling algorithm to improve the convergence rate, which brings us great challenges.

In addition, most power SCADA risk assessments focus on the system itself, ignoring that cyber attacks are becoming a major factor affecting system security. Thus, we propose a novel power system risk assessment algorithm that takes into account cyber attacks. The major contributions of the work are four-fold:

- We propose an optimal sampling algorithm based on multiple integration models and variational problems, which realizes optimal sampling of the random state for improving the sampling efficiency and the indexes accuracy.
- To provide more efficient selection of parsing variables, we propose a selective parsing algorithm based on the projection variance, which overcomes the shortcomings of the parsing algorithm for the excessive analytical number.
- We combine the optimal sampling algorithm and the selective parsing algorithm into an improved hybrid algorithm for risk assessment of three attack types, which is the first attempt in the field. The improved hybrid algorithm combines the advantages of both algorithms.
- To assess the effectiveness of the improved hybrid algorithm, we conducted an error analysis of the risk assessment index and performed an experimental comparison on the UNSW-NB15 dataset. Experiments show that the algorithm can achieve better performance than other algorithms.

2   Related Work

The study of power system risk assessment algorithms has continuously been concerned by researchers.

Roslan [5] proposed sequential Monte Carlo (SMC) and non-sequential Monte Carlo (NSMC). They found that the SMC algorithm is more suitable to assess the distribution system. Zhang [6] proposed an improved SMC algorithm approach to substation connection risk assessment. Wu [7] adopted the SMC algorithm based on the minimal path sets to assess the risk of the distribution network. [8–10] proposed improved SMC algorithms to assess the risk of power systems respectively. However, the traditional Monte Carlo algorithm is memory-intensive, which leads to inefficiency.

Liu and Shen [11] used the improved important sampling algorithm, which meets the needs of assessment speed and accuracy. Bavajigari [12] presented the importance sampling algorithm to improve the computational efficiency of Monte Carlo sampling. Guo and Feng [13] calculated the security risk of the power system by the Latin hypercube sampling algorithm. Liu and Li [14] proposed a new algorithm combining Latin hypercube sampling (LHS) and Monte Carlo sequential simulation. The probability density functions adopted by these improved algorithms are superior to traditional sampling algorithms, but they are still far from the optimal distribution.

To overcome the shortcomings of the above algorithms, we propose a risk assessment algorithm that combines optimal sampling and selective parsing algorithms. The context of the assessment is that the power SCADA suffers cyber attacks. We aim to compare the performance of the risk indexes obtained by different algorithms and thus validate the superiority of the algorithm. The algorithm quantifies the impact of cyber attacks on power SCADA more accurately as well as has good engineering application value.

3 Preliminaries

3.1 SCADA Cyber Attack Types

Reports in [15] show an increasing number of security incidents and cyber attacks against SCADA in recent years. We have investigated the Repository of Industrial Security Incidents (RISI) [16] and SCADA cyber attacks that have occurred in the last 20 years [17]–[21] all over the world.

The three attacks that appear most frequently and bring us the biggest security challenges are *Analysis*, *DDoS*, and *Worm*. Specifically, *Analysis* contains the port scan, spam, and HyperText Mark-up Language (HTML) file penetrations. Attackers can use analysis tools to identify active ports and prepare for subsequent attacks. *DDoS* blocks the communication network by sending a large number of attack packets. Legitimate network packets are flooded with fake attack packets and can not reach the control center, while the network packets sent down from the control center can not be transmitted to the next layer of the network. *Worm* attacks Programmable Logic Controller (PLC) and other computers in the control center. Once the *Worm* infects the PLC, it can replicate itself to spread to other computers.

3.2 Traditional Risk Assessment Algorithm

To quantify the impact of three cyber attack types on the system, we take the 32 generators of the test system IEEE RTS-79 [22] as the example for the risk assessment. In the paper, we study the circuit breakers and generators of the power system as a whole object. Note that the circuit breakers and generators of the power system are treated as a whole object.

The forced outage rate (for) of a generator is the probability of an outage occurring when a component is forced out of operation immediately due to a fault. for of the power system generator i corrected under conditions of cyber attack for_i.

The traditional Monte Carlo simulation algorithm samples each component and determines the component state. The combination gives the state of the entire system.

For the generator i, consider two states of normal operation (denoted by 1) and fault (denoted by 0):

$$x_i = \begin{cases} 0 & 0 \le U_i \le for_i \\ 1 & for_i < U_i \le 1, \end{cases} \tag{1}$$

where x_i is the state of generator i. U_i is a random number that obeys a uniform distribution U(0, 1) generated by a computer. By comparing U_i with for_i, the generator state x_i can be determined.

$LOLP$ (Loss of Load Probability) is the probability that the available capacity of a generation system will not be able to meet the annual maximum load demand of the system:

$$LOLP = \frac{1}{N} \sum_{i=1}^{N} F_{LOLP}(\vec{X}_i), \tag{2}$$

where N denotes the number of random states for the system. F_{LOLP} is the test function of $LOLP$. $\vec{X}_i$ is the system random state vector. When the system is in condition $\vec{X}_i$ without a load cut, then $F_{LOLP}(\vec{X}_i)=0$. Otherwise, $F_{LOLP}(\vec{X}_i)=1$.

$EDNS$ (Expected Demand Not Supplied) is the expected value of load demand power reduction due to generation capacity shortage in a given time range of the system, which is measured in MW:

$$EDNS = \frac{1}{N} \sum_{i=1}^{N} F_{EDNS}(\vec{X}_i), \tag{3}$$

F_{EDNS} is the test function of $EDND$. $F_{EDNS}(\vec{X}_i)$ represents the active power of the system in the random state $\vec{X}_i$ in accordance with the cut-off power.

$LOLP$ and $EDNS$ are both risk assessment indexes. The smaller value of both, the lower the risk value of the system. The higher the risk value of cyber attacks means the greater the threat to power SCADA.

4 Improved Risk Assessment Algorithm

The disadvantages of traditional sampling algorithms are low sampling efficiency and slow convergence. As a useful supplement to the sampling algorithm, the parsing algorithm can speed up the convergence rate. However, the number of parsing algorithm is excessive, increasing exponentially with the number of system components. We improve the two algorithms and combine them into an improved hybrid algorithm, as shown in Fig. 1.

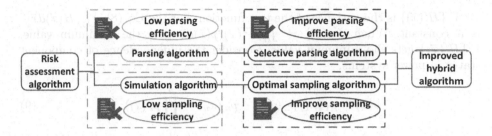

Fig. 1. The framework of the improved hybrid algorithm.

4.1 Multiple Integral Models for Risk Assessment

To reduce the variance of the test function, we need to optimize the probability distribution function of the system state variables. Rewrite the test function in the form of a random number vector $\vec{x}$ as the independent variable.

$$F(\vec{X}) = H(\vec{x}), \tag{4}$$

The element x_i of the vector $\vec{x}$ is a continuous variable.

$$R = E[F(\vec{X})] = E[H(\vec{x})] = \int_{\Omega} H(\vec{x})d\vec{x}, \tag{5}$$

where R is the risk assessment index. Ω is an n-dimensional hypercube surrounded by planes $x_1 = 0$, $x_1 = 1$, $x_2 = 0$, $x_2 = 1$, $...x_n = 0$, $x_n = 1$. $d\vec{x} = dx_1 dx_2 ... dx_n$. We transform the power SCADA risk assessment problem into a multiple integral model.

4.2 Optimal Sampling Algorithm

Optimal Sampling Density Function. According to [11]–[14], reducing the variance $V\{H(\vec{x})\}$ of the test function can improve sampling efficiency and computational speed. Calculate the estimated value $\widehat{R}$ of the risk assessment index.

$$\widehat{R} = \frac{1}{N} \sum_{k=1}^{N} H'(\vec{x}_k), \tag{6}$$

$p(\vec{x})$ is the probability density function.
The probability density function of sample $\vec{x_k}$ is $p(\vec{x_k})$.

$$H'(\vec{x}) = \frac{H(\vec{x})}{p(\vec{x})}, \tag{7}$$

$H'(\vec{x})$ is the corresponding test function of sample $\vec{x_k}$. $\vec{x}$ takes continuous values in the integration region.

$$V\{H'(\vec{x})\} = \int_{\Omega} \left[H^2(\vec{x})/p(\vec{x}) \right] d\vec{x} - \left[\int_{\Omega} H(\vec{x})d\vec{x} \right]^2, \tag{8}$$

$V\{H'(\vec{x})\}$ is the variance of the test function. For the Eq. (8), $\left[\int_{\Omega}H(\vec{x})d\vec{x}\right]^2$ is a constant. When $J[p(\vec{x})] = \int_{\Omega}H^2(\vec{x})/p(\vec{x})d\vec{x}$ gets the minimum value, $V\{H'(\vec{x})\}$ gets the minimum value. Consider the independence of component states in power systems.

$$p(\vec{x}) = p_1(x_1)p_2(x_2)\cdots p_n(x_n) = \prod_{i=1}^{n} p_i(x_i). \tag{9}$$

The problem of minimizing the variance of the test function is transformed into a variational problem $J = \min\{J[p]\}$.

$$\begin{cases} J[p] = \int_{\Omega}\left[H^2(\vec{x})/\prod_{i=1}^{n}p_i(x_i)\right]d\vec{x} \\ \int_0^1 p_i(x_i)\,dx_i = 1(i = 1, 2, \ldots, n). \end{cases} \tag{10}$$

According to the variational principle, the optimal edge distribution density of the i_{th} $(i = 1, 2, \ldots n)$ dimension is:

$$p_i(x_i) = \frac{\sqrt{\int_{\Omega_i}\left[H^2(\vec{x})/\prod_{\substack{j=i \\ j\neq i}}^{n}p_j(x_j)\right]d\vec{x}_{(i)}}}{\int_0^1\sqrt{\int_{\Omega_i}\left[H^2(\vec{x})/\prod_{\substack{j=1 \\ j\neq i}}^{n}p_i(x_i)\right]d\vec{x}_{(i)}}dx_i}, \tag{11}$$

$d\vec{x}_{(i)} = dx_1 dx_2 \ldots dx_{i-1} dx_{i+1} \ldots dx_n$. Ω_i is a subspace surrounded by planes $x_1 = 0$, $x_1 = 1$, $x_2 = 0$, $x_2 = 1$, $\ldots x_{i-1} = 0$, $x_{i-1} = 1$, $x_{i+1} = 0$, $x_{i+1} = 1, \ldots x_n = 0$, $x_n = 1$.

Optimal Sampling Algorithm. We set $I_i(x_i)$:

$$I_i(x_i) = \int_{Q_i}\left[H^2(\vec{x})/\prod_{\substack{j=1 \\ j\neq i}}^{n}p_j(x_j)\right]d\vec{x}_{(i)}, \tag{12}$$

The piecewise function $I_i(x_i)$ is constant in subintervals $[0, for_i)$ and $[for_i, 0]$:

$$I_i(x_i) = \begin{cases} I_{i1} & x_i \in [0, for_i) \\ I_{i2} & x_i \in [for_i, 1] \end{cases}, \tag{13}$$

Calculate the estimated value $\widehat{I_{i1}}$, $\widehat{I_{i2}}$ of I_{i1} and I_{i2}:

$$\hat{I}_{i1} = \frac{1}{N_1}\sum_{k=1}^{N_1}\left[\frac{H(\vec{x}_k)}{\prod_{\substack{j=1 \\ j\neq i}}^{n}p_j(x_j)}\right]^2\Bigg|_{x_i\in(0, for_i)}, \tag{14}$$

$$\hat{I}_{i2} = \frac{1}{N_2} \sum_{k=1}^{N_2} \left[\frac{H(\bar{x}_k)}{\prod_{\substack{j=1 \\ j \neq i}}^{n} p_j(x_j)} \right]^2 \Bigg|_{x_i \in (for_i, 1)}, \tag{15}$$

N_1, N_2 are the number of samples that satisfy the two subintervals respectively. The expression of the optimal sampling density function is:

$$p_i(x_i) = \begin{cases} p_{i1} & x_i \in [0, for_i) \\ p_{i2} & x_i \in [for_i, 1] \end{cases}, \tag{16}$$

$$p_{i1} \approx \frac{\sqrt{\hat{I}_{i1}}}{for_i \sqrt{\hat{I}_{i1}} + (1 - for_i) \sqrt{\hat{I}_{i1}}}, \tag{17}$$

$$p_{i2} \approx \frac{\sqrt{\hat{I}_{i2}}}{for_i \sqrt{\hat{I}_{i2}} + (1 - for_i) \sqrt{\hat{I}_{i2}}}. \tag{18}$$

The whole algorithm is divided into two stages: pre-sampling and formal sampling. The purpose of pre-sampling is to obtain the optimal density function for each sub-interval by iterative calculation. Then, we sample the random states of the system according to the optimal density function during formal sampling by Eq. (17) and (18). Finally, the risk index of the power SCADA is assessed by Eq. (5).

4.3 Selective Parsing Algorithm

The selective parsing algorithm uses the projected variance to quantify the effect of the randomness of the variables on the variance of the test function. The variables with high impact are selected for parsing to effectively reduce the variance.
We set $K_i(x_i)$:

$$K_i(x_i) = \frac{\int_{\Omega_i} H(\vec{x}) d\vec{x}_{(i)}}{p_i(x_i)}. \tag{19}$$

Transform Eq. (6):

$$R = \int_0^1 dx_i \int_{\Omega_i} H(\vec{x}) d\vec{x}_{(i)} = \int_0^1 K_i(x_i) p_i(x_i) dx_i, \tag{20}$$

$$\hat{R}_i = \frac{1}{N} \sum_{j=1}^{N} K_i(x_{ij}). \tag{21}$$

The accuracy of $\hat{R}$ depends on the variance of $K_i(x_{ij})$:

$$V\{K_i\} = \int_0^1 \{K_i(x_i) - E[K_i(x_i)]\}^2 p_i(x_i) dx_i, \tag{22}$$

$V\{K_i\}$ represents the effect of the randomness for the variable x_i on the variance of the risk assessment index, called the projected variance of x_i.

Analogous to $I_i(x_i)$, the piecewise function $K_i(x_{ij})$ is constant in subintervals $[0, for_i)$ and $[for_i, 0]$:

$$K_i(x_i) = \begin{cases} K_{i1} & x_i \in [0, for_i) \\ K_{i2} & x_i \in [for_i, 1] \end{cases}. \tag{23}$$

Calculate the estimated value $\widehat{K_{i1}}$, $\widehat{K_{i2}}$:

$$\hat{K}_{i1} = \frac{1}{N_1} \sum_{k=1}^{N_1} \left[\frac{H(\vec{x}_k)}{\prod_{j=1}^{n} p_j(x_j)} \right] \Bigg|_{x_i \in (0, for_i)}, \tag{24}$$

$$\hat{K}_{i2} = \frac{1}{N_2} \sum_{k=1}^{N_2} \left[\frac{H(\vec{x}_k)}{\prod_{j=1}^{n} p_j(x_j)} \right] \Bigg|_{x_i \in (0, for_i)}, \tag{25}$$

The projected variance of x_i is:

$$V\{K_i\} \approx \left\{ \hat{K}_{i1} - E[K_i(x_i)] \right\}^2 for_i p_{i1} + \left\{ \hat{K}_{i2} - E[K_i(x_i)] \right\}^2 (1 - for_i) p_{i2}, \tag{26}$$

$$E[K_i(x_i)] \approx for_i p_{i1} \hat{K}_{i1} + (1 - for_i r_i) p_{i2} \hat{K}_{i2}. \tag{27}$$

Similar to the optimal sampling algorithm, the selective parsing algorithm is divided into two stages: pre-sampling and formal sampling. Pre-sampling calculates the projection variances and arranges them in order of magnitude, which is used to select the parsing variables. The optimal set of parsing variables is determined in this order. The optimal parsing variables are analyzed in the formal sampling stage. We can improve parsing efficiency by the selective parsing algorithm.

4.4   Improved Hybrid Algorithm

We combine optimal sampling with selective parsing algorithms and propose an improved hybrid algorithm. The optimal sampling algorithm improves the efficiency of sampling calculation by optimizing the sampling density function. The selective parsing algorithm improves the efficiency of parsing calculation by optimizing parsing variables.

Figure 2 shows the flow chart of the proposed algorithm. First, we enter the system state, set the pre-sampling iterations and the sampling number to set the initial sampling density to 1. Then iteratively calculate the optimal density function for each dimension and interval in pre-sampling 1. Calculate the projection variance of variables according to the optimal density function and rank them in order of magnitude to determine the optimal parsing variables in pre-sampling 2. Next, sample the random states of the simulated variables according to the optimal density function and enumerate the states of the parsing variables to obtain the system states in the formal sampling until sampling completes. Finally, count risk assessment indicators, test function variances and coefficients of variance, and output the assessment results.

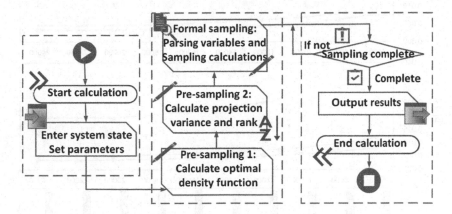

Fig. 2. Flow chart of the improved hybrid algorithm.

5   Example Analysis

5.1   Optimal Sampling Algorithm Assessment Results

To verify the sampling efficiency of the optimal sampling algorithm, we take 32 generators of IEEE-RTS79 as the object.

We conduct an error analysis of the reliability assessment indexes. Figure 3 shows β_{LOLP}, β_{EDNS}, V_{LOLP}, V_{EDNS} under different sampling number for four sampling algorithms. β_{LOLP}, β_{EDNS} is the variance of $LOLP$ and $EDNS$. V_{LOLP}, V_{EDNS} are the variances of the test function for $LOLP$ and $EDNS$. The pre-sampling of the optimal algorithm consists of two iterations of the calculation, each with 2000 samples. The number of samples starts from 6000.

It can be seen that the values of β_{LOLP}, β_{EDNS} of four sampling algorithms decrease as the number of samples increases. It means that the accuracy of the reliability index increases with the number of samples. The curves smooth out when the number of sampling reaches 20,000. At this point, the four sampling algorithms have the highest sampling efficiency and the most accurate calculation accuracy. Tests have shown that a sampling density function with minimal variance is obtained after 2 iterations for the optimal sampling algorithm.

As can be seen from the bar charts, the latter three improvements all reduce the sampling variance to some extent compared to the traditional algorithm. In particular, the optimal sampling algorithm has the largest reduction. It not only has the smallest variance of the test function under the same sampling number, but also the variance of the test function tends to decrease with each iteration. This proves that the index accuracy and sampling efficiency of the optimal sampling algorithm are the highest among the four algorithms.

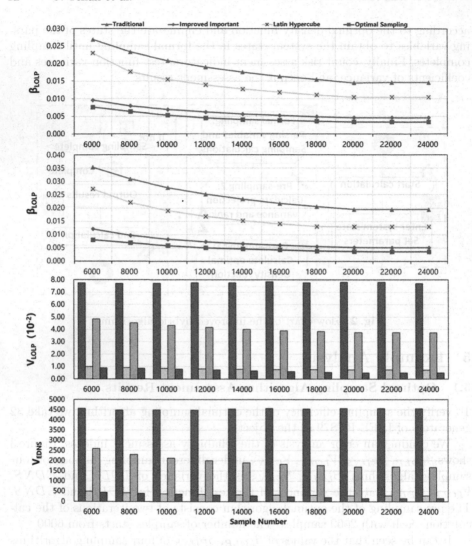

Fig. 3. β_{LOLP}, β_{EDNS}, V_{LOLP}, V_{EDNS} for four algorithms

5.2 Improved Hybrid Algorithm Assessment Results

To verify the performance of the improved hybrid algorithm, we assessed the selective parsing algorithm in combination with traditional and optimal sampling algorithms respectively. Based on the conclusion in Sect. 6.1, we selected a sample number of 20,000 for comparison. We consider the effect of the projection variance of the system state variables on reliability, which takes 32 generators of IEEE-RTS79 as the parsing variables.

Our experiment is divided into three stages.

In the first stage, we combine selective parsing with the traditional sampling algorithm to obtain an improved traditional algorithm. The pre-sampling is carried out according to the traditional sampling algorithm, which consists of two iterations of the calculation, each with 2000 samples. The projection variance of the variables is calculated from the obtained sampling density function by the selective parsing algorithm and the 32 generators are reordered according to the magnitude of the projection variance. In the formal sampling process, the reordered parsed variables are parsed. The variance of the test function is calculated to obtain the results of the improved traditional algorithm.

In the second stage, we combine selective parsing with the optimal sampling algorithm to obtain the improved hybrid algorithm. The traditional algorithm of the first stage is replaced with the optimal sampling algorithm. Repeat the steps of the first stage and obtain the results of the improved hybrid algorithm.

In the third stage, the performance of the improved algorithms are verified by comparing the variance of the test functions obtained in Sect. 5.1.

Figure 4 shows the comparison results of four algorithms. The abscissa is the generator number reordered according to the projected variance. The smaller the number, the larger the projected variance. We can conclude that V_{LOLP} and V_{EDNS} decrease as the projection variance increases. It means that parsing variables with larger projected variances have a greater impact on the variance of the test function. The greater the projection variance of the parsing variables, the more efficient the parsing of the selective parsing algorithm. Selecting parsing variables with large projection variance for parsing can reduce the variance of the test function and improve the parsing efficiency. The improved hybrid algorithm further improves the performance of the optimal sampling algorithm, which has the highest sampling efficiency in Sect. 5.1.

The number of samples is set to 20,000. We compare the assessment results of the five algorithms in Table 1. Note that $Time(/s)$ is the parsing time. From Table 1, compared to the other algorithms, we can conclude that β_{LOLP}, β_{EDNS}, V_{LOLP}, V_{EDNS} of the improved hybrid algorithm are minimum, which means that the improved hybrid algorithm has the highest sampling efficiency and the assessment indexes obtained are the most accurate. In addition, the improved hybrid algorithm greatly reduces the parsing time of algorithms due to the selective parsing algorithm's improved parsing efficiency. The parsing time improved 94.545% compared to the traditional algorithm. It is of great significance in the reliability assessment of modern large-scale power systems.

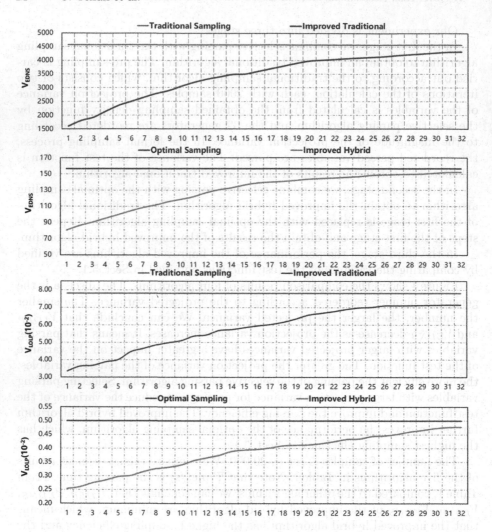

Fig. 4. V_{EDNS}, V_{LOLP} for improved algorithms

Table 1. The assessment results of five algorithms

Algorithm	$LOLP(10^{-2})$	$V_{LOLP}(10^{-2})$	$\beta_{LOLP}(10^{-2})$	$EDNS$	V_{EDNS}	$\beta_{EDNS}(10^{-2})$	Time
Traditional	8.43019	7.81100	1.45035	15.2672	4568.45	1.94486	165
Improved Important	8.49715	0.72946	0.45807	15.0129	289.65	0.52224	21
Latin Hypercube	8.50148	3.74545	1.04238	15.1606	1692.56	1.29878	132
Optimal Sampling	8.32678	0.50213	0.003406	14.5367	156.483	0.00369212	17
Improved Hybrid	**8.30146**	**0.32541**	**0.001534**	**14.5246**	**102.152**	**0.00161354**	**9**

Table 2. $LOLP(10^{-2})$ for cyber attack

Type	Traditional	Improved Important	Latin Hypercube	Optimal Sampling	Improved Hybrid
Primary value	8.4302	8.4972	8.5015	8.3268	**8.3015**
Worms	16.1869	16.3136	16.3459	15.8672	**15.9496**
DDoS	15.3428	15.4124	15.4423	15.1454	**15.0887**
Analysis	16.6942	16.8568	16.8154	16.5478	**16.4983**

Table 3. $EDNS(/MW)$ for cyber attack

Type	Traditional	Improved Important	Latin Hypercube	Optimal Sampling	Improved Hybrid
Primary value	15.2672	15.0129	15.1606	14.5367	**14.5246**
Worms	30.0572	29.5787	29.8675	28.6785	**28.6033**
DDoS	31.5478	31.1878	31.4865	30.1853	**30.1502**
Analysis	33.9645	33.3752	33.7457	32.3458	**32.3071**

5.3 Risk Assessment for Cyber Attack

The UNSW-NB15 dataset [23] is used to generate attacks for evaluation. $LOLP$ and $EDNS$ are obtained for cyber attack in Table 2 and Table 3. Note that the primary values for the assessment index are obtained without cyber attacks. As a result of the five algorithms calculations, we can conclude that $LOLP$ and $EDNS$ values of *Analysis* attack are the largest among the three attack types. Through our error analysis it is clear that although the five algorithms produce consistent conclusions, the other four are not sufficiently precise in their indexes. To maximize the accuracy of the calculation, we have adopted the assessment indexes of the improved hybrid algorithm calculation. *Analysis* attack has the largest $LOLP$ and $EDNS$ values among the three attack types, meaning it has the greatest impact on the reliability of the system. The value of $LOLP$ increases 98.74% and $EDNS$ increases 122.43% compared to the primary value. For *Worms* attack, the value of $LOLP$ increases 92.13% and $EDNS$ increases 96.93%. For *DDoS* attack, the value of $LOLP$ increases 81.76% and $EDNS$ increases 107.58%. As a result of our precise assessment, the risk value of *Analysis* attack is the maximum, meaning it is the most dangerous for the power SCADA.

6 Conclusion

In this paper, we first propose an optimal sampling algorithm based on multiple integration models and variational problems, which improves sampling efficiency and indexes accuracy. Besides, a selective parsing algorithm based on the projection variance is proposed to provide a more efficient selection of parsing variables for improving parsing efficiency. Then, we combine the two improved algorithms to form an improved hybrid algorithm for risk assessment of three attack types. After error analysis and experimental comparisons, we can confirm that the improved hybrid algorithm outperforms the traditional and existing algorithms. The assessment results accurately quantify the impact of cyber attacks on SCADA security, which show that the *Analysis* attack has the greatest risk value. It is extremely well predicted that *Analysis* attack is the greatest threat to power SCADA, providing insights into the establishment of the power system security enhancement strategies.

References

1. Darshana, U., et al.: An efficient key management and multi-layered security framework for SCADA systems. IEEE Trans. Netw. Serv. Manage. **19**(1), 642–660 (2021)
2. He, Hailei., et al.: Reliability evaluation based on modified latin hypercube sampling and minimum load-cutting method. In: 2015 5th International Conference on Electric Utility Deregulation and Restructuring and Power Technologies (DRPT). IEEE, 2015
3. Gonzalez-Fernandez, R.A., Leite da Silva, A.M.: Reliability assessment of time-dependent systems via sequential cross-entropy Monte Carlo simulation. IEEE Trans. Power Syst. **26**(4), 2381–2389 (2011)
4. Bie, Z., Wang, X.: The application of Monte Carlo method to reliability evaluation of power systems. Autom. Electr. Power Syst. **21**(6), 68–75 (1997)
5. Roslan, N.N.R.B., Fauzi, N.F.B.M., Ridzuan, M.I.M.: Sequential and nonsequential monte carlo in assessing reliability performance of distribution network. In: 2020 Emerging Technology in Computing, Communication and Electronics (ETCCE). IEEE (2020)
6. Zhang, K., et al.: Improved sequential monte carlo method approach to substation connection reliability assessment. In: 2020 IEEE 4th Conference on Energy Internet and Energy System Integration (EI2). IEEE (2020)
7. Wu, L., et al.: Reliability assessment of AC/DC hybrid distribution network based on sequential monte carlo method. In: 2020 5th Asia Conference on Power and Electrical Engineering (ACPEE). IEEE (2020)
8. Weibo, L., et al.: Risk assessment technology of ship power system based on improved time series algorithm. In: 2020 7th International Conference on Information Science and Control Engineering (ICISCE). IEEE (2020)
9. Li, L., et al.: Risk assessment for renewable energy penetrated power systems considering battery and hydrogen storage systems. In: 2021 Power System and Green Energy Conference (PSGEC). IEEE (2021)
10. Tang, S., Liu, Z., Wang, L.: Power system reliability analysis considering external and insider attacks on the SCADA system. In: 2020 IEEE/PES Transmission and Distribution Conference and Exposition (T&D). IEEE (2020)
11. Liu, J., Shen, H., Yang, F.: Reliability evaluation of distribution network power supply based on improved sampling monte carlo method. In: 2020 5th Asia Conference on Power and Electrical Engineering (ACPEE). IEEE (2020)
12. Bavajigari, S.K.K., Singh, C.: Investigation of computational advantage of using importance sampling in monte carlo simulation. In: 2019 North American Power Symposium (NAPS). IEEE (2019)
13. Guo, J., et al.: Security risk assessment of power system based on latin hypercube sampling and daily peak load forecasting. In: 2020 IEEE 4th Conference on Energy Internet and Energy System Integration (EI2). IEEE (2020)

14. Aibin, L., Wenyi, L.: Reliability evaluation of distribution network with distributed generation based on latin hypercube sequential sampling. In: 2020 3rd International Conference on Electron Device and Mechanical Engineering (ICEDME). IEEE (2020)
15. Miller, B., Rowe, D.: A survey SCADA of and critical infrastructure incidents. In: Proceedings of the 1st Annual Conference on Research in Information Technology (2012)
16. RISI-The Repository of Industrial Security Incidents, Apr 2020. [online] Available: http://www.risidata.com/
17. Pliatsios, D., et al.: A survey on SCADA systems: secure protocols, incidents, threats and tactics. IEEE Commun. Surv. Tutorials **22**(3), 1942–1976 (2020)
18. Moore, D., et al.: Inside the slammer worm. IEEE Secur. Priv. **1**(4), 33–39 (2003)
19. Levy, E.: The making of a spam zombie army. dissecting the Sobig worms. IEEE Secur. Priv. **1**(4), 58–59 (2003)
20. Langner, R.: Stuxnet: dissecting a cyberwarfare weapon. IEEE Secur. Priv. **9**(3), 49–51 (2011)
21. Samdarshi, R., Sinha, N., Tripathi, P.: A triple layer intrusion detection system for SCADA security of electric utility. In: 2015 annual IEEE India Conference (INDICON). IEEE (2015)
22. Stamp, J., McIntyre, A., Ricardson, B.: Reliability impacts from cyber attack on electric power systems. In: 2009 IEEE/PES Power Systems Conference and Exposition. IEEE (2009)
23. The UNSW-NB15 Dataset, Intelligent Security Group UNSW Canberra, June 2021 [online] Available: https://research.unsw.edu.au/projects/unsw-nb15-dataset

A Visual Tool for Interactively Privacy Analysis and Preservation on Order-Dynamic Tabular Data

Fengzhou Liang[1], Fang Liu[2(✉)], and Tongqing Zhou[3]

[1] Sun Yat-Sen University, Guangzhou 510000, China
liangfzh@mail2.sysu.edu.cn
[2] Hunan University, Changsha 410000, China
fangl@hnu.edu.cn
[3] National University of Defense Technology, Changsha 410000, China
zhoutongqing@nudt.edu.cn

Abstract. The practice of releasing individual data, usually in tabular form, is obligated to prevent privacy leakage. With rendered privacy risks, visualization techniques have greatly prompted the user-friendly data sanitization process. Yet, we point out, for the first time, the attribute order (i.e., schema) of tabular data inherently determines the risk situation and the output utility, while is ignored in previous efforts. To mitigate this gap, this work proposes the design and pipeline of a visual tool (TPA, Tabular Privacy Assistant) for nuanced privacy analysis and preservation on order-dynamic tabular data. By adapting data cube structure as the flexible backbone, TPA manages to support real-time risk analysis in response to attribute order adjustment. Novel visual designs, i.e., data abstract, risk tree, integrated privacy enhancement, are developed to explore data correlations and acquire privacy awareness. We demonstrate TPA's effectiveness with a case study on the prototype and qualitatively discuss the pros and cons with domain experts for future improvement.

Keywords: Interactive system · Visualization · Privacy analysis

1 Introduction

We are all providers and beneficiaries of the collection and release of individual data. Generally maintained as multi-attribute tables, the collected data can be used in various learning, statistic, and decision-making tasks (e.g., disease diagnosing, product recommendation). Alongside the well-known benefits, privacy issues in the publish of data have raised massive concerns recently, as more and more real-world safety violation caused by data leakage and abuse are witnessed [21,28] and the promulgation of regulations (e.g., GDPR).

The privacy risk stems from the fact that individual identity, although usually anonymized, is correlated and may be re-identified by the other seemingly harmless attributes. As a result, it is obligated for data holders (e.g., organizations,

H. Gao et al. (Eds.): CollaborateCom 2022, LNICST 461, pp. 18–38, 2022.
https://doi.org/10.1007/978-3-031-24386-8_2

companies) to properly sanitize data before releasing it. Research communities have responded to this critical requirement with many privacy protection techniques, including anonymity [16], differential privacy [9], and synthetic data mixture [1, 36]. With such technical basis, visualization has been introduced recently to facilitate illustrative, understandable, and easy-to-use privacy analysis tools on behalf of the users [6, 7, 31–33, 35]. For example, in [33], visual presentations on privacy exposure level and utility preservation degree are provided for detecting and mitigating privacy issues in tabular data.

Previous visual methods for privacy analysis build on the setting of fixed attribute order, i.e., the target table has fixed columns. However, we find that **the currently unexplored attribute order (i.e., schema) inherently determines the privacy risk situation and the output utility** (Detail analysis in Sect. 3.2). For example, in the process of checking K-anonymity privacy constraints [30] on a sheet, whereas we may find privacy breach on the 3rd attribute and have 5 values changed during protection in an order of 'Age, Work, Disease', we would face a totally different (thornier) privacy context, like privacy breach on the 1st attribute with 10 values changed, in order 'Work, Disease, Age'. As a result, randomly choosing an attribute order, as the existing proposals do, may unfortunately lead to over-protection and unnecessary utility losses.

We are thus motivated to design a flexible visual tool (TPA) that can support and explore order adjustment for nuanced (user-specific, reactive) privacy investigation. The most challenging part for dynamic order is that one should dynamically re-perform risk analysis (e.g., equivalent class parsing) according to the new attribute order. This can be a disaster for existing implementations as it involves aggregation calculations for all combinations under additive prefixes, especially when the sheet owns vast amounts of data items and lots of attributes, indicating significant interaction latency. As a remedy, we adapt the data cube structure with flexibly pre-aggregation to organize the table and use an operation tree to handle order adjustment in real-time (Sect. 4.1).

Combined with various privacy enhancement technologies, TPA guides data holders on the risks in their data, and prompt utility losses of preserving operations. The main contributions are as follows:

- We identify the impact of tabular attribute order on privacy analysis, utility loss, and processing costs. We propose a new tool to explore such a property by adopting data cube to guarantee real-time interaction.
- We leverage multi-dimensional value distance to measure utility change at the back-end. We use abstract extraction for inter-attribute relationship analysis and design an intuitive risk tree that semantically bonded with data items for interactive privacy analysis preservation at the front-end.
- We implement the prototype of TPA and evaluate its effectiveness with use a case from the medical domain, respectively. A qualitative interview points out the pros and cons of TPA from the perspective of domain experts.

2   Related Work

In this section, we provide the background of the privacy preserving and review the literature on visualization.

2.1   Privacy Preserving Techniques

Data providers sanitize the data before before making it public. There are three dominant technologies:

Anonymity Method. The most widely used technique for dealing with linking attacks is k-anonymity [30], which is one of the most representative methods. K-anonymity calls all records with the same quasi-identifier an equivalence class. It requires each equivalence class has at least k records. The k-anonymity avoids attackers to identify users by quasi-identifiers with a confidence level no more than $\frac{1}{k}$. However, it cannot prevent homogeneity attacks. For example, the sensitive attributes in a equivalence classes are identical, and the attackers can still confirm their sensitive information. Hence, l-diversity was proposed [19]. If a sensitive attribute of an equivalence class has at least l well-represented count, then the equivalence class is said to be l-diversity. Similarly, if all the equivalence classes meet l-diversity, the dataset can be considered to meet l-diversity. If the distance between the distribution of the sensitive attribute in the equivalence class and the distribution of the sensitive attribute in the whole dataset does not exceed the threshold t, it is considered to meet t-closeness [17]. In addition, there are many other variants based on these three methods [15,29].But anonymity methods are parameter sensitive, and apply to specific constraints.

Differential Privacy. Differential privacy [9] is widely used which has no disadvantages of anonymous methods (only applicable to attackers with specific background knowledge). If the absence of a data item does not significantly affect the output result, the function conforms differential privacy definition. For example, if there is a function that queries 100 items in a certain way and results in the same results as queries for the 99 items, there is no way for an attacker to find information about the 100th item. Therefore, the core idea of differential privacy is that there is only one record for the difference between two data sets, making the probability of the result is almost the same.

Synthetic Data. The intuitive advantage of synthetic data is that it is 'artificial data', so synthetic data does not contain real information. Synthesizing data is also presented to protect publishing data from traditional attacks [1,23,36]. Therefore, many studies [2,4,27] work on similarity between real and synthetic records to measure privacy leakage in synthetic datasets. True, these techniques avoid exposing real data, but as Stadler argues [27], these studies seriously overestimate the ability of privacy preserving. They can't always prevent attacks. Synthetic data is far from the holy grail of privacy preserving data publishing.

2.2   Privacy Visualization

Privacy preserving is a part of data processing. Visualization plays a key role in data analysis and processing. Recent literature proves that visualization is gaining momentum in the domain of privacy preserving. Much work has assimilated and expanded the concept of privacy and data mining, analyzed how to reduce privacy leaks, maintain utility, and provide the preserving pipeline.

Visualization in Data Analysis. Data analysis [18,34] mainly analyzes the relationship between samples from the perspective of distribution, correlation and clustering. Many visualization tools, such as Hierarchical Cluster Explorer [26], PermutMatrix [5] and Clustergrammer [11], are used to analyze the relationship between samples.

Tabular is the primary way to represent data attribute relationships. Tabular visualization [12,13,24] is extremely scalable because cells in table can be divided into many pixels to show more information about data. Tagging is a critically acclaimed tool [12], which is an item-centric (cells in the sheet) visualization technique that provides a seamless combination of details through data-driven aggregation.

Visualization for Privacy Analysis. In recent years, a growing number of studies focus on visualizing-specific contributions for privacy preserving. Chou et al. proposed a visualization tool to help avoid privacy risks in vision, and designed a visual method based on anonymity technology for social network graphs [6] and time series [7]. GraphProtector [32] guides users to protect privacy by using graphical interactive visualizations to the connection of sensitive and non-sensitive nodes and observe structural changes in the graph of utility.

There are also some studies [3,8,37] that analyze how existing visualizations of privacy preserving affect data and how effective they are. Dasgupta et al. analyze the disclosure risks associated with vulnerabilities in privacy-preserving parallel coordinates and scatter plots [8], and present a case study to demonstrate the effectiveness of the model. Zhang et al. investigate visual analysis of differential privacy [37]. They analyze effectiveness of task-based visualization techniques and a dichotomy model is proposed to define and measure the success of tasks.

Visualization for Privacy Preserving. The preserving pipeline is designed to provide users with a complete processing framework from analysis to protection. Xiao et al. proposed a visualization tool named VISEE [35] to help protect privacy in the case of sensor data sharing. VISEE makes a trade-off between utility and privacy by visualizing the degree of mutual information between different pairs of variables. Overlook [31] was developed for differential privacy preserving of big data. It allows data analysts and data administrators to explore noised data in the face of acceptable delays, while ensuring query accuracy comparable to other synopsis-based systems. Wang et al. [33] propose UPD-Matrix (utility preservation degree matrix) and PER-Tree (privacy exposure risk tree) and developed a visualization tool for multi-attribute tabular based on them. It provides a five-step pipeline of user interaction and iterative processing of data.

These visualization tools are designed to help users troubleshoot potential risks. However, most of them are based on a single exploration domain or automatic algorithms. We find that different schema has great difference in risk analysis and handling (Sect. 3.2). Our approach allows users to explore the tabular data of different attribute order more flexibly and support different granularity of privacy preserving operations.

3   Preliminaries, Motivations, and Requirements

For ease of exposition, we first denote the relevant entities: 1) **Individuals** whose information are recorded in a sheet. One individual can correspond to several items. 2) **Data holders**[1] (e.g., institutions, administrators) that own, maintain, and release the sheet.

3.1   Preliminaries on Tabular Privacy

The basic privacy risk of sharing tabular data is that individual identity is correlated and may be revealed by the other seemingly harmless attributes. We denote such a unique combination of attributes a **quasi-identifier** for individual privacy. We first give some key definitions in this privacy context.

(Definition 1) **Equivalent Class**: A subset of items with equal values on all the focused attributes.

For example, in Fig. 1, if 'Gender' is the focused attribute, then all the items with value 'M' form an equivalent class, while all items with 'F' form another class. According to K-anonymity argument, if the size of a equivalent class is smaller than k, then the inside items form quasi-identifiers that identify their owners' identities.

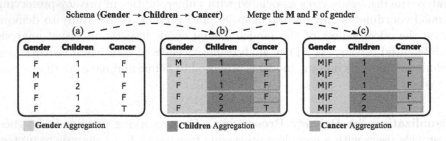

Fig. 1. Aggregation for privacy analysis under a schema example. (a) Original sheet. (b) Reordered records by schema. (c) Privacy-enhanced sheet based on merging attribute values.

Given a tabular set, a general privacy analysis process (e.g., [33]) involves calculating the size of equivalent classes under additive attribute prefix. For

---
[1] We use data holder and user interchangeably.

example, measuring the size of equivalent class of prefix 'Gender=F' and raising a privacy risk if the number is smaller than k; then checking prefix 'Gender=F, Children−1', et al.

(Definition 2) **Schema**: The order of attributes assigned for measuring the size of equivalent class to find a privacy breach.

We denote the process of finding equivalent classes according to the schema as **aggregation**, so that **privacy investigation turns into aggregation in the given order of attributes**. Figure 1 shows the aggregation under a specific schema (from the left column to the right ones). Attribute of the left-most column (*Gender*) is first investigated by measuring the equivalent class of Male ('M') and Female ('F') separately. Wherein, the 'M' class would breach K-anonymity if $k > 1$, which can be mitigated by merging values 'M' and 'F' together to loose the quasi-identifier ($k = 5$). Then the next dimension (*Children*) is measured by counting items under prefix 'M, 1', 'F, 1', and 'F, 2' separately.

3.2   Motivations: Self-defined and Dynamic Schema

Previous studies use a fixed schema during privacy analysis for that analyzing equivalent class for a tabular set is computation complex, especially when there are large amounts of data items with many attributes. As a result, they usually perform analysis according to the original attribute order in the sheet. However, we find that:

Remark: *Different schema will yield different privacy risk situations, facilitate distinguished privacy-preserving granularity, and introduce distinct risk handling overhead.*

Taking the merging operation as an example, different schemas correspond to different aggregations and result in different equivalence classes after merging. In the case of Fig. 2, O1 and O2 are the same sheet with different schema. When checking the first attribute, O1 will merge the 'Gender' into $M|F$ (operation a), whereas 'Children' in O2 satisfies $k = 2$-anonymity and will be retained. Then, O1 continues to check 'Children' without merging operation and merge 'Cancer' under the prefix of 'Gender-Children'. O2, on the other hand, merges the 'Cancer' and 'Gender' attributes under the prefix of 'Children'. Finally, O1 has 10 values altered, while O2 got eight changed during aggregation. That is, the schema has a explicit impact on the privacy situations and enhancement level.

In particular, we note that the latter attribute in the schema order has a higher chance of breaching privacy as the equivalent class of a longer prefix (finer granularity) gradually gets smaller, namely, easier to go below the constraint k. As a result, the latter attribute may be heavily merged for privacy preserving, losing more utility. Considering this, we point out that **the schema should be assigned by the data holder according to their privacy/utility preference**, e.g., subjectively retaining information of some attributes by putting them in the front. Furthermore, as we will show in Sect. 6, **data holders will dynamically adjust the schema to analyze the risky attributes in coarser granularity** for flexible merging operations. For example, instead of studying

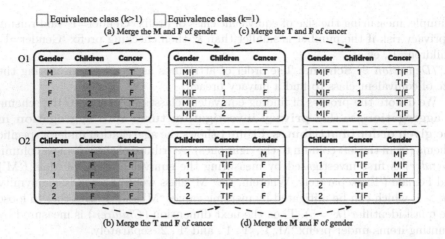

Fig. 2. An example of performing equivalent class merging for privacy enhancement under different schemas (O1 and O2). Obviously, the yielded sheets are different.

many equivalent classes for a latter attribute, one can move it to the front to perform merging on fewer classes.

Yet, existing visualization cannot meet the above dynamic schema intentions, as the change in schema requires a new round of aggregation, which will cause significant latency in online interaction. We are thus motivated to design a new privacy visualization tool that supports schema dynamics.

3.3   Requirement Analysis

Through meetings with domain experts, we acknowledge that they are familiar with common privacy enhancement technologies, such as k-anonymity and differential privacy. In fact, they have actively applied these techniques to mitigate risk before data released. On this basis, we discussed the insufficiency in current privacy practice and have identified four main requirements:

R1: Ability to Control Schema. As indicated above, different order of attributes shows different preference on attributes and has different granularity when applying privacy preserving operations. Flexible support for adjustable schema is widely required.

R2: Multidimensional Data Analysis. Users' prior knowledge is important in risk analysis. Even professional data analysts cannot find relation between attributes by simply glancing at a sheet. Heuristic algorithms for risk assessing do not know the semantic knowledge and their results are unreliable. Therefore, domain experts believe that a sketch view on for exploring attribute relations is beneficial.

R3: Intuitive Risk Cue. Prior privacy preserving studies have addressed visual designs for privacy risk. In these realizations, users are reminded that there are risks somewhere without mapping directly to the specific records on the sheet. Thus, it is expected to provide an integrated process for risk presentation and mitigation.

R4: Operation-Granularity Utility Evaluation. The sanitization of data inevitably discard some information details. It would blur the data, deviate the statistics, and reduce releasing utility. In particular, as different schema and sanitization operations lead to different utilities, users generally want to attain the utility outputs of the current settings for further involvement.

4 Back-End Engine

This section introduces the key techniques of TPA and how they are used in the system.

4.1 Data Structure for Order-dynamic Schema

Section 3 discusses the necessity and challenges of adjusting schema dynamically. We propose to adapt data cube as the basis for data management, which has efforts in addressing **R1** and **R2**. With data cube, we design the operation tree and facilitate users to change schema and perform operations with almost no perceptible latency.

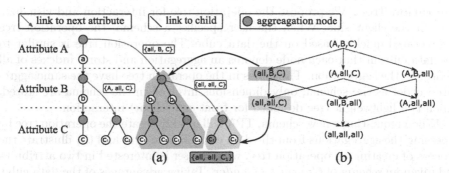

Fig. 3. Data cube of a dataset with attributes $D = A, B, C$. (a) Tree-based data cube. (b) Aggregation relationships of the data cube.

Data Cube. Data Cube [14] is well suited to handle online analytical processing queries. It is a data processing form for statistics of data, such as SUM, MIN, MAX and AVERAGE. Queries have low latencies by pre-aggregated. We introduce the data cube into TPA, and pre-calculated aggregations are used to reduce query latency.

As shown in Fig. 3, (a) shows a tree-based data cube. Similar to a search tree, records are added as a node based on the value of each dimension. However, the data cube also stores the aggregated results (i.e., the subtree pointed to by the blue arrows). The aggregation results store records when a dimension value was ignored. When a query does not care about the values of specific dimensions, data cube can response quickly by access aggregation. For example, The user wants to find all records which attribute C is c_1 and doesn't care about other attributes. The result can be obtained by accessing the aggregation of $\{all, all, c_1\}$, which is the green node in the figure.

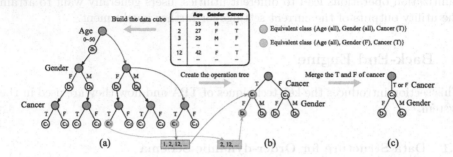

Fig. 4. An illustration of creating and updating the operation tree. (a) Data cube is built at the back-end based on the tabular data above. (b) Operation tree is generated based on the data cube. (c) An example of updating the operation tree.

Operation Tree. We propose the operation tree for interaction and visualization on the client side. When the user specifies a schema, the operation tree is generated quickly based on the data cube. The operation tree is similar to the data cube in that each node denotes an aggregation and stores indexes of all records in the aggregation. The nodes in the operation tree have the same aggregated order as the schema, only dimensions involved in the schema are stored, which is a lightweight tree designed for front-end (client) interaction.

When requesting a new schema, TPA will quickly create the operation tree by accessing the aggregations from the data cube. Figure 4 (a) and (b) illustrate the process of creating an operation tree, when a user is interested in two attributes and given an schema of $Cancer \rightarrow Gender$. Taking advantages of the data cube, TPA does not need to traverse all records to build the operation tree. TPA can quickly find out records of each node (operation tree) just by looking at aggregations of the data cube. TPA is able to create the operation tree with little overhead, even if the user frequently reorders the dimensions.

When we apply certain preserving operations, they are directly performed to the operation tree. Figure 4 (c) show how the operation tree updated after a merging operation performed. Updating may add or delete nodes and branches, and update the values of node records. Since these changes only tweak the tree structure, they do not incur much computing overhead on the client side, while changes to the operation tree are synchronized to the data cube of the server side, again with no additional delay in interaction.

4.2   Utility Quantification

Utility is a summary term describing the value of a given data release as an analytical resource [10], which is essentially a measure of the information obtained from the dataset. There is no accepted measure of utility and few studies focus on utility quantification of tabular data. According to the definition of utility, we consider using **distance** and **distribution** to measure the utility loss. For any values $f_a(x)$ in original dataset (where $f_a(x)$ is the value of the attribute a) and handling values $f_a'(x)$ which is obtained after privacy preserving, we use $L_{distance}(F_a, F_a')$ and $L_{distribution}(F_a, F_a')$ to denote the utility loss according to the difference in distance and distribution between them. We propose different algorithms to calculate utility losses for numerical data and categorical data, respectively.

Numerical Distance. Inspired by EMD [25], Earth Mover's Distance is used to compare the distance between two datasets. Sort all records of two datasets, and calculate the distance of the corresponding records:

$$L_{distance}(F_a, F_a') = \sum_{i=1}^{n} \frac{|i - j|}{n}, \tag{1}$$

where i and j refer to the sorted index of $f_a(x)$ and $f_a'(x)$ and n is the number of records.

Categorical Distance. Since the Categorical data may be fuzzy, the value of $f_a(x)$ is actually a set. For example, $f_{gender} = \{male, female\}$ represents an uncertain value that the gender of this record may be male or female. First, we calculate I of these two fuzzy sets, where I denotes the number of individual values that can only be taken from one of the sets. Taking $\{a, b, c\}$ and $\{b, c, d\}$ as an example, a and d are individual values, hence the I is 2. Then the distance between sets can be calculated by:

$$L_{distance}(F_a, F_a') = \sum_{i=1}^{n} \frac{2I}{|f_a(x)| + |f_a'(x)|}, \tag{2}$$

where $|f_a(x)|$ refers to the size of the set (i.e., the number of fuzzy values contained).

Numerical Distribution. As a nonparametric test method, K-S test [20] is applicable to compare the distribution of two datasets when the distribution is unknown. We use the K-S test to measure the distribution of numerical distribution and use the p-value to represent the utility loss:

$$L_{distribution}(F_a, F_a') = 1 - p. \tag{3}$$

Categorical Distribution. To measure the distribution of fuzzy sets, we first get the global distribution of all possible values. For an attribute a, count the number of occurrences of all values $C = \{c_{a_1}, c_{a_2}, \ldots, c_{a_n}\}$, where c_{a_n} refers to the number of values with a_n. Given a fuzzy set $f_a(x)$, counting each possible value a_n by $c_{a_n} = c_{a_n} + \frac{1}{|f_a(x)|}$. After getting the global count, the distance of each value can be calculated by:

$$L_{distribution}(F_a, F_a') = \sum_{i=1}^{n} \frac{|C - C'|}{n}. \tag{4}$$

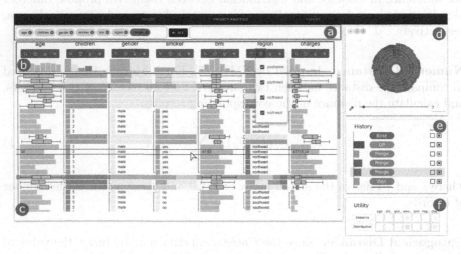

Fig. 5. Tabular Privacy Assistant (TPA), a visual tool for the risk analysis and privacy preservation of tabular data with dynamic attribute order. (a) A widget that allows personalized attribute order setting and dynamic adjustment. (b) Statistics of different attributes for overall distribution analysis. (c) The main view for tabular data presentation (box plot means abstract of several items) and interactive privacy enhancement (e.g., choosing five items to merge). (d) Privacy risk tree under the current attribute order (red: privacy breach items on K-anonymity). (e) Historical privacy enhancement operations (allowing backtrack and comparison). (f) Data utility dynamics during interactions.

5   Front-End Visualization

We implemented the TPA prototype system, as shown in the Fig. 5. The front-end of TPA works in 5 steps (Fig. 6): importing, building data cube, privacy analysis, privacy preserving, and exporting. Among them, (c) privacy analysis and (d) privacy preserving are of the most concern for data holders. Being at the heart of visualization and interaction, these two steps work iteratively by presenting risks and performing enhancement until privacy and utility are both satisfactory.

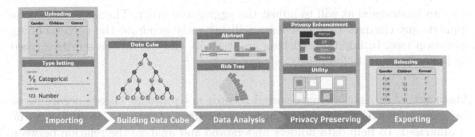

Fig. 6. TPA visualization framework, a 5-step pipeline: import the data sheet, build the data cube, iterate to analyze and deal with privacy risks, and finally export the data sheet.

5.1   Importing and Building Data Cube

As the first step in the pipeline, the user needs to upload the data sheet here. TPA will attempt to automatically identify the attributes type (categorical or numeric), and user can correct possible misjudgments by manually setting the type. Once the attribute type is determined, it cannot be modified in subsequent steps.

After receiving the sheet uploaded at the first step, TPA will build the data cube for management and create a session. The session created is used to respond to requests for schemas and to keep track of updates to the operation tree.

5.2   Privacy Analysis

Figure 5 (a) shows how the schema is modified. This widget has two boxes (left and right), and user changes the order by moving the attributes in these two boxes. The first time at this step all the attributes are in the right side area, and users can select the interested attributes and move them to the left. Users can also add or remove interested attributes at any time. The attributes of the left

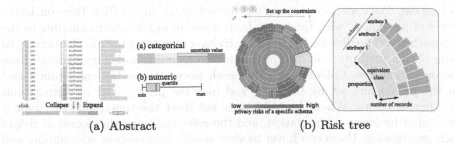

(a) Abstract   (b) Risk tree

Fig. 7. Abstract: Performance on the building time and response time. (a) Linkube's building time on the Flight dataset. (b) The response time of 10,000 queries on the Twitter dataset. (c) The response time of Linkube with the arrival of queries. **Risk tree**: A risk tree design for intuitive perception of privacy risks in aggregations.

box can be dragged at will to adjust the aggregated order. Thanks to data cube applied, any changes to the schema will instantly generate the corresponding operation tree. In addition, clicking an attribute can mark it as sensitive (used for l-diversity and t-closeness).

Abstract. Aggregations have sorted records in equivalent classes according to the schema, but dozens or even hundreds of lines of records are hardly to be summarized. To help data holders understand and analyze the relation between attributes (**R2**), we design the visual abstract. As shown in Fig. 5 (b), TPA provides a global abstract, which shows the distribution and proportion of values. In addition to the global summary, TPA supports draw abstract for any aggregation selected. Clicking on the left of the record to collapse or expand the aggregation, and draw abstract for the collapse one. There are two types of the abstracts, as shown in Fig. 7(a):

- The categorical abstract in (a). Its value distribution is represented by the percentage of color block. For fuzzy values, such as null values and uncertain values, are bisected among all possible blocks. The light (upper) part of the color block refers to the uncertain value. By observing the proportion of the light part, users can know how many records apply the merging operation.
- The numeric abstract in (b), based on a box-plot design. The box-plot clearly shows the extreme, quartile, and mean values of the aggregation.

With summaries by the abstract, users can quickly get the information of the selected aggregation and the relation between the data of different attributes, which is helpful for data analysis.

Privacy Risk Tree. Abstract can guide data analysis, and help to explore data relations, but users also like the system to tell them directly where the privacy risks are (**R3**). We came up with a more intuitive visual design, the risk tree, locating privacy risks according to anonymity technologies. Figure 7(b) illustrates the risk tree widget. A selector on the top left of the widget allow user to select a specific anonymity technology from k-anonymity, l-diversity and t-closeness. The constraint parameters are set by the slider. Risk Tree consists of layers of pie charts, with the layers from inside to outside corresponding to the given schema. The division of piece at each layer represents the distribution of the value of this attribute, and each piece is a corresponding node (aggregation) from the operation tree. Calculate whether each piece satisfies the constraint based on the parameters set by the user, and map the privacy risk of aggregations to different colors. When the block does not meet the constraint, the color is calculated by linear interpolation, and the color can relay the degree of risk of each aggregation. Users can hover to view specific aggregation information, and click to quickly jump to its location in the main view.

Due to the different granularity of each layer, the actual priority of risks are different. Obviously, the aggregation node of the outer layer has fewer records, exposing fine-grained privacy risk easily. On the contrary, the high risk color of the inner aggregation indicates that the aggregation has large-scale leakage and should be paid more attention to. A simple understanding is that the risk of inner aggregations means that an attacker can use less information to identify items and should be dealt with first.

5.3 Privacy Preservation

The privacy risks identified in the previous step could be addressed in the this step. TPA provides four operations for privacy enhancement: merging, noise injection, fake data injection, and removing. Operations other than merging require a selection of records. As shown in Fig. 8(a) (b), user can select records by ctrl+clicking equivalent classes or records.

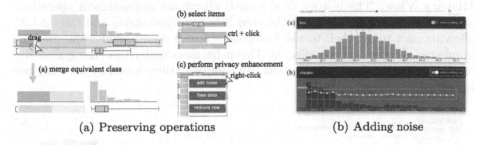

(a) Preserving operations   (b) Adding noise

Fig. 8. Preserving operations: (a) Merging operation. (b) Select records. (c) Open operations menu. **Adding noise**: A visual design for adding noise.

Merging. Merging is the primary preserving operation, which prevents an attacker from identifying items by making the value fuzzy. Two equivalent classes can be merged when all prior attributes of them have same values (i.e., the two nodes in the operation tree have the same parent node). As shown in Fig. 8(a), dragging one folded class onto another to merge them. The value of these two classes will be updated from a concrete value to an uncertain value ($\mathbf{A|B}$). Besides, the two aggregations that are merged will exist as a new class in the operation tree, so user can continue to merge it with other classes which have the same parent.

Adding Noise. The noise operation applies to numeric attributes. By clicking the 'Add noise' of the menu, a new view for noise operation is shown in Fig. 8(b). The view shows the histogram for all numeric attributes, and the number of bars in the histogram determines the granularity of bins, which can be set by tweaking the slider above. The noise operation adds Laplace noise to the data based on differential privacy. One can click the switch in the upper right corner to set the noise parameter, and drag the white dot in Fig. 8(a) (b) to set λ of Laplace for each bin that how much noise to add. After parameters are set, view will prompt some red lines which denote the fluctuations of each bin after adding noise.

Adding Fake Data. The fake operation uses CTGAN [36] to generate synthetic records and adds these records into sheet to confuse attackers. After clicking 'Generate fake data' in the menu, TPA will use the selected records as training inputs to generate synthetic records. Synthetic data is not always effective in preventing leakages, but it provides a method that does not require other prior knowledge. Since the synthetic data have similar distribution as the training inputs, the utility loss can be controlled to some extent.

Removing Records. Sometimes, users want to remove records directly (e.g., outlier data). The removing operation can be applied to remove the selected records from the sheet.

History View. The history view records all privacy enhancement operations applied. As shown in Fig. 9(a), the view lists historical states and their detail, allowing user to go back to the historical state. It also provides the user the number of records that are affected. This helps users understand the granularity of each operation. In addition, users can compare utility losses by selecting two historical states.

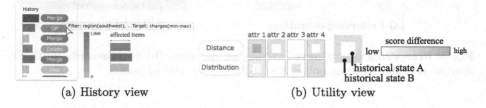

(a) History view   (b) Utility view

Fig. 9. History view: The history view records the historical states. **Utility view**: Comparison of two historical states, indicating the difference in utility loss.

Utility Analysis. For any preserving operation, whether it is modifying the original value or adding/removing records, will result in a loss of utility. Thus, user wants to see how utility changes with each operation (**R4**). TPA uses the measure introduced in Sect. 5.2 to estimate the utility loss by calculating the distance and distribution. To compare utility changes in each operation, we propose the utility comparison view (Fig. 9(b)). Users can select two historical states at history view to compare. When we select a historical state, TPA will compute the result from applying the first operation to the operation selected, and then calculates the difference in utility between selected state and the original sheet.

To compare two different states, we utilize a **superimposed matrix** to visualize the changes in two historical states. The rows represent algorithms to be compared and the columns represent attributes. Each cell is divided into an outer region and an inner region, with the background color saturation representing the difference of the utility in two different state. The higher the saturation, the more the differs from the original data in this attribute (high utility loss). The view is designed to help users understand changes in utility.

5.4 Exporting

The analysis and preserving loop stops if data holder considers the privacy and utility situation are satisfactory. The corresponding sheet is such downloaded and released.

6 Case Study

We conduct a case study with the prototype of TPA. This dataset comes from the CDC (Centers for Disease Control and Prevention) [22], which collects data on the health of U.S. residents. Each record has 300 attributes, including various indicators of the body. According to a CDC report, heart disease is the leading cause of death in the United States. Considering indicators related to heart disease, we narrowed it down to 12 attributes and randomly selected 20,000 records for this example.

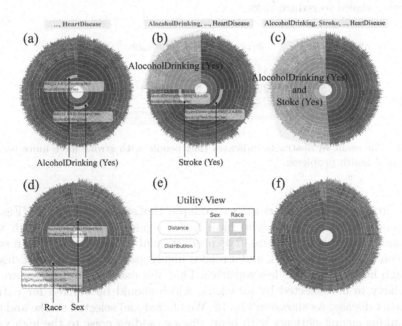

Fig. 10. For a hight-dimensional complex dataset, t-clossness is used to explore dimensional correlations and locate high risk aggregations. (a), (b) and (c) Iterate through the schema to find high correlated attributes. (d) and (e) Compare the utility loss after using the preserving operation on 'Race' and 'Sex'. (f) Result of applying preserving operations.

Patients certainly don't want to expose their disease. In this example, we focus on analyzing and dealing with privacy risks related to 'HeartDisease' attribute. From the perspective of publishers, we should first find out what other attributes are related to the disease. We set the 'HeartDisease' as a sensitive attribute and adjust it to the end of the order. As a result in Fig. 10 (a), the t-closeness view in risk-tree points out that the distribution of heart disease among drinkers was clearly different from the global distribution. It can be considered that drinking is highly correlated with heart disease. We move 'AlcoholDrinking' to the front of the order and look at the risk-tree again. The new view (b) shows that "Stroke" also has a significant effect on the distribution. Thus, we move 'Stroke' after 'AlcoholDrinking'.

We have moved high correlated attributes to the front of the order, and adjusted schema is easier to locate risks than a random schema (c). After switching to the K-anonymity view, we find some aggregations with salient high risk in branches of the 'Sex' and 'Race'. To reduce risk, we merge aggregations of 'Sex', which is shown in Fig. 10(d). Jump to the high risk aggregation and try to deal with two attributes separately by merging operation. Figure 10 (e) indicates the comparison of the feedback from utility view, we find that to merge 'Sex' has less utility loss than to merge 'Race'. Therefore, merging aggregations of 'Sex' is a better choice to reduce risks.

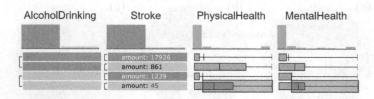

Fig. 11. The result of abstracts indicates that people with stroke have more physical and mental health problems.

To further explore the risks, we collapse the attribute 'Stroke' (Fig. 11). Abstracts show that people who have had a stroke tend to have high value of mental and physical problems. The proportion of people who had both stroke and alcohol drinking is small, and stroke is highly associated with heart disease. Although health scores are less sensitive. That also means health scores are also more likely to be collected by attackers, which should be blurred for patients with heart disease. As shown in Fig. 12, We filtered and selected stroke and alcohol drinking among patients with heart disease, adding noise to the high values of mental and physical problems.

For a dataset with 12 dimensions and 20,000 records, taking a long time to calculate once aggregations. Taking advantage of the data cube, even such a high-dimensional dataset can still interact in real-time and dynamically adjust the aggregated order.

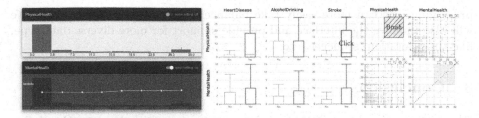

Fig. 12. Add noise to blur the health score and protect the privacy of people who smoke, stroke and have heart disease.

7   Qualitative Discussions

We conducted interview with four domain experts on the applicability of TPA in real-world scenarios. These users are experienced in data analysis and often work with tabular data. They commented positively on our work and indicated suggestions for improvement.

Effectiveness. Interviewees agreed that TPA was effective in data analysis, especially in aggregation abstract that help them to grasp the value distribution of attributes and the correlation between attributes in the dataset (**R2**). They favored the function that they could adjust the schema in real-time (**R1**), and also appreciated TPA's capability to efficiently handle big datasets. One of the users said that *it was difficult to effectively analyze the risks of data sets in the past when faced with high-dimensional data sets.* When used in conjunction with risk tree, dynamic adjustment order were considered to help perceive privacy risks intuitively (**R3**). In addition, TPA saved them a lot of time than other visualization tools, by providing more preserving operations and allowing them to control the granularity of them (**R4**).

Limitations. However, some users pointed out that the interaction design of the prototype was not good enough, even though we instructed users how to use TPA in prior. Further, some supposed that the utility view may be of limited use. While the utility view could remind them of the differences between the current state and the original one, they still don't understand how those differences mean. Some users also suggested providing a recommendation scheme function to help to carry out privacy enhancement operations. This indicates that, whereas TPA is designed to provide users with high flexibility, they can often get lost in the choices, thus providing some recommended actions shall be a good way to get started quickly.

Future Work. Considering that data will be shared to work for specific analysis tasks, we plan to extract patterns for those tasks (e.g., extreme values of samples, clustering, etc.). By indicating the pattern differences before and after privacy preserving, one can more easily take balance between privacy and utility. We will also improve the interface and provide support for more diverse data type, like time, location, sequence, etc.

8   Conclusion

We propose a visual tool, TPA, for privacy protection of tabular data. Our design helps users analyze multidimensional data relationships and identify potential privacy issues. In addition, we provide users with some preserving operations to reduce privacy risks and a utility view is designed to help control the utility loss of operations. By introducing data cube, we have implemented a system that support user exploring any aggregated order in real-time, allowing users to analyze privacy risks from different perspectives and flexibly control the granularity of preserving operations. We use a real dataset to demonstrate that TPA can handle all kinds of data, including big datasets and high dimensional datasets.

Acknowledgment. This work is supported by National Natural Science Foundation of China (62172155, 62072465).

References

1. Abay, N.C., Zhou, Y., Kantarcioglu, M., Thuraisingham, B., Sweeney, L.: Privacy preserving synthetic data release using deep learning. In: Berlingerio, M., Bonchi, F., Gärtner, T., Hurley, N., Ifrim, G. (eds.) Machine Learning and Knowledge Discovery in Databases, pp. 510–526. Springer International Publishing, Cham (2019)
2. Abowd, J.M., Vilhuber, L.: How protective are synthetic data? In: Domingo-Ferrer, J., Saygın, Y. (eds.) Privacy in Statistical Databases, pp. 239–246. Springer, Berlin Heidelberg, Berlin, Heidelberg (2008)
3. Bhattacharjee, K., Chen, M., Dasgupta, A.: Privacy-preserving data visualization: reflections on the state of the art and research opportunities. In: Computer Graphics Forum. vol. 39, pp. 675–692. Wiley Online Library (2020)
4. Bolón-Canedo, V., Sánchez-Maroño, N., Alonso-Betanzos, A.: A review of feature selection methods on synthetic data. Knowl. Inf. Syst. **34**(3), 483–519 (2013)
5. Caraux, G., Pinloche, S.: Permutmatrix: a graphical environment to arrange gene expression profiles in optimal linear order. Bioinformatics **21**(7), 1280–1281 (2005)
6. Chou, J.K., Bryan, C., Ma, K.L.: Privacy preserving visualization for social network data with ontology information. In: 2017 IEEE Pacific Visualization Symposium (PacificVis), pp. 11–20. IEEE (2017)
7. Chou, J.K., Wang, Y., Ma, K.L.: Privacy preserving visualization: a study on event sequence data. In: Computer Graphics Forum. vol. 38, pp. 340–355. Wiley Online Library (2019)
8. Dasgupta, A., Kosara, R., Chen, M.: Guess me if you can: A visual uncertainty model for transparent evaluation of disclosure risks in privacy-preserving data visualization. In: 2019 IEEE Symposium on Visualization for Cyber Security (VizSec), pp. 1–10. IEEE (2019)

9. Dwork, C.: Differential privacy: a survey of results. In: Agrawal, M., Du, D., Duan, Z., Li, A. (eds.) Theory and Applications of Models of Computation, pp. 1–19. Springer, Berlin Heidelberg, Berlin, Heidelberg (2008)

10. Elliot, M., Hundepool, A., Nordholt, E.S., Tambay, J.L., Wende, T.: Glossary on statistical disclosure control. In: Monograph on Official Statistics, pp. 381–392. Eurostat (2006)

11. Fernandez, N.F., et al.: Clustergrammer, a web-based heatmap visualization and analysis tool for high-dimensional biological data. Scientific data 4(1), 1–12 (2017)

12. Furmanova, K., et al.: Taggle: combining overview and details in tabular data visualizations. Inf. Vis. 19(2), 114–136 (2020)

13. Furmanova, K., et al.: Taggle: Scaling table visualization through aggregation. In: Poster@ IEEE Conference on Information Visualization (InfoVis' 17), p. 139 (2017)

14. Gray, J., et al.: Data cube: a relational aggregation operator generalizing group-by, cross-tab, and sub-totals. Data Min. Knowl. Disc. 1(1), 29–53 (1997)

15. LeFevre, K., DeWitt, D.J., Ramakrishnan, R.: Mondrian multidimensional k-anonymity. In: 22nd International Conference on Data Engineering (ICDE'06), pp. 25–25. IEEE (2006)

16. Li, B., Erdin, E., Gunes, M.H., Bebis, G., Shipley, T.: An overview of anonymity technology usage. Comput. Commun. 36(12), 1269–1283 (2013)

17. Li, N., Li, T., Venkatasubramanian, S.: t-closeness: Privacy beyond k-anonymity and l-diversity. In: 2007 IEEE 23rd International Conference on Data Engineering, pp. 106–115. IEEE (2007)

18. Li, T., Li, N.: On the tradeoff between privacy and utility in data publishing. In: Proceedings of the 15th ACM SIGKDD International Conference on Knowledge Discovery and Data Mining, pp. 517–526 (2009)

19. Machanavajjhala, A., Kifer, D., Gehrke, J., Venkitasubramaniam, M.: l-diversity: Privacy beyond k-anonymity. In: ACM Transactions on Knowledge Discovery from Data (TKDD) 1(1), 3-es (2007)

20. Massey, F.J., Jr.: The kolmogorov-smirnov test for goodness of fit. J. Am. Stat. Assoc. 46(253), 68–78 (1951)

21. de Montjoye, Y.A., Hidalgo, C.A., Verleysen, M., Blondel, V.D.: Unique in the crowd: the privacy bounds of human mobility. Sci. Rep. 3(1), 1376 (2013)

22. Pytlak, K.: Personal key indicators of heart disease. https://www.kaggle.com/datasets/kamilpytlak/personal-key-indicators-of-heart-disease/metadata (2022)

23. Rajabiyazdi, F., Perin, C., Oehlberg, L., Carpendale, S.: Exploring the design of patient-generated data visualizations. In: Proceedings of Graphics Interface 2020, pp. 362–373. GI 2020 (2020)

24. Rao, R., Card, S.K.: The table lens: merging graphical and symbolic representations in an interactive focus+ context visualization for tabular information. In: Proceedings of the SIGCHI conference on Human factors in computing systems, pp. 318–322 (1994)

25. Rubner, Y., Tomasi, C., Guibas, L.J.: The earth mover's distance as a metric for image retrieval. Int. J. Comput. Vision 40(2), 99–121 (2000)

26. Seo, J., Shneiderman, B.: Interactively exploring hierarchical clustering results [gene identification]. Computer 35(7), 80–86 (2002)

27. Stadler, T., Oprisanu, B., Troncoso, C.: Synthetic data-anonymisation groundhog day. arXiv preprint arXiv:2011.07018 (2021)

28. Sweeney, L.: Simple demographics often identify people uniquely (2000)

29. Sweeney, L.: Achieving k-anonymity privacy protection using generalization and suppression. Internat. J. Uncertain. Fuzziness Knowl.-Based Syst. 10(05), 571–588 (2002)

30. Sweeney, L.: k-anonymity: a model for protecting privacy. Internat. J. Uncertain. Fuzziness Knowl.-Based Syst. **10**(05), 557–570 (2002)
31. Thaker, P., Budiu, M., Gopalan, P., Wieder, U., Zaharia, M.: Overlook: Differentially private exploratory visualization for big data. arXiv preprint arXiv:2006.12018 (2020)
32. Wang, X., et al.: Graphprotector: a visual interface for employing and assessing multiple privacy preserving graph algorithms. IEEE Trans. Visual Comput. Graph. **25**(1), 193–203 (2018)
33. Wang, X., et al.: A utility-aware visual approach for anonymizing multi-attribute tabular data. IEEE Trans. Visual Comput. Graph. **24**(1), 351–360 (2017)
34. Wu, F.T.: Defining privacy and utility in data sets. U. Colo. L. Rev. **84**, 1117 (2013)
35. Xiao, F., et al.: An information-aware visualization for privacy-preserving accelerometer data sharing. HCIS **8**(1), 1–28 (2018). https://doi.org/10.1186/s13673-018-0137-6
36. Xu, L., Skoularidou, M., Cuesta-Infante, A., Veeramachaneni, K.: Modeling tabular data using conditional gan. In: Advances in Neural Information Processing Systems, vol. 32 (2019)
37. Zhang, D., Sarvghad, A., Miklau, G.: Investigating visual analysis of differentially private data. IEEE Trans. Visual Comput. Graph. **27**(2), 1786–1796 (2020)

Prevention of GAN-Based Privacy Inferring Attacks Towards Federated Learning

Hongbo Cao[1], Yongsheng Zhu[2,3], Yuange Ren[1], Bin Wang[4], Mingqing Hu[5], Wanqi Wang[3], and Wei Wang[1(✉)]

[1] Beijing Key Laboratory of Security and Privacy in Intelligent Transportation, Beijing Jiaotong University, No.3 Shangyuancun, Beijing 100044, China
{hongbo.cao,19125226,wangwei1}@bjtu.edu.cn
[2] School of electronic information engineering, Beijing Jiaotong University, No.3 Shangyuancun, Beijing 100044, China
[3] Institute of Computing Technologies, China Academy of Railway Sciences Corporation Limited, Beijing 100081, China
{zhuys,wangwq}@rails.cn
[4] Zhejiang Key Laboratory of Multi-dimensional Perception Technology, Application and Cybersecurity, Hangzhou 310053, China
bin_wang@zju.edu.cn
[5] iFLYTEK Co., Ltd,Hefei, China
mqhu3@iflytek.com

Abstract. With the increasing amount of data, data privacy has drawn great concern in machine learning among the public. Federated Learning, which is a new kind of distributed learning framework, enables data providers to train models locally to protect privacy. It solves the problem of privacy leakage of data by enabling multiple parties, each with their training dataset, to share the model instead of exchanging private data with the server side. However, there are still threats of data privacy leakage in federated learning. In this work, we are motivated to prevent GAN-based privacy inferring attacks in federated learning. For the GAN-based privacy inferring attacks, inspired by the idea of gradient compression, we propose a defense method called Federated Learning Parameter Compression (FLPC) which can reduce the sharing of information for privacy protection. It prevents attackers from recovering the privacy information of victims while maintaining the accuracy of the global model. Comprehensive experimental results demonstrated that our method is effective in the prevention of GAN-based privacy inferring attacks.

Keywords: Federated learning · Inferring attacks · Generative adversarial network · Intrusion detect · Parameter compress

1 Introduction

Deep learning, which is the most popular machine learning method driven by big data, has been widely used in various domain like image recognition [1],

© ICST Institute for Computer Sciences, Social Informatics and Telecommunications Engineering 2022
Published by Springer Nature Switzerland AG 2022. All Rights Reserved
H. Gao et al. (Eds.): CollaborateCom 2022, LNICST 461, pp. 39–54, 2022.
https://doi.org/10.1007/978-3-031-24386-8_3

social networks [2], speech technology [3], natural language process [4] and face detection [5]. However, the centralized data storage currently has many problems. First, if all training data is stored and trained in a centralized manner, the transmission of data requires a very large communication cost. Second, training learning algorithms on large dataset requires higher performance computing equipment. Third, many scenarios cannot be relied on because of the absence of trust boundaries. If personal information is submitted to the outside, users will face privacy leakage risks because they cannot control how their data will be used after sharing, which will directly disclose important personal privacy information and may cause serious privacy problems [6]. Therefore, it is important to run a machine learning in a way that protects sensitive data from privacy leakage.

Federated learning (FL) [7,8] is a novel machine learning paradigm to solve this problem. In federated learning, the data owner must participate in the whole learning process instead of relying on a trusted third party. Federated learning was first proposed by Google [7]. It is a server-client architecture consisting of a parameter server and multiple clients. The server and the client carry out multiple rounds of iterative communication and collaborate to train a global model. Private data is stored in a locally isolated device and will not be shared with other parties during the training process, which not only guarantees users' privacy and data security but also solves the problem of data fragmentation and isolation.

Although FL shows superb performance in privacy-preserving and breaks data silos effectively, it's still surprisingly susceptible to GAN-based data reconstruction attacks [9], which is a kind of privacy inference attack [10] in the training phase of FL.

Existing relatd work show that differential privacy (DP) [11] is regarded as one of the strongest defense methods against these attacks. The core idea of DP is introducing random noise into the privacy information, but DP often adds so sufficient noise that the accuracy of the global model is reduced notably.

To address this problem, we focus on the inference attacks toward Non-i.i.d federated learning. In addition, we conduct various experiments to evaluate the privacy leakage that the adversary can get from the parameter of the global model during the training phase and understand the relationship between the reconstruction sample and global model information leakage. Thus, we find parameter compression is an effective defense method against GAN-based reconstruction attacks toward federated learning.

Our contributions can be summarized as the follows:

- We reveal that the gan-based privacy inferring attacks toward federated learning is defensible.
- We propose an efficient defense method to protect sensitive data against inferring attacks toward federated learning.
- We compare our method with the current defense method that adds noise to the parameter and the experiment result shows our method is better.

2   Related Work

2.1   Overview of Federated Learning

It has been well recognized that FL is a peculiar form of collaborative machine learning technique. FL allows the participants to train their model without exchanging data to a centralized server, which combats the problems of privacy concerned about central machine learning and communication costs.

A traditional FL system is built by a central server to aggregate and exchange parameters and gradients. The end-user devices train their local model and exchange their parameter or gradient periodically without uploading data to ensure that there is no privacy leakage concern.

Generally, the whole process of FL can be expressed as follows.

(1) Client Initialization: The participants download the parameter from the central server to initialize their local global.
(2) Local training: Every client uses the private data to train the model and upload parameters to the central server at last.
(3) Parameter Aggregation: The central server gathers the uploaded parameter from every participant and generates a new global model by robust aggregation and SGD.
(4) Broadcast model: The central parameter server broadcasts the global model to all the participants.

Categorization of Federated Learning. Based on the characteristics of the data distribution [10], federated learning can be classified into three general types.

HFL, which is also called homogeneous federated learning, usually occurs in the situation where the training data of the clients have overlapping identical feature space but have disparate sample space. Most research, which focuses on FL, assumes that the model is trained in HFL.

VFL, which is also called heterogeneous federated learning, is suitable for the situation where the participants have the Non-i.i.d datasets [12]. Meanwhile, sample space is shared between participants who have different label spaces or feature spaces.

FTL [13] is suitable for situations similar to that of traditional transfer learning [14], which aims to leverage knowledge from previously available source tasks to solve new target tasks.

Threats in Federated Learning. FL is vulnerable to adversarial attacks such as unauthorized data-stealing or debilitating global model [15]. The adversary mainly focuses on both the privacy attacks and robustness attacks towards centralized federated learning.

In privacy attacks that often occur in the training phase, the target of the adversary can be the sample reconstruction. This is an inferring attack that aims to reconstruct the training sample and/or associated labels used by other FL participants. The privacy leakage of the sample reconstruction attacks may come from model gradients [16], loss function [17] or model parameters [9]. Furthermore, the sample reconstruction attacks are considered not only on the client-side but on the server-side [18]. Besides, Fu et al. [19] proposed a label inference attack which is in a special and interesting Non-i.i.d. federated learning setting. Existing relatd work regard differential privacy as an efficient method to defend the privacy inference attack [20]. In the local differential privacy, the FL clients add Gaussian noise to the local gradients or parameters.

Another main attack toward federated learning is the robustness attack which aims to corrupt the model. Due to the characteristic of the inaccessibility of local training data in a typical FL system, poisoning attacks are easy to implement which causes FL to be even more vulnerable to poisoning attacks than classic centralized machine learning [21]. The goal of the adversary is to diminish the performance and the convergence of the global model. These misclassifications may cause serious security problems.

Besides, the backdoor attack [22] is known for its higher impact of its capabilities to set the trigger. It's an effective targeted method to attack FL system. Various robust aggregation algorithms are proposed to defend against poisoning attacks towards FL, such as Krum [23], Bulyan [24], Median [25] and Fang [26].

There also exist related work on the prevention of Android malware [27–33], on the detection of software vulnerabilities [34], on the detection of network anomalies [35], or on enhancing the privacy in other scenarios like communications of smart vehicles [36].

2.2   Generative Adversarial Networks

In the field of deep learning, generative adversarial networks (GANs) [37] have recently been proposed, and they are still in a highly developed and researched stage [38]. Various GANs has been proposed. They can be used to generate deepfake face [39], generate image by text [40]. The goal of GAN is not to classify images into different categories, but to generate samples that are similar to the samples in the training dataset and have the same distribution without touching the original samples.

The training of GAN network is a typical game confrontation process of finding the maximum and minimum values. The game between discriminator and generator is shown as in formula 1.

$$\min_{G} \max_{D} V(G, D) = E_{x \sim p_{data}(x)} log[D(x)]$$
$$+ E_{z \sim p_z(z)} log[1 - D(x)] \tag{1}$$

When the discriminator D cannot distinguish between the samples in the original data and the samples generated by the generator G, the training process ends.

Hitaj et al. [9] first proposed a GAN-based reconstruction attack. In the attack, malicious participants in the system steal the private data information of other honest participants. The attacker only needs to train a GAN locally to simulate the victim's training samples and then injects fake training samples into the system over and over again. Without anyone in the system noticing,

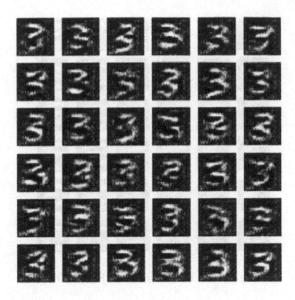

Fig. 1. The image recovered by the attacker

the attacker can trick the victim into releasing more information about their training data, and eventually recover the victim's sample data.

For the GAN-based privacy inferring attacks, Yan et al. [41] proposed to detect the GAN-based privacy inferring attacks by setting hidden points on the parameter server side, and adjusting the parameters of the model to make the training model GAN invalid. Since GAN must alternately optimize G and D to achieve the optimal synchronization, G may collapse if the optimal balance between G and D is not reached. Since the learning rate has a great influence on the training process, this method disrupts the training process of GAN and makes it invalid by changing the learning rate.

The GAN-based privacy inferring attacks aim to reconstruct recognizable data images from the victim's personal data information. The GAN effectively learns the distribution of training data. In order to prevent such attacks, Luo et al. [42] proposed an Anti-GAN framework to prevent attackers from learning the true distribution of victim data by adding fake images into the source real image. The victim first inputs the personal training data into the GAN generator, and then inputs the generated fake images into the global model for training of federated learning. Besides, the author designed a new loss function so that the images generated by the victim's GAN not only have classification features similar to the original training data, but also have indistinguishable visual features to prevent privacy inferring attacks.

Fig. 2. Defense result when R% = 90%

2.3   Compression

Distributed Stochastic Gradient Descent algorithm has been widely used in the training of large-scale deep learning models, and the communication cost between working nodes has become a new system bottleneck.

Gradient compression is a solution that improves communication efficiency by compressing the gradient of transmission. In general, the gradient change of the model parameters in each iteration is relatively small, most of the parameters are still the same as before. So there will be a lot of redundant parameters during the transmission process, but the attacker can use the redundancy parameters updates to reconstruct the sample. Gradient compression uses this feature to compress the gradient generated in each iteration. This method reduces the amount of gradient in communication and reduces the burden on bandwidth by sending a sparse vector of a subset of important values in the gradient.

There are many optimization algorithms for Gradient Compression. For example, Lin et al. [43] proposed the Deep Gradient Compression algorithm to preserve the model accuracy in the gradient compression process. In order to reduce the gradient sparsification time, Shi et al. [44] proposed an optimal algorithm to find the trade-off between communication cost and sparsification time cost. There are also optimization algorithms of adaptive compression ratios to increase the flexibility of compression schemes [45], etc.

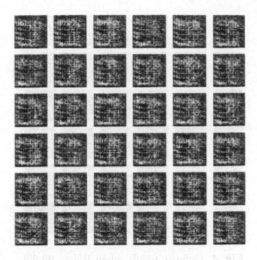

Fig. 3. Defense result when R% = 99%

3   Defense Against GAN-Based Privacy Inferring Attacks

3.1   Threat Model of GAN-Based Privacy Inferring Attacks

In federated learning, all participants have their own data, and they train a global model with a common learning goal, which means that each participant knows the data labels of the other participants. The central server is authoritative and trustworthy, it cannot be controlled by any attacker.

The attacker pretends to be an honest participant in the federated learning system, but tries to extract information about local data owned by other participants. The attacker builds a GAN model locally. At the same time, the attacker follows a protocol that is agreed upon by all participants. He uploads and downloads the correct number of gradients or parameters according to the agreement. The attacker influences the learning process without being noticed by other participants. He tricks the victim into revealing more information about his local data.

Adversary A participates in the collaborative deep learning protocol. All such participants agree in advance on a common learning objective, which means that they agree on the type of neural network architecture and labels on which the training would take place. Let V be another participant (the victim) that declares labels [a,b]. The adversary A declares labels [b,c]. Thus, while b is in common, A has no information about class a. The goal of the adversary is to infer as much useful information as possible about class a [42].

The attack begins when the test accuracy of both the global model and the local model of the server is greater than a threshold. The attack process is as follows. First, V trains the local model and uploads the model parameters to the central server. Second, A downloads the parameters and updates his

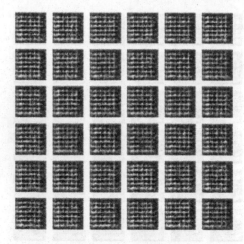

Fig. 4. Defense result when R% = 99.9%

discriminator of GAN accordingly. A then generates samples of class a from GAN and marks it as class c. A trains his local model with these fake samples and uploads these parameters to the global model on the server side. Then A tricks victim V to provide more information about class a. Finally, A can reconstruct images of class a that are very similar to V's own original images.

Algorithm 1. Parameter Compression on client C

Require: *parameters* $w = \{w[0], w[1], ..., w[n]\}$
1: **for** $j = 0$ to n **do**
2:    $diff \Leftarrow w_t[j] - w_{t-1}[j]$
3:    $count \Leftarrow |diff|$
4:    $k \Leftarrow count \cdot (1 - R\%)$
5:    $w_{compressed}[j] \leftarrow top_k(abs(diff)) + w_{t-1}[j]$
6: **end for**
7: C *submit* $w_{compressed}$ *to server*

3.2 Parameter Compression Method

There is a gradient compression method in distributed learning, which reduces the communication overhead by compressing the gradient in each communication round. Gradient sparsification is a kind of gradient compression. The sparsification algorithm decides to send a small part of the gradient to participate in the parameter update, and most of the gradients with small changes are temporarily updated. The widely used gradient sparsification method is to select the gradient according to the compression rate $R\%$. In this method, the gradient with a

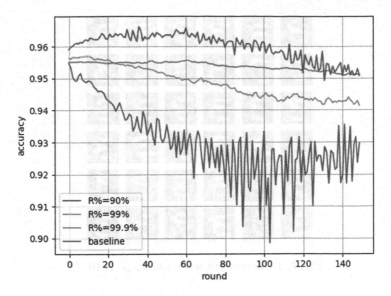

Fig. 5. Test accuracy of global model

maximum change of 1-$R\%$ was finally chosen. Usually, the compression ratio is 90% , 99% and 99.9%.

Parameter Compression (PC) method takes advantage of the idea of gradient compression. Since the parameters of the model contain the key information about the training data, compressing the parameters is equivalent to truncating some parameters, which reduces the data information leaked to the attacker and achieves the purpose of privacy protection.

The algorithm of parameter compression of a single client model is presented in Algorithm 1. In the tth round, for the jth parameter component, it calculates the difference $diff$ between round t and the previous round t-1. Then the k largest parameters are selected from the absolute value of $diff$. Finally, it can obtain the compression parameters of the jth parameter component by adding these k parameters and the parameter of the round t-1. When all the parameter components are compressed, the final compressed parameters of the model can be obtained. Define R% as the compression ratio. If R% is 90%, it means that only the first 10% (1-R%) of the absolute value of the difference e will be updated.

The parameter compression scheme is applied to the GAN-based privacy inferring attacks. Before uploading the local model parameters, each client compresses the parameters and uploads them to the server. The server keeps its aggregation algorithm unchanged, and still uses the federated average algorithm (FedAvg) to aggregate all parameters.

Fig. 6. Defense result when $noise_{scale}$ is 10^{-4}

3.3 Experiments

Datasets and CNN Architectures MNIST Dataset: It consists of handwritten gray-scale images of digits ranging from 0 to 9. Each image is 28 × 28 pixels. The dataset consists of 60,000 training data samples and 10,000 testing data samples [46]. This experiment used a convolutional neural network (CNN) based architecture on the MNIST dataset. The layers of the networks are sequentially attached to one another based on the keras.Sequential() container so that layers are in a feed-forward fully connected manner. The neural networks are trained by Tensorflow.

Results. The defense of GAN-based privacy inferring attacks takes the attack experiment of reconstructing the digital image of "3" as an example. Figure 1 shows the victim's data finally reconstructed by the attacker. It can be seen that the attacker recovers a very clear image.

The results of the parameter compression scheme are as follows. When R% = 90%, the image finally recovered by the attacker is shown in Fig. 2. As can be seen, the image is much more blurred than the original image recovered by the attacker, but the number 3 in the image is still recognizable. Thus, this compression ratio isn't high enough to prevent information leakage.

When R% = 99%, the attacker eventually recovers an image like Fig. 3. The image is too fuzzy for the number to be recognized, but there are some outlines, which means some valid information is still leaked.

When R% = 99.9%, the image recovered by the attacker is shown in Fig. 4. It can be seen that no valid data information can be seen at all. Therefore, when compression rate is 99.9%, the privacy leakage can be completely prevented.

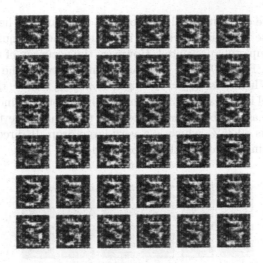

Fig. 7. Defense result when $noise_{scale}$ is 10^{-3}

Global Model Accuracy. In order to test whether the accuracy of the global model is influenced after the parameters of the client are compressed, the accuracy of the global model on the test dataset is calculated during each round of federated learning. Figure 5 shows the accuracy change of the global model on the test dataset: the final accuracy of the global model with different compression rates is above 94%. Compared with the baseline of the original attack without compression, it has no significant effect on the accuracy of the global model.

3.4 Compare with Gaussian Noise

Local differential privacy is often used to defend against this attack, but it may negatively impact the model performance if the strength of the noise is not appropriate.

Experiments. Adding noise is a common way to disturb the information. When all clients upload updated parameters, they first add Gaussian noise to the updated parameters to protect their data information from leaking. In the experiments, the mean of Gaussian noise is set to 0, and the standard deviation of different noise is marked as $noise_{scale}$. And $noise_{scale}$'s value is set as 10^{-4}, 10^{-3}, 10^{-2}.

When $noise_{scale} = 10^{-4}$, the noise added is the smallest. It can be seen that it cannot prevent the leakage of data information, as shown in Fig. 6. When $noise_{scale} = 10^{-3}$, the final image recovered by the attacker is shown in Fig. 7. Although the image is more noisy than when $noise_{scale} = 10^{-4}$, there are very few outlines of the number three. When $noise_{scale} = 10^{-2}$, the image finally recovered by the attacker is shown in Fig. 8. At this time, the content of the image is completely invisible. The attacker can not obtain any valuable information about the digital image 3, which indicates that the attack failed.

From the above experiments, it can be seen that only in the situation where the Gaussian noise standard deviation is greater than or equal to 10^{-2}, data leakage can be completely prevented. However, the accuracy of the global model is greatly affected. Figure 9 is the accuracy change curve of the global model on the test dataset. When $noise_{scale} = 10^{-3}$ and $noise_{scale} = 10^{-4}$, the final accuracy of the global model is similar to that of the baseline, both around 95%. But when $noise_{scale} = 10^{-2}$, as the blue curve shown in the figure, the final accuracy of the global model is 80.35%, which is a very large drop. It directly destroys the training and learning process of the global model.

Fig. 8. Defense result when $noise_{scale}$ is 10^{-2}

Analysis of Privacy Protection. From the above experiments, it can be seen that although noise can be added to the parameters when the noise is small, it is not enough to cover up the information of the real samples. When the noise is large, it directly decreases the accuracy of the global model. Therefore, adding noise to the parameters is not a desirable defense method. In the parameter compression defense method, not only the private information is protected from leaking, but no great influence on the accuracy of the global model is exerted when the compression rate is 99.9%. Therefore, parameter compression is a desirable and efficient defense method. In GAN-based privacy inferring attacks, the premise on which the attacker's GAN network takes effect is that the model at the server and both local models have reached an accuracy that is higher than a certain threshold [9]. When the parameters are compressed, the accuracy of the model has reached a relatively high level and the accuracy of the model cannot be greatly affected. In the Gaussian noise defense method, adding larger noise is equivalent to directly making larger changes to the model parameters, which has a great impact on the accuracy of the global model. Therefore, parameter

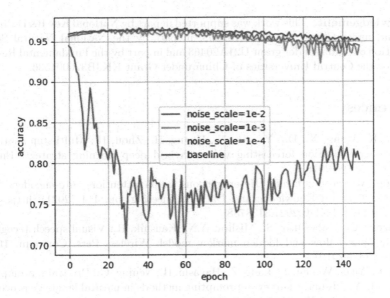

Fig. 9. Test accuracy of global model

compression is an efficient defense method that prevents GAN-based privacy inferring attacks.

4   Conclusion

For the GAN-based privacy inferring attacks, experimental results demonstrate that our proposed parameter compression method, which uploads part of the parameters with the largest changes in each round, is effective in protecting data privacy.

In this way, the sharing of information is reduced to prevent private information leakage. By adopting Gaussian noise defense method, although privacy can be protected when the noise is large enough, the accuracy of the global model is reduced. Therefore, parameter compression is a better defense method, as it guarantees the accuracy of the model to a great extent by sharing only the important parameter updates.

The core idea of the parameter compression defense method proposed in this paper is gradient compression which was originally proposed to reduce communication costs by reducing the gradient amount to compress the gradient. The Parameter compression method also reduces the exposure of data information by reducing the shared parameters so as to achieve the role of defending against GAN privacy inference attack. Therefore, studying whether the idea of gradient compression can prevent other privacy leakage problems in federated learning, and how to optimize this compression algorithm to protect information can be our future work.

Acknowledgement. This work was supported in part by National Key R&D Program of China, under Grant 2020YFB2103802, in part by the National Natural Science Foundation of China, under grant U21A20463 and in part by the Fundamental Research Funds for the Central Universities of China under Grant KKJB320001536.

References

1. Yan, K., Wang, X., Du, Y., Jin, N., Huang, H., Zhou, H.: Multi-step short-term power consumption forecasting with a hybrid deep learning strategy. Energies **11**(11), 3089 (2018)
2. Wang, W., et al.: Hgate: Heterogeneous graph attention auto-encoders. IEEE Transactions on Knowledge and Data Engineering, pp. 1–1 (2021). https://doi.org/10.1109/TKDE.2021.3138788
3. Sharma, U., Maheshkar, S., Mishra, A.N., Kaushik, R.: Visual speech recognition using optical flow and hidden markov model. Wireless Pers. Commun. **106**(4), 2129–2147 (2019)
4. Liu, P., Yuan, W., Fu, J., Jiang, Z., Hayashi, H., Neubig, G.: Pre-train, prompt, and predict: A systematic survey of prompting methods in natural language processing. arXiv preprint arXiv:2107.13586 (2021)
5. Ranjan, R., Bansal, A., Zheng, J., Xu, H., Gleason, J., Lu, B., Nanduri, A., Chen, J.C., Castillo, C.D., Chellappa, R.: A fast and accurate system for face detection, identification, and verification. IEEE Trans. Biomet., Behav. Identity Sci. **1**(2), 82–96 (2019)
6. Shokri, R., Shmatikov, V.: Privacy-preserving deep learning. In: Proceedings of the 22nd ACM SIGSAC conference on computer and communications security, pp. 1310–1321 (2015)
7. McMahan, B., Moore, E., Ramage, D., Hampson, S., y Arcas, B.A.: Communication-efficient learning of deep networks from decentralized data. In: Artificial intelligence and statistics, pp. 1273–1282. PMLR (2017)
8. Liu, M., Ho, S., Wang, M., Gao, L., Jin, Y., Zhang, H.: Federated learning meets natural language processing: A survey. arXiv preprint arXiv:2107.12603 (2021)
9. Hitaj, B., Ateniese, G., Perez-Cruz, F.: Deep models under the gan: information leakage from collaborative deep learning. In: Proceedings of the 2017 ACM SIGSAC Conference on Computer and Communications Security, pp. 603–618 (2017)
10. Lyu, L., Yu, H., Ma, X., Sun, L., Zhao, J., Yang, Q., Yu, P.S.: Privacy and robustness in federated learning: Attacks and defenses. arXiv preprint arXiv:2012.06337 (2020)
11. Naseri, M., Hayes, J., De Cristofaro, E.: Toward robustness and privacy in federated learning: Experimenting with local and central differential privacy. arXiv e-prints pp. arXiv-2009 (2020)
12. Zhu, H., Xu, J., Liu, S., Jin, Y.: Federated learning on non-iid data: a survey. Neurocomputing **465**, 371–390 (2021)
13. Saha, S., Ahmad, T.: Federated transfer learning: concept and applications. Intelligenza Artificiale **15**(1), 35–44 (2021)
14. Maschler, B., Weyrich, M.: Deep transfer learning for industrial automation: a review and discussion of new techniques for data-driven machine learning. IEEE Ind. Electron. Mag. **15**(2), 65–75 (2021)
15. Liu, P., Xu, X., Wang, W.: Threats, attacks and defenses to federated learning: issues, taxonomy and perspectives. Cybersecurity **5**(1), 4 (2022)

16. Zhao, B., Mopuri, K.R., Bilen, H.: idlg: Improved deep leakage from gradients. arXiv preprint arXiv:2001.02610 (2020)

17. Sannai, A.: Reconstruction of training samples from loss functions. CoRR abs/1805.07337 (2018), http://arxiv.org/abs/1805.07337

18. Wang, Z., Song, M., Zhang, Z., Song, Y., Wang, Q., Qi, H.: Beyond inferring class representatives: User-level privacy leakage from federated learning. In: IEEE INFOCOM 2019-IEEE Conference on Computer Communications, pp. 2512–2520. IEEE (2019)

19. Fu, C., Zhang, X., Ji, S., Chen, J., Wu, J., Guo, S., Zhou, J., Liu, A.X., Wang, T.: Label inference attacks against vertical federated learning. In: 31st USENIX Security Symposium (USENIX Security 22), Boston, MA (2022)

20. Triastcyn, A., Faltings, B.: Federated learning with bayesian differential privacy. In: 2019 IEEE International Conference on Big Data (Big Data), pp. 2587–2596. IEEE (2019)

21. Shejwalkar, V., Houmansadr, A.: Manipulating the byzantine: Optimizing model poisoning attacks and defenses for federated learning. In: NDSS (2021)

22. Bagdasaryan, E., Veit, A., Hua, Y., Estrin, D., Shmatikov, V.: How to backdoor federated learning. In: International Conference on Artificial Intelligence and Statistics, pp. 2938–2948. PMLR (2020)

23. Blanchard, P., El Mhamdi, E.M., Guerraoui, R., Stainer, J.: Machine learning with adversaries: Byzantine tolerant gradient descent. In: Advances in Neural Information Processing Systems, vol. 30 (2017)

24. Guerraoui, R., Rouault, S., et al.: The hidden vulnerability of distributed learning in byzantium. In: International Conference on Machine Learning, pp. 3521–3530. PMLR (2018)

25. Yin, D., Chen, Y., Kannan, R., Bartlett, P.: Byzantine-robust distributed learning: Towards optimal statistical rates. In: International Conference on Machine Learning, pp. 5650–5659. PMLR (2018)

26. Fang, M., Cao, X., Jia, J., Gong, N.: Local model poisoning attacks to {Byzantine-Robust} federated learning. In: 29th USENIX Security Symposium (USENIX Security 20), pp. 1605–1622 (2020)

27. Wang, W., Wang, X., Feng, D., Liu, J., Han, Z., Zhang, X.: Exploring permission-induced risk in android applications for malicious application detection. IEEE Trans. Inf. Forensics Secur. 9(11), 1869–1882 (2014)

28. Wang, W., Zhao, M., Wang, J.: Effective android malware detection with a hybrid model based on deep autoencoder and convolutional neural network. J. Ambient Intell. Human. Comput. 10(8), 3035–3043 (2018)

29. Fan, M., Liu, J., Wang, W., Li, H., Tian, Z., Liu, T.: DAPASA: detecting android piggybacked apps through sensitive subgraph analysis. IEEE Trans. Inf. Forensics Secur. 12(8), 1772–1785 (2017)

30. Wang, W., Li, Y., Wang, X., Liu, J., Zhang, X.: Detecting android malicious apps and categorizing benign apps with ensemble of classifiers. Future Gener. Comput. Syst. 78, 987–994 (2018)

31. Su, D., Liu, J., Wang, W., Wang, X., Du, X., Guizani, M.: Discovering communities of malapps on android-based mobile cyber-physical systems. Ad Hoc Netw. 80, 104–115 (2018)

32. Wang, X., Wang, W., He, Y., Liu, J., Han, Z., Zhang, X.: Characterizing android apps' behavior for effective detection of malapps at large scale. Future Gener. Comput. Syst. 75, 30–45 (2017)

33. Liu, X., Liu, J., Zhu, S., Wang, W., Zhang, X.: Privacy risk analysis and mitigation of analytics libraries in the android ecosystem. IEEE Trans. Mob. Comput. **19**(5), 1184–1199 (2020)

34. Wang, W., Song, J., Xu, G., Li, Y., Wang, H., Su, C.: ContractWard: Automated vulnerability detection models for ethereum smart contracts. IEEE Trans. Netw. Sci. Eng. **8**(2), 1133–1144 (2021)

35. Wang, W., Shang, Y., He, Y., Li, Y., Liu, J.: Botmark: automated botnet detection with hybrid analysis of flow-based and graph-based traffic behaviors. Inf. Sci. **511**, 284–296 (2020)

36. Li, L., et al.: Creditcoin: a privacy-preserving blockchain-based incentive announcement network for communications of smart vehicles. IEEE Trans. Intell. Transp. Syst. **19**(7), 2204–2220 (2018)

37. Goodfellow, I., Pouget-Abadie, J., Mirza, M., Xu, B., Warde-Farley, D., Ozair, S., Courville, A., Bengio, Y.: Generative adversarial nets. In: Advances in Neural Information Processing Systems, vol. 27 (2014)

38. Hinz, T., Fisher, M., Wang, O., Wermter, S.: Improved techniques for training single-image gans. In: Proceedings of the IEEE/CVF Winter Conference on Applications of Computer Vision, pp. 1300–1309 (2021)

39. Karras, T., Laine, S., Aittala, M., Hellsten, J., Lehtinen, J., Aila, T.: Analyzing and improving the image quality of stylegan. In: Proceedings of the IEEE/CVF Conference on Computer Vision and Pattern Recognition, pp. 8110–8119 (2020)

40. Ding, M., et al.: Cogview: mastering text-to-image generation via transformers. Adv. Neural. Inf. Process. Syst. **34**, 19822–19835 (2021)

41. Yan, X., Cui, B., Xu, Y., Shi, P., Wang, Z.: A method of information protection for collaborative deep learning under gan model attack. In: IEEE/ACM Transactions on Computational Biology and Bioinformatics (2019)

42. Luo, X., Zhu, X.: Exploiting defenses against gan-based feature inference attacks in federated learning. arXiv preprint arXiv:2004.12571 (2020)

43. Lin, Y., Han, S., Mao, H., Wang, Y., Dally, W.J.: Deep gradient compression: Reducing the communication bandwidth for distributed training. arXiv preprint arXiv:1712.01887 (2017)

44. Shi, S., Wang, Q., Chu, X., Li, B., Qin, Y., Liu, R., Zhao, X.: Communication-efficient distributed deep learning with merged gradient sparsification on gpus. In: IEEE INFOCOM 2020-IEEE Conference on Computer Communications, pp. 406–415. IEEE (2020)

45. Chen, C.Y., Choi, J., Brand, D., Agrawal, A., Zhang, W., Gopalakrishnan, K.: Adacomp: Adaptive residual gradient compression for data-parallel distributed training. In: Proceedings of the AAAI Conference on Artificial Intelligence, vol. 32 (2018)

46. Deng, L.: The mnist database of handwritten digit images for machine learning research. IEEE Signal Process. Mag. **29**(6), 141–142 (2012)

ACS: An Efficient Messaging System with Strong Tracking-Resistance

Zhefeng Nan[1,2], Changbo Tian[1,2(✉)], Yafei Sang[1,2], and Guangze Zhao[3]

[1] Institute of Information Engineering, Chinese Academy of Sciences,
Beijing 100093, China
{nanzhefeng,sangyafei}@iie.ac.cn
[2] School of Cyber Security, University of Chinese Academy of Sciences,
Beijing 100049, China
tianchangbo@iie.ac.cn
[3] Chinese Asset Cybersecurity Technology CO., Ltd, Beijing 100041, China

Abstract. The increasingly rampant network monitoring and tracing bring a huge challenge on the privacy protection, because even if the message data is encrypted, the communication privacy is difficult to be hidden. Existing anonymous systems sacrifice anonymity for efficient communication, or vice versa. In this paper, we present *ACS*, an efficient messaging system which leverages a two-layer framework to provide tracking-resistance. The first layer is the *entry layer*, which consists of *entry servers* to relay messages. The second layer is the *exchange layer*, which consists of *exchange servers* to exchange messages. Users divide its message into different shares and send each share to exchange server via a randomly chosen entry server. Users only provide their pseudonyms to exchange servers for message exchange. Then, entry servers have no information about the message exchange, and exchange servers have no information about users' identities. The exchange servers also provide message storage service in case that the receiver of these messages are offline, in which way, the communication becomes more simple and flexible. The experimental results show that our proposed system guarantees the strong tracking-resistance and high communication efficiency.

Keywords: Anti-tracking network · Anonymous communication · Message segmentation · Offline messaging · Privacy protection · Cyber security

1 Introduction

The security of communication privacy attracts more and more attention due to the disclosure of extensive mass surveillance programs [1–4], especially, some network surveillance and censorhip programs are participated or dominated by

Supported by the National Key Research and Development Program of China under Grant No.2019YFB1005205.

H. Gao et al. (Eds.): CollaborateCom 2022, LNICST 461, pp. 55–74, 2022.
https://doi.org/10.1007/978-3-031-24386-8_4

the state. The protection of communication privacy and users' identities in the Internet has become an increasingly important security requirement.

To address this problem, anonymous network has been proposed as the countermeasure to fight against the network surveillance and censorship [5]. Tor, a practical manifestation of Onion-routing, has become the most popular anonymous network. Unfortunately, the Onion-routing based anonymous networks are susceptible to traffic analysis attack [6–8] by an adversary that can monitor or tamper with network traffic between nodes. Mix-net [9] based anonymous networks are message-oriented systems which confuse the network traffic through mix nodes to improve anonymity. Due to the high latency and computation overhead of mixing, they can hardly accommodate real-time and high bandwidth communication. DC-net [10,11] based anonymous networks allow multiple parties to implement a broadcast channel to prevent each party from distinguishing the message sender and receiver. However, they sacrifice the bandwidth for the anonymity.

With the development of network technologies, the techniques of network surveillance and censorship become more diverse and sophisticated. And the adversary may have a global view of network and continuously monitor the Internet backbone. Furthermore, the adversary may take the active attack to crack down the anonymous system, such as the DDoS attack or information tampering. So, A successful system needs to resist powerful active and passive attacks, and provide efficient and secure communication.

In this paper, we propose an anti-tracking messaging system called ACS. ACS system contains two kinds of servers: entry server and exchange server which construct the two-layer framework of ACS. The entry server is only used to relay the messages between the user and exchange layer. In this way, the entry server breaks the direct relationship between the user and exchange server. Hence, each user only needs to provide its pseudonym to exchange server for message exchange. The message exchange is implemented only according to the users' pseudonyms.

To avoid information leakage, each sender divides its message into different shares and sends each message share to one exchange server for message exchange. Only received all the message shares from the exchange servers, the receiver can reconstruct the original message. The entry server and exchange server can not get any valid information from each message share.

Each message share is delivered by a randomly chosen entry server to improve security and anti-tracking in network communication. The exchange server also stores the valid message shares if the receiver is offline. When the receivers access ACS system again, they can receive the message stored in the exchange servers. The offline messaging avoids the negotiation and confirmation between the communicating parties, which provides a more flexible transmission mechanism.

The contributions of this paper are outlined as follows:

- We design an anti-tracking messaging system (ACS), which divides the messaging process into message forwarding and message exchange through two-layer (entry layer and exchange layer) messaging framework. Entry layer hides the users' identities from the exchange layer and the exchange layer hides the communication relationship from the entry server. ACS provides low-latency communication and high tracking-resistance.

- ACS system provides offline messaging which makes the communication more flexible. The communicating parties need no negotiation and confirmation with each other. Then, each user doesn't need to stay online in ACS system all the time to wait for the possible messaging process. Also, offline messaging makes the messaging process happen in different time, which improves the difficulty in traffic analysis of communication relationship.
- ACS system reduces the information leakage to the minimum level through message segmentation mechanism. The original message will be split into different shares, and each message share will be sent to different exchange server via different entry server. Only received all the message shares, the receiver can reconstruct the original message.

The rest of the paper proceeds as follows. In Sect. 2, we introduce the noticeable anonymous networks and technologies. In Sect. 3, we introduce the threat model and give an overview of ACS system. In Sect. 4, we elaborate on the architecture of ACS system. After that, Sect. 5 analyzes the ACS system in detail from the resistance to active and passive attacks. Section 6 evaluates ACS system with its communication and anti-tracking performance. Finally, we conclude our work in Sect. 7.

2 Related Works

All the anonymous networks share the common goal of hiding users' identities and communication patterns from the adversary. Anonymous networks can be mainly divided into three categories: (i) Multi-hop based methods, (ii) Mix-net based methods, (iii) DC-net based methods.

2.1 Multi-Hop Based Methods

Multi-hop based methods use several relay nodes to transfer information and each relay node only knows its direct communication nodes to hide the whole transmission path. Tor, as the most popular anonymous network, provides sender anonymity through multi-hop onion routing. Considering the limitations of Tor, such as the directory server, untrusted volunteer ndoes et al., many systems propose the improvement methods based on Tor. PIR-Tor [12] is an architecture for the Tor network in which users obtain information about only a few onion routers using private information retrieval techniques(PIR), and the security of PIR-Tor depends on the security of PIR schemes. SGX-Tor [13] is a practical approach to effectively enhance the security and privacy of Tor by utilizing Intel SGX, a commodity trusted execution environment. SGX-Tor can prevent code modification and limits the information exposed to untrusted parties. Herd [14] is an anonymous network where a set of dedicated, fully interconnected cloud-based proxies yield suitably low-delay circuits, while untrusted superpeers add scalability. Herd provides caller/callee anonymity among the clients within a trust zone and under a strong adversarial model. HORNET [15] enables high-speed end-to-end anonymous channels by leveraging next generation network architectures. HORNET is designed as a low-latency onion routing system that operates at the network layer thus enabling a wide range of applications. HORNET uses only symmetric cryptography for data forwarding yet requires no per-flow state on intermediate nodes. TresMep [16] uses node ring to relay message and each node ring randomly chooses the exit node to deliver the message. TresMep achieves a dynamic multi-hop communication path to improve tracking-resistance at the cost of communication latency.

Multi-hop based methods have the advantage in network scalability and low-latency communication, but these methods are vulnerable to traffic analysis [17,18] and malicious node infiltration [7,19,20]. Network traffic on anonymous communication has its special features that can be distinguished from the background traffic. The adversary can monitor the network traffic, recognize the anonymous traffic through its features and trace its transmission path. Moreover, it is also difficult to prevent the malicious nodes from infiltrating in the communication channel. Then, the malicious nodes can observe the communication relationship to break the anonimity.

2.2   Mix-Net Based Methods

Mix-net based methods use mix nodes to shuffle the traffic and output them in a reshuffled form. Then, the input-output relation between different traffic can be hidden, such that an adversary is not able to establish a correlation between input and output traffic. Vuvuzela [21] is a new scalable messaging system that offers strong privacy guarantees, hiding both message data and metadata. Vuvuzela is secure against adversaries that observe and tamper with all network traffic, and that control all nodes except for one server. But Vuvuzela operates in rounds, and offline users lose the ability to receive messages and all messages must traverse a single chain of relay servers. Stadium [22] and Anon-Pop [23] improve the Vuvuzela by making the routing of messages dependent on the dynamics of others. Loopix [24] provides bi-directional "third-party" sender and receiver anonymity and unobservability by leveraging cover traffic and brief message delays. Loopix allows offline users to receive messages and uses parallel mix nodes to improve the scalability of the network. Riffle [25] consists of a small set of anonymity servers and a large number of users, and guarantees anonymity as long as there exists at least one honest server. Riffle uses a new hybrid verifiable shuffle technique and private information retrieval for bandwidth and computation-efficient anonymous communication. But Riffle can not handle network churn.

Mix-net based methods can effectively resist the traffic analysis and correlation analysis. But, the computation overhead in mix nodes may result in the high latency in communication. In general, the mix nodes need to be deployed specially, so that mix-net based methods is vulnerable to the single point failure.

2.3 DC-Net Based Methods

DC-net protocol offers non-interactive anonymous communication using secure multi-party computation with information-theoretically secure anonymity, guaranteeing sender anonymity while enabling all participants to verify the final outcome [26].

Dissent [27,28] offers provable anonymity with accountability for moderate-size groups, and efficiently handles unbalanced loads where few members wish to transmit in a given round. Each DC-net run transmits the variable-length bulk data comprising one member's message, using the minimum number of bits required for anonymity. BAR [29] combines broadcasting features of DC-net with layered encryption of Mix-net. The main advantage of BAR over other broadcast systems is bandwidth configurability and it can significantly reduce the required bandwidth for a small increase in latency, without affecting anonymity. Atom [30] is an anonymity system that protects against traffic-analysis attacks and avoids the scalability bottlenecks of traditional anonymity systems. Atom consists of a distributed network of mix servers connected with a carefully structured link topology. Atom is designed for latency tolerant unidirectional anonymous communication applications with only sender anonymity in mind.

DC-Net based methods protect the users against traffic analysis attacks effectively, but sacrifice the bandwidth. The DC-net protocol lacks the flexibility in anonymous communication, which needs all participants' cooperations, and allows only one user to communicate in one protocol round.

3 Overview of ACS

3.1 Threat Model

The main goal of ACS system is to hide the users' network identities and communication patterns from the adversary. So, ACS considers adversaries with the following capabilities.

Firstly, the adversary has a global view of the network to observe all network traffic between users, entry servers and exchange servers. This adversary is able to observe the entire network infrastructure, launch network attacks or conduct indirect observations. Secondly, the adversary has the ability to corrupt the servers of ACS system. If the adversary controls the entry server, it will get the communication relationship between the users and exchange servers. If the adversary control the exchange servers, it will know the message exchange among the user' pseudonyms. But, we assume only a fraction of entry servers and exchange servers can be corrupted or be operated by the adversary. Finally, the adversary has the ability to participate in ACS system as a compromised user, who may deviate from the protocol of ACS system. But we assume that the adversary can only control a limited number of such users.

We also consider the adversary has the limited computational resources so that it cannot break the security of cryptography. In ACS system, the only leaked information is whether an user is online or offline. This information is impossible to hide from the adversary, and hence it is the minimum level of information leakage.

3.2 The Overview

The ACS system's architecture contains of two layers, entry layer and exchange layer, as illustrated in Fig. 1. We consider a population of U users communicating through ACS, each of which can act as sender and receiver, denoted by indices s_i and r_i, where $i \in \{1, ..., U\}$. Each sender creates different shares of the message using additive secret sharing scheme [31] and sends the message shares to different entry servers randomly. The entry servers are used for grouping the received message shares and forwarding them to/from exchange servers. For anonymity, the users only provide their pseudonyms to exchange servers, and negotiate the symmetric keys with exchange servers via identity-based cryptography [32–34] to encrypt the message shares. So, all users need to register in exchange servers with pseudonyms, and exchange servers achieve the message exchange according to the pseudonyms of the communicating parties.

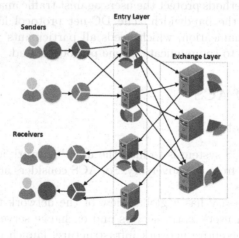

Fig. 1. The ACS system's architecture.

The exchange servers can be viewed as "information center" to exchange the message secretly and anonymously. The exchange servers also provide storage service to achieve the offline messaging. If the senders forward the message shares to exchange servers, but no receivers request for them. Exchange servers will store these message shares and wait for the requests from the receivers until the storage service of these message shares is expired. Storage service of message shares reduces the process of communication handshake between senders and receivers which makes the anti-tracking communication more flexible and efficient.

ACS contains the following three steps to implement its functionality:

- **User Registration.** At the beginning, each user u_i registers in the exchange servers with a unique pseudonym. Each exchange server takes the role of Key Generation Center (KGC) to generate the secret key for each user using a master secret key through identity-based key arrangement protocol (ID-based KAP) [32–34].
- **Anti-tracking Communication.** ACS system works in rounds. In each round of communication, all the online users need to send messages (the real messages or the cover messages) to exchange servers. The real messages contain the pseudonyms of the sender and the receiver for message exchange. The cover messages contain no useful information, but show the online status to exchange servers. All the messages will be divided into different shares, and sent to exchange servers through different entry servers. The exchange servers output the new message shares according to the content of the received message shares, and send them back to the corresponding users. After each user collects all the message shares from exchange servers, it can reconstruct the complete message.
- **Offline Messaging.** The message exchange is implemented only by the pseudonyms of users and the content of message shares. Because the exchange servers cannot receive the message shares from offline users, the messages sent to the offline users cannot be transmitted successfully. In this case, the exchange servers provide the storage service for these messages and wait the corresponding users go online. Storage service makes that the communication between the sender and receiver does not have to happen in one same round of ACS, which also improves the tracking-resistance.

4   The ACS Architecture

In this section, we will introduce the architecture of ACS system in details. For the convenience of discussion, we assume that ACS consists of three exchange servers in exchange layer: MS_1, MS_2, MS_3, and four entry servers in entry layer: ES_1, ES_2, ES_3, ES_4. We denote n as the number of users.

4.1   User Registration

At the beginning, each exchange server $MS_l, l \in \{1, 2, 3\}$, plays the role of KGC to generate the master secret key msk_l according to ID-based KAP [32–34]. Each user u_i generates a unique pseudonym UN_i of 64 bits, and sends its UN_i to each exchange server. According to the pseudonym of each user, each exchange server MS_l generates the secret key $sk_{i,l}$ for each user u_i and sends $sk_{i,l}$ to u_i. For the convenience of key agreement between users and exchange servers, each exchange server also generates its pseudonym SN_l and computes the corresponding secret key sk_{MS_l} using the master secret key msk_l. Then, each exchange server publishes its pseudonym SN_l to each user for the key agreement.

When registration is completed, each user u_i will get three secret keys: sk_1, sk_2, sk_3, and the corresponding pseudonyms of exchange servers: SN_1, SN_2,

SN_3. Each exchange server will get the list of all registered users' pseudonyms: $C_{UN} = \{UN_1, UN_2, ..., UN_n\}$. Then, users and exchange servers only use the pseudonyms to recognize each other.

4.2   Anti-tracking Communication

Anti-tracking communication is the core function of ACS. In each communication round r, the main phases of anti-tracking communication are outlined as follows.

Input preparation. In each round r, all users have to play one of the following roles: (i) the sender, which send message to a specific user, (ii) the receiver, which check the message from a specific user, and (iii) the cover, which send the cover message to exchange servers in order to circumvent the threat of traffic analysis and show the online status to ACS system.

According to the three role types, we define the message block as the form (L, u_i, u_j, M) in which L denotes the role type, u_i denotes the source user of this message, u_j denotes the target user of this message, and M denotes the context of communication. In ACS system, $L = S$ denotes the sender, $L = R$ denotes the receiver, and $L = C$ denotes the cover. We can set $M = m_c$ (m_c denotes the cover message), if no message need to be delivered, and $u_j = 0$ when the covers create the message block because the covers only send the redundant traffic.

Each sender s_i first creates three shares of its message m_i using additive secret sharing scheme. The additive secret sharing scheme works in a ring $\mathbb{Z}_N$, where a secret value $x \in \mathbb{Z}_N$ which will be shared among n parties. The n shares of x can be created by first choosing $n - 1$ random numbers modulo N and the last share is computed by subtracting the $n - 1$ random numbers from x and then modulo N:

$$
\begin{aligned}
x_1 &\leftarrow random() \ (mod \ N) \\
x_2 &\leftarrow random() \ (mod \ N) \\
&\cdots \\
x_n &\leftarrow x - x_1 - \cdots - x_{n-1} \ (mod \ N)
\end{aligned}
\tag{1}
$$

So that, $m_i = m_{i,SM_1} + m_{i,SM_2} + m_{i,SM_3}$ according to additive secret sharing scheme, and m_{i,SM_l} denotes the share will be delivered to exchange server SM_l.

Assume the sender s_i intends to send message m_i to receiver r_j, then it creates the message share $(S, s_i, r_j, m_{i,SM_l})$, $l \in \{1, 2, 3\}$. The receiver r_j creates the message share $(R, r_j, s_i, 0)$ which denotes r_j has message request from s_i. Each cover c_k creates the message share $(C, c_k, 0, 0)$.

According to ID-based KAP, each user u_i computes the encrypted keys $k_{i,l}$ with its secret key sk_i and the pseudonym SN_l of exchange server MS_l. The exchange server MS_l can also compute the encrypted key $K_{i,l}$ with its secret key sk_{MS_l} and the pseudonym UN_i of each user u_i. Then, each user u_i uses secret key $k_{i,l}$ to encrypt the message share which will be sent to exchange server MS_l.

Anti-Tracking Communication. Users and exchange servres have no identity information about each other except their pseudonyms. So, the entry servers relay the messages between users and exchange servers by mapping the pseudonyms to the real addresses.

Each user u_i randomly sends its message share to an entry servrer, then the entry server will get different message shares from different users. Entry servers record the corresponding relationship between users and message shares. Likewise, exchange servers record the corresponding relationship between entry servers and message shares. In this way, entry servers break the direct links between users and exchange servers and exchange servers only use the users' pseudonyms to complete the message exchange.

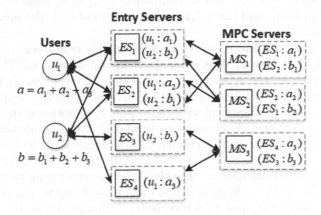

Fig. 2. The communication between users and exchange servers via entry servers.

In Fig. 2, a simple example of communication between users and exchange servers via entry servers is presented. The entry servers forward the message shares to exchange servers, and the exchange servers can recognize that each message share belongs to which entry server. After the message exchange is completed by the exchange servers, each exchange server computes the output message shares which contain the result of messaging, and sends them back to the corresponding entry servers. Then, the entry servers send these message shares to the relevant users according to the pseudonym in each message share.

Message Exchange. $MS_l (l \in \{1, 2, 3\})$ will receive one message share from each online user. To check the consistency of the message shares received by each exchange server, the exchange server first sorts the message shares according to the users' pseudonyms using the oblivious quicksort algorithm [35]. Then, each exchange server computes a hash value of the pseudonyms in the order they appear in the above sequence, as $H_{MS_l} = H(UN_1 || UN_2 || ... || UN_n)$. Each exchange server MS_l compares its H_{MS_l} with the hash value computed by other exchange servers. If the hash values are equal, all the exchange servers receive the right message shares. Otherwise, the malicious operations are taken place in either entry servers or exchange servers.

The message shares of the *sender*, *receiver* and *cover* are respectively denoted as: $b_s = (S, s_i, r_j, m)$, $b_r = (R, r_j, s_i, 0)$, and $b_c = (C, c_k, 0, 0)$.

According to the role type and the users' pseudonyms, the exchange servers implement the message exchange process among different message shares. We conclude five cases in the message exchange process as follows:

(1) $b_s = (S, u_i, u_j, m)$ and $b_r = (R, u_j, u_i, m_{req})$. In this case, b_s and b_r have the same communicating parties, which denote user u_i and u_j wish to exchange messages. The exchange server computes the output message shares, $b'_s = (S, u_i, u_j, m_{req})$ and $b'_r = (R, u_j, u_i, m)$, and sends b'_s and b'_r to user u_i and u_j respectively. The fourth component m_{req} of b'_s denotes the request information of u_j, and the fourth component m of b'_r is the message which will be sent to u_j.

(2) $b_s = (S, u_i, u_j, m)$ and $b_c = (C, u_j, 0, 0)$. In this case, user u_i sends message to u_j, but user u_j does not request messages from u_i. The exchange server computes the output message shares, $b'_s = (S, u_i, j_j, infos)$ and $b'_c = (C, u_j, u_i, m)$, and sends b'_s and b'_c to user u_i and u_j respectively. b'_s changes its fourth component with $infos$ from b_s to notice u_i the completion of message exchange, b'_c changes its third and fourth components with u_i and m from b_c respectively to notice u_j that u_i has sent the message m.

(3) $b_r = (R, u_i, u_j, m_{req})$ and $b_c = (C, u_j, 0, 0)$. In this case, user u_i has a message request from user u_j, then the exchange server computes the output message shares, $b'_r = (R, u_i, u_j, info_r)$ and $b'_c = (C, u_j, u_i, m_{req})$, and sends b'_r and b'_c to user u_i and u_j respectively. b'_r changes its fourth component with $info_r$ from b_r to notice u_i that its request information has been sent to u_j, b'_c changes its third and fourth components with u_i and m_{req} from b_c respectively to notice u_j that u_i has a request message m_{req}.

(4) $b_s = (S, u_i, u_j, m)$, but no message shares come from u_j. In this case, we think user u_j is offline. Then, the exchange server stores the message share from u_i until b_s is expired. Also, the exchange server computes the output message share $b'_s = (S, u_i, u_j, info_{off})$ and sends b'_s to user u_i to notice the offline status of user u_j.

(5) $b_r = (R, u_i, u_j, m_{req})$, but no message shares come from u_j. In this case, the exchange server stores the message share from u_i, computes the output message share $b'_r = (R, u_i, u_j, info_{off})$ and sends b'_r to user u_i to notice the offline status of user u_j.

In fact, the above process of message exchange is implemented among the received message shares and the stored message shares in each exchange server. The detailed message exchange process will be discussed in the following section.

4.3   Message Storage

In each round r, all online users need to send messages to ACS system. In other words, if the exchange servers do not receive the message share from user u_k, we believe user u_k is offline. If the valid message shares, $b_s = (S, s_i, r_j, m_{i,SM_l})$ and

$b_r = (R, r_j, s_i, 0)$, do not match the corresponding users, the exchange servers will store them for the future message exchange.

The message exchange between the received message shares and the stored message shares in each exchange server is the key problem for offline messaging. Assume that $Seq_r = (a_1, a_2, ..., a_n)$ and $Seq_s = (b_1, b_2, ..., b_m)$ denote the sequences of received message shares and stored message shares respectively. $Source(x)$ and $Target(x)$ denote the source user and target user of message share x respectively. We discuss the offline messaging from the following cases:

(1) Exist $a_i \in Seq_r(1 \le i \le n)$, $b_j \in Seq_s(1 \le j \le m)$, $Source(a_i) = Target(b_j)$. But for other $a_k \in Seq_r(1 \le k \le n, k \ne i)$, $Source(a_i) \ne Target(a_k)$. In this case, the message exchange only exists between the received message shares and stored message shares. As illustrated in Fig 3a, the exchange server extracts the valid information from the stored message shares, and computes the output message shares according to the communicating message shares.

(2) Exist $a_i, a_k \in Seq_r(1 \le i, k \le n, i \ne k)$, $b_j \in Seq_s(1 \le j \le m)$, $Source(a_i) = Target(a_k)$ and $Source(a_i) = Target(b_j)$. In this case, the received message share and stored message share have the same user for messaging. As illustrated in Fig 3b, the exchange message outputs two message shares, one is to carry the valid information of the received message share, the other is to carry the valid information of the stored message share.

In each messaging round, the exchange server deletes the stored message shares when their valid information has been transmitted or they are expired.

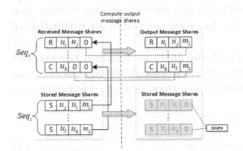 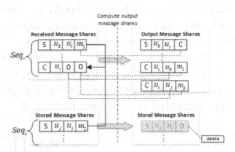

(a) A case of message exchange which only exists between received message shares and stored message shares.

(b) A case of message exchange in which both the received message share and stored message share have the same user for messaging.

Fig. 3. The two cases of message exchange between the received message shares and the stored message shares.

5   System Analysis

In this section, we present the analysis of ACS' security and argure its resistance to active attack and passive attack.

5.1   Resistance to Active Attack

Security of Entry Server. In the architecture of ACS, users and exchange servers have no valid information with each other except their pseudonyms. They recognize and communicate with each other only through their pseudonyms. Then, entry servers take the role of "middleman" in the communication between users and exchange servers. The advantage of entry servers is concluded as follows:

- The identities of users and exchange servers are protected by entry servers.
- The message can be mixed and shuffled by entry servers which foil the network monitors from learning about the correspondences between the users and exchange servers.
- The entry servers facilitate the synchronization and consistency of different exchange servers.

All the communication between users and exchange servers rely on entry servers, once the entry servers are corrupted by the adversary, the performance of trakcing-resistance of ACS would be threatened. So, the security of entry servers has to be taken into account. To this end, we guarantee that the number of entry servers is n_e, the number of exchange servers is n_x, and $n_e >> n_x$. The message from each user should be divided into n_m shares, and each share can only be delivered by one entry server. In this way, we can reduce the risk of collusion of corrupted entry servers.

Assume the adversary can not corrupt all the entry servers and the number of corrupted entry servers is $n_c(1 \le n_c \le n_e)$. Each user randomly chooses one entry server for one share, then the probability of that all chosen entry servers are corrupted is P_c shown in Equ. 2.

$$P_c = \prod_{i=1}^{n_c} \frac{n_c - (i-1)}{n_e - (i-1)} \tag{2}$$

Only $n_c \approx n_e$, then $P_c \approx 1$. In other words, if most of the entry servers are corrupted, adversary can control the communication between the users and exchange servers in high probability. But in practical application, it is difficult for the adversary to control all the entry servers.

Even some of the entry servers may be corrupted, the corrupted entry servers can not collect all the shares from one user. Then, every malicious operation, such as tamper or discard the message shares, will be detected by exchange servers because at least one honest entry server will forward the correct information to exchange servers.

Security of Exchange Server. We consider the corrupted exchange servers which provide the wrong outputs to destroy the reconstruction of messages. Then, at least one honest exchange server can guarantee the security of ACS. Before the message exchange, each exchange server will check the consistency of all its received message shares with other exchange servers. The corrupted exchange servers which provide the wrong verification information will be detected by other exchange servers.

Each user gets different sets of ID-based KAP from different exchange servers, and encrypts the message share sent to the exchange server MS_i with the agreed upon key which is generated by MS_i. In this way, the exchange server cannot decrypt the message shares sent to other exchange servers. So, ACS guarantees the security of message shares sent to different exchange servers and deters the collusion of corrupted exchange servers.

5.2   Resistance to Passive Attack

ACS system relies on the entry servers to provide the unlinkability between the users and exchange servers. Every online user sends the messages to exchange servers, and receives the corresponding output messages from the exchange servers in each messaging round. No matter whether the users have the messaging tasks or not, they have the same communication behaviors which provide high resistance to traffic analysis and correlation attack.

Each user has no information about the exchange servers, and communicate with them only via their pseudonyms. Only entry servers know the communication relationship between the users and exchange servers. But, entry servers have no information about the message exchange process.

ACS system relies on the exchange servers to break the communication relationship between different users. All the message exchange process is completed by the exchange servers. The exchange servers provide the following advantages: (i) No information about message exchange will be leaked without the control of exchange servers. Only the exchange servers know the communication relationship among different pseudonyms of users. (ii) The message exchange only relies on users' pseudonyms, without the collusion of entry servers, no adversary can trace the communication relationship of different users. (iii) Each exchange server also provides the message storage service for offline messaging, so the message exchange process may not happen in one messaging round of ACS system. It is nearly impossible for the adversary to trace the communication of different users which happens in different messaging rounds.

The messages transmitted in ACS system may be the real or the cover messages. All the messages will be created into different shares and encapsulated into the same form (L, u_i, u_j, M) which has been mentioned above. All message shares are padded to the same length and end-to-end encrypted to make sure the adversary can not distinguish the real message from the cover message, and also learn no information from the encrypted messages.

6   Experiments and Evaluation

We implement a prototype of the ACS system which contains 5 exchange servers which are deployed on the computer with a 12-core 4 GHz CPU and 64 GB RAM, and 10 entry servers which are deployed on Cloud platforms with a 2-core 4 GHz CPU and 48 GB RAM. We run a simulation program on a computer with a 8-core 3 GHz CPU and 64 GB RAM to simulate the independent users to communicate with the ACS system.

We evaluate the ACS prototype system from its system performance and anti-tracking ability.

6.1   Performance Evaluation

We first evaluate the latency overhead of ACS system in consideration of the various number of users and the different message size. In this experiment, all users send the messages to a randomly chosen target in each round, and the message size is set with $1KB, 2KB, 4KB$ and $8KB$ respectively. After the prototype system completes the communication, we measure the running time to evaluate the latency overhead. In the following experimental results, we use $|M|$ to indicate the message size.

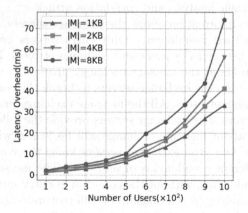

Fig. 4. Latency overhead of ACS system where 100 to 1000 users simultaneously send message with different size.

As shown in Fig. 4, with the increasing of the number of users and the message size, we can see that the latency overhead of the prototype system grows exponentially. In the current system configuration, when the number of users is less than 500, the latency overhead of all the four cases is in a reasonable range.

But, when the number of users exceeds 500, the latency overhead grows sharply. There are two aspects which may affect the communication efficiency of ACS system: (i) the performance of message forwarding of entry servers, and (ii) the performance of message exchange in exchange servers. Next, we will evaluate the performance of the entry servres and exchange servers respectively to find out the bottleneck of ACS system in communication efficiency.

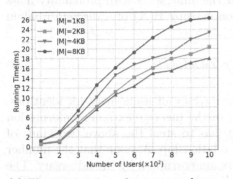 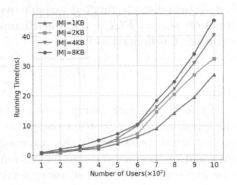

(a) The running time of message exchange of all exchange servers in different message size.1

(b) The running time of Entry servers in different message size.

Fig. 5. The running time of entry servers and exchange servers in different message size.

To evaluate the performance of exchange servers, we directly send the message shares to exchange servers and measure the running time when exchange servers complete the message exchange. As shown in Fig. 5a, all the curves grow sharply when the number of users exceeds 500. The message exchange in each exchange server uses the oblivious Quicksort algorithm [35] which needs $O(log(n))$ steps to sort n inputs when executed in parallel [36]. So, the complexity of message exchange computation is in logarithm relation with the number of inputs. The exchange servers need more computation cost to match the communicating users and computes the output messages when the number of users is increased.

To evaluate the performance of entry servers, we only implement the function of entry servers to relay the message shares. The exchange servers do not take any operations and directly send back the received messages to entry servers as the outputs. Then, we measure the running time of entry servers when they complete the transmission of all the upstream and downstream messages. As shown in Fig 5b, with the increasing of the number of users, the running time of entry servers grows exponentially. Compared with the experimental results of latency overhead evaluation, the performance of entry servers in message forwarding has a direct effect on the communication efficiency of ACS system. In our prototype system, we only set five entry servers to relay the messages between the users and exchange servers. With the increasing of users, entry servers need to process more transmission requests from users. The entry servers also need extra time to mix, label the message shares and correlate the pseudonyms with their real network addresses.

6.2 Anti-tracking Evaluation

To effectively evaluate the anti-tracking performance of ACS, we introduce a measuring method of tracking-resistance based on information entropy [37,38]. Let X be a discrete random variable over the finite set $\mathbb{F}$ with probability mass function $p(x) = P(X = x)$. The Shannon entropy H(X) of a discrete random variable X is defined as Equ. 3.

$$H(X) = -\sum_{x \in X} p(x)log(p(x)) \tag{3}$$

In ACS, the entry server protects the privacy of users' network identities, the exchange server protects the privacy of the message exchange information among users' pseudonyms. An adversary has to steal the above two kinds of information to trace the communication relationship. Assume that the number of entry servers is n_e and n'_e entry servers are corrupted by the adversary. The number of exchange servers is n_x, and n'_x exchange servers are corrupted. The corrupted entry server can analyze the message shares and distinguish the sender and target exchange server of each message share, but cannot decrypt the message share encrypted by the secret key of each exchange server. The corrupted exchange server knows the pseudonyms in communication. So, the path between two communicating users contains three hops: $v_e \rightarrow v_x \rightarrow v_e$, in which v_e denotes the entry server and v_x denotes the exchange server. The traceable probability of ACS, denoted by P_{trace}, is defined by Eq. 4.

$$P_{trace} = (\frac{n'_e}{n_e})^2 \frac{n'_x}{n_x} \tag{4}$$

We consider that the messaging behavior of each user is independent in probability, and each user randomly chooses the entry servers to forward the message shares. Then, the distribution of traced users can regard as Binomial Distribution. For n communicating users, k of them can be traced by the adversary, then the probability of traced users is defined by Eq. 5.

$$P\{X = k\} = \binom{n}{k}(P_{trace})^k(1 - P_{trace})^{n-k} \tag{5}$$

The traceable rate R_{trrace} indicates the probability of tracing the communicating users via the corrupted servers. We use the entropy of traced users' distribution to describe R_{trace}. So, R_{trace} can be calculated by Eq. 6.

$$R_{trace} = -\sum_{k=1}^{n}(P\{X = k\})log(P\{X = k\}) \tag{6}$$

We simulate 1000 users to communicate with each other via ACS prototype system. Through the increase of n'_e and n'_x, we evaluate the tracking-resistance of ACS according to its traceable rate R_{trace}. In Fig. 6a, we increase n'_e from 1 to 10, and compare R_{trace} under different n'_x. In Fig. 6b, we increase n'_x from 1 to 5, and compare R_{trace} under different n'_e. From the experimental results, R_{trace} increases in logarithm relation with both of n'_e and n'_x. The adversary can reach an efficient traceable rate R_{trace} only when both of the entry servers and exchange servers are compromised in high probability. So, the anti-tracking ability lies in the double protection of entry server and exchange server. On the contrary, it's not sufficient for the adversary to trace the communicating users if they only compromise one kind of servers.

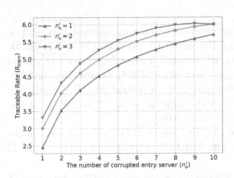 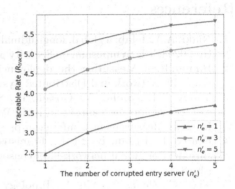

(a) Traceable rate w.r.t. corrupted entry servers.

(b) Traceable rate w.r.t. corrupted exchange servers.

Fig. 6. The tracking-resistance evaluation with increasing number of corrupted entry servers and corrupted exchange servers.

7   Conclusion

In this paper, we present ACS system to achieve the anti-tracking messaging. In the design of ACS system, ACS contains two layers: entry layer and exchange layer, which separates the two process of message forward and message exchange. The entry servers are only used to relay messages between the users and exchange servers. The exchange servers are only used to exchange the message shares. To improve the anti-tracking performance, all the users use pseudonyms to label their messages, and exchange servers have no information about the users' real identities. Even the entry servers know the identities of the users, but they have no information about the message exchange process. So, the adversary has to corrupt both the entry servers and exchange servers to trace the communicating users. In addition, message storage is also provided to achieve offline messaging.

We evaluate the prototype system of ACS of its communication latency and anti-tracking performance. From the experimental results, ACS has a acceptable communication latency and a strong anti-tracking ability. Only when both of the entry servers and exchange servers are corrupted, the adversary can trace the communicating users effectively. But in practical application, it is difficult for the adversary to corrupt both of the entry server and exchange server.

Acknowledgment. The authors would like to thank the anonymous reviewers for their insightful comments and suggestions on this paper. This work was supported in part by the National Key Research and Development Program of China under Grant No.2019YFB1005205.

References

1. Niaki, A.A.: Iclab: a global, longitudinal internet censorship measurement platform. In: 2020 IEEE Symposium on Security and Privacy (SP), pp. 135–151. IEEE (2020)
2. Raman,R.S.: Measuring the deployment of network censorship filters at global scale. In: Network and Distributed Systems Security (NDSS) Symposium (2020)
3. Yadav, T.K., Sinha, A., Gosain, D., Sharma, P.K., Chakravarty, S.: Analyzing web censorship mechanisms in india Where the light gets. In: Proceedings of the Internet Measurement Conference, pp. 252–264 (2018)
4. Pearce, P., Ensafi, R., Li, F., Feamster, N., Paxson, V.: Toward continual measurement of global network-level censorship. IEEE Security Privacy **16**(1), 24–33 (2018)
5. Tian, C., Zhang, Y., Yin, T.: Topology self-optimization for anti-tracking network via nodes distributed computing. In: Gao, H., Wang, X. (eds.) CollaborateCom 2021. LNICST, vol. 406, pp. 405–419. Springer, Cham (2021). https://doi.org/10.1007/978-3-030-92635-9_24
6. Johnson, A., Wacek, C., Jansen, R., Sherr, M., Syverson, P:. Users get routed: Traffic correlation on tor by realistic adversaries. In: Proceedings of the 2013 ACM SIGSAC conference on Computer and communications security, pp. 337–348 (2013)
7. Sun, Y.: {RAPTOR}: Routing attacks on privacy in tor. In: 24th {USENIX} Security Symposium ({USENIX} Security 15), pp. 271–286 (2015)
8. Tian, C., Zhang, Y., Yin, T.: A feature-flux traffic camouflage method based on twin gaussian process. In: 2021 IEEE 20th International Conference on Trust, Security and Privacy in Computing and Communications (TrustCom), pp. 959–966. IEEE (2021)
9. Danezis, G., Dingledine, R., Mathewson, N.: Mixminion: Design of a type iii anonymous remailer protocol. In 2003 Symposium on Security and Privacy, 2003, pp. 2–15. IEEE (2003)
10. Borges, F., Buchmann, J., Mühlhäuser, M.:.Introducing asymmetric dc-nets. In: 2014 IEEE Conference on Communications and Network Security, pp. 508–509, IEEE (2014)
11. Golle, P., Juels, A.: Dining cryptographers revisited. In: Cachin, C., Camenisch, J.L. (eds.) EUROCRYPT 2004. LNCS, vol. 3027, pp. 456–473. Springer, Heidelberg (2004). https://doi.org/10.1007/978-3-540-24676-3_27
12. Mittal, P., Olumofin, F.G., Troncoso, C., Borisov, N., Goldberg, I.: Pir-tor: Scalable anonymous communication using private information retrieval. In: USENIX Security Symposium, pp. 31–31 (2011)

13. Kim, S., Han, J., Ha, J., Kim, T., Han, D.: Sgx-tor: a secure and practical tor anonymity network with sgx enclaves. IEEE/ACM Trans. Netw. **26**(5), 2174–2187 (2018)
14. Blond, S.L., Choffnes, D., Caldwell, W., Druschel, P., Merritt, N.: Herd: A scalable, traffic analysis resistant anonymity network for voip systems. In: Proceedings of the 2015 ACM Conference on Special Interest Group on Data Communication, pp. 639–652 (2015)
15. Chen, C., Asoni, D.E., Barrera, D., Danezis, G., Perrig, A.: Hornet: High-speed onion routing at the network layer. In: Proceedings of the 22nd ACM SIGSAC Conference on Computer and Communications Security, pp. 1441–1454 (2015)
16. Tian, C., Zhang, Y., Yin, T., Tuo, Y., Ge, R.: Achieving dynamic communication path for anti-tracking network. In: 2019 IEEE Global Communications Conference (GLOBECOM), pp. 1–6. IEEE (2019)
17. Montieri, A., Ciuonzo, D., Aceto, G., Pescapé, A.: Anonymity services tor, i2p, jondonym: classifying in the dark (web). IEEE Trans. Dependable Secure Comput. **17**(3), 662–675 (2018)
18. Kwon, A., AlSabah, M., Lazar, D., Dacier, M., Devadas, S.: Circuit fingerprinting attacks: Passive deanonymization of tor hidden services. In: 24th {USENIX} Security Symposium ({USENIX} Security 15), pp. 287–302 (2015)
19. Evans, N.S., Dingledine, R., Grothoff, C.: A practical congestion attack on tor using long paths. In: USENIX Security Symposium, pp. 33–50 (2009)
20. Winter, P., Ensafi, R., Loesing, K., Feamster, N.: Identifying and characterizing sybils in the tor network. In 25th {USENIX} Security Symposium ({USENIX} Security 16), pp. 1169–1185 (2016)
21. Van Den Hooff, J., Lazar, D., Zaharia, M., Zeldovich, N.: Vuvuzela: Scalable private messaging resistant to traffic analysis. In: Proceedings of the 25th Symposium on Operating Systems Principles, pp. 137–152 (2015)
22. Tyagi, N., Gilad, Y., Leung, D., Zaharia, M., Zeldovich, N.: Stadium: A distributed metadata-private messaging system. In: Proceedings of the 26th Symposium on Operating Systems Principles, pp. 423–440 (2017)
23. Gelernter, N., Herzberg, A., Leibowitz, H.: Two cents for strong anonymity: the anonymous post-office protocol. In: Capkun, S., Chow, S.S.M. (eds.) CANS 2017. LNCS, vol. 11261, pp. 390–412. Springer, Cham (2018). https://doi.org/10.1007/978-3-030-02641-7_18
24. Piotrowska, A.M., Hayes, J., Elahi, T., Meiser, S., Danezis, G.: The loopix anonymity system. In: 26th {USENIX} Security Symposium ({USENIX} Security 17), pp. 1199–1216 (2017)
25. Kwon, A., Lazar, D., Devadas, S., Ford, B.: Riffle: an efficient communication system with strong anonymity. Proc. Privacy Enhanc. Technol. **2016**(2), 115–134 (2016)
26. Shirazi, F., Simeonovski, M., Asghar, M.R., Backes, M., Diaz, C.: A survey on routing in anonymous communication protocols. ACM Comput. Surv. (CSUR), **51**(3), 1–39 (2018)
27. Corrigan-Gibbs, H., Ford, B.: Dissent: accountable anonymous group messaging. In: Proceedings of the 17th ACM Conference on Computer and Communications Security, pp. 340–350 (2010)
28. Wolinsky, D.I., Corrigan-Gibbs, H., Ford, B., Johnson, A.: Dissent in numbers: Making strong anonymity scale. In: 10th {USENIX} Symposium on Operating Systems Design and Implementation ({OSDI} 12), pp. 179–182 (2012)

29. Kotzanikolaou, P., Chatzisofroniou, G., Burmester, M.: Broadcast anonymous routing (bar): scalable real-time anonymous communication. Int. J. Inf. Secur. **16**(3), 313–326 (2017)
30. Kwon, A., Corrigan-Gibbs, H., Devadas, S., Ford, B.: Atom: Horizontally scaling strong anonymity. In: Proceedings of the 26th Symposium on Operating Systems Principles, pp. 406–422 (2017)
31. Gelernter, N., Herzberg, A., Leibowitz, H.: Two cents for strong anonymity: the anonymous post-office protocol. In: Capkun, S., Chow, S.S.M. (eds.) CANS 2017. LNCS, vol. 11261, pp. 390–412. Springer, Cham (2018). https://doi.org/10.1007/978-3-030-02641-7_18
32. Paterson., Srinivasan, S.: On the relations between non-interactive key distribution, identity-based encryption and trapdoor discrete log groups. Designs, Codes Cryptograph. **52**(2), 219–241 (2009)
33. Chen, L., Cheng, Z., Smart, N.P.: Identity-based key agreement protocols from pairings. Int. J. Inform. Security **6**(4), 213–241 (2007)
34. Wu, L., Zhang, Y., Raymond Choo, K.-K., He, D.: Efficient and secure identity-based encryption scheme with equality test in cloud computing. Future Gen. Comput. Syst. **73**, 22–31 (2017)
35. Bogdanov, D., Laur, S., Talviste, R.: A practical analysis of oblivious sorting algorithms for secure multi-party computation. In: Bernsmed, K., Fischer-Hübner, S. (eds.) NordSec 2014. LNCS, vol. 8788, pp. 59–74. Springer, Cham (2014). https://doi.org/10.1007/978-3-319-11599-3_4
36. Alexopoulos, N., Kiayias, A., Talviste, R., Zacharias, T.: Mcmix: Anonymous messaging via secure multiparty computation. In: 26th {USENIX} Security Symposium ({USENIX} Security 17), pp. 1217–1234 (2017)
37. Serjantov, A., Danezis, G.: Towards an information theoretic metric for anonymity. In: Dingledine, R., Syverson, P. (eds.) PET 2002. LNCS, vol. 2482, pp. 41–53. Springer, Heidelberg (2003). https://doi.org/10.1007/3-540-36467-6_4
38. Díaz, C., Seys, S., Claessens, J., Preneel, B.: Towards measuring anonymity. In: Dingledine, R., Syverson, P. (eds.) PET 2002. LNCS, vol. 2482, pp. 54–68. Springer, Heidelberg (2003). https://doi.org/10.1007/3-540-36467-6_5

Anti-Clone: A Lightweight Approach for RFID Cloning Attacks Detection

Yue Feng[1,2], Weiqing Huang[1,2,3], Siye Wang[1,2,3(✉)], Yanfang Zhang[1,2], Shang Jiang[1,2], and Ziwen Cao[1,2]

[1] Institute of Information Engineering, Chinese Academy of Sciences, Beijing, China
{fengyue,huangweiqing,zhangyanfang,jiangshang,
caoziwen,wangsiye}@iie.ac.cn
[2] School of Cyber Security, University of Chinese Academy of Sciences,
Beijing, China
[3] School of Computer and Information Technology, Beijing Jiaotong University,
Beijing, China

Abstract. Millions of radio frequency identification (RFID) tags are pervasively used all around the globe to identify a wide variety of objects inexpensively. However, the tag cannot use energy-hungry cryptography due to the limit of size and production costs, and it is vulnerable to cloning attacks. A cloning attack fabricates one or more replicas of a genuine tag, which behave the same as the genuine tag and can deceive the reader to obtain legitimate authorization, leading to potential economic loss or reputation damage. Among the existing solutions, the methods based on radio frequency (RF) fingerprints are attractive because they can detect cloning attacks and identify the clone tags. They leverage the unique imperfections in the tag's wireless circuitry to achieve largescale RFID clone detection. However, training a high-precision detection model requires a large amount of data and high-performance hardware devices. And some methods require professional instruments such as oscilloscopes to collect fine-grained RF signals. For these reasons, we propose a lightweight clone detection method Anti-Clone. We combine convolutional neural networks (CNN) with transfer learning to combat data-constrained learning tasks. Extensive experiments on commercial off-the-shelf (COTS) RFID devices demonstrate that Anti-Clone is more lightweight than the existing methods without sacrificing detection accuracy. The detection accuracy reaches 98.4%, and the detection time is less than 5 s.

Keywords: Radio frequency identification (RFID) · Cloning detection · Fingerprint · Transfer learning

1 Introduction

Radio frequency identification (RFID) technology is a non-contact automatic identification technology through spatial coupling or backscattering of radio frequency signals. The advantages of low cost, lightness, and long-distance identification of multiple targets make RFID technology widely used in every corner

H. Gao et al. (Eds.): CollaborateCom 2022, LNICST 461, pp. 75–90, 2022.
https://doi.org/10.1007/978-3-031-24386-8_5

of our life. Such as payment systems, object monitoring, and continuous health monitoring through implantation [14, 16–20, 26, 27, 29, 30]. However, since RFID can be attached to cash and other valuable objects and implanted into animals and people, their widespread usage has raised severe security and privacy concerns. More importantly, the low cost and small size of tags make some excellent cryptographic algorithms and security mechanisms unable to be applied to existing RFID systems. For these reasons, RFID tags are vulnerable to attack.

This paper considers the tag cloning attack, where the attacker extracts data from the corrupted tag to other tag chips or rogue devices called clone tags. The clone tag saves all the valid data the same as the genuine tag and has the same permissions as the genuine tag. Intuitively, the resilience of RFID tags to cloning attacks is strongly correlated to their applicability in critical applications. For example, by injecting clone tags into the logistics or drug supply chain, the company will lose the tracking of assets [31]. By injecting clone tags into e-passports to ensure national borders' security, terrorists or illegal immigrants will enter a country undetected. By injecting clone tags into the access control system, unauthorized personnel will enter the control area at will. More importantly, clone tags may cause severe damage to human health and safety because RFID technology is used in the medical field.

Approach. To solve the cloning problem of low-cost tags without relying on cryptography, some prior work has proposed approaches based on radio frequency (RF) fingerprints [2, 7, 11, 24, 25, 32]. RF fingerprints leverage the common individual differences in the RFID tag circuit. By extracting the features of the received signal and associating them with a given tag, the unique identification of the tag can be obtained. These features are generated in the production process and cannot be controlled by human beings. We call them RF fingerprints. Existing methods rely on protocol-specific feature-extraction techniques, such as minimum power response [25], spectral characteristics [32], and dynamic wavelet fingerprints [1], which can only be applied to a specific tag type. And these methods need professional equipment such as oscilloscopes and universal software radio peripheral (USRP) to collect fine-grained fingerprints, which is beyond the capacity of existing commercial off-the-shelf (COTS) readers. In contrast, in this paper, we use machine learning (ML), especially convolutional neural networks (CNNs), to create RF fingerprint classifiers to detect clone tags. Compared with traditional ML, the main advantage of CNN is that it uses many parameters and can distinguish high device populations.

Existing Issues. A fundamental challenge in training any CNN model comes from the need for large data sets. This challenge is severe in our environment due to the limited public RF fingerprint data sets. A naive solution is to continuously collect the data of each tag for a long time. However, it is difficult to obtain large-scale and high-quality data in actual scenarios due to cost, privacy, environmental constraints, and other issues. Therefore, to reduce the cost of model training and adapt the neural network to the learning task with limited data, this paper introduces transfer learning into CNN and proposes a lightweight method Anti-Clone for detecting clone tags.

Technical Contributions. We summarize the novel contributions of Anti-Clone to the current status of cloning detection:

1. We entirely use the limited processing capacity of passive RFID tags and introduce Anti-Clone, which can detect cloned tags in real-time. Anti-Clone only requires COTS devices and no additional hardware devices.
2. We use the non-replicable physical layer signal to establish the tag RF fingerprint, creatively convert the signal sequence into images, and build the fingerprint database of genuine tags based on CNN. Then combined with transfer learning to reduce the cost of model training and simultaneously make the network adapt to the learning task with limited data.
3. We implemented a prototype and conducted extensive experiments. Our results show that Anti-Clone has high detection accuracy. Extensive experiments show that the detection accuracy reaches up to 98.4%, and the detection time overhead is minimal. The fastest is less than 5 s.

The rest of this paper is organized as follows. Section 2 introduces the related work. Section 3 provides an overview of the cloning attack threat model, the theoretical and experimental basis for Anti-Clone's work, and the challenges and solutions of clone detection. Section 4 describes the Anti-Clone in detail. Section 5 evaluates the performance of Anti-Clone. Section 6 concludes this paper.

2 Related Work

Aiming at the risk of cloning attacks faced by RFID technology, how to quickly and effectively detect clone tags has attracted much attention. Current scholars focus on synchronization keys, collision detection, trajectory analysis, and RF fingerprints.

2.1 Synchronization Keys

Synchronization keys are double authentication for a tag by loading different random numbers into a low-cost tag. Lehtonen [15] investigated a method to pinpoint tags with the same ID. It writes a new random number on the tag's memory every time the tag is scanned. A back-end that issues these numbers detect tag cloning attacks as soon as the genuine and the cloned tag are scanned. Okpara [21] proposed a detection method based on chaos theory used to generate random numbers. These methods increase the communication delay and require tag memory space.

2.2 Collision Detection

The method based on the collision principle to detect clone tags was proposed by Bu et al. [3–5]. The conflict caused by a genuine tag and a cloned tag with the same ID is used for clone tag detection, which is driven by the Aloha communication protocol. However, these methods were later overturned by Burmester et al. [6]. They proved that these methods are impossible in practice by analyzing the protocol.

2.3 Trajectory Analysis

The trajectory-based detection method indicates whether the trajectory to be measured matches the normal trajectory. Normal trajectories can be predefined trajectories or statistical features based on historical trajectories.

Ouafi and Vaudenay [22] proposed Pathchecker. When the final trajectory is not equal to the defined target trajectory, it is regarded as abnormal. This method has high detection accuracy. However, storing the correct trajectory requires a large amount of memory, which is a high requirement for tags.

Feng et al. [10,12] proposed the deClone, which obtained the features of normal trajectories through statistics on many historical trajectories and then found anomalies through matching. Wang et al. [28] also contributed to this field. These methods are highly portable. However, they could only detect the presence of a cloning attack in the system, not identify which one is the cloning tag.

2.4 RF Fingerprints

The method based on RF fingerprint can distinguish individual tags. In detail, it can identify which is the genuine tag and which is the clone tag. The seminal work applies RFP to 50 HF tags, achieving a 2.43% error rate [8]. Among others, the features used are based on the Hilbert transform. Zanetti et al. [32] use the time and spectrum level domain to fingerprint 70 UHF tags, achieving 71% accuracy. To improve detection accuracy, Piva et al. [23] combine CNN and federated learning. However, these methods ignore the difficulty of collecting data. Therefore, for learning tasks with limited data, we combine CNN with transfer learning. Without loss of detection accuracy, our method is more lightweight than other methods.

3 Overview of Anti-Clone

3.1 Threat Model

In RFID systems, a cloning attack is to create one or more copies of genuine tags, which are called clone tags and have the same valid data as genuine tags. The clone tag saves all the valid data the same as the genuine tag and has the same permissions as the genuine tag. Since most RFID applications use the authenticity of tags to verify the authenticity of tagged objects, clone tags may harm the entity. Therefore, this paper aims to identify clone tags with the COTS devices.

3.2 Basic Idea

The application layer data (such as EPC and ID) stored in the tag memory can be cloned by the attacker. The physical layer RF signal is difficult to clone because the RF signal is affected by many factors, including device diversity, multipath effect, tag position, and direction. Different environments and hardware devices significantly impact the RF signal, which makes the RF signal unpredictable and is widely used in wireless sensing. The received signal strength (RSS) and phase are two basic physical-layer metrics of RF signals. The received signal strength indication (RSSI) reflects the value of RSS. An RFID reader can directly read RSSI and phase.

In this section, we first model the RF signal and theoretically deduce the influence of different tags on the signal. Then, we prove our derivation through experiments.

RSS/Phase Model. RSS model. Received signal strength (RSS) measures the power present in a received RF signal. Phase reflects the offset degree between the received signal and the sent signal. According to the Friis equation [9], we can quantify the effect of different tags on RSS.

$$RSS = 10 \lg \left(\frac{P_{T,\,\text{reader}}}{1\,mW} G_{\text{reader}}{}^2 G_{tag}{}^2 \left(\frac{\lambda}{4\pi d} \right)^4 T_b \right) \tag{1}$$

where $P_{T,reader}$ is the transmission power of the reader antenna, G_{reader} is the gain of the reader antenna, G_{tag} is the gain of the tag antenna, d is the distance from the reader antenna to the tag, λ is the working wavelength of the RFID system, and T_b is a constant representing the backscattering loss.

In the same environment, when the readers are the same and the distance between the readers and tags is the same, RSS depends on the gain of the tag antenna. And the gain varies with different devices.

Phase model. The phase reading ϕ reported by the RFID reader contains three parts.

$$\phi = \phi_{\text{tag}} + \phi_{\text{pro}} + \phi_{\text{cir}} \tag{2}$$

where ϕ_{tag} is the phase shift caused by the tag and is related to the tag antenna impedance Za. ϕ_{pro} is caused by the distance d that the signal travels in the air. ϕ_{cir} is the phase shift introduced by the RFID reader circuit. All three parts are unknown.

When the readers and their distance from the tag are the same, ϕ_{pro} and ϕ_{cir} are fixed. ϕ_{tag} is the phase shift caused by the tag and is related to the tag antenna impedance Za and tag diversity. And many studies have shown that the object material will have an impact on the impedance.

RSS/Phase Changes for Different Tags. We show the impact of different tags on RF signals through a toy experiment. In the same environment, we placed five different tags with the same type at the same location and observed the RSSI and phase. The results are shown in Fig. 1. The abscissa is the phase, and the ordinate is the RSSI. Different colors represent different tags. Although the experimental environment and deployment conditions remain unchanged, the RF signal measurement results of different tags differ. Hardware differences cause this. These results confirm the significant influence of tag diversity on RF signals. We can distinguish tags by RF signal.

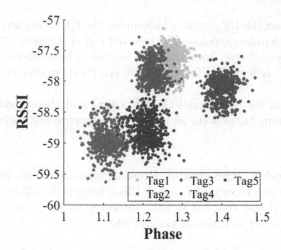

Fig. 1. Tag diversity.

3.3   Observation and Challenges

When the tag reports its ID to the reader, the reader measures RSSI and phase. Therefore, for tags with different IDs, we can easily classify the physical layer signal according to the IDs. However, when a cloning attack occurs, the clone tag has the same valid data as the genuine tag, including ID. The measured RSSI and phases mix even though they come from different tags (a genuine tag and its clone tags). The preliminary studies show that RF signals can distinguish different tags.

However, we still face challenges. First, the difference between tags is minimal, and RF signals are highly couple. A simple classification algorithm makes it difficult to distinguish the tags accurately. Second, collecting a large amount of data requires a lot of human and financial resources, and it needs to design an efficient classifier for the learning task with limited data. Third, tags are usually attached to the surfaces of the objects. The surface material of the object will affect the RF signal.

To overcome these challenges, we combined two physical layer indicators. We convert the sequence data into two-dimensional images classified through CNN. We combine CNN with transfer learning to adapt to the learning task with limited data and design a lightweight clone detection method, Anti-Clone. In the experimental evaluation stage, we considered the impact of different material types of attachments on the experimental results.

4   Anti-Clone Design

To achieve our goal of detecting the clone tag, we propose Anti-Clone, which operates as shown in Fig. 2.

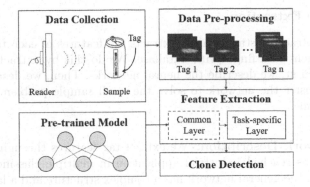

Fig. 2. Overview of Anti-Clone.

4.1 Data Pre-processing

In this section, we will pre-process the data. We transform the sequence into the form of images to better distinguish the tags.

We divide the data sequence of a tag into multiple data blocks and then form multiple images containing the same amount of data. However, due to the different sampling rates of devices and the interference of the environment, it is impossible to ensure that the amount of data collected is the same in the same collection time. In addition, for the network, the larger the amount of data, the higher the accuracy of the model. Therefore, we use the sliding window to divide the data sequence into blocks with the same amount of data as much as possible. In order to make the images contain more effective information and ensure that the same class has the same reference, we take the maximum and minimum values of all the data by a tag as the boundary of this class of heat map. Figure 3 shows the heat map generated by four different tags.

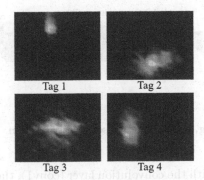

Fig. 3. Heatmap of different tags.

4.2 Feature Extraction

The feature extraction stage mainly extracts the features of each tag to realize the establishment of a fingerprint database. We do this by extracting features from images. First, we describe the neural networks. Then, we describe how to effectively transfer the network to solve the small sample problem and reduce the training time.

Neural Network Description. We extract tag features through CNN. Currently, CNN has reached industrial application in multiple classification problems. However, the general network has a complex structure and a large amount of computation, which is incompatible with a large amount of data and reasonable real-time. This paper decides to use the lightweight network SqueezeNet for image classification.

SqueezeNet was proposed by Forrest et al. in 2017 [13]. It has fewer parameters while ensuring the same recognition accuracy, which means that the architecture requires less communication with the server in distributed training. SqueezeNet is more suitable for deployment on devices with limited performance.

The fire module is the basic building module in SqueezeNet, which is composed of a squeeze module and expand module. The squeeze module comprises a set of 1×1 continuous convolution. The expand module contains a set of 1×1 continuous convolution and 3×3 convolutions in the spatial ascending superposition. The schematic diagram is shown in Fig. 4.

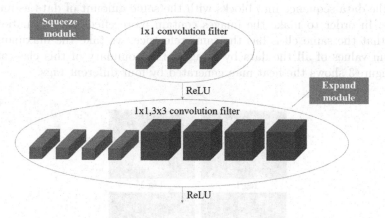

Fig. 4. Fire module schematic diagram.

SqueezeNet starts with the convolution layer (conv1), then uses 8 fire modules (fire2-9), and ends with the convolution layer (conv10). Figure 5 depicts the structure of SqueezeNet.

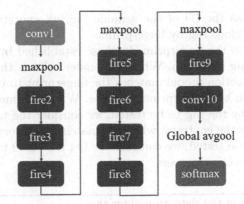

Fig. 5. SqueezeNet model flow diagram.

Extending to New Tasks. We hope to expand the network to new classification tasks efficiently to reduce the training network's consumption. For example, after training the classifier with a large data set, we want to extend it to the learning task with limited data to detect clone tags. Therefore, we adopt transfer learning to transfer training knowledge from a well-trained source domain to a new target domain.

The networks described in the previous section are composed of multiple layers. Some of them are used for feature extraction or coding. At the same time, others are used for classification. The feature extraction layer can be further divided into a common layer and a task-specific layer. The common layer can be directly transferred from the trained classifier to the target domain as a freezing layer. This dramatically reduces the number of parameters that the new task needs to learn, thus reducing the size of the data set required to achieve high accuracy. We freeze the previous layer and replace the last two-dimensional convolution layer "conv10" and classification layer "softmax". And then retrain the network.

4.3 Clone Detection

We have introduced the classification model based on transfer learning in detail. This model realizes the feature extraction of genuine tags and can establish the legal fingerprint database of genuine tags. When the tag to be tested is read, we will match the fingerprint of the tag to be tested with the fingerprint database to complete the cloning detection. In this section, we will introduce this process in detail.

During the cloning attack, the attacker clones the valid application data, including the ID used for identification. The fingerprint signal used for data transmission in the communication process depends on the device itself and cannot be predicted and cloned. Therefore, when the clone tag appears, although the ID is the same as the ID of the genuine tag, we can still distinguish the genuine tag and the clone tag by fingerprints.

In detail, based on the fingerprint database established by the genuine tag, we carry out clone tag detection. When the reader collects the tag information to be tested, the detection model matches the fingerprint to be tested with the genuine fingerprint in the fingerprint database. When the matched category is the same as the ID by the tag to be tested, we consider the tag to be tested to be a genuine tag. On the contrary, when the matched category is different from the ID by the tag to be tested, we consider the tag is a clone tag. See Algorithm 1 for the detailed detection process.

Algorithm 1. Cloning tag detection algorithm

Input:
> The ID of the tag, which means the category: ID
> RSSI of the tag to be detected: R
> Phase of the tag to be detected: P

Output:
> The status of the tag to be detected: clone or genuine

1: *image*: An image transformed from a sequence of the tag to be detected
2: *pred*: The prediction category of the model on the image
3: *image* = toImage(R, P)
4: *pred* = classify(*image*)
5: **if** *pred* $\neq$ *ID* **then**
6:    The tag is cloned.
7: **else**
8:    The tag is genuine.
9: **end if**

---

5 Implementation and Evaluation

In this section, we present the implementation and evaluation of our system.

5.1 Experimental Setup

We implemented Anti-Clone in the indoor environment of a typical office building. We use COTS RFID devices to build a system prototype. As shown in Fig. 6. An Impinj Speedway R420 reader connects to a larid S9028 antenna to collect the physical layer signal of each tag. The reader continuously broadcasts signals. When the tag responds to ID, the reader simultaneously records the RSSI and phase information of the tag.

We collected data with three types of tags to evaluate the impact of tag types on Anti-Clone performance. Tags were pasted on objects with four types of materials. We collected them to evaluate the effects of different material types on detection performance. We used 500 tags for the experiment and carried out a cloning attack on each tag in turn.

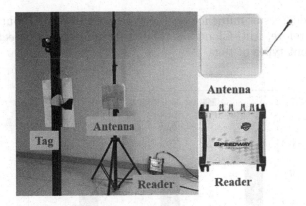

Fig. 6. System deployment.

5.2 Efficiency of Anti-Clone

Overall Performance. We study the effectiveness of Anti-Clone against cloning attacks, which helps remind users and avoid potential economic losses. We use the accuracy rate, false positive rate (FPR), and false negative rate (FNR) to display the results. FPR means a false alarm rate. FNR means miss alarm rate. The detection results show that the detection accuracy of Anti-Clone for cloning attack is 98.4%.

We evaluated the classification model separately. This model realizes the feature extraction of tag individuals and is the primary determinant of the detection effect of Anti-Clone. We use the traditional machine learning classifier quadratic discriminant analysis (QDA), K-nearest neighbor (KNN) clustering algorithm, and SqueezeNet for comparison. The results are shown in the following table. The results show that the classification model is superior to other methods in terms of classification effect (Table 1).

Table 1. Comparison of the results of different classifiers

Approach	QDA	KNN	SqueezeNet
Accuracy	58.23%	69.63%	**99.4%**

Performance with Different Types of Tags. In the RFID application system, different tags are designed according to the protected objects' types, shapes and materials, and planned costs. We evaluated the impact of different tag types on the effectiveness of Anti-Clone and selected three commonly used typical tags in the experiment, including NXP U8, Impinj R6, and imping M4E. We compared the performance in Fig. 7. The results show that different types of tags have different degrees of influence on the experimental results, but the effect is negligible. Therefore, Anti-Clone has robustness in clone tag detection and can adapt to different types of tags.

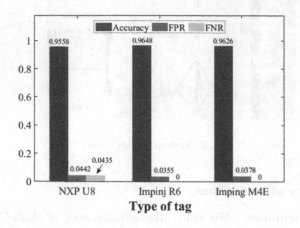

Fig. 7. Accuracy v.s. type of tags.

Performance with Different Material Types of Objects. In the RFID application system, the effect of the surface material of the protected object on the tag signal has been proved by experiments. In this section, we evaluate the effects of objects with different materials on the clone detection effect. We selected four typical materials commonly used in the system, including paper, plastic and rubber. Figure 8 shows the experimental results. The abscissa indicates different types of attached objects, and the ordinate indicates the accuracy rate, FPR, and FNR. We can see that the detection accuracy is over 96% for different types of attached objects. Therefore, the different materials of the tag protection object have no impact on the Anti-Clone, which has good robustness in the clone tag detection.

5.3   Time Overhead

Model Training Time. At the stage of establishing a fingerprint database, we combine CNN with transfer learning to combat small sample learning, make the network lightweight, and reduce the dependence on hardware resources. In this section, the lightweight is demonstrated by using the training time of the network before and after the transfer learning. We used the same data to train the network. The results show that 23 min can be saved by using transfer learning with a 1.8% loss of detection accuracy.

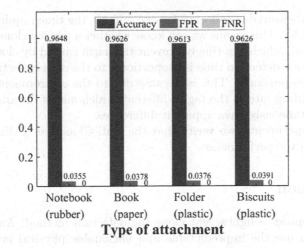

Fig. 8. Accuracy v.s. type of attachment.

Clone Detection Time. Cloning attacks detection system usually needs high real-time performance and requires administrators to respond quickly to clone tags. Therefore, the shorter the detection time and the loss can be reduced as much as possible.

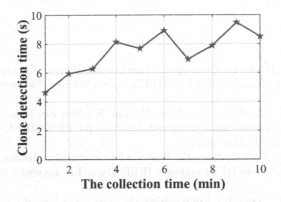

Fig. 9. Clone detection time overhead.

In this paper, the construction of the fingerprint database is offline, and the modeling time will not affect the detection time. Therefore, in this section, we only consider the time cost in the online detection stage. We built a system prototype on a laptop with common performance. The following figure shows the impact of different data volumes on the detection time. The abscissa represents the data collection time. The ordinate represents the clone detection time. When the data to be measured is collected for one minute, the time required for detection is less than 5 s. This means we can know whether a tag is a cloned tag within 5 s after it is read, which can timely prevent the harm caused by cloning attacks. In Fig. 9, the clone detection time is proportional to the data collection time, but it is not fully proportional. This is because due to the environment's influence, the reader's reading rate to the tag is different, which makes the amount of data collected simultaneously have apparent differences.

Through experiments, we verify that the Anti-Clone has a slight detection delay and real-time performance.

6   Conclusion

This paper proposes a lightweight clone tag detection method, Anti-Clone. Its basic idea is to use the unpredictable and unclonable physical layer signal to describe each tag with COTS RFID devices. We combined CNN with transfer learning to overcome the challenges of limited data and high signal coupling. A large number of experimental results show that the detection accuracy of Anti-Clone can reach 98.4% without any software or hardware modifications needed.

Our future work will be conducted on the extension of Anti-Clone to arbitrary environments. We try to design a detection method with environment robustness.

Acknowledgment. This work was supported by the Strategic Priority Research Program of Chinese Academy of Sciences, Grant No. XDC02040300

References

1. Bertoncini, C., Rudd, K., Nousain, B., Hinders, M.: Wavelet fingerprinting of radio-frequency identification (rfid) tags. IEEE Trans. Industr. Electron. **59**(12), 4843–4850 (2012)
2. Bu, K., Weng, M., Zheng, Y., Xiao, B., Liu, X.: You can clone but you cannot hide: a survey of clone prevention and detection for RFID. IEEE Commun. Surv. Tutor. **19**(3), 1682–1700 (2017)
3. Bu, K., Liu, X., Luo, J., Xiao, B., Wei, G.: Unreconciled collisions uncover cloning attacks in anonymous RFID systems. IEEE Trans. Inf. Forensics Secur. **8**(3), 429–439 (2013)
4. Bu, K., Liu, X., Xiao, B.: Approaching the time lower bound on cloned-tag identification for large RFID systems. Ad Hoc Netw. **13**, 271–281 (2014)
5. Bu, K., Xu, M., Liu, X., Luo, J., Zhang, S., Weng, M.: Deterministic detection of cloning attacks for anonymous RFID systems. IEEE Trans. Industr. Inf. **11**(6), 1255–1266 (2015)
6. Burmester, M., Munilla, J., Ortiz, A.: Comments on "unreconciled collisions uncover cloning attacks in anonymous RFID systems". IEEE Trans. Inf. Forensics Secur. **13**(11), 2929–2931 (2018)
7. Chen, X., Liu, J., Wang, X., Zhang, X., Wang, Y., Chen, L.: Combating tag cloning with cots rfid devices. In: 2018 15th Annual IEEE International Conference on Sensing, Communication, and Networking (SECON), pp. 1–9. IEEE (2018)

8. Danev, B., Heydt-Benjamin, T.S., Capkun, S.: Physical-layer identification of RFID devices. In: USENIX Security Symposium, pp. 199–214 (2009)
9. Dobkin, D.: The RF in RFID: uhf RFID in practice. Newnes (2012)
10. Feng, Y., Huang, W., Wang, S., Zhang, Y., Jiang, S.: Detection of RFID cloning attacks: a spatiotemporal trajectory data stream-based practical approach. Comput. Netw. **189**, 107922 (2021)
11. Han, J., et al.: Geneprint: generic and accurate physical-layer identification for UHF RFID tags. IEEE/ACM Trans. Networking **24**(2), 846–858 (2016)
12. Huang, W., Zhang, Y., Feng, Y.: Acd: an adaptable approach for RFID cloning attack detection. Sensors **20**(8), 2378 (2020)
13. Iandola, F.N., Han, S., Moskewicz, M.W., Ashraf, K., Dally, W.J., Keutzer, K.: Squeezenet: Alexnet-level accuracy with 50x fewer parameters and < 0.5 mb model size. arXiv preprint arXiv:1602.07360 (2016)
14. Ilie-Zudor, E., Kemény, Z., Blommestein, F.V., Monostori, L., Meulen, A.: A survey of applications and requirements of unique identification systems and RFID techniques. Comput. Ind. **62**(3), 227–252 (2011)
15. Lehtonen, M., Ostojic, D., Ilic, A., Michahelles, F.: Securing RFID systems by detecting tag cloning. In: Tokuda, H., Beigl, M., Friday, A., Brush, A.J.B., Tobe, Y. (eds.) Pervasive 2009. LNCS, vol. 5538, pp. 291–308. Springer, Heidelberg (2009). https://doi.org/10.1007/978-3-642-01516-8_20
16. Liu, J., Chen, M., Chen, S., Pan, Q., Chen, L.: Tag-compass: determining the spatial direction of an object with small dimensions. In: IEEE INFOCOM 2017-IEEE Conference on Computer Communications, pp. 1–9. IEEE (2017)
17. Liu, J., Zhu, F., Wang, Y., Wang, X., Pan, Q., Chen, L.: RF-scanner: shelf scanning with robot-assisted RFID systems. In: IEEE INFOCOM 2017-IEEE Conference on Computer Communications, pp. 1–9. IEEE (2017)
18. Liu, X., et al.: Multi-category RFID estimation. IEEE/ACM Trans. Networking '**25**(1), 264–277 (2016)
19. Liu, X., et al.: RFID estimation with blocker tags. IEEE/ACM Trans. Networking **25**(1), 224–237 (2016)
20. Liu, X., Xiao, B., Zhu, F., Zhang, S.: Let's work together: fast tag identification by interference elimination for multiple RFID readers. In: 2016 IEEE 24th International Conference on Network Protocols (ICNP), pp. 1–10. IEEE (2016)
21. Okpara, S.: Detecting cloning attack in low-cost passive RFID tags. In: An Analytic Comparison between KILL Passwords and Synchronized Secrets Obinna (2015)
22. Ouafi, K., Vaudenay, S.: Pathchecker: an RFID application for tracing products in supply-chains. Technical report (2009)
23. Piva, M., Maselli, G., Restuccia, F.: The tags are alright: Robust large-scale RFID clone detection through federated data-augmented radio fingerprinting. In: Proceedings of the Twenty-second International Symposium on Theory, Algorithmic Foundations, and Protocol Design for Mobile Networks and Mobile Computing, pp. 41–50 (2021)
24. Romero, H.P., Remley, K.A., Williams, D.F., Wang, C.M.: Electromagnetic measurements for counterfeit detection of radio frequency identification cards. IEEE Trans. Microwave Theory Techniques **57**(5), 1383–1387 (2009)
25. Senthilkumar, C., Thompson, D.R., Di, J.: Fingerprinting RFID tags. IEEE Trans. Depend. Secure Comput. **8**(6), 938–943 (2011)
26. Shahzad, M., Liu, A.X.: Fast and reliable detection and identification of missing RFID tags in the wild. IEEE/ACM Trans. Networking **24**(6), 3770–3784 (2016)

27. Wang, C., Xie, L., Wang, W., Xue, T., Lu, S.: Moving tag detection via physical layer analysis for large-scale RFID systems. In: IEEE INFOCOM 2016-The 35th Annual IEEE International Conference on Computer Communications, pp. 1–9. IEEE (2016)
28. Wang, P., Zhou, Y., Zhu, C., Huang, J., Zhang, W.: Analysis on abnormal behavior of insider threats based on accesslog mining. CAAI Trans. Intell. Syst **12**, 781–789 (2017)
29. Xie, L., Sun, J., Cai, Q., Wang, C., Wu, J., Lu, S.: Tell me what i see: recognize RFID tagged objects in augmented reality systems. In: Proceedings of the 2016 ACM International Joint Conference on Pervasive and Ubiquitous Computing, pp. 916–927 (2016)
30. Xie, L., Wang, C., Liu, A.X., Sun, J., Lu, S.: Multi-touch in the air: concurrent micromovement recognition using rf signals. IEEE/ACM Trans. Networking **26**(1), 231–244 (2017)
31. Zanetti, D., Fellmann, L., Capkun, S.: Privacy-preserving clone detection for RFID-enabled supply chains. In: 2010 IEEE International Conference on RFID (2010)
32. Zanetti, D., Danev, B., apkun, S.: Physical-layer identification of uhf RFID tags. In: Proceedings of the Sixteenth Annual International Conference on Mobile Computing and Networking, pp. 353–364 (2010)

A Privacy-Preserving Lightweight Energy Data Sharing Scheme Based on Blockchain for Smart Grid

Xinyang Li[1], Yujue Wang[1], Yong Ding[1,2(✉)], Shiye Ma[3], Bei Xiao[3],
Zhihong Guo[3], Xiaorui Kang[3], Xiaohui Ma[3], and Jia Mai[3]

[1] Guangxi Key Laboratory of Cryptography and Information Security,
School of Computer Science and Information Security,
Guilin University of Electronic Technology, Guilin, China
[2] Cyberspace Security Research Center, Pengcheng Laboratory, Shenzhen, China
stone_dingy@126.com
[3] Shanghai Energy Technology Development Co., Ltd, Shanghai, China

Abstract. As many users join the smart grid system, energy companies
need user energy data to manage and improve energy delivery. However,
while enjoying the services provided by energy companies, the energy
data submitted by users may lead to the risk of privacy leakage. To
solve this problem, this paper proposes a privacy-preserving scheme for
smart grid based on blockchain and multi-receiver encryption (PPBME).
The scheme utilizes lightweight multi-receiver encryption, blockchain,
and smart contract technologies to solve the problem of privacy leakage
when user data are shared. Also, our PPBME construction employs off-
chain storage technology to improve the scalability of the blockchain, so
that reducing the storage pressure of the blockchain. This paper also proposes a compensation mechanism for the loss of user privacy. According
to the security analysis and computational cost analysis, our PPBME
scheme is efficient and secure in supporting smart grid applications.

Keywords: Smart grid · Blockchain · Lightweight · Multi-receiver
encryption · Off-chain storage

1 Introduction

Nowadays, as people pay attention to renewable energy power generation, there
is an urgent need for an intelligent system that evaluates and prices electricity in
real-time, which cannot be offered by the classic power distribution system. The
smart grid was introduced in the early 2000s s to integrate the two-way communication infrastructure into the traditional power grid [12], which provides
functions such as digital communication between users and suppliers, and monitoring, updating, and reliable distribution of electrical energy for smart meters.
It is necessary to provide security mechanism on user data [3].

© ICST Institute for Computer Sciences, Social Informatics and Telecommunications Engineering 2022
Published by Springer Nature Switzerland AG 2022. All Rights Reserved
H. Gao et al. (Eds.): CollaborateCom 2022, LNICST 461, pp. 91–110, 2022.
https://doi.org/10.1007/978-3-031-24386-8_6

With the popularization of smart grids and smart home appliances, the data generated and transmitted in smart grids has grown tremendously. Regarding companies responsible for supplying and transmitting electricity, the data collected by smart meters can help them improve system performance and enhance the user experience. Nevertheless, users want a great service experience without their privacy being gained by any entity other than the company they trust [18]. Also, the information transmission between smart meters and service providers faces security and privacy challenges [24]. In the process of data sharing, how to protect the privacy, security and verifiability of user energy data is a problem that smart grids need to solve. Tampering with energy data may mislead service providers and lead to financial losses. In addition, the adversary's long-term analysis of energy data may reveal the user's daily behavior, leading to the leakage of user privacy.

1.1 Our Contributions

To address the privacy and security problems of energy data sharing in smart grid, this paper proposes a privacy-preserving scheme based on blockchain and multi-receiver encryption (PPBME). User data includes the usage data of various types of energy for a period of time, which may contain the user's private information. These data are required for the service providers to adjust resource allocation and regulate prices. Since in the process of data sharing over the public network, user energy data may subject to common known attacks such as eavesdropping and tampering, our PPBME construction is designed to ensure the confidentiality and integrity of the data by utilizing blockchain and data encryption technologies. PPBME also employs off-chain storage technology to store the original data in the cloud. The blockchain stores the relevant credentials for data usage, thereby improving the scalability of the blockchain. Due to the limit computing power of smart meters, the encryption scheme of PPBME in data sharing uses lightweight multi-receiver encryption, which can better achieve fine-grained access control. In order to incentivize users to share their private energy data, the smart contracts are used to generate contract accounts, and service providers will compensate users for privacy leakage by paying to the contract accounts.

The security analysis demonstrates that the proposed PPBME construction can protect the privacy and security of user energy data, as well as resist traditional attacks. Theoretical and experimental analysis show that the computing cost of the proposed PPBME construction is significantly reduced compared with related solutions.

1.2 Related Works

To address the privacy protection issues of communications between suppliers and users in smart grids, many cryptographic schemes have been proposed. Ding et al. [4] presented an efficient metering data aggregation scheme, which supports batch verification of collectors and power service providers, and ensures the privacy and integrity of metering data. Chen et al. [2] proposed a privacy protection scheme based on the certificateless aggregate signcryption technology, where masking random numbers are used to hide the consumption data of users. Wei et al. [14] presented to apply the blind signature to smart grid to achieve conditional anonymity so that malicious users can be identified. Li et al. [16] further proposed a scheme using conditional anonymous group blind signatures to protect data privacy in smart grids. Yu et al. [25] proposed an EC-ElGamal encryption supporting double trapdoor decryption in smart grid to ensure data privacy.

Due to the limited computing power of smart meter, many studies have proposed lightweight algorithms to protect data privacy at the smart meter side. Liu et al. [17] proposed a lightweight authentication communication scheme, which uses XOR operation to encrypt data and Lagrangian interpolation for identity authentication. However, the XOR operation does not provide sufficient security, so some schemes have been proposed to improve the security of their scheme while ensuring data privacy with only lightweight operations.

Zhang et al. [26] designed a lightweight anonymous authentication key agreement scheme for smart meters and service providers, which simultaneously realizes authentication and key sharing. Moghadam et al. [5] established a low-cost and secure two-way handshake communication using an ECC-based authentication and key exchange protocol. Gope et al. [8,9] used a physically unclonable function (PUF) to provide a smart meter-to-service provider authenticated key exchange protocol. The difference is that [9] solves the security problem of the modeling attack faced by [8]. Cao et al. [1] also used PUF to implement a lightweight privacy-preserving authentication data collection scheme. The experiments show that this scheme has high efficiency and low communication cost.

As an emerging technology, blockchain has the advantages of decentralization, data immutability, and traceability. Zhang et al. [27] used blockchain to realize secure signing of multi-party electronic contracts. Their scheme also uses an identity-based encryption algorithm to ensure the confidentiality of the contract and fairness in signing contracts. Wen et al. [23] constructed a blockchain supervision framework in a multi-party environment, which uses a double-chain structure to supervise the data in the blockchain. Blockchain technology can also be employed to realize privacy-preserving and verifiable billing in smart grid systems [28]. Gao et al. [7] proposed using blockchain technology to monitor smart grid, which can ensure user data privacy and transparently provide users with electricity consumption details. Gai et al. [6] adopted consortium chains to protect the privacy of energy transactions in smart grids.

However, the scalability of the blockchain is still a problem to be considered. If the storage space of all nodes is used to store data, the vast data redundancy will cause a significant burden on the blockchain nodes. Wang et al. [21] proposed an on-chain and off-chain coordination management system based on a consortium blockchain. In this system, the blockchain only stores the hash value and response records of the data, while a large amount of raw data is stored in an off-chain database. Wang et al. [22] designed a blockchain-based smart grid data sharing scheme, which provides immutability and transparency through cloud and blockchain as off-chain storage space and authentication platform, respectively. Although off-chain storage can solve the blockchain scalability problem, the security provided by on-chain storage cannot be replaced entirely. For example, there is no guarantee that data stored off-chain has not been tampered with.

2 Preliminaries

2.1 Blockchain

Blockchain is a peer-to-peer network technology for building and maintaining a distributed ledger or database of records [20]. Participants in the blockchain need to be verified by a specific consensus mechanism before uploading data to the blockchain for storage. The data blocks on the blockchain are linked in the chronological order of their respective generation in the form of chains and are copied and stored on different nodes. It has the characteristics of decentralization, immutability, and so on. With these characteristics, blockchain can ensure the reliability of recorded data.

Smart contract was first proposed by Nick Szabo [19] in 1994, which is essentially a piece of software code on the blockchain. It usually runs in a virtual environment, and the application can interact with the smart contract through the virtual machine's interface. The smart contract will strictly execute this code to complete the operations defined by the code.

2.2 Mathematical Difficulties on Elliptic Curves

Discrete Logarithm (DL) Problem. Let G be an elliptic curve group of prime order q, and P be a generator of G. Given a tuple (x, xP) with unknown $x \in Z_q^*$, computing x is difficult in any polynomial algorithm.

Decision Diffie-Hellman (DDH) Problem. Let G be an elliptic curve group of prime order q, and P be a generator of G. Given $X = xP$ and $Y = yP$ with unknown $x, y \in Z_q^*$, determining whether $Q = xyP \in G$ holds is difficult in any polynomial algorithm.

3 System Model and Security Requirements

This section presents the system model of PPBME and summarizes its security requirements.

3.1 System Model

As shown in Fig. 1, a PPBME system consists of five types of entities, namely, key generation center (KGC), smart meter (SM), energy company (EC), cloud and blockchain (BC).

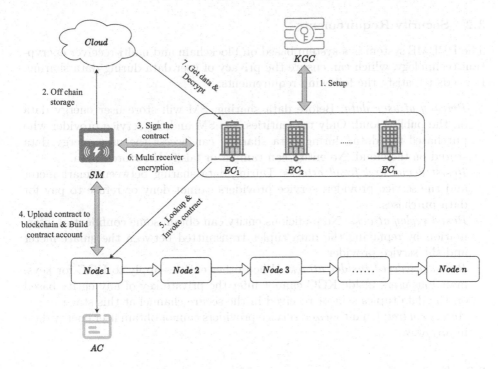

Fig. 1. System model of PPBME.

- **KGC:** KGC is a trusted third party that is mainly responsible for generating and distributing members' public and private keys.
- **SM:** The smart meter belongs to the sender in the system, which has the ability to collect energy data from various household energy-consuming appliances, is responsible for generating data information, and can generate ciphertext using the recipients' identities and public keys. Also, each smart meter can create a contract account AC, so that all nodes in the blockchain can access to pay privacy compensation.
- **EC:** The energy company belongs to the receiver in the system and is an energy service provider in the smart grid. This entity hopes to obtain the data collected by the user's smart meter to improve service quality and reduce costs. It can decrypt the ciphertext with its private key. By paying for contract accounts, energy companies can compensate users for privacy loss when sharing data.
- **Cloud:** The cloud is responsible for storing user energy data in encrypted form, and providing cloud storage services for users to store data off-chain to improve system efficiency.
- **BC:** The blockchain is responsible for storing data such as the transaction between SM and EC. Note that the original data is not stored on blockchain.

3.2   Security Requirements

The PPBME system is a system based on blockchain and multi-receiver encryption technology, which can ensure the privacy of user data during data sharing. It needs to satisfy the following requirements.

- *Privacy of user data*: Before data sharing, SM will store user energy data on the public cloud. Only two entities, the SM and the service provider who purchased the data, during data sharing, can access the user energy data stored on the cloud. No entity can tamper or falsify the stored data.
- *Resist denial and fraud attacks*: During data sharing between smart meter and the service provider, service providers cannot deny or refuse to pay for data purchases.
- *Resist replay attacks*: No malicious entity can obtain some confidential information by replaying the data tuples transmitted between the smart meter and the service provider.
- *Resist privileged-insider attack*: When other entities apply to KGC for keys, malicious users inside KGC cannot infer the private key of any entity based on the data tuples sent or received in the secure channel at this stage.
- *Access control*: Unauthorized service providers cannot obtain user energy data in any way.

3.3   System Framework

A PPBME construction consists of eight procedures, namely, Setup, KeyGen$_{EC}$, KeyGen$_{SM}$, OffChainSto, TransApp, TransPro, MulEnc, and Dec.

- **Setup**$(1^\lambda) \rightarrow \Omega$: The system setup procedure is executed by KGC, which takes the security parameter 1^λ as input and outputs the system public parameters Ω.
- **KeyGen$_{EC}$**$(\Omega, ID_i) \rightarrow (pk_i, sk_i, d_{EC_i}, X_{EC_i})$: The key generation procedure of EC is executed by KGC, which takes the system public parameters Ω and EC's identity ID_i as input, and outputs the public-private key pair (pk_i, sk_i) and signing key pair (d_{EC_i}, X_{EC_i}) for EC.
- **KeyGen$_{SM}$**$(\Omega, ID_{SM}) \rightarrow (d_{SM}, X_{SM})$: The key generation procedure of SM is executed by KGC, which takes the system public parameters Ω and SM's identity ID_{SM} as input and outputs the signing key pair (d_{SM}, X_{SM}) for SM.
- **OffChainSto**$(\Omega, M) \rightarrow (k, CK, site, D)$: Off-chain storage procedure is executed by SM, which takes the system public parameters Ω and user energy data M as input and outputs symmetric key k, ciphertext CK of data M under symmetric key k, the storage transaction D and the storage location *site*.
- **TransApp**$(\Omega, ID_i, contract_i) \rightarrow (Y_i, O)$: The transaction application procedure is executed by EC and SM. EC takes the system public parameter Ω, EC's identity ID_i and purchase contract $contract_i$ as input, outputs the transaction request data Y_i, and sends Y_i to SM. SM takes the system public

parameter Ω and the transaction request data Y_i of EC as input and outputs transaction data O.

- **TransPro**$(\Omega, O) \rightarrow (\{L_i\}_{i=1}^n, AC, \delta_{com})$: The transaction processing procedure is executed by SM, which takes the system public parameters Ω and transaction data O as input. SM initiates a smart contract through the transaction data O, and the smart contract creates the transaction $\{L_i\}_{i=1}^n$ of both parties. When all nodes successfully verify the transaction through the consensus algorithm, the transaction will be recorded in the blockchain. At the same time, SM creates a contract account AC that all nodes in the blockchain can access. EC pays enough contract currency to contract account AC as "compensation", AC closes the payment channel, changes the status of the contract account, and returns a payment completion flag δ_{com}.

- **MulEnc**$(\Omega, \{ID_i\}_{i=1}^n, \{pk_i\}_{i=1}^n, k) \rightarrow CT$: The multi-receiver encryption procedure is executed by SM, which takes the system public parameters Ω, symmetric key k, the identities of all participant ECs $\{ID_i\}_{i=1}^n$ and their public keys $\{pk_i\}_{i=1}^n$ as input and outputs the ciphertext CT under the symmetric key k and a multi-receiver encryption scheme.

- **Dec**$(\Omega, CT, site, pk_i, sk_i) \rightarrow (k, M)$: The decryption procedure is executed by EC, which takes the system public parameters Ω, ciphertext CT, EC's public-private key pair (pk_i, sk_i) and the data storage location $site$ in the cloud as input. The EC decrypts the ciphertext CT using the multi-receiver encryption scheme to obtain the symmetric key k, then finds the storage transaction D according to the storage location $site$ in the cloud, and finally decrypts the ciphertext CK in D with the symmetric key k to obtain the user energy data M.

A correct PPBME construction should satisfy the following conditions: If all participants faithfully follow the procedures, then

- Each EC can successfully validate the key pair generated by KGC.
- Each EC can successfully decrypt the ciphertext generated by SM.

4   PPBME Construction

This section introduces a PPBME construction.

4.1   System Initialization

Setup. KGC takes the security parameter 1^λ as input and outputs $p, q, E, G, G_p, G_q, P, Q$, where p, q are two distinct prime integers, E is an elliptic curve defined on F_p, G is the additive group on the elliptic curve E, G_p is a subgroup of G with prime order p, G_q is a subgroup of G with prime order q, $P \in G_p$ is a generator of G_p, and $Q \in G_q$ is a generator of G_q.

KGC chooses a random integer $x \in Z_p^*$ as the master private key, and calculates $P_{pub} = x \cdot P$ as the corresponding public key. KGC selects five collision-resistant hash functions $H_i : \{0,1\}^* \to Z_p^*$ for $i = 1, 2, 3$, $H_4 : \{0,1\}^* \to Z_q^*$ and $H_5 : \{0,1\}^* \to \{0,1\}^{l_1}$, where l_1, l_2 are determined by the security parameter λ. KGC chooses a secure multi-receiver encryption algorithm I, a secure symmetric encryption scheme $\Pi = (KeyGen, Enc, Dec)$ (e.g., AES) and a function $F(\cdot)$ that maps from point to value [13]. KGC publishes the system public parameters $\Omega = \{p, q, E, G, G_p, G_q, P, P_{pub}, Q, H_1, H_2, H_3, H_4, H_5, I, \Pi, F, l_1, l_2\}$.

KeyGen$_{EC}$. Each EC_i randomly selects an integer $t_i \in Z_p^*$, and calculates

$$T_i = t_i \cdot P$$

Then, EC_i sends dataset $set_1 = \{T_i, ID_i\}$ to KGC, where ID_i is EC_i's identity.

KGC computes the encryption and signing keys for EC_i according to the dataset set_1 and the system parameters Ω. KGC randomly selects integers $r_i, v_i \in Z_p^*$, $d_{EC_i} \in Z_q^*$, calculates

$$R_i = r_i \cdot P$$
$$V_i = v_i \cdot T_i$$
$$X_{EC_i} = d_{EC_i} \cdot Q$$
$$b_i = H_1(R_i \| V_i \| ID_i)$$
$$c_i = r_i + b_i x \pmod{p}$$

and sends the dataset $set_2 = \{R_i, V_i, c_i, v_i, d_{EC_i}, X_{EC_i}\}$ to EC_i through a secure channel.

After receiving the dataset set_2, EC_i first verifies it by checking the following equality

$$R_i + H_1(R_i \| V_i \| ID_i)P_{pub} \stackrel{?}{=} c_i \cdot P \tag{1}$$

If it holds, set_2 is valid, and then EC_i calculates $u_i = t_i \cdot v_i$. Thus, the public key of EC_i is $pk_i = (R_i, V_i)$, and the private key is $sk_i = (c_i, u_i)$. At the same time, EC_i obtains the public-private key pair (d_{EC_i}, X_{EC_i}) for signing.

KeyGen$_{SM}$. Similarly, SM applies to KGC for a pair of signing keys, sends the SM's identity ID_{SM} to KGC.

KGC randomly selects an integer $d_{SM} \in Z_q^*$, calculates

$$X_{SM} = d_{SM} \cdot Q$$

and sends the dataset $set_4 = \{d_{SM}, X_{SM}\}$ to SM through a secure channel.

Therefore, SM obtains the public-private key pair (d_{SM}, X_{SM}) for signing.

4.2   Off-Chain Storage

With the secure symmetric encryption scheme Π, SM generates the symmetric key k, and encrypts the user energy data M to obtain ciphertext CK as follows.

$$k \leftarrow \Pi.KeyGen(1^\lambda)$$
$$CK = \Pi.Enc_k(M)$$

SM generates current timestamp T_1, selects a random integer $\dot{a} \in Z_q^*$, and calculates a signature tuple $\dot{\sigma}_{SM} = (\dot{A}, \dot{B})$ as follows.

$$\dot{A} = F(\dot{a} \cdot Q) \pmod{q}$$
$$\dot{B} = \dot{a} - H_4(CK\|T_1) \cdot d_{SM} \pmod{q}$$

SM outputs a storage transaction $D = \{CK, T_1, \dot{\sigma}_{SM}\}$. Then, SM stores D on the public cloud and records the data storage location $site$.

4.3   Transaction Processing

TransApp. Each EC_i generates a purchase contract $contract_i$ and current timestamp $T_{2,i}$, selects a random integer $a_i \in Z_q^*$, and calculates a signature tuple $\sigma_{EC,i} = (A_i, B_i)$ as follows.

$$A_i = F(a_i \cdot Q) \pmod{q}$$
$$B_i = a_i - H_4(contract_i\|T_{2,i}\|ID_i\|X_{EC_i}) \cdot d_{EC_i} \pmod{q}$$

EC_i sends a request data Y_i to SM, where

$$Y_i = \langle contract_i, T_{2,i}, ID_i, X_{EC_i}, \sigma_{EC,i} \rangle$$

After receiving the request data Y_i, SM first checks whether $T_{now} - T_{2,i} \leq \varepsilon$ holds, where T_{now} is the current time, and ε is the maximum transmission delay. Then, if SM approves the purchase contract of EC_i, it returns an approval response and generates a timestamp T_3. Next, SM selects a random integer $\ddot{a} \in Z_q^*$, and calculates a signature tuple $\ddot{\sigma}_{SM} = (\ddot{A}, \ddot{B})$ as follows.

$$\ddot{A} = F(\ddot{a} \cdot Q) \pmod{q}$$
$$\ddot{B} = \ddot{a} - H_4((Y_1, Y_2, \cdots, Y_n)\|T_3\|X_{SM}) \cdot d_{SM} \pmod{q}$$

Then, SM outputs the transaction data O, where

$$O = \langle Y_1, Y_2, \cdots, Y_n, T_3, X_{SM}, \ddot{\sigma}_{SM} \rangle$$

TransPro. SM initiates a smart contract through O, as shown in Algorithm 1. The smart contract verifies the signature in O as follows

$$F(\ddot{B} \cdot Q + H_4((Y_1, Y_2, \cdots, Y_n)\|\mathcal{T}_3\|X_{SM}) \cdot X_{SM}) \stackrel{?}{=} \ddot{A} \qquad (2)$$

and, for each Y_i, checks the signature as follows.

$$F(B_i \cdot Q + H_4(contract_i\|\mathcal{T}_{2,i}\|ID_i\|X_{EC_i}) \cdot X_{EC_i}) \stackrel{?}{=} A_i \qquad (3)$$

If all are satisfied, the transaction L_i between EC_i and SM is constructed and recorded in the blockchain. At the same time, a contract account AC is created, and all nodes in the blockchain can access the contract account.

Algorithm 1. Create Transaction and Contract Accounts

Input: $O = \langle Y_1, Y_2, \cdots, Y_n, \mathcal{T}_3, X_{SM}, \ddot{\sigma}_{SM} \rangle$
Output: $L_i; AC; \delta_{com}$
 1: **if** $Time.now() - \mathcal{T}_3 \leq \varepsilon$ **Then**
 2: **Verify** $\langle Y_1, Y_2, \cdots, Y_n\|\mathcal{T}_3\|X_{SM} \rangle = Ver_{X_{SM}}(\ddot{\sigma}_{SM})$ is true
 3: **end if**
 4: $T_{trans} \leftarrow Time.now(); value = 0; status = 1$
 5: **While** $i \leq n$ **do**
 6: $i := i + 1$
 7: **Verify** $(contract_i\|\mathcal{T}_{2,i}\|ID_i\|X_{EC_i}) = Ver_{X_{EC_i}}(\sigma_{EC,i})$ is true **Then**
 8: $L_i \leftarrow (Y_i, value_{contract_i}, T_{trans})$
 9: $AC \leftarrow (value, status)$
10: $p \leftarrow AC.getpayment()$
11: $AC.updata(value = value + p)$
12: **if** $Time.now() - T_{trans} \leq \varepsilon$ **Then**
13: L_i completed
14: **Verify** $value \geq \sum value_{contract_i}$ is true **Then**
15: Receive δ_{com} from Blockchain
16: **if Verify** $\delta_{com} = true$ **Then**
17: $AC.updata(status = 0)$
18: **end if**

EC_i synchronizes blockchain data and detects the status of contract account AC. EC_i needs to pay the purchase amount in the purchase contract $contract_i$ to the contract account AC. After AC receives the purchase amount, it determines whether the amount is sufficient. If satisfied, it changes the status of the AC and returns a payment completion flag δ_{com}.

4.4   Data Sharing

SM synchronizes blockchain data and checks the status and identity of the contract account AC. When all ECs have executed the contract, the SM encrypts the symmetric key k using a multi-receiver encryption scheme.

MulEnc. With the identities $\{ID_i\}_{i=1}^n$ of $\{EC_i\}_{i=1}^n$ and their public keys $\{pk_i\}_{i=1}^n$, SM encrypts the symmetric key k, and shares the ciphertext and cloud storage address with participating ECs as follows. SM randomly chooses $\omega \in \{0,1\}^{l_2}$, and computes

$$s = H_2(k\|\omega)$$
$$S = s \cdot P$$

For each EC_i, SM calculates

$$b_i = H_1(R_i\|V_i\|ID_i)$$
$$U_i = s \cdot (R_i + b_i P_{pub} + V_i)$$
$$\mu_i = H_3(U_i\|ID_i\|R_i\|V_i)$$

randomly chooses an integer $e \in Z_p^*$, and computes a polynomial $f(y)$ with degree n as follows.

$$f(y) = \prod_{i=1}^n (y - \mu_i) + e \quad (\text{mod } p)$$

Next, SM calculates

$$\gamma = (k\|\omega) \oplus e$$
$$C = H_5(S\|e) \oplus H_5(k\|\omega)$$

and uploads ciphertext $CT = (S, f, \gamma, C)$ and the data storage location $site$ to blockchain.

Dec. After EC_i obtains $\{CT, site\}$ from the blockchain, it finds the cloud storage transaction D through $site$. Then, EC_i verifies the timestamp on the transaction D, and checks the following equality

$$F(\dot{B} \cdot Q + H_4(CK\|T_1) \cdot X_{SM}) \stackrel{?}{=} \dot{A} \tag{4}$$

If it holds, it indicates that D is a storage transaction created by SM; otherwise, D is an invalid transaction. After EC_i has successfully verified the signature, EC_i computes

$$U_i' = (c_i + u_i) \cdot S$$
$$\mu_i' = H_3(U_i'\|ID_i\|R_i\|V_i) \tag{5}$$
$$e = f(\mu_i') \quad (\text{mod } p)$$

and checks the following equality

$$H_5(e \oplus \gamma) \stackrel{?}{=} H_5(S\|e) \oplus C \tag{6}$$

If it is not satisfied, the decryption process aborts; otherwise, EC_i outputs the symmetric key k.

EC_i decrypts the ciphertext CK in D and outputs the SM energy data M as follows.

$$M = \Pi.Dec_k(CK)$$

Theorem 1. *The proposed PPBME construction is correct.*

Proof. To prove the correctness of the proposed PPBME construction, it is necessary to prove that the Eqs. (1)–(6) are satisfied.

For the dataset set_2 issued by KGC, equality (1) satisfies as follow:

$$R_i + H_1(R_i\|V_i\|ID_i)P_{pub}$$
$$= r_i \cdot P + H_1(R_i\|V_i\|ID_i)x \cdot P$$
$$= (r_i + H_1(R_i\|V_i\|ID_i)x) \cdot P$$
$$= c_i \cdot P$$

For the signature $\ddot{o}_{SM}$ from SM, equality (2) satisfies as follow:

$$F(\ddot{B} \cdot Q + H_4((Y_1, Y_2, \cdots, Y_n)\|T_3\|X_{SM}) \cdot X_{SM})$$
$$= F((\ddot{a} - H_4(Y_1, Y_2, \cdots, Y_n) \cdot d_{SM}) \cdot Q$$
$$+ H_4((Y_1, Y_2, \cdots, Y_n)\|T_3\|X_{SM}) \cdot X_{SM})$$
$$= F(\ddot{a} \cdot Q)$$
$$= \ddot{A}$$

The Eqs. (3) and (4) can be proved similar to the Eq. (2)

In order to decrypt the energy data M from ciphertext CK, the Eq. (5) satisfies as follow:

$$U_i' = (c_i + u_i) \cdot S$$
$$= (c_i + u_i) \cdot s \cdot P$$
$$= s \cdot (c_i \cdot P + u_i \cdot P)$$
$$= s \cdot ((r_i + b_i x) \cdot P + t_i \cdot v_i \cdot P)$$
$$= s \cdot (r_i \cdot P + b_i x \cdot P + v_i \cdot T_i)$$
$$= s \cdot (R_i + b_i P_{pub} + V_i) = U_i$$

For U_i calculated by SM and U_i' calculated by EC_i, we have

$$f(\mu_i) = f(H_3(U_i\|ID_i\|R_i\|V_i)) = e \pmod{p}$$

and

$$f(\mu_i') = f(H_3(U_i'\|ID_i\|R_i\|V_i)) = e \pmod{p}$$

Therefore, $k\|\omega = e \oplus \gamma$, which means EC can correctly decrypt the symmetric key k and further decrypt ciphertext CK.

In order to verify the correctness of the ciphertext CT decryption, the Eq. (6) satisfies as follow:

$$H_5(e \oplus \gamma) = H_5(k\|\omega) = H_5(S\|e) \oplus C$$

5   System Security Analysis

This section analyzes the security and performance of the proposed PPBME construction.

Theorem 2. *Suppose the symmetric encryption scheme Π is secure. In the PPBME construction proposed in this paper, any entity (including the cloud) except the key owner cannot obtain or infer the original data stored on the cloud. Also, the key owner cannot maliciously modify the data stored in the cloud.*

Proof. In the off-chain storage phase of PPBME, only SM with the symmetric key k can decrypt the ciphertext stored in the cloud. Only by obtaining the symmetric key k and the data storage location *site* can the attacker decrypt the private data through the decryption algorithm $\Pi.Dec_k(\cdot)$. At the same time, SM needs to sign the ciphertext and the current timestamp and store them in the cloud together. If the encryption party maliciously modifies the data, it will be detected and traced in time.

Theorem 3. *In the proposed PPBME construction, the transaction application and processing between SM and EC can effectively resist denial and fraud attacks.*

Proof. In PPBME, transaction processing between EC and SM is performed by smart contracts in a prescribed manner. EC's transaction and data usage are publicly recorded in the blockchain ledger, which means EC cannot deny or refuse to pay compensation. If the EC has fraudulent or false transactions, the real identity of EC will be discovered and traced. Therefore, the PPBME system proposed in this paper can effectively resist denial and fraud attacks.

Theorem 4. *The proposed PPBME construction is resistant to replay attacks. Any adversary cannot extract some valuable information by replaying the request data Y or transaction data O transmitted between EC and SM.*

Proof. The PPBME construction is proposed in a synchronous environment, and the massages between EC and SM are processed with the current timestamp. Thus, any adversary cannot efficiently perform replay attacks on the system. If the adversary tries to launch a replay attack by pretending to be a participant, when the smart contract creates transaction information and contract accounts, it will detect whether there are old messages through the timestamp attached to the messages.

Theorem 5. *The proposed PPBME construction can resist the privileged insider attack.*

Proof. In the KeyGen phase, the internal attacker may know the dataset $set_2 = \{R_i, V_i, c_i, v_i\}$ sent by KGC to EC. However, it cannot obtain r_i, v_i, t_i and the master private key x if the DL assumption holds in probabilistic polynomial time. Also, the attacker cannot obtain u_i in EC's private key $sk_i = (c_i, u_i)$, without knowing t_i and v_i. Thus, the PPBME construction can resist privileged insider attacks.

6   Comparison and Analysis

In this section, we compare the proposed PPBME scheme with the ones proposed by Kumar et al. [15], He et al. [11], and Guan et al. [10] in terms of security, functional characteristics, and computational cost.

6.1   Comparison on Security and Functionality Features

In Table 1, the schemes in [10,11,15] and our PPBME scheme are compared under five attributes such as simulated attack, denial and fraud attacks, replay attack, privileged insider attack and access control. The analysis shows that only our PPBME scheme can resist all these attacks and support access control mechanism, thus, our PPBME construction is more secure than other related schemes in [10,11,15].

Table 1. Security and functional features.

Properties	[15]	[11]	[10]	PPBME scheme
Simulated attack	Yes	Yes	Yes	Yes
Denial and fraud attacks	No	No	Yes	Yes
Replay attack	Yes	No	No	Yes
Privileged insider attack	—	Yes	Yes	Yes
Access control	No	Yes	Yes	Yes

In Kumar et al.'s scheme [15], a session key is generated for each pair of participants in the smart grid who wish to trade to ensure the confidentiality of the communication between two parties. Their scheme also uses timestamps to prevent replay attacks. However, this scheme does not support supervision on transaction party and allow the trusted third party to register for the two parties, thus, malicious users may conduct fake transactions, or launch denial and fraud attacks. Also, in one-to-many transactions, the scheme of Kumar et al. [15] cannot achieve access control well.

He et al.'s scheme [11] achieves system privacy protection through a multi-receiver encryption scheme, where the original data was directly encrypted and transmitted. For big data, it would be a major problem for devices with limited computational resources such as smart meters. Also, their scheme cannot resist denial and fraud attacks among users.

Guan et al.'s scheme [10] provides users with fine-grained access control through ciphertext-policy attribute-based encryption (CP-ABE). The service provider can determine whether the data is the one to be purchased through an access policy verification. However, their scheme is designed in bilinear groups, which seriously decreases the efficiency of data encryption and decryption.

The PPBME scheme proposed in this paper can solve the shortcomings of [10,11,15]. Our PPBME scheme uses the blockchain to store transaction information and smart contracts to control the completion of transactions, preventing the appearance of fraudulent or false transactions by participants and effectively resisting denial and fraud attacks. Also, we consider the scalability of the blockchain and store the encrypted data on the public cloud for off-chain storage. During transaction processing, the smart contract will authenticate the transaction parties and the transaction content to ensure that the transaction is valid, prevent the simulated attack and replay attack, and protect the security of transactions. Moreover, our PPBME scheme uses lightweight multi-receiver encryption technology to achieve access control and data privacy protection during transmission. Therefore, our PPBME scheme provides more security protection mechanisms than related one in smart grid.

6.2 Theoretical Analysis

As shown in Table 2, we analyze and compare the computing cost of our PPBME construction and the schemes in [10, 11, 15], where G_1, G_2 are multiplicative cyclic groups, and $\hat{G}$ is additive groups on nonsingular elliptic curves.

Suppose n ECs are wishing to obtain energy data from SM. In order to achieve energy data sharing, Kumar et al.'s scheme [15] requires SM to perform $3n$ multiplication operations on $\hat{G}$, $5n$ hash operations, $3n$ symmetric encryption operations and n XOR encryption operations. Therefore, the transaction and encryption time on the SM side is $3nT_{sm-\hat{G}} + 5nT_{gh} + 3nT_{Enc/Dec} + nT_{sc}$. The EC side needs to implement 5 multiplication operations on $\hat{G}$, 8 hash operations, one XOR operation and 3 symmetric encryption operations. Therefore, the transaction and decryption time on EC side is $5T_{sm-\hat{G}} + 8T_{gh} + 2T_{sc} + 3T_{Enc/Dec}$.

In He et al.'s scheme [11], the SM side needs to perform $3n+1$ multiplication operations on $\hat{G}$, n addition operations on $\hat{G}$, $4n+2$ hash operations, n XOR encryption operation and one symmetric encryption operation. Therefore, the transaction and encryption time on SM side is $(3n+1)T_{sm-\hat{G}} + nT_{add-\hat{G}} + (4n+2)T_{gh} + nT_{sc} + T_{Enc/Dec}$. The EC side needs to implement 3 multiplication operations on $\hat{G}$, 7 hash operations, two XOR operations and one symmetric encryption operation. Therefore, the transaction and decryption time on EC side is $3T_{sm-\hat{G}} + 7T_{gh} + 2T_{sc} + T_{Enc/Dec}$.

In Guan et al.'s scheme [10], the SM side needs to perform $n+2$ exponentiation operations on G_1, one bilinear pair matching operation and two exponentiations on G_2. Therefore, the transaction and encryption time on SM side is $(n+2)T_{exp-G_1} + T_{bp} + 2T_{exp-G_2}$. EC side needs to implement $2n+3$ bilinear pairing operations, n exponentiation operations on G_2, one exponentiation operation on G_1, one hash operation and one ECDSA signing operation. Therefore, the transaction and decryption time on EC side is $(2n+3)T_{bp} + nT_{exp-G_2} + T_{exp-G_1} + T_{gh} + T_{sig}$.

Table 2. Calculation cost comparison.

Schemes		Smart meter side	Service provision side
[15]	K_1	—	$2T_{sm-\hat{G}} + T_{gh}$
	K_2	$2nT_{sm-\hat{G}} + 3nT_{gh} + nT_{Enc/Dec} + nT_{sc}$	$T_{sm-\hat{G}} + 4T_{gh} + T_{Enc/Dec}$
	K_3	$nT_{sm-\hat{G}} + 2nT_{gh} + 2nT_{Enc/Dec}$	$2T_{sm-\hat{G}} + 2T_{Enc/Dec} + 3T_{gh} + T_{sc}$
[11]	K_1	—	$T_{sm-\hat{G}}$
	K_2	$(3n+1)T_{sm-\hat{G}} + 4nT_{gh} + nT_{add-\hat{G}} + nT_{sc}$	—
	K_3	$2T_{gh} + T_{Enc/Dec}$	$2T_{sm-\hat{G}} + 7T_{gh} + 2T_{sc} + T_{Enc/Dec}$
[10]	K_1	—	$T_{gh} + T_{sig}$
	K_2	$(n+2)T_{exp-G_1}$	—
	K_3	$T_{bp} + 2T_{exp-G_2}$	$(2n+3)T_{bp} + nT_{exp-G_2} + T_{exp-G_1}$
PPBME scheme	K_1	—	$2T_{sm-\hat{G}} + T_{add-\hat{G}} + T_{gh}$
	K_2	$T_{Enc/Dec} + 2T_{sig}$	T_{sig}
	K_3	$(2n+1)T_{sm-\hat{G}} + 2nT_{add-\hat{G}} + (2n+3)T_{gh} + 2T_{sc}$	$T_{sm-\hat{G}} + 3T_{gh} + 2T_{sc} + T_{Enc/Dec} + T_{ver}$

Notes: K_1: System initialization, K_2: Off-chain storage and data processing, K_3: Data sharing. T_{bp}: Bilinear mapping time ($e : G_1 \times G_1 \rightarrow G_2$), T_{exp-G_1}: Exponentiation operation time on group G_1, T_{exp-G_2}: Exponentiation operation time on group G_2, $T_{sm-\hat{G}}$: Multiplication operation time of group $\hat{G}$, $T_{add-\hat{G}}$: Addition operation time of group $\hat{G}$, T_{gh}: Hash operation time, T_{sc}: XOR operation time, $T_{Enc/Dec}$: Symmetric encryption/decryption time, T_{sig}: ECDSA signature operation time, T_{ver}: ECDSA authentication operation time.

In our PPBME scheme, the SM side needs to perform $2n + 1$ multiplication operations on $\hat{G}$, $2n$ addition operations on $\hat{G}$, $2n + 3$ hash operations, two XOR encryption operations, one symmetric encryption operation and two ECDSA signing operations. Therefore, the transaction and encryption time on SM side is $(2n+1)T_{sm-\hat{G}} + 2nT_{add-\hat{G}} + (2n+3)T_{gh} + 2T_{sc} + T_{Enc/Dec} + 2T_{sig}$. EC side needs to implement 3 multiplication operations on $\hat{G}$, one addition operation on $\hat{G}$, 4 hash operations, two XOR operations, one ECDSA signing operation, one ECDSA verification operation and one symmetric encryption operation. Therefore, the transaction and decryption time on EC side is $3T_{sm-\hat{G}} + T_{add-\hat{G}} + 4T_{gh} + 2T_{sc} + T_{sig} + T_{ver} + T_{Enc/Dec}$.

6.3   Experimental Analysis

In this section, we evaluated the experimental performance of the proposed PPBME construction in an environment with a quad-core Xeon processor, 16G memory, and the 2021.3.3 version of the Goland software. The PBC and Crypto libraries are used to support crypto operations, where the elliptic curve is of Type E ($y^3 = x^3 + ax + b$) such that q and the element size in G are all 256 bits, and the encryption algorithm is AES-256-CBC. All hash functions are SHA-256. The experimental results of key operations are summarized in Table 3. According to Table 2 and Table 3, it is easy to get the running time at the smart meter side and the service provider side of these schemes, which are shown in Table 4.

Table 3. Running time of key operations.

Notations	Runtime (milliseconds)
T_{bp}	28.353
T_{exp-G_1}	1.352
T_{exp-G_2}	1.725
$T_{sm-\hat{G}}$	2.806
$T_{add-\hat{G}}$	0.016
T_{gh}	0.002
T_{sc}	0.001
$T_{Enc/Dec}$	0.042
T_{sig}	2.945
T_{ver}	5.871

Table 4. Running time (milliseconds).

Scheme	Smart meter side	Service provider side
Kumar et al. [15]	$8.555n$	14.174
He et al. [11]	$8.443n + 2.852$	8.476
Guan et al. [10]	$1.352n + 34.507$	$58.431n + 89.358$
PPBME scheme	$5.648n + 8.746$	17.302

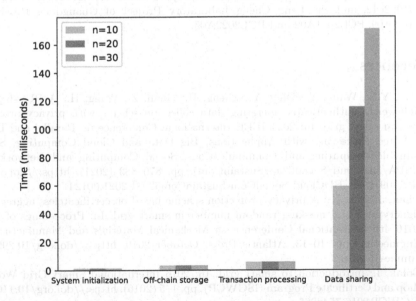

Fig. 2. Time cost at smart meter side.

We evaluated the time spent at the smart meter side of the proposed PPBME scheme in the system initialization phase, off-chain storage phase, transaction processing phase, and data sharing phase when the number of service providers $n = 10, 20, 30$, respectively, which are shown in Fig. 2. These results are consistent with those in Table 4. Therefore, the proposed PPBME scheme enjoys higher efficiency than other related schemes.

7   Conclusion

In order to solve the privacy leakage problem caused by data sharing in smart grid systems, this paper proposed a privacy protection system based on blockchain and multi-receiver encryption. The elliptic curve encryption and off-chain storage technologies are used to improve the system's efficiency in processing data. Before data sharing, energy companies deposit the compensation to the contract account to compensate for the leakage of user data in the future. Users can achieve control access on energy data for energy companies through smart meters with a multi-recipient encryption technology. The security and performance analysis showed that the proposed PPBME construction is secure and efficient.

Acknowledgment. This article is supported in part by the National Key R&D Program of China under project 2020YFB1006004, the Guangxi Natural Science Foundation under grants 2019GXNSFFA245015 and 2019GXNSFGA245004, the National Natural Science Foundation of China under projects 62162017, 62172119, 61862012 and 61962012, and the Peng Cheng Laboratory Project of Guangdong Province PCL2021A09, PCL2021A02 and PCL2022A03.

References

1. Cao, Y.N., Wang, Y., Ding, Y., Zheng, H., Guan, Z., Wang, H.: A PUF-based lightweight authenticated metering data collection scheme with privacy protection in smart grid. In: 2021 IEEE International Conference on Parallel and Distributed Processing with Applications, Big Data and Cloud Computing, Sustainable Computing and Communications, Social Computing and Networking (ISPA/BDCloud/SocialCom/SustainCom), pp. 876–883 (2021). https://doi.org/10.1109/ISPA-BDCloud-SocialCom-SustainCom52081.2021.00124
2. Chen, J., Ren, X.: A privacy protection scheme based on certificateless aggregate signcryption and masking random number in smart grid. In: Proceedings of the 2016 4th International Conference on Mechanical Materials and Manufacturing Engineering, pp. 10–13. Atlantis Press, October 2016. https://doi.org/10.2991/mmme-16.2016.3
3. Colak, I.: Introduction to smart grid. In: 2016 International Smart Grid Workshop and Certificate Program (ISGWCP), pp. 1–5 (2016). https://doi.org/10.1109/ISGWCP.2016.7548265
4. Ding, Y., Wang, B., Wang, Y., Zhang, K., Wang, H.: Secure metering data aggregation with batch verification in industrial smart grid. IEEE Trans. Industr. Inf. **16**(10), 6607–6616 (2020). https://doi.org/10.1109/TII.2020.2965578
5. Farhdi Moghadam, M., Mohajerzdeh, A., Karimipour, H., Chitsaz, H., Karimi, R., Molavi, B.: A privacy protection key agreement protocol based on ECC for smart grid. In: Choo, K.-K.R., Dehghantanha, A. (eds.) Handbook of Big Data Privacy, pp. 63–76. Springer, Cham (2020). https://doi.org/10.1007/978-3-030-38557-6_4

6. Gai, K., Wu, Y., Zhu, L., Qiu, M., Shen, M.: Privacy-preserving energy trading using consortium blockchain in smart grid. IEEE Trans. Industr. Inf. **15**(6), 3548–3558 (2019). https://doi.org/10.1109/TII.2019.2893433
7. Gao, J., et al.: GridMonitoring: secured sovereign blockchain based monitoring on smart grid. IEEE Access **6**, 9917–9925 (2018). https://doi.org/10.1109/ACCESS.2018.2806303
8. Gope, P., Sikdar, B.: Privacy-aware authenticated key agreement scheme for secure smart grid communication. IEEE Trans. Smart Grid **10**(4), 3953–3962 (2019). https://doi.org/10.1109/TSG.2018.2844403
9. Gope, P., Sikdar, B.: A privacy-aware reconfigurable authenticated key exchange scheme for secure communication in smart grids. IEEE Trans. Smart Grid **12**(6), 5335–5348 (2021). https://doi.org/10.1109/TSG.2021.3106105
10. Guan, Z., Lu, X., Yang, W., Wu, L., Wang, N., Zhang, Z.: Achieving efficient and privacy-preserving energy trading based on blockchain and ABE in smart grid. J. Parallel Distrib. Comput. **147**, 34–45 (2021)
11. He, D., Wang, H., Wang, L., Shen, J., Yang, X.: Efficient certificateless anonymous multi-receiver encryption scheme for mobile devices. Soft. Comput. **21**(22), 6801–6810 (2016). https://doi.org/10.1007/s00500-016-2231-x
12. Kabalci, E., Kabalci, Y.: Introduction to smart grid architecture. In: Kabalci, E., Kabalci, Y. (eds.) Smart Grids and Their Communication Systems. Energy Systems in Electrical Engineering, pp. 3–45. Springer, Singapore (2019). https://doi.org/10.1007/978-981-13-1768-2_1
13. Katz, J., Lindell, Y.: Introduction to Modern Cryptography. CRC Press, Boca Raton (2020)
14. Kong, W., Shen, J., Vijayakumar, P., Cho, Y., Chang, V.: A practical group blind signature scheme for privacy protection in smart grid. J. Parallel Distrib. Comput. **136**, 29–39 (2020)
15. Kumar, P., Gurtov, A., Sain, M., Martin, A., Ha, P.H.: Lightweight authentication and key agreement for smart metering in smart energy networks. IEEE Trans. Smart Grid **10**(4), 4349–4359 (2019). https://doi.org/10.1109/TSG.2018.2857558
16. Li, X., Sun, X., Li, F.: A group blind signature scheme for privacy protection of power big data in smart grid. In: Tan, Y., Shi, Y., Zomaya, A., Yan, H., Cai, J. (eds.) DMBD 2021. CCIS, vol. 1453, pp. 23–34. Springer, Singapore (2021). https://doi.org/10.1007/978-981-16-7476-1_3
17. Liu, Y., Cheng, C., Gu, T., Jiang, T., Li, X.: A lightweight authenticated communication scheme for smart grid. IEEE Sens. J. **16**(3), 836–842 (2016). https://doi.org/10.1109/JSEN.2015.2489258
18. Su, Z., Wang, Y., Xu, Q., Fei, M., Tian, Y.C., Zhang, N.: A secure charging scheme for electric vehicles with smart communities in energy blockchain. IEEE Internet Things J. **6**(3), 4601–4613 (2019). https://doi.org/10.1109/JIOT.2018.2869297
19. Szabo, N.: Formalizing and securing relationships on public networks. First Monday **2**(9) (1997). https://doi.org/10.5210/fm.v2i9.548, https://firstmonday.org/ojs/index.php/fm/article/view/548
20. Underwood, S.: Blockchain beyond bitcoin. Commun. ACM **59**(11), 15–17 (2016). https://doi.org/10.1145/2994581
21. Wang, K., Yan, Y., Guo, S., Wei, X., Shao, S.: On-chain and off-chain collaborative management system based on consortium blockchain. In: Sun, X., Zhang, X., Xia, Z., Bertino, E. (eds.) ICAIS 2021. CCIS, vol. 1423, pp. 172–187. Springer, Cham (2021). https://doi.org/10.1007/978-3-030-78618-2_14

22. Wang, Y., et al.: SPDS: a secure and auditable private data sharing scheme for smart grid based on blockchain. IEEE Trans. Industr. Inf. **17**(11), 7688–7699 (2021). https://doi.org/10.1109/TII.2020.3040171

23. Wen, B., Wang, Y., Ding, Y., Zheng, H., Liang, H., Wang, H.: A privacy-preserving blockchain supervision framework in the multiparty setting. Wirel. Commun. Mob. Comput. **2021** (2021). https://doi.org/10.1155/2021/5236579

24. Yang, L., Xue, H., Li, F.: Privacy-preserving data sharing in smart grid systems. In: 2014 IEEE International Conference on Smart Grid Communications (Smart-GridComm), pp. 878–883 (2014). https://doi.org/10.1109/SmartGridComm.2014.7007759

25. Zhan, Y., Zhou, L., Wang, B., Duan, P., Zhang, B.: Efficient function queryable and privacy preserving data aggregation scheme in smart grid. IEEE Trans. Parallel Distrib. Syst. **33**(12), 3430–3441 (2022). https://doi.org/10.1109/TPDS.2022.3153930

26. Zhang, L., Zhao, L., Yin, S., Chi, C.H., Liu, R., Zhang, Y.: A lightweight authentication scheme with privacy protection for smart grid communications. Future Gener. Comput. Syst. **100**, 770–778 (2019)

27. Zhang, T., Wang, Y., Ding, Y., Wu, Q., Liang, H., Wang, H.: Multi-party electronic contract signing protocol based on blockchain. IEICE Trans. Inf. Syst. **E105.D**(2), 264–271 (2022). https://doi.org/10.1587/transinf.2021BCP0011

28. Zhao, M., Ding, Y., Tang, S., Liang, H., Wang, H.: A blockchain-based framework for privacy-preserving and verifiable billing in smart grid. Peer-to-Peer Netw. Appl. (2022). https://doi.org/10.1007/s12083-022-01379-4

Dynamic Trust-Based Resource Allocation Mechanism for Secure Edge Computing

Huiqun Yu[1,2]([⊠]), Qifeng Tang[1], Zhiqing Shao[1]([⊠]), Yiming Yue[1], Guisheng Fan[1]([⊠]), and Liqiong Chen[3]

[1] Department of Computer Science and Engineering,
East China University of Science and Technology, Shanghai, China
{yhq,zshao,gsfan}@ecust.edu.cn
[2] Shanghai Key Laboratory of Computer Software Evaluating and Testing,
Shanghai, China
[3] Shanghai Institute of Technology, Shanghai 201418, China

Abstract. Edge computing plays an important role in processing and storing data. By offloading tasks to the edge server, mobile users can access necessary computing resources on demand. However, security of edge computing service is still a major concern. This paper proposes an edge computing resource allocation mechanism based on dynamic trust. First, security problems due to lack of reliability in the resource allocation process are solved based on the trust mechanism. This mechanism considers the resource allocation process between the mobile user node and the edge server as a transaction, according to the trading behavior in the transaction process of server to give its corresponding trust. Second, a trust mechanism is used for dynamic credit granting. Mobile users with similar behaviors form a group, where a representative is elected to trade resources and bundle information into a block and attach it on the chain. At the same time, the delay problem is added as a constraint to the trust calculation. Finally, the simulation experiment shows that the mechanism improves security of edge computing.

Keywords: Edge computing · Security · Trust · Blockchain · Resource allocation

1 Introduction

Edge computing technology has emerged with the development of innovative edge devices, such as the Internet of Things and smart phones. In order to

This work was partially supported by National Natural Science Foundation of China No.62276097, Shanghai Municipal Natural Science Foundation under Grant No.21ZR1416300, Capacity building project of local universities Science and Technology Commission of Shanghai Municipality No.22010504100.

improve the efficiency of computing resources and optimize performance indicators, edge computing resource allocation and task scheduling have received widespread attention [1]. At the same time, edge computing also faces many security problems, its nodes are exposed at the edge of the network [2], computing power and storage capacity are limited, which make equipment and network resources favor by attackers easily [3].

The attackers pose threats to different infrastructures in edge computing network architectures, such as user devices, server nodes, and network resources. In order to improve the security of edge computing in resource allocation, a reasonable trust mechanism can be established to filter the infrastructure in the network. To construct the evaluation mechanism including resource trust, identity trust and behavior trust, it is necessary to integrate the historical information, the matching degree of resources to different requirements.

For the design of trust mechanism, the credibility mechanism included in blockchain technology has been relatively mature in the calculation of trust, so it can be introduced to edge computing. The blockchain technology adopts the method of distributed data storage, in essence, it can be seen as a decentralized database. We can think of blockchain as an intermediary responsible for resource allocation transactions, account management and currency exchange, which is jointly managed and maintained by users. Therefore, compared with the traditional centralized database, the consensus mechanism, encryption algorithm, smart contract and other technologies included in it make it have the characteristics of multi-party maintenance, immutability, openness and transparency [4], and data security and high availability are well guaranteed [5]. Therefore, with the help of its immutable property, it can be considered to store the relevant information in the transaction process of edge computing resources on the chain, which can be monitored and viewed by users, and is not easy to be changed.

This paper studies the security of edge computing resource allocation and proposes a dynamic trust-based edge computing resource allocation mechanism (DTERAM). This mechanism regards the resource application process between the edge server and the mobile user as a transaction, and dynamically grants credit based on the behavior of the edge server in the resource transaction process. At the same time, in order to reduce the number of interactions between the edge server and mobile users and the cost of mobile users to purchase resources, the DTERAM divides mobile users into groups and realizes resource sharing within the group. Mobile users apply for resources to edge servers on a group basis, preferentially select edge servers with a high degree of trust for transactions, and group members share the cost of purchasing resources. The DTERAM takes the security of resource transactions as the evaluation standard, realizes resource allocation between edge servers and mobile users, and improves the security of the transaction process.

The main contributions of this paper are as follows:

(1) A trust model is established to realize the resource transaction process between edge servers and mobile users, which improves the security of resource allocation. The server pricing process takes into account the relationship between

price and user needs, and uses a greedy algorithm to solve the trust model to improve the security in the process of resource transactions.

(2) An edge computing resource allocation mechanism based on dynamic trust of blockchain is proposed. Two aspects of historical trust degree and dynamic trust degree are considered. Adding trust in the evaluation of the server status is more conducive for mobile users to select edge servers with high security.

The remainder of this paper is organized as follows. In Sect. 2, related work is reviewed. Section 3 introduces the system model. Section 4 introduces the DTERAM resource allocation mechanism. Section 5 carries on the experimental results and related analysis and the conclusion is given in Sect. 6.

2   Related Work

In recent years, there has been a lot of research work on resource allocation in edge computing. Dong et al. [6] presented a task priority-oriented resource allocation method for mobile edge computing, and assigned corresponding priorities to tasks based on their average processing value to achieve the effect of reducing overall delay and energy consumption. Li et al. [7] proposed a joint resource allocation and task scheduling algorithm, which improved the peak load capacity of the edge and reduced user delay. Xue et al. [8] established a joint convex optimization goal based on computational offloading and task allocation, and used Lagrangian multiplier method to iterate update to get the optimal solution. Yang et al. [9] proposed a joint optimization scheme for task offloading and resource allocation in a 5G communication network based on edge computing, and transformed the problem of task offloading and resource allocation into a joint optimization problem of time delay and energy consumption. Alfakih T et al. [10] proposed a state-action-state-action (RL-SARSA) algorithm based on reinforcement learning to solve the resource management problem of edge servers. Liao et al. [11] proposed a resource allocation and task scheduling optimization scheme based on service emergency priority. Samrat Nath et al. [12] studied the dynamic caching, computing shunting, and resource allocation problems in the cache-assisted multiuser MEC system with random task arrival. Wang et al. [13] studied the problem of effectively allocating and adjusted edge resources in the case of high dynamics brought about by user mobility in edge computing.

The main focus of the above-mentioned research is on the algorithm optimization of the edge computing resource allocation process, which is continuously improved under the premise of considering the characteristics of delay and mobility, but the security issues are ignored. However, the Internet technology is becoming more and more perfect, security issues such as data leakage and personal information privacy appear to be particularly important. Therefore, improving the security in the process of resource allocation has become an urgent problem to be solved in related fields.

As the underlying technology of the Bitcoin system, blockchain technology has been more and more used in recent years due to its high security. With the development of blockchain technology research, there are more researches on the application of blockchain in the field of non-digital currency [14], such as in applying it to edge computing to solve security problems. Ref. [15] proposed an edge computing distributed trusted authentication system based on blockchain technology. Xu et al. [16] aimed at the problem of lack of trust in sharing the data generated in edge computing among stakeholders, developed a blockchain-based big data sharing framework, and a new type of blockchain transaction including Express. Zhang et al. [17] aimed at the security problem of the consensus algorithm vulnerable to attacks in blockchain-based mobile edge computing, proposed a group signature scheme to verify the generated blocks of the blockchain and verify the identity of mobile users. Wu et al. [18] introduced an incentive mechanism and a decentralized accountability mechanism to establish a trust and reputation system for CEC stakeholders, and used smart contracts to verify correctness and automatically punish them in case of failure. Nabil EI Loini et al. [19] established a trusted orchestration management framework based on blockchain, which supports the identification, traceability and orchestration of all participants, and achieves complete tracking and verification of data. Huang et al. [20] used blockchain technology to improve the security of edge computing resource allocation, while taking into account the fairness cost (FDC) and node mobility (RDC). In the reputation based consensus mechanism (PoR) included in the D2D-ECN framework proposed in Ref. [21], the device with the highest reputation score is responsible for packaging the resource transactions and reputation records of the blockchain.

For the existing research on improving the security of edge computing with the help of blockchain technology, the trust degree is mainly based on identity verification, data storage and verification, but the behavior trust of participants is only an evaluation value based on historical information. Therefore, we consider a dynamic trust evaluation of participants behavior, and evaluate trust from two aspects: historical information and real-time transaction behavior.

3   System Model

First, an example of edge computing resource trading is given to describe the process of resource trading. The process consists of four parts: pricing, bidding, selection and negotiation, transaction and feedback. When a transaction occurs, the sequence of steps performed is as follows:

(1) The edge server sets the price of a unit resource with reference to the overall demand put forward by the mobile user, and the unit resource price is inversely proportional to the overall demand of the mobile user.

(2) After negotiation within the group, mobile users give their own bids based on their actual conditions.

(3) Mobile users select the target server based on the trust level, the resource pricing and the resource capacity of the edge server, then negotiate the final price with the target server, and the final price must be higher than the cost price of the resource. The negotiation process is divided into three types: 1) If the mobile user bid is not less than the selling price of the edge server, the final price is the mobile user bid; 2)If the mobile user bid is less than the selling price of the edge server and greater than the resource cost price, the final price is the

selling price; 3)If the mobile user's bid is less than the cost price of the resource, then the transaction failed.

(4) The mobile user group and the edge server conduct transactions at the final price determined in step 3. After the transaction is completed, the mobile user will give feedback on the quality of experience during the transaction.

The specific process is shown in Fig. 1. The mobile users are divided into different groups. The members in the group have the same preference for resources and the group is used as a unit to apply for resources. In order to improve the security in the resource allocation process, the mobile users select edge servers for transactions based on factors such as trust and price. The resource transactions involve a group of edge servers (sellers) and mobile user groups (buyers). The edge server sets its own selling price according to the overall needs of users. The user makes a choice with reference to the trust and selling price of the edge server. During the transaction, mobile users do not know each other's bids, and edge servers do not know each other's selling prices, and the information is stored on the blockchain. According to resource demand, trust and price, complete the mapping of edge server and mobile user group to realize resource service.

As shown in Fig. 1, we model the process of resource allocation between edge servers and mobile users as trust transactions, and design a high security feasible solution for j mobile user groups to allocate i edge server resources. The solution considers that the resources provided by different servers are heterogeneous, because the same type of resources provided by different servers are different due to factors such as trustworthiness, service quality, and price.

In the transaction process between the edge server and the mobile user, in order to obtain the maximum utility, the edge server acts as the seller and sets the resource selling price according to the resource cost and demand. As a buyer, in order to reduce costs and the number of interactions with edge servers, the mobile users form a group with the same hobbies, share the resources and distribute the cost evenly. Additionally, the representative selected by group conduct transactions with the edge server. In the selection process of the edge

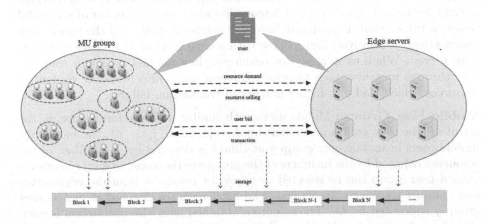

Fig. 1. Trading model of resource allocation mechanism based on dynamic trust

Table 1. Parameters of the system model

Symbol	Description
I	The set of edge servers
J	The set of mobile user groups
C_i	Capacity of edge server i
B_i	Bandwidth of edge server i
p_i	Unit resource final price of edge server i
s_i	Unit resource selling price of edge server i
c_i	Unit resource cost price of edge server i
val_j	Unit resource bid of mobile user group j
D_j	Total resource demand of mobile user group j
$m_{i,j}$	Resources demand by mobile user group j from edge server i
$trust_i$	Trust of edge server i
$\Delta_{i,j}$	State evaluation by mobile user group j for edge server i

server, although each edge server has its own resources, due to the difference in service quality, the user group will first evaluate the status value of the server through the trust level, resource capacity and resource price of the edge server, then select the server with the best status value for resource service. The main symbols involved in the transaction model are explained in Table 1.

Edge Servers: Edge server provides mobile users with the resources they request, the set of edge servers is denoted by $I = \{1, 2, \ldots, i, \ldots, m\}$, the capacity of edge server i is denoted by C_i and the bandwidth of edge server i is denoted by B_i. Different edge servers have different quality of service when providing resources to users. The trust degree of the edge servers is evaluated, the initial trust degree is set to 0.5, and the upper limit is set to 1. The edge servers are divided into three categories through trust changes: high-quality, low-quality, and malicious edge servers. Edge servers with a degree of trust between [0.5,1] provide high-quality services, with a large number of successful transactions, reasonable resource prices, and low transaction delays; Edge servers with a degree of trust between [0.2, 0.5) provide low-quality services, the number of successful resource transactions is moderate, resource prices are high, and the transaction process delay is relatively high; Those with a trust level of [0, 0.2) are malicious edge servers. When users apply for resources, they conduct malicious competition through measures such as price reduction, or tamper with the content of resources, which lead to a higher number of transaction failures.

Mobile User Groups: Mobile users with similar interests form a group, the set of mobile user groups is denoted by $J = \{1, 2, \ldots, j, \ldots, n\}$, the number of mobile users in mobile user group j at time t is denoted by $n_j(t)$. Most of the resources required by the members of the group are the same, so a representative from a user group can be selected to apply for resources from the edge server and conduct resource transactions. The total resource demand of mobile user group j is denoted by D_j. The resources obtained after the transaction is completed can be shared and exchanged within the group, which can improve their QoE. In addition, the members of the group equally share the costs required in

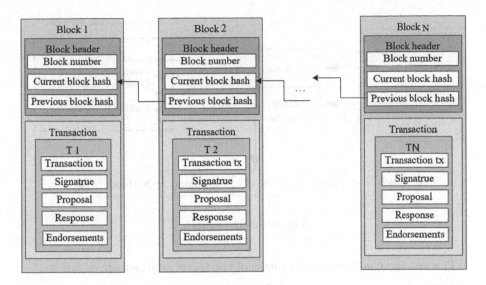

Fig. 2. Blockchain structure

the resource transaction process, which not only reduces the number of interactions between the user and the server, avoids repeated applications for the same resource, but also reduces the cost for users to obtain the required resources.

Blockchain: Blockchain can be divided into public chain and private chain. Public affairs can be verified by all independent participants, and private affairs need to be processed by authorized participants. In this paper, a public chain is used to record the resource transaction process between edge servers and mobile users. The block structure is shown in Fig. 2. Each block contains two parts: Block header and Transaction. The Block header realizes the connection between blocks through the included hash value, and Transaction is responsible for storing the relevant information of each transaction. Members of the same mobile user group can view and verify the information on the blockchain. Representatives selected by each group are responsible for packaging the relevant transaction records of each resource application and uploading them to the blockchain.

Smart Contract: The smart contract is a set of commitments defined in digital form, and an agreement that includes contract participants to implement these commitments. Smart contracts can be introduced in the transaction process, and information such as pricing, payment, storage, and delivery can be processed through smart contracts. As shown in Fig. 3, each smart contract is assigned a unique address, which can be triggered by sending a transaction. Different events are triggered by processes in the smart contract, and related transactions will be recorded on the blockchain in the order of timestamps. The use of smart contracts can enable entities to write transaction rules according to certain specifications of their own conditions, and achieve the purpose of maximizing utility through time and transaction prices. In addition, using smart contracts to execute transactions does not need to rely on trusted third parties (banks, Government, etc.).

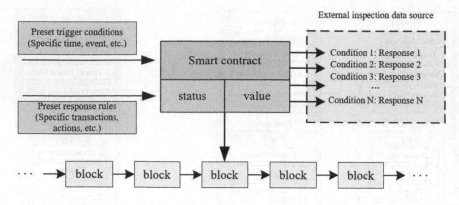

Fig. 3. Smart contract

The specific conditions and process of the smart contract are as follows:

Initialization: 1) Initial settings for resource transactions. The capacity C_i, cost price c_i, selling price p_i and trust $trust_i$ of edge server i; The resource demand D_j, resource bid val_j of mobile user group j; Transaction deployment time $dTime$. 2)The edge server i and the mobile user group j negotiate smart contract transaction rules.

Creation: After the edge server i and the mobile user group j agree on the smart contract transaction rules, use the create function to deploy smart contracts on the blockchain. The output of this function is the address of the smart contract on the blockchain, which is public to all edge servers and mobile users, so each entity can be selective Interact with the contract. In addition, in order to ensure the smooth progress of the smart contract, both the edge server i and the mobile user group j must put some deposits in their accounts into the smart contract to prevent malicious behavior. The smart contract will return the deposit after the transaction is over.

Transaction: If a smart contract is deployed on the blockchain, the transaction function is executed, resource transactions between edge server i and the mobile user group j will start after time $t > dTime$. The mobile user group j calculates status $\Delta_{i,j}$ based on the trust $trust_i$, the resource capacity C_i, and the unit resource selling price p_i of the edge server i, choose the server with the largest value of $\Delta_{i,j}$ to apply for resource transactions. The edge server i determines the resource selling price according to the total resource demand of mobile users in order to obtain the maximum utility u_i. In addition, smart contracts can supervise content delivery between mobile user group j and edge server i. If any party does not abide by the signed agreement, the function $Penally()$ will be called. Finally, if the smart contract reaches the service period, financial settlement is performed, and all assets owned by it are recovered.

Threat Model: We also consider the harm of untrusted edge servers and mobile user groups. First, the edge server maliciously participates in the competition of

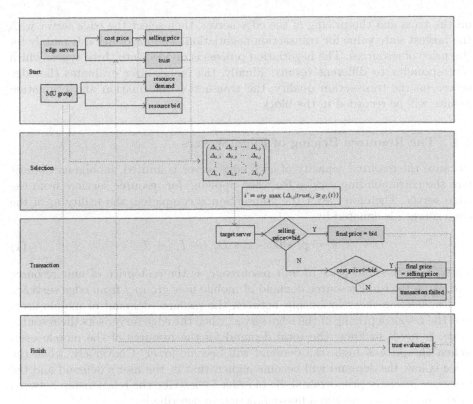

Fig. 4. Transaction process

resource transactions, such as malicious bidding that interferes with the transaction, resulting in a waste of time or resources. Second, attackers may use them to return malware or viruses to the requesting program to gain potential intent. Third, a malicious mobile user group may refuse the resource service of the edge server and thus refuse to pay. Similar to the existing blockchain-based applications, this paper uses a reputation mechanism to grant dynamic trust, and uses trust as an important reference condition in the resource transaction process to ensure security.

4   Dynamic Trust-Based Edge Computing Resource Allocation Mechanism

The specific process of the dynamic trust-based edge computing resource allocation mechanism is shown in Fig. 4. There are four stages including Start, Selection, Transaction, and Finish. Among them, the Start stage is mainly the pricing stage of the edge server, the pricing process is based on the total demand of mobile users. Selection, Transaction and Finish are three stages of the transaction process. In this three processes, mobile users will calculate state values based on the trust and the pricing of the edge server, then select the edge server with the largest state value for transaction negotiation. The negotiation is mainly for the price of resources. The negotiation process is divided into three types, which corresponding to different results. Finally, the mobile user evaluates the edge server on the transaction quality, the transaction information and evaluation results will be recorded in the block.

4.1   The Resource Pricing of Edge Servers

Because the resource capacity of each edge server is limited, mobile users must pay the corresponding service fee when applying for resource services from the edge server. Therefore, after the transaction is completed, the utility u_i of the edge server i is denoted by:

$$u_i = p_i * D_j - c_i * D_j; i \in I, j \in J \tag{1}$$

where p_i is the final price of unit resource, c_i is the cost price of unit resource and D_j is the total resource demand of mobile user group j from edge server i.

Considering the relationship between the resource demand of mobile users and the resource pricing of the edge server, when the edge server sets the resource price, it needs to know the total demand for the resource of the mobile user. When the price is high, the demand will become lower. Conversely, when the price is low, the demand will become higher, that is, the user's demand and the price are inversely proportional. So in order to describe the relationship between price and demand, we use a linear function to describe it.

$$D_j = \begin{cases} C_i - \xi_i * s_i, s_i \leq \frac{C_i}{\xi_i} \\ 0, s_i > \frac{C_i}{\xi_i} \end{cases} \tag{2}$$

where C_i is the resource capacity of the edge server i, s_i is the selling price of unit resource and ξ_i is the price reference value of edge server i when pricing. The ξ_i is related to many factors, including the number of mobile users, the size of the resource applied for, and the popularity of the resource. Therefore, the calculation method of the ξ_i in reference [22] takes into account the relationship between the price of edge server resources and the demand of mobile users, and rewrites the utility of the edge server i as

$$u_i = (p_i - c_i) * (C_i - \xi_i * s_i); \forall i \in I \tag{3}$$

In this process, the malicious edge server can have two kinds of attack behaviors. The first type of behavior is that a malicious edge server deletes, modifies, or replaces the resource content applied by the mobile user to achieve some of its potential intentions. The second type of behavior is that the edge server has been destroyed, thereby injecting viruses or malware into mobile users requesting resources from themselves. If an attack is to be implemented here, mobile users need to select a malicious edge server to apply for resources. In the solution proposed in this paper, the choice of edge server is related to trust and resource prices. Therefore, in order to attract more mobile users, each malicious edge server needs to obtain a higher degree of trust, and need to set a lower resource price, but this will not maximize the utility. At the same time, after a transaction is over, the feedback of mobile users will reduce the trust value of the malicious edge server, making it unable to have a higher trust value, then it will not continue to be selected. Therefore, our proposed scheme can avoid these two attack methods.

4.2   Mobile User Groups

In the process of resource transactions, the attack of malicious edge servers may cause mobile users to be unable to obtain the required resources for security. Therefore, in order to improve the security in the transaction process, we have added the concept of trust to enable mobile users to obtain reliable and trust-worthy resource services. We assign a trust value to each edge server, and use the trust value to indicate the credibility of the edge server. The higher the value, the higher the credibility of the server and the safer and more reliable the resource services provided.

According to the interactive behavior and result of the resource transaction process with the edge server, the mobile user can evaluate the service quality of the edge server. If the user is satisfied with the service, they can send a high-level feedback, and the user can achieve dynamic credit to the edge server based on the real-time feedback of each service quality, update its trust value in time, and ensure high security at any time.

According to the processing method in reference [23], the DTERAM mechanism divides the entire process into a series of epoch from the running time, each epoch completes a resource transaction and generates a block, which is divided into three parts in the process of calculating the trust degree of the edge server.

(1) The initial trust $trust_i(his)$ based on the historical records before the start of each epoch;

(2) The trust $trust_i(t-1)$ of the last transaction at the current transaction moment t;

(3) The delay time $Latency$ obtained by the calculation method of delay in reference [24].

First, based on the logistic regression model, the calculation method of the initial trust degree of the edge server is given.

$$trust_i(his) = \frac{1}{1 + e^{-\alpha(\sum_{x=0}^{n-1} \nu_x - \gamma \times \sum_{x=0}^{n-1} \varphi_x)}} \tag{4}$$

where $trust_i(his)$ is the initial trust given to the edge server i based on the previous behavior of i at the beginning of the current transaction, n is the current nth transaction, α is the total number of transactions that the server has participated in, ν_x is whether edge server i is trading normally during the xth transaction, normally is 1 and otherwise is 0. And φ_x is whether edge server i is trading maliciously during the xth transaction, maliciously is 1 and otherwise is 0, γ is the penalty weight for malicious transactions performed by the edge server, which can be set by the user. The greater the weight, the greater the penalty for malicious transactions. At the same time, the initial trust level is specified as $trust_i(0) = \frac{1}{1+e^{-\alpha(0-0)}} = 0.5$.

The logistic regression model has a rapid increase in the trust value during the logarithmic growth period. It is not reasonable to judge the trust value purely based on the model. Therefore, this paper balances the trust of current transaction based on the historical and the trust of the last transaction. At the same time, considering the delay of edge computing, the formula for calculating the trust of the transaction is finally obtained.

$$trust_i(t) = \beta \times trust_i(his) + (1 - \beta)trust_i(t - 1) + \frac{\lambda}{Latency} \tag{5}$$

where $trust_i(t)$ is the trust of the edge server i in the tth epoch resource transaction. Here, parameter β issued to modify the rate of increase of trust to avoid the centralization of trust in the initial stage caused by excessive growth. The initial value of β is 1, because at the beginning it is not known whether the edge server will be prone to malicious transactions. Parameter λ is to weight the delay, the delay and the trust have an inverse relationship. The smaller the delay, the greater the trust degree value. Conversely, the greater the delay, the lower the trust degree value.

The change of parameter β is determined by the cumulative trust deviation $\nu_t * ttrust_i$, and the specific relationship is

$$\beta = threshold + c \times \frac{\delta_t * trust_i}{1 + \nu_t * trust_i} \tag{6}$$

Initially, $\nu_0 * trust_i = 0$, parameter c can be defined by the user to control the weight of the reaction to the recent behavior of the edge server. $threshold$ is a threshold set to prevent β transition saturation from tending to 1, the initial value is set to 0.25, $\delta_t * trust_i$ is the trust degree deviation, the calculation method is,

$$\delta_t * trust_i = |trust_i(t - 1) - trust_i(his)| \tag{7}$$

At the tth epoch transaction, the trust degree deviation of edge server i is equal to the difference between the current initial trust degree and the absolute value of the trust degree in the $t - 1$th epoch transaction, therefore, the calculation method of the cumulative trust deviation $\nu_t * trust_i$ in the tth epoch transaction is

$$\nu_t * trust_i = c \times \delta_t * trust_i + (1 - c)\nu_{t-1}trust_i \tag{8}$$

The larger the value of the parameter c, it means that the weight of the recent trust deviation given by the mobile user is more important than the previous cumulative trust deviation weight.

Latency is the delay time, which is inversely related to the trust. Here the delay time is divided into four parts, namely the bidding time of mobile user group bid^j, the bidding time of edge server $charge^i$ and the time of negotiate $Cond_i^j$.

$$Latency = \{bid^j, charge^i, Cond_i^j\} \tag{9}$$

After obtaining the trust of the edge server, the mobile user group will choose the edge server with the best trust according to their needs. There are two criteria for mobile users to choose the best edge server: 1)The optimal edge server selected should have a high degree of trust and be able to provide safe, reliable, and high-quality resource services; 2)The resource price of the optimal edge server should be low and the capacity should be large. Therefore, each mobile user group will establish a trust threshold to judge whether the edge server is trustworthy. The trust threshold is calculated as:

$$v_{i,j}(t) = \omega_{tr} trust_{i,j}^{max}(t) + \alpha \times log(1 + \frac{n_j(t)}{n_j^{max}(t)}) \tag{10}$$

$trust_{i,j}^{max}(t)$ is the maximum trust of the mobile user group j to the edge server i from the initial time to the current time t, $n_j(t)$ represents the number of users in mobile user group j at time t, $n_j^{max}(t)$ represents the maximum number of users in the mobile user group in time$[0,t]$, α is a weighting parameter, and ω_{tr} is a threshold adjustment parameter.

Each mobile user group calculates the resource status of the edge server, and then selects an optimal server for resource transactions. We define the resource status of the server as the ratio between trust level, resource capacity and resource price. Then for the mobile user group j, the resource status of the edge server i is

$$\Delta_{i,j} = \frac{\eta * trusti, j + \mu * C_i}{s_i} \tag{11}$$

where η and μ are the weighted parameters of trust level and resource capacity respectively, according to the resource status of each edge server, the mobile user group j selects the best edge server for transactions.

$$i^* = argmax_i\{\Delta_{i,j}|trust_{i,j} \geq \zeta(t)\} \tag{12}$$

After the mobile user group j selects the edge server i^* corresponding to the maximum state value $\Delta_{i,j}$, the two will negotiate the resource price of the transaction. The negotiation process is:

$$p_i = \begin{cases} val_j, val_j > s_j \\ s_i, c_i \leq val_j \leq s_i \\ fail; val_j < c_i \end{cases} \tag{13}$$

On the other hand, trust can be used as a reward for edge servers to provide high-quality services, and it is also a manifestation of edge server reputation. In order to maintain the number of edge servers participating in the resource transaction process, trust consumption is introduced. In addition, based on the characteristics of the Logistics regression model, the trust level of the edge server is limited by the upper limit. Here, the reference to trust consumption is to ensure the participation of edge servers. If few edge servers participate in the transaction process, the resource allocation mechanism based on dynamic trust is of little significance. As long as the edge server participates in the bidding and selection of resource transactions, regardless of whether it is selected by the mobile user in the end, there will be no trust consumption. On the contrary, if the edge server does not participate, then its trust will be consumed. The calculation formula for the trust consumption of the edge server i is

$$trust_i(his) = \begin{cases} \frac{1}{1+e^{-\alpha(\sum_{x=0}^{n-1} \nu_x - \gamma \times \sum_{x=0}^{n-1} \varphi_x)}}, & \Delta_B = 0 \\ trust_i(t) \times e^{-D \times \Delta_B}, & otherwise \end{cases} \tag{14}$$

where Δ_B represents the block interval, that is the interval between the last participating transaction and the current participating transaction (starting from 0), the calculation method is $\Delta_B = B_{cur} - B_{pre}$. If two transactions are consecutive, then $\Delta_B = 0$, at this time, the edge server participates in the calculation and transactions with the current trust level, and the trust consumption function will not be executed, which greatly ensures that the edge server actively participates in resource transactions. The value of D will be dynamically adjusted according to the transaction quality, and the final resource transaction quality will be maintained at a stable level. The increase in transaction difficulty will make transactions require more trust weighting. High-quality servers will choose not to participate in the transaction temporarily, in order to find that the difficulty is reduced, and the opportunities will increase to participate in the transaction, but when the participation of the edge server is too low, the probability of the malicious edge server's success becomes higher. At the same time, the increase in difficulty will increase the trust consumption of edge servers that do not participate in transactions, which will help increase the participation of edge servers.

4.3   DTERAM Algorithm Implementation

The Algorithm 1 is the implementation process of the proposed DTERAM, DTERAM is mainly composed of two main parts, the user's choice of edge server (SelectEdgeServer) and the utility calculation of the edge server (Edgeserversutility). The DTERAM algorithm takes edge servers I, resource cost price c_i, resource selling price s_i, initial trust $trust_i(his)$, delay time T_i, mobile user group J, resource demand D_j and resource bid val_j as input. In each round of transactions, the mobile user group j will read the trust level of the edge server i^*, then calculate the service status $\delta_{i,j}$ of i, next sort the edge server status values in descending order, and select the server i^* with the highest status value, and then conduct price negotiation to get the transaction price p_i^*. After completing the transaction with price p_i^*, the mobile user group j evaluates the server i^*, and the server i^* calculates its own utility.

The DTERAM algorithm mainly uses blockchain-related technologies to improve the security of edge computing in the process of resource allocation. However, while using blockchain technology, the process of generating blocks and put the block on the chain will consume a part of the time. Therefore, the mechanism needs to be optimized in terms of time performance. The next step can be to reduce time consumption and improve the performance.

5   Experimental Results and Analysis

In this section, we evaluate the proposed method through simulation experiments. First, we introduce the relevant settings of the simulation experiment, and then analyze the results of the experiment.

5.1   The Setup of Simulation Experiment

First, 5 mobile user groups and 10 edge servers are deployed in the network. The number of users in each mobile user group is randomly determined between [5,10], the resource demand of resources is randomly determined between [1,10] Mb, and the resource capacity of each edge server is randomly determined between [10,50] Mb. The initial trust level of each edge server is set to 0.5, and the edge servers are preliminarily divided into three types: high quality, low quality and malicious. The proportions of the three types are 0.4, 0.3 and 0.3 respectively. Other parameter configurations are: $\zeta(i,j) = 0.4$, $\gamma=2$, $\alpha = 1$, $threshold = 0.25$, $\eta = 0.3$, $\mu = 0.4$.

Algorithm 1. Dynamic Trust-Based Edge Computing Resource Allocation Mechanism

Require:

The edge servers I, the resource cost price c_i, the resource selling price s_i, the initial trust $trust_i(his)$, the delay time T_i, the mobile user group J, the resource demand D_j and the resource bid val_j.

Ensure:

The set of redundant service DWS_f and the set of active execution service for tasks in user request U_f;

1: Initial: $t = 0$, $trust_i(his) = 0.5$, $p_i = 0$.
2: **for** $t = 1 \longrightarrow T$
3: **procedure** SelectEdgeServer
4:     get $trust_i(his)$ of each edge servers by using blockchain
5:     calculate $trust_i(t)$ by Eq.(5)
6:     **for** $i = 1 \longrightarrow I$
7:         **for** $j = 1 \longrightarrow J$
8:             $\frac{\eta * trusti, j + \mu * C_i}{s_i}$
9:             **if** $trust_{i,j} \geq \eta(t)$
10:                 $i^* \longleftarrow max \Delta_{i,j}$
11:             **end if**
12:         **end for**
13:     **end for**
14:     **for** $j = 1 \longrightarrow J$
15:         **if** $val_j > s_i^*$
16:             $p_i^* \longleftarrow val_j$
17:             Transaction
18:         **else if** $val_j < s_i^*$ and $val_j > c_i^*$
19:             $p_i^* \longleftarrow s_j$
20:             Transaction
21:         **else if** $val_j < c_i^*$
22:             Transaction failure
23:         **end if**
24:     **end for**
25:     Each social group updates its current trust for Edge Server by Eq.(4)
26:     **return** updated $trust_i(t)$
27: **end procedure**
28: **procedure** Edgeserversutility
29:     **for** $i = 1 \longrightarrow I$
30:         $\mu_{i,j} \longleftarrow (p_i - c_i) \times D_j$ or 0
31:         $\mu_i \longleftarrow \sum_{j=1}^{J} \mu_{i,j}$
32:     **end for**
33: **end procedure**
34: $t \longleftarrow t + 1$
35: **end for**

5.2   The Analysis of Simulation Experiment Results

Figure 5 illustrates the relationship between the edge server unit resource price and the number of transactions. It can be seen from the figure that the unit resource price of a highquality edge server increases with the increase in the number of transactions, and eventually stabilizes. The unit resource prices of low-quality edge servers and malicious edge servers both increase at the beginning, but will gradually decrease in the future and eventually stabilize. It can be understood that the initial trust of all edge servers is the same at the beginning, the mobile user group will prefer lower-priced servers when choosing, so the resource prices of low-quality and malicious edge servers that have lower-priced will increase. However, as the transaction progresses, trust is an important basis for the selection of mobile user groups, low-quality edge servers and malicious edge servers will be exposed, users gradually turn to high-quality edge servers, which will cause the resource prices of high-quality edge servers to gradually rise to achieve greater utility. When the trust tends to stabilize, the price tends to stabilize accordingly and this time the utility of the edge server reaches its maximum value. At the same time, lowquality and malicious edge servers can only participate in the competition by lowering resource prices due to the decline in trust. However, since trust is an important basis for selection, the effect is not great. Figure 6 is the relationship between the resource demand and resource price of the mobile user group when the edge servers are 10, 20, 30, and 40 respectively. It can be seen that when the number of edge servers is different, as the mobile Fig. 6. unit resource price-resource requirements. user groups demand for resources increases, the price gradually increases. At the same time, when the resource demand of mobile users is the same, the fewer the number of edge servers, the higher the resource price. It can be understood that when the demand for mobile users increases, edge servers will increase resource prices to obtain greater profits. In addition, when there are more edge servers, the edge servers will participate in the competition by reducing prices to attract more mobile users to conduct resource transactions. Therefore, the more edge servers there are, the lower the resource price will be.

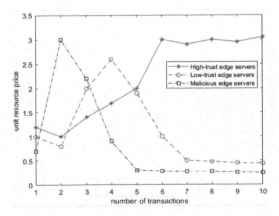

Fig. 5. Unit resource price-number of transactions

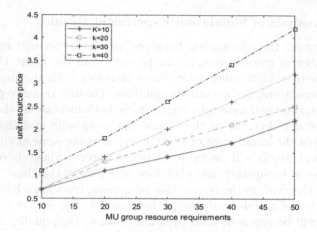

Fig. 6. Unit resource price-resource requirements

Figure 7 shows the relationship between the average trust of edge servers and the number of transactions. This paper calculates the average values of the trust levels of highquality, low-quality, and malicious edge servers respectively. The initial value of trust is 0.5, therefore, the initial values of the average trust levels of the three types of servers are all 0.5. It can be seen from the figure that the average trust of highquality edge servers increases with the increase in the number of transactions, and then gradually stabilizes. Conversely, the trust of low-quality and malicious edge servers will decrease over time. It can be understood that high-quality edge servers provide high-quality resource services. Due to high-quality services, mobile users' trust evaluation of the server during the transaction process will also increase, and as the number of transactions increases, the server's average trust level will stabilize. On the contrary, low-quality and malicious edge servers provide low-quality services that will cause mobile users to lower their trustworthiness, which leads to their average trust-worthiness gradually decreasing as the number of transactions increases.

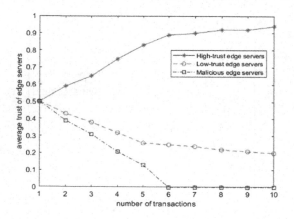

Fig. 7. The average trust-number of transactions

Figure 8 shows the relationship between the overall trust of high-quality edge servers and the number of transactions when the c are 0.1, 0.5, and 0.9 respectively. Since the high-quality ratio among the 10 edge servers is 0.4, the initial overall trust level is 2, and the upper limit of trust level is 4. It can be seen from the figure that the c value is different, the corresponding trust rate growth rate is also different, but in the end it will be close to the upper limit. The larger the value of c, it means that the trust growth rate in recent transactions accounts for a larger proportion of the overall trust growth rate, that is, the real-time trust changes reflected in the transaction process have a greater impact on the trust calculation. After the transaction, the trust of the edge server will be maintained at a stable level.

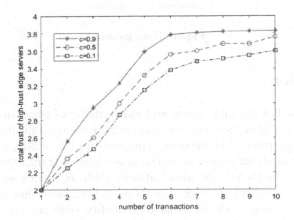

Fig. 8. Total trust-number of transactions

Figure 9 shows the decline process of the overall trust of edge servers. This process assumes that all edge servers remain offline when their trust reaches their peak, that is, if they do not participate in resource transactions, then the entire transaction will no longer be safe. It can be seen from the figure that if all edge servers do not participate in resource transactions, the trust level of the first few transactions remains basically stable, but after the fifth transaction, the trust level has dropped significantly, and the decline process is non-linear. After the seventeenth transaction, it gradually tends to zero.

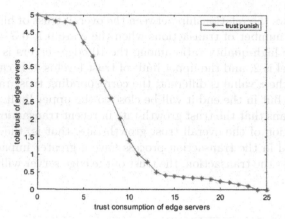

Fig. 9. Trust punish

6   Conclusion

In view of the malicious competition and vulnerability of edge computing in the process of resource allocation, an edge computing resource allocation mechanism based on dynamic trust of blockchain is proposed in this study, regarding trust as an important basis for selection, at the same time all transaction information is stored on the blockchain to avoid attacks such as malicious tampering of information. It is verified through simulation experiments that as the number of transactions increases, the trust of high-quality edge servers will gradually increase to a stable state, while the trust of low-quality and malicious edge servers will gradually decrease as the number of transactions increases. Mobile users choose high-quality edge nodes for resource services, and transaction information is stored on the blockchain, which greatly improves security.

This paper addresses the security of edge computing in the process of resource allocation, taking into account the security of mobile users when making choices and the security of information storage, using smart contract technology to process the transaction process. However, the use of smart contracts is still on the surface. Later, we will consider in-depth study of smart contract technology and borrow smart contract technology to better improve the security of edge computing resource allocation.

References

1. Wang, L., Wu, C., Fan, W.: Summary of edge computing resource allocation and task scheduling optimization. J. Syst. Simul. **33**(3), 509–520 (2020)
2. Zhuang, X., Yang, B., Wang, X., et al.: Research on mobile edge computing security. Telecommun. Eng. Technol. Standard. **31**(12), 38–43 (2018)
3. Chen, L., Tang, H., You, W., Bai, Y.: Research on mobile edge computing security defense. J. Netw. Inf. Secur. **7**(1), 130–142 (2021)

4. Guo, S., Wang, R., Zhang, F.: Overview of the principles and applications of blockchain technology. Comput. Sci. **48**(2), 271–281 (2021)
5. Zhang, L., Liu, B., Zhang, R., et al.: Overview of blockchain technology. Comput. Eng. **45**(5), 1–12 (2019)
6. Dong, S., Wu, J., Li, H., et al.: Resource allocation method of mobile edge computing for priority tasks. Comput. Eng. **46**(3), 18–23 (2020)
7. Li, J., Zhang, Y., Pang, L., Ding, W., Sun, G., Yu, H.: Resource allocation and task scheduling methods in mobile edge computing. J. Chongqing Univ. Technol. (Nat. Sci.) **440**(11), 164–171 (2020)
8. Xue, J., An, Y.: New task offloading and resource allocation strategy based on edge computing. Comput. Eng. Sci. **42**(6), 959–965 (2020)
9. Yang, S.: A joint optimization scheme for task offloading and resource allocation based on edge computing in 5G communication networks. Comput. Commun. **160**, 759–768 (2020)
10. Alfakih, T., Hassan, M., Gumaei, A., et al.: Task offloading and resource allocation for mobile edge computing by deep reinforcement learning based on SARSA. IEEE Access **8**, 54074–54084 (2020)
11. Liao, J., Xian, W., et al.: Resource allocation and task scheduling scheme in priority-based hierarchical edge computing system. In: 2020 19th International Symposium on Distributed Computing and Applications for Business Engineering and Science (DCABES) (2020)
12. Nath, S., Wu, J.: Dynamic computation offloading and resource allocation for multi-user mobile edge computing. In: GLOBECOM 2020–2020 IEEE Global Communications Conference. IEEE (2020)
13. Wang, L., Jiao, L., Li, J., et al.: MOERA: mobility-agnostic online resource allocation for edge computing. IEEE Trans. Mob. Comput. **18**(8), 1843–1856 (2019)
14. Shen, S., Mao, Y., Li, L.: A general application scheme of blockchain for non-digital currency. J. Nanjing Univ. Posts Telecommun. Nat. Sci. Ed. **39**(1), 1–11 (2019)
15. Hu, X., Guo, S., Guo, S., et al.: Blockchain meets edge computing: a distributed and trusted authentication system. IEEE Trans. Industr. Inf. **16**(3), 1972–1983 (2020)
16. Xu, C., Wang, K., Li, P., et al.: Making big data open in edges: a resource-efficient blockchain-based approach. IEEE Trans. Parallel Distrib. Syst. **30**(4), 870–882 (2019)
17. Zhang, S., Lee, J.: A group signature and authentication scheme for blockchain-based mobile-edge computing. IEEE Internet Things J. **7**(5), 4557–4565 (2019)
18. Wu, B., Xu, K., Li, Q., et al.: Toward blockchain-powered trusted collaborative services for edge-centric networks. IEEE Netw. **34**(2), 30–36 (2020)
19. Ioini, N., Pahl, C.: Trustworthy orchestration of container based edge computing using permissioned blockchain. In: 2018 Fifth International Conference on Internet of Things: Systems, Management and Security, pp. 147–154 (2018)
20. Huang, Y., Zhang, J., Duan, J., et al.: Resource allocation and consensus on edge blockchain in pervasive edge computing environments. In: 2019 IEEE 39th International Conference on Distributed Computing Systems (ICDCS). IEEE, pp. 1476–1486 (2019)
21. Qiao, G., Leng, S., Chai, H., et al.: Blockchain empowered resource trading in mobile edge computing and networks. In: ICC 2019–2019 IEEE International Conference on Communications (ICC). IEEE (2019)
22. Xu, Q., Su, Z., Yang, Q.: Blockchain-based trustworthy edge caching scheme for mobile cyber-physical system. IEEE Internet Things J. **7**(2), 1098–1110 (2020)

23. Huang, J., Xia, X., et al.: Trust degree certification mechanism based on dynamic authorization. J. Softw. **30**(9), 2593–2607 (2019)
24. Song, J., Gu, T., Ge, Y., et al.: Smart contract-based computing ResourcesTrading in edge computing. In: 2020 IEEE 31st Annual International Symposium on Personal, Indoor and Mobile Radio Communications (2020)

A Stochastic Gradient Descent Algorithm Based on Adaptive Differential Privacy

Yupeng Deng[1], Xiong Li[2(✉)], Jiabei He[3], Yuzhen Liu[1], and Wei Liang[1]

[1] School of Computer Science and Engineering,
Hunan University of Science and Technology, Xiangtan 411201, China
`wliang@hnust.edu.cn`
[2] School of Computer Science and Engineering,
University of Electronic Science and Technology of China, Chengdu 611731, China
`lixiong@uestc.edu.cn`
[3] College of Computer Science, Nankai University, Tianjin 300071, China
`hejiabei@mail.nankai.edu.cn`

Abstract. The application of differential privacy (DP) in federated learning can effectively protect users' privacy from inference attacks. However, privacy budget allocation strategies in most DP schemes not only fail to be applied in complex scenarios but also severely damage the model usability. This paper designs a stochastic gradient descent algorithm based on adaptive DP, which allocates a suitable privacy budget for each iteration according to the tendency of the noise gradients. As the model parameters keep optimizing, the scheme adaptively controls the noise scale to match the decreased gradients, resizing the allocated privacy budget when too small. Compared with other DP schemes, our scheme flexibly reduces the negative effect of added noise on model convergence and consequently improves the training efficiency of the model. We implemented the scheme on five datasets (Adult, BANK, etc.) with three models (SVM, CNN, etc.) and compared it with other popular schemes in the classification accuracy and training time. Our scheme proved to be efficient and practical, which achieved 2% better than the second one in model accuracy, costing merely 4% of its training time with the 0.05 privacy budget.

Keywords: Differential privacy · Stochastic gradient descent · Empirical risk minimization · Machine learning

1 Introduction

In recent years, big data-driven artificial intelligence (AI) has burst into great potential, accomplishing large-scale complex task learning in many fields such as finance, medical care, urban planning, and autonomous driving. Machine learning, as the core technology of AI, is also widely concerned about its performance and privacy. Traditional machine learning requires centralized training by service providers after collecting user data. However, user data is closely related

© ICST Institute for Computer Sciences, Social Informatics and Telecommunications Engineering 2022
Published by Springer Nature Switzerland AG 2022. All Rights Reserved
H. Gao et al. (Eds.): CollaborateCom 2022, LNICST 461, pp. 133–152, 2022.
https://doi.org/10.1007/978-3-031-24386-8_8

to the individual user and may contain sensitive information such as personal age, race, and disease. As privacy concerns grow, users are less willing to share their data. Paradoxically, AI technologies must rely on large amounts of data collection and fusion. Without access to the unlimited wealth of information to train models and develop technologies, the development of AI applications will be severely limited.

Federated learning (FL) emerged in the context of the contradiction between data silos and the need for data fusion. In 2017, Google first introduced the concept of federated learning [23], in which multiple data holders (e.g., cell phones, IoT devices, or financial or medical institutions) collaborate to train models without directly sharing data and only exchange training parameters in the intermediate stage. Ideally, federated learning results in a shared model similar to or better than a model trained on a central server with the universal set of all users' data [22]. As a result, companies can fuse data to extract information legally and efficiently. At the same time, individuals or other data-holding organizations can still enjoy the AI services companies provide while retaining data control.

For the sake of dealing with federated learning in data-rich scenarios, the stochastic gradient descent (SGD) algorithm is exploited as a very efficient method due to its ability to extend to the parallel mode in computation. Initially, SGD accesses all data records of a dataset in random order and updates the corresponding model approximation by the local gradient of the loss function associated with each record. Due to its tractability and scalability, SGD has become a method efficient of choice for large-scale data training [5]. To improve the convergence efficiency, some researchers have proposed the mini-batch SGD algorithm [10,11]. It uses partial samples to calculate the gradient instead of a single sample or all samples during the training iteration. Compared with the randomized algorithm, the mini-batch SGD algorithm uses multiple samples to calculate the gradient, which can reduce the variance of the randomized gradient and thus improve the convergence speed of the algorithm to some extent.

Although federated learning achieves natural protection for data privacy by avoiding direct data exposure to third parties, it's still facing three significant risks of privacy leakage: First, federated learning requires the exchange of intermediate parameters for collaborative training, which may compromise privacy. Second, unreliable participants exacerbate the risk of the privacy breach. Finally, attackers can steal user privacy by inferring the user data through the trained model.

To reduce the risk of privacy leakage from passing intermediate parameters, the differential privacy mechanism is introduced. In 2006, Dwork et al. [13,14] proposed differential privacy, which is a practical approach to guarantee a quantifiable level of privacy. Among them, the ϵ-differential privacy model has received extensive research attention. It ensures privacy in theory and is robust to known attacks (e.g., those involving auxiliary information) [16], while implementation requires perturbing the data by adding noise.

Transforming the gradient in the training process can protect data privacy and security but it meanwhile reduces the usability of the model. In earlier work on differential privacy SGD [8,18,25,31], the learning rate was set to a constant and the privacy budget was equally distributed to each iteration. For example, suppose the budget is ϵ and the maximum number of iterations is T, then the privacy budget allocated to each iteration is $\epsilon_t = \frac{\epsilon}{T}$, $(t = 1, 2, \ldots, T)$. Under this privacy budget allocation scheme, the convergence is strictly limited by the preselection parameter T. If T is too small, the optimal solution has not been obtained at the end of the iterative process; if T is too large, it means that the privacy budget allocated to each iteration is small and the corresponding interference noise added to the gradient is large, and the accuracy cannot be guaranteed.

The optimal problem of differential privacy SGD iterations in the machine learning training process is the empirical risk minimization (ERM): Let $D = \{d_1, \ldots, d_n\}$ be an input database of n independent observations. Each observation $d_i = (x_i, y_i)$ is composed of $x_i \in R_p$ and $y_i \in R$. The ERM problem can be expressed in the following form: $\min_{w \in C} f(w; D) := \frac{1}{n} \sum_{i=1}^{n} L(w, d_i) + \frac{\lambda}{2} \|w\|_2^2$, where L is a loss function and C is a convex set. Note that the regularization term $\frac{\lambda}{2} \|w\|_2^2$ does not affect the privacy guarantee since it is independent of the data.

To solve the private ERM problem, a large number of works have conducted relevant research on privacy budget allocation strategies. Abadi et al. [1] proposed a new mechanism for tracking privacy loss, called moments accountant, which permits tight automated analysis of the privacy loss of complex composite mechanisms and significantly improves the accuracy of the model under a suitable privacy budget. Lee et al. [21] designed an adaptive privacy budget allocation scheme to assign appropriate privacy budgets for each iteration separately to satisfy zero-concentrated differential privacy (zCDP) while improving the accuracy of the model. However, both methods (especially [21]) require more computational overhead to enhance the usability of the model compared to earlier work. Also, in scenarios with small privacy budgets, the scheme of Abadi et al. [1] cannot work due to its mechanism.

It is not hard to discover two critical points in solving the private ERM problem: proper privacy budget strategies and criteria to judge the effectiveness of the noise gradient. Wang et al. [28] proposed a new differential privacy budget allocation scheme in the tree index. The privacy budget allocated during the iteration is an arithmetic progression. Inspired by their scheme, we propose an improved differential privacy budget allocation scheme. When t is small, the gradient value of the model is larger and can withstand greater noise; as t increases, the gradient value of the model decreases, and a larger privacy budget needs to be allocated to reduce the effect of noise and ensure the convergence of the model. And our scheme ensures that each noise gradient conforms to the direction of gradient descent, i.e., that the value of the loss function continues to decrease. It was mentioned in [21] that the noise gradient may be in the direction of descent even if the norm of the noise gradient is much larger than the norm of the true gradient. Our solution is to take in a set of weights obtained from different learning rates, compute their loss function values, and choose the learning rate corresponding to the smallest loss function value. If the selected learning rate is 0, this noise gradient does not fit the gradient descent direction. The algorithm will discard it and reallocate a larger privacy budget to compute a new noise gradient.

Combining the above solution ideas for the two critical problems, we propose a differential privacy SGD algorithm with adaptive privacy budget allocation. Our contributions are summarized as follows:

- We proposed a stochastic gradient descent algorithm based on adaptive differential privacy. It can flexibly choose a suitable privacy budget for each iteration to guarantee model usability and accelerate the training process.
- Unlike previous works, we designed a learning rate selection mechanism. It can select the optimal learning rate in a set of learning rate, which ensures that the model parameters keep optimizing and ultimately achieve higher accuracy.
- We perform extensive experiments on real datasets against other popular ERM algorithms. Experimental results show that our scheme achieves 2% higher model accuracy than the second one, costing only 4% of its training time with a 0.05 privacy budget, which means that our scheme is efficient and practical.

The rest of this paper is organized as follows. In Sect. 2, we review related work. In Sect. 3, we provide preliminaries on differential privacy and machine learning. We introduce the specific implementation of our scheme in Sect. 4. Section 5 contains the experimental results on real datasets.

2   Related Work

Applying differential privacy in federated learning can effectively protect data privacy, but the usability of models perturbed by noise will unavoidably be destroyed, so solving the private ERM problem becomes a complex problem. So far, many works have been trying to solve the private ERM problem in machine learning, and their methods can be mainly concluded into three types: output perturbation, objective perturbation, and gradient perturbation.

The output perturbation [8,18,32] is the addition of perturbations to the results, in which noise is added to the output of the underlying deterministic algorithm. The form of added noise depends on the sensitivity of the underlying algorithm, which measures the maximum change in the algorithm's output when an element in the input data set changes. Simply put, the principle of output perturbation is to find the exact convex minimizer and then add noise. Chaudhuri et al. [8] implemented the ERM with output perturbation and proved that adding noise to the output result can play a specific role in artifacts. Zhang et al. [32] used algorithmic stability arguments to bound the L_2 sensitivity of the whole batch gradient descent algorithm to determine the amount of noise that must be added to outputs partially optimize the objective function. In general, the noise generated by output perturbation algorithms is usually inaccurate because the noise is calibrated to the worst-case analysis.

The objective perturbation [8,17,19] is to add noise to the objective function. Unlike the output perturbation, this is not a random disturbance classifier but a disturbance to the objective of algorithm minimization. The study of Chaudhuri et al. [8] showed that objective perturbation performs better than output perturbation. Kifer et al. [19] used approximate differential privacy instead of pure differential privacy, effectively improving the utility of objective perturbation methods. Although objective perturbation is more effective, its privacy guarantee is based on the premise that the problem can be solved exactly, but most time optimization problems are solved approximately in practice.

The iterative gradient perturbation method [3,30] and their variants [27,29, 32] are very popular method. Bassily et al. [3] proposed a (ϵ, δ)-differentially private version of stochastic gradient descent (SGD) algorithm. At each iteration, their algorithm perturbs the gradient with Gaussian noise and applies the advanced composition [15] together with the privacy amplification result [4] to get an upper bound on the total privacy loss. Later, Talwar et al. [26] improved those lower bounds on the utility for the Least absolute shrinkage and selection operator (LASSO) problem. In [27], the gradient perturbation method is combined with the stochastic variance reduced gradient (SVRG) algorithm, and the resulting algorithm is near-optimal with less gradient complexity. Abadi et al. [1] proposed a new mechanism for tracking privacy loss, called moments accountant, which permits tight automated analysis of the privacy loss of complex composite mechanisms and significantly improves the accuracy of the model under a suitable privacy budget. Lee et al. [21] designed an adaptive privacy budget allocation scheme to assign appropriate privacy budgets for each iteration separately to satisfy zero-concentrated differential privacy (zCDP) while improving the accuracy of the model. Du et al. [12] extended the Gaussian DP's central limit theorem (CLT), and proposed a novel dynamic DP-SGD algorithm for this case. Cheng et al. [9] proposed a gradient-based algorithm with distributed differential privacy in which try to expand the number of iterations instead of the fixed. It combines the Analytic Gaussian Mechanism with linear search method to broaden the definition domain of ϵ and obtain a relatively compact variance bound.

3 Preliminaries

In this section, we briefly recall the definition of differential privacy, introduce essential theorems, and then overview the basic principles of machine learning using SGD.

3.1 Differential Privacy

Definition 1 ((ϵ, δ)-Differential Privacy [13]). *A randomized mechanism* $M : D \to R$ *with domain D and range R satisfies (ϵ, δ)-DP if for any two adjacent inputs $d, d' \in D$ and for any subset of outputs $S \subseteq R$ it holds that*

$$\Pr[M(d) \in S] \leq e^\epsilon \Pr[M(d' \in S)] + \delta \tag{1}$$

The non-negative parameter ϵ is the privacy budget, which indicates the degree of privacy protection. As ϵ is set smaller, the privacy protection becomes greater. When ϵ tends to zero, the probability distribution of M outputting the same result on the adjacent data sets D and D' tends to be the same, and the less information M may disclose. The δ is also a non-negative parameter, which indicates the probability that the difference between the outputs of M on D and D' exceeds e^ϵ, i.e., the probability of violating differential privacy protection. Obviously, the smaller the δ, the higher the degree of privacy protection.

In particular, when $\delta = 0$, the algorithm M provides the strictest ϵ - differential privacy protection.

Theorem 1 (Privacy amplification via sampling [4]). Over a domain of data sets D^n, if an algorithm M is $\epsilon' < 1$ differentially private, then for any data set $D' \in D^n$, executing M on uniformly random γn entries of D' ensures $2\gamma\epsilon'$-differential privacy.

Theorem 2 (Navie composition [14]). The class of ϵ-differentially private mechanisms satisfies $k\epsilon$-differential privacy under k-fold adaptive composition.

Theorem 3 (Strong composition [15]). Let $\epsilon, \delta' > 0$. The class of ϵ-differentially private algorithms satisfies (ϵ', δ')-differential privacy under k-fold adaptive composition for $\epsilon' = \sqrt{2k\ln(1/\delta')} + k\epsilon(e^\epsilon - 1)$.

Lemma 1 [6]. If two mechanisms satisfy (ϵ_1, δ)-DP and (ϵ_2, δ)-DP, then their composition satisfies $(\epsilon_1 + \epsilon_2, \delta)$-differential privacy.

Definition 2 (L_2sensitivity). For the adjacent data sets D and D', let $Q : D^n \to R^d$ be the query function, and the L_2 sensitivity of the query function Q is defined as follows:

$$\Delta_2(Q) = \max_{D \sim D'} \|Q(D) - Q(D')\|_2 \tag{2}$$

The L_2 sensitivity represents the maximum range of variation of the query function Q over the adjacent data set.

Theorem 4 (Gaussian Mechanism [14]). Let $\epsilon \in (0, 1)$ be arbitrary and f be a query function with L_2 sensitivity of $\Delta_2(Q)$. The Gaussian Mechanism, which returns $f(D) + N(0, \sigma^2)$, with

$$\sigma \geq \frac{\Delta_2(Q)}{\epsilon} \sqrt{2\ln(1.25/\delta)} \tag{3}$$

is (ϵ, δ)- differential privacy.

3.2   Machine Learning

Machine learning is a general term for a class of algorithms that try to attempt to mine large amounts of historical data for implied patterns and use them for prediction or classification. More specifically, machine learning can be thought of as finding a function where the input is sample data and the output is the desired outcome.

To ensure the correctness of the function found by the machine learning algorithm, we define a loss function L that represents the penalty for mismatching the training data. The loss $L(w)$ on parameters w is the average of the loss over the training examples $\{d_1, \ldots, d_n\}$, so $L(w) = \frac{1}{N} \sum_i L(w; xd_i)$. We want to find w in the training, which produces the minimum loss (though in practice we seldom expect to reach an exact global minimum).

For complex algorithms, like neural networks, the loss function L is usually non-convex and difficult to minimize. In practice, the minimization is often done by the mini-batch stochastic gradient descent (SGD) algorithm. SGD also known as incremental gradient descent, is an iterative method for optimizing differentiable objective functions. The method iteratively updates weights and biases by calculating the gradient of loss function on small batch data. For example, at iteration t, SGD randomly selects a small set of data $D_t \subset D$ and calculates the corresponding gradient $\nabla L(w_t; D_t)$. $-\nabla L(w_t; D_t)$ may not be the correct update direction, but it is the expected update direction since $E(\nabla L(w_t; D_t))|w_t = \nabla L(w_t)$. SGD goes far beyond the naive gradient descent method on the highly nonconvex loss surface, which has dominated most modern machine learning algorithms. In this algorithm, at each step, one forms a batch B of random examples and computes $g_B = \frac{1}{|B|} \sum_{d \in B} \nabla L(w; d)$ as an estimation to the gradient $\nabla L(w)$. Then w is updated following the gradient direction $-g_B$ towards a local minimum.

4 Proposed Scheme

In this section, we first describe the main idea of the proposed algorithm and then present the details of its four main components.

4.1 The Main Idea

As shown in Algorithm 1, during the t-th epoch training, after obtaining the gradient by training the model on the dataset, the algorithm first clips the gradient to obtain the original gradient g_t. Subsequently, the corresponding noise is calculated according to the assigned privacy budget and added to the original gradient to get the noise gradient $\tilde{g}_t$. Then, it determines whether the noise gradient conforms to the gradient descent direction. If it does, the algorithm calculates the weight w for the next iteration by the corresponding learning rate. If not, the algorithm assigns a larger privacy budget and recalculates the noise gradient until the noise gradient conforms to the gradient descent direction. The above processes repeat until the end of the training, and the notations used in our scheme are shown in Table 1.

Table 1. Notations

Notation	Description
d	The data for training
w	The model weight
$L(\cdot)$	The loss function
$\tilde{g}_t$	The noise gradient
σ	The noise scale
C_{grad}	The gradient norm bound
ϵ	The privacy budget
a	The privacy budget increase rate
ρ	The a increase rate
η	The learning rate
Φ	The set of learning rate
λ	The learning rate decay rate

Algorithm 1: Differential Privacy SGD Algorithm

Input: $\{d_1, \ldots, d_n\}$, $L(w)$, ϵ, C_{grad}, ρ, λ

1 Initialize w_0 and Φ
2 **while** $t \leq T$ **do**
3 　　$g_t \leftarrow \sum_{i=1}^{n} (\nabla L(w_t; d_i) / \max(1, \frac{\|L(w_t)\|_2}{C}))$
4 　　$\epsilon_t \leftarrow A + \frac{B}{1 + e^{-at+b}}$
5 　　$\sigma \leftarrow 1/\epsilon_t$
6 　　$\tilde{g}_t \leftarrow \bar{g}_t + N(0, \sigma^2 C_{grad}^2 I)$
7 　　$idx \leftarrow 0$
8 　　**while** $idx = 0$ & $t < \frac{T+1}{2}$ **do**
9 　　　　$\Omega = \{L(w_t - \eta \tilde{g}_t) : \eta \in \Phi\}$
10 　　　$idx \leftarrow \arg \min\{\Omega\}$
11 　　　**if** $idx > 0$ **then**
12 　　　　　$\eta_t \leftarrow \eta_{idx}$
13 　　　　　$w_{t+1} \leftarrow w_t - \eta_t \tilde{g}_t$
14 　　　**end**
15 　　　**else**
16 　　　　　$a \leftarrow \rho \cdot a$
17 　　　　　$\epsilon_t \leftarrow A + \frac{B}{1 + e^{-at+b}}$
18 　　　　　$\sigma \leftarrow 1/\epsilon_t$
19 　　　　　$\tilde{g}_t \leftarrow \bar{g}_t + N(0, \sigma^2 C_{grad}^2 I)$
20 　　　**end**
21 　　**end**
22 　　**if** $t\%\tau = 0$ **then**
23 　　　$\eta_{max}^{t+1} = \lambda \cdot max(\eta_1, \eta_2, \ldots, \eta_t)$
24 　　**end**
25 **end**
26 **return** w

4.2 Private Gradient Approximation

In each iteration, the noise gradient $\tilde{g}_t = \nabla L(w_t) + N(0, \sigma^2)$ can be obtained by adding Gaussian noise with variance σ^2 to $\nabla L(w_t)$. According to Theorem 4, the magnitude of the noise σ^2 depends on the maximum change in the output value of the query function Q when one individual data changes. To Bound this quantity, some works [8, 19] assume $\|x\| \leq 1$. Instead, we adopted the scheme of Abadi et al. [1], clip the gradient in L_2 norm by dividing it by $\max(1, \frac{\|L(w_t)\|_2}{C_{grad}})$.

4.3 Adaptive Privacy Budget Allocation

Varying from the equal allocation in previous privacy budget allocation schemes, our scheme considers the privacy protection needs of each iteration. It continuously adjusts the size of the allocated privacy budget as the training progresses. In the model training process, as the training progresses, the model's accuracy increases, and the impact of adding noise becomes greater, so more privacy budget is needed to ensure that the model's accuracy is not affected.

We divide the training process into three stages: Model initialization, Model training, and Model convergence. In the first stage, the model is just trained, and the accuracy requirement is not high, so we can allocate a small privacy budget and increase the privacy budget by a small amount, and finally obtain a model with low accuracy. After entering the second stage, the privacy budget is increased by a large margin so that the model can be steadily improved until it is close to convergence. Finally, in the third stage, the near-convergence model can converge faster under the maximum privacy budget.

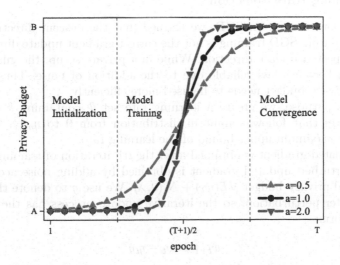

Fig. 1. Allocated privacy budget per epoch

For the t-th iteration, the allocated privacy budget is calculated according to Eq. 4, i.e., the privacy budgets ϵ_1, ϵ_2, ..., ϵ_T are assigned to the iterations from 1 to T respectively (assuming the total number of iterations is T).

$$\epsilon_t = \epsilon_{min} + \frac{\epsilon_{max}}{1 + e^{-at+b}}, 1 \leq t \leq T \tag{4}$$

where ϵ_t is the privacy budget at iteration t, the constants ϵ_{min} and ϵ_{max} jointly control the maximum and minimum values of the privacy budget during training, and the constants a and b control the growth rate of the privacy budget.

From Eq. 4 and Fig. 1, we can find that the value of a determines the trend of each privacy budget value assigned throughout the training process when the constants ϵ_{min}, ϵ_{max} and b are fixed. The smaller the value of a, the closer the difference between neighboring privacy budgets; conversely, the larger the value of a, the larger the difference between neighboring privacy budgets. Therefore, an appropriate a value can assign a reasonable privacy budget for each iteration and ensure the improvement of model accuracy.

Our scheme changes the size of the allocated privacy budget by dynamically adjusting the value of a during the training process. As shown in Fig. 1, when $t < \frac{T+1}{2}$, the smaller a is in the same iteration, the larger the corresponding privacy budget is. So when the algorithm finds that the current privacy budget is too small, it updates $a = \rho \cdot a, 0 < \rho < 1$, where ρ is the decay coefficient, and reallocates the privacy budget. After half of the training process is completed, i.e., $t > \frac{T+1}{2}$, when the privacy budget has reached a high level, keep a constant and complete the subsequent privacy budget allocation according to Eq. 4.

4.4   Learning Rate Selection

In the previous section on SGD, we learned that the descent direction of the gradient g_t during SGD training is not the correct gradient update direction but it is the expected update direction. While in a private setup, the guarantee in expectation becomes less reliable due to the addition of noise. Thus the per-iteration privacy budget needs to be used more efficiently.

For this purpose, we create a learning rate set Φ containing k candidate learning rates that follow a uniform distribution from 0 to η_{max}. The η_{max} denotes the maximum upper bound of the learning rate.

The updated gradient is obtained after the tth iteration of training $\nabla L(w_t)$, and the perturbed updated gradient is obtained by adding noise according to the assigned privacy budget $\nabla L(w_t) + N_t(0, \lambda)$. We use $\tilde{g}$ to denote the update gradient after perturbation, so the iterative update process has the following simplified form:

$$w_{t+1} = w_t - \eta_t \tilde{g} \tag{5}$$

For the best case, the model parameters are close to the optimal solution for each iteration. Therefore, we need to select the most appropriate learning rate from the learning rate candidate set Φ for the current noise level.

In our scheme, the element in Ω is the value of the loss function $L(w_t - \eta\tilde{g})$, i.e. $\Omega = \{L(w_t - \eta\tilde{g}) : \eta \in \Phi\}$. Then we locate the minimum value $L(w_t - \eta_{idx}\tilde{g})$ in Ω, and the corresponding learning rate η_{idx} is the best learning rate we aim to find. If the learning rate η_{idx} is 0, it means that this noise gradient does not match the gradient descent direction; the algorithm will reallocate a larger privacy budget and recalculate the noise gradient. Until the learning rate η_{idx} is not 0, the model is updated using the selected learning rate.

4.5   Adjusting the Learning Rate Selection Range

Generally, the SGD algorithm with a constant learning rate does not guarantee convergence to the optimum. In order to control the variance of private gradient estimation, the range of learning rate selection needs to be updated. After every τ iteration, we update η_{max} according to the following rule:

$$\eta_{max}^{t+1} = \lambda \cdot max(\eta_1, \eta_2, \ldots, \eta_t), 0 < \lambda < 1 \tag{6}$$

where η_{max}^{t+1} is the maximum learning rate at the $t+1$th iteration, λ is the decay coefficient, η_t denotes the learning rate chosen at iteration t. This allows our algorithm to adaptively change the learning rate range based on the relative position of the current iteration.

4.6   Correctness of Privacy

The correctness of the algorithm depends on (ϵ, δ)-differential privacy composition (Lemma 1) and accounting for the privacy cost of each primitive.

Proof To maintain the total privacy budget as our pre-set value ϵ, let $\epsilon_t + \epsilon_{T-t+1} = 2 \cdot \frac{\epsilon}{T}$. According to the Lemma 1, the total privacy budget ϵ can be expressed as:

$$\epsilon_{total} = \sum_{t=1}^{T} \epsilon_t = \frac{T}{2}(\epsilon_t + \epsilon_{T-t+1}) = T \cdot \frac{\epsilon}{T} = \epsilon \tag{7}$$

To keep the correctness of Eq. 7, the sum of parameters ϵ_{min} and ϵ_{max} will be constant as $2 \cdot \frac{\epsilon}{T}$, and parameter b will be a fixed value $\frac{aT}{2}$.

Since our scheme adjusts the value of a during training, we need to discuss whether $\epsilon_{total} \leq \epsilon$ holds in this scenario. We assume that k operations to update the value of a occur, where $k \leq \lfloor \frac{T+1}{2} \rfloor$. When $k = 0$, Eq. 7 still holds. And when $k > 0$, take $k = 1$ as an example, the value of a is updated from a_0 to a_1, where $a_1 < a_0$. Figure 1 shows that when $t > \frac{T+1}{2}$, the smaller a is, the smaller the corresponding privacy budget is; thus, we have $\epsilon_t(a_1) < \epsilon_t(a_0)$ for each iteration.

Therefore, the total privacy budget satisfies the following condition:

$$
\begin{aligned}
\epsilon_{total} &= \sum_{t=1}^{T} \epsilon_t \\
&= \sum_{1}^{\frac{T+1}{2}} \epsilon_t + \sum_{\frac{T+1}{2}+1}^{T} \epsilon_t \\
&= \sum_{1}^{\frac{T+1}{2}} \epsilon_t + \epsilon_{\frac{T+1}{2}+1}(a_1) + \ldots + \ldots + \epsilon_T(a_1) \\
&< \sum_{1}^{\frac{T+1}{2}} \epsilon_t + \epsilon_{\frac{T+1}{2}+1}(a_0) + \ldots + \epsilon_{t'}(a_0) + \epsilon_{t'+1}(a_1) + \ldots + \epsilon_T(a_1) \\
&= \epsilon
\end{aligned}
$$

In summary, the privacy budget consumed in our scenario does not exceed the total set privacy budget.

5   Experimental Results

In this section, we apply the scheme to the classical machine learning algorithms: support vector machines (SVM) and logistic regression. We compare our scheme with other popular schemes in model classification accuracy and training time to show that our scheme has better accuracy and higher efficiency. Finally, we apply our scheme to a more complex convolutional neural network (CNN) to illustrate that our scheme is also excellently suited for complex models.

5.1   Experiment on SVM and Logistic Regression

In this part, we experiment with SVM and Logistic Regression on the four UCI datasets and compare them with other schemes. The dataset we use is as follows: (i) Adult [2,7] dataset contains 48,842 records of individuals from the 1994 US Census. (ii) BANK [2] contains 45,211 records of marketing campaign-related information about customers of a Portuguese banking institution. (iii) IPUMS-BR and (iv) IPUMS-US datasets are also Census data extracted from IPUMS-International [24], and they contain 38,000 and 40,000 records, respectively. Table 2 summarizes the characteristics of datasets used in our experiments.

Baseline Model. We compare our scheme against four baseline algorithms, namely, SGD-Adv [3], SGD-MA [1], DP-AGD [21] and NonPrivate. SGD-Adv is a differentially private version of SGD algorithm, it implements differential privacy protection under SGD algorithm by advanced composition theorem with privacy amplification results. SGD-MA also implements differential privacy protection under SGD, except that it uses a combinatorial approach called moments

Table 2. Characteristics of datasets

Dataset	Size (n)	Dime	Label
Adult	48,842	124	Is annual income >50k?
BANK	45,211	33	Is the product subscribed?
IPUMS-BR	38,000	53	Is monthly income >$300?
IPUMS-US	40,000	58	Is annual income >25k?

accountant, tailored for Gaussian noise distribution. DP-AGD is an adaptive privacy budget allocation scheme that dynamically adjusts the size of the privacy budget for the current iteration during the training process. NonPrivate is an optimization algorithm that does not satisfy differential privacy.

In the comparison experiment, we report the classification accuracy (i.e., the proportion of correctly classified examples in the test set) and the time spent on training the model. All reported results are averaged over 10 iterations of 5-fold cross-validation.

Parameter Setting. When there are known default parameter settings for the prior works, we use the same settings. Throughout all the experiments, the value of privacy parameter δ is fixed to 10^{-8} for the Adult, BANK, IPUMS-BR, and IPUMS-US datasets. According to the common practice in optimization, the sizes of mini-batches for SGD-Adv and SGD-MA are set to $\sqrt{n}$. The parameter settings of DP-AGD refer to the values given in the article [3], where the gradient crop value C_{grad} is set to 3.0, the objective function crop value C_{obj} is set to 3.0, and the attenuation parameter γ is set to 0.1.

Since the parameters of our scheme can be dynamically adjusted during training, we just need to consider a few parameters, and the most important of which is the gradient clipping norm C_{grad}. If C_{grad} is set to a too low value, it significantly reduces the sensitivity, but at the same time, it can cause too much information loss in the estimates. Conversely, if C_{grad} is set too high, the sensitivity becomes high, resulting in adding too much noise to the estimates. On the other hand, increasing the norm bound C forces us to add more noise to the gradients (and hence the parameters) since we add noise based on σC. In practice, a good way to choose a value for C is by taking the median of the norms of the unclipped gradients over the course of training. Based on experiments in testing the effect of different C_{grad} on classification accuracy, we finally determined the value of C_{grad} to be 3.0.

Experimental Results on SVM. Support vector machine (SVM) is one of the most effective tools for classification problems. The SVM classification problem is formulated as an optimization problem:

$$\min_{w} \frac{\lambda}{2}\|w\|_2^2 + \frac{1}{n}\sum_{i=1}^{n}\max\{1 - y_i w^T x_i, 0\},$$

where $x_i \in R^{p+1}$ and $y_i \in -1, +1$ for $i \in [n]$.

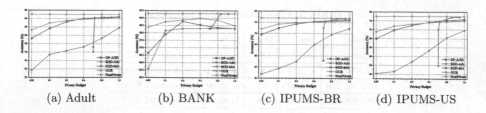

(a) Adult	(b) BANK	(c) IPUMS-BR	(d) IPUMS-US

Fig. 2. Classification accuracies of SVM by varying the ϵ

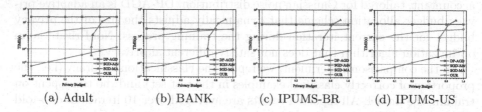

(a) Adult	(b) BANK	(c) IPUMS-BR	(d) IPUMS-US

Fig. 3. Training time of SVM by varying ϵ

Figure 2 shows the classification accuracy of the SVM model on the four real data sets, and Fig. 3 shows the training time of the SVM. Taking the experiments on the Adult dataset as an example, in Fig. 2(a), we can see that when the privacy budget was small (e.g., $\epsilon = 0.05$ and $\epsilon = 0.1$), our scheme was able to achieve a higher classification accuracy compared to the other three schemes. The reason was that adaptive privacy budget allocation provides a tighter privacy loss and enables our scheme to withstand a higher number of iterations, this can also be reflected in Fig. 3(a), our scheme took a longer time than SGD-Adv to complete an iteration. However, we improved the classification accuracy by about 10% compared to SGD-Adv. Also, compared to DP-AGD, which also performed well with a small privacy budget, our scheme achieved higher classification accuracy in less time. When $\epsilon = 0.05$, our scheme spent 0.94 s to obtain 71.05% classification accuracy, while the DP-AGD scheme spent 25.86s to obtain 67.93 % classification accuracy.

As the privacy budget increases, we no longer have a clear advantage in classification accuracy. After $\epsilon \geq 0.2$, DP-AGD obtained an approximate accuracy with our scheme. When $\epsilon = 0.2$, our scheme spent 2.68s to access 83.50% classification accuracy, while the DP-AGD scheme spent 25.55s to get 83.23 % classification accuracy. SGD-MA worked properly when $\epsilon = 0.58$ and led other differential privacy schemes at $\epsilon = 0.95$ and $\epsilon = 1.32$. When $\epsilon = 0.8$, our scheme spent 4.30 s to obtain 84.05% classification accuracy, while the DP-AGD scheme spent 26.93 s to access 84.25% classification accuracy, and the SGD-MA scheme spent 11.76 s to acquire 84.22% classification accuracy. The reason was that the moments accountant mechanism used by SGD-MA can provide a tight bound on the privacy loss, which, combined with the privacy amplification effect due to subsampling, enables SGD-MA to withstand a higher number of iterations.

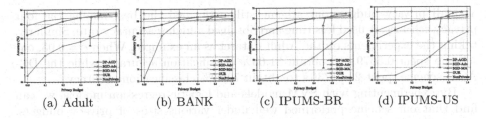

Fig. 4. Classification accuracies of logistic regression by varying ϵ

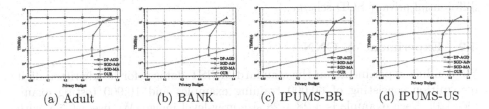

Fig. 5. Training time of logistic regression by varying ϵ

However, the disadvantage is that when the privacy budget is small, it is difficult to use the moment accountant scheme due to the insufficient number of iterations. When δ was fixed as 10^{-8}, a single iteration of SGD-MA consumed a privacy budget of about 0.58. And a lower privacy budget implies a higher level of privacy protection, so it is difficult for the moments accountant scheme to achieve a high level of privacy protection. However, our scheme still had significant strength in training time.

The experimental results on other datasets were basically consistent with the performance on the Adult dataset as well. It is worth noting that in Fig. 2(b) and Fig. 3(b), we noticed that when conducting experiments on BANK dataset, the classification accuracy decreases and the training time was large when the privacy budget was large (e.g., $\epsilon = 0.8$ and $\epsilon = 1.6$). After analysis, we believed that it is because the structure of the BANK dataset is very simple. Hence, the model reaches convergence too early, and finding a noisy gradient to match the gradient descent direction can be more difficult. Maybe this problem can be improved by adjusting the number of training iterations.

Experimental Results on Logistic Regression. We also applied our algorithm to a regularized logistic regression model in which the goal is

$$\min_{w} \frac{\lambda}{2}\|w\|_2^2 + \frac{1}{n}\sum_{i=1}^{n} \log(1 + exp(-y_i w^T x_i)),$$

where $x_i \in R^{p+1}$, $y_i \in -1, +1$ and $\lambda > 0$ is a regularization coefficient.

The performance of the logistic regression model on the four datasets in Fig. 4 and Fig. 5 was generally consistent with that of the SVM model. Under a small privacy budget, our scheme still performed the best among the four privacy schemes, it used less time and obtained a higher accuracy rate. Similarly, taking the experiments on the Adult dataset as an example. When $\epsilon = 0.05$, our scheme spent 0.5679 s to obtain 81.63% classification accuracy, while the DP-AGD scheme spent 25.91736 s to obtain 79.00% classification accuracy.

By experimenting with SVM models and logistic regression models, we can find that our scheme performed well under various sizes of privacy budgets, especially under small privacy budgets, it can get a higher classification accuracy in a shorter training time. This shows that our scheme is a practical and efficient differential privacy SGD scheme.

5.2   Experiment on CNN

We conduct experiments on the standard MNIST dataset for handwritten digit recognition consisting of 60,000 training examples and 10,000 testing examples [20]. Each example is a 28×28 size gray-level image. We use a CNN with ReLU units and softmax of 10 classes (corresponding to the 10 digits) with cross-entropy loss.

Baseline Model. Our baseline model is a CNN model consisting of two convolutional layers and one Fully-Connected layer, using ReLU as the activation function. Using the batch size 128, we can reach an accuracy of 98.34% in about 10 epochs as shown in Fig. 6(a).

Parameter Setting. In this part of the experiment, the key parameter we need to determine remains the gradient clipping norm C_{grad}. Based on experiments in testing the effect of different C_{grad} on classification accuracy, we finally determined the value of C_{grad} to be 5.0.

Experiment Results on CNN. For a differentially private model, we experiment with the same model on MNIST. To limit sensitivity, we clip the gradient norm of each layer at 5.0. We report results for three choices of the privacy budget, which we call small ($\epsilon = 0.5$), medium ($\epsilon = 2$), and large ($\epsilon = 8$). Meanwhile, the δ-values are all set to 10^{-5}.

Figure 6(b) 6(c) 6(d) shows the results for different privacy budget. Each plot shows the evolution of training accuracy and loss function value as a function of the number of epochs. We achieved 89%, 95%, and 96% test set accuracy for (0.5, 10^{-5}) (2, 10^{-5}), and (8, 10^{-5})-differential privacy respectively. In Fig. 6(b) we can see that the loss function value fluctuates more during the descent and the final model had a lower classification accuracy at $\epsilon = 0.5$ compared to the other two cases. This was because using a small privacy budget requires adding a larger amount of noise to the gradient. Benefiting from the fact that our algorithm determines whether the noise gradient according to the direction of gradient descent during training, the value of the loss function decreased and the accuracy

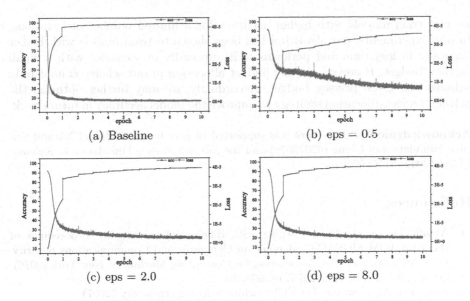

Fig. 6. Results on the accuracy for different noise levels on the MNIST dataset

improved. Also thanks to the adaptive privacy budget allocation, a larger privacy budget can be allocated to ensure the convergence of the model in the later stages of training. Combining Fig. 6(c) and Fig. 6(d), the training process of the model is smoother and the final accuracy is higher after increasing the privacy budget. The final model accuracy of our scheme was only 1% away from the SGD-MA scheme, which performed well on CNN.

In addition, in our experiments, a substantial improvement in accuracy occurred at the start of a new epoch of training, which can be also demonstrated in Fig. 6. The problem also appeared in non-privacy-preserving training and was slowly corrected in subsequent training, so we believe it caused little influence on the final result.

By experimenting on a CNN, we are able to find that our scheme still has excellent performance even on a more complex model, which indicates the suitable generalization of our scheme.

6   Conclusion

The private ERM problem in machine learning has been a tough problem since it sacrifices too much utility and accuracy for privacy preservation. Solving the privacy ERM problem can enhance the usability of the model while protecting users' privacy, which has considerable positive significance for the popularization and practicality of federated learning. According to the problem above, we design a stochastic gradient descent algorithm based on adaptive differential privacy: it allocates a privacy budget for each iteration incrementally based on the current iteration and evaluates the suitability of each added noise. Thus, in our scheme, we can train models with higher accuracy for a limited number of iterations. In our experiments, our algorithm has been shown to train models with higher accuracy in less time and performs well, especially in scenarios with a small privacy budget. However, privacy budget allocation in our scheme cannot fully exhaust the given privacy budget. Accordingly, we may further optimize the privacy budget allocation strategy to improve the model accuracy in future work.

Acknowledgments. This work was supported in part by the National Natural Science Foundation of China (62072078) and the Natural Science Foundation of Sichuan, China (2022NSFSC0550).

References

1. Abadi, M., et al.: Deep learning with differential privacy. In: Proceedings of the 2016 ACM SIGSAC Conference on Computer and Communications Security. CCS 2016, pp. 308–318. Association for Computing Machinery, New York (2016). https://doi.org/10.1145/2976749.2978318
2. Asuncion, A., Newman, D.: UCI machine learning repository (2007)
3. Bassily, R., Smith, A., Thakurta, A.: Private empirical risk minimization: efficient algorithms and tight error bounds. In: 2014 IEEE 55th Annual Symposium on Foundations of Computer Science, pp. 464–473. IEEE, October 2014. https://doi.org/10.1109/FOCS.2014.56
4. Beimel, A., Kasiviswanathan, S.P., Nissim, K.: Bounds on the sample complexity for private learning and private data release. In: Micciancio, D. (ed.) TCC 2010. LNCS, vol. 5978, pp. 437–454. Springer, Heidelberg (2010). https://doi.org/10.1007/978-3-642-11799-2_26
5. Bottou, L., Cun, Y.: Large scale online learning. In: Thrun, S., Saul, L., Schölkopf, B. (eds.) Advances in Neural Information Processing Systems, vol. 16. MIT Press, Cambridge (2003)
6. Bun, M., Steinke, T.: Concentrated differential privacy: simplifications, extensions, and lower bounds. In: Hirt, M., Smith, A. (eds.) TCC 2016. LNCS, vol. 9985, pp. 635–658. Springer, Heidelberg (2016). https://doi.org/10.1007/978-3-662-53641-4_24
7. Chang, C.C., Lin, C.J.: LibSVM: a library for support vector machines **2**(3) (2011). https://doi.org/10.1145/1961189.1961199
8. Chaudhuri, K., Monteleoni, C., Sarwate, A.D.: Differentially private empirical risk minimization. J. Mach. Learn. Res. **12**(null), 1069–1109 (2011). https://doi.org/10.5555/1953048.2021036
9. Cheng, J., et al.: Adaptive distributed differential privacy with SGD. In: Workshop on Privacy-Preserving Artificial Intelligence, vol. 6 (2020)
10. Cotter, A., Shamir, O., Srebro, N., Sridharan, K.: Better mini-batch algorithms via accelerated gradient methods. In: Proceedings of the 24th International Conference on Neural Information Processing Systems. NIPS 2011, pp. 1647–1655. Curran Associates Inc., Red Hook (2011)
11. Dekel, O., Gilad-Bachrach, R., Shamir, O., Xiao, L.: Optimal distributed online prediction using mini-batches. J. Mach. Learn. Res. **13**(null), 165–202 (2012). https://doi.org/10.5555/2188385.2188391
12. Du, J., Li, S., Feng, M., Chen, S.: Dynamic differential-privacy preserving sgd. arXiv preprint arXiv:2111.00173 (2021)

13. Dwork, C., McSherry, F., Nissim, K., Smith, A.: Calibrating noise to sensitivity in private data analysis. In: Halevi, S., Rabin, T. (eds.) TCC 2006. LNCS, vol. 3876, pp. 265–284. Springer, Heidelberg (2006). https://doi.org/10.1007/11681878_14
14. Dwork, C., Roth, A.: The algorithmic foundations of differential privacy. Found. Trends Theor. Comput. Sci. 9(3–4), 211–407 (2014). https://doi.org/10.1561/0400000042
15. Dwork, C., Rothblum, G.N., Vadhan, S.: Boosting and differential privacy. In: 2010 IEEE 51st Annual Symposium on Foundations of Computer Science, pp. 51–60. IEEE, October 2010. https://doi.org/10.1109/FOCS.2010.12
16. Ganta, S.R., Kasiviswanathan, S.P., Smith, A.: Composition attacks and auxiliary information in data privacy. In: Proceedings of the 14th ACM SIGKDD International Conference on Knowledge Discovery and Data Mining. KDD 2008, pp. 265–273. Association for Computing Machinery, New York (2008). https://doi.org/10.1145/1401890.1401926
17. Hua, J., Xia, C., Zhong, S.: Differentially private matrix factorization. IJCAI 2015, pp. 1763–1770. AAAI Press (2015). https://doi.org/10.5555/2832415.2832494
18. Jain, P., Kothari, P., Thakurta, A.: Differentially private online learning. In: Conference on Learning Theory, pp. 24–31. JMLR Workshop and Conference Proceedings (2012)
19. Kifer, D., Smith, A., Thakurta, A.: Private convex empirical risk minimization and high-dimensional regression. In: Mannor, S., Srebro, N., Williamson, R.C. (eds.) Proceedings of the 25th Annual Conference on Learning Theory. Proceedings of Machine Learning Research, vol. 23, pp. 25.1-25.40. PMLR, Edinburgh, 25–27 June 2012
20. Lecun, Y., Bottou, L., Bengio, Y., Haffner, P.: Gradient-based learning applied to document recognition. Proc. IEEE 86(11), 2278–2324 (1998). https://doi.org/10.1109/5.726791
21. Lee, J., Kifer, D.: Concentrated differentially private gradient descent with adaptive per-iteration privacy budget. In: Proceedings of the 24th ACM SIGKDD International Conference on Knowledge Discovery and Data Mining. KDD 2018, pp. 1656–1665. Association for Computing Machinery, New York (2018). https://doi.org/10.1145/3219819.3220076
22. Li, T., Sahu, A.K., Talwalkar, A., Smith, V.: Federated learning: challenges, methods, and future directions. IEEE Sig. Process. Mag. 37(3), 50–60 (2020). https://doi.org/10.1109/MSP.2020.2975749
23. McMahan, H.B., Moore, E., Ramage, D., Hampson, S., Arcas, B.A.: Communication-efficient learning of deep networks from decentralized data. In: International Conference on Artificial Intelligence and Statistics (2016)
24. Ruggles, S., Genadek, K., Goeken, R., Grover, J., Sobek, M.: Integrated public use microdata series, Minnesota Population Center (2018)
25. Song, S., Chaudhuri, K., Sarwate, A.D.: Stochastic gradient descent with differentially private updates. In: 2013 IEEE Global Conference on Signal and Information Processing, pp. 245–248. IEEE, December 2013. https://doi.org/10.1109/GlobalSIP.2013.6736861
26. Talwar, K., Thakurta, A., Zhang, L.: Nearly-optimal private lasso. In: Proceedings of the 28th International Conference on Neural Information Processing Systems. NIPS 2015, vol. 2, pp. 3025–3033. MIT Press, Cambridge (2015). https://doi.org/10.5555/2969442.2969577
27. Wang, D., Ye, M., Xu, J.: Differentially private empirical risk minimization revisited: faster and more general. In: Advances in Neural Information Processing Systems, vol. 30 (2017). https://doi.org/10.48550/arXiv.1802.05251

28. Wang, X., Han, H., Zhang, Z., Yu, Q., Zheng, X.: Budget allocation method for tree index data differential privacy. Comput. Appl. **38**(7), 1960–1966 (2008)
29. Wang, Y.X., Fienberg, S.E., Smola, A.J.: Privacy for free: posterior sampling and stochastic gradient Monte Carlo. In: Proceedings of the 32nd International Conference on International Conference on Machine Learning. ICML 2015, vol. 37, pp. 2493–2502. PMLR, JMLR.org (2015). https://doi.org/10.5555/3045118.3045383
30. Williams, O., McSherry, F.: Probabilistic inference and differential privacy. In: Proceedings of the 23rd International Conference on Neural Information Processing Systems. NIPS 2010, vol. 2, pp. 2451–2459. Curran Associates Inc., Red Hook (2010). https://doi.org/10.5555/2997046.2997169
31. Wu, X., Li, F., Kumar, A., Chaudhuri, K., Jha, S., Naughton, J.: Bolt-on differential privacy for scalable stochastic gradient descent-based analytics. In: Proceedings of the 2017 ACM International Conference on Management of Data. SIGMOD 2017, pp. 1307–1322. Association for Computing Machinery, New York (2017). https://doi.org/10.1145/3035918.3064047
32. Zhang, J., Zheng, K., Mou, W., Wang, L.: Efficient private ERM for smooth objectives. In: Proceedings of the 26th International Joint Conference on Artificial Intelligence. IJCAI 2017, pp. 3922–3928. AAAI Press (2017). https://doi.org/10.5555/3172077.3172437

Evading Encrypted Traffic Classifiers by Transferable Adversarial Traffic

Hanwu Sun[1,2], Chengwei Peng[3], Yafei Sang[1,2(✉)], Shuhao Li[1,2],
Yongzheng Zhang[4], and Yujia Zhu[1,2]

[1] Institute of Information Engineering, Chinese Academy of Sciences, Beijing, China
{sunhanwu,sangyafei,lishuhao,zhuyujia}@iie.ac.cn
[2] School of Cyber Security, University of Chinese Academy of Sciences,
Beijing, China
[3] National Computer Network Emergency Response Technical Team/Coordination
Center of China, Beijing, China
pengchengwei@cert.org.cn
[4] China Assets Cybersecurity Technology Company, Beijing, China
zhangyongzheng@iie.ac.cn

Abstract. Machine learning algorithms have been widely leveraged in
traffic classification tasks to overcome the challenges brought by the
enormous encrypted traffic. On the contrary, ML-based classifiers introduce adversarial example attacks, which can fool the classifiers into giving wrong outputs with elaborately designed examples. Some adversarial attacks have been proposed to evaluate and improve the robustness of ML-based traffic classifiers. Unfortunately, it is impractical for
these attacks to assume that the adversary can run the target classifiers locally (white-box). Even some GAN-based black-box attacks still
require the target classifiers to act as discriminators. We fill the gap
by proposing FAT (We use FAT rather than TAT to imporove readabil-
ity.), a novel black-box adversarial traffic attack framework, which generates the transFerable Adversarial Traffic to evade ML-based encrypted
traffic classifiers. The key novelty of FAT is two-fold: i) FAT does not
assume that the adversary can obtain the target classifier. Specifically,
FAT builds proxy classifiers to mimic the target classifiers and generates transferable adversarial traffic to misclassify the target classifiers.
ii) FAT makes adversarial traffic attacks more practical by translating
adversarial features into traffic. We use two datasets, CICIDS-2017 and
MTA, to evaluate the effectiveness of FAT against seven common ML-
based classifiers. The experimental results show that FAT achieves an
average evasion detection rate (EDR) of 86.7%, which is higher than the
state-of-the-art black-box attack by 34.4%.

Keywords: Transferable adversarial traffic · Encrypted traffic
classifiers · Adversarial example attack · Black-box attack

© ICST Institute for Computer Sciences, Social Informatics and Telecommunications Engineering 2022
Published by Springer Nature Switzerland AG 2022. All Rights Reserved
H. Gao et al. (Eds.): CollaborateCom 2022, LNICST 461, pp. 153–173, 2022.
https://doi.org/10.1007/978-3-031-24386-8_9

1 Introduction

Network traffic classification is a critical and fundamental task in network management and cyberspace security [1]. With the widespread use of encryption technology, the volume of encrypted traffic is ballooning (Google reports that 95% of its products use encrypted communication [2]). Unfortunately, encrypted network traffic brings enormous challenges to traditional payload-based traffic classifiers [3]. To overcome these challenges, Machine Learning (ML) algorithms have been widely leveraged in encrypted traffic classification tasks and have become the mainstream method in many applications, such as quality of service (QoS) [4], application classification [5] and malicious traffic detection [6], etc.

While excellent performances are shown, ML-based encrypted traffic classifiers introduce new vulnerabilities named *adversarial example attacks* [7,8]. An adversarial example is formed by adding a well-designed and tiny perturbation to the normal example, which can fool the ML-based classifier into giving a wrong classification output with high confidence. To evaluate and improve the robustness of ML-based classifiers, the computer vision community proposes several adversarial example attacks, such as FGSM [8] and C&W [9]. Nevertheless, these attacks are specifically designed for images and are not well suited for disrupting network traffic. Due to the limitations of the complex TCP/IP protocols, not all bytes in the encrypted traffic can be modified at will. Additionally, extracting features from traffic is non-differentiable, making most gradient-based adversarial example generation methods unsuitable for two-step ML classifiers.

Some works have attempted to remove gaps between the data and exploit the adversarial vulnerability of encrypted traffic classifiers [10–12]. Unfortunately, the assumptions are too strong to perform these adversarial attacks. Firstly, most existing adversarial example attacks assume that the adversary can obtain copies of the target classifiers and run them locally. Even some methods [11, 12] use the target classifier as the discriminator of the Generative Adversarial Network(GAN) [13] architecture to generate adversarial examples and do not require the target classifier to backpropagate gradient. The target classifiers are still needed to participate in the entire calculation process. This requirement still seems harsh for the adversary. Secondly, some works choose to directly perform adversarial perturbations on feature vectors to avoid the non-differentiability problem of feature extraction. It is impractical to assume that the adversary can manipulate the feature vectors directly. Hence, a more practical adversarial attack is required to evaluate and improve ML-based encrypted traffic classifiers.

In this paper, we fill the gap by proposing FAT with more reasonable assumptions. FAT is a novel and practical black-box adversarial traffic attack framework, which is capable of generating the transFerable Adversarial Traffic to evade the ML-based encrypted traffic classifiers. The key novelty of FAT consists of two parts. Firstly, FAT does not assume that the adversary is able to obtain the copies of the target classifiers and run them locally. FAT barely requires any knowledge of the target encrypted classifiers except the prediction results. It is not harsh for the adversary to obtain the prediction result from a commercial encrypted traffic classifier. Proxy classifiers are built locally in FAT to mimic the target classifiers, and transferable adversarial traffic is generated to misclassify the target classifiers. Secondly, FAT makes the adversarial traffic attack more practical by translating the time-related features and packet-length-related features into traffic.

Our contributions can be briefly summarized as follows:

(1) We propose FAT, a novel and practical black-box adversarial traffic attack framework, which is able to effectively misclassify the encrypted traffic classifiers without controlling or obtaining the target classifiers. FAT is the first adversarial traffic attack assuming that the adversary does not obtain the copies of the target classifier to the best of our knowledge.

(2) We transform the time-related and packet-length-related adversarial features into real adversarial traffic, which can run on existing network infrastructure normally. It is more practical to perform an adversarial attack by the adversarial traffic than the adversarial feature vectors.

(3) We evaluate the effectiveness of FAT on two popular datasets(CICIDS-2017 and MTA). The results show that FAT can achieve an average evasion detection rate(EDR) of 86.7%, which is 51.6% and 34.4% higher than the state-of-the-art white-box and black-box attacks, respectively.

(4) We demonstrate that the architecture of the proxy classifier and the dataset on which the proxy classifier is trained are two key factors affecting the transferability of the adversarial traffic.

2   Related Work

Encrypted Traffic Classifiers. Sun *et al.* [14] propose a hybrid approach combining signature and statistical features, using the signature method to identify TLS traffic and then using the statistical feature-based method to identify different applications. Liu *et al.* [15] designed a set of packet-level statistic features and fed them into a semi-supervised algorithm to distinguish different encrypted flows. Okada *et al.* proposed and evaluated 49 statistical features and analyzed how these features differentiated between unencrypted and encrypted traffic. Liu *et al.* [16] proposed an end-to-end model that leverages the powerful representational capabilities of the DL algorithm to learn useful features from packet sequences automatically. Moreover, they use autoencoder to strengthen this feature learning process. Finally they use several layers of MLP as a classifier to classify the learned features and achieve very high classification accuracy. As described, methods using ML and DL techniques have become the mainstream.

Adversarial Examples Attack. The concept of adversarial examples was first proposed by Szegedy *et al.* [7]. They design L-BFGS to maliciously add imperceptible subtle perturbations to the input samples, which cause the target model to output incorrect classification results with high confidence. Goodfellow *et al.* [8] proposed a Fast Gradient Sign Method(FGSM) to generate adversarial examples efficiently and quickly. FGSM solved the problem of the low efficiency of L-BFGS.

In the field of traffic, the most primitive attack is traffic obfuscation against a traffic classifier. Stinson *et al.* [17] escaped the detection of the classifiers by making some random perturbations to the traffic. But such attacks didn't exploit the adversarial vulnerabilities of machine learning. Hashemi *et al.* [11] introduced the adversarial example technique to the field of anomaly detection and designed an adversarial attack against traffic classifiers. Nonetheless, such attacks based on the white-box assumption are not very practical. Lin *et al.* [10] designed an adversarial traffic features generation method based on GAN architecture. However, this method can only generate adversarial feature sets but cannot be converted into adversarial traffic and has limited practicality. While Novo *et al.* [18] implemented adversarial examples in the traffic space by adding adversarial proxy at both hosts of the C&C communication link, it is still a while-box attack. Han *et al.* [12] proposed a sophisticated black-box adversarial traffic attack also using GAN. Unfortunately, these GAN-based methods still require the target model to act as the discriminator, which is still harsh for the adversary to some extent.

3   Preliminaries

In this section, we sequentially introduce the adversarial examples attack, our motivation and define our problem and goals.

Table 1. List of the notations

Notations	Meaning	Notations	Meaning
X	Traffic flow set	ψ_t	Target classifier
$X_{m/b}$	A malicious/benign flow in X	ψ_p	Proxy classifier
$X^{adv/c}$	A adversarial/clean flow in X	α	Gradient scaling factor
x_i	The i-th feature of flow X	θ	Parameters of a classifier ψ
$Y_{m/b}$	Actual malicious/benign label	η	Adversarial perturbation
$Z_{m/b}$	Prediction of target classifiers	$\mathcal{L}$	Cross-Entropy loss
$A_{m/b}$	Prediction of proxy classifiers	ε	Perturbation constraint

3.1   Adversarial Examples

An adversarial example is a maliciously modified input, which causes the victim ML&DL-based classifier ψ to make a wrong prediction. Usually, adversarial examples are also generated by minimizing the loss function $\mathcal{L}$. However, unlike training a neural network, when generating adversarial examples, the parameters θ of the target classifier are kept fixed and modify the input samples.

$$X^{adv} = \arg \min_{d(X, X^{adv}) \leq \varepsilon} \mathcal{L}(X, Y_{targeted}, Y_{true}; \theta) \tag{1}$$

In a targeted adversarial attack, the loss function usually consists of two cross-entropy losses $\mathcal{C}$. Minimizing the first cross-entropy loss to keep the predicted label Z far away from the actual label Y_{true}, and minimizing the second cross-entropy loss to ensure the predicted labels are as close as possible to the targeted label $Y_{targeted}$.

$$\mathcal{L}(X, Y_{targeted}, Y_{true}; \theta) = -\mathcal{C}(\psi(X; \theta), Y_{true}) + \mathcal{C}(\psi(X; \theta), Y_{targeted}) \quad (2)$$

Given the classifier prediction distribution Z and label Y, the cross-entropy loss is as follows: $I(Y = c)$ is one if $Y = c$; otherwise, it is zero.

$$\mathcal{C}(Z, Y) = -\frac{1}{N} \sum_{i}^{N} \sum_{c=1}^{C} I(Y = c) \log Z_c^i \quad (3)$$

Additionally, we use the L-infinity norm distance function to measure the degree of perturbation.

$$d(X, X^{adv}) = ||X^{adv} - X||_{\infty} \quad (4)$$

3.2 Motivation

Adversarial attacks essentially move normal examples across the classifier's decision boundary by perturbing. Consequently, we need the parameters of the target classifier to calculate the direction in which the examples are moving. Unfortunately, it seems impractical for the adversary to get the complete parameters of a black-box classifier.

Inspired by this limitation, we attempt to locally build a proxy classifier with a similar decision boundary as the target classifier. Thus the proxy classifier guides a similar moving direction for the adversarial examples as the target classifier. Additionally, the architecture and training data are two key factors affecting the decision boundary of a classifier. Classifiers with similar architectures trained on data which have similar distributions have closer decision boundaries. Therefore, we need to search or a suitable architecture for the proxy classifier and collect data with the same or similar distributions as the target classifier used.

As shown in Fig. 1, when we build a proxy classifier that meets the requirements, the remaining work is to move the examples to cross the proxy classifier's decision boundary. By controlling the moving distance, the samples will also cross the decision boundary of the target classifier. We consider such adversarial examples to be transferable.

3.3 Problem Definition

This paper focus on the task of malicious encrypted traffic detection. Therefore, the adversarial example attack is to generate adversarial traffic to misclassify the target malicious traffic classifier. A raw traffic flow can be represented as a feature vector. In a specific attack scenario, given a malicious but clean(not be perturbed) flow $X_m^c = [x_1, x_2, \cdots, x_n], X_m^c \in \mathbb{X}$, where x_i is the i-th feature

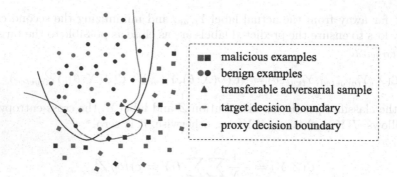

Fig. 1. The motivation of the transferable adversarial examples

of the malicious flow, and $\mathbb{X}$ is the traffic flow set. The target malicious traffic classifier ψ_t classifies the malicious flow as malicious label Z_m.

Our approach is divided into two steps. First, we need to train a proxy classifier ψ_p to mimic the target classifier. And the proxy classifier can also classify the malicious flow normally $\psi^p(X_m^c) \rightarrow Z_m$. The second step is to generate adversarial traffic flow X_m^{adv}. And the adversarial traffic flow not only can misclassify the proxy classifier $\psi_p(X_m^{adv}) \rightarrow Z_b$, but also can be transferred to misclassify the target classifier $\psi_t(X_m^{adv}) \rightarrow Z_b$ to output the benign label. Table 1 list the notations used in this paper.

4   Proposed Method

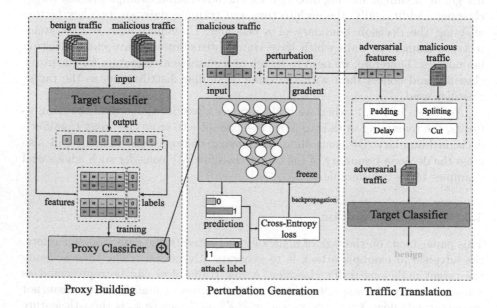

Fig. 2. The general framework of our approach.

This section first discuss the threat models in adversarial traffic attack scenarios, which contains some assumptions about the adversary and the detectors. And then, our approach will be introduced. The approach mainly consists of three steps, as shown in Fig. 2. Firstly we feed a batch of traffic samples into the target classifier and collect the output. Afterwards we use the output as the labels of these traffic samples to train a proxy classifier. Secondly, we conduct a gradient-based adversarial attack on the proxy classifier and generate the adversarial perturbation. Finally, we translate the adversarial features into the original malicious traffic and perform adversarial attack on the target encrypted traffic classifier.

4.1   Thread Model

The thread model for adversarial traffic attack is shown in Fig. 3. Entities related to it are as follows.

1) *The victim*. A victim is a host that is infected with malware or controlled by malware, also known as a zombie host, leaking information to the outside world or receiving instructions through encrypted command and control(C&C) channel.
2) *The detector*: The detectors are malicious encrypted traffic classifiers which are located in some communication nodes between the victim hosts and the hackers. They are usually viewed as black-box models and are passive in capturing the packets from the link.
3) *The adversary*: The adversaries are usually the ones who control the victim host, so they can manipulate the traffic generated by the malware and access the communication link. Furthermore, we assume that the adversaries can obtain the detection result of the detectors. It isn't a strong assumption to obtain the results of the detector compared to obtaining the copy of the detector or requiring the detector to participate in the calculation. Many commercial detectors, such as MTD [19] and GuardDuty [20], provide the service of querying detection results.

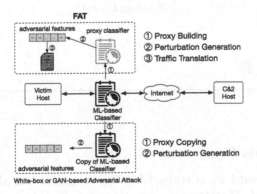

Fig. 3. Threat model for adversarial traffic attack scenarios

4.2 Proxy Building

The first and critical step of our approach is the proxy model building. In this step, we try to build a proxy classifier that has a similar decision boundary with the target classifier.

First of all, we prepare a batch of data X containing benign traffic and malicious traffic and its actual label Y. For the k-th traffic sample X_k, feed it to the target classifier ψ_t and collect its output Z_k. Note that Z_k is a category of X_k, not the probability distribution, which make it is more practical to implement. Next, we focus on training the proxy classifier ψ_p. For the j-th traffic sample X_j, we feed it into the proxy classifier and obtain the output a_j. And then calculate the cross-entropy loss(as shown in Eq. 3) of a_j and Z_j. Finally, we update the parameters θ of the proxy classifier by backpropagating. The entire process of transfer training is shown as Algorithm 1.

The adversary could control the victim host to run the malware and generate corresponding malicious traffic in a practical attack scenario. It should be noted that most online detectors have a proper delay, so there needs to be a time interval between running the malware twice on the victim host. Thus, it is time-consuming and laborious work. In the experimental environment, we directly input the prepared traffic to the target classifier.

Algorithm 1. Proxy Building

Input: Encrypted traffic samples: $X \in \mathbb{X}$; Target detector: ψ_t; Learning rate: lr; Train epoch size: $epoch$; Samples number: N

Output: proxy model: $\psi_p^* = \underset{\theta \in \psi_p}{\arg\min} \, \mathcal{J}(\psi_p(X), \psi_t(X))$

  for $k \leftarrow 1$ **to** N **do**
    $Z_k \leftarrow \psi_t(X_k)$
  end for
  for $i \leftarrow 1$ **to** $epoch$ **do**
    $L \leftarrow 0$
    for $j \leftarrow 1$ **to** N **do**
      $a_j \leftarrow \psi_p(X_j)$
      $loss \leftarrow -(Z_j \cdot log(a_j) + (1 - Z_j) \cdot log(1 - a_j))$
      $L \leftarrow L + loss$
    end for
    $L \leftarrow \frac{L}{N}$
    $\theta_{i+1} = \theta_i - lr \cdot \frac{\partial L}{\partial \theta_i}$
  end for

4.3 Perturbation Generation

Since the proxy model ψ_p is trained locally, we can obtain all the parameters of the proxy model. Therefore, we can generate adversarial perturbations with gradient-based methods.

Given a malicious traffic sample X_m, we need to turn it into adversarial malicious traffic X_m^{adv}. Firstly, we obtain the output A of the proxy classifier for X_m. And then calculate the cross-entropy loss of A and attack target label Y_b(means that the adversary wants the proxy classifier to misclassify X as benign). Finally, we update X_m with the gradient obtained by backpropagation. We cyclically repeat the above steps until the proxy classifier predicts X_m as benign, at which point we get the adversarial traffic X_m^{adv}. The generation of X_m^{adv} is shown in Algorithm 2.

There are two points to pay special attention to. On the one hand, unlike the training of ψ_p, we need to fix the parameters θ of the proxy classifier ψ_p and modify the input samples guided by the gradient. On the other hand, our perturbation to the traffic samples needs to be limited under ε, and the distance function d we use here is the L-infinity norm to control the cost of translating adversarial traffic.

Algorithm 2. Generate Adversarial Example

Input: proxy detector: ψ_p; Malicious but clean traffic: X_m^c; Scaling factor: α; Perturbation constraint: ϵ; Max epoch size: *epoch*;

Output: Adversarial malicious traffic: X_m^{adv}

$X_m^{adv} \leftarrow X_m$

$A \leftarrow \psi_p(X_m^{adv})$

$num \leftarrow 0$

while $A \neq Y_b$ and $num \leq epoch$ **do**

$\quad loss \leftarrow -(Y_b \cdot log(A) + (1 - Y_b) \cdot log(1 - A))$

$\quad \eta \leftarrow \frac{\partial loss}{\partial X_m^{adv}}$

$\quad X_m^{adv} \leftarrow X_m^{adv} + \alpha \cdot \eta$

$\quad X_m^{adv} \leftarrow clip(X_m^{adv}, \varepsilon)$ **s.t.** $d(X_m^c, X_m^{adv}) \leq \varepsilon$

$\quad A \leftarrow \psi_p(X_m^{adv})$

$\quad num \leftarrow num + 1$

end while

4.4   Traffic Translation

The adversarial traffic samples X^{adv} we generate so far are feature vectors. As mentioned before, an adversarial attack on features is meaningless to the adversary. So our main task in this part is to translate the adversarial features sequences X_m^{adv} into real adversarial traffic.

There are two kinds of features commonly used in ML&DL-based encrypted traffic classifiers. Traditional ML classifiers generally use manually extracted statistical features as input, while DL classifiers automatically learns useful information from sequential features. We used *CICFlowMeter* [21] to extract 77-dimensional flow-based statistical features[1], and use two sequential features:

---

[1] The 77-dimensional feature list extracted by CICFlowMeter can be obtained from https://github.com/ahlashkari/CICFlowMeter.

packet-length sequence and time-interval sequence. In this paper, we divide existing features into three categories according to the operations of translating adversarial feature into traffic. Features used in this paper are shown in Table 2

Packet Length-Related Features. Packet length-related features include various packet length-related statistical features and sequential features, such as mean packet length, max packet length, packet length sequence and so on. Time-related features such as packet interval are greatly affected by hardware, so they can generally be artificially increased but not reduced.

- *Padding*. The adversary would pad meaningless data, such as 0x00, to the end of the packet to increase the packet's length. When the C&C server receives the data, it will remove the padding data at the end, so this operation will not affect the regular communication of the malware.
- *Splitting*. The adversary would split a packet into two smaller packets to reduce the length of some large packets. For the C&C server, it is equivalent to receiving two smaller packets.

Time-Related Features. Time-related features include various time-related statistical features and time-related sequential features, such as flow duration, mean packet interval, time interval sequence and so on. For translating time-related features into traffic, the following operations are used. Note that we only operate the application layer data in order to ensure the normal transmission of the traffic.

- *Delay*. The adversary would delay a packet until the interval time between two packets meets the requirements.

5   Experimental Evaluation

In this section, we first introduce our experimental settings in detail, including the datasets, proxy&target classifier architectures, evaluation metrics and experimental environment. Then we search for the optimal hyperparameters and the optimal proxy classifier architectures for each target classifier. Based on optimal hyperparameters and proxy classifier, we evaluate the effectiveness of FAT and compare it with the state-of-the-art black-box and white-box adversarial attacks. Finally, we visualize the adversarial traffic and explain why it works.

5.1   Experimental Settings

Datasets. We use two popular traffic datasets(CICIDS-2017 and MTA) to evaluate the effectiveness of FAT. *CICIDS-2017* [22] dataset contains benign and the most up-to-date common attack traffic, which resembles true real-world data. We selected five common attack traffic as positive samples and the same amount of

Table 2. Summary of features

Statistical features					Sequence features
	No.	Name	Attributes	Direction	Name
Time-related features	0	Flow duration	-	Both	Time interval sequence
	15–28	Time between two packets	Avg, Std, Max, Min	Both	
			Sum, Avg, Std, Max, Min	Fwd	
			Sum, Avg, Std, Max, Min	Bwd	
	69–76	Active time	Avg, Std, Max, Min	Both	
		Idle time	Avg, Std, Max, Min	Both	
Packet- length-related features	1–12	Packet count	–	Both	Packet length sequence
		Total length	–	Fwd, Bwd	
		Packet length	Avg, Std, Max, Min	Fwd, Bwd	
	37–41	Packet length	Avg, Std, Max, Min, Var	Both	
Others	13–14 50–68	Rate	–	–	–
	29–36 42–49	TCP flag	–	–	

benign traffic in the same period as negative samples. *MTA* [23] dataset provides a large amount of C&C communication traffic captured from sandbox environments for up to 10 years. We collected 1621 pcap files provided by MTA from 2013 to 2022. Then we filtered out all encrypted flows and labelled each SSL flow by comparing its SHA1 fingerprint of the certificate and the *SSL Blacklist project* [24]. Finally, we selected the traffic of five malware families with enough flows as positive samples and the same number of benign traffic as negative samples. Table 3 describes the malicious type and the number of flows of the datasets we used.

In each dataset, we split the dataset into a target training set (40%), a proxy training set (40%) and a test set (20%). The target training set is used to train the target classifiers, and the proxy training set contains only features and no labels. The test set is used to generate adversarial traffic and test the performance of the target classifiers. We use 5-fold cross-validation to reduce overfitting.

Target Classifiers. To evaluate the effectiveness of FAT against ML-based malicious encrypted traffic classifiers. We use the seven most common ML-based classifiers with different architectures as the target classifiers. Logistics Regression (LR), Decision Tree (DT) and Support Vector Machine (SVM) represent common supervised learning classifiers. Multi-Layer Perceptron (MLP) represents neural network-based classifiers. Isolation Forest (IF) is the representative of unsupervised classifiers. Additionally, Long Short-Term Memory (LSTM) [25] and FS-Net [16] are representatives of end-to-end classifiers that exploit the sequential features of traffic.

Table 3. Summary of datasets in evaluation

Datasets	Features type	Malicious type	# Flows
CICIDS-2017	Statistical features	Botnet	1,966
		Fuzzing	231,073
		PortScan	127,537
		BruteForce	13,835
		DDoS	97,718
MTA	Statistical features sequence features	Tofsee	22,947
		Dridex	8,165
		Quakbot	706
		TrickBot	657
		Gozi	585

Proxy Classifiers. To explore the effect of proxy classifiers using different algorithmic architectures and features on the effectiveness of FAT, we selected three proxy classifiers with different architectures. MLP is representative of traffic classifiers using statistical features, and LSTM and FS-Net are representatives of classifiers using sequential features. At the same time, they also represent common traffic classifiers with DNN and RNN structures. Note that the adversarial traffic is formed by modifying the original malicious traffic according to the back-propagated gradient of the proxy classifier, so the proxy classifier is limited to neural network-based classifiers.

Table 4. The classification result confusion matrix

True label	Predicted label	
	Z_m	Z_b
Y_m	True Positive (TP)	False Negative (FN)
Y_b	False Positive (FP)	True Negative (TN)

Metrics. For each category, according to the true label Y and predicted label Z of each sample, samples can be divided into four categories, as shown in Table 4. For each target classifier, we use macro *Precision, Recall, F1-Score* to evaluate its classification performance.

We focus on whether the target classifier can correctly identify malicious samples, so we use the macro *Evasion Detection Rate*(EDR) as the metric to evaluate our attack. EDR, aka False Negative Rate (FNR), refers to the ratio of the number of samples that are actually malicious but predicted to be benign to the total number of actual malicious samples.

$$EDR_i = \frac{FN_i}{TP_i + FN_i}, EDR = \frac{1}{N}\sum_{i=1}^{N} EDR_i \qquad (5)$$

Experimental Environment. The core part of the proxy/target model and adversarial perturbing are implemented with the Sciket-learn and PyTorch frameworks. We used a machine that has a Xeon processor with 32 cores running at 2.3 GHz and 128 GB RAM.

5.2 Proxy Classifier and Hyperparameter Selection

Impact of Perturbation Limit(ε). Like other traffic obfuscation methods, adversarial traffic attacks also have a trade-off between the degree of perturbation and the evasive effectiveness. In order to search for the optimal ε, we designed the following experiments.

Firstly, when both the target classifier and the proxy classifier are FS-Net, the evasive effectiveness of FAT with different ε is shown in Fig 4(a). For all malware families in the MTA dataset, FAT's evasion detection rate(EDR) increases with the perturbation degree ε. When $\varepsilon = 0.03$, the EDR of all malware families are above 90%. What's more, Fig. 4(b) shows the evasive effectiveness of adversarial traffic for different target classifiers with different ε. Taking Trickbot as an example, when $\psi_p = LSTM$ and $\varepsilon = 0.10$, the adversarial traffic has excellent evasive effectiveness on DL-based classifiers such as FS-Net and LSTM but has weak evasive effectiveness on traditional ML-based classifiers such as SVM and LR. The reason is that the architecture of the proxy classifier and the target classifier are too different. The influence of the algorithm architecture between the proxy classifier and the target classifier will be explored later. However, even if the classifier architectures are quite different, when $\varepsilon = 0.3$, the adversarial traffic can achieve acceptable evasive effectiveness.

Additionally, it can be seen from Fig. 4(a) that the variations of the evasive effectiveness on the proxy model and the target model are similar. So the adversary can fine-tune ε based on the feedback from the proxy model until the best one is found.

Impact of Training Data. For an ML&DL-based classifier, the distribution of training data dramatically affects the shape of its decision boundary or decision hyperplane. By collecting the output of the target classifier, we try to build a training dataset with a similar distribution to the target. The more data we collect, the more similar its distribution is to the original distribution. We use different number of collected samples to train the proxy classifier ($\psi_p = LSTM$) separately and then generate adversarial traffic. The evasive effectiveness of FAT for FS-Net is shown in Fig. 5. From our experimental results, it can be seen that the more data we collect, the higher the probability of adversarial traffic evading the target classifier.

Proxy Classifier Selection. There are two key factors to guide us in choosing an appropriate proxy classifier. One is the architecture of the target classifier, and the other is the type of features used by the target classifier.

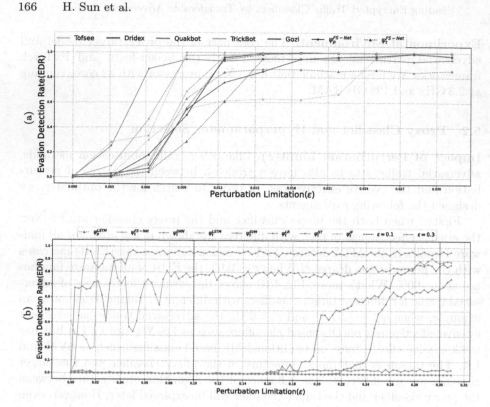

Fig. 4. The evasion effectiveness of the adversarial traffic with different ε. (a) shows different malware families and (b) shows different target architectures.

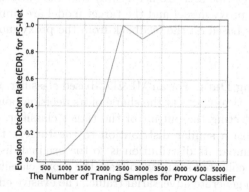

Fig. 5. The evasive effectiveness of adversarial traffic generated by LSTM classifier trained with different number of training samples.

To figure out the transferability of FAT between classifiers with different architectures, we chose three proxy classifiers (MLP, LSTM, FS-Net) and seven target classifiers and conducted 21 sets of experiments. At the same time, in order to explore the impact of different types of features on FAT, we extract two type of features from MTA dataset for experiment. Note that FS-Net is not included in the experiments of statistical features since FS-Net cannot handle statistical features.

When the $\varepsilon = 0.1$, the experimental result is shown in Table 5. When the proxy and target classifiers use the same architecture, FAT achieves the best EDR even if their parameters are different. When the proxy and target classifiers use different but similar architecture, for example, FS-Net and LSTM, the evasive effectiveness is acceptable for the adversary. On the contrary, if the proxy classifier uses a significantly different architecture from the target classifier, such as LSTM and IF, the evasive effectiveness is poor. Thus we can conclude that **adversarial traffic transfer better between the classifier with more similar architectures**.

From the experimental results, we also find that FAT can be transferred well between classifiers using the same type of features. For example, if MLP is used as the proxy classifier, the EDR of FAT against classifiers using sequential features is significantly higher than those using sequential features. This is because such RNN-based classifiers are designed to analyse sequential data, which are different from traditional ML algorithms. In contrast, MLP is closer to traditional ML algorithms and can better fit statistical features.

We attempt to explain from the perspective of the decision boundary. There are two main factors that determine the decision boundary of a classifier, one is the algorithm architecture, and the other is the distribution of the training data. Classifiers with similar architectures contain more similar mapping functions and are more likely to learn similar decision boundaries. For example, both FS-Net and LSTM contain RNN structure, which is very different from DNN, so the adversarial traffic generated based on LSTM has good evasive effectiveness for FS-Net, but is poor for DNN classifier. What's more, some ML algorithms like DT and IF do not apply gradients to update parameters, so the gradient-based adversarial traffic seems to be less effective for evading these classifiers.

Table 5. Transferability of adversarial traffic between classifiers with different architectures ($\varepsilon = 0.1$).

Feature type	Proxy classifiers (ψ_p)	EDR against target classifiers (ψ_t)						
		MLP	FS-Net	LSTM	LR	DT	SVM	IF
Sequence features	MLP	**65.62**	32.84	27.43	20.63	15.1	0.46	**49.06**
	FS-Net	8.9	**99.94**	**96.19**	30.03	**100**	0.46	21.36
	LSTM	7.06	96.68	82.58	**42.26**	71.63	0.55	24.136
Statistical features	MLP	**69.05**	–	41.67	**72.96**	**63.69**	**51.03**	**21.74**
	LSTM	34.62	–	**75.97**	38.52	50.48	34.84	0.89

5.3 Attack Effectiveness for Different Target Classifiers

Based on the above observations and findings, the attack effectiveness experiments of FAT are set up as follows. For the sequential feature, we choose FS-Net as the proxy classifier, and for the statistical feature, we use MLP as the proxy classifier. We calculate the detection performance of four ML-based classifiers and two DL-based classifiers, respectively, and the EDR of FAT against the above seven target classifiers.

When the perturbation limitation $\varepsilon = 0.1$, the experimental results are shown in Table 6. When the target classifiers use sequential features, the adversarial traffic generated by FS-Net achieves more than 95% evasion detection rate on LSTM and FS-Net while having poor evasive effectiveness on MLP, LR, SVM and IF. DT seems odd, mainly because the tree-related classifiers can change the classification result as long as one suitable feature is modified.

When the target classifiers use statistical features, the adversarial traffic generated by MLP has more than 50% EDR for most ML classifiers except IF. The reason is that IF is different from other classifiers and does not use indicators such as distance or density to describe the difference between a sample and other samples, so modifying features in a small range may not work well for IF.

Table 6. Detection effectiveness of target classifiers and evasing effectiveness of adversarial traffic.

Target classifier (ψ_t)	Sequence features ($\psi_p =$ FS-Net)				Statistical features ($\psi_p =$ MLP)			
	Detection			Evasion	Detection			Evasion
	P	R	F1	EDR	P	R	F1	EDR
MLP	97.78	98.43	98.11	8.90	94.84	95.00	94.80	**69.05**
FS-Net	99.98	99.98	99.98	**99.94**	–	–	–	–
LSTM	96.88	97.09	96.85	**96.19**	94.40	94.47	94.35	41.67
LR	99.75	99.87	99.81	30.03	89.75	99.06	94.09	**72.96**
DT	100.00	100.00	100.00	**100.00**	99.61	99.53	99.57	63.69
SVM	99.85	98.99	99.42	0.46	96.43	99.24	97.77	**51.03**
IF	82.84	52.71	64.35	21.36	76.54	48.22	59.16	**21.74**

5.4 Comparison Experiments

Comparison Attack. To fully evaluate the effectiveness of FAT, we compare it with the state-of-the-art white-box and black-box adversarial traffic work. The baseline and SOTA works are summarized as follows.

– **Baseline.** Applying random perturbations to the traffic can also misclassifies the target classifiers [17], which is also adversarial to the target classifier to some extent. *R-T* randomly inserts interval time between packets; *R-D* randomly duplicates partial original traffic.

- **White-box.** Hashemi *et al.* [11] introduced adversarial attacks into network intrusion detection systems for the first time. They design a white-box adversarial attack assuming that the adversary has all knowledge about the target classifiers.
- **Black-box.** Han *et al.* [12] designed a black-box adversarial attack based on the GAN architecture and used the same CICIDS-2017 dataset as ours for evaluation.

Furthermore, to evaluate the effectiveness of our method in feature-constrained scenarios, we divide FAT into four groups according to the features. All statistical features in the first group can be modified(FAT-A). The second and third groups only modify time-related features(FAT-T) and packet length-related features(FAT-L), respectively. The last group modifies both time-related features and packet-length-related features.

Table 7. Comparative experimental results with $\psi_p = MLP$

Target	Detection			Comparison attack				Our FAT			
	P	R	F1	EDR				EDR			
				R-D	R-T	White-box	Black-box	A	T	L	T+L
MLP	99.62	98.52	99.16	12.96	7.15	27.03	47.89	94.89	73.99	58.37	**95.02**
LR	99.46	94.54	96.92	13.88	15.73	57.54	62.67	84.83	59.41	74.39	**80.38**
DT	99.88	99.86	99.87	14.02	15.90	56.70	65.11	99.99	100.00	100.00	**99.99**
SVM	99.41	96.47	97.71	15.39	13.65	33.89	59.93	99.63	81.86	65.59	**92.78**
IF	90.72	57.45	70.46	0.38	6.58	0.26	25.67	54.19	44.11	10.32	**55.33**
AVG	97.82	89.37	92.82	11.33	11.80	35.08	52.25	86.71	71.35	61.73	**82.12**

Comparison Results. The comparison results are shown in Table 7. As shown in the experimental results, when all features can be modified arbitrarily, our attack achieves an average EDR of 86.7%, which is higher than the state-of-the-art black-box attack by 34.4%. Even when only time-related features or packet length-related features are modified, our attack can achieve an average EDR of 71.3% and 61.7%, and if both types of features are used, the average EDR can reach 82.1%.

Comparing our second and third groups of attacks, we find that the performance of MLP, SVM, and IF is more dependent on time-related features, while LR is more dependent on packet-length-related features.

5.5   Adversarial Traffic Visualization

To intuitively explain why FAT can evade encrypted traffic classifiers and can be transferred between classifiers with similar architecture, we conduct the following visualization experiments.

Effectiveness of FAT. For benign traffic and malicious traffic of each attack in the CICIDS-2017 dataset, we extract their 77-dimensional statistical features and generate adversarial features for malicious traffic under the guidance of the MLP proxy classifier. Finally, we use PCA to reduce the three sets of statistical features to 2 dimensions and draw their corresponding scatter plots.

The result is shown in Fig. 6. For each malicious attack, the distribution of the adversarial traffic is far different from its original malicious traffic and is closer to the benign traffic. In other words, FAT looks more like benign traffic to the classifiers based on spatial distance. This phenomenon is more obvious on Botnet, BruteForce and PortScan. Adversarial perturbation essentially changes the distribution of traffic in space, and once it crosses the decision boundary of the classifier, the adversarial traffic can misclassify the classifiers.

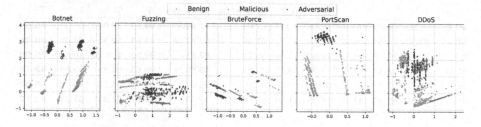

Fig. 6. Adversarial traffic visualization ($\psi_p = MLP$ and $\varepsilon = 0.1$).

Transferability of FAT. To demonstrate the transferability of FAT between classifiers with different architecture, we conduct the following experiments. For each target classifier, we take the prediction of the target classifier as the ground truth label, and combine the prediction of the proxy classifier to get the confusion matrix.

The results is shown in the Fig. 7 Fewer FPs and FNs indicate that the prediction results of the proxy classifier are closer to the target classifier. The experimental results show that the prediction results of MLP are closer to LR, SVM and DT, but quite different from IF. This means that the decision boundary of MLP is more similar with LR, SVM and DT, and FAT can be better transferred among them. Combined with the results in Table 7, it can be seen that the FAT generated by MLP has better evasion effectiveness against LR, SVM and DT, but the evasion effectiveness against IF is poor.

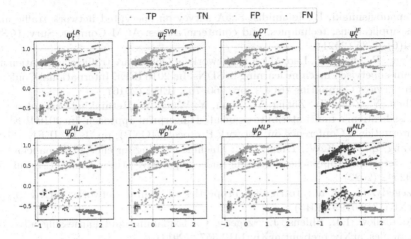

Fig. 7. Prediction results of classifiers with different architectures.

6   Conclusions and Future Work

This paper proposed a novel adversarial traffic attack framework named FAT, which can effectively misclassify the ML-based traffic classifiers without controlling or obtaining the target classifier. Firstly, we built a proxy classifier with a similar decision boundary to the target classifier. And then, we generate adversarial features via the proxy classifier to misclassify the target classifier. Finally, we translated the adversarial features into real adversarial traffic. Experimental results showed that under appropriate settings, transferable adversarial traffic can achieve an average EDR of 86.7% for unknown target classifiers, which is higher than the state-of-the-art black-box attack by 34.4%.

For future work, we will try to generate transferable adversarial traffic based on more complex features and attempt to propose a practical approach to defense the adversarial traffic attacks.

Acknowledgements. We thank the anonymous reviewers for their insightful comments. This work was supported by the National Key Research and Development Program of China (No. 2019YFB1005201, No. 2019YFB1005203 and No. 2019YFB1005205).

References

1. Tahaei, H., Afifi, F., Asemi, A., Zaki, F., Anuar, N. B.: The rise of traffic classification in IoT networks: a survey. J. Netw. Comput. Appl. **154**, 102538 (2020)
2. Google Transparency Report. https://transparencyreport.google.com/https/overview. Accessed 20 Mar 2022

3. Papadogiannaki, E., Ioannidis, S.: A survey on encrypted network traffic analysis applications, techniques, and countermeasures. ACM Comput. Surv. (CSUR) **54**(6), 1–35 (2021)

4. Wang, P., Lin, S. C., Luo, M.: A framework for QoS-aware traffic classification using semi-supervised machine learning in SDNs. In: 2016 IEEE International Conference on Services Computing (SCC), pp. 760–765. IEEE (2016)

5. Chen, Y., Zang, T., Zhang, Y., Zhou, Y. Wang, Y.: Rethinking encrypted traffic classification: a multi-attribute associated fingerprint approach. In: 2019 IEEE 27th International Conference on Network Protocols (ICNP), pp. 1–11. IEEE (2019)

6. Wang, Z., Fok, K.W., Thing, V.L.: Machine learning for encrypted malicious traffic detection: approaches, datasets and comparative study. Comput. Secur. **113**, 102542 (2022)

7. Szegedy, C., et al.: Intriguing properties of neural networks. arXiv preprint arXiv:1312.6199 (2013)

8. Goodfellow, I.J., Shlens, J., Szegedy, C.: Explaining and harnessing adversarial examples. arXiv preprint arXiv:1412.6572 (2014)

9. Carlini, N., Wagner, D.: Towards evaluating the robustness of neural networks. In: 2017 IEEE Symposium on Security and Privacy (SP), pp. 39–57. IEEE (2017)

10. Lin, Z., Shi, Y., Xue, Z.: IdsGAN: generative adversarial networks for attack generation against intrusion detection. arXiv preprint arXiv:1809.02077 (2018)

11. Hashemi, M.J., Cusack, G., Keller, E.: Towards evaluation of NIDSS in adversarial setting. In: Proceedings of the 3rd ACM CoNEXT Workshop on Big DAta, Machine Learning and Artificial Intelligence for Data Communication Networks, pp. 14–21 (2019)

12. Han, D., et al.: Evaluating and improving adversarial robustness of machine learning-based network intrusion detectors. IEEE J. Sel. Areas Commun. **39**(8), 2632–2647 (2021)

13. Goodfellow, I., et al.: Generative adversarial nets. In: Advances in Neural Information Processing Systems, vol. 27 (2014)

14. Sun, G.L., Xue, Y., Dong, Y., Wang, D., Li, C.: An novel hybrid method for effectively classifying encrypted traffic. In: 2010 IEEE Global Telecommunications Conference GLOBECOM 2010, pp. 1–5. IEEE (2010)

15. Liu, H., Wang, Z., Wang, Y.: Semi-supervised encrypted traffic classification using composite features set. J. Netw. **7**(8), 1195 (2012)

16. Liu, C., He, L., Xiong, G., Cao, Z., Li, Z.: Fs-net: a flow sequence network for encrypted traffic classification. In: IEEE INFOCOM 2019-IEEE Conference on Computer Communications, pp. 1171–1179. IEEE (2019)

17. Stinson, E., Mitchell, J.C.: Towards systematic evaluation of the evadability of bot/botnet detection methods. WOOT **8**, 1–9 (2008)

18. Novo, C., Morla, R.: Flow-based detection and proxy-based evasion of encrypted malware c2 traffic. In Proceedings of the 13th ACM Workshop on Artificial Intelligence and Security, pp. 83–91 (2020)

19. Managed Threat Detection. https://www.huaweicloud.com/product/mtd.html. Accessed 11 Aug 2022

20. Amazon GuardDuty. https://aws.amazon.com/cn/guardduty/. Accessed 11 Aug 2022

21. Davis, J.J., Clark, A.J.: Data preprocessing for anomaly based network intrusion detection: a review. Comput. Secur. **30**(6–7), 353–375 (2011)

22. Sharafaldin, I., Lashkari, A.H., Ghorbani, A.A.: Toward generating a new intrusion detection dataset and intrusion traffic characterization. ICISSp **1**, 108–116 (2018)

23. Malware Traffic Analysis. https://malware-traffic-analysis.net/. Accessed 20 Mar 2022

24. SSL Blacklist Project. https://sslbl.abuse.ch/. Accessed 20 Mar 2022

25. Zhu, X., Sobihani, P., Guo, H.: Long short-term memory over recursive structures. In: International Conference on Machine Learning, pp. 1604–1612 (2015)

A Secure Auction Mechanism for Task Allocation in Mobile Crowdsensing

Dan Li[1], Tong Liu[1,2]($\boxtimes$), and Chengfan Li[1,2]

[1] School of Computer Engineering and Science, Shanghai University, Shanghai, China
{ld19721539,tong_liu}@shu.edu.cn
[2] Shanghai Engineering Research Center of Intelligent Computing System, Shanghai, China

Abstract. Mobile crowdsensing has attracted widely attention as a new sensing paradigm, in which mobile users collect sensing data by their devices embedded various sensors. To motivate mobile users participating in sensing tasks, a number of auction mechanisms have been proposed. In our work, we focus on the task allocation problem with multiple constraints for the auction-based crowdsensing system to maximize profit of the central platform, which has been proved to be NP-hard. To solve the problem, a greedy-based task allocation algorithm with $(1+\gamma)$-approximation solution is proposed, in which the bid improving profit of the platform most is selected as the winning bid greedily in each iteration. However, bids for all tasks of a user submitted to the platform might let out location of the user unexpectedly. Therefore, we further design a secure auction mechanism with secret-sharing-based task allocation protocol, where each user can submit at most a winning bid to the platform instead of all bids for tasks to prevent locations of users from being inferred. The effectiveness of task allocation and location privacy protection based on our proposed secure auction mechanism is verified by theoretical analysis and simulations.

Keywords: Mobile crowdsensing · Privacy protection · Auction mechanism · Secret sharing

1 Introduction

With the improvement of 5G technology, Internet of Things (IOT) devices interact with each other at low delay and high rate to provide services such as intellisense, recognition and pervasive computing. As a new sensing paradigm of IOT, mobile crowdsensing [1] collects data through large-scale smart mobile devices embedded sensors like accelerator, camera, GPS, etc. Generally, a crowdsensing system consists of many mobile user devices to collect sensing data and a central platform resided on the cloud to extract valuable information from received sensing data. Compared with the traditional data acquisition method which takes advantage of purchasing and installing sensors, mobile user devices have more

© ICST Institute for Computer Sciences, Social Informatics and Telecommunications Engineering 2022
Published by Springer Nature Switzerland AG 2022. All Rights Reserved
H. Gao et al. (Eds.): CollaborateCom 2022, LNICST 461, pp. 174–193, 2022.
https://doi.org/10.1007/978-3-031-24386-8_10

flexibility to collect a large amount of data in different regions in crowdsensing system. Thanks to the effectiveness of mobile crowdsensing, it has been applied in many fields such as health care [11], environmental monitoring [9], traffic prediction [14,16].

In order to ensure the quality of service for mobile crowdsensing applications, it is important to stimulate mobile users to participant in sensing tasks. Moreover, assigning tasks to users for execution (i.e., task allocation) is a critical step to impact profit of the platform, which has become a major concern. So far, many task allocation methods have been proposed to address the problem of motivating users based on auction mechanisms [19,22,24]. Normally, a mobile user should transmit bid data including bids for all tasks to the platform for task allocation. However, the sensitive information such as location of each user might be revealed unexpectedly in an auction-based crowdsensing system without trusted third parties when raw bid data of users are submitted to the platform. The intuition of location leakage is that the smaller the bid for a task in bid data submitted by a user, the distance between the user and the task is shorter. If mobile crowdsensing applications fail to effectively protect location privacy of mobile users, users will be reluctant to take part in sensing tasks. Thus, it is vitally important to protect sensitive information of users for a crowdsensing system.

Nowadays, a number of literature is committed to protect the location privacy of mobile users for crowdsensing systems. Some location privacy protection mechanisms are proposed for crowdsensing with third trusted parties by applying encryption and differential privacy (DP). For these encryption approaches [2,4,7,20], they always assume there is a trusted authority in the crowdsensing system which is responsible for key generation and distribution to collaborate with smart mobile users to encrypt sensitive data. Differently, DP-based methods [6,18] perturb the original sensitive data of smart device users by a trusted platform to keep privacy information from leakage. However, it is not realistic to assume that there is a completely trusted third party. Fortunately, both location differential privacy (LDP) and secret-sharing method are effective tools for crowdsensing without a trusted third party. Compared to DP-based approaches, LDP-based methods [5,12,17,23] perturb sensitive data by mobile users locally instead of the platform. Differently, the research based on the secret sharing scheme [21] divides private data into multiple shares and send these shares to other users to compute collaboratively and safely through interactive communication. However, there are few methods considering location privacy leakage of users by bid information for task allocation in the auction-based crowdsensing system without any trusted third party.

Although these researches have protected the private locations of mobile users, it is very difficult for them to be applied to our proposed model. *Firstly*, we must ensure that the location privacy information cannot be inferred based on bids submitted by users during the auction mechanism for our mobile crowdsensing system, meanwhile the task allocation decisions should be decided. However, it is ignored by many existing works. *Secondly*, the DP and LDP schemes inevitably lead to performance degradation of results by adding noise. Thus, it is unjustified to adopt the methods to protect privacy for the NP-hard problem in our work which can only obtain an approximate solution in polynomial time. *Finally*, although existing works based on encryption schemes can achieve the homomorphism of the calculation to ensure the validity of decisions, they set up an authority agency to generate and distribute keys in the crowdsensing system. Moreover, encryption will generate a huge computational cost, which greatly increases the computation delay of privacy protection.

To solve the problem of task allocation for auction-based crowdsensing system, we firstly propose the greedy-based task allocation (GBTA) algorithm. Then, a secure auction mechanism utilizing secret-sharing-based task allocation (SSTA) protocol is designed, in which each user only submits the winning bid to the platform. For the auction mechanism based on GBTA algorithm, each user submits bid data for all tasks to the platform and the algorithm greedily selects a winning bid which can most improve profit of the platform in each iteration. However, as the bid data of a user should be enclosed and submitted to the untrusted platform, the location of the user might be inferred. Thus, we apply secret sharing technology to design a secure auction mechanism, in which each mobile user splits one bid into multiple polynomial bid shares and sends them to other users. After these users complete security multi-party computation according to SSTA protocol, all users will return the decision shares they hold for restoration. In the end, each user only needs to upload the price request for the assigned task, not for all tasks. As the platform cannot infer the distance relationship between tasks and a user according to the submitted winning bid of the user based on our secure auction mechanism, the location privacy of users can be well protected.

The main contributions of our work are summarized in the following:

- we consider the task allocation problem in the auction-based crowdsensing system, in which one task can be allocated to multiple users under budget constraint of the task. Meanwhile, the attack model which can infer locations of users based on bid data is presented. We prove the task allocation problem is NP-hard, then the GBTA algorithm is designed to obtain an approximate solution.
- To protect the location information of users during the auction process, a secure auction mechanism incorporating the SSTA protocol is proposed for crowdsensing without a trusted third party, in which each mobile user can only submit at most one winning bid to the platform. Moreover, the SSTA protocol can obtain the same approximate solution as GBTA. We prove that the location privacy of users is well protected from being disclosed to third parties during the execution of SSTA.
- We conduct simulations to evaluate the effectiveness of task allocation and location privacy protection level of the proposed mechanism. The results show that our method can effectively protect the location privacy of users while ensuring the profit of the platform.

This paper is organized as follows. We first discuss related works in Sect. 2. Then, we present our system model, attack model and problem formulation in

Sect. 3. The GBTA algorithm and the secure auction mechanism utilizing SSTA protocol with a logarithmic approximation ratio are proposed in Sect. 4. Finally, simulation results are presented in Sect. 5, and the paper is concluded in Sect. 6.

2   Related Work

In this section, we present briefly several location privacy-preserving mechanisms for mobile crowdsensing which can be classified into two categories including of trusted third party (TTP) assisted mechanisms and TTP-free mechanisms.

There are some works [2,4,6,7,18,20] focus on crowdsensing systems with TTPs. The approach proposed in [2] can prevent leakage of geo-tagged sensing data for crowdsensing with fog nodes effectively by applying Paillier encryption, in which the users send ciphertext of sensing data encrypted with a key distributed by the TTP. In [4], locations of users and regions of sensing tasks can be encrypted into a set of prefixes after key distribution by the trusted authority based on prefix encoding method. Moreover, both [7,20] are committed to design secure reverse auction mechanisms to protect locations of users by preventing bid leakage during auction period for crowdsensing with a TTP distributing keys to users. Li et al. [6] obfuscate position correlation weights between mobile users through trusted edge nodes based on differential privacy for edge computing. Wei et al. [18] assume that the cellular service provider is a TTP, and service requesters and mobile users send raw location data to the TTP for adding noise.

In other works [5,12,17,21,23], researchers assume that there is no TTP in the proposed crowdsensing system. Obviously, this assumption is more realistic. To recruit mobile users, Li et al. [5] guarantee the crowdsensing coverage meanwhile protecting locations of users based on LDP methods. Mobile users need upload one of frequently visited obfuscated-locations and find a set of users to maximize future crowdsensing coverage based on these perturbed locations in [17]. A novel location privacy-preserving mechanism is designed in [23] to protect the location of users in the space dimension and spatiotemporal activity. For the field of Internet of Vehicles, Qian et al. [12] propose a location-preserving task allocation method meanwhile improving task quality by perturbing locations on mobile devices. Different from above works, Xiao et al. [21] protect the sensing quality of each user to prevent location privacy leakage based on secret sharing scheme.

However, there are few works which are commited to location privacy protection at the auction stage for the crowdsensing system without any TTP.

3   System Model and Problem Formalization

In this section, we introduce our crowdsensing system model which consists of a semi-honest central platform and plenty of semi-honest mobile users. Then, a security model is introduced to measure the computation security under semi-honest model in our crowdsensing system and an attack model is presented to infer locations of users based on the received bid data. Finally, the task allocation problem formalization is given.

3.1 Crowdsensing System Model

We consider there is a central platform to announce many sensing tasks $\mathcal{T} = \{t_1, t_2, \cdots, t_m\}$ and some mobile users $\mathcal{U} = \{u_1, u_2, \cdots, u_n\}$ participate in sensing tasks in our crowdsensing system. Moreover, the platform and users are semi-honest, which means they may extract extra information from received data. After the platform announces sensing tasks, a user can be allocated at most one task to execute and each task may be allocated to multiple users so that the platform can obtain an accurate estimated value of the task based on a mass of sensing data collected by these users. For sake of convenience, geographical locations can be represented by two-dimensional grid coordinates in a 2D space. Thus, each task is denoted by a tuple $t_j \overset{\text{def}}{=} <l_j, B_j>$, where l_j is the grid coordinate location of the sensing task t_j, and B_j is the total budget of t_j.

If a user u_i's location is inconsistent with the location of the task t_j to be performed, the user should move to the location of the task to collect sensing data. The cost of the movement is denoted by c_i^j, which is positively correlated with the distance d_i^j between user u_i and task t_j. Compared to the cost of movement, the cost of performing tasks can be neglected so that the bid of user u_i performing task t_j is equivalent to the cost of movement and can be also denoted by c_i^j. That is to say, the bid increases as the distance between the user and the task increases. After the sensing data collected by user u_i of task t_j is transmitted to the platform, the platform will make a profit $\alpha_i G_j - c_i^j$, in which $\alpha_i \in [0, 1]$ represents the credit of user u_i for completing tasks according to quality of historical sensing data and G_j is the basic earning of task t_j provided by the platform.

As shown as Fig. 1, the auction process for our auction-based crowdsensing system can be divided into five steps: (1) The platform publishes m location-sensitive tasks with location tags and budget constraints. (2) Each user generates the bid set $C_i = \{c_i^1, c_i^2, \cdots, c_i^j\}$ based on the distance to tasks and submits these bid data to the platform. (3) The platform allocates tasks to users to maximize the profit of the platform according to received bid sets of all users $\mathcal{C} = \{C_1, C_2, \cdots, C_n\}$. (4) Each user submits the results of allocated sensing task to the platform. (5) The platform pays some rewards to users according to the winning bids.

However, as the raw bid sets are uploaded to the central platform in the auction-based crowdsensing system, the platform may infer the location of a user according to the distance between the user and each task contained in the bid set. Therefore, a secure auction mechanism for crowdsensing without any TTP will be designed in the Sect. 4.4 to prevent the location of each user from being revealed.

3.2 Security Model

In our work, both the platform and mobile users are semi-honest. On the one hand, the platform and mobile users follow the task allocation protocol, showing the honest aspect. On the other hand, they may infer the location privacy

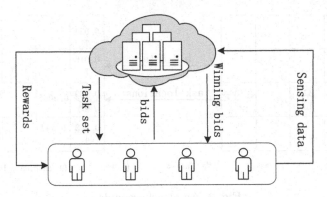

Fig. 1. An auction-based crowdsensing system model.

according to the received bid data in the course of auction, showing the dishonest aspect. Moreover, if each semi-honest party in system cannot extract extra information from the received data during execution of protocol, we can consider the computation in the protocol to be private. The private computation under semi-honest model can be defined in the following:

Definition 1 (Private computation under semi-honest model [3]). *Suppose there is a function $\mathcal{F}$ that is computed jointly by n parties, we let x_i be the input of the i-th party, and $\mathcal{F}_i$ is the output of the i-th party, i.e., $\mathcal{F}(x_1, x_2, \cdots, x_n) = (\mathcal{F}_1, \mathcal{F}_2, \cdots, \mathcal{F}_n)$. Especially, let $1 \le i \le n$ represent n mobile users. The view of the i-th party during the execution of the protocol is $VIEW_i = (x_i, r, m_i)$, where r represents the outcome of the i-th party's internal coin tosses and m_i represents the messages that the user has received. For $\mathcal{I} = \{i_1, i_2, \cdots, i_k\} \subset \{1, 2, \cdots, n\}$, the outcomes of these parties $\mathcal{F}_{i_1}, \mathcal{F}_{i_2}, \cdots, \mathcal{F}_{i_k}$ can be denoted by $\mathcal{F}_{\mathcal{I}}$. Moreover, the view of $\mathcal{I}$ is $VIEW_{\mathcal{I}} \stackrel{def}{=} (\mathcal{I}, VIEW_{i_1}, VIEW_{i_2}, \cdots, VIEW_{i_k})$. Then, for any party subset $\mathcal{I}$, the computation protocol can compute the function $\mathcal{F}$ privately if there exists a polynomial time algorithm $\mathcal{A}$ satisfying the following relationship:*

$$\mathcal{A}(\mathcal{I}, (x_{i_1}, x_{i_2}, \cdots, x_{i_k}, \mathcal{F}_{\mathcal{I}})) = VIEW_{\mathcal{I}}. \tag{1}$$

According to Eq. (1), what is acquired from a party's view can be obtained entirely from the input and output of this party. That is to say, any party in our system cannot infer the location information from they received data as long as a private computation protocol is designed.

3.3   Attack Model

For the crowdsensing system, we introduce an attack model to infer the location of a user according to bid data submitted by the user. For the convenience of expression, the candidate locations, where the distance to tasks increases as the bid increases, are denoted by $\mathcal{L}$. Then, the attacker infers the location of a user

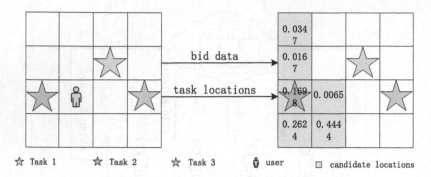

Fig. 2. An attack example.

by calculating the Euclidean distance similarity between the normalized distance vector from a candidate location to tasks and the normalized bid vector.

For example, there is a region divided to $4*4$ grids and a user at location (1,1), three tasks located at (2,2), (0,1), (3,1) respectively as shown as Fig. 2. Suppose the original bid vector is set as (2,1,4) computed by the square function. Firstly, the candidate locations $\mathcal{L}$ can be determined as coloured areas in the figure. That is to say, the distances from a location in $\mathcal{L}$ to task 2, task 1, and task 3 are monotonically increasing and the user must be in one of these candidate locations. Next, the Euclidean distance similarity between the normalized distance vector of each candidate grid and normalized bid vector can be obtained. Finally, we can find that the value of grid (1,1) is smallest which means the user is most likely to be in the location. So far, an attacker may infer the location of a user based on the received bid information.

3.4 Problem Formalization

In the work, we focus on the secure task allocation problem in the auction-based mobile crowdsensing under the semi-honest model to maximize the total profit of the platform. Then, the problem can be formalized as follows:

$$Maximize: \quad \sum_{j=1}^{m} \sum_{i=1}^{n} (\alpha_i G_j - c_i^j) x_i^j \tag{2}$$

$$Subject\ to: \quad \sum_{i=1}^{n} c_i^j x_i^j \leq B_j \tag{3}$$

$$\sum_{j=1}^{m} x_i^j \leq 1 \tag{4}$$

$$x_i^j \in \{0,1\} \tag{5}$$

$$Eq.(1) \quad holds \tag{6}$$

Here, Eq. (3) represents the budget constraint, which means the total cost of multiple users performing a task cannot exceed budget of the task and Eq. (4) indicates that each user can be allocated at most one task. Equation (5) shows the task allocation decision x_i^j is binary. If the task t_j is allocated to the u_i (i.e., bid c_i^j is one of winning bids), the decision variable $x_i^j = 1$, otherwise $x_i^j = 0$. To protect the location of each user from being revealed, Eq. (6) should be satisfied so that additional location information of users can not be inferred during the execution of a secure computation protocol.

4 Methodology

In this section, we first introduce a GBTA algorithm for the system without security guarantee, and we analyse theoretically the approximation ratio achieved by the GBTA algorithm. Moreover, a secure auction mechanism with SSTA protocol is designed on this basis. Finally, we prove that the location of each user can be preserved well during the execution of SSTA and the accuracy of this method is same as GBTA algorithm.

4.1 Problem Complexity Analysis

Theorem 1. *The task allocation problem is NP-hard.*

Proof. We consider a special case of the task allocation problem, in which there is only one task to be allocated, i,e., $| \mathcal{T} |= 1$. Thus, each user u_i will generate a bid c_i for the task. Moreover, the credit of user u_i is denoted by α_i, G is the basic earning of the task provided by the platform and the budget of the task is B. Then, we should select some users $\mathcal{U}' \subseteq \mathcal{U}$ performing the task to maximize $\sum_{u_i \in \mathcal{U}'} (\alpha_i G - c_i)$, while the total bid of users $\mathcal{U}'$ is no more than the budget B. Obviously, the special problem is regarded as 0–1 knapsack problem equivalently which is a classic NP-hard problem: Given a knapsack with capacity B and an item set $\mathcal{U}$, the value of item u_i is $\alpha_i G - c_i$ and the weight is c_i, select some items to put into the knapsack to maximize the total value within the capacity of the knapsack. Accordingly, the general task allocation problem in our work is at least NP-hard.

4.2 Greedy-Based Task Allocation Algorithm

As the task allocation problem is NP-hard, an algorithm based on greedy strategy is designed to obtain an approximate solution in polynomial time. Firstly, let $\mathcal{X}$ be the set of decision variable x_i^j whose initial value is 0. The GBTA algorithm contains multiple iterations and the algorithm always selects the bid which most improves the profit of the platform within the budget constraints of tasks in each iteration. That is to say, if there is a bid c_i^j that makes $\alpha_i G_j - c_i^j$ the largest non-negative value, the task t_j will be allocated to user u_i, i,e., $x_i^j = 1$. Moreover, if there is no bid to meet the budget constraint or make non-negative profit in bid data of a user, the user will be not assigned tasks. Since each user is assigned at most one task, the user u_i should be removed from the user set $\mathcal{U}$ after a task is allocated to the user and GBTA terminates when the user set is empty.

Algorithm 1: Greedy-Based Task Allocation algorithm

Input: $\mathcal{U}, \mathcal{S}, \mathcal{C}, \{\alpha_i \mid i \in \mathcal{U}, j \in \mathcal{T}\}, \{B_j, G_j \mid j \in \mathcal{T}\}$
Output: $\mathcal{X}$

    initialization: $\mathcal{X} = 0, max = -1$
1: **while** $\mathcal{U} \neq \varnothing$ **do**
2:     **for** each user i in $\mathcal{U}$ **do**
3:         construct task set of each user u_i:
            $T_i' = \{t_j \mid c_i^j \leq B_j, \alpha_i G_j - c_i^j \geq 0\}$
4:     **if** $T_i' = \varnothing$ **then**
5:         $\mathcal{U} = \mathcal{U} \backslash u_i$;
6:     **for** each user i in $\mathcal{U}$ **do**
7:         **for** each task j in T_i' **do**
8:             **if** $\alpha_i G_j - c_i^j > max$ **then**
9:                 $max = \alpha_i G_j - c_i^j$
10:                 $allocTask = j$
11:                 $selUser = i$
12:     $x_{selUser}^{AllocTask} = 1$
13:     $\mathcal{U} = \mathcal{U} \backslash selUser$
14:     $B_{allocTask} = B_{allocTask} - c_i^j$
15: **return** task allocation decision $\mathcal{X}$

The detailed GBTA algorithm is as shown as Algorithm 1. From step 2 to step 5, we construct a candidate task set for each user, in which each task has enough budget and the profit of the platform will be improved by assigning the task to the user. If the candidate task set of a user u_i is empty, the user will not be assigned any task. Then, a winning bid which produces largest non-negative profit $\alpha_i G_j - c_i^j$ within task budget constraint is determined in step 6–11 for each iteration and we record the index of the winning bid. When a bid c_i^j is winning bid, the task t_j will be allocated to the user u_i. Thus, we remove the user who has been assigned a task from the user set and update the budget of the task t_j in step 12–14.

4.3 Approximation Performance Analysis

Theorem 2. *Suppose the profit produced by Algorithm 1 is F_{alg} and the profit generated by the optimal solution is F_{opt}. They satisfy the following equation:*

$$\frac{F_{opt}}{F_{alg}} \leq 1 + \gamma, \text{ where } \gamma = max\{\frac{B_j}{c_i^j} \mid t_j \in \mathcal{T}, u_i \in \mathcal{U}\} \tag{7}$$

Proof. Then, we can prove Eq. (7) by adopting mathematical induction method.

(1) Firstly, when $\mid \mathcal{U} \mid = 1$, we can find obviously that the greedy solution is same as optimal solution and $F_{opt}/F_{alg} = 1 (< 1 + \gamma)$.

(2) Next, suppose $F_{opt}/F_{alg} \leq 1 + \gamma$ holds when $\mid \mathcal{U} \mid = n$.

(3) Given $\mid \mathcal{U} \mid = n+1$. Without loss of generality, we assume that $\alpha_1 G_1 - c_1^1 = max\{\alpha_i G_j - c_i^j \mid u_i \in \mathcal{U}, t_j \in \mathcal{T}\}$ and the value is non-negative. According to the

GBTA algorithm, u_1 must be assigned task t_1, i,e., $x_i^j = 1$. Now, we consider two cases in the following:

In the Optimal Solution, Task t_1 is also Allocated to User u_1. Consider the sub-problem P' in which the user set is $\mathcal{U}' = \mathcal{U} - \{u_1\}$ and the budget of task t_1 is $B_1' = B_1 - c_1^1$. After running the GBTA algorithm for the sub-problem P', we can get the profit $F_{alg|P'}$. Moreover, the profit generated by optimal solution for the sub-problem is denoted by $F_{opt|P'}$. Then, we have $F_{alg} = F_{alg|P'} + (\alpha_1 G_1 - c_1^1)$ and $F_{opt} = F_{opt|P'} + (\alpha_1 G_1 - c_1^1)$ based on optimal structure of our problem. According to the step (2) of the mathematical induction, we find $F_{opt|P'} \leq (1 + \gamma) F_{alg|P'}$. Accordingly, we have:

$$\frac{F_{opt}}{F_{alg}} = \frac{F_{opt|P'} + (\alpha_1 G_1 - c_1^1)}{F_{alg|P'} + (\alpha_1 G_1 - c_1^1)} \leq 1 + \gamma \tag{8}$$

In the Optimal Solution, Task t_1 is Not Allocated to User u_1. Thus, the task t_1 is assigned to other users $\mathcal{U}_{opt}^{(1)}$ and the profit generated by the allocated task t_1 based on optimal solution is denoted by $F_{opt}^{(1)}$. Then, we have:

$$F_{opt}^{(1)} = \sum_{u_i \in \mathcal{U}_{opt}^{(1)}} (\alpha_i G_1 - c_i^1) \leq \gamma(\alpha_1 G_1 - c_1^1) \tag{9}$$

Without loss of generality, we assume the user u_1 is allocated task t_2 in optimal solution. Consider the sub-problem P'' in which the user set is $\mathcal{U}'' = \mathcal{U} - \{u_1\} - \mathcal{U}_{opt}^{(1)}$, the task set is $\mathcal{T}'' = \mathcal{T} - \{t_1\}$ and the budget of task t_2 is $B_2 - c_1^2$. The profit produced by optimal solution for the sub-problem can be denoted by $F_{opt|P''}$. Then, we have:

$$F_{opt} = F_{opt|P''} + F_{opt}^{(1)} + (\alpha_1 G_2 - c_1^2) \tag{10}$$

It should be noted that the sub-problem P'' is contained in problem P' so that $F_{opt|P''} \leq F_{opt|P'}$. Moreover, as $|\mathcal{U}'| = n$ in sub-problem P', we can get $F_{opt|P'} \leq (1 + \gamma) F_{alg|P'}$. Thus, the following inequality exists:

$$F_{opt|P''} \leq (1 + \gamma) F_{alg|P'} \tag{11}$$

From Eq. (9) to Eq. (11) and $\alpha_1 G_1 - c_1^1 = max\{\alpha_i G_j - c_i^j \mid u_i \in \mathcal{U}, t_j \in \mathcal{T}\}$, we have:

$$\begin{aligned} \frac{F_{opt}}{F_{alg}} &= \frac{F_{opt|P''} + F_{opt}^{(1)} + (\alpha_1 G_2 - c_1^2)}{F_{alg|P'} + (\alpha_1 G_1 - c_1^1)} \\ &\leq \frac{(1 + \gamma) F_{alg|P'} + \gamma(\alpha_1 G_1 - c_1^1) + (\alpha_1 G_2 - c_1^2)}{F_{alg|P'} + (\alpha_1 G_1 - c_1^1)} \\ &\leq 1 + \gamma \end{aligned} \tag{12}$$

So far, Theorem 2 is proved. That is to say, GBTA algorithm can achieve $(1+\gamma)$-approximation solution where $\gamma = max\{\frac{B_j}{c_i^j} \mid t_j \in \mathcal{T}, u_i \in \mathcal{U}\}$.

4.4   A Secure Auction Mechanism for Task Allocation

For the basic auction-based crowdsensing system, the location of a user could be leaked out as the bid set of the user is submitted to the platform to execute the GBTA algorithm. To protect the bid information from third parties, we apply the secret sharing scheme to the GBTA. Firstly, we introduce the preliminaries of a well-known Shamir secret sharing scheme and then a secure auction mechanism with SSTA protocol is designed for protecting sensitive information and assigning tasks to users.

Preliminaries

Definition 2 (Shamir secret sharing). *Let p be an odd prime and $\mathbb{Z}_p$ be a prime field. A secret $s \in \mathbb{Z}_p$ means that $s \in \{0, 1, 2, \cdots, p - 1\}$. If a secret s is shared among n parties based on a random polynomial $f_s = s + \alpha_1 x + \alpha_2 x^2 + \cdots + \alpha_t x^t \bmod p$ with randomly chosen $\alpha_k \in \mathbb{Z}_p$ for $1 \leq k \leq t \leq \frac{n}{2}$, $[s]_p = \{f_s(i) \mid 1 \leq i \leq n\}$ is a share set of the secret $s \in \mathbb{Z}_p$. Moreover, the share of secret s received by party i in the $[s]_p$ is denoted by $[s]_p^i$.*

Suppose that there are two secrets a, b to be shared and the random polynomials with degree t of them are $f_a = a + a_1 x + a_2 x^2 + \cdots + a_t x^t \bmod p$ and $f_b = b + b_1 x + b_2 x^2 + \cdots + b_t x^t \bmod p$, respectively. For the sake of writing, we use $[\cdot]$ instead of $[\cdot]_p$ in the following. Then, there are some mathematical operations of secure multi-party computation to calculate one function based on Shamir secret sharing scheme. The addition operation and subtraction operation can be redefined and computed as follows:

$$[a] + [b] \triangleq [(a + b) \bmod p] = ([a] + [b]) \bmod p \tag{13}$$

$$[a] - [b] \triangleq [(a - b) \bmod p] = ([a] - [b]) \bmod p \tag{14}$$

The Eq. (13) above can be established as $f_a + f_b = (a + b) + (a_1 + b_1)x + (a_2 + b_2)x^2 + \cdots + (a_t + b_t)x^t \bmod p$ and in a similar way, Eq. (14) is correct. Obviously, we can find that each user u_i can calculate the redefined addition and subtraction of own shares locally by the received share $[a]_p^i$ and share $[b]_p^i$.

However, the multiplication operation $[a] * [b] \triangleq [(a*b) \bmod p]$ and comparison operation $Comp([a], [b])$ can not be realized locally for any party. Let l be the bit size of the prime p. In our work, $[a] * [b]$ is computed by communicating with other parties according to the secure distributed multiplication protocol [8] based on Newton's interpolation theorem, in which the computation complexity is $O(n^2 l)$ bit-operations per user and the communication complexity is $O(nl)$. To compare the value a and value b, a multiparty comparison computation protocol [10] is proposed, in which the communication complexity is $279l + 5$ times as large as the multiplication operation and the computation complexity depends on 15 rounds of performing the multiplication protocol in parallel. Note that if $a \leq b$, the comparison protocol determines $Comp([a], [b]) = [1]$, otherwise $Comp([a], [b]) = [0]$. Then, the max selection operation $Max([a], [b]) \triangleq [max(a, b)]$ can be calculated by $[a] + (Comp([a], [b]) * ([b] - [a]))$.

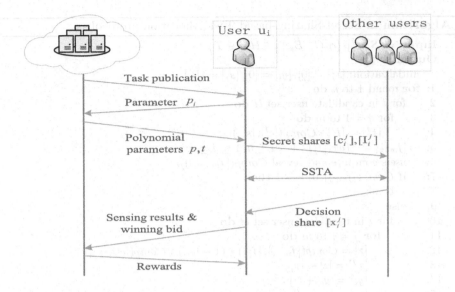

Fig. 3. A secure auction mechanism for crowdsensing system.

Design for Secure Auction Mechanism. In auction-based crowdsensing system, if only the winning bid of a user is submitted to the platform, the platform can not infer location of the user according to the distance relationship between the user and tasks contained in bid set of the user. This gives us the inspiration to design our secure auction mechanism to maximize total profit of the platform by task allocation. The main steps of our secure auction mechanism are as shown as Fig. 3.

(1) *Task Publication:* The platform publishes m tasks, the location l_j and the budget B_j of each task $t_j, 1 \leq j \leq m$. Moreover, the platform computes the value of $\alpha_i G_j$ and sends the value to each user u_i.

   (2) *Parameters Generation:* Each user u_i submits an odd prime p_i which is larger than $max(c_i^1, \cdots, c_i^m)$. Then, the platform determines the odd prime p which is larger than $max(\alpha_i G_j + 1, \{p_i \mid u_i \in \mathcal{U}\}, \{B_j \mid t_j \in \mathcal{T}\})$ and the degree of polynomial is $t(\leq n)$. The parameters including the odd prime p and degree t are released to all users.

   (3) *Secret Sharing:* Each user u_i computes function I_i^j according to the received value $\alpha_i G_j$ and bid c_i^j as follows:

$$I_i^j = \begin{cases} \alpha_i G_j - c_i^j + 1, & \text{if } \alpha_i G_j - c_i^j \geq 0 \\ 0, & \text{if } \alpha_i G_j - c_i^j < 0. \end{cases}$$

Then, each user u_i generates a share set $[c_i^j]$ of secret c_i^j and a share set $[I_i^j]$ of secret I_i^j and transmits the shares $[c_i^j]_p^{i'}, [I_i^j]_p^{i'}$ to each other user $u_{i'}$.

Algorithm 2: Secret-Sharing-based Task Allocation protocol

Input: $\mathcal{U}, \mathcal{S}, [c_i^j], \{\alpha_i G_j, B_j \mid i \in \mathcal{U}, j \in \mathcal{T}\}$
Output: $[\mathcal{X}]$
    initialization: $[x_i^j] = [0], [y_i] = [0], [s_j] = [B_j]$
1: **for** round 1 to n **do**
2:    **for** i in candidate user set $\mathcal{U}$ **do**
3:       **for** $j = 1$ to m **do**
4:          $[f_i^j] = [I_i^j] * Comp([c_i^j], [s_j])$
5:      $[f_{max}] = Max([f_i^j] \mid 1 \le i \le n, 1 \le j \le m)$
6:      users compute and reveal $Comp([f_{max}], 0)$.
7:      **if** $Comp([f_{max}], 0) == 1$ **then**
8:         break;
9:      **else**
10:       **for** i in candidate user set $\mathcal{U}$ **do**
11:         **for** $j = 1$ to m **do**
12:           $[z] = Comp([f_{max}], [f_i^j]) * (1 - [y_i]) * Comp([c_i^j], [s_j])$
13:           $[x_i^j] = [z] + [x_i^j]$
14:           $[y_i] = [y_i] + [z]$
15:           $[s_j] = [s_j] - ([z] * [c_i^j])$
           each user $u_{i'}$ send $[y_i]_p^{i'}$ to user u_i for restoration,
16:       **if** $y_i = 1$ **then**
17:         the user u_i communicates with the platform, then the platform updates
        and broadcasts the candidate user set $\mathcal{U} = \mathcal{U} - \{u_i\}$ to all users.
18:       **else**
19:         continue;
20: **return** polynomial decision share $[\mathcal{X}]$

---

(4) *Task Allocation:* This step is also regarded as the process of selecting winning bids. Users jointly make the task allocation decision share $[\mathcal{X}] = \{[x_i^j] \mid \forall u_i \in \mathcal{U}, \forall t_j \in \mathcal{T}\}$ according to SSTA protocol.

Specially, Users compute jointly the function $[f_i^j], \forall u_i \in \mathcal{U}, \forall t_j \in \mathcal{T}$. If the bid c_i^j is larger than the budget B_j, SSTA determines the function $[f_i^j] = [0]$, otherwise $[f_i^j] = [I_i^j]$ in step 2–4. Step 5–8 indicates that the maximum value of the function is determined as f_{max} privately and the protocol will be terminated in advance if $f_{max} < 0$. From step 12–17, users determine the winning bid and make task allocation decisions. If the function f_i^j is largest and user u_i has not been assigned a task on the condition that the budget of t_j is adequate, users determine the decision share set $[x_i^j] = [1]$ and execution flag of the user is $[y_i] = [1]$. Then, the budget of task t_j should be updated and the user u_i should be removed from the candidate user set. Moreover, the decision share set $[\mathcal{X}]$ can be decided after at most n iterations. When the $[\mathcal{X}]$ is decided, each user $u_{i'}$ sends $\{[x_i^j]_p^{i'} \mid \forall t_j \in \mathcal{T}\}$ to user u_i. Then, the task allocation decision $\{x_i^j \mid \forall t_j \in \mathcal{T}\}$ can be derived by user u_i according to decision share $[x_i^j]$ based on Newton's interpolation theorem.

(5) *Task Submission:* If the task allocation decision $x_i^j = 1$, user u_i arrives the location of task t_j. Moreover, the user sends the sensing data of task t_j and the winning bid c_i^j to the platform. Note that the platform only obtains the winning bid and the allocated task of each user so that the locations of users can be protected.

(6) *Reward Users:* The platform pays rewards for each user u_i according to the winning bid c_i^j submitted by the user.

Theorem 3. *The SSTA protocol in the secure auction mechanism can protect location of each user from being revealed to other semi-honest mobile users and the platform, even if $t-1$ users are monitored at the same time by other attackers.*

Proof. In the step 1 and step 2 of our proposed mechanism, each user submits some random numbers which are independent of the user's location. Then, each user receives some bid polynomial shares uploaded by other users in step 3. As the coefficients of polynomials are random, users cannot infer bid information from received bid shares. Thus, the inputs of SSTA will not leak the bid information of each user. Since the multiplication operation and comparison operation have been proved to be secure [8,10], we just focus on proof of the computation security of SSTA protocol itself. Let $\mathcal{I} = \{i_1, i_2, \cdots, i_k\} \subset \{1, \cdots, n\}$ represent any $k = t - 1$ users selected from mobile users $\mathcal{U}$. According to the SSTA protocol, we can obtain the received message of user i_h, denoted by $m_{i_h} = \{[f_i^j]_p^{i_h}, [z]_p^{i_h}, [x_i^j]_p^{i_h}, [y_i]_p^{i_h}, [s_j]_p^{i_h}, [f_{max}]_p^{i_h}\}$. Thus, the view of user i_h is $VIEW_{i_h} = (\{n, m, c_{i_h}^j, \alpha_i G_j, B_j\}, r, m_{i_h})$. Then, the view of user set $\mathcal{I}$ can be denoted as $VIEW_{\mathcal{I}} = \{\mathcal{I}, VIEW_{i_1}, \cdots, VIEW_{i_k}\}$. In $VIEW_{\mathcal{I}}$, the number of shares of each secret is no larger than the degree t, so that information of these secrets cannot revealed by these shares according to the secret sharing scheme. Moreover, the platform obtains only some flags 0 or 1 independent of locations of users to determine whether the protocol can be terminated in advance. Thus, Eq. (6) holds and the whole SSTA protocol is secure.

Theorem 4. *The SSTA protocol can also produce $(1 + \gamma)$-approximation solution, where $\gamma = max\{\frac{B_j}{c_i^j} \mid t_j \in \mathcal{T}, u_i \in \mathcal{U}\}$.*

Proof. Originally, the SSTA protocol applies secret sharing scheme based on the GBTA algorithm to protect sensitive information of users. By analysis of GBTA and SSTA, we can find that both of them select a bid which can most improve profit of the platform as the winning bid in each iteration. Thus, SSTA protocol can obtain the same task allocation decisions as GBTA, and then the Theorem 4 is proved.

5   Evaluation

In this section, we first introduce compared algorithms and simulation settings, and then the SSTA protocol is evaluated in two perspectives, i,e., task allocation performance measured by total profit of the platform and privacy protection level evaluated by location privacy leakage rate.

5.1   Algorithms for Comparison

Although many existing researches have focused on task allocation in mobile crowdsensing, the various crowdsensing models and problems in these works are not exactly same as ours. Generally, greedy strategies are often adopted to deal with NP-hard task allocation problems. In order to measure the validity of task allocation results of GBTA algorithm and SSTA protocol, we design two task allocation algorithms in the following based on the basic idea of algorithms proposed by [13, 15] for comparison, which can be applied to our work.

The first comparison method is Minimum Bid First (MBF) task allocation algorithm, in which the platform selects the smallest bid in each iteration for task allocation. Another approach is Maximum Profit per Cost First (MPCF) algorithm, where the bid with the largest platform profit obtained by unit cost is decided as a winning bid in each round of execution, i,e., $max\{\frac{\alpha_i G_j - c_i^j}{c_i^j} \mid$ $u_i \in \mathcal{U}, t_j \in \mathcal{T}\}$. In addition, we compare the task allocation algorithm without privacy protection GBTA and SSTA protocol to analyse the impact of secret-sharing-based privacy protection approach applied in SSTA on the total profit of the platform.

5.2   Simulation Settings

In our simulations, we conduct the experiments on geographic areas which are divided into $50*50$ grids. The basic earning of task G_j is constrained in the range $[20, 100]$. To obtain bids by mobile users, four basic monotonically increasing functions are considered as follows:

$$c_i^j = f_i(d_i^j) = \begin{cases} a_i * d_i^j & \text{if } u_i \text{ selects linear function} \\ a_i * d_i^{j^2} & \text{if } u_i \text{ selects square function} \\ a_i * \sqrt{d_i^j} & \text{if } u_i \text{ selects square root function} \\ a_i * \log\left(1 + d_i^j\right) & \text{if } u_i \text{ selects logarithmic function} \end{cases} \quad (15)$$

where $a_i \in (0, 20]$.

Table 1. Parameter Settings

Parameter name	Values
Number of users n	$100, 200, \mathbf{300}, 400, 500$
Number of tasks m	$50, \mathbf{100}, 150, 200, 250$
Range of task budget B	$[50, 60], [50, 70], \mathbf{[50, 80]}, [50, 90], [50, 100]$
Mean of user credit α	$0.5, 0.6, \mathbf{0.7}, 0.8, 0.9$

Moreover, we consider four variable parameters including the number of users n, the number of tasks m, the range of task budget B and the mean of user credit

α. The values of these parameters are shown in Table 1, in which default values of the parameters are highlighted in bold. When we change one of the variable parameters, the other parameters will remain as the default values.

5.3   Evaluation on Task Allocation Performance

To evaluate the influence of the number of users and the number of tasks on task allocation performance, we compare the total profit of the platform obtained by MBF, MPCF, GBTA and SSTA. The results are depicted as Fig. 4 and Fig. 5.

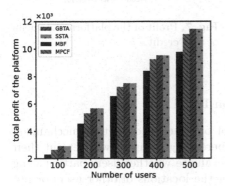

Fig. 4. Total profit of the platform v.s. number of users.

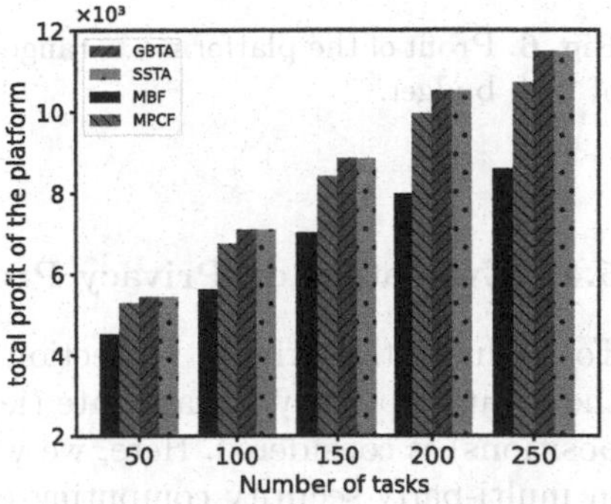

Fig. 5. Total profit of the platform v.s. number of tasks.

On the one hand, we can find that our approach GBTA and SSTA can achieve more profit than MBF and MPCF when the number of users participating sensing tasks increases from 100 to 500 or the number of tasks increases from 50 to 250. This is because MBF only takes the cost of the platform into consideration but ignores the benefits obtained by the platform. Moreover, only if a winning bid is less than 1, the profit obtained by MPCF will be greater than that of GBTA and SSTA. On the other hand, we can observe that the profit of the platform increases significantly as the number of users and tasks increases. Additionally, the results obtained by GBTA are consistent with those obtained by SSTA due to the same basic idea which is discussed in Theorem 4.

In addition, we also report experimental results of profit of the platform with different range of task budget and various mean of user credit in Fig. 6 and Fig. 7, respectively. With the changes of the two parameters B and α, we can find that the results of SSTA and GBTA are superior to the comparison methods MBF and MPCF. Moreover, we can observe that the profit of the platform obtained by our approach improves in either situation. In particular, when the range of task budget extends, the profit obtained by MPCF, GBTA, SSTA slightly but steadily increases. This is because the task allocation decisions change only when the budget of a task is insufficient.

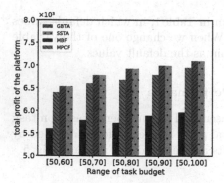
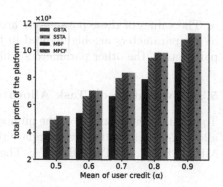

Fig. 6. Profit of the platform v.s. range of task budget.

Fig. 7. Profit of the platform v.s. mean of user credit.

5.4   Evaluation on Privacy Protection Level

To evaluate the privacy protection level of our proposed auction mechanism, the location privacy leakage rate (i,e., the percentage of users who let out their positions) is considered. Here, we will not evaluate whether users participating in multi-party security computing can infer the locations of other users or not during the execution of SSTA since the security has been proved in Theorem 3. Specifically, when the privacy protection method is not adopted, the platform infers location of each user based on the original bids for all tasks of the user according to attack model mentioned in Sect. 3.3. Moreover, the platform can only obtain the results of the auction including the winning bid and an assigned task of a user in the case of applying our mechanism so that the platform can only infer the location of a user by blindly assuming that the location of the assigned task is the user's location.

As shown as Fig. 8, we can observe that the privacy leakage rate with our approach remains around 0.02 while the locations of 98% of users are exposed to the platform without any protection method as the number of users increases. The essence of stability is that a constant number of bids submitted by a user does not allow the platform to extract more location information during the auction without protection. Naturally, the increase of users may lead to an increase in the number of users consistent with the location of the assigned task. However, the privacy leakage rate keeps stable by adopting our effective mechanism in the crowdsensing system.

In Fig. 9, although there are only 50 tasks in the region of crowdsensing system, the location privacy of users is revealed with probability 0.963. Moreover, the privacy leakage rate is closer to 1 which means almost all locations of users can be inferred by the platform as the number of tasks increases. This is because the platform may deduce the location of a user according to more bid information, in which the number of bids is consistent with the number of tasks. We also report the privacy leakage rate for our auction mechanism with protection

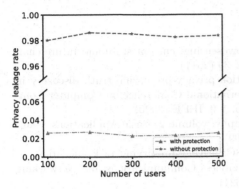

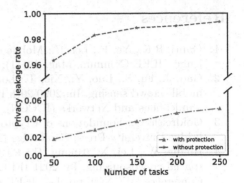

Fig. 8. Profit of the platform v.s. number of users.

Fig. 9. Profit of the platform v.s. number of tasks.

in the figure, and we can find that the probability of location privacy disclosure increases slowly and monotonously as the number of tasks increases. The reason is that an increase in the number of tasks makes it more likely that users and tasks are in the same location. However, when there are 250 tasks, the privacy leakage rate descends about 95% by adopting the proposed auction.

6 Conclusion

In this paper, we consider the problem of task allocation with location privacy protection in an auction-based crowdsensing system without any trusted third party. We first formalize the problem as a NP-hard problem and propose GBTA algorithm with $(1 + \gamma)$-approximation solution for task allocation without the security constraint. However, the bid information of a user is positively and strongly correlated with the distance from the user to tasks, which may lead to the location leakage of the user in the crowdsensing based on the attack model. Thus, we next design a secure auction mechanism by applying SSTA protocol to assign tasks privately which can achieve the same results as GBTA. It is proved that the security of the auction mechanism is guaranteed. Finally, the simulation results show that our approach has excellent performance in task allocation and it can protect location privacy of users effectively.

Acknowledgements. This work is supported by Grant No. 20CG47 from Shanghai Chen Guang Program and Grant No. 22ZR1423700 from Shanghai Committee of Science and Technology. This work is also supported by the Shanghai Foundation for Development of Science and Technology, China (No. 21142202400). We also appreciate the High Performance Computing Center of Shanghai University and Shanghai Engineering Research Center of Intelligent Computing System for providing the computing resources.

References

1. Ganti, R.K., Ye, F., Lei, H.: Mobile crowdsensing: current state and future challenges. IEEE Commun. Mag. **49**(11), 32–39 (2011)
2. Gao, J., Fu, S., Luo, Y., Xie, T.: Location privacy-preserving truth discovery in mobile crowd sensing. In: 2020 29th International Conference on Computer Communications and Networks (ICCCN), pp. 1–9. IEEE (2020)
3. Goldreich, O.: Foundations of Cryptography: volume 2, Basic Applications. Cambridge University Press, Cambridge (2009)
4. Huang, W., Lei, X., Huang, H.: PTA-SC: privacy-preserving task allocation for spatial crowdsourcing. In: 2021 IEEE Wireless Communications and Networking Conference (WCNC), pp. 1–7. IEEE (2021)
5. Li, L., Zhang, X., Hou, R., Yue, H., Li, H., Pan, M.: Participant recruitment for coverage-aware mobile crowdsensing with location differential privacy. In: 2019 IEEE Global Communications Conference (GLOBECOM), pp. 1–6. IEEE (2019)
6. Li, M., Li, Y., Fang, L.: ELPPS: an enhanced location privacy preserving scheme in mobile crowd-sensing network based on edge computing. In: 2020 IEEE 19th International Conference on Trust, Security and Privacy in Computing and Communications (TrustCom), pp. 475–482. IEEE (2020)
7. Liu, T., Zhu, Y., Wen, T., Yu, J.: Location privacy-preserving method for auction-based incentive mechanisms in mobile crowd sensing. Comput. J. **61**(6), 937–948 (2018)
8. Lory, P.: Secure distributed multiplication of two polynomially shared values: enhancing the efficiency of the protocol. In: 2009 Third International Conference on Emerging Security Information, Systems and Technologies, pp. 286–291. IEEE (2009)
9. Mun, M., et al.: Peir, the personal environmental impact report, as a platform for participatory sensing systems research. In: Proceedings of the 7th International Conference on Mobile Systems, Applications, and Services, pp. 55–68 (2009)
10. Nishide, T., Ohta, K.: Multiparty computation for interval, equality, and comparison without bit-decomposition protocol. In: Okamoto, T., Wang, X. (eds.) PKC 2007. LNCS, vol. 4450, pp. 343–360. Springer, Heidelberg (2007). https://doi.org/10.1007/978-3-540-71677-8_23
11. Pryss, R., Reichert, M., Herrmann, J., Langguth, B., Schlee, W.: Mobile crowd sensing in clinical and psychological trials-a case study. In: 2015 IEEE 28th International Symposium on Computer-Based Medical Systems, pp. 23–24. IEEE (2015)
12. Qian, Y., Ma, Y., Chen, J., Wu, D., Tian, D., Hwang, K.: Optimal location privacy preserving and service quality guaranteed task allocation in vehicle-based crowdsensing networks. IEEE Trans. Intell. Transp. Syst. **22**(7), 4367–4375 (2021)
13. Song, T., et al.: Trichromatic online matching in real-time spatial crowdsourcing. In: 2017 IEEE 33rd International Conference on Data Engineering (ICDE), pp. 1009–1020. IEEE (2017)
14. Thiagarajan, A., et al.: Vtrack: accurate, energy-aware road traffic delay estimation using mobile phones. In: Proceedings of the 7th ACM Conference on Embedded Networked Sensor Systems, pp. 85–98 (2009)
15. To, H., Ghinita, G., Shahabi, C.: A framework for protecting worker location privacy in spatial crowdsourcing. Proc. VLDB Endow. **7**(10), 919–930 (2014)
16. Wan, J., Liu, J., Shao, Z., Vasilakos, A.V., Imran, M., Zhou, K.: Mobile crowd sensing for traffic prediction in internet of vehicles. Sensors **16**(1), 88 (2016)

17. Wang, L., Qin, G., Yang, D., Han, X., Ma, X.: Geographic differential privacy for mobile crowd coverage maximization. In: Thirty-Second AAAI Conference on Artificial Intelligence (2018)
18. Wei, J., Lin, Y., Yao, X., Zhang, J.: Differential privacy-based location protection in spatial crowdsourcing. IEEE Trans. Serv. Comput. **15**(1), 45–58 (2022). https://doi.org/10.1109/TSC.2019.2920643
19. Wen, Y., et al.: Quality-driven auction-based incentive mechanism for mobile crowd sensing. IEEE Trans. Veh. Technol. **64**(9), 4203–4214 (2014)
20. Xiao, M., et al.: SRA: secure reverse auction for task assignment in spatial crowdsourcing. IEEE Trans. Knowl. Data Eng. **32**(4), 782–796 (2019)
21. Xiao, M., Wu, J., Zhang, S., Yu, J.: Secret-sharing-based secure user recruitment protocol for mobile crowdsensing. In: IEEE INFOCOM 2017-IEEE Conference on Computer Communications, pp. 1–9. IEEE (2017)
22. Xu, Q., Su, Z., Dai, M., Yu, S.: APIs: privacy-preserving incentive for sensing task allocation in cloud and edge-cooperation mobile internet of things with SDN. IEEE Internet Things J. **7**(7), 5892–5905 (2019)
23. Yang, Q., Chen, Y., Guizani, M., Lee, G.M.: Spatiotemporal location differential privacy for sparse mobile crowdsensing. In: 2021 International Wireless Communications and Mobile Computing (IWCMC), pp. 1734–1741 (2021). https://doi.org/10.1109/IWCMC51323.2021.9498951
24. Zhang, Q., Wen, Y., Tian, X., Gan, X., Wang, X.: Incentivize crowd labeling under budget constraint. In: 2015 IEEE Conference on Computer Communications (INFOCOM), pp. 2812–2820. IEEE (2015)

Deep Learning and Application

A Pareto-Efficient Task-Allocation Framework Based on Deep Reinforcement Learning Algorithm in MEC

Wenwen Liu, Sinong Zhao, Zhaoyang Yu, Gang Wang[✉],
and Xiaoguang Liu[✉]

College of Computer Science, TJ Key Lab of NDST, Nankai University,
Tianjin, China
{liuww,zhaosn,yuzz,wgzwp,liuxg}@nbjl.nankai.edu.cn

Abstract. Mobile-edge computing (MEC) has emerged as a promising paradigm that moves tasks running in the cloud to edge servers. In MEC systems, there are various individual requirements, such as less user-perceived time and lower energy consumption. In this case, substantial efforts have been paid to task allocation, aiming at enabling lower latency and higher resource utilization. However existing studies on multiple-objectives task allocation algorithms rarely consider the Pareto efficient problem, where no objective could be further improved without vitiating the other objectives optimization. In this paper, we propose a Pareto-efficient task-allocation framework based on a deep reinforcement learning algorithm. We give the formal formulations for objectives and construct a multi-objectives' optimization model for task allocation. Then a Pareto efficient algorithm is proposed to solve the problem of conflicting among multi-objectives. By coordinating multi-objectives parameters get from Pareto efficient algorithm, the deep reinforcement learning model takes a Pareto-efficient task allocation to improve real-time and resource utilization performance. We evaluate the proposed framework over various real-world tasks and compare it with existing allocating tasks models in edge computing networks. By using the proposed framework, we can get an accuracy that not be lower than 90% under the 0.6 s latency requirement. The simulation results also show that the proposed framework achieves lower latency and higher resource utilization compared to other task allocation methods.

Keywords: Mobile edge computing · Pareto-efficient · Task-allocation framework · Deep reinforcement learning algorithm

This research is supported in part by the National Science Foundation of China under Grant 62141412 and Grant 61872201, in part by the Science and Technology Development Plan of Tianjin under Grant 20JCZDJC00610, in part by the Key Research and Development Program of Guangdong under Grant 2021B0101310002, and in part by the Fundamental Research Funds for the Central Universities.

H. Gao et al. (Eds.): CollaborateCom 2022, LNICST 461, pp. 197–213, 2022.
https://doi.org/10.1007/978-3-031-24386-8_11

1   Introduction

With the development of Internet of Things (IoT) and Artificial Intelligence (AI), the number of terminal tasks has increased violently. This caused the increasing energy consumption and latency. Mobile Edge Computing system (MEC) [2, 13,14] extends the tasks running in the cloud into edge servers to guarantee QoS requirements. It integrates computing resources, storage space and network bandwidth to ensure system lower latency [6,22], higher resource efficiency [30], and better security [23,26,28]. This new kind of computing paradigm encounters some new challenges. For example, it is an urgent issue that how to guarantee the normal operation of tasks under limited resource capacity and response time.

Some research has addressed the above issue and put forward effective task allocation solutions. Zhang et al. [27] designed a Load-Aware Resource Allocation and Task Scheduling (LA-RATS) algorithm to deal with both delay-tolerant and delay-sensitive mobile applications. They first formulated a resource allocation model for delay-sensitive and delay-tolerant requirements, and then proposed a task back filling mechanism that has two merits: (1) by using a backward shifting strategy, it could full use of the idle resource, (2) by avoiding unnecessary queue growth for VMs to save energy consumption and running time. Wang et al. [20] proposed a unified Mobile-Edge Computing and Wireless Power Transfer model (MEC-WPT model) that addressed the latency-limited practical scenario. It improves the MEC performance by jointly optimizing (1) the energy transmit beamforming at the AP, (2) the CPU frequencies, (3) the offloaded bit numbers, and (4) the time allocation among users. Based on the above work, they developed an optimal resource allocation scheme that minimizes the total energy consumption under the constraint that users' individual computation latency. Jiao et al. [21] proposed an online resource optimization algorithm that points at a gap-preserving transformation of the problem. It offers a feasible solution with a designed logarithmic objective for edge cloud resource allocation over time.

However, the current task-allocation algorithms rarely consider the Pareto efficient problem among multiple-objectives. The principal reason is that the conflicts among different objectives, and it's difficult for us to optimize multi-objectives at the same time. In an edge computing system, the CPU utilization rate and task running time are not entirely consistent.

To address the issues aforementioned, in this paper we study Pareto-efficient task allocation and present a **P**areto-efficient task allocation framework for improving resource **U**tilization and **R**eal-timing in **E**dge computing networks, we call it **Pure**. The contributions of this paper are summarized as follows:

- First, we formulate the objectives (response time and CPU energy consumption) and construct a multi-objectives optimization model for task allocation in edge computing networks.
- Second, we propose a Pareto efficient algorithm to solve the problem of conflict among multi-objectives. It uses the scalarization method to transform the multi-objectives problem into a single objective problem and gets QoS optimization.

- Third, by coordinating multi-objectives parameters get from Pareto efficient algorithm, the deep reinforcement learning model takes a Pareto-efficient task allocation to improve real-time and resource utilization performance.
- Finally, we evaluate Pure over various real-world tasks and compare it with three existing popular models in a simulation environment. The simulation results show that Pure's better performance in terms of latency, accuracy and resource utilization.

The rest of the paper is organized as follows. Section 2 provides related work and Sect. 3 describes the detailed design of Pure that includes Pure's architecture overview, quantifying the performance objectives and construction of the multi-objectives optimization model, the description of the Pareto efficient algorithm and the DRL-based Pareto-efficient task allocation model. The evaluations and analysis are displayed in Sect. 4. Section 5 concludes this paper.

2   Related Work

Task allocation is one of the main challenges in MEC, and a variety of research interests are emerging. In this section, we mainly focus on two aspects of multi-objectives task allocation: the content of multiple objectives and how to solve the multi-objectives model.

In the prior work, different optimization objectives and solution methods are considered in task allocation. In [19], the authors provided a multi-objectives task allocation mechanism in a multi-robot system. They mainly considered the tasks' actual energy and completion time objectives. Based on these, they built the multi-robot dynamic task allocation problem and used a genetic algorithm to solve the problem. Although the proposed algorithm is so flexibility that it can be implemented in other domains, its computational complexity is very high, and the tasks allocation could require high computational resources. Dinh et al. [4] proposed an optimization framework of offloading from a single mobile server to multiple edge servers. They built a multi-objectives model to minimize the execution latency and the edge servers' energy consumption objectives. A linea relaxation-based approach and a semidefinite relaxation (SDR)-based approach were proposed and be used to achieve the near optimal performance. The evaluation results demonstrated the framework's performance improvement in terms of energy consumption and execution latency when multiple edge servers and CPU frequency are considered. However, this paper was not considered about the Pareto-efficient of multi-objectives model. In [17], Ziwen Sun et al. proposed an Attack Localization Task Allocation (ALTA) algorithm in edge sensor networks. They mainly focused on the total task execution time, total energy consumption and load balance objectives. In the algorithm, the multi-objectives binary particle swarm optimization method is used to determine the nodes joining to locate attacks in order to prolong the lifetime of networks during locating attacks' position. Same as before, this paper was not considered about the Pareto-efficient of multi-objectives model.

In particular, some work paid more attention to resource scheduling in edge task allocation. In [16], Yan Sun et al. proposed a two-level resource scheduling model to achieve a resource scheduling scheme. The scheme constructs multi-objectives problems that optimizing the service latency and the overall stability of task execution. In order to solve multi-objectives optimization problems, they proposed a novel resource scheduling scheme using an improved Non-dominated Sorting Genetic Algorithm II (NSGA-II). Although the scheme could reduce the service latency and improve the stability, it did not consider how to reduce the cost of resource. In [12], Liqing Liu et al. proposed a multi-objectives optimization problem that minimizes the energy consumption, execution delay, and payment cost. They used the scalarization method to transform the multi-objectives optimization problem into a single-objective optimization problem. And Interior Point Method (IPM) was applied to solve the a single-objective optimization problem. The simulation results showed that the proposed model could reduce the accumulated error and improve the calculation accuracy effectively. But it also could not consider the Pareto-efficient problem of multi-objectives model. Chu-ge Wu et al. proposed a fuzzy logical offloading strategy based on multi-objectives resource allocation in edge computing [12]. The optimization objectives is both agreement index and robustness. A multi-objective Estimation of Distribution Algorithm (EDA) was designed to solve and optimize the fuzzy offloading strategy. Similarly, it was also not consider the Pareto-efficient problem of multi-objective model.

To sum up, it can be inferred that the energy consumption and latency are important factors that need to be optimized in edge scenarios. Most of the above references have optimized these two factors. But these previous works were rarely considered the Pareto-efficient problem of multi-objectives model. However the Pareto-efficient problem can be further improve the efficiency between delay and resource utilization. In this paper, we present the quantitative formulas of response time and CPU energy consumption, and construct a multi-objectives optimization model for task allocation. Further, we achieve the parameters for transforming the multi-objectives problem into a single-objective problem by Pareto efficient algorithm and get the efficient tasks' collocation by the DRL algorithm. The details are as follows.

3   The Pure Framework

3.1   The Architecture Overview

Generally, a MEC system involves three tiers: 1) the terminal device tier contains end users, mobile devices and sensors, 2) the edge server tier contains multiple interconnected edge servers, such as cloudlets, and 3) the cloud tier acts as a monitor of the whole system. Here we mainly pay attention to the edge server tier. Pure aims to take task allocation to improve edge server CPU utilization and reduce the task execution time. There are three steps of Pure:

– **Quantifying the performance objectives and constructing the multi-objectives optimization model.** We quantify the performance objectives that affects QoS requirement, including the response time and the energy consumption of CPU of each task. Based on this, we construct a multi-objectives optimization model for task allocation.

- **The Pareto efficient algorithm.** This step we use scalarization technique to achieve the parameters for transforming the multi-objectives problem into a single-objective problem. This also makes Pareto-efficiency be guaranteed, where no objective can be further optimized without weakening other objectives.
- **The deep reinforcement learning-based Pareto-efficient task allocation model.** Based on the single-objective model gets from the Pareto efficient algorithm, in this step we introduce how to adapt deep reinforcement learning technology completing the Pareto-efficient task allocation model.

We will detail each step in the following subsections.

3.2 Quantifying the Performance Objectives and Constructing the Multi-objectives Optimization Model

Interdependent Tasks Model. This part, we mainly introduce the interdependent tasks model.

Symbols representation of corresponding variables are explained in Table 1. Given a task set $N = \{1, 2, ..., n\}$, an edge server set $M = \{1, 2, ..., m\}$. For an edge server $j(1 \leq j \leq m)$, its dominant frequency is f_j. For an task $i(1 \leq i \leq n)$, the amount of data to be input during execution is d_i^U, the total number of CPU clock cycles required during execution is c_i, the average upload rate from task i to edge server j is v_{ij}^U, the average download rate is v_{ij}^D. And there is an allocation indication variable set $L = l_{i,j}(1 \leq i \leq n, 1 \leq j \leq m)$, i.e.,

$$l_{i,j} = \begin{cases} 1, & \text{if task } i \text{ is allocated to edge server } j, \\ 0, & \text{otherwise.} \end{cases}$$

The Execution Time Model. In this part, we mainly focus on the execution time. We can get the execution time of task i from following equation:

$$t_i = \sum_{j=1}^{m} l_{ij} * (c_i/f_i). \tag{1}$$

And the whole application' (including n tasks) execution time can be calculated as following equation:

$$T = \sum_{i=1}^{n} (\sum_{j=1}^{m} l_{ij} * (c_i/f_i)). \tag{2}$$

The Computational Energy Consumption Model. Considering that CPU is the most energy consuming factor in edge servers, we take the CPU utilization

Table 1. Table of notations and descriptions.

Notation	Description
N	The set of the tasks
M	The set of the edge servers
f_j	The dominant frequency of edge server j
d_i^U	The amount of data to be input during execution task i
c_i	The total number of CPU clock cycles required during execution task i
v_{ij}^U	The average upload rate from task i to edge server j
v_{ij}^D	The average download rate from task i to edge server j
L	The allocation indication variable set
$l_{i,j}$	The allocation indication variable when task i is allocated into edge server j ($1 \leq i \leq n, 1 \leq j \leq m$)

as the computational energy consumption model in system. The dynamic power calculation model of CPU in edge server j is given in [3,25], that is

$$P_j(s) = \sigma + \mu s^\alpha, \tag{3}$$

where σ is the static power, μ and α are constants that relate to the specific hardware device, and $\alpha \geq 1$, s is the running speed of edge server j, which is proportional to the frequency.

Thus the energy consumption of task i running in edge server j is

$$P_i = \sum_{j=1}^{m} l_{ij} * P_j(s). \tag{4}$$

And the whole application' (including n tasks) energy consumption is

$$P = \sum_{i=1}^{n} (\sum_{j=1}^{m} l_{ij} * P_j(s)). \tag{5}$$

Multi-objectives Optimization Model. To sum up, this paper constructs the following multi-objectives function,

$$\min \Gamma(T, P) \tag{6}$$

$$\Gamma(T, P) = \gamma T + (1 - \gamma)P \tag{7}$$

$$\text{s.t.} \quad \gamma \in [0, 1], \tag{8}$$

$$T \leq \epsilon, \tag{9}$$

$$P_i \in [P_{min}, P_{max}], \tag{10}$$

$$\sum_{j \in m} l_{ij} = 1. \tag{11}$$

where ϵ denotes the execution time threshold. P_{min}, P_{max} represent the minimum and maximum energy consumption that the current edge server can load.

Objective functions (6) and (7) represent to minimize the application's execution time and computational energy consumption. We use a customized weighted product method [18] to approximate Pareto solutions, with multi-objectives fusion and optimization goal. Constraint (8) limits the range of γ, and γ is the balance factor of T and P. Constraint (9) guarantees the whole application's execution time is not to exceed the time threshold ϵ. Constraint (10) keeps the energy consumption of task i cannot exceed the upper and lower limits of the edge server's capacity. Constraint (11) indicates that each task is allocated and can only be allocated to a unique edge server.

In the above multi-objectives optimization model, the goal of task allocation is to map n tasks to m edge servers, so as to minimize the energy consumption on the premise of reducing the task execution time as much as possible. In this way, given a set of tasks and edge servers, under the execution time and server energy consumption thresholds, the multi-objectives optimization problem is transformed into an optimal task allocation problem to minimize execution time and energy consumption. Therefore, how to get a solution that optimizes for two objectives in the sense that no objective can be further improved without vitiating the other objectives optimization is introduced as the following subsection.

3.3   The Pareto Efficient Algorithm

Currently, the existing solutions for Pareto optimization mainly includes two categories: the heuristic search method and scalarization method [11]. In order to obtain the Pareto efficient solution of the multi-objectives model in Subsect. 3.2, we use scalarization method to transform multi-objectives problem into single objective problem, and then solve the value of γ.

There we assume that there are δ optimization objectives in the multi-objectives optimization model. $\Gamma(\theta)$ represents the model to optimize all objectives (corresponding the objective function (6)). Suppose δ objectives have δ differentiable loss functions $l_i(i \in (1, 2, ..., \delta))$ correspondingly, then the loss function $L(\theta)$ of δ objectives is:

$$L(\theta) = \sum_{i=1}^{\delta} \gamma_i l_i. \tag{12}$$

Based on above, we optimize δ objectives that is equal to minimizing $L(\theta)$. We use scalar technology to combine multiple objectives into one objective, and then solve it, get the value of γ. The problem is transformed into solving the minimization loss function $L(\theta)$ process:

$$\min \quad || \sum_{i=1}^{\delta} \gamma_i \nabla_\theta l_i ||_2^2 \tag{13}$$

$$\text{s.t.} \quad \sum_{i=1}^{\delta} \gamma_i = 1, \gamma_i \geq c_i, \forall i \in 1, 2, ..., \delta. \tag{14}$$

This is a non-negative least squares problem, paper [11] gave the whole solution to this problem. Due to page limited, we omit the details of the solution process. From the result of the solution, we get the generated Pareto Frontier set, the solution with minimum requirement to get the γ value. Finally, we get the single objective model depending on the choice of fairness. Solving it $\gamma = 0.73$. Unless explicitly stated we use $\gamma = 0.73$ in our experiments. Next subsection will describe the DRL-based Pareto-efficient task allocation model.

3.4   The DRL-Based Pareto-Efficient Task Allocation Model

Deep Reinforcement Learning (DRL) [9,10] is one of the machine learning techniques that combines the perception ability of deep learning with the decision-making ability of reinforcement learning. It drives agent(s) learning to maximize reward while interacting with an uncertain and varying environment in deep learning networks. We choose it to take tasks allocation for three reasons. Firstly, DRL is a Markov decision process, in which future strategies are only related to the present state, not past state. Secondly, the well-trained DRL model is running fast, while the edge task allocation also requires real-time characteristic. Thirdly, the DRL has the advantages of scalability and versatility. Our well-trained DRL model can adapt to current scenario through corresponding training dataset, and we can cope with the change of various scenarios by changing corresponding training dataset.

In order to deal with the task allocation in the case of edge servers, we apply Deep Q-Learning Network (DQN) [5].

A Markov Decision Progress (MDP) of our problem is defined as a five-tuple $< S, A, P(s, a), R(s, a), s_0 >$, S is a finite set of states appeared in the environment, A is a finite set of actions, $P(s, a)$ is a next state transition probability matrix gets from action a in the state s, $R(s, a)$ is the reward function that indicates how well the agent is doing after taking the action a in the state s, and s_0 is the initial state in the environment.

Next, we describe the adaptive DRL task allocation approach including state space, action space, reward function, offline training and online allocation.

State Space: Given the state set $S : \{s_0, s_1, ..., s_t, ..., s_\omega\}$, s_0 is the initial state, ω denotes the states number. For the current task i allocation, we want to deal with how to minimize the energy consumption while ensuring less execution time according to the definition of function (6–7), constraints (8–11)). We adopt the initial state s_0 is the state that all servers is unoccupied and no tasks has been assigned, and $s_t = L_t$, L_t is an $n * m$ matrix representing n tasks' allocation scheme in m edge servers at state t. If task $i(i \in n)$ is allocated to edge server $j(j \in m)$, $l_{i,j}$ is 1, otherwise it is 0. So L is a (0,1) allocation matrix that makes up of $l_{i,j}$.

Action Space: At each state, assuming that n tasks come to our system to be allocated, there are m edge processors. Hence, each task has m optional processing positions to be allocated, the action space size is n^m. This leads to unbearable amount of computation and training time on edge processors. In our model, for each task i to be allocated, we keep the agent to take only one action (0 or 1, 0 denotes task i is not allocated into the current edge server, 1 denotes i is allocated into the current edge server). Therefore the task i action space is $\{a_1, a_2, ..., a_m\}$, and n tasks action space size is $n * m$.

Reward Function: The reward function $R(s, a)$ indicates how well the agent is doing after taking the action a in the states s, it helps the learner learn the feedback value of action and impacts the network learning quality highly.

Our goal is to get tasks allocation through solving the multi-objectives optimization model in Subsect. 3.3. Base on the execution time and energy consumption optimization objectives, we define a reward function about them. We denote T_i and P_i as the sum of execution time and energy consumption of entire tasks from state $i-1$ to state i. Then we normalize them to get the reward value in state i which has a regular form for DRL algorithms.

$$r_i = \gamma * \frac{T_{i-1} - T_i}{T_0} + (1 - \gamma) * \frac{P_{i-1} - P_i}{P_0}. \tag{15}$$

In Eq. (15), we first get the execution time T_0 and energy consumption P_0 in initial state s_0, and take them as baseline. To have a comparison with the last state s_{i-1}, we do the corresponding values in state s_{i-1} minus the values in state s_i, then divide the result by s_0's corresponding value. This reward function returns the reward value of the state i. Obviously, a higher value of r_i stands for the greater reward, the more execution time and energy consumption the current state save compared to the prior state s_i, and the more effective the current action is.

Offline Training. Based on the above, the well-trained model could be generated offline. Algorithm 1 illustrates the training process. In Algorithm 1, we set x epochs(that makes the training process converge enough), and each epoch of training has y steps. At the beginning of the algorithm, we require the tasks queue Q_{task}, the execution time constraint ϵ and the limit of energy consumption $[P_{min}, P_{max}]$ as the input factors. Then the s_0 and empty task allocation matrix L are initialized. We run the tasks in FIFO order from Q_{task}, and periodically sample the edge servers' resource conditions. Then allocate the task according to the actions and compute the rewards after the actions are performed. At last update the parameters of the neural network. Repeat the step and epoch until convergence or getting the maximum epoch threshold. The DRL model is well-trained.

Algorithm 1. DRL Training

Require:
   Build the DRL neural network architecture A;
   Put tasks into priority queue Q_{task} according to FIFO;
   $[P_{min}, P_{max}] \leftarrow$ the limit of energy consumption;
   $\epsilon \leftarrow$ the execution time constraint;
Ensure: The well-trained DRL model.
 1: Initialization:
   Replay memory B to capacity C_B;
   $s_0 \leftarrow$ initial state;
   $L \leftarrow$ the task allocation matrix;
 2: **for** $epoch \leftarrow 1$ to x **do**
 3:    Get the current task from Q_{task};
 4:    Update the current state s;
 5:    Update the task allocation matrix L;
 6:    **for** $step \leftarrow 1$ to y **do**
 7:       **if** $e < \epsilon$ **then**
 8:          Select the action a by running A;
 9:          Get the next state s_{step+1} and compute the next edge reward r;
10:          Store transition(s, a, r, s_{step+1}) in B;
11:          Update the network by sampling transitions;
12:          $s = s_{step+1}$.
13:       **end if**
14:    **end for**
15: **end for**

After all the epochs are performed or the model gets convergence, the reinforcement learning neural network is adjusted to the best state. And the models in different epochs are saved. We can obtain a well-trained model which has been loaded and use it inference without retraining. The algorithm time complexity is $\mathcal{O}(x * y)$.

To avoid the problem of hard convergence in training, we get experience replay method to alleviate correlation in the sample sequence (the detailed operation is not described here, refer to [24]).

Online Allocation. After the training process, we obtain a well-trained model, with the network parameters corresponding to each action. However, what we need is the current task's optimal allocation of the inference system. When a new task starts coming into task queuing by FIFO, the trained model periodically observes the system states and takes corresponding actions online. Repeat the process until all the epochs are performed or the model gets convergence, then return the final task allocation matrix L.

4   Evaluations

In this section, we evaluate the performance of Pure with simulation experiments in edge computing scenarios.

4.1 Experiments Setup

We use the cloudlet-discovery project [15] to establish our edge computing simulation environment, and 2-tier architecture was simulated, which includes edge tier and cloud tier. VMware 12 tool is used to install multiple virtual machines to mimic edge servers. We simulate three edge servers in edge tier and one cloud server in cloud tier, their configuration is listed in Table 2, and they are all inter-connected via WiFi. The Network Time Protocol (NTP) tool is applied to synchronize time among edge servers and cloud server. The *perf* tool is used to monitor the hardware performance in Linux. The bandwidth is set to 8Mbps according to Internet connection speeds in different countries in [1].

In order to catch the CPU features, we use tested tasks are divided from autonomous driving applications. We choose Image classification, Real-time positioning, Feature extraction and Object detection application domains under different models and datasets to enrich the number of tasks, such as image classification applications under Resnet-50, Yolo, MobileNet-v3 (etc.) models used Imagenet, Cifar-100, and KITTI [7] (etc.) datasets. And eventually we get 216 tasks in different types.

Baselines. We employ the following task allocation methods as baselines.

- **The shortest distance task allocation strategy (SD)** [15]: It selects the closest edge server to requesting terminal device. Although the shortest distance method reduces the network transmission distance, it does not consider whether the shortest distance edge server is suitable for task execution or not. Therefore, it may lead to multiple allocations, so as to prolong the delay.
- **The prioritized task scheduling strategy (PS)** [8]: It prioritizes the tasks according to a priority policy. Generally, the task with tighter time limits should have higher priority to be allocated. The latest allowable start time (LAST) of task is defined as priority score. That is the task with earlier LAST should have higher priority, and be allocated to edge server preferentially.
- **Greedy algorithm (GA)** [29]: For each task, GA takes out the maximum resource capacity by greedy algorithm, then places them into the corresponding edge server under the QoS requirements, at last updates allocated servers tasks combination and resource capacity.

Table 2. Hardware configurations

Equipment	CPU frequency	No. core	Memory
Laptop	3.6 GHz	4 cores	8 GB
Edge server A	2.4 GHz	2 cores	4 GB
Edge server B	2.4 GHz	4 cores	8 GB
Edge server C	1.2 GHz	2 cores	1 GB

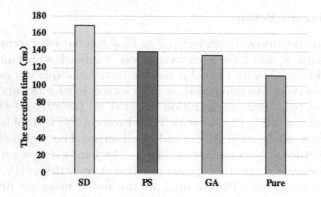

Fig. 1. The comparison of four task allocation strategies' execution time

4.2　The Execution Time Evaluation

Latency is an important metric in edge computing scenarios. Here we mainly focus on the execution time in formula (2). Figure 1 shows the execution time of different task allocation strategies. It can be seen that when performing tasks, Pure achieves the lowest execution time and the SD task allocation strategy's execution time is rather high. The execution time of PS and GA are lower than that SD and higher than Pure.

The reason for this is that SD only considers the distance between mobile device and edge server, it does not consider whether the closest server meets the network congestion and insufficient computing resources, re-allocation is possible. Compared with SD, PS takes consideration of the tasks' running time and the available resources of servers, so it ensures the tasks with stricter time constraints are allocated with more sufficient computing resources, thereby reducing overall execution time. GA gets greedy algorithm to select the current most suitable edge server under the execution time threshold. Compared with above three baselines, the Pure leverages the Pareto efficient algorithm and well-trained DRL allocation algorithm to take allocation. Online selection edge server time is short. Therefore, Pure obtains the minimum execution time.

4.3　The Reliability in Mobile Scenario Evaluation

To better understand of the reliability in mobile scenario, we explore the accuracy ratio of image recognition tasks, that is, the probability of correct image recognition ratio. Figure 2 plots the accuracy ratio of four strategies under the 0.6s latency requirement while meeting the mobility demand. The reliability is measured by accuracy under three states of the mobile terminals including static, low mobility and high mobility. The speed of mobile terminal at low mobility is 10 miles per hour (MPH) and the speed at high mobility is 35 MPH. The corresponding observations and analysis are as follows.

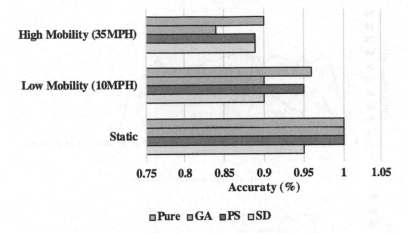

□Pure □GA ■PS □SD

Fig. 2. The comparison of reliability of four task allocation strategies in mobile scenario

First, the accuracy ratios decrease as the speeds of the mobile device increase. The reason is obvious. On the one hand, the higher speed of mobile terminal makes the wireless network unstable. On the other hand, the quality of the network link between different cellular unit may decrease in the mobile environment.

Second, for four strategies, we can see that the reliability of Pure is higher than the others at various moving speed. Compared with SD, the Pure allocates the edge server with sufficient computing resources while ensuring the execution time in the mobile process, however the SD may have the problem of insufficient computing resources and network congestion, therefore the Pure's result is higher than SD. On the other hand, for the PS and GA, no matter how fast the mobile terminal moves, it will select the edge server in the current link range, so their accuracy rates will not be affected largely. And Pure will select the edge server of network transmission quality in the process of moving. Furthermore, at the latency requirement of 0.6 s, the reliability of Pure is able to achieve not be lower than 90%, which maintains the highest reliability at different moving speeds.

4.4 The CPU Cost of Edge Servers

In this subsection, we monitor the CPU utilization of the four strategies in the dynamic time situation. There we run the 10 tasks to record the changes in CPU utilization of SD, PS, GA and Pure strategies, which is shown in Fig. 3. Analysis for each algorithm is as follows.

For SD, from the start time of the task (CPU utilization up to non-zero value, we can get this from abscissa) in Fig. 3 (a), (b), (c), the first task is allocated to edge server A, then to edge server B and finally to edge server C. According to the duration running time of edge servers, there are more tasks performed on edge servers A and B compared with edge server C. In addition, because resource

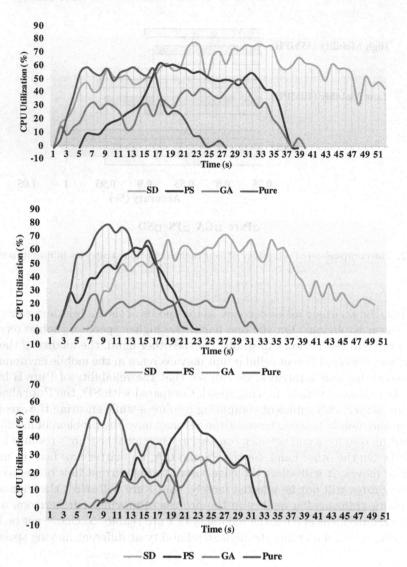

Fig. 3. The CPU utilization of (a) Edge server A (b) Edge server B and (c) Edge server C.

optimization is not considered, the total CPU resource loads (the shadow part covered by the blue curve in three figures) on the servers are very high.

For PS, we get from PS's curve that it first allocates task to edge server B based on the time constraints and available resources on the edge server. Since the resources of edge server B are occupied by the first task, the other tasks are allocated to edge servers A and C successively, which have more available computing resources. Judging from the duration running time, the CPU load is more balanced than SD and GA, and the time to finish all the tasks is also shorter them.

For GA, it uses the greedy algorithm to assign tasks to the server A, server B, and server C in time order. The tasks' execution time of GA is longer than PS and Pure, because GA is not taking much more consideration on execution time, the same is true for imbalance CPU utilization.

Last but not least, for Pure, three servers start executing tasks almost simultaneously and the completion time is about 39 s (we get the longest running time in three servers). In addition, the total CPU load (the shadow area covered by purple curves) is much smaller and more balanced than other baselines. It shows that the proposed algorithm Pure can balance decreasing execution time and CPU utilization well.

5 Conclusions

In this paper, we present Pure framework to ensure that tasks with various demands run efficiently in MEC system. It constructs a multi-objectives optimization model for task allocation, and a Pareto efficient algorithm is proposed to solve the problem of conflict among multi-objectives. Then a deep reinforcement learning model takes a Pareto-efficient task allocation for improving real-time and resource utilization performance. The evaluations were presented to illustrate the effectiveness of the Pure framework and demonstrate the superior performance over the existing traditional task-allocation strategies. Specifically, Pure could get much lower latency, more accurate result and lower CPU cost.

In the future, some other issues could be considered. We will try to take Pure test more types resources, such as I/O, bandwidth and so on.

References

1. List of countries by internet connection speeds (2020). https://en.wikipedia.org/wiki/List_of_countries_by_Internet_connection_speeds, accessed May
2. Ahmed, A., Ahmed, E.: A survey on mobile edge computing. In: International Conference on Intelligent Systems and Control (2016)
3. Albers, S.: Energy-efficient algorithms. Commun. ACM **53**(5), 86–96 (2010)
4. Dinh, T.Q., Tang, J., La, Q.D., Quek, T.Q.S.: Offloading in mobile edge computing: task allocation and computational frequency scaling. IEEE Trans. Commun. **65**(8), 3571–3584 (2017). https://doi.org/10.1109/TCOMM.2017.2699660
5. Fan, J., Wang, Z., Xie, Y., Yang, Z.: A theoretical analysis of deep q-learning. In: Learning for Dynamics and Control, pp. 486–489. PMLR (2020)
6. Feng, M., Krunz, M., Zhang, W.: Joint task partitioning and user association for latency minimization in mobile edge computing networks. IEEE Trans. Veh. Technol. **70**(8), 8108–8121 (2021)
7. Geiger, A., Lenz, P., Stiller, C., Urtasun, R.: Vision meets robotics: the kitti dataset. Int. J. Robot. Res. (IJRR) (2013)
8. Geng, Y., Yang, Y., Cao, G.: Energy-efficient computation offloading for multicore-based mobile devices. In: IEEE INFOCOM 2018-IEEE Conference on Computer Communications, pp. 46–54. IEEE (2018)

9. Lei, C.: Deep reinforcement learning. In: Lei, C. (ed.) Deep Learning and Practice with MindSpore. CIR, pp. 217–243. Springer, Singapore (2021). https://doi.org/10.1007/978-981-16-2233-5_10

10. Li, Y.: Deep reinforcement learning: an overview. arXiv preprint arXiv:1701.07274 (2017)

11. Lin, X., et al.: A pareto-efficient algorithm for multiple objective optimization in e-commerce recommendation. In: Proceedings of the 13th ACM Conference on Recommender Systems, pp. 20–28 (2019)

12. Liu, L., Chang, Z., Guo, X., Mao, S., Ristaniemi, T.: Multiobjective optimization for computation offloading in fog computing. IEEE Internet Things J. **5**(1), 283–294 (2018). https://doi.org/10.1109/JIOT.2017.2780236

13. Mach, P., Becvar, Z.: MEC: a survey on architecture and computation offloading. IEEE Commun. Surv. Tutor. (2017)

14. Mukherjee, M., Lei, S., Di, W.: Survey of fog computing: fundamental, network applications, and research challenges. IEEE Commun. Surv. Tutor. **20**(3), 1826–1857 (2018)

15. Satyanarayanan, M., Bahl, P., Caceres, R., Davies, N.: The case for VM-based cloudlets in mobile computing. IEEE Pervasive Comput. **8**(4), 14–23 (2009)

16. Sun, Y., Lin, F., Xu, H.: Multi-objective optimization of resource scheduling in fog computing using an improved NSGA-II. Wireless Pers. Commun. **102**(2), 1369–1385 (2018)

17. Sun, Z., Liu, Y., Tao, L.: Attack localization task allocation in wireless sensor networks based on multi-objective binary particle swarm optimization. J. Netw. Comput. Appl. **112**, 29–40 (2018). https://doi.org/10.1016/j.jnca.2018.03.023. https://www.sciencedirect.com/science/article/pii/S1084804518301103

18. Tan, M., et al.: MnasNet: platform-aware neural architecture search for mobile. In: Proceedings of the IEEE/CVF Conference on Computer Vision and Pattern Recognition, pp. 2820–2828 (2019)

19. Tolmidis, A.T., Petrou, L.: Multi-objective optimization for dynamic task allocation in a multi-robot system. Eng. Appl. Artif. Intell. **26**(5), 1458–1468 (2013). https://doi.org/10.1016/j.engappai.2013.03.001. https://www.sciencedirect.com/science/article/pii/S0952197613000377

20. Wang, F., Xu, J., Wang, X., Cui, S.: Joint offloading and computing optimization in wireless powered mobile-edge computing systems. IEEE Trans. Wireless Commun. **17**(3), 1784–1797 (2017)

21. Wang, L., Jiao, L., Li, J., Mühlhäuser, M.: Online resource allocation for arbitrary user mobility in distributed edge clouds. In: 2017 IEEE 37th International Conference on Distributed Computing Systems (ICDCS), pp. 1281–1290. IEEE (2017)

22. Wang, S., Zhao, Y., Huang, L., Xu, J., Hsu, C.H.: QoS prediction for service recommendations in mobile edge computing. J. Parallel Distrib. Comput. **127**, 134–144 (2019)

23. Wang, S., Li, J., Wu, G., Chen, H., Sun, S.: Joint optimization of task offloading and resource allocation based on differential privacy in vehicular edge computing. IEEE Trans. Comput. Soc. Syst. **9**(1), 109–119 (2021)

24. Xu, Z., et al.: Experience-driven networking: a deep reinforcement learning based approach. In: IEEE INFOCOM 2018-IEEE Conference on Computer Communications, pp. 1871–1879. IEEE (2018)

25. Yao, F., Demers, A., Shenker, S.: A scheduling model for reduced CPU energy. In: Proceedings of IEEE 36th Annual Foundations of Computer Science, pp. 374–382. IEEE (1995)

26. Yi, S., Qin, Z., Li, Q.: Security and privacy issues of fog computing: a survey. In: Xu, K., Zhu, H. (eds.) WASA 2015. LNCS, vol. 9204, pp. 685–695. Springer, Cham (2015). https://doi.org/10.1007/978-3-319-21837-3_67
27. Zhang, F., et al.: A load-aware resource allocation and task scheduling for the emerging cloudlet system. Futur. Gener. Comput. Syst. **87**, 438–456 (2018)
28. Zhang, P., Wang, Y., Kumar, N., Jiang, C., Shi, G.: A security and privacy-preserving approach based on data disturbance for collaborative edge computing in social IoT systems. IEEE Trans. Comput. Soc. Syst. **9**(1), 97–108 (2021)
29. Zhou, J., Zhao, X., Zhang, X., Zhao, D., Li, H.: Task allocation for multi-agent systems based on distributed many-objective evolutionary algorithm and greedy algorithm. IEEE Access **8**, 19306–19318 (2020)
30. Zhou, S., Jadoon, W.: Jointly optimizing offloading decision and bandwidth allocation with energy constraint in mobile edge computing environment. Computing 1–27 (2021)

An Adaptive Ensembled Neural Network-Based Approach to IoT Device Identification

Jingrun Ma[1,2], Yafei Sang[1,2(✉)], Yongzheng Zhang[3], Xiaolin Xu[4],
Beibei Feng[1,2], and Yuwei Zeng[5]

[1] Institute of Information Engineering, Chinese Academy of Sciences, Beijing, China
{majingrun,sangyafei}@iie.ac.cn
[2] School of Cyber Security, University of Chinese Academy of Sciences,
Beijing, China
[3] China Assets Cybersecurity Technology Co., Ltd., Beijing, China
[4] National Computer Network Emergency Response Technical Team/Coordination
Center of China, Beijing, China
[5] State Key Laboratory of Mathematical Engineering and Advanced Computing,
Zhengzhou, China

Abstract. The Internet of Things (IoT) has developed rapidly in recent years and has been widely used in our daily life. An online report claimed that the connected IoT devices will reach the scale of 14.4 billion globally at the end of 2022. With the rapid and large-scale deployment of such devices, however, some severe security problems and challenges arised as well, especially in the field of IoT device management. Device identification is a prerequisite procedure to mitigate the above issues. Therefore, accurately identifying the deployed IoT devices plays a vital role in network management and cyber security. In this work, we come up with a spatio-temporal-based method that characterizes IoT device behaviors by leveraging the packet sequence features of IoT traffic, which is able to automatically extract the high-level features from raw IoT traffic. The further evaluation indicates that our method is capable of identifying diverse IoT devices with satisfactory accuracy.

Keywords: IoT Identification · Traffic classification

1 Introduction

IoT refers to the tens of billions of low-cost devices that communicate with each other and remote servers on the Internet autonomously, which contains a great diversity of types, and it comprises devices, such as IP cameras, motion sensors, and Internet of Vehicles devices. According to an authoritative report, the number of connected IoT devices will reach 14.4 billion by the end of 2022 [1]. The number of IoT devices connected to the Internet has exploded, making the home smarter by providing convenient services. However, with the popularization of IoT devices, security risks caused by the potential vulnerable IoT devices arise as well.

© ICST Institute for Computer Sciences, Social Informatics and Telecommunications Engineering 2022
Published by Springer Nature Switzerland AG 2022. All Rights Reserved
H. Gao et al. (Eds.): CollaborateCom 2022, LNICST 461, pp. 214–230, 2022.
https://doi.org/10.1007/978-3-031-24386-8_12

It is known that IoT devices are easy to be penetrated and exploited due to the architecture design [12,17]. There are lots of works referred that adversary tends to exploit the vulnerable IoT devices to conduct network attacks [3,11,19, 20]. It is important for the network manager to accurately identify the network-connected IoT devices, especially the vulnerable ones, while it is not a trivial thing. An automatic identification method is able to facilitate the management of connected IoT devices, which would minimise the threat of cyber-attack on enterprise network to some extents.

There is a variety of works on IoT device identification based on network traffic analysis using machine learning techniques. They establish machine learning frameworks by leveraging various network traffic characteristics to identify IoT devices on a network. Sivanathan et al. [21] inspect the payload of packets to extract domain names, port numbers and other numerical features from network flow in a time window, and then builds a two-state classifier to identify the IoT devices. Thangavelu et al. [22] propose a distributed IoT device fingerprinting technique that can identify the presence of common devices, and find new devices, by clustering device fingerprints. Hamad et al. [9] analyze packet sequence from high-level network traffic, and creates IoT device fingerprint by leveraging flow-based features. Pinheiro et al. [18] propose a solution that uses packet length statistics including mean, standard deviation, and the number of bytes to identify IoT devices and events.

These machine learning-based methods conduct the analysis relying on the statistical characteristics of network traces, which need expert knowledge to carry out feature engineering. Moreover, some methods need to inspect the payload of packets to extract features, which may bring privacy risks and will be useless when encrypted traffic introduced.

In this paper, we address the above problem by developing an adaptive ensembled neural network-based method that exploits spatio-temporal features to classify IoT devices. Our method is able to identify IoT devices efficiently as it relys only on the length and TCP window size of a few packets without any statistical computation and inspecting payloads. A traffic flow refers to a packet sequence that consists of multiple packets. We can extract multiple characteristics from each packet. Therefore, we represent a flow as a collection of characteristics sequence, which can characterize each IoT device from spatial dimension and temporal dimension, respectively. In the temporal domain, we use bi-LSTM to learn the timing relationship and extract temporal features between packets for each characteristics sequence. In the spatial domain, we use an adaptive ensemble of multiple bi-LSTM to learn the correlation between different characteristics sequences. In this paper, we use packet length sequence and TCP window size sequence for accurate IoT device identification. In general, other characteristics sequences can be used in the same way which makes the method scalable.

In this paper, we propose a robust approach to identify IoT devices. Our contributions are as follows:

- We analyze packet characteristic sequences such as packet length sequence and TCP window size sequence, and use them to characterize IoT devices.

- We propose an spatio-temporal-based approach that exploits the packet sequence features from spatial dimension and temporal dimension, respectively. It can characterize the behavior of IoT devices without inspecting packet payloads, which can avoid privacy leakage risks.
- We build an adaptive ensemble of neural networks to identify IoT devices, which is scalable.
- Our method reach the accuracy of 99% on multiple datasets.

The rest of this paper is organized as follows: Sect. 2 describes relevant prior work. In Sect. 3 we present the preprocess of IoT traffic data and analysis of packet sequence features. We introduce the model architecture detailedly in Sect. 4. Section 5 presents the experiments and results. Finally, Sect. 6 concludes this paper.

2   Related Work

With the widespread application of IoT devices, there is a lot of work in IoT device identification. Previous methods in this field mainly fall into two categories: fingerprint-based methods and machine learning-based methods.

Fingerprint-Based Methods. The fingerprint-based methods profile IoT devices by exploiting plaintext information in the IoT traffic or features from network protocols. They generate fingerprints for each type of IoT device and identify them in the network by leveraging these fingerprints. Feng et al. [7] proposed a method to identify IoT device types by leveraging plaintext in banner grabbing. They scaned ports in the network and analyzed the response information that includes device vendor name and device product model. However, they assumed that the IoT device information are included in the response packet. Their method would be less effective when the device does not respond or device information are not included in the response packet. Yang et al. [24] gave an observation that different IoT device manufacturers have a diversity of implementation for the same network service. In addition, they extracted features from three network layers and generate fingerprints by using a neural network. Trimananda et al. [23] proposed a solution that can automatically extract packet-level signatures to identify IoT devices. These signatures which can be generated without prior knowledge consisted of sequences of packet lengths and directions.

Machine Learning-Based Methods. There are a lot of methods relying on building machine learning models using statistics of IoT traffic. These methods usually leverage supervised learning to characterize traffic patterns for each IoT device. Sivanathan et al. [21] collected a dataset in a testbed environment, and analyzed the features which can profile the IoT device. They build a two-stage classifier by leveraging both plaintext features and statistical features. Nguyen et al. [16] proposed a unsupervised learning-based method to identify compromised IoT devices by utilizing a self-learning federated learning approach, which can profile IoT devices without labeled data. Ma et al. [13] proposed a solution that leverage CNN to learn spatio-temporal traffic fingerprints to identify the IoT devices, which also can identify the devices that hidden behind NAT. Duan et al. [6] only used the frequency distribution of bidirectional packet length to characterize IoT devices, and classified IoT devices with the k-NN algorithm, which can work extensively and adaptively. Marchal et al. [14] proposed a method that leverages periodic communication traffic to characterize IoT devices. This method can identify previously unseen IoT devices without expert knowledge or labeled data by leveraging an unsupervised learning method. Yin et al. [25] proposed a deep learning-based method to identify IoT devices. They build an automatic end-to-end framework based on CNN and bi-LSTM model in the face of identifying IoT devices.

3   Data Preprocess and Feature Analysis

In this paper, a flow is considered as a detection sample. A flow is a collection of multiple associated packets [5] between two computer addresses using a particular protocol on a particular pair of ports. Packets with the same tuple of information (source IP, destination IP, source port, destination port, protocol) belong to the same flow. The flow is bidirectional which includes packets that client to server and server to client.

3.1   Data Preprocess

We extract packet features from pcap files of IoT traffic and reconstruct flows by leveraging 5-tuple information. Each flow consists of multiple packet feature sequences, which our sequence models will learn representative features from.

Moreover, the number of packets in traffic flows are not always the same, which may conflict with the requirement of our classification model which needs a uniform size of input data. Hence, the flows that we reconstruct before need to be processed into same format. The following unified preprocessing measures including padding and segmentation are applied to make input flows have a uniform size:

- If the number of packets in a flow exceeds a certain threshold that we set, we select the first M packets in a flow to represent it as a whole.
- If the number of packets in a flow is less than the threshold, we pad the characteristics sequence with zeros.

A traffic flow is preprocessed according to the above rules, which allows for reducing the amount of data and unifying the data size.

3.2   Packet Feature Analysis

In this paper, we choose two packet characteristics sequences to identify the IoT device correctly, which is scalable and other feature sequences can be added without major changes. The method exploits packet length sequence and TCP window size sequence derived from traffic flow, which is unnecessary to compute

Table 1. The breakdown of TMC-18

ID	IoT devices	Flow(#)	Connection type
1	Withings Monitor	5,591	Wired
2	Withings Sensor	3,584	Wireless
3	Samsung SmartCam	15,906	Wireless
4	TP-Link Cloud Camera	1,109	Wireless
5	HP Printer	151	Wireless
6	Amazon Echo	20,903	Wireless
7	Triby Speaker	149	Wireless
8	iHome	177	Wireless
9	Insteon Camera	4,073	Wired
10	Belkin Wemo Switch	7,642	Wireless
11	TP-Link Smart Plug	232	Wireless
12	Belkin Wemo Motion Sensor	78,761	Wireless
13	Netatmo Weather Station	2,347	Wireless
14	Netatmo Welcome	2,682	Wireless
15	PIX-STAR	1,139	Wireless

statistical features of flows. The premise is that packet length patterns of different IoT devices are distinct, which can be used to characterize the device [15]. In addition, TCP window size is also a distinction for different IoT traffic. TCP can govern the amount of data sent between client and server by using window size. The window size indicates an ability to receive data that can be buffered during a connection [2]. Different IoT devices have different capabilities of processing data and buffering data, and their corresponding servers are also diverse. We analyze these two packet characteristics in terms of size and sequence change on part data from [21] which is also used in the evaluation. The list of IoT devices are shown in Table 1.

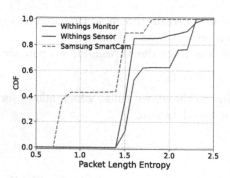
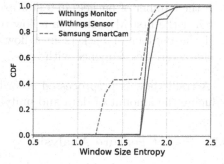

(a) Packet length entropy distribution.   (b) Window size entropy distribution.

Fig. 1. Entropy distribution of three selected devices.

We select three devices including Withings Monitor, Withings Sensor and Samsung SmartCam from Table 1, and analyze their packet characteristics distribution. Among these three devices, Withings Monitor and Withings Sensor are two types of product with different functions from the same vendor. Withings Monitor and Samsung SmartCam are the same types of product which have similar functions from different vendors.

Here, we use entropy to measure the distribution of packet characteristics in a flow. Figure 1 shows the Cumulative Distribution Function (CDF) of packet length entropy and window size entropy. We can see that Withings Monitor and Withings Sensor have more similar packet characteristics distribution compared with Samsung SmartCam. Even though Withings Monitor and Samsung Smart-Cam are the same types of product, they have obvious differences in packet length distribution and window size distribution. For the same vendor's devices, there is an obvious distinction between Withings Monitor and Withings Sensor in the packet length distribution, but the distribution of the window size is not so obvious between these two devices. Next, we analyze these two packet characteristics on all the IoT devices in Table 1.

Packet Length. Different IoT devices carry a diversity of services, so the packet length may express different patterns when they communicate with the server. For example, smart camera devices usually generate flows with lots of packets and large packet lengths to transfer video streams. On the contrary, smart plug devices generate flows that consist of a few amount of packets and small packet lengths. We calculate the mean packet length of each flow for all IoT devices. Figure 2(a) illustrates the boxplot of mean packet length of each IoT device. We can see that the packet length of some devices is not obviously different, such as Withings Monitor, Triby Speaker, Belkin Wemo Switch, Belkin Wemo Motion Sensor, and Netatmo Weather Station. On the contrary, devices like TP-Link Cloud Camera and Netatmo Welcome have a conspicuous difference compared with other devices. It is confusing for those devices with similar mean packet length distribution. So we don't only use the packet length but introduce the packet length sequence which can reflect the change of the packet length over time. Figure 2(b) illustrates the boxplot of entropy of packet length for each IoT device. As shown in Fig. 2(b), entropy of packet length sequence is distinct between those confusing devices.

Window Size. The data processing ability of different IoT devices is different, so they have different patterns in window size. Because of low computing resources, IoT devices usually provide a relatively single service which leads to that they communicate with only a few servers. The window size characterizes the communication patterns between IoT devices and their servers. We also calculate the mean window size of each flow for all IoT devices. Figure 3(a) illustrates the boxplot of mean window size of each IoT device and Fig. 3(b) shows the boxplot of entropy of window size sequence. Most IoT devices have different patterns in window size and entropy of window size. We can see that devices

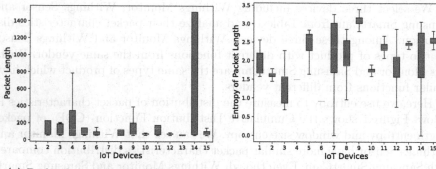

(a) Packet length of each IoT devices.   (b) Entropy of packet length sequence.

Fig. 2. Various packet length patterns of different IoT devices.

with similar mean window size have different entropy of window size such as Belkin Wemo Switch and Belkin Wemo Motion Sensor. And devices with similar entropy of window size have different mean window size such as Withings Sensor and Amazon Echo.

These two characteristic sequences can work together for accurate IoT device identification.

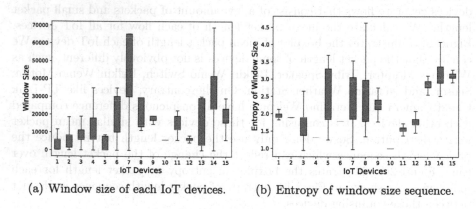

(a) Window size of each IoT devices.   (b) Entropy of window size sequence.

Fig. 3. Various window size patterns of different IoT devices.

4   Model Methodology

In this section, we build a adaptive ensembled neural network model based on deep learning. We introduce the overall structure of the model and the main network layers.

4.1 Overview

Our adaptive ensembled neural network is a hierarchical model as shown in Fig. 4. The packet length sequence and TCP window size sequence are extracted from flows during data preprocessing. Subsequently, the packet characteristics sequence is transformed into embedding vectors. Then the adaptive ensemble of sequence networks is designed to process the embedding feature to extract spatio-temporal features at the flow level. Finally, discrimination results are output through the fully connected network. Experiments show that this combination of multiple packet characteristics sequence can effectively classify IoT devices.

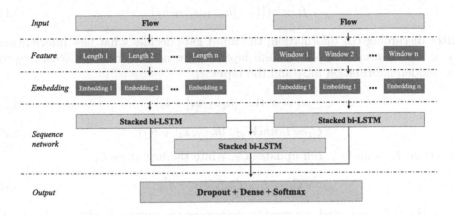

Fig. 4. Architecture of the neural network.

4.2 Embedding Layer

The input of embedding layer consists of a packet characteristic sequence. Inspired by embedding in natural language processing, we consider the sequence as a sentence, and convert the value of the characteristic sequence into a vector as the output of this layer.

Given a packet characteristic sequence with n elements $x = [F_1, F_2, ..., F_n]$ and dimension d of element embedding vectors, each element F_i, $i \in [1, n]$ need to be converted into a d-dimension vector. Finally, we can obtain the embedding matrix $E \in \mathbb{R}^{n \times d}$ for each packet characteristic sequence.

Converting the packet characteristic sequences into embedding vectors can integrate a large amount of valuable information, which can improve the ability of learning representative features and boost the performance of identifying IoT devices.

4.3 Adaptive Ensemble of Sequence Network

Network traffic is the conversation between the client and the server, which means that the packet sequence is naturally temporal. LSTM is a special kind of Recurrent Neural Network (RNN) which can process sequence of inputs. Traditional RNNs have the disadvantages of long-term dependency problem which will result in gradient disappearance or explosion. LSTM uses gate structure to remember or forget information to avoid the long-term dependency problem. An LSTM has three gates to control the cell state including forget gate, input gate and output gate.

Before adding new information, The forget gate decides what information to be discarded from previous sequence. f_t outputs a value between 0 and 1 according to the hidden information h_{t-1} and the input x_t. The current cell keeps more information if f_t is close to 1 otherwise less.

$$f_t = \sigma(W_f \cdot [h_{t-1}, x_t] + b_f) \tag{1}$$

After discarding the information, the input gate decides what new information to be stored in current cell. A tanh layer creates new information according to the hidden information h_{t-1} and the input x_t.

$$i_t = \sigma(W_i \cdot [h_{t-1}, x_t] + b_i) \tag{2}$$

$$\tilde{C}_t = tanh(W_C \cdot [h_{t-1}, x_t] + b_C) \tag{3}$$

Based on f_t, i_t and $\tilde{C}_t$, cell updates C_{t-1} into the new state C_t.

$$C_t = f_t \times C_{t-1} + i_t \times \tilde{C}_t \tag{4}$$

After the cell is updated, we need to determine the output h_t of the cell, which is controlled by the output gate o_t.

$$o_t = \sigma(W_o \cdot [h_{t-1}, x_t] + b_o) \tag{5}$$

$$h_t = o_t \times tanh(C_t) \tag{6}$$

To learn sequential features from both forward and backward directions, we use bidirectional LSTM (bi-LSTM) to incorporate the contextual features of the packet characteristics sequence. To improve the representation of the model, we adopt multi-layer bi-LSTM to learn the low-level and high-level features at the same time.

Many sequential features can be extracted from the traffic flow and we use multiple stacked bi-LSTM to learn different sequential features respectively. We use two stacked bi-LSTM to learn temporal features from packet length sequence and window size sequence. Moreover, another stacked bi-LSTM is used to learn spatial features. It takes the outputs of other stacked bi-LSTM as input, as shown in Fig. 4. This can learn the correlation between different packet characteristics sequence in the spatial dimension.

These stacked bi-LSTM form an adaptive ensemble of sequential neural networks. It learns spatio-temporal features from multiple packet characteristic sequences, which can characterize traffic patterns of different IoT devices. Moreover, it is scalable and other characteristic sequence can be added in easily.

4.4   Dense Layer

The last part of the model includes a dropout layer and a fully-connected layer followed by a softmax function to obtain a prediction vector $\hat{y}_{ij}$. We then use the cross-entropy loss function for calculating the loss L of the result, which can be expressed as:

$$L = -\sum_{i=1}^{n}\sum_{j=1}^{c} y_{ij} \log \hat{y}_{ij} \tag{7}$$

where y_{ij} is the true label vector, $\hat{y}_{ij}$ is the prediction vector.

5   Evaluation

In prior sections, we analyze the traffic of IoT devices and preliminarily introduce the architecture of the model. This section sequentially introduces the experiment-used datasets, the evaluation metrics, and the performance comparison between the prior work and ours.

5.1   Datasets

We conduct experiments on four public datasets to verify the effectiveness of the method. Next, we give a brief description of these datasets. Table 2 shows the breakdown of these datasets.

Sivanathan et al. [21] publish a 20-day IoT traffic dataset, TMC-18, that collected in an experimental environment. To fit our experiment, we discard both the non-IoT device flows and the devices that own only a few flows here. Finally, 15 IoT devices, as shown in Table 1, are left to use in this experiment.

Hamza et al. [10] publish a 44-day IoT traffic dataset, SOSR-19, which includes attack traffic and benign traffic. Its collection environment is similar to TMC-18, and we select the benign traffic to evaluate our method.

Garcia et al. [8] create a labeled dataset with malicious and benign IoT network traffic. We also use benign IoT traffic to complete the evaluation.

Dadkhah et al. [4] generate a dataset for profiling, behavioural analysis of different IoT devices. It also has malicious and benign IoT traffic, and we evaluate on the benign IoT traffic.

Table 2. The breakdown of the datasets

Dataset	Devices (#)	Flow (#)	Public year
TMC-18 [21]	15	144,446	2018
SOSR-19 [10]	15	578,533	2019
IoT-23 [8]	3	559	2020
CIC-IoT [4]	37	199,033	2022

5.2   Metrics

Here, we use precision, recall, F1-score, and accuracy to evaluate the effectiveness of our approach. In our setting, for each IoT device, a correctly identified flow is treated as a true positive (TP); a flow identified as belonging to this device but actually not is treated as a false positive (FP); a flow of this device identified to other devices is treated as a false negative (FN). Based on these three definitions, three metrics are defined for each device as follows.

$$Precision = \frac{TP}{TP + FP} \tag{8}$$

$$Recall = \frac{TP}{TP + FN} \tag{9}$$

$$F1 = \frac{2 * Precision * Recall}{Precision + Recall} \tag{10}$$

We use macro averages of these three metrics and accuracy in evaluation. Accuracy is defined as follows.

$$Accuracy = \frac{\# \ of \ correct \ identification}{\# \ of \ total \ identification} \tag{11}$$

5.3   Experimental Setting

We take the packet feature sequences as the input of the model. The packet number is set to 32. The dimension of the packet feature embedding vector is set to 256. Besides, we set the dimension of hidden states of each bi-LSTM to 256 and take the 2 layer bi-LSTM in each sequence. Moreover, we take dropout with a 0.3 ratio to avoid over-fitting, and use 0.0001 as the learning rate of Adam optimizer. We implement our approach with pytorch and deploy it on a server with 32 CPU cores and 128 GB memory. The server uses a NVIDIA 1080Ti for accelerating computing.

5.4   Experiments and Results

Here, we use four well-known IoT traffic datasets to evaluate the performance of our method in terms of precision, recall, F1, and accuracy. After extracting features from IoT devices traffic to generate training and testing samples, we have randomly split these instances into three groups, one containing 80% of the instances for training, one containing 10% of the instances for validating, and the other containing 10% of the instances for testing. The adaptive ensemble of the sequence network is trained, and then evaluate to distinguish IoT devices. The evaluation includes fine-grained classification, and coarse-grained classification. The former distinguishes each single IoT device, and the latter distinguishes IoT device type. IoT devices with the same vendor and type are regarded as one class in the IoT device type identification. Moreover, we investigate the feature distribution on the IoT devices with the same vendor and type.

Table 3. Experiments on multiple datasets

Method	TMC-18				SOSR-19				IoT-23				CIC-IoT			
	A (%)	P (%)	R (%)	F1 (%)	A (%)	P (%)	R (%)	F1 (%)	A (%)	P (%)	R (%)	F1 (%)	A (%)	P (%)	R (%)	F1 (%)
KNN	74.59	77.03	55.87	57.68	91.25	85.23	68.75	73.13	99.86	99.32	98.43	98.86	40.30	53.46	38.60	36.90
DT	79.97	78.41	62.70	65.40	91.25	86.08	70.38	75.22	99.85	99.18	98.51	98.84	43.23	55.60	41.21	40.70
RF	79.32	79.30	62.61	65.37	91.25	86.48	70.13	75.34	**99.89**	**99.39**	**98.99**	**99.14**	43.56	55.38	41.70	40.55
SVM	50.24	30.35	18.70	16.53	66.38	26.74	14.38	13.65	90.89	90.65	46.69	53.63	13.80	10.54	6.27	4.32
MV	79.30	79.43	62.38	65.40	91.23	86.02	68.96	74.85	99.86	99.14	98.70	98.92	43.05	56.39	41.30	40.70
IoT ETEI	99.54	95.46	92.89	93.39	99.88	88.91	81.85	82.02	98.24	98.99	98.61	98.78	85.79	60.48	54.83	53.13
Our method	**99.97**	**96.73**	**93.47**	**94.61**	**99.99**	**98.12**	**98.68**	**98.18**	98.21	99.05	98.41	98.70	**86.06**	**65.73**	**65.81**	**64.59**

Fine-Grained Identification. Table 3 presents the experiment results on four datasets. Our method reaches the accuracy of 99.7%, 99.99%, and 98.21% on TMC-18, SOSR-19, and IoT-23 datasets, respectively. Precision, recall, and F1-score all exceed 93.47% on TMC-18, SOSR-19 and IoT-23. The evaluation on CIC-IoT dataset reaches an accuracy of 86.06%.

IoT devices in TMC-18 and SOSR-19 datasets are the same devices. We aggregate these two datasets and test our method on the mixed dataset. Figure 5 shows the confusion matrix on mixed dataset, in which rows represent actual labels and columns represent predictions. The diagonal values show the correct classifications. Figure 5 illustrates that our method performs well on each device and only a few samples are not correctly identified. Our method has reached an identifying accuracy of over 99.4% on most IoT devices. The experimental results clearly show that our approach has the ability to conduct accurate IoT device identification.

From Table 3 we can see that accuracy, precision, recall, and F1-score for fine-grained identification on CIC-IoT dataset is 86.06%, 65.73%, 65.81%, and 64.59%, respectively, which is obviously lower than on other datasets.

Coarse-Grained Identification. Our method performs a bit poor on the CIC-IoT dataset. Figure 6 illustrates the confusion matrix on CIC-IoT dataset. IoT Devices with low identification rates such as Gosund ESP series devices, are the same type of product that share the same vendor. And Amazon Echo Dot, and Yutron Plug series devices, are the same. Figure 7 shows the packet length entropy distribution of these three type devices. The entropy distribution is similar in each group. As for Amazon Echo Dot, entropy distribution is almost identical. Thus, IoT devices that are the same type of product from same vendor, use similar communication patterns making it difficult to identify. These products are not upgraded during the iterative process considering the communication protocol or mechanism, which causes the traffic generated during network communication is almost identical.

We regard devices with the same vendor and type as one class of device, to carry out coarse-grained identification. For example, we regard Gosund ESP_1 Socket, Gosund ESP_2 Plug, Gosund ESP_3 Socket, Gosund ESP_4 Plug, Gosund ESP_5 Socket, Gosund ESP_6 Plug, and Gosund ESP_7 Plug as one class, Gosund ESP Plug Series, and we carry out same operations on other IoT

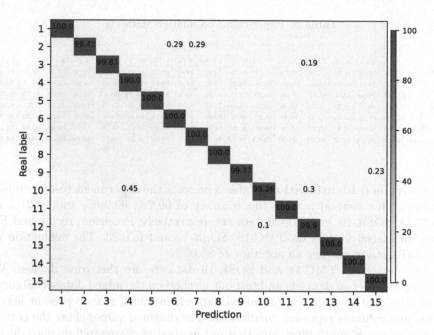

Fig. 5. Confusion matrix on TMC-18 and SOSR-19 dataset.

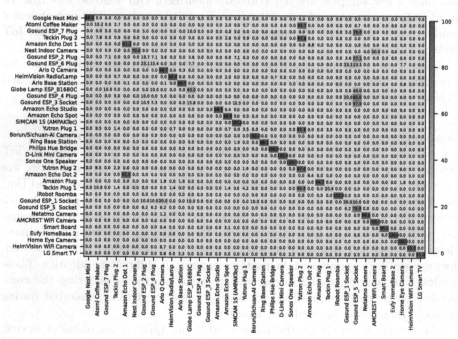

Fig. 6. Confusion matrix on CIC-IoT dataset.

devices which are the same type of product of same vendor. After merging the labels, there are 23 IoT devices left. The accuracy, precision, recall, and F1-score reaches 99.05%, 96.11%, 94.37%, and 94.19%, respectively in coarse-grained identification, which is much higher than before.

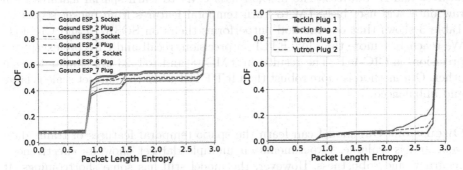

(a) Packet length distribution of Gosund devices.

(b) Packet length distribution of Plug devices.

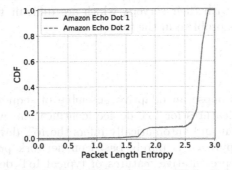

(c) Packet length distribution of Echo Dot devices.

Fig. 7. Packet length entropy distribution of confusing devices in CIC-IoT dataset.

Comparison with Prior Work. Pinheiro et al. [18] propose a solution that also uses packet length statistics to identify IoT devices. The solution uses only the statistical mean, the standard deviation, and the number of bytes transmitted over a one-second window. The solution carries out the identification by using five classification algorithm, including k-Nearest Neighbors (KNN), Decision Tree (DT), Random Forest (RF), Support Vector Machine (SVM) and Majority Voting (MV). Table 3 shows the corresponding comparison results. Our method outperforms the prior work on TMC-18, SOSR-19, and CIC-IoT, while slightly lags behind the RF method on IoT-23. The problem lies in the fact that the scale of the IoT-23 dataset is a bit small, which contains only 3 devices and 559 traffic flows. However, with the increasing of dataset scale, the performance of the RF method has declined gradually. Moreover, SVM reached the worst results in all scenarios.

Yin et al. [25] propose IoT ETEI, a deep learning-based method which leveraging CNN and bi-LSTM model to extract spatio-temporal features. It takes raw bytes of traffic flows as input, and removes irrelevant fields, such as MAC address and IP address. The method uses CNN to learn spatial features from raw data, and uses bi-LSTM to learn temporal features from packet sequence. Table 3 shows that our method outperforms theirs on SOSR-19 and CIC-IoT. We reach 10% more than IoT ETEI on precision, recall and F1-score except for precision on CIC-IoT. The results on TMC-18 and IoT-23 are similar to each other. Our method is more robust than IoT ETEI when the dataset scale is large and unbalanced.

Discussion. Our model can learn the spatio-temporal features of traffic data well, and is scalable. Experiments on multiple dataset show its effectiveness, accuracy, and robustness. However, the model still has some shortcomings. It performs a bit poor in fine-grained identification of IoT devices on the CIC-IoT dataset. IoT devices with same type and vendor follow similar traffic patterns when communicate with their servers, which are difficult to be identified. We need to improve this problem in the future.

6   Conclusion

In this paper, we propose an adaptive ensemble of sequence networks based on spatio-temporal features for IoT device identification, which takes network packet traces as input and automatically infers the IoT device type of the network traces. Our approach is purely based on network packet traces, and it jointly learns the representative features of typical IoT devices from the raw flow sequences. It takes stacked bi-LSTM to learn the representation of the flow sequence. Moreover, it can be easily extended with multi-attribute sequences as the input. It works well with both encrypted and plaintext flows. Our further evaluation demonstrates that our method is able to effectively identify the type of each IoT device from the mixed network traffic with high accuracy.

Acknowledgements. We thank the anonymous reviewers for their insightful comments. This work is supported by The National Key Research and Development Program of China under Grant No. 2019YFB1005201, No. 2019YFB1005203 and No. 2019YFB1005205.

References

1. Number of connected IoT devices growing 18% to 14.4 billion globally. https://iot-analytics.com/number-connected-iot-devices/
2. RFC 793 - transmission control protocol. https://datatracker.ietf.org/doc/html/rfc793

3. Antonakakis, M., et al.: Understanding the mirai botnet. In: 26th USENIX Security Symposium (USENIX Security 2017), pp. 1093–1110 (2017)
4. Dadkhah, S., Mahdikhani, H., Danso, P.K., Zohourian, A., Truong, K.A., Ghorbani, A.A.: Towards the development of a realistic multidimensional IoT profiling dataset. In: 2022 19th Annual International Conference on Privacy, Security & Trust (PST), pp. 1–11. IEEE (2022)
5. Dainotti, A., Pescape, A., Claffy, K.C.: Issues and future directions in traffic classification. IEEE Network 26(1), 35–40 (2012)
6. Duan, C., Gao, H., Song, G., Yang, J., Wang, Z.: ByteIoT: a practical IoT device identification system based on packet length distribution. IEEE Trans. Netw. Service Manag. (2021)
7. Feng, X., Li, Q., Wang, H., Sun, L.: Acquisitional rule-based engine for discovering internet-of-thing devices. In: Proceedings of the 27th USENIX Conference on Security Symposium, pp. 327–341 (2018)
8. Garcia, S., Parmisano, A., Erquiaga, M.J.: IoT-23: a labeled dataset with malicious and benign IoT network traffic. Stratosphere Lab., Praha, Czech Republic, Technical report (2020)
9. Hamad, S.A., Zhang, W.E., Sheng, Q.Z., Nepal, S.: IoT device identification via network-flow based fingerprinting and learning. In: 2019 18th IEEE International Conference on Trust, Security and Privacy in Computing and Communications/13th IEEE International Conference on Big Data Science and Engineering (TrustCom/BigDataSE), pp. 103–111. IEEE (2019)
10. Hamza, A., Gharakheili, H.H., Benson, T.A., Sivaraman, V.: Detecting volumetric attacks on lot devices via SDN-based monitoring of mud activity. In: Proceedings of the 2019 ACM Symposium on SDN Research, pp. 36–48 (2019)
11. Li, J., Li, Z., Tyson, G., Xie, G.: Your privilege gives your privacy away: an analysis of a home security camera service. In: IEEE INFOCOM 2020-IEEE Conference on Computer Communications, pp. 387–396. IEEE (2020)
12. Loi, F., Sivanathan, A., Gharakheili, H.H., Radford, A., Sivaraman, V.: Systematically evaluating security and privacy for consumer IoT devices. In: Proceedings of the 2017 Workshop on Internet of Things Security and Privacy, pp. 1–6 (2017)
13. Ma, X., Qu, J., Li, J., Lui, J.C., Li, Z., Guan, X.: Pinpointing hidden IoT devices via spatial-temporal traffic fingerprinting. In: IEEE INFOCOM 2020-IEEE Conference on Computer Communications, pp. 894–903. IEEE (2020)
14. Marchal, S., Miettinen, M., Nguyen, T.D., Sadeghi, A.R., Asokan, N.: AuDI: toward autonomous IoT device-type identification using periodic communication. IEEE J. Sel. Areas Commun. 37(6), 1402–1412 (2019)
15. Miettinen, M., Marchal, S., Hafeez, I., Asokan, N., Sadeghi, A.R., Tarkoma, S.: IoT sentinel: automated device-type identification for security enforcement in IoT. In: 2017 IEEE 37th International Conference on Distributed Computing Systems (ICDCS), pp. 2177–2184. IEEE (2017)
16. Nguyen, T.D., Marchal, S., Miettinen, M., Fereidooni, H., Asokan, N., Sadeghi, A.R.: Dïot: a federated self-learning anomaly detection system for IoT. In: 2019 IEEE 39th International Conference on Distributed Computing Systems (ICDCS), pp. 756–767. IEEE (2019)
17. Notra, S., Siddiqi, M., Gharakheili, H.H., Sivaraman, V., Boreli, R.: An experimental study of security and privacy risks with emerging household appliances. In: 2014 IEEE Conference on Communications and Network Security, pp. 79–84. IEEE (2014)

18. Pinheiro, A.J., Bezerra, J.D.M., Burgardt, C.A., Campelo, D.R.: Identifying IoT devices and events based on packet length from encrypted traffic. Comput. Commun. **144**, 8–17 (2019)
19. Ren, J., Dubois, D.J., Choffnes, D., Mandalari, A.M., Kolcun, R., Haddadi, H.: Information exposure from consumer IoT devices: a multidimensional, network-informed measurement approach. In: Proceedings of the Internet Measurement Conference, pp. 267–279 (2019)
20. Sadeghi, A.R., Wachsmann, C., Waidner, M.: Security and privacy challenges in industrial internet of things. In: 2015 52nd ACM/EDAC/IEEE Design Automation Conference (DAC), pp. 1–6. IEEE (2015)
21. Sivanathan, A., et al.: Classifying IoT devices in smart environments using network traffic characteristics. IEEE Trans. Mob. Comput. **18**(8), 1745–1759 (2018)
22. Thangavelu, V., Divakaran, D.M., Sairam, R., Bhunia, S.S., Gurusamy, M.: Deft: a distributed IoT fingerprinting technique. IEEE Internet Things J. **6**(1), 940–952 (2018)
23. Trimananda, R., Varmarken, J., Markopoulou, A., Demsky, B.: Packet-level signatures for smart home devices. In: Network and Distributed Systems Security (NDSS) Symposium, vol. 2020 (2020)
24. Yang, K., Li, Q., Sun, L.: Towards automatic fingerprinting of IoT devices in the cyberspace. Comput. Netw. **148**, 318–327 (2019)
25. Yin, F., Yang, L., Wang, Y., Dai, J.: IoT ETEI: end-to-end IoT device identification method. In: 2021 IEEE Conference on Dependable and Secure Computing (DSC), pp. 1–8. IEEE (2021)

Fine-Grained Head Pose Estimation Based on a 6D Rotation Representation with Multiregression Loss

Jin Chen[1], Huahu Xu[1(✉)], Minjie Bian[1,2], Jiangang Shi[3], Yuzhe Huang[1],
and Chen Cheng[1]

[1] School of Computer Engineering and Science, Shanghai University, Shanghai, China
huahuxu@163.com
[2] State Grid Shanghai Municipal Electric Power Company, Shanghai, China
[3] Shanghai Shangda Hairun Information System Co., Ltd., Shanghai, China

Abstract. Estimating the head pose is vital in action evaluation since it has extensive applications such as in automobile driver-assistance systems, performance evaluations of athletes and customers' attention in retail stores. It is difficult to predict the head orientation from an RGB image by deep learning more accurately. We propose 6DHPENet, a fine-grained 6D head pose estimation network, to estimate the 3D rotations of the head. First, the model adopts a 6D rotation representation for 3D rotations as training objective to guarantee effective learning. 6D rotation representation is a continuous and one-to-one mapping function for 3D rotations. Second, achieving 3D facial landmarks from real-time activities consumes more time and is subject to frontal views. We drop the 3D facial landmarks to enhance the adaptability and generalization ability in various application scenes. Third, after the last convolution extraction layer, a squeeze-and-excitation module is introduced to construct both the local spatial and global channel-wise facial feature information by explicitly modeling the interdependencies between the feature channels. Finally, a multiregression loss function is presented to improve the accuracy and stability for a full-range view of the head pose estimation. In addition, our method is compact and efficient for mobile devices because of the lightweight CNN backbone. The quantitative experiment results trained on 300W-LP datasets show the superior performance of our 6D rotation representation-based multiregression fine-grained method on the AFLW2000 and BIWI datasets.

Keywords: Head pose estimation · 6D rotation · Fine-grained image analysis · Multiregression loss · Landmark-free method

1 Introduction

Head pose estimation (HPE) estimates the 3D rotations of heads from a single RGB image or videos. It has a wide range of applications, such as the evaluation of athletes' performance [5] in sports such as diving and skiing, head orientation estimations for

H. Gao et al. (Eds.): CollaborateCom 2022, LNICST 461, pp. 231–249, 2022.
https://doi.org/10.1007/978-3-031-24386-8_13

occluded pedestrians for the intention recognition of pedestrians [4], virtual and augmented reality [3] and other human attention modeling. For instance, in an automobile driver-assistance system [3], head pose estimation of the driver is an essential method to monitor whether the driver is engaged in fatigued driving or inattentive behavior. Due to the high practical value of HPE, it is a crucial task in the field of computer vision, especially in the area of action evaluation.

The camera-relative HPE is defined as the computation of the 3D rotation matrix for a head pose in the projection from the 3D space to the image plane. One of the important steps in the work is to compute the rigid Euclidean transformation from the 3D points in the world coordinate system to the corresponding 2D points in the camera coordinate system [1]. Inspired by the advancements in deep learning technology, many approaches have leveraged convolutional neural networks (CNNs) to address the problem of HPE. Overall, the research approaches can be classified into two main strategies: one is with 3D facial landmarks, and the other is without 3D facial landmarks. Some researches [3, 6] use facial landmark detection to establish a 2D-3D correspondence matching regression between the image and the 3D ground-truth landmarks. A standard human head 3D model [7] is used to imitate the real 3D face parameters, and then the 3D rotations of the heads are computed. However, this strategy has difficulty extracting key feature points from large poses such as profile views because of the occlusion of the facial features, which leads to more computation and larger models.

As a consequence, many landmark-free approaches [8–10] have been proposed to solve this issue. The head pose is estimated directly from a single image by the CNN regression models. Instead of predicting the 3×3 rotation matrix directly, they always choose other representations for the 3D rotations, as formulated in the 3D or 4D representations, such as the Euler angles and quaternions. Euler angles [11] are the most widely used because of their intuitiveness and simplicity of expression with only three elements, the angle of yaw, pitch and roll. However, there are some limitations for Euler angles. One is the ambiguity problem in terms of the gimbal lock [1]. Gimbal locking means that when two rotating axes become parallel, one degree of freedom (DOF) will be lost. Second, choosing different rotation orders will lead to different value of angles. Third, non-stationary properties [5] exist because the facial features do not change smoothly with respect to the angle size. The quaternion representation for 3D rotations has the antipodal problem [12]. When defining the representation space, $(q \in R^4, ||q||_2 = 1)$, q and $-q$ correspond to the same 3D rotation. In addition, the results from [13] proved that the 3D and 4D representations for 3D rotations are unsuitable for regression networks because of discontinuity. As demonstrated in these studies, using Euler angles or quaternion representations to annotate the head orientation is inappropriate for the regression in the CNN model. To solve these problems, we take the continuous representations (the 5D or 6D rotation matrix) to express the 3D rotation matrix to lower the error rate in neural networks. Furthermore, since real-time inferencing is necessary for many applications, including motion capture and generating attention maps for retail stores [14], it is necessary to adopt a more lightweight and mobile-friendly network as the CNN backbone to achieve faster speeds.

In this paper, we present a fine-grained 6D head pose estimation network (6DHPENet) that adopts a 6D rotation representation for 3D rotations as the training objective and make inferences from a single RGB image without 3D facial landmarks. The 6DHPENet predicts the value of the 3D rotation matrix of a head pose. It is trained on 300W-LP datasets and achieves the best result with an average mean absolute error (MAE) of 3.63 on the BIWI and AFLW2000 datasets. Specifically, the total MAE improves by 3.2% in the AFLW2000 datasets. There are four main innovations in the construction of the proposed 6DHPENet. First, the 6D rotation representation is composed by simply dropping the last column vector of the original 3×3 rotation matrix. Then a Gram-Schmidt-like process is used for mapping the 6D rotation representation to the original space. Second, to be friendly to mobile devices, we choose two lightweight CNN models, EfficientNet [15] and RepVGG [16], as the CNN backbone to extract the shallow and deep facial features. Third, to gain the fine-grained facial feature, the squeeze-and-excitation (SE) [17] module is embedded after the last CNN layer. To construct the local spatial and global channel-wise information, the SE module explicitly models the interdependencies between the feature channels. Finally, we use a multiregression loss function that contains the geodesic loss and the orthogonal loss to compute the difference between the predicted value and the ground-truth value in the training process for a gradient descent regression. The geodesic loss minimizes the angular difference between the ground-truth rotation matrix and the predicted one. The orthogonal loss constrains the orthogonality of the predicted rotation matrix caused by the calculation error in the Gram-Schmidt-like process to obtain better stability. In conclusion, our research contributions can be summarized as follows.

- **6D Rotation Representation for 3D Rotations**. The continuity of the 6D representation reduces the misleading neural networks, and dropping 3D facial landmarks enhances the generalization performance of the method.
- **Extraction of Fine-grained Feature Information**. The lightweight CNN backbone is introduced, and the SE module is embedded to construct local spatial and global channel-wise facial fine-grained feature information.
- **A Novel Multi-Regression Loss Function**. It contains the geodesic loss and the orthogonal loss. It improves accuracy and stability for the full-range view of the HPEs.
- **Excellent experiment results**. This shows that our approach based on a 6D rotation representation combined with the SE module and multiregression loss, is effective and suitable for fine-grained head pose estimation.

The remainder of the paper is organized as follows: Sect. 2 gives a brief review of the state-of-the-art head pose estimation methods. Section 3 presents the framework of proposed method and details of each part. Section 4 shows an experiment implementation and analysis on several public datasets. Finally, conclusions from our work are discussed in Sect. 5.

2 Related Work

2.1 Approaches for Discontinuous Representations

Head pose estimation has been actively researched over the past 25 years. For the research on monocular RGB images, there are several kinds of methods including classical methods [37, 38], geometric & deformable landmark-based methods [2] and regression & classification landmark-free methods [8–10, 18, 36, 41]. The traditional classical methods include template matching and cascaded detectors. Their characteristically take the discretized pose as a template compared to the input images. The geometric methods [39, 40] are also called the perspective to point (PnP) problems with 3D facial landmarks. In the existing landmark-free approaches, most of them are used to predict head pose from a discretized set of poses by regression and classification methods or multitasks methods [8–10, 18, 36]. In conclusion, these methods usually choose discontinuous annotations as the training objective of a head pose estimation.

For instance, Euler angles and quaternions are utilized as the training regression objective for most state-of-the-art methods. Hopenet [8] proposed a CNN model combined with a multiloss to predict head pose Euler angles directly from image intensities without key points. The multiloss network is composed of a pose bin classification and a regression component. Based on the same strategy as Hopenet WHENet [18] introduced a wrapped loss to improve the yaw accuracy for anterior views in a full-range HPE. Similarly, QuatNet [9] designs a multiregression loss that combines L2 regression with ordinal regression loss to address the non-stationary property in a HPE. Bin et al. [36] introduce a method using two-stage ensembles with average top-k regression. Despite the intuitiveness of Euler angles, it has been proven that four or fewer dimensional representations are discontinuous representations for 3D rotations.

2.2 Continuous Representations of 3D Rotations

In neural networks, the theoretical [23, 24] results suggest that functions that are smoothly or strongly continuous have a lower approximation error for a given number of neurons. Therefore, many researchers devote themselves to studying the theory of continuous representations of 3D rotations.

Wu et al. [21] studied the problem of restoring the orthonormality of a noisy rotation matrix by finding its nearest correct rotation matrix. Zhou et al. [13] present continuous representations for a general case of the n dimensional rotation group $SO(n)$, which is suitable for neural networks and shows that it needs at least 5 dimensions of information to achieve a continuous representation of rotations in 3D rotation space. Another innovation for Zhou et al. [13] is to propose a geodesic loss to minimize the angle error between two rotations. 6DRepNet [19] follows the approach by Zhou et al. [13] and engages a network to predict the 6D rotation representation for 3D rotations. Furthermore, Zhi et al. [20] proposed a deep network pipeline based on vector representation for a 3D rotation matrix with vector orthogonal constraints. Cao et al. [20] used three-vector annotations and illustrated that the Euler angle annotation has issues of discontinuity.

2.3 Fine-Grained Head Pose Estimation

To obtain better HPE accuracy by deep CNN networks, it is desirable to enhance feature aggregation and extract more effective local and global context information. There are several fine-grained HPE methods. Yang et al. [10] proposed a classification method that learns a fine-grained structure mapping for spatially grouping features before aggregation. Wu et al. [21] studied learning from a synergy process of 3D morphable models (3DMMs) and facial landmarks to predict complete 3D facial geometry, including 3D alignment, face orientation, and 3D face modeling.

For extraction of the fine-grained features, the existing methods need more annotations or more complex construction of networks. To explicitly model the interdependencies between the feature channels simply, Shen et al. [17] proposed a squeeze-and-excitation network (SENet) with an SE block that adaptively recalibrates the channel-wise feature responses. It has a more understandable network structure.

3 Model Framework

3.1 6DHPENet Overview

AS shown in Fig. 1, 6DHPENet is a solution to end-to-end 2D image-to-3D rotation correspondence learning for head pose estimation without 3D landmarks. It mainly consists of five modules.

CNN Backbone for Encoding Feature Space. The input of this network is a single RGB image I, which shows a cropped head. For the input image I, a CNN backbone is utilized to extract the shallow and deep facial features from the image and encode a feature space K, where $K \in R^{H \times W \times C}$. We choose RepVGG-b1g2 [15] and EfficientNet-B0 [16] as the CNN backbone.

Squeeze-and-Excitation Module for Embedding Fine-Grained Features. The feature space $K (K \in R^{H \times W \times C})$ is passed into a squeeze-and-excitation module to obtain

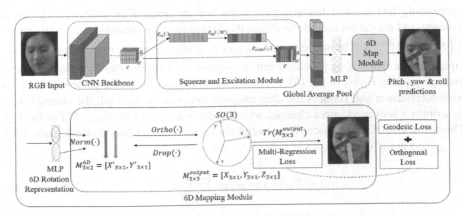

Fig. 1. An overview of 6DHPENet.

the fine-grained and reweighted feature space $\tilde{K}\left(\tilde{K} \in R^{H \times W \times C}\right)$. The squeeze-and-excitation module contains three steps: First, the input feature space K is squeezed into a channel-wise feature descriptor s by the average pooling function $F_{sq}(\cdot)$. Second, the channel-wise feature descriptor s is excited into a channel-wise weight descriptor z by $F_{ex}(\cdot, W)$. Third, the input feature space K is reweighted into the fine-grained feature space $\tilde{K}$ by $F_{scale}(\cdot, \cdot)$. In Sect. 3.2, we will introduce the details of $\tilde{K} = SE(K)$.

Output of a 6D Rotation Representation. After embedding the fine-grained feature space $\tilde{K}$, $\tilde{K}$ is sized into the feature space $F\left(F \in R^{1 \times 1 \times C}\right)$ by global average pooling (GLP) and reshaped into the fused feature vector f ($f \in R^C$). The fused feature vector f is sent into a multilayer perceptron (MLP) called the fully connected layer Z_{linear} that outputs 6 dims of neurons, called m_6. The output tensor m_6 is viewed as a 6D rotation representation matrix $M_{3 \times 2}$. In Sect. 3.3, we will give the definition of 6D representation for 3D rotations.

6D Mapping Module. Through a Gram-Schmidt-like process $Ortho(\cdot)$ to map the 6D Matrix $M_{3 \times 2}$ into the 3D rotations, $M_{3 \times 3}(M_{3 \times 3} \in SO(3), M_{3 \times 3}M_{3 \times 3}^T = I, \det(M_{3 \times 3}) = 1)$, finally the Euler angles (the angles of yaw, pitch, roll) are computed by $Tr(M_{3 \times 3}^{output})$ from the 3D rotations $M_{3 \times 3}$. In Sect. 3.4, we introduce the details of the 6D mapping process.

Multiregression Loss Function. The multiregression loss function contains the geodesic loss L_{geo} and the orthogonal loss L_{ortho}. L_{geo} minimizes the angular difference between the ground-truth rotation matrix and the predicted rotation matrix. L_{ortho} constrains the orthogonality of the predicted rotation matrix caused by a calculation error by the Gram–Schmidt-like process to obtain better stability. The multiregression loss function computes the difference between the predicted value and the ground-truth value in the training process for the gradient descent regression.

3.2   SE Module for Embedding Fine-Grained Features

Embedding fine-grained features passes the feature space $K\left(K \in R^{H \times W \times C}\right)$ into a squeeze-and-excitation module to obtain the fine-grained and reweighted feature space $\tilde{K}\left(\tilde{K} \in R^{H \times W \times C}\right)$. The squeeze-and-excitation module contains three steps: First, the input feature space K is squeezed into a channel-wise feature descriptor s by global average pooling $F_{sq}(\cdot)$ in Eq. (6). $F_{sq}(\cdot)$ sums out the global feature information by no parameterization and reduces the characteristic dimensions. Second, the channel-wise descriptor s is excited into a channel-wise weight descriptor z by $F_{ex}(\cdot, W)$ in Eq. (7). Third, the input feature space K is reweighted into the fine-grained feature space $\tilde{K}$ by $F_{scale}(\cdot, \cdot)$ in Eq. (8).

$$s = F_{sq}(K) = \frac{1}{H \times W} \sum_{i=1}^{H} \sum_{j=1}^{W} K(i,j) \tag{6}$$

$$z = F_{ex}(s, W) = \sigma(g(z, W)) = \sigma(W_2(\delta(W_1(z, W)))) \tag{7}$$

$$\tilde{K} = F_{scale}(K, z) \tag{8}$$

In Eq. (7), σ is the sigmoid function, δ is the ReLU function, $W_i (i = 1, 2)$ is the ith fully connected layer, and W is the weight of excitation. $F_{ex}(\cdot, W)$ obtains the channel-wise weight z by reducing the channel dimensions by increasing the channel dimensions to achieve a more nonlinear processing capability. In Eq. (8), z is resized to the same size as K, and then a pixel-wise multiplication is conducted to reweight the feature space K into the fine-grained feature space $\tilde{K}$.

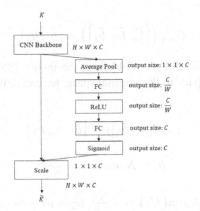

Fig. 2. Flowchart of the squeeze-and-excitation module.

The flowchart of the SE module is shown in Fig. 2. For the inputting feature space K, there are two stages for generating the output feature space $\tilde{K}$. In the first stage, the input feature space K is squeezed into a channel-wise feature descriptor $s \in R^{1 \times 1 \times C}$ by global average pooling $F_{sq}(\cdot)$ in Eq. (6). $F_{sq}(\cdot)$ sums out the global feature information on the $H \times W$ dimensions. Second, the channel-wise descriptor s is excited into a channel-wise weight descriptor $z \in R^{1 \times 1 \times C}$ by $F_{ex}(\cdot, W)$ in Eq. (7). There are four steps in $F_{ex}(\cdot, W)$. The factor W is set to 16 by experiment practice. The first step is an MLP layer that outputs $\frac{C}{W}$ dims of neurons to fuse the channel characteristics. The second step is a ReLU activation function. The third step is an MLP layer that outputs c dims of neurons to extract the channel-wise attention. The fourth step is a sigmoid function to normalize the value between[0, 1]. Finally, the channel-wise weight descriptor z is reshaped into $1 \times 1 \times C$ for the preparation of the pixel-wise multiplication. In the second stage, the input feature space K is reweighted into the fine-grained feature space $\tilde{K}$ by conducting a pixel-wise multiplication $F_{scale}(\cdot, \cdot)$ between the input feature space K and the channel-wise weight z in Eq. (8).

3.3 6D Representation for the 3D Rotations

Zhou et al. [13] presented continuous representations for the general case of the n dimensional rotation group $SO(n)$. We discuss the definition of the 6D rotation representation.

It is a continuous one-to-one mapping relationship between 6D rotation representation $M_{3\times2} = [\vec{a}_1, \vec{a}_2]$ and the 3D rotations $M_{3\times3} = [\vec{b}_1, \vec{b}_2, \vec{b}_3]$, where $\vec{a}_i, \vec{b}_i, i = 1, 2, \ldots., n$ are column vectors.

First, let the original space be $X = SO(3)$ and the representation space be $R = \mathbb{R}^{3\times2}$. Given the 3D rotation matrix $M_{3\times3}$, we know that it is an orthogonal matrix and meets the conditions: $M \in R^{3\times3}, M_{3\times3} \in SO(3), M_{3\times3}M_{3\times3}^T = I, \det(M_{3\times3}) = 1$. Therefore, the 6D rotation representation $M_{3\times2}$ should contain an orthogonalization process in the representation itself. Then we can define a mapping $G_{map}(\cdot)$ from the original space to the representation space by simply dropping the last column vector of the input 3D rotation matrix:

$$G_{map}\left([\vec{b}_1, \vec{b}_2, \vec{b}_3]\right) = [\vec{b}_1, \vec{b}_2] \tag{1}$$

The set $G_{map}(\cdot)$ is a Stiefel manifold from the theory [25]. For the mapping f_{map} from the representation space to the original space, we can define the following Gram–Schmidt-like process:

$$f_{map}([\vec{a}_1, \vec{a}_2]) = [\vec{b}_1, \vec{b}_2, \vec{b}_3] \tag{2}$$

$$\vec{b}_1 = Norm(\vec{a}_1) = \frac{\vec{a}_1}{||\vec{a}_1||} \tag{3}$$

$$\vec{b}_2 = Norm\left(\vec{U}_2\right) = \frac{\vec{U}_2}{||\vec{U}_2||}, \vec{U}_2 = \vec{a}_2 - \vec{b}_1 \cdot \vec{a}_2\vec{b}_1 \tag{4}$$

$$\vec{b}_3 = \vec{b}_1 \times \vec{b}_2 \tag{5}$$

Norm($\cdot$) denotes a normalization function by the L2-Norm. The third vector $\vec{b}_3$ can be calculated by the ordinary cross product $\vec{b}_1 \times \vec{b}_2$ in Eq. (5). The process of the Proof: for every $M_{3\times3} \in SO(3)$, $f_{map}\left(G_{map}(M_{3\times3})\right) = M_{3\times3}$ has been verified by the induction and the properties of the orthonormal basis vectors in [13, 26].

3.4 6D Mapping Module

From Sect. 3.3, we note that the 6D rotation matrix can be transformed into the 3×3 rotation matrix by a one-to-one mapping function $Ortho(\cdot)$ which equals Eqs. (2) and $Drop(\cdot)$ which equals Eq. (1). Thus, we introduce the steps of the 6D mapping process by using the theory of the definition of the 6D Representation for the 3D Rotations.

As shown in Algorithm 1, specifically, we split the output of the MLP layer into two column vectors $M_{3\times2}^{6D} = [X_{3\times1}', Y_{3\times1}']$ and then use a Gram–Schmidt-like process $Ortho(\cdot)$ in Eq. (2,3,4,5) to map the 6D rotation Matrix $M_{3\times2}$ into the 3D rotations $M_{3\times3}(M \in R^{3\times3}, M_{3\times3} \in SO(3), M_{3\times3}M_{3\times3}^T = I, \det(M_{3\times3}) = 1)$. The Gram–Schmidt-like process $Ortho(\cdot)$ has several steps. First, $X_{3\times1}$ is normalized by using Eq. (3) with $X_{3\times1}'$. Second, the second vector $Z_{3\times1}'$ is generated by using Eq. (4). Third, $Z_{3\times1}$ is normalized by using Eq. (3) with $Z_{3\times1}'$. Fourth, the third vector $Y_{3\times1}$ is generated by using Eq. (5). Fifth, the third vector $Y_{3\times1}$ is generated by using Eq. (5). Finally, $X_{3\times1}, Y_{3\times1}$ and $Z_{3\times1}$ are aggregated into the 3D rotation matrix $M_{3\times3}^{output}$.

Algorithm 1. 6D Map Module

Input: The 6 dims of neurons m_6 (output by the MLP layer).
Output: The 3D rotation matrix $M_{3\times3}^{output}$.

1: Split the m_6 into two column vectors $X'_{3\times1}, Y'_{3\times1}$.
2: Normalize $X'_{3\times1}$ into $X_{3\times1}$ using Equation (3) $X_{3\times1} = norm(X'_{3\times1})$.
3: Generate the second vector $Z'_{3\times1}$ using Equation (4) $Z'_{3\times1} = CrossProduct(X_{3\times1}, Y'_{3\times1})$
4: Normalize $Z'_{3\times1}$ into $Z_{3\times1}$ using Equation (3) $Z_{3\times1} = norm(Z'_{3\times1})$.
5: Generate the third vector $Y_{3\times1}$ using Equation (5) $Y_{3\times1} = CrossProduct(Z_{3\times1}, X_{3\times1})$
6: Aggregate $X_{3\times1}, Y_{3\times1}, Z_{3\times1}$ into the rotation matrix $M_{3\times3}$
7: **return** the 3D rotation matrix $M_{3\times3}^{output}$

Finally, to compare the result with other methods, the 3D rotation maxtrix $M_{3\times3}^{output}$ is transformed into the Euler angles, the angles of yaw, pitch and roll by $Tr(M_{3\times3}^{output})$. $Tr(M_{3\times3}^{output})$ means computing the Euler angles from a rotation matrix and the details have been shown in Slabaugh et al. [11].

3.5 Multiregression Loss Function

Our method is trained end-to-end. During the training process, we employed a novel multiregression loss function that contains the geodesic loss L_{geo} and the orthogonal loss L_{ortho} for the training objective. As shown in Eq. (9), the total loss is the addition of the L_{geo} and L_{ortho} with a weighted term α that is set to a small number whose range is between [0.1, 0.5].

$$L = L_{geo}(M_{predict}, M_{ground}) + \alpha \cdot L_{ortho}(M_{predict}) \tag{9}$$

Geodesic Loss. For a given 3D rotation matrix M, $M \in SO(3)$, can be represented by a rotation axis $\vec{\mu}$ and rotation angle θ according to Rodrigues' rotation formula [27]. Figure 3 shows the relationship between M and θ that equals Eq. (10).

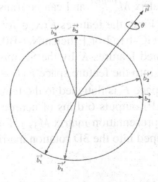

Fig. 3. Geodesic loss geometric meaning.

$$tr(M) = 1 + cos2\theta \tag{10}$$

Then the geodesic loss is defined as the minimal angular difference between two 3×3 rotation matrices, which calculates the angle between the predicted rotation matrix $M_{predict}$ and the ground truth matrix M_{ground}. It can be defined as:

$$L_{geo} = \cos^{-1}(\frac{\left(M_{00}'' + M_{11}'' + M_{22}'' - 1\right)}{2}) \tag{11}$$

$$M'' = M_{predict} M_{ground}^{T} \tag{12}$$

Orthogonal Loss. L_{ortho} constrains the orthogonality of the predicted rotation matrix caused by the calculation error on the Gram–Schmidt-like process. Given the predicted rotation matrix $M_{predict} = \left[\vec{b}_1, \vec{b}_2, \vec{b}_3\right]$, where $\vec{b}_i, i = 1, 2, \ldots, n$ are column vectors, $M_{predict} \in R^{3\times3}, \vec{b}_i \in R^{3\times1}$, the loss term is shown as follows:

$$L_{ortho} = MAE\left(\vec{b}_i \vec{b}_j, 0\right)(i \neq j, i \in [1, 2, 3], j \in [1, 2, 3]) \tag{13}$$

$$M_{predict} = \left[\vec{b}_1, \vec{b}_2, \vec{b}_3\right] \tag{14}$$

In Eq. (13), we adopt the mean absolute error loss function for the orthogonal loss to minimize the difference between the cross product of the column vectors and the zero value. If a calculation error does not exist, the cross product of the column vectors should be zero because the column vectors in the rotation matrix are mutually orthogonal.

3.6 Complete Structure of 6DHPENet

AS shown in Algorithm 2, for a single RGB image, we trained an end-to-end network 6DHPENet to predict the value of head pose $M_{3\times3}^{output}$. The raw form of the head pose is defined as the 3D rotation matrix $M_{3\times3}^{output}$ and can be transformed into other representations, such as Euler angles. First, the features $K(K \in R^{H \times W \times C})$ are extracted from I by the CNN backbone RepVGG-b1g2 or EfficientNet-B0. Second, the features K are reweighted into the fine-grained features $\tilde{K}$ by the SE module. The details are shown in Sect. 3.2. Third, $\tilde{K}$ is sized into the feature space $F(F \in R^{1 \times 1 \times C})$ by global average pooling. Fourth, the feature space F is flattened to the feature vector f ($f \in R^{C}$). Fifth, a Multilayer Perceptron (MLP) outputs 6 dims of neurons, called m_6. The tensor m_6 is viewed as a 6D rotation representation matrix $M_{3\times2}$. Finally, the 6D rotation representation matrix $M_{3\times2}$ is mapped into the 3D rotation matrix $M_{3\times3}^{output}$. The 6D mapping process is shown in Sect. 3.4.

Algorithm 2. Complete Structure of 6DHPENet

Input: A single RGB image I with a cropped face.
Output: The 3D rotation matrix $M_{3\times3}^{output}$.

1: Extract features $K(K \in R^{H \times W \times C})$ from I by the CNN backbone.

2: Reweight the features K into the fine-grained feature $\tilde{K}$ by SE module: $\tilde{K} = SE(K)$.

3: Size the $\tilde{K}$ into feature space F ($F \in R^{1 \times 1 \times C}$) by global average pooling.

4: Reshape feature space F into the feature vector f ($f \in R^C$).

6: The tensor $m_6 = Z_{linear}(f)$ by the Multilayer Perceptron (MLP) that outputs 6 dims of neurons.

7: m_6 is viewed as a 6D rotation representation matrix $M_{3\times2}^{6D} = [X'_{3\times1}, Y'_{3\times1}]$.

8: $M_{3\times3}^{output} = Ortho(M_{3\times2}^{6D})$ by a 6D mapping module in **Algorithm 1**.

9: **If** on the training process, **then**:

10:   use the multiregression loss function L for the gradient descent regression.

11: **return** the 3D rotation matrix $M_{3\times3}^{output}$

4 Experiment and Analysis

4.1 Datasets and Data Preprocessing

There are three popular public benchmark datasets, 300W-LP [2], AFLW2000 [2] and BIWI [28]. According to most of the previous research work, we choose the 300W-LP dataset as the training dataset and the AFLW2000 and BIWI datasets as the testing datasets. What's more, we retain the images with Euler angles θ of three rotations, including the angles where the yaw, pitch, and roll, are between $[-99°, 99°]$ and convert the annotations of the Euler angles into a 3D rotation matrix.

300W-LP. The 300W-LP dataset was derived from the 300 W dataset [29] which unifies several datasets including AFW [30], HELEN [31], IBUG [29] and LFPW [32], for face alignment with 68 landmarks. It generates 61,225 samples through face profiling with 3D image meshing across large poses and further expands to 122,450 samples with a flipping transformation.

AFLW2000. The AFLW2000 dataset contains the first 2,000 images of the AFLW dataset [33] by providing ground-truth 3D faces and the corresponding 68 landmarks. The faces in the dataset have been processed in large pose variations with various illumination conditions and facial appearances.

BIWI. The BIWI dataset is composed of 24 videos of 20 subjects in a controlled indoor environment. There are a total of approximately 15,000 frames in the dataset. The faces in the dataset are detected by MTCNN [34] to obtain face bounding box results.

For the data preprocessing for training the network, we perform three kinds of data augmentation transformations. First, the image is cropped so that it leaves a margin from the head bounding box $(X_{min}, Y_{min}, X_{max}, Y_{max})$ by a random loose factor $\gamma \in [0.1, 0.5]$. The crop function is equal to Eqs. 15, 16, 17 and 18. Second, the image is randomly flipped horizontally by a probability factor $p \in [0, 1]$. If $p > 0.5$, the image is flipped.

Third, the image is randomly blurred by a probability factor $q \in [0, 1]$. If $q > 0.5$, make the image blurred. Finally, before the image is fed into the network, we resize the image into the uniform size 224×224 and normalize the pixel values into $[0, 1]$.

$$X'_{min} = X_{min} - |\gamma * (X_{max} - X_{min})| \tag{15}$$

$$Y'_{min} = Y_{min} - |\gamma * (Y_{max} - Y_{min})| \tag{16}$$

$$X'_{max} = X_{max} + |\gamma * (X_{max} - X_{min})| \tag{17}$$

$$Y'_{max} = Y_{max} + |\gamma * (Y_{max} - Y_{min})| \tag{18}$$

4.2 Experiment Environment

We use PyTorch to implement our proposed network. For data augmentation in the training process, the raw images are randomly cropped into a loose size with a scale factor k, randomly flipped by a probability factor p and randomly blurred by a probability factor q. The details are shown in Sect. 4.1.

We use an Adam optimizer with a learning rate of 1e-4. We set the batch size to 128 and use 80 epochs to train the network. The experiments were performed on a computer with a GTX3090Ti GPU. For experiments practice, at the beginning of the backpropagation, we only use the geodesic loss function before the 30th epoch. After the 30th epoch, we use the multiregression loss combined with the orthogonal loss and set the factor of orthogonal loss to 0.1 in experiment.

4.3 Results and Analysis

Experiment 1: Experiment 1 is implemented here with the factor settings in Sect. 4.2. Our 6DHPENet is composed of the CNN backbone of RepVGG-b1g2 and the squeeze-and-excitation module and outputs the 3D rotation matrix. 6DHPENet is trained on the 300W-LP datasets. Because the 3D rotation matrix is nonintuitive and most works choose Euler angles as output, we convert the predicted rotation matrix to Euler angles for comparison. As shown in Fig. 4, we present some sample results of head pose estimations using the proposed trained method by visualizing the Euler angles. The red

Fig. 4. Sample results of head pose estimation using the proposed method.

line indicates the pitch angle on the x-axis. The green line indicates the yaw angle on the y-axis, and the blue line indicates the roll angle on the z-axis.

On the evaluation of the experiment results, we take the mean absolute error (MAE) to calculate the error between the predicted Euler angles and the ground-truth Euler angles. The MAE is calculated by Eq. (19).

$$MAE = \sum_{\theta=yaw,pitch,roll} \left(|\theta_{prdeict} - \theta_{ground-truth}| \right) \qquad (19)$$

A summary of the results is given in Table 1 below. It achieves the best result of an average mean absolute error (Avg MAE) of 3.63 on the BIWI and AFLW2000 datasets. Specifically, the MAE of the sum of the three angles is improved by 3.2% in the AFLW2000 datasets.

Table 1. Summary of results: Avg[2] MAE denotes the average of the BIWI and AFLW2000 datasets overall results. The Full Range[1] denotes whether the method allows full range predictions.

Method	Full Range[1]	Params ($\times 10^6$)	BIWI MAE	AFLW2000 MAE	Avg[2] MAE
3DDFA [2]	N	–	19.07	7.393	13.231
Hopenet [8]	N	23.9	4.895	6.155	5.525
SSR-Net-MD [35]	N	**0.2**	4.650	6.010	5.330
FSA-Caps-Fusion [10]	N	1.2	4.000	5.070	4.535
WHENet-V [18]	N	4.4	3.475	4.834	4.155
WHENet [18]	Y	4.4	3.814	5.424	4.619
QuatNet [9]	N	–	4.146	4.503	4.325
6DRepNet [19]	Y	4.3	3.470	3.970	3.720
TriNet [20]	Y	–	4.290	4.669	4.480
6DHPENet(ours)	Y	4.4	**3.420**	**3.840**	**3.630**

As shown in Table 2, we make comparisons with the state-of-the-art methods on the BIWI and AFLW2000 datasets in detail by the MAE on each rotation of the head pose and the angles of yaw, pitch and roll. On the BIWI datasets, the MAE on the pitch is 4.01, and the total MAE of the three angles is 3.42. On the AFLW2000 datasets, the MAE on the pitch is 4.68, and the total MAE of the three angles is 3.84. The results show that our 6DHPENet obtains the best result both on the pitch angle and the total MAE of the three angles. This means that our method is adapted to the general scenarios. Although 6DHPENet does not always perform the best, with MAE values of 3.51, 3.65 and 2.74 for the yaw and roll angles, respectively. However, in contrast to other methods, the difference is small, and equals 0.57, 0.02 and 0.06, respectively. Although the MAE on the yaw angle is higher than that of the QuatNet by a difference value of 0.57 (3.51–2.94) in the comparisons, the MAE on the other angles is lower than that of the QuatNet by an average value of 0.88. The reason is probably the lack of enough full-view samples and the influence of visual instability for the various head poses, especially the yaw and roll angles, which have not yet been eliminated.

Table 2. Comparisons with state-of-the-art methods on the BIWI and AFLW2000 datasets.

Method	BIWI				AFLW2000			
	Yaw	Pitch	Roll	MAE	Yaw	Pitch	Roll	MAE
3DDFA [2]	36.20	12.30	8.78	19.10	5.40	8.53	8.25	7.39
Hopenet ($\alpha = 1$) [8]	4.81	6.61	3.27	4.90	6.92	6.64	5.67	6.41
Hopenet ($\alpha = 2$) [8]	5.12	6.98	3.39	5.12	6.47	6.56	5.44	6.16
FSA-Net [10]	4.27	4.96	2.76	4.00	4.50	6.08	4.64	5.07
HPE [36]	3.12	5.18	4.57	4.29	4.80	6.18	4.87	5.28
WHENet-V [18]	3.60	4.10	2.73	3.48	4.44	5.75	4.31	4.83
WHENet [18]	3.99	4.39	3.06	3.81	5.11	6.24	4.92	5.42
QuatNet [9]	**2.94**	5.49	4.01	4.15	3.97	5.62	3.92	4.50
6DRepNet [19]	3.24	4.48	**2.68**	3.47	**3.63**	4.91	3.37	3.97
TriNet [20]	4.11	4.76	3.05	3.97	4.04	5.77	4.20	4.67
6DHPENet (ours)	3.51	**4.01**	2.74	**3.42**	3.65	**4.68**	**3.18**	**3.84**

Experiment 2: We conduct an error analysis of two landmark-free methods (WHENet and 6DHPENet) on the AFLW2000 datasets. The error analysis visualizes the MAE on the total angle of yaw, pitch and roll, or the difference in each angle by predicting the head pose when a single RGB image is inputted that is generated by WHENet and 6DHPENet. Both methods are trained on 300W-LP. We convert the predicted rotation matrix to Euler angles for comparison. The results are shown in Fig. 5 and Fig. 6.

As shown in Fig. 5, we take some examples on the AFLW2000 datasets from the frontal to the profile views. On the first line, we put some original images and draw the ground-truth annotations of the Euler angles below the image as in $\left[\theta_{yaw}, \theta_{pitch}, \theta_{roll}\right]$. On the second line, we show the result by using WHENet and print the total MAE of the three angles below the image. On the third line, we show the result by using the proposed method 6DHPENet and print the total MAE of the three angles below the image. The frontal views of a human face are shown in the first and fourth columns. The predicted results by 6DHPENet make for a total MAE of 2.207° and 2.731°, whereas the predicted results by WHENet make for a total MAE of 4.518° and 8.837°. The profile views of a human face are shown in the second and third columns. The predicted results by 6DHPENet make for a total MAE of 5.981° and 5.631°, whereas the predicted results by WHENet make for a total MAE of 11.945° and 8.494°. Based on observations of the visualization results, it can be concluded that the smaller the total MAE is, the better accuracy the head pose estimation has. The proposed method has good generalization ability from the frontal to the profile views of the head pose. Contrary to our method based on the 6D rotation representation, the traditional landmark-free methods of directly predicting the Euler angles from images have a large accuracy error.

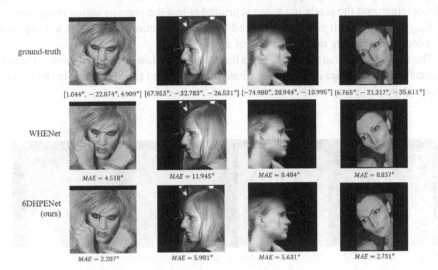

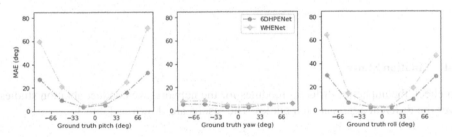

Fig. 5. Comparison of head pose estimation results on AFLW2000 images.

Fig. 6. MAE on AFLW2000 using the landmark-free methods. All were trained on 300W-LP.

As shown in Fig. 6, we draw the lines of the MAE values. The Euler angles' range $\theta \in [-99°, 99°]$ is equally divided into intervals in a span of 33°. The first picture shows the trend in the MAE of a pitch angle between six intervals ($[-99°, -66°), [-66°, -33°)$, $[-33°, 0°), [0°, 33°), [33°, 66°), [66°, 99°]$). The second picture shows the trend in the MAE of the yaw angle between the same six intervals. The third picture shows the trend in the MAE of the roll angle between the same six intervals. The red curve represents the prediction MAE of 6DHPENet, and the yellow curve represents the prediction MAE of WHENet. On the rotation of pitch, yaw and roll, all the MAE curves of 6DHPENet are significantly lower than those of the WHENet. Therefore, it proves that the continuity of 6D rotation representation makes the network learn better and achieve better accuracy.

Experiment 3: We evaluated the effect of resolutions by the trained 6DHPENet on 300W-LP. An image is picked up randomly from the AFLW2000 dataset. The image is downsampled by a Gaussian kernel. The indicated downsampling factor includes 4X, 16X and 64X. Then, the downsampled images are reshaped to the original size by bilinear interpolation before being supplied to the 6DHPENet. As shown in Fig. 7, the first image is the original, and the predicted value is printed below the corresponding image formed in $[\theta_{yaw}, \theta_{pitch}, \theta_{roll}]$. It can be concluded that the prediction accuracy is not seriously degraded by aggressive downsampling of up to 64X.

The result proves that the 6DHPENet has stability for low-resolution scenes. It can be inferred that 6DHPENet extracts the effective fine-grained facial features in the training process depending on the CNN backbone and SE module.

[22.437°, −3.179°, −3.578°]   [23.466°, −1.912°, −3.000°]   [23.686°, −2.559°, −2.744°]   [18.978°, −3.808°, −4.056°]

Fig. 7. Downsampling factor vs. the angles of yaw, pitch & roll. The ground-truth values are $[19.495°, 2.322°, −4.536°]$.

4.4 Ablation Study

To check the impact of different modules for the network, we conduct ablation studies over the different aggregation modules. The results are shown in Table 3.

Table 3. Ablation study over different aggregation modules. (with/without the squeeze-and-excitation module, geodesic loss function or orthogonal loss function).

ID	Modules			AFLW2000			
	SE module	Geodesic loss	Orthogonal loss	Yaw	Pitch	Roll	MAE
1	✓	✓		3.773	4.699	**3.154**	3.874
2		✓	✓	3.666	4.782	3.359	3.936
3		✓		3.692	4.812	3.460	3.988
4	✓	✓	✓	**3.650**	**4.689**	3.180	**3.840**

Test ID1 is composed of an SE module and geodesic loss. Its result is better than the other test without the SE module and it improves by 2.8% over the worst MAE of 3.988. This shows that the SE module generates fine-grained features and is beneficial to the regression of the network. Test ID2 and test ID3 are without the SE module, one is with orthogonal loss while the other is without orthogonal loss. Observed from the results, the test with orthogonal loss scores a lower MAE of 3.936 as compared to the other one of 3.988. This shows that it is necessary to constrain the calculation error caused by Gram–Schmidt-like process. Test ID4 is composed of all the modules and it obtains the best result of a total MAE of 3.840. It can be inferred that our approach, combined with the SE module and multiregression loss function, is effective and suitable for fine-grained head pose estimation.

Table 4. Comparisons with different CNN backbones.

	CNN backbone	BIWI				AFLW2000			
		Yaw	Pitch	Roll	MAE	Yaw	Pitch	Roll	MAE
1	Efficientnet-b0	3.837	4.230	2.762	3.609	4.020	4.963	3.666	4.216
2	Repvgg-b1g2	**3.510**	**4.012**	**2.738**	**3.420**	**3.650**	**4.689**	**3.180**	**3.840**

As shown in Table 4, we use the Efficientnet-b0 and the Repvgg-b1g2 network separately as the CNN backbone for the 6DHPENet. The experiment results show that Repvgg-b1g2 is better than Efficientnet-b0. There is a phenomenon that the SE module does not obtain a better score even if it is embedded in Efficientnet-b0. We assume that the squeeze-and-excitation module added after the last CNN layer may be more conducive to the spatial integration of the local and global information in the CNN network, as well as the channel relationship for head pose estimation.

5 Conclusions

In this paper, we present a 6D head pose estimation network (6DHPENet) to solve the problem of predicting a head pose without 3D facial landmarks by end-to-end deep learning. The 6DHPENet adopts a 6D rotation representation for 3D rotations as the training objective without 3D facial landmarks. The squeeze-and-excitation module is introduced to construct the local spatial and global channel-wise information by explicitly modeling the interdependencies between the feature channels. A novel multiregression loss function is designed to improve the accuracy for the full-range view of a HPE. The experiment results show that the 6D rotation representation for 3D rotations outperforms the other methods.

In the future, to improve the efficiency of the network, it is promising to extend the larger full-view datasets to train the network. In addition, due to the applications that usually need to be deployed on mobile devices, we expect to study more lightweight networks and improve the corresponding speeds.

References

1. Vincent, L., Pascal, F.: Monocular model-based 3D tracking of rigid objects: a survey, now (2005)

2. Xiangyu, Z., Zhen, L., Xiaoming, L., Hailin, S., Stan, Z.L.: Face alignment across large poses: a 3D solution. In: 2016 IEEE Conference on Computer Vision and Pattern Recognition (CVPR), pp. 146–155. IEEE (2016)
3. Murphy-Chutorian, E., Trivedi, M.M.: Head pose estimation and augmented reality tracking: an integrated system and evaluation for monitoring driver awareness. IEEE Trans. Intell. Transp. Syst. 11(2), 300–311 (2010)
4. Rehder, E., Kloeden H., Stiller, C.: Head detection and orientation estimation for pedestrian safety. In: Proceedings IEEE International Conference Intelligent Transportation Systems 2014, pp. 2292–2297 (2014)
5. Pirsiavash, H., Vondrick, C., Torralba, A.: Assessing the quality of actions. In: Fleet, D., Pajdla, T., Schiele, B., Tuytelaars, T. (eds.) ECCV 2014. LNCS, vol. 8694, pp. 556–571. Springer, Cham (2014). https://doi.org/10.1007/978-3-319-10599-4_36
6. Adrian, B., Georgios, T.: How far are we from solving the 2D & 3D face alignment problem? (and a dataset of 230,000 3D facial landmarks). In: Proceedings of International Conference on Computer Vision (ICCV) (2017)
7. Blanz, V., Vetter, T., Rockwood, A.: A morphable model for the synthesis of 3D faces. In: SIGGRAPH 1999: Proceedings of the 26th Annual Conference on Computer Graphics and Interactive Techniques, pp. 187–194(1999)
8. Ruiz, N., Chong, E., Rehg, J.M.: Fine-grained head pose estimation without keypoints. In: 2018 IEEE/CVF Conference on Computer Vision and Pattern Recognition Workshops (CVPRW), pp. 2155–215509 (2018)
9. Hsu H., Wu, S T., Sheng, W., Wing, H.W., Lee C.: QuatNet: quaternion-based head pose estimation with multiregression loss. IEEE Trans. Multimedia 21(4), 1035–1046 (2019)
10. Tsun-Yi, Y., Yi-Ting, C., Yen-Yu, L., Yung-Yu, C.: FSA-Net: learning fine-grained structure aggregation for head pose estimation from a single image. In: 2019 IEEE/CVF Conference on Computer Vision and Pattern Recognition (CVPR), pp. 1087–1096 (2019)
11. Slabaugh, G.G.: Computing Euler angles from a rotation matrix (1999)
12. Ashutosh, S., Justin, D., Andrew, Y.N.: Learning 3-D object orientation from images. In: 2009 IEEE International Conference on Robotics and Automation, pp. 794–800. IEEE (2009)
13. Zhou, Y., Barnes, C., Jingwan, L., Yang, J., Hao, L.: On the continuity of rotation representations in neural networks. In: 2019 IEEE/CVF Conference on Computer Vision and Pattern Recognition (CVPR), pp. 5738–5746 (2019)
14. Yi, S., Xiaogang W., Xiaoou T.: Deep convolutional network cascade for facial point detection. In: Proceedings of the IEEE Conference on Computer Vision and Pattern Recognition, pp. 3476–3483 (2013)
15. Mingxing, T., Quoc, V.L.: EfficientNet: rethinking model scaling for convolutional neural networks. arXiv preprint arXiv:1905.11946 (2019)
16. Xiaohan, D., Zhang, X., Ningning, M., Jungong, H., Guiguang, D., Jian, S.: RepVGG: making VGG-style ConvNets great again. In: 2021 IEEE/CVF Conference on Computer Vision and Pattern Recognition (CVPR), pp. 13728–13737 (2021)
17. Jie, H., Li, S., Gang, S., Albanie, S.: Squeeze-and-Excitation Networks. IEEE Trans. Pattern Anal. Mach. Intell. 99 (2017)
18. Zhou, Y., Gregson , J.: WHENet: real-time fine-grained estimation for wide range head pose. In: 2020 British Machine Vision Conference (BMVC) (2020)
19. Hempel, T., Abdelrahman, A. A., Al-Hamadi A.: 6D rotation representation for unconstrained head pose estimation. arXiv e-prints (2022)
20. Zhi, C., Zong, C., Dong, L., Ying, C.: A vector-based representation to enhance head pose estimation. In: 2021 IEEE Winter Conference on Applications of Computer Vision (WACV), pp. 1187–1196 (2021)
21. Wu, C.Y., Xu, Q., Neumann, U.: Synergy between 3DMM and 3D Landmarks for Accurate 3D Facial Geometry (2021)

22. Soheil, S., Arya, S., Josep, M.P., Federico, T.: On closed-form formulas for the 3-d nearest rotation matrix problem. IEEE Trans. Robotics **36**(4), 1333–1339 (2020)
23. Kendall, A., Cipolla, R., et al.: Geometric loss functions for camera pose regression with deep learning. In: Proceedings CVPR, vol. 3, p. 8 (2017)
24. Li, F.J., Xu, Z.B.: The essential order of approximation for neural networks. Sci. China Ser. F Inf. Sci. **194**(1), 120–127 (2004)
25. Stiefel manifold. https://en.wikipedia.org/wiki/Stiefel_manifold
26. Bloom, D.M.: Linear algebra and geometry. CUP Archive (1979)
27. Rodrigues, O.: Journal de Math'ematiques 5, 380 (1840)
28. Gabriele, F., Matthias, D., Juergen, G., Andrea, F., Luc, V.G.: Random forests for real time 3D face analysis. Int. J. Comput. Vision **101**(3), 437–458 (2013)
29. Christos, S., Georgios, T., Stefanos, Z., Maja, P.: 300 faces in-the-wild challenge: the first facial landmark localization challenge. In: Proceedings of the IEEE International Conference on Computer Vision Workshops, pp. 397–403 (2013)
30. Xiangxin, Z., Deva, R.: Face detection, pose estimation, and landmark localization in the wild. In: 2012 IEEE Conference on Computer Vision and Pattern Recognition, pp. 2879–2886. IEEE (2012)
31. Erjin, Z., Haoqiang, F., Zhimin, C., Yuning, J., Qi, Y.: Extensive facial landmark localization with coarse-to-fine convolutional network cascade. In: Proceedings of the IEEE International Conference on Computer Vision Workshops, pp. 386–391 (2013)
32. Peter, N.B., David, W.J., David, J.K., Neeraj, K.: Localizing parts of faces using a consensus of exemplars. IEEE Trans. Pattern Anal. Mach. Intell. **35**(12), 2930–2940 (2013)
33. Peter, M., Roth, M.K., Paul, W., Horst, B.: Annotated facial landmarks in the wild: a large-scale, real-world database for facial image analysis. In: Proceedings First IEEE International Workshop on Benchmarking Facial Image Analysis Technologies (2011)
34. Kaipeng, Z., Zhanpeng, Z., Zhifeng, L., Yu, Q.: Joint face detection and alignment using multitask cascaded convolutional networks. IEEE Signal Process. Lett. **23**(10), 1499–1503 (2016)
35. Tsun-Yi, Y., Yi-Hsuan, H., Yen-Yu, L., Pi-Cheng, H., Yung-Yu, C.: SSR-Net: a compact soft stagewise regression network for age estimation. In: IJCAI, vol. 5, p. 7 (2018)
36. Bin, H., Renwen, C., Wang, X., Qinbang, Z.: Improving head pose estimation using two-stage ensembles with top-k regression. Image Vis. Comput. **93**, 103827 (2020)
37. Jamie, S., Shaogang, G., Eng-Jon, O.: Understanding pose discrimination in similarity space. In: BMVC, pp. 1–10 (1999)
38. Jeffrey, N., Shaogang, G.: Composite support vector machines for detection of faces across views and pose estimation. Image Vis. Comput. **20**(5–6), 359–368 (2002). https://doi.org/10.1016/S0262-8856(02)00008-2
39. Cai, Q., Gallup, D., Zhang, C., Zhang, Z.: 3D deformable face tracking with a commodity depth camera. In: Daniilidis, K., Maragos, P., Paragios, N. (eds.) ECCV 2010. LNCS, vol. 6313, pp. 229–242. Springer, Heidelberg (2010). https://doi.org/10.1007/978-3-642-15558-1_17
40. Ruigang, Y., Zhengyou, Z.: Model-based head pose tracking with stereo vision. In Proceedings of Fifth IEEE International Conference on Automatic Face Gesture Recognition, pp. 255–260. IEEE (2002)
41. Srinivasan, S., Boyer, K.L.: Head pose estimation using view based eigenspaces. In: Object Recognition Supported by User Interaction for Service Robots, vol. 4, pp. 302–305. IEEE (2002)

Purpose Driven Biological Lawsuit Modeling and Analysis Based on DIKWP

Yingtian Mei[1], Yucong Duan[1(✉)], Lei Yu[2], and Haoyang Che[3]

[1] School of Computer Science and Technology, Hainan University, Haikou, China
duanyucong@hotmail.com
[2] Department of Computer Science, Inner Mongolia University, Hohhot, China
[3] User Digitization Department, Zeekr Group, Hangzhou, China

Abstract. Towards an innovative automatic resolution on disputations involving essentially inconsistent, incomplete, inaccurate, inexpressible resources in biological lawsuits, we propose to integrate the modeling and processing the semantics embodied in the inconsistent, incomplete, inaccurate and inexpressible Data, Information, Knowledge, Wisdom, Purpose (DIKWP) representing the stakeholders' cognitive understandings, uniformly as DIKWP (stakeholder), and the multiple modal documentary content, uniformly as DIKWP (content). We firstly map the content in the sample lawsuit input, transaction, communication and juridical output as DIKWP (content) Graphs including DIKWP Content Graph from the objective material literally. Thereafter we proposed a purpose driven or oriented traversing of the pursues along with reasoning and documenting the subjective DIKWP of the stakeholders as DIKWP (stakeholder) Graphs including DIKWP Cognition Graph. Traversing among DIKWP (content) and DIKWP (stakeholder) based on our proposed Essence Computation and Reasoning, Existence Computation and Reasoning, Purpose Computation and Reasoning allows the integration of the subjective and objective semantics to bridge the gaps leaved by previously processing inconsistent, incomplete, inaccurate, inexpressible resources besides great potential on crossing modals DIKWP validations. Computationally DIKWP promises enhanced understand ability and reduced complexity with shorten cognitive distances and reasoning distances.

Keywords: DIKWP · Purpose driven · Essence computation and reasoning · Existence computation and reasoning · Purpose computation and reasoning · Semantic computation · Biological lawsuit

Supported by Hainan Province Key R&D Project (ZDYF2022GXJS007, ZDYF2022 GXJS010), Hainan Province Key Laboratory of Meteorological Disaster Prevention and Mitigation in the South China Sea, Open Fund Project (SCSF202210) and Hainan Province Higher Education and Teaching Reform Research Project (Hnjg2021ZD-3).

H. Gao et al. (Eds.): CollaborateCom 2022, LNICST 461, pp. 250–267, 2022.
https://doi.org/10.1007/978-3-031-24386-8_14

1   Introduction

Semantics [1] is the essential cognitive content for people to think and communicate using a language composed of conceptual symbols. The cognitive interpretation of finding concepts can be mapped to the existence confirmation, dependency relationship and pattern discovery from Concept Space to Semantic Space. A large number of DIKW resources are gathered in biological legal cases. During the construction and application of DIKW maps, Duan et al. [2] proposed to formalize DIKW elements, and classify content objects and relationships into typed DIKW content with a unified standard. Mapping semantic element entities or relationships in related resources to multimodal conceptual model levels such as DIKW through intent-oriented fusion, experience systemization, and ontology formalization [3].

Current AI solutions lack effective strategies, which can combine machine learning, subjective judgment information, expert knowledge, and smart strategies. Under the background of incomplete data, insufficient information, incomplete knowledge, and unbalanced wisdom strategies, the mixed subjective and objective [4-6] DIKW content faces great challenges in technologies such as interpretable and trusted semantic representation and responsible AI service system construction. Through the interaction and integration of DIKW services, the innovation of concepts, theories and model mechanisms in interdisciplinary fields can be realized. The theoretical basis is the integration, transformation and sharing of DIKW concepts and semantics.

The innovation of DIKW service integration and interaction based on subjective objectification [7,8] helps to solve this series of problems. The difference between relations and entities in the conceptualization process can be revealed through relations or semantics, and can also be used as a basis for distinguishing types of data resources and information resources in subsequent work. Using the Axiom of Consistency of Semantics (CS), Axiom of Conservation of Existence Set (CEX), Axiom of Consistency of Compounded Essential Set (CES), Axiom of Inheritance of Existence Semantics (IHES) and other axiom systems based on Existence Computation and Reasoning (EXCR) [9] and Existence Computation and Reasoning (ESCR) [10] to reveal the semantic space of the points, lines and surfaces of the Euclidean space, and then complete the stipulation proof of the Four Color Theorem [11], Semantic modeling and cognitive reduction analysis of Goldbach's Conjectur [12] and Collatz Conjecture [13]. For large-scale concept-semantic expression fuzzy and mixed semantic content fusion, especially the fusion scene where semantic content is time-sensitive and continuously evolving. Based on the fusion of EXCR exist semantics and cross-DIKW modalities, the Essential Semantic Relationship Defined Everything of Semantics (RDXS) [14,15] is constructed. By associating the EXCR existence semantics of content descriptive and executable contradictory goals with the ESCR essential semantics, DIKW Graphs supports more complete conceptual, semantic modeling and processing [16] of multimodal categories. Based on the EXCR and ESCR mechanisms, the meta-model [17] of DIKW Graphs is designed, which is also applied in intelligent form filling [18], emotional communication [19], Privacy Protection

[20], Internet of Things [21], Cloud Computing [22], Electronic Commerce [23] and so on.

2   Architecture Design

Starting from the natural language of incomplete, imprecise, inconsistent data, information, knowledge and wisdom concepts, semantics. The multi-dimensional, multi-modal, and multi-scale subjective and objective content service interaction expressed in machine language is used to identify the semantics of uncertain concepts, subjective and objective formal modeling, formal expression and value fusion processing, and construct purpose-driven fusion data and information., knowledge and wisdom case modeling and judgment.

There are a large number of relevant Biological Lawsuit Resource (BLRES) on the Internet, but the real and complete resources are always different from individual and local resources. Its specific manifestations are incomplete, inconsistent, inaccurate and inexpressible. We found two paragraphs of text in the network, the first paragraph of text, we deleted it, and got individual local resources. By comparing the two, it is easy to see that there is a huge difference in the meaning of the two sentences. The protagonist of the second paragraph of text has the same name, but does different things. It is not difficult to see that the attributes of the protagonist are different.

Example 1

Complete Resource: There is a group of white animals waiting quietly on the ice surface. Suddenly the group of animals moved **quickly** and rushed towards a certain part of the ice. They move faster than humans and are **not afraid** of the cold. This animal can survive by **reducing** its caloric needs **when food is completely unavailable**. What is a target to identify?

Individual Resource: There is a group of white animals waiting quietly on the ice surface. Suddenly the group of animals moved **slowly** and rushed towards a certain part of the ice. They move faster than humans and are **afraid** of the cold. This animal can survive by **increasing** its caloric needs. What is a target to identify?

Example 2

Role	Text
A	Shylock is mysterious. Initially discovered in February 2011 by security firm, Shylock delivers web injects into victims' browsers and logs keystrokes. Shylock is so contagious that it can be infected by sending a mail. What is Shylock?
B	Shylock is mysterious. In September 2011, Shylock walked to the shop, bought a knife and killed a doctor. He eluded the police for three years by relying on his keen insight. What is Shylock?

The inconsistency, incompleteness, inaccuracy, and inexpressivenes to express the essential data, information, and knowledge between individual resources and complete resources make AI unable to make accurate decisions, and even lead to wrong judgments. Confusion of subjective and objective semantic categories of the subject expression content, insufficient degree of objectification of subjective semantics, lack of semantic correlation, inaccurate semantics, inconsistency of semantics, drift of concept-semantic mapping, redundancy of semantic-concept mapping, etc. Realize the automation of inter-service services and improve the efficiency of intelligent interaction.

From the DIKWP (content) Graphs and the DIKWP (stakeholder) Graphs, the data, information, knowledge, wisdom and purpose mapping of the content involved in the text are carried out, and the recognition result is obtained by driving the Purpose. The Cognition Graph is mainly descriptive content, the Content Graph supports executable processing, and the two graphs can be represented in tabular form.

DIKWP (content) Graphs include Data Content Graph, Information Content Graph, Knowledge Content Graph, Wisdom Content Graph and Purpose Content Graph.

$$DIKWP_{CT} ::= < DG_{CT}, IG_{CT}, KG_{CT}, WG_{CT}, PG_{CT} > \tag{1}$$

DIKWP (stakeholder) Graphs include Data Cognition Graph, Information Cognition Graph, Knowledge Cognition Graph, Wisdom Cognition Graph and Purpose Cognition Graph.

$$DIKWP_{CG} ::= < DG_{CG}, IG_{CG}, KG_{CG}, WG_{CG}, PG_{CG} > \tag{2}$$

Define the text content of Example 1, Example 2A and Example 2B as content(C1), content(C2) and content(C3), respectively, and define user(A) and user(B) for multiple users. For content(C1), content(C2), user(A), user(B), corresponding expressions are:

$$DIKWP_{CT}(C1) ::= < DG_{CT}(C1), IG_{CT}(C1), KG_{CT}(C1), WG_{CT}(C1), PG_{CT}(C1) >$$
$$DIKWP_{CT}(C2) ::= < DG_{CT}(C2), IG_{CT}(C2), KG_{CT}(C2), WG_{CT}(C2), PG_{CT}(C2) >$$
$$DIKWP_{CG}(A) ::= < DG_{CG}(A), IG_{CG}(A), KG_{CG}(A), WG_{CG}(A), PG_{CG}(A) >$$
$$DIKWP_{CG}(B) ::= < DG_{CG}(B), IG_{CG}(B), KG_{CG}(B), WG_{CG}(B), PG_{CG}(B) >$$
$$\tag{3}$$

For the understanding of content(C1) by user(A), the cognitive DIKWP in user(A) is denoted as:

$$DIKWP_{CG}(A(C1)) ::=$$
$$< DG_{CG}(A(C1)), IG_{CG}(A(C1)), KG_{CG}(A(C1)), WG_{CG}(A(C1)), PG_{CG}(A(C1)) > \tag{4}$$

For the understanding of content(C1) by user(B), the cognitive DIKWP in user(B) is denoted as:

$$DIKWP_{CG}(B(C1)) ::=$$
$$< DG_{CG}(B(C1)), IG_{CG}(B(C1)), KG_{CG}(B(C1)), WG_{CG}(B(C1)), PG_{CG}(B(C1)) > \tag{5}$$

The final combined DIKWP of semantics, denoted as DIKWP (semantic (stakeholder, content)), is the integration of objective DIKWP (content) and subjective cognitive DIKWP (stakeholder).

$$DIKWP_S ::= < DG_S, KG_S, KG_S, WG_S, PG_S >$$
$$DIKWPS$$
$$::= DIKWPCT + DIKWPCG$$
$$::= < DG_{CT}, IG_{CT}, KG_{CT}, WG_{CT}, PG_{CT} > + \tag{6}$$
$$< DG_{CG}, IG_{CG}, KG_{CG}, WG_{CG}, PG_{CG} >$$
$$::= < (DG_{CT} + DG_{CG}), (IG_{CT} + IG_{CG}), (KG_{CT} + KG_{CG}),$$
$$(WG_{CT} + WG_{CG}), (PG_{CT} + PG_{CG}) >$$

For the understanding of content(C1) by user(A), the final combined semantic DIKWP is denoted as:

$$DIKWP_S(A(C1))$$
$$::= DIKWP_{CT}(C1) + DIKWP_{CG}(A(C1))$$
$$::= < DG_S(A(C1)), IG_S(A(C1)), KG_S(A(C1)), WG_S(A(C1)), PG_S(A(C1)) >$$
$$::= < (DG_{CT}(A(C1)) + DG_{CG}(C1)),$$
$$(IG_{CT}(A(C1)) + IG_{CG}(C1)), (KG_{CT}(A(C1)) + KG_{CG}(C1),$$
$$(WG_{CT}(A(C1)) + WG_{CG}(C2)), (PG_{CT}(A(C1)) + PG_{CG}(C1)) > \tag{7}$$

For the understanding of content(C1) by user(B), the final combined semantic DIKWP is denoted as:

$$DIKWP_S(B(C1))$$
$$::= DIKWP_{CT}(C1) + DIKWP_{CG}(B(C1))$$
$$::= < DG_S(B(C1)), IG_S(B(C1)), KG_S(B(C1)), WG_S(B(C1)), PG_S(B(C1)) >$$
$$::= < (DG_{CT}(B(C1)) + DG_{CG}(C1)), \tag{8}$$
$$(IG_{CT}(B(C1)) + IG_{CG}(C1)), (KG_{CT}(B(C1)) + KG_{CG}(C1)),$$
$$(WG_{CT}(B(C1)) + WG_{CG}(C1)), (PG_{CT}(B(C1)) + PG_{CG}(C1)) >$$

3   Resource Mapping

Taking the complete resource as an example, it is divided according to the part of speech, and the specific meaning is mapped to the data resource, such as noun, number, time, etc. Mappings that contain some kind of information into information resources, for example, verbs, adjectives, etc. Combined with context semantic structure, as well as data resources and information resources, knowledge resources are derived. According to the semantic structure expressed by the context in the paragraph, the observed relationship, and combined with the data, information, and knowledge resources, the purpose resources are obtained. Wisdom resources are stored in the form of a value system, and it is necessary to judge the feasibility of intentions through the value system.

Complete Resource

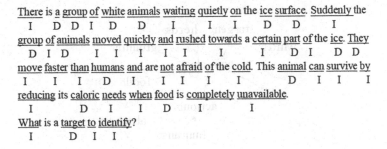

Map resources to corresponding data, information, knowledge, wisdom, and purpose as shown in Table 1.

Table 1. Partial resource mapping

D	I	K	W	P
target	here	$no(food) \rightarrow$	animal,	$what(target)$
a	of	$reducing(caloric)$	survivable	survive
group	waiting	$\rightarrow survive$		
white	quietly			
animals	on			
ice	suddenly			
surface	moves			
they	quickly			
humans	and			
caloric	rushed			
part	towards			

3.1 Data Mapping

The nodes of the data graph are connected by time sequence, concept and semantic relationship to form a connected structure. Part of the data further forms a topological structure through the partial order relationship. Topological structure is represented by physical connections on the graph, and its specific meaning will change due to different partial order relationships, such as ring topology, tree topology and other structures. Using the joint structure and topological structure in the graph can well represent and calculate the relationship between the data, such as in-out degree, distance, frequency weight, etc.

Data Content Graph

The way the content data model is handled is defined based on dimensions and frequency. We map the text from Example 1 to the data resource to get the Data Content Graph, as shown in Fig. 1.

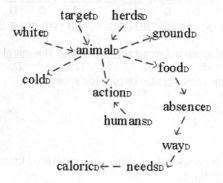

Fig. 1. Data content graph-Example 1

We map the A and B fragments of Example 2 to the data resources to obtain the Data Content Graph, as shown in Fig. 2.

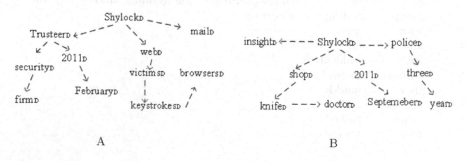

Fig. 2. Data content graph-Example 2

Data Cognition Graph

Data Cognition Graph is the cognition of concepts and the processing of probability. Different people in Example 1 have different Cognition Graph. Assuming three bodies user(A), user(B), and user(C), combined with the white, animal, and ground nodes of the Data Content Graph, user(A) will think that the white land animals may be white swans, white cows, white sheep, white horses, arctic wolves, and user(B) will think they may be white cows, white sheep, white horse, polar bear, and user(C) will think it is white cow, white sheep, white horse, arctic wolf, polar bear, then the corresponding Data Cognition Graph is shown in the Fig. 3.

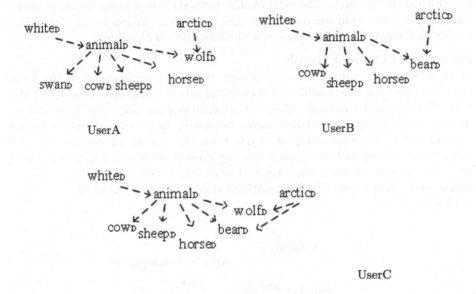

Fig. 3. Data cognition graph-Example 1

According to the Data Content Graph of the two fragments in Example 2, the Shylock node of the A text fragment is directly connected to the web node, and indirectly connected to the security and firm nodes, and the Shylock node of the B text fragment is directly or indirectly connected to the nodes such as police, shop, and insight. Suppose that if Shylock of Example 2 is a person, it is a character in Shakespeare, and it is the protagonist of the detective Sherlock. If it is an item, it can be something, and if it is a virtual item, it can be a virus. The Data Cognition Graph is shown in the Fig. 4.

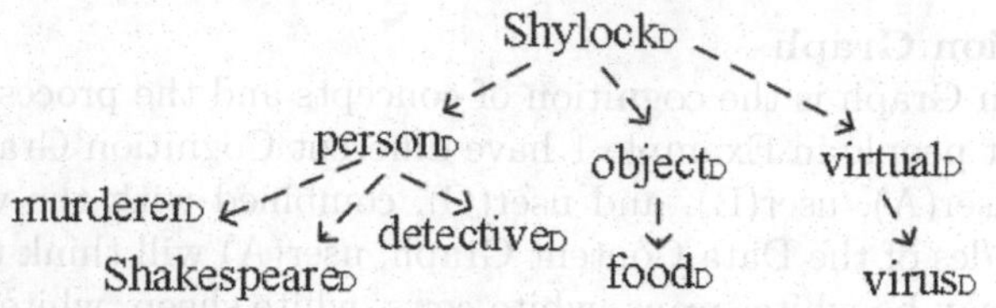

Shylock_D

person_D   object_D   virtual_D

murderer_D   detective_D   food_D   virus_D

Shakespeare_D

Fig. 4. Data cognition graph-Example 2

3.2 Information Mapping

In information resources, the relationship between information, in addition to the general connection method, some also need to be linked across data. The content information model exists in a partial order relationship.

Information Content Graph

In traditional text information extraction, it is often represented in the form of triples, and the relationship between entities is determined according to the text. This method can easily filter out some important data and information, resulting in incomplete and inaccurate resources, and even expressing wrong meanings. Our resource mapping starts from the essence of various types of resources, and does not easily filter out any type of resources. The five types of resources have a certain connection with each other, and this connection is not extracted from the text. The Information Content Graph of Example 1 is shown in the Fig. 5.

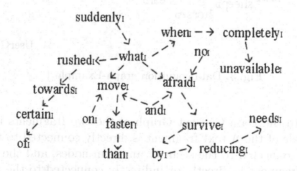

Fig. 5. Information content graph-Example 1

The Information Content Graph is obtained from the two paragraphs of text mapping information resources in Example 2 (Fig. 6).

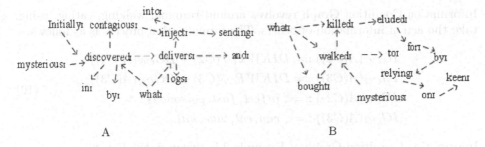

A   B

Fig. 6. Information content graph-Example 2

Information Cognition Graph

Example 1 according to human cognition, combined with text, determine the semantic map of information cognition. The animal node in the data cognition graph, combined with the action, cold nodes, and cognition in the content data graph, can obtain the Information Cognition Graph node fast and ice node, thereby obtaining nodes such as move, walk, run, and immediately.

$$IG_{CG}(A(C1)) ::= DIKWP_{CT}(C1) + DG_{CT}(A(C1))$$
$$IG_{CG}(A(C1)) ::=< move, run, walk, fast.. >$$

(9)

Information Cognition Graph of Example 1 is shown in the Fig. 7.

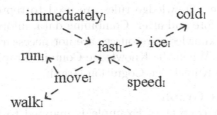

Fig. 7. Information cognition graph-Example 1

The protagonists of the two fragments in Example 2 have the same name, but they express different things. Combined with our cognition, they form different information cognitive semantic models.

According to the Shylock, security, web nodes in the content data graph of segment A, the virtual and virus nodes in the data cognitive semantic graph, and the contagious, inject, and into nodes in the content information graph, it can be seen that the Information Cognition Graph revolves around infection, fast, spread and other information.

The Shylock, shop, knife, doctor nodes in the Data Content Graph of segment B, the person node in the data cognitive semantic graph, and the walk, kill and other nodes in the Information Content Graph, it can be seen that the

Information Cognition Graph revolves around running, walking, eating, using, take the action information of others. The formalization process is as follows.

$$IG_{CG}(A(C2)) ::= DIKWP_{CT}(C2) + DG_{CG}(A(C2))$$
$$IG_{CG}(A(C3)) ::= DIKWP_{CT}(C3) + DG_{CG}(A(C3))$$
$$IG_{CG}(A(C2)) ::=< infect, fast, poisonous.. >$$
$$IG_{CG}(A(C3)) ::=< run, eat, take, kill... >$$

(10)

Information Cognition Graph of Example 2 is shown in the Fig. 8.

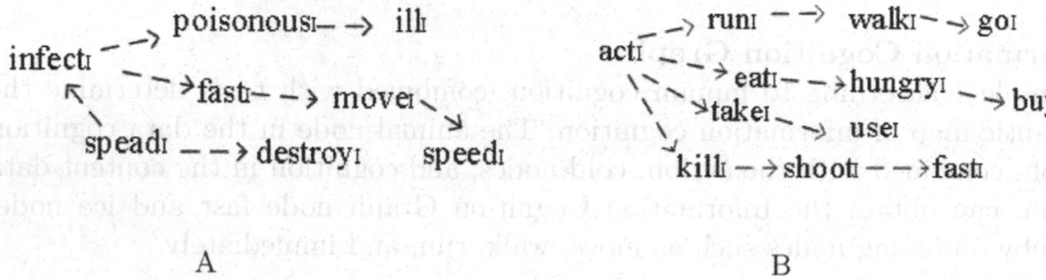

Fig. 8. Information cognition graph-Example 2

3.3   Knowledge Mapping

In knowledge resources, knowledge rules are used to represent, and there is a logical relationship before and after. Combining data, information resources and context, the deduced knowledge resources are not necessarily correct, and some of them are unproven. When the Knowledge Content Graph cannot handle it, it can be filled from the Knowledge Cognition Graph.

Knowledge Content Graph

According to the text content of Example 1, mapped to knowledge resources, the Knowledge Content that can be obtained is as follows, indicating that in the absence of food, it is possible to survive by reducing calories (Table 2).

Table 2. Knowledge content-Example 1

	Knowledge content
K	$no(food) \rightarrow reducing(caloric) \rightarrow survive$

The content of the two fragments of Shylock in Example 2 is mapped to its knowledge resources respectively, and the Knowledge Content table is obtained (Table 3).

Table 3. Knowledge content-Example 2

	A	B
K	$and(contagious(Shylock),$ $sending(mail))$ $\rightarrow infect(Shylock)$	$and(killed(doctor),$ $relying(keen(insight)))$ $\rightarrow for(eluded(police), threeyears)$

Knowledge Cognition Graph

Combining Data, Information Cognition Graph, and related text, on the basis of personal cognition, the Knowledge Cognition Graph is obtained. In Example 1, user(A), user(B), user(C) three objects have different Knowledge Cognition Graph. For example, the white, animal, and ground nodes in the Data Content Graph of user(A), the arctic and wolf nodes in the Data Cognition Graph, the move, fast and other nodes in the Information Content Graph, and the move, run, and fast nodes in the Information Cognition Graph, combined with recognition, get K_1, and so on. The Knowledge Cognition table is shown in Table 4, and the analysis is as follows.

$$KG_{CG}(A(C1)) ::= DIKWP_{CT}(C1) + DG_{CG}(A(C1)) + IG_{CG}(A(C1))$$
$$KG_{CG}(B(C1)) ::= DIKWP_{CT}(C1) + DG_{CG}(B(C1)) + IG_{CG}(B(C1)) \quad (11)$$
$$KG_{CG}(C(C1)) ::= DIKWP_{CT}(C1) + DG_{CG}(C(C1)) + IG_{CG}(C(C1))$$

Table 4. Knowledge cognition-Example 1

	Knowledge cognition	Meaning
K(user(A))	$speed(arctic\ wolf) \rightarrow up(65\,km/h)$	Arctic wolves can run as fast as 65 km/h.
	$sheep \rightarrow noafraid(cold)$	Sheep are not afraid of cold.
	$speed(Sam) \rightarrow run(15\,min, 5\,km)$	Sam ran the 5 km half marathon in 15 min
	$arctic\ wolf \rightarrow stored(food)$	Arctic wolves can store food
K(user(B))	$speed(arctic\ bear) \rightarrow up(60km/h)$	Arctic bears can run as fast as 60 km/h.
	$arctic\ bear \rightarrow stored(food)$	Arctic bears can store food.
	$arctic\ bear \rightarrow reducing(caloric)$ $\rightarrow survive$	Arctic bears can survive by cutting calories minutes
	$speed(Bolt, Olympic)$ $\rightarrow run(9.58\,s, 100\,m)$	Bolt, who ran the 100-meter dash with a world record of 9.58 s at the 2008 Beijing Summer Olympics
K(user(C))	$arctic\ bear \rightarrow noafraid(cold)$	Arctic bears are not afraid of cold
	$speed(arctic\ bear) \rightarrow up(60\,km/h)$	Arctic bears can run as fast as 60 km/h
	$arctic\ bear \rightarrow reducing(caloric)$ $\rightarrow survive$	Arctic bears can survive by cutting calories minutes
	$arctic\ wolf \rightarrow stored(food)$	Arctic wolves can store food

In the cognitive, the Data Content Graph nodes security, firm, Trusteer, victims, browsers, keystrokes in the A segment of Example 2, and the Information Content Graph nodes contagious, inject, inject and other resources, we know that Shylock may be a virus. In segment B, the Data Content Graph nodes shop, knife, doctor and the Information Content Graph nodes walked, bought, kill and other resources indicate that Shylock may be a murderer. The Knowledge Cognition table is shown in Table 5.

Table 5. Knowledge cognition-Example 2

	A	B
K	$and(Shylock, infect(victims, browser))$ $\rightarrow is(Shylock, virus)$	$kill(Shylock, doctor))$ $\rightarrow is(Shylock, murderer)$

3.4   Purpose Mapping

In the purpose resource, purpose can be divided into main purpose and sub-purpose according to the fineness. Different purpose maps obtained by the same main purpose will have different effects on the establishment of the model due to the difference in content bias and dominant type.

Purpose Content Graph
According to the text content of Example 1 and Example 2, it is mapped to the purpose resource, and the Purpose Content that can be obtained is as follows (Table 6).

Table 6. Purpose content

	Example 1	Example 2
P_1	$what(target)$	$what(Shylock)$
P_2	$survive$	

Purpose Cognition Graph
In cognition, the purpose of animals is observed, and the purpose is not consistent in different fields. For example, in the classroom, Purpose Cognition is learning. In recessive activities, Purpose Cognition may be a game. From the perspective of teachers, individual Purpose Cognition may be education. The Purpose Cognition table for Example 1 is as follows (Table 7).

Table 7. Purpose cognition-Example 1

	Purpose cognition
P_1	$what(target)$
P_2	$study(knowledge)$
P_3	$play(game)$
P_4	$educate(student)$

In Example 2, the content intent in segment A is what Shylock is, combined with Data Content Graph nodes security, victims, etc., Information Content Graph nodes what, inject, etc. According to Knowledge Cognition Graph nodes, we know that Shylock is a virus. Integrating our cognition, the purpose can be to benefit from viruses, obtain personal information, and obtain bank card passwords. The partial order relationship between them is more beneficial than personal information is greater than passwords. The Purpose Content in segment B is what Shylock is, combined with Data Content Graph nodes shop, knife, doctor, etc., Information Content Graph nodes walk, kill, etc. According to Knowledge Cognition Graph node, we know that Shylock is a murderer. Combining our cognition, purpose can be manslaughter or intentional homicide. Combined with the content of the acquired resources, the partial order relationship between intentional homicide is greater than that of negligent homicide. The Purpose Cognition table for Example 2 is as follows (Table 8).

Table 8. Purpose cognition-Example 2

	A	B
P_1	$get(benefit)$	$intentional(homicide)$
P_2	$get(information)$	$negligent(homicide)$
P_3	$get(password)$	

3.5 Wisdom Mapping

Wisdom resources are mainly constructed according to the value model. After the system obtains the purpose, it needs to judge the feasibility of the purpose through the value model. The two-tuple (type, extreme value) corresponding to the boundary of a specific goal is set to represent the wisdom resource.

Wisdom Content Graph
Combined with the text of Example 1, animals can survive by reducing their own calories without food, indicating that the animal has a high survival rate. The Wisdom Content of Example 1 is as follows (Table 9).

Table 9. Wisdom content-Example 1

	Wisdom content
W	animal, survivable

Wisdom Cognition Graph

In cognition, for example, entrepreneurs value efficiency more and consider economic contribution more important, while philanthropists place more value on reputation and consider individual happiness more important than contribution. In Example 1, different people have different perceptions. For example, businessmen value economic value, but scientists think it has research value. The Wisdom Cognition Graph is shown in the figure below (Fig. 9).

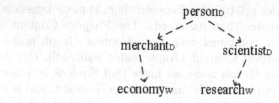

Fig. 9. Wisdom cognition graph-Example 1

In Example 2, text A is in cognition, combined with Knowledge Cognition Graph, Shylock is fast and has high commercial value, while text B is in cognition, Shylock is too cruel. The Wisdom Cognition in Example 2 is as follows (Table 10).

Table 10. Wisdom cognition-Example 2

	A	B
W_1	Shylock, fast	business, high
W_2	business, high	

3.6   Purpose Driven Processing

In Example 1, according to the purpose input (target), the output (animal) is obtained by combining Data Graph, Information Graph, Knowledge Graph or DIKW derivation. user(A), user(B) and user(C) draw different conclusions under different Cognition Graph. It is necessary to find the output results that satisfy the intention in the existing cognitive system. When data, information, knowledge, and wisdom are inconsistent, incomplete, inaccurate and inexpressible, the conclusions drawn directly affect judgment. For example, the individual resource in Example 1. The formal analysis process of user(A), user(B) and user(C) is as follows.

Example 1

$$user(A)$$
$$INPUT: what(target), DIKWP_S(A(C1))$$
$$OUTPUT: arctic\ wolf$$

$$user(B)$$
$$INPUT: what(target), DIKWP_S(B(C1)) \hspace{2cm} (12)$$
$$OUTPUT: arctic\ bear$$

$$user(C)$$
$$INPUT: what(target), DIKWP_S(C(C1))$$
$$OUTPUT: arctic\ bear$$

In Example 2, although the protagonists of both A and B are Shylock, they are actually saying different things. This conclusion is also drawn through content data, information, knowledge, wisdom and its cognitive semantics. The specific formal analysis process is as follows.

Example 2

$$Fragment\ A$$
$$INPUT: what(Shylock), DIKWP_S(A(C2))$$
$$OUTPUT: is(Shylock, virus)$$

$$(13)$$

$$Fragment\ B$$
$$INPUT: what(Shylock), DIKWP_S(A(C3))$$
$$OUTPUT: is(Shylock, person)$$

Different people have different cognitions and different judgment results for the same affairs. The same person has different judgment results for different affairs. So in the context of incompleteness, inconsistency, inaccuracy, and inexpressibility, the results are also incomplete, inconsistent, imprecise, and inexpressible. The difference between the cognitive understandings of content(C1) by user(A) and user(B) is as follows.

$$DIFF(DIKWP_{CG}((user(A), user(B)), content(C1)))$$
$$::= DIKWP_{CG}(A(C1)) - DIKWP_{CG}(B(C1)) \hspace{1cm} (14)$$

The difference between the understood semantics of content(C1) by user(A) and user(B) is as follows.

$$DIFF(DIKWP_S((user(A), user(B)), content(C1)))$$
$$::= DIKWP_S(A(C1)) - DIKWP_S(B(C1))$$
$$::= (DIKWP_{CT}(C1) + DIKWP_{CG}(A(C1))) \tag{15}$$
$$- (DIKWP_{CT}(C1) + DIKWP_{CG}(B(C1)))$$

4   Conclusion

We map the objective materials in biological legal cases to the Data Content graph, Information Content Graph, Knowledge Content Graph, Wisdom Content Graph and Purpose Content Graph. Combine the Cognition of stakeholders to form Data Cognition Graph, Information Cognition Graph, Knowledge Cognition Graph, Wisdom Cognition Graph and Purpose Cognition Graph. Traversing among DIKWP (content) and DIKWP (stakeholder) based on our proposed Essence Computation and Reasoning, Existence Computation and Reasoning and Purpose Computation and Reasoning allows the unprecedented integration of the subjective and objective semantics to bridge the gaps leaved by previously processing inconsistent, incomplete, inaccurate and inexpressible resources besides great potential on crossing modals DIKWP validations. The model uses DIKWP modal transformation for shortening the cognitive and computational reasoning distance between problem input and processed result, thus reducing the errors caused by incomplete, inconsistent, inaccurate and inexpressible resources input.

References

1. Millikan, R.G.: Varieties of Meaning. Studies in Cognitive Systems, pp. 287–326 (2004)
2. Duan, Y., Zhan, L., Zhang, X., Zhang, Y.: Formalizing DIKW architecture for modeling security and privacy as typed resources. In: Gao, H., Yin, Y., Yang, X., Miao, H. (eds.) TridentCom 2018. LNICST, vol. 270, pp. 157–168. Springer, Cham (2019). https://doi.org/10.1007/978-3-030-12971-2_10
3. Duan, Y.: Towards a periodic table of conceptualization and formalization on state, style, structure, pattern, framework, architecture, service and so on. In: SNPD 2019, pp. 133–138 (2019). https://doi.org/10.1109/SNPD.2019.8935653
4. Duan, Y.: The end of Objective mathematics as a return to Subjective, February 2022. https://doi.org/10.13140/RG.2.2.36171.87841
5. Duan, Y., Cruz, C., Nicolle, C.: Identifying objective true/false from subjective yes/no semantic based on OWA and CWA. J. Comput. **8**(7), 1847–1852 (2013)
6. Duan, Y.: Research Proposal on Purpose/Intention Driven Objectification of Subjective Content, August 2022. https://doi.org/10.13140/RG.2.2.24622.38720
7. Benjamin, J.: An outline of intersubjectivity: the development of recognition. Psychoanal. Psychol. **7**(S), 33 (1990)

8. Saini, A.: Want to do better science? Admit you're not objective. Nature **579**(7798), 175–175 (2020)
9. Duan, Y.: Applications of relationship defined everything of semantics on existence computation. In: 2019 20th IEEE/ACIS International Conference on Software Engineering, Artificial Intelligence, Networking and Parallel/Distributed Computing (2019)
10. Duan, Y.: Existence Computation and Reasoning (EXCR) and Essence Computation and Reasoning (ESCR) based revelation of the semantics of point, line and plane, February 2022. https://doi.org/10.13140/RG.2.2.32383.89767
11. Duan, Y.: A constructive semantics revelation for applying the four color problem on modeling. In: 2010 Second International Conference on Computer Modeling and Simulation, Sanya, pp. 146–150. IEEE (2010). https://doi.org/10.1109/ICCMS.2010.113
12. Duan, Y., Shao, L., Hu, G.: Specifying knowledge graph with data graph, information graph, knowledge graph, and wisdom graph. Int. J. Softw. Innov. (IJSI) **6**(2), 10–25 (2018)
13. Duan, Y.: A stochastic revelation on the deterministic morphological change of 3x+1. In: SERA 2017, London, pp. 333–338. IEEE (2017). https://doi.org/10.1109/SERA.2017.7965748
14. Duan, Y.: Existence computation: revelation on entity vs. relationship for relationship defined everything of semantics. In: SNPD 2019, pp. 139–144 (2019). https://doi.org/10.1109/SNPD.2019.8935728
15. Duan, Y.: Applications of relationship defined everything of semantics on existence computation. In: SNPD 2019, pp. 184–189 (2019). https://doi.org/10.1109/SNPD.2019.8935701
16. Duan, Y., Cruz, C.: formalizing semantic of natural language through conceptualization from existence. Int. J. Innov. Manag. Technol. **2**(1), 37–42 (2011)
17. Duan, Y., Sun, X., Che, H., et al.: Modeling data, information and knowledge for security protection of hybrid IoT and edge resources. IEEE Access **7**, 99161–99176 (2019)
18. Huang, Y., Duan, Y.: Towards purpose driven content interaction modeling and processing based on DIKW. In: 2021 IEEE World Congress on Services (SERVICES), pp. 27–32 (2021). https://doi.org/10.1109/SERVICES51467.2021.00032
19. Hu, T., Duan Y.: Modeling and measuring for emotion communication based on DIKW. In: 2021 IEEE World Congress on Services (SERVICES), pp. 21–26 (2021). https://doi.org/10.1109/SERVICES51467.2021.00031
20. Duan, Y., Lu, Z., Zhou, Z., et al.: Data privacy protection for edge computing of smart city in a DIKW architecture. Eng. Appl. Artif. Intell. **81**, 323–335 (2019)
21. Gao, H., Duan, Y., Shao, L., et al.: Transformation-based processing of typed resources for multimedia sources in the IoT environment. Wireless Netw. **27**(5), 3377–3393 (2021)
22. Song, Z., Duan, Y., Wan, S., et al.: Processing optimization of typed resources with synchronized storage and computation adaptation in fog computing. Wirel. Commun. Mob. Comput. 1–13 (2018)
23. Gao, H., Huang, W., Duan, Y.: The cloud-edge-based dynamic reconfiguration to service workflow for mobile ecommerce environments: a QoS prediction perspective. ACM Trans. Internet Technol. (TOIT) **21**(1), 1–23 (2021)

Research on Depth-Adaptive Dual-Arm Collaborative Grasping Method

Hao Zhang[1], Pengfei Yi[1], Rui Liu[1], Jing Dong[1], Qiang Zhang[1,2],
and Dongsheng Zhou[1,2(✉)]

[1] The Key Laboratory of Advanced Design and Intelligent Computing,
Ministry of Education, School of Software Engineering, Dalian University,
Dalian, People's Republic of China
zhouds@dlu.edu.cn
[2] School of Computer Scicence and Technoloy, Dalian University of Technology,
Dalian, People's Republic of China

Abstract. Among the existing dual-arm cooperative grasping methods,
the dual-arm cooperative grasping method based on RGB camera is the
mainstream intelligent method. However, these methods often require
predefined depth, difficult to adapt to changes in depth without modification. To solve this problem, this paper proposes a dual-arm cooperative grasping method based on RGB camera, which is suitable for scenes
with variable depth, to increase the adaptability of dual-arm cooperation. Firstly, we build a mathematical model based on RGB camera,
and use the markers attached to the target to obtain the depth information of the target. Then the 3D pose of the target under the robot
world coordinate system is obtained by combining the depth information and pixel information. Finally, the task is assigned to the left and
right robotic arms, and the target grabbing task is realized based on the
main-auxiliary control. The proposed approach is validated in multiple
experiments on a Baxter robot under different conditions.

Keywords: Dual-arm collaboration · Target localization · Robotics

1 Introduction

The dual-arm collaboration [15,21] is an important part of the robotics field.
Since some tasks will exceed the capabilities of a single robotic arm, dual-arm are
required to cooperate and can be used in various tasks. For example, it is used to
automated minimally invasive suturing [27], sorting of surgical instruments [23],
harvesting of aubergine [19], as well as performing high-precision tasks [20]. It can
also perform grasping and placing tasks that are laborious for human workers,
non-fixed-point grasp to achieve autonomous assembly tasks and improve work
efficiency by working with dual-arm.

Existing dual-arm collaboration methods still have some limitations. Using
predefined paths and manual intervention methods to complete collaborative

H. Gao et al. (Eds.): CollaborateCom 2022, LNICST 461, pp. 268–285, 2022.
https://doi.org/10.1007/978-3-031-24386-8_15

tasks with a fixed target pose or by manipulating the arms in real time is not very intelligent. With the development of computer vision, a vision-guided dual-arm collaborative approach has emerged. Compared with the above methods, this method has higher intelligence and can estimate the pose information of the target through visual information when the depth information is known. Most of these methods use a fixed depth scene. However, when the depth is not fixed, these methods often resort to additional depth cameras to acquire the target's pose. This approach increases the cost of use while making deployment and integration more difficult.

Aiming at the limitation of the dual-arm cooperative method when the depth is variable, in order to improve the adaptability of the dual-arm cooperative grasping method based on the RGB camera, this paper proposes a dual-arm cooperative grasping method that only relies on the RGB camera. This method can be applied to scenes with varying depths. Depth information is lost when only RGB cameras are used, and depth information is difficult to obtain due to the lack of a known standard to measure depth changes. Inspired by the single-arm approach to grasping objects, we use mathematical modeling to obtain a deep informative model. Then the depth value is obtained from the depth information model and combined with the image information to estimate the position and pose information of the target. Finally, the target is grasped through the cooperation of the dual-arm. The main work of this paper is as follows:

- In this paper, we propose a dual-arm collaborative grasp method based on RGB cameras to obtain depth information through the established mathematical model, without relying on additional devices such as depth cameras.
- We propose a target position localization method based on a monocular RGB camera and a method to estimate the target pose from image information.
- We designed a dual-arm collaborative control strategy based on main-auxiliary control. It can steadily control the dual-arm to collaboratively grasp the target object.

2   Related Work

In industrial production, dual-arm achieve collaborative tasks by means of pre-defined paths, such as completing the board burr removal [16]. The advantage of this method is that it is more efficient, it can achieve interruption-free work, and can meet the production requirements, which plays an important role in industrial production. However, the robot performs repetitive operations, the arms cannot be flexibly adjusted. In addition, dual-arm collaboration methods are broadly classified into human intervention-based dual-arm collaboration and computer vision-based dual-arm collaboration. In the following, we will first introduce the human intervention-based and computer vision-based methods. Since there are many common problems in single-arm grasping and dual-arm grasping, the idea of single-arm grasping method to solve the problem is very worthy of reference. Then we will introduce the methods related to single-arm grasping. The introductions are respectively as follows.

2.1 Dual-Arm Collaboration Based on Human Intervention

Liang et al. [9] proposed a bilateral teleoperating system, where the operator can control the 6DOF pose and gripper width of each arm through an intuitive bilateral manipulator. Using the double-sided manipulator, the operation of the robotic arms on both sides is independent and does not affect each other, which is convenient for control. Tung et al. [22] proposed a method for remotely controlling robotic arm collaboration. Multiple users in different locations use mobile phones to control the robot arms. Since the delay of each user's network connection is different, it is adopted to wait for all mobile phone connections to receive new mobile phone information, and then start all robotic arms to ensure the coordination of multiple robotic arms. Laghi et al. [8] presented an alternative method for remotely manipulating robots. Not only independent control can be achieved, but also shared control can be achieved. Lipton et al. [10] proposed a method to control a dual-arm robot through a VR device, and the user could control the robot remotely. Bai et al. [1] presented a strategy of the dual-arm coordinated control for twisting manipulation. One of the robotic arms is controlled through predefined planning. The operator observes through the camera and controls the other arm in real time via teleoperation to complete the dual-arm collaboration.

Yu et al. [25] proposed a cooperative control strategy. The operator operates the master arm movement and returns the movement information of the master arm to the control terminal, and the control terminal controls the slave robot arm movement based on this information to achieve the effect that the slave arm follows the master arm movement. Ibarguren et al. [6] proposed a trajectory-driven cooperative task execution architecture. When the operator guides the robot, it follows a given trajectory to move smoothly. And impedance control is added to allow the operator to adjust the path.

2.2 Dual-Arm Collaboration Based on Computer Vision

Rastegarpanah et al. [17] described the realization of different grasping tasks based on computer vision. Firstly, by controlling the motion of the main arm, the double-arm operation is realized based on the method of motion tracking. The target is then grasped using the dual arms cooperatively based on a fixed depth and moved along a defined path. Medjram et al. [13] proposed a vision-based method for estimating the pose of a carton using edge features and perspective methods. Grasp point information is obtained by using a depth camera and modeling perspective changes. Zahavi et al. [26] presented use of dual-arm to perform pick and place tasks while using a single overhead camera system. It is used to detect and grasp the areas on both sides of the industrial robot, and classify it and place them in a specified location. The implemented machine visual algorithm can identify the color and shape of the target.

2.3   Single-Arm Based Grasping Methods

Yang et al. [24] presented a single-arm target grasping method, which can quickly recognize the attribute information of the object and complete the grasping. Griffin et al. [5] designed a framework to extract the pixel information of the target through video object segmentation technology, and calculate the depth value of the target through RGB camera motion, and then perform a single-arm grasp operation on the target. Lundell et al. [12] presented a top grasp planning method, in dense sampling of the scene, the grasp directions are selected from directly above the target and from five oblique angle positions, which utilize markers for position calibration. Du et al. [3] summarized the robot grasping method based on computer vision. It is divided into three parts, including the target positioning method, the target attitude estimation method, and the target grasping estimation method. Cai et al. [2] presented a grasp training system. The system can select the correct grab target according to the defined correction strategy.

In summary, the method based on predefined paths has stricter requirements for target position and lower ability to adapt to changes. The human intervention-based method has a high operator dependence, when operators become insufficient concentration during prolonged operations, this can lead to unnecessary hazards. The dual-arm collaborative method based on RGB camera has high intelligence, but there is difficulty in handling depth changes. To improve this situation, inspired by the single-arm grasping target methods. Firstly, we estimate the depth information based on the RGB camera using visual information combined with markers of known width. And the estimated depth information is calibrated by the established depth information model to obtain a more accurate depth value. Then the position and pose of the target are calculated based on the depth information. Finally, a dual-arm collaborative grasping of the target object is achieved based on the main-auxiliary control strategies.

3   Methods

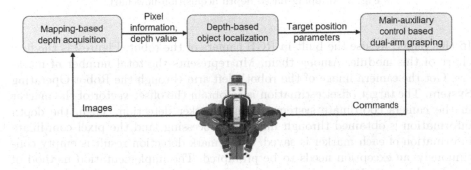

Fig. 1. Overview of the method.

This paper proposes a dual-arm cooperative grasping method suitable for depth-variable scenes. Based on the RGB camera, the dual-arm cooperate to grasp targets of different depths and different poses. The method is implemented as follows (see Fig. 1): the robot obtains the image of the workspace (with known internal parameters) through the left arm camera. The depth information of the target is first obtained through the generated mapping model. Then the target is located based on the depth information and pixel coordinate information to obtain the 3D positional parameters of the target. Finally, based on the main-auxiliary control, control commands are sent to both robot arms to realize collaborative grasp by dual-arm.

3.1   Mapping-Based Depth Acquisition

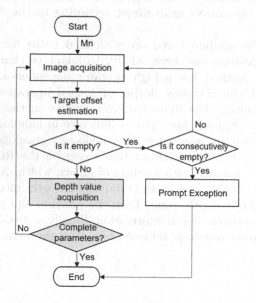

Fig. 2. Mapping-based depth acquisition flowchart.

In this paper, we use the built-in RGB camera of the robot. Figure 2 is the flow chart of this module. Among them, Mn represents the total number of markers. Get the camera image of the robot's left arm through the Robot Operating System. The target offset estimation is to obtain the offset vector of the marker in the camera coordinate system through marker detection. Then, the depth information is obtained through mapping processing, and the pixel coordinate information of each marker is saved. If the mark detection result is empty continuously, an exception needs to be prompted. The implementation method of depth value acquisition and parameter integrity judgment is described below.

Depth Value Acquisition. Obtaining accurate depth information is mission-critical. This paper uses the offset of the marker with respect to the Z axis of the left-arm camera coordinate system as approximate depth information. And the steps of first reducing volatility of depth information and then increasing accuracy are used to obtain more accurate depth values.

In order to obtain a more stable depth value, the mean method is used to reduce the volatility, and the sample mean S_a is calculated as shown in Eq. 1.

$$S_a = (\sum_{m=0}^{n} val_n)/(n+1) \tag{1}$$

where m is the counter, n is the set threshold, and val is the Z-axis offset of the marker in the camera coordinate system. When a marker information is detected in a frame of image, the value of the counter m is incremented by one, and the val is accumulated and stored in the sum. If a frame of pictures is invalid, the values of m and sum will not be changed. When the counter reaches the threshold, record S_a as the sample value, then set both m and sum to zero.

In order to obtain a more accurate depth value, the real depth is changed according to a certain rule, and a sample value corresponding to the depth value is collected. There is a certain difference between the sample value and the real value. Since the fluctuation of the sample value is reduced by Eq. 1 processing, the sample value under the same depth value is relatively stable. The corresponding relationship model is obtained by curve fitting the collected multiple sets of sample values and the real depth values. $f_d(S_a)$ represents the relationship between the depth value and the sample mean.

$$f_d(S_a) = p_1 \cdot (S_a)^3 + p_2 \cdot (S_a)^2 + p_3 \cdot (S_a) + p_4 \tag{2}$$

where S_a denotes the sample mean and p_1, p_2, p_3, p_4 are the coefficients. The mean value S_a is re-acquired as an independent variable, and the depth information d is obtained through relational model processing.

In the subsequent calculation of the 3D pose of the target, depth information and pixel information need to be used. The pixel information of the complete grab point needs to be saved here. As in the marker detection, there is a failure to detect all markers. In order to ensure the completeness of parameters, we create a parameter judger (P_J) to solve the problem of incomplete parameters, and the expression is as follows.

$$P_J = \begin{cases} 1, \forall m_i \neq 0 \\ 0, otherwise \end{cases} \tag{3}$$

where m_i represents the element in the parameter vector M, and the parameter vector M is input into the parameter judger. When P_J returns 1, it means that the parameters are complete, and when it returns 0, it means that the parameters are missing, and the image needs to be re-acquired, and the detection is performed until the complete parameters are obtained.

3.2 Depth-Based Object Positioning

Object positioning includes target location positioning and target pose estimation. The target location positioning is to obtain the position of the object in the robot world coordinate system, and the target pose estimation is to obtain the rotation vector from the robot's world coordinate system to the object's own coordinate system. Details are described below.

Target Location Positioning. The depth information obtained by the above method is combined with pixel coordinates to calculate the three-dimensional coordinate position of the target in the camera coordinate system, and then converted into coordinates in the robot world coordinate system. Take the marked center point as the target position P. Obtain the pixel coordinates P' of the center point of the marker through the pixel coordinates of the corner points of the marker.

In the image coordinate system, c' is the "center" point of the image corresponding to the optical axis, and the length of the coordinate difference between p' and c' as Eq. 4.

$$L(\Delta i)|_{i=u,v} = \Delta i \cdot dx \tag{4}$$

where u, v represent the image coordinate axes, Δi represents the coordinate difference between p' and c', and dx represents the width of the square pixel.

In the camera coordinate system (three-dimensional coordinates), based on the principle of optical imaging, according to the correspondence between the left-arm camera coordinate axis and the image coordinate axis, the target is in the camera coordinate system, about the coordinates of the X and Y axes The values are $X_{w(u)}, X_{w(v)}$.

$$X_w(i)|_{i=u,v} = d \cdot L(\Delta i)/f \tag{5}$$

where d represents the depth of the target from the camera (Eq. 2), f represents the focal length of the camera.

By calibrating the camera, the position of the target under the camera coordinate system can be derived as C_p based on the camera internal reference.

$$C_p = [X_w(u), X_w(v), d]^T \tag{6}$$

where $X_w(u), X_w(v)$ see Eq. 5, d denotes the depth information see Eq. 2.

According to the value of f_x in the camera internal reference, the value of $L(\Delta i)/f$ near the center of the image is less than 1. Therefore, the influence of the depth value error on the coordinate value will be reduced, the coordinates of the target in the camera coordinate system about the X-axis and Y-axis will be more accurate. Then convert the target position to the robot world coordinate system, and the position of the target in the world coordinate system is represented as P_w.

$$P_w = P_0 + R_{cw} \cdot C_p + R_{gw} \cdot G_c \tag{7}$$

where P_0 denotes the starting position of the left-arm planar gripper end under the robot world coordinate system. R_{cw} denotes the rotation matrix of the conversion from the camera coordinate system to the robot world coordinate system. C_p denotes the position of the target in the camera initial position coordinate system. R_{gw} denotes the rotation matrix of the conversion from the left arm planar gripper coordinate system to the robot world coordinate system. G_c denotes the position of the left-arm camera in the left-arm plane gripper coordinate system. Since the positions of the left-arm camera and the left-arm plane gripper are relatively fixed, G_c is a constant value.

Target Pose Estimation. Figure 3 shows the rotational change of the marker in the image. The upper left corner indicates the origin of the image coordinate system, the horizontal direction indicates the u-axis, and the vertical direction indicates the v-axis. The second column shows the cases when the marker is not deflected and deflected by 180°, and the pose of the marker when $v_i = v_j$ is set as the initial pose. The first column indicates that the marker is rotated counterclockwise with respect to the initial pose, and the third column indicates that the marker is rotated clockwise with respect to the initial pose. The angle marked by the red line is the angle of marker deflection.

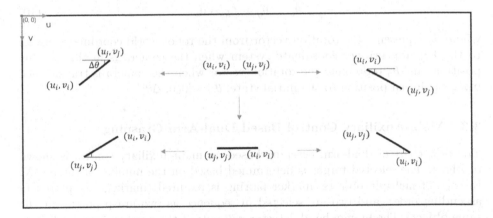

Fig. 3. Different rotation states of markers.

Since the positions of the corner points of the marker are relatively fixed, the deflection angle $\Delta\theta$ of the marker with respect to the initial pose is calculated using the fixed corner points.

$$\Delta\theta = \arctan \frac{|\Delta v_{ij}|}{|\Delta u_{ij}|} \tag{8}$$

where Δv_{ij} denotes the change of longitudinal coordinates of corner point i and corner point j, Δu_{ij} denotes the change of transverse coordinates of corner point i and corner point j, and $arctan$ represents the inverse tangent function.

When the marker is deflected counterclockwise, the slope of the line where corner point i and corner point j are located is negative in the image coordinate system. On the contrary, when the marker is deflected clockwise with respect to the initial pose, the slope of the line where corner point i and corner point j are located is positive. The direction of rotation is expressed as f_{dor}.

$$f_{dor} = \begin{cases} 1, if \Delta u_{ij} \cdot \Delta v_{ij} < 0 \\ -1, otherwise \end{cases} \tag{9}$$

where Δv_{ij} indicates the difference between the longitudinal coordinates of corner point i and corner point j, and Δu_{ij} indicates the difference between the lateral coordinates of corner point i and corner point j. A f_{dor} of 1 indicates that the marker is deflected counterclockwise with respect to the initial pose, and a f_{dor} of -1 indicates that the marker is deflected clockwise with respect to the initial pose.

In the camera coordinate system, when the marker is in the initial pose, the relative states of the camera and the marker are called the initial state. The rotation vector of the left-arm gripper coordinate system in the world coordinate system is denoted as θ_w. When controlling the robot, the θ_w parameter Euler angles need to be converted into Quaternion to control the plane gripper state.

$$\theta_w = \theta_g + f_{dor} \cdot \theta_o \tag{10}$$

where θ_g represents the rotation vector from the robot world coordinate system to the left arm gripper coordinate system when the camera is in the starting position, and θ_o represents the rotation vector when the camera is transformed from the initial position to the initial state, $\theta_o = [0, 0, \Delta\theta]^T$.

3.3   Main-Auxiliary Control Based Dual-Arm Grasping

The flow chart of dual-arm grasping based on main-auxiliary control is shown in Fig. 4. The selected target is determined based on the number of targets N. In case of multiple objects, marker pairing is required (markers are placed in ascending order, and two are selected in sequence as two grasp points for the same object). The human hand detector will output the pixel center coordinates of the hand. If the object selection condition is satisfied in three consecutive frames, the object is determined. Based on the pixel coordinates of the two grasping points of the object, it is judged whether the positional parameters need to be exchanged, and then the two grasping point position parameters of the object are assigned to the left and right robotic arms. The object selection conditions and the dual-arm cooperative control method are described as follows.

Object Selection. N is the number of the target object T. The target is determined according to whether there are multiple target objects. If N is greater

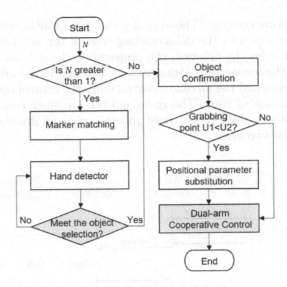

Fig. 4. Main-auxiliary control based dual-arm grasping.

than 1, since each object T_n occupies a pair of marks, where $n \in [1, N]$. The coordinates of the two marked center pixels of the object T_n are (u_{n_1}, v_{n_1}) and (u_{n_2}, v_{n_2}). In the image coordinate system, the pixel coordinate value of the right arm of the robot is smaller than the value of the left arm. And according to the rules for storing the coordinate parameters, it is necessary to compare the pixel coordinates of the two grasping points to decide whether the pose parameters should be swapped.

$$T_{grasp}(N) = \begin{cases} T_1, if N = 1 \\ T_a, otherwise \end{cases} \tag{11}$$

where $a = \{n | h(u_h, v_h) \in [u_{n_1} : u_{n_2}, v_{n_1} : v_{n_2}]\}, [u_{n_1} : u_{n_2}, v_{n_1} : v_{n_2}]$ represents a rectangular pixel frame consisting of (u_{n_1}, v_{n_1}) and (u_{n_2}, v_{n_2}) as diagonal points. $h(u_h, v_h)$ represents the pixel center point of the hand.

Dual-Arm Cooperative Control. The timing schematic for main-auxiliary control is shown in Fig. 5. In this paper, the main-auxiliary control (unified control clock) is used to achieve synchronization of dual-arm collaborative operation. The method uses main-auxiliary control for the control of the left and right robotic arms. The main control enables the control of both robotic arms, while the auxiliary control is used to control the right robotic arm only. The main control and auxiliary control are used simultaneously only when the cooperative operation is performed. A communication connection is used between the main and the auxiliary control. The main control transmits the joint angle of the right arm to the auxiliary control, and the auxiliary control returns the identification information after the right arm task is completed. For cooperative operation, it is necessary to unify the main and the auxiliary control clocks, which is done by a delayed waiting strategy. Theoretically, the delay waiting time of the main control should be equal to the delay waiting time of the auxiliary control plus the propagation delay. In practice, the propagation delay is so small as to be negligible when the main control transmits information to the auxiliary control. Therefore, the main and the auxiliary control unify the control clocks by waiting for the same amount of time. The main and the auxiliary control then sends control commands to the left and right robotic arms simultaneously to ensure the synergy of the two arms.

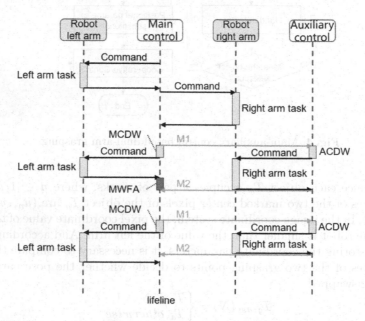

Fig. 5. The timing schematic for main-auxiliary control. ACDW: Auxiliary control delay waiting. MCDW: Main control delay waiting. MWFA: The main control waits for the auxiliary control. M1: Right arm joint angles. M2: Identifying characters.

4   Results

To verify the effectiveness of our proposed method, we conducted multiple sets of experiments with the Baxter robot as an example. The experimental configuration will be described in Subsect. 4.1. In Subsect. 4.2 we describe the experimental design. In Subsect. 4.3, we will present the experimental results and analyze the results.

4.1   Experimental Configuration

Throughout the experiments, a computer, an experimental workbench with variable height, target objects with locally graspable features and markers [4,14,18] of known width were used. And a Baxter robot with a parallel gripper equipped with an RGB camera (1280 × 800 pixels) on its left arm, as shown in Fig. 6.

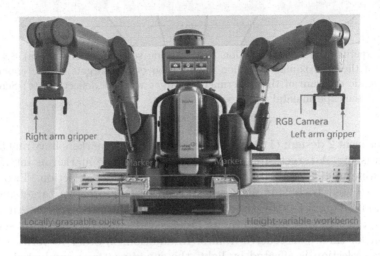

Fig. 6. Experimental scene diagram.

4.2   Experimental Design

In order to quantitatively evaluate the influence of different depths, different poses, and different environments on the dual-arm cooperative grasping method, we verify the effectiveness and interference resistance of the method in two parts. The first part is to verify the effectiveness of the method under different depths, different lighting conditions, and different positional conditions. The second part is to verify the robustness of the method under the conditions of redundant marker interference and multiple target selection.

Experiment 1 design: (1) To verify whether the method can grasp targets of different depths by collaborating with dual-arm, we set the height of the workbench to five different heights (constrained by the working space of the robot arms, the height of the worktable surface from the camera is controlled within 30–70 cm, and five different heights are set within this range). (2) To verify whether the method can successfully grasp the target in different poses on the workbench, the target attitude is divided into target without deflection and with deflection angle (as shown in Fig. 7(b) (c)), and the target position is changed according to the distribution position of Fig. 7(a). (3) To verify whether the method is affected by light conditions, five sets of experiments with different depth conditions were conducted under both natural light and light conditions.

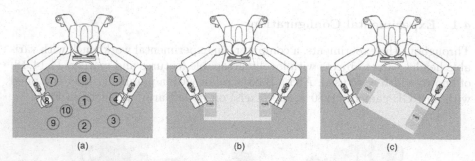

(a)   (b)   (c)

Fig. 7. Experimental target position and attitude setting schematic. (a) Schematic diagram of the approximate location distribution of the targets in the experiment. (b) Schematic diagram of the experimental target without deflection. (c) Schematic diagram of the experimental target with deflection.

Experiment 2 design: (1) Verify whether redundant markers have an effect on target grasping. A target object, three markers, and one marker as interference marker were used. (2) Verify the effectiveness of target selection. Two target objects are used with four markers, and since there are two targets, human interaction is required at this time, and the target to be grasped is determined by detecting the manually selected target objects and satisfying the target selection condition for three consecutive frames. In addition, in order to verify whether the target selection is affected by light, the experiment was conducted in a set of experiments under natural lighting and lighting conditions. The human hand detection uses Yolov5 [7] as the detection framework and weights [11].

Description: It is necessary to detect multiple frames of images when acquiring depth information (the threshold is set to 20 in this experiment). During the experiment, each set of experiments (ten grasp experiments) only acquired depth information once at the beginning, and used this depth information to complete ten grasp tasks. Since the method involves marker pairing, the following usage rules need to be defined for markers. (1) The left and right edges of the marker need to be in the same direction as the edge of the local graspable point, as shown in Fig. 8. (2) If more than two markers are used, the markers need to be ranked in ascending order by serial number, and two consecutive markers from the first one are used for the same target object.

Graspable local features

Graspable local features

Fig. 8. Marker usage rules.

4.3   Experimental Results and Analysis

Table 1. Experiment 1 results statistics. NL_di($i = 1, 2, \ldots, 5$): The height difference between the work surface and the camera under natural light conditions. EL_di($i = 1, 2, \ldots, 5$): The height difference between the workbench and the camera under lighting conditions. SG_n: The target is not deflected, only its position is changed, and the target grasp success rate is counted. SG_y: The target is deflected and changes its position, and the target grasp success rate statistics. RS: After placing the target, when the arms return to the initial position, sometimes due to the deviation between the distance between the dual-arm grippers and the actual width of the target, the plane gripper will take one end of the target away from the experimental desktop. RS indicates that this does not happen. NSR said that such a situation occurred. ASR: Average success rate.

Ec	SG_n	RS	SG_y	RS	ASR	
NL_d1	10/10	10/10	10/10	6/10	100%	80%
NL_d2	10/10	7/10	10/10	10/10	100%	85%
NL_d3	10/10	9/10	10/10	10/10	100%	95%
NL_d4	9/10	8/10	10/10	10/10	95%	90%
NL_d5	10/10	9/10	10/10	10/10	100%	95%
EL_d1	10/10	9/10	10/10	10/10	100%	95%
EL_d2	10/10	8/10	10/10	8/10	100%	80%
EL_d3	10/10	10/10	10/10	9/10	100%	95%
EL_d4	10/10	9/10	10/10	10/10	100%	95%
EL_d5	10/10	10/10	10/10	10/10	100%	100%
ASR	99%	89%	100%	93%	99.5%	91%

The results of Experiment 1 are shown in Table 1. Overall, the grasping success rate was 99.5% and the RS success rate was 91%. One grasping failure occurred. (1) In the experiments with different heights of the table for the grasping situation, it can be seen that (d4, d5) RS success rate is slightly higher than (d1, d2). The reason is that the target is closer to the camera under d1 condition, and the target position changes by the same distance under d1 condition, which is more obviously affected by the camera distortion. Although the experimental results of each group are slightly different, the difference is not obvious, indicating that the method is equally effective under different depth conditions. (2) The success rates of RS were 89% and 93% under the conditions of target changing position without deflection and deflection, respectively, indicating that there was no significant difference in the results when the target was in different positions, indicating that the method can be applied to targets in different positions. (3) Under the natural light and light illumination environment, the grasping success rate and RS success rate are also 89% and 93%, which indicates that the lighting effect also has no obvious effect on the method, and the method is applicable to different lighting environments. In the case of failure to grasp during experiment 1, the right arm gripper rotates during the ascent of the dual-arm grasping target. The reason is that the optimal solution path from point A to point B is different from the optimal solution path obtained from point B to point A during the inverse kinematics solution process. When it has been adjusted by reusing the joint angle of point A, this situation does not occur anymore.

Table 2. Experiment 2 results statistics. NL_i(i = 3, 4): Use three markers under natural light conditions. EL_4: Use four markers under lighting conditions. MP: Markers pairing. TS: The correct number of times of target selection by detecting human hands. SG: The number of successful grasps of the target. RS and ASR are the same as Table 1.

Ec	MP	TS	SG	RS	ASR
NL_3	10/10	0	9/10	9/10	90%
NL_4	10/10	10/10	10/10	8/10	80%
EL_4	10/10	10/10	10/10	9/10	90%

The results of Experiment 2 are shown in Table 2. The overall task success rates were 90%, 80%, and 90%, respectively. (1) NL_3 verified the redundant marker interference situation, and the MP success rate was 100%, indicating that the redundant interference markers did not affect the results. (2) In NL_4 and EL_4 experiments, the success rates of TS, MP, and SP were 100%. This indicates that the target selection method was effective, and the illumination environment did not significantly affect the target selection. The success rates of RS in the three experiments were 90%, 80%, and 90%, respectively, which were not significantly different from the results of experiment 1. There was a grasp failure during experiment 2. The reason was that when changing the target position, the position during the move was recorded instead of the target position.

The common problems of Experiments 1 and 2, the main reasons for NRS: (1) When solving the three-dimensional coordinates, the solution is only performed once, and sometimes the solution is not accurate enough. (2) Since rubber pads are used on both sides of the flat gripper of the robotic arm, the gripper is opened, and the rubber pad will have a certain elasticity, which will also affect the placement of the target. (3) There is also a certain error in the movement of the robot arm, and each movement will be slightly deviated. Next, it is necessary to further improve the calculation accuracy of the target pose through position verification.

The method proposed in this paper was not compared with other vision-based dual-arm collaboration methods. The reason is the other methods using RGB cameras with fixed depth or using depth camera acquisition. Also due to the different experimental specific settings between us, the evaluation criteria of the results are different. Therefore, this paper is not compared with other methods.

5   Disscussion

This paper proposes a dual-arm collaboration grasp method based on RGB cameras. Firstly, the depth information model is established by RGB camera, and using the markers attached to the target to obtain the depth information of the target. Then the 3D position of the target in the robot world coordinate system is calculated. Finally, the target object is grasped by the cooperation of both arms. This method does not depend on the depth camera and can be applied to the scene with varying depth, which improves the applicability of the dual-arm collaboration method based on RGB camera. The method can be applied to depth-variant grasping tasks and autonomous assembly tasks in industrial scenes using only RGB cameras.

However, this method also has certain limitations. First, a mark needs to be attached to the local graspable point of the object, and the mark must be used according to the rules. The main reason for these limitations is that the pixel information of the local graspable points needs to be obtained through marker detection to calculate the pose. Secondly, since this method only calculates the pose change of the target on the workbench, it is not applicable when the target is inclined. Therefore, future work focuses on edge detection methods as well as target 6D grasp point estimation methods. The edge detection method is used to determine the local graspable point pixel coordinate information, and the 6D pose estimation is used to obtain the object's pose in order to expand the applicability of the method.

Acknowledgement. This work was supported by the Project of NSFC (Grant No. U1908214), Special Project of Central Government Guiding Local Science and Technology Development (Grant No. 2021JH6/10500140), the Program for Innovative Research Team in University of Liaoning Province (LT2020015), the Support Plan for Key Field Innovation Team of Dalian (2021RT06), the Science and Technology Innovation Fund of Dalian (Grant No. 2020JJ25CY001), the Support Plan for Leading Innovation Team of Dalian University (Grant No. XLJ202010) and Dalian University Scientific Research Platform Project (No. 202101YB03).

References

1. Bai, W., et al.: Dual-arm coordinated manipulation for object twisting with human intelligence. In: 2021 IEEE International Conference on Systems, Man, and Cybernetics (SMC), pp. 902–908. IEEE (2021)
2. Cai, J., Cheng, H., Zhang, Z., Su, J.: Metagrasp: data efficient grasping by affordance interpreter network. In: 2019 International Conference on Robotics and Automation (ICRA), pp. 4960–4966. IEEE (2019)
3. Du, G., Wang, K., Lian, S., Zhao, K.: Vision-based robotic grasping from object localization, object pose estimation to grasp estimation for parallel grippers: a review. Artif. Intell. Rev. **54**(3), 1677–1734 (2021)
4. Garrido-Jurado, S., Muñoz-Salinas, R., Madrid-Cuevas, F.J., Medina-Carnicer, R.: Generation of fiducial marker dictionaries using mixed integer linear programming. Pattern Recogn. **51**, 481–491 (2016)

5. Griffin, B.A., Corso, J.J.: Learning object depth from camera motion and video object segmentation. In: Vedaldi, A., Bischof, H., Brox, T., Frahm, J.-M. (eds.) ECCV 2020. LNCS, vol. 12352, pp. 295–312. Springer, Cham (2020). https://doi.org/10.1007/978-3-030-58571-6_18

6. Ibarguren, A., Eimontaite, I., Outón, J.L., Fletcher, S.: Dual arm co-manipulation architecture with enhanced human-robot communication for large part manipulation. Sensors 20(21), 6151 (2020)

7. Jocher, G., et al.: ultralytics/yolov5: v5. 0-yolov5-p6 1280 models aws supervise. ly and youtube integrations. Zenodo 11 (2021)

8. Laghi, M., et al.: Shared-autonomy control for intuitive bimanual tele-manipulation. In: 2018 IEEE-RAS 18th International Conference on Humanoid Robots (Humanoids), pp. 1–9. IEEE (2018)

9. Liang, J., Mahler, J., Laskey, M., Li, P., Goldberg, K.: Using DVRK teleoperation to facilitate deep learning of automation tasks for an industrial robot. In: 2017 13th IEEE Conference on Automation Science and Engineering (CASE), pp. 1–8. IEEE (2017)

10. Lipton, J.I., Fay, A.J., Rus, D.: Baxter's homunculus: virtual reality spaces for teleoperation in manufacturing. IEEE Robot. Autom. Lett. 3(1), 179–186 (2017)

11. Liu, D., et al.: A novel and efficient distance detection based on monocular images for grasp and handover. In: Gao, H., Wang, X. (eds.) CollaborateCom 2021. LNICST, vol. 406, pp. 642–658. Springer, Cham (2021). https://doi.org/10.1007/978-3-030-92635-9_37

12. Lundell, J., Verdoja, F., Kyrki, V.: Beyond top-grasps through scene completion. In: 2020 IEEE International Conference on Robotics and Automation (ICRA), pp. 545–551. IEEE (2020)

13. Medjram, S., Brethe, J.F., Benali, K.: Markerless vision-based one cardboard box grasping using dual arm robot. Multimedia Tools Appl. 79(31), 22617–22633 (2020)

14. Muñoz-Salinas, R., Marín-Jimenez, M.J., Yeguas-Bolivar, E., Medina-Carnicer, R.: Mapping and localization from planar markers. Pattern Recogn. 73, 158–171 (2018)

15. Ott, C., Nakamura, Y.: Employing wave variables for coordinated control of robots with distributed control architecture. In: 2008 IEEE International Conference on Robotics and Automation, pp. 575–582. IEEE (2008)

16. Punlum, V., Srisertpol, J., Khaengkam, S.: The application of double arms scara robot for deburring of PCB support plate. In: 2017 International Conference on Circuits, Devices and Systems (ICCDS), pp. 1–5. IEEE (2017)

17. Rastegarpanah, A., Marturi, N., Stolkin, R.: Autonomous vision-guided bi-manual grasping and manipulation. In: 2017 IEEE Workshop on Advanced Robotics and its Social Impacts (ARSO), pp. 1–7. IEEE (2017)

18. Romero-Ramirez, F.J., Muñoz-Salinas, R., Medina-Carnicer, R.: Speeded up detection of squared fiducial markers. Image Vis. Comput. 76, 38–47 (2018)

19. Sepúlveda, D., Fernández, R., Navas, E., Armada, M., González-De-Santos, P.: Robotic aubergine harvesting using dual-arm manipulation. IEEE Access 8, 121889–121904 (2020)

20. Silvério, J., Clivaz, G., Calinon, S.: A laser-based dual-arm system for precise control of collaborative robots. In: 2021 IEEE International Conference on Robotics and Automation (ICRA), pp. 9183–9189. IEEE (2021)

21. Smith, C., et al.: Dual arm manipulation-a survey. Robot. Auton. Syst. 60(10), 1340–1353 (2012)

22. Tung, A., et al.: Learning multi-arm manipulation through collaborative teleoperation. In: 2021 IEEE International Conference on Robotics and Automation (ICRA), pp. 9212–9219. IEEE (2021)

23. Wu, Q., Li, M., Qi, X., Hu, Y., Li, B., Zhang, J.: Coordinated control of a dual-arm robot for surgical instrument sorting tasks. Robot. Auton. Syst. **112**, 1–12 (2019)
24. Yang, Y., Liu, Y., Liang, H., Lou, X., Choi, C.: Attribute-based robotic grasping with one-grasp adaptation. In: 2021 IEEE International Conference on Robotics and Automation (ICRA), pp. 6357–6363. IEEE (2021)
25. Yu, X., Zhang, S., Sun, L., Wang, Y., Xue, C., Li, B.: Cooperative control of dual-arm robots in different human-robot collaborative tasks. Assem. Autom. **40**(1), 95–104 (2019)
26. Zahavi, A., Haeri, S.N., Liyanage, D.C., Tamre, M.: A dual-arm robot for collaborative vision-based object classification. In: 2020 17th Biennial Baltic Electronics Conference (BEC), pp. 1–5. IEEE (2020)
27. Zhong, F., Wang, Y., Wang, Z., Liu, Y.H.: Dual-arm robotic needle insertion with active tissue deformation for autonomous suturing. IEEE Robot. Autom. Lett. **4**(3), 2669–2676 (2019)

Collaborative Working

Semantic SLAM for Mobile Robot with Human-in-the-Loop

Zhenchao Ouyang[1,2]([✉])(iD), Changjie Zhang[2], and Jiahe Cui[1,2](iD)

[1] Beihang Hangzhou Innovation Institute Yuhang, Beihang University,
Yuhang, Hangzhou 311100, Zhejiang, China
ouyangkid@buaa.edu.cn
[2] School of Computer Science and Engineering, Beihang University,
Beijing 100191, China

Abstract. Mobile robots are an important participant in today's modern life, and have huge commercial application prospects in the fields of unmanned security inspection, logistics, express delivery, cleaning and medical disinfection. Since LiDAR is not affected by ambient light and can operate in a dark environment, localization and navigation based on LiDAR point clouds have become one of the basic modules of mobile robots. However, compared with traditional binocular vision images, the sparse, disordered and noisy point cloud poses a challenge to efficient and stable feature extraction. This makes the LiDAR-based SLAM have more significant cumulative errors, and poor consistency of the final map, which affects tasks such as positioning based on the prior point cloud map. In order to alleviate the above problems and improve the positioning accuracy, a semantic SLAM with human-in-the-loop is proposed. First, the interactive SLAM is introduced to optimize the point cloud pose to obtain a highly consistent point cloud map; then the point cloud segmentation model is trained by artificial semantic annotation to obtain the semantic information of a single frame of point cloud; finally, the positioning accuracy is optimized based on the point cloud semantics. The proposed system is validated on the local platform in an underground garage, without involving GPS or expensive measuring equipment.

Keywords: Semantic SLAM · Robot · Point cloud segmentation · Human-in-the-loop · Interactive SLAM

1 Introduction

With the rapid development of technology, the related applications of mobile robots are gradually entering daily life from the research stage. Especially during the fight against the COVID-19, mobile robots have undertaken a series of tasks such as material distribution, disinfection and sterilization, service, and cleaning. At the same time, as China enters an aging society, the birth rate continues to decline, the demographic dividend disappears, and the labor shortage will

H. Gao et al. (Eds.): CollaborateCom 2022, LNICST 461, pp. 289–305, 2022.
https://doi.org/10.1007/978-3-031-24386-8_16

become increasingly significant [1]. The demand for unmanned operations in society and the market continues to rise, and mobile robots [2] will become one of the important guarantees to fill the workforce gap.

Autonomous environment perception and self-positioning are the basic functions of mobile robots. Robots need to complete the acquisition of their own poses before they can carry out more complex mobile tasks. The current mainstream autonomous positioning of robots includes Simultaneous Localization and Mapping (SLAM) [3], odometer of wheel speed encoder [4], Ultra-Wide-Band (UWB) [5], GPS [6], and multi-sensor fusion solutions [7]. Among them, GPS cannot locate targets in occluded environments or indoors; UWB requires construction on the environment; wheel speedometers are easily affected by slippage and wear, and dynamic modeling of the robot chassis is required, and the estimation accuracy of the rotational pose is also poor. The SLAM algorithm based on open-loop control is less dependent on equipment, and has a wider range of stability and applicable scenarios.

Based on environmental perception sensors and data structures, existing SLAM algorithms can be roughly divided into two categories: vision [8] and LiDAR-based SLAM. LiDAR based on active perception is not affected by ambient light and can perceive in a dark environment, which can provide reliable guarantees for mobile robots. LiDAR-based SLAM technology [9] can provide mobile robots with localization and stable environment-dense mapping information, which is the key module of robot mobility. However, the sparseness and randomness of LiDAR point clouds make the registration features much lower than stereo-based images [10], thus introducing more significant cumulative errors, resulting in the degradation of the point cloud map and poor consistency of the final map. This in turn affects prior map-based localization and a range of downstream tasks.

Although a series of optimization methods have been carried out for the front-end and back-end of the SLAM system, the existing algorithms are still not comparable to the human perception ability. One main reason is that the current SLAM algorithm lacks the ability to understand semantic information of the environment–human cognition. Existing systems [11] try to optimize SLAM systems by introducing environmental semantic information to simulate primary human-like cognition, which is the recently developed semantic SLAM. However, due to the scarcity of point cloud-based semantic segmentation datasets for large-scale scenes, the development of deep learning models has just begun. Annotation of sparse point cloud data, especially for low-cost LiDAR is also extremely challenging.

To solve the above problems, a semantic SLAM with human-in-the-loop is proposed in this paper, we focus on improving mobile robot localization with only low cost LiDAR for the indoor environment. The system takes human collaboration into consideration from the following two aspects: 1) we first introduce the interactive SLAM [12] to refine normal SLAM results, and generate corrected pose based on global point cloud map. 2) Then the point clouds with high global consistency are manually labeled with target-level semantics. By labeling the overlapped map [13] instead of a single point cloud frame, not only the labeling efficiency is greatly improved, but fewer errors are introduced. 3) The point cloud segmentation model [14] is trained for the extraction of semantic labels, and 4) a novel semantic prior map-based localization method is proposed. The algorithm utilizes point cloud semantic label information to optimize the global map search and local pose estimation of the localization process, and is validated in a large local underground parking garage.

2   Related Works

Considering we only focus on SLAM with semantic information, this section briefly summarized the recent development of semantic visual and LiDAR SLAM.

2.1   Visual Semantic SLAM

Zhang et al. [15] presented a semantic SLAM system for RGB-D cameras under the ORB-SLAM2 [16] framework. The YOLO [17] is introduced as an obstacle detector to extract object-level features in the scene. With this operation, unstable features belonging to moving objects are removed, and the localization accuracy is improved. They also use the fast line rasterization algorithm to speed up the construction of Octomap. However, Yolo can only provide bounding box (BBox)-level detection accuracy, especially when the irregular target is close to the lens, the detection frame will contain a lot of background information. This means that the features in the background will also be eliminated, resulting in the failure of inter-frame registration. Wang et al. [18] use depth map-based flood filling to extract the contour of objects, and acquire highly precise semantic segmentation results.

Kang et al. [19] tried to reduce the error introduced by the BBox while providing the 3D space information of the targets with a robust edge detector. The edge detector divides indoor objects into two wrappers-cuboid or cylinder, and uses 2D-3D transformation to generate the object into 3D landmarks for later usage. But their work only considered a simple indoor environment with limited targets.

PSPNet-SLAM [20] is another improved version of ORB-SLAM2 framework. In this system, the image segmentation-based pyramid-structured PSPNet [21] is used to get a segmentation mask instead of a bounding box for each object. The masks of moving objects can effectively reduce the background introduced by the bounding boxes, thereby increasing the registration features to improve the overall accuracy and system robustness. Zhao et al. [22] follow the same workflow of PSPNet-SLAM while adding the GPS and landmarks from google map to enable the system to be used in outdoor scenarios for self-driving vehicles.

Kimera [23] built a local mesh of the scene based on multi-frame stereo data to guarantee globally-consistent trajectory estimation, but is also not suitable for open areas.

Other visual semantic SLAM [24–27] follow the same trends of using different deep learning based object detection [28, 29] or segmentation models [30, 31] as a filter to remove the unstable object and get a refined local image/depth map.

Some researchers try to use other sensor information to help visual SLAM adapt to outdoor environments. However, the unstable light and limited FOV make visual SLAM unable to meet safety requirements for self-driving vehicles.

2.2 LiDAR Semantic SLAM

Although RGB-D camera and stereo parallax estimation can offer point clouds, they are either within a short distance or inaccurate under bad light conditions. Only the LiDAR (multi-beam) based point cloud is considered.

Since there are almost no point cloud-based segmentation dataset, early algorithms, such as LIMO [32] and [33], fused the camera and LiDAR to get the semantic information of point clouds. The moving targets are first detected or segmented from the image view, and their BBoxes or masks are projected into the 3D point cloud for later filtering based on the external parameter matrix [10] of camera-LiDAR calibration system. On the one hand, the inherent difference between the FOV of the camera and the LiDAR will introduce projection errors. On the other hand, the camera FOV is relatively limited and can only filter part of dynamic targets, especially for 360-degree ring-like LiDAR.

To achieve fast segmentation for 3D sparse point clouds in large distances without involving camera image, LiSeg [34] follows the RangeNet++ [35] which directly deployed the segmentation on the 2D spherical mapping of raw point cloud. And then, the point cloud after removing the dynamic target is projected back to the 3D space for subsequent SLAM. SUMA++ [11] combines the multi-class flood fill with RangeNet++ to refine the 2D segmentation result of the spherical projection map. With semantic constraints from above operations, the projected scans matching through ICP are improved, and SUMA++ is able to work with very few static structures on the highway. OverlapNet [36] also benefits from the segmentation results of RangeNet++, and combines the semantic class probability with other point cloud cues for prediction of overlap of the current map and heading yaw of the agent.

Recurrent-OctoMap [37] uses a Nap-LSTM model to learn the semantic state transition between different time-scales of observation for the long term SLAM requirement. Different processing strategies will be used to construct different maps based on dynamic objects, such as moving and potential moving vehicles. The test shows that the OctoMap built from 7-day-long mapping data can maintain semantic memory using long-term experience. But long-term SLAM mapping ignores fine-grained spatial features, which makes real-time positioning accuracy poor.

With the release of the SemanticPOSS [38] and SemanticKITTI [13], it is possible to directly perform 3D point cloud semantic segmentation [14,39], and related semantic SLAM. The model directly performs semantic segmentation in three-dimensional space, which can effectively use the complete spatial information without additional projection and back-projection operations. The artifacts introduced back-projection can also be avoided.

3 System Workflow

Our workflow consists of the following four main steps (as shown in Fig. 1). 1) A normal SLAM-based data collection and refinement based on offline interactive SLAM is first adopted, the later operation involved human collaboration in closed-loop optimization. 2) The point clouds are then overlapped based on the refine posed from the last step, and the human is involved again in labeling the point cloud with cognitive prior knowledge. This operation generates both a point cloud map (through voxelization) and a per-frame labeled point cloud dataset with predefined semantic labels. 3) A point cloud segmentation model is then trained based on the collected and labeled dataset. 4) Finally, each scan is first fed into the segmentation model to get per-point labels, and matching to the semantic map in a 'global-local' paradigm.

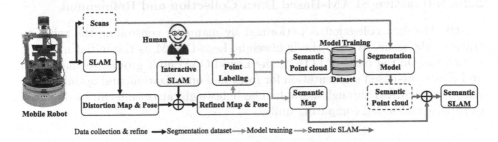

Fig. 1. The workflow of the semantic SLAM for mobile robots with human-in-the-loop.

With the involvement of human cooperation, we can refine the robot pose and final map without GPS positioning information or high-end laser trackers (such as Leica and Focus). At the same time, the point cloud is batch-labeled, based on the cumulative point cloud map instead of a single frame, with the help of human cognition. This greatly improves the labeling efficiency. Through the collaboration between human and the mobile robot, the subsequent semantic SLAM can be carried out. Next, the specific workflow will be introduced based on the local mobile robot and experimental environment.

3.1 Local Robot Platform

Our mobile robot is a differential two-wheel chassis equipped with a low-cost LiDAR with 16 beams@10 Hz and 360° (Robosense, RS-16), a monitor and embedded computer unit (Nvidia Jetson AGX), as shown in Fig. 2(a). The experimental environment is a large underground parking garage (about 328 m long), GPS signals cannot be received in this environment. A comparison between the bird's-eye view above ground building map based on UAV image stitching and the underground point cloud map optimized by this algorithm is shown in Fig. 2(b), it can be found that the final point cloud map has a high match with the surface scene.

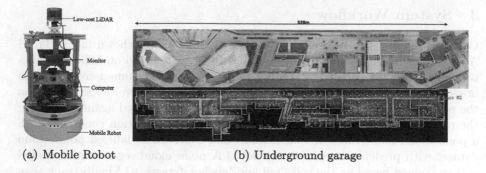

(a) Mobile Robot   (b) Underground garage

Fig. 2. Local experiment platform and environment.

3.2 Interactive SLAM-Based Data Collection and Refinement

Firstly, the data collection is performed by manually controlling the robot to traverse the scene. We use the lightweight Lego-LOAM as the initial mapping algorithm. On the basis of LOAM, the Lego-LOAM adds ground segmentation and clustering-based segmentation for front-end optimization, and optimizes the back-end of SLAM through a graph. The lightweight algorithm can be deployed in robotic embedded computing units.

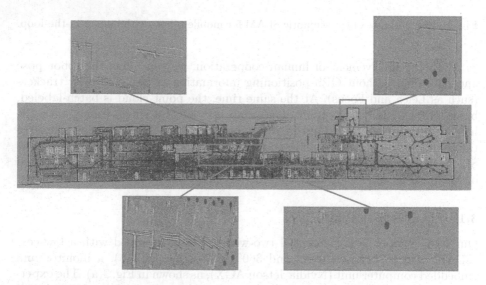

Fig. 3. The point cloud map output by the algorithm contains some significant mapping errors.

Due to the large size of the scene, the pose estimation bias will be introduced during robot motion (especially rotation), resulting in the shift or degradation of the final point cloud map. Some large pose offsets or long-term accumulated errors can lead to closed-loop detection errors and failures. For man-made buildings, mapping errors are easily observed (as shown in Fig. 3), such as excessively thick walls, wall ghosting, ground noise, etc. At the same time, for the lower wall of the entire map, it can also be seen that there are obvious arcs instead of straight lines.

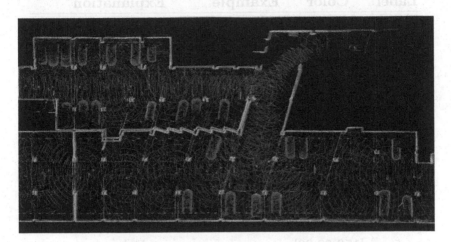

Fig. 4. The point cloud map output by the algorithm contains some significant mapping errors.

However, these errors can be easily detected by a human. Therefore, the offline interactive SLAM is introduced by adding closure and other pose constraints through a human operator during the back-end optimization. The interactive SLAM [12] mainly realizes map correction by introducing manual closed-loop detection in back-end optimization. Figure 4 shows the corrected results for the most heavily drifted region in Fig. 3. The whole process requires constant human-in-the-loop iterative optimization, and the specific optimization time depends on factors such as the scene size and the scale of draft areas. Finally, we get a refined pose for each frame, and a map from overlapped and voxelized point clouds.

3.3 Semantic Point Cloud Labeling and Segmentation Model Training

We then separately label the overlapped point cloud and the voxelized map according to the predefined classes with **Point Labeler**[1]. Table 1 illustrates the eight common targets appearing in the local underground garage, they can be roughly divided into stable senses (road, column, wall and ceiling), moving subjects (vehicle, motorcycle, pedestrian), and unrecognized noise. In the current

---

[1] https://github.com/jbehley/point_labeler.

stage, manual collaboration is introduced again, and data annotation is performed with the help of human cognition, which is used to build a semantic point cloud dataset and a global map with semantic labels.

Table 1. The predefined semantic labels for underground garage.

Label	Color	Example	Explanation
0	[0,0,0]	null	unlabeled noise or outliers
1	[0,0,255]		Vehicle
2	[245,150,100]		Motorcycle
3	[245,230,100]		Pedestrian
4	[250,80,100]		Road
5	[150,60,30]		Column
6	[255,0,0]		Wall
7	[180,30,80]		Ceiling

The **Point Labeler** organized the point cloud and corresponding relative pose ($[x, y, z, roll, pitch, yaw]$) as input, and overlapped the point cloud into a scene, and divided the whole scene into smaller square cells. Therefore, during the labeling process, the complete structure based on the nearest neighbor point cloud can give a more complete target space shape. And at the same time, with the help of the pose information optimized by interactive SLAM, batch annotation (relative to a single frame) can be easily and quickly performed. Figure 5 illustrates an example of the labeling tool UI with corresponding sense from the image, the annotator can easily identify the class of the object through the map-level point cloud (first annotate and filter the ground and ceiling).

We divide the labeled data into two disjoint subsets, one is used for model training, and the other is used for model evaluation. Comprehensively considering both computational efficiency and segmentation accuracy, the following three models are considered in the current study, i.e., RandlaNet [39], PolarNet [14], and Cyclinder3D [40].

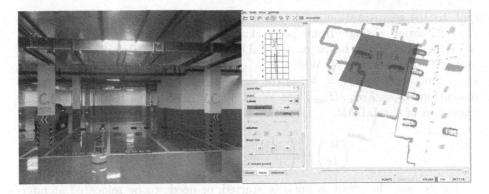

Fig. 5. The underground sense (left) and related point cloud map by removing ground and ceiling in **Point Labeler** (right).

3.4   Location Based on Semantic Point Cloud

Before starting work, the robot may start from different locations (for example, get items from different sources for delivery, or wake up from any map location for clearing), and it is critical to obtain an accurate current location through the prior semantic map. To further optimize the storage and subsequent searching of the point cloud map, the point cloud normal are calculated, and the point cloud is rasterized to obtain the triangular mesh-grid representation. This operation is done offline before integration into the robot localization system (Fig. 6).

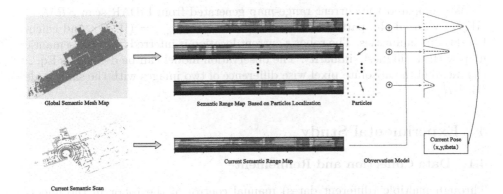

Fig. 6. A mesh grid based global semantic map is first generated from the labeled point cloud map. And the local semantic range-map is used for coarse localization with MCL.

As the point cloud segmentation model is trained, we encapsulate the semantic cognitive ability of humans to point clouds into the map and per-frame point cloud. Each time the robot gets a new scan, the point clouds are first sent to the segmentation model, and the point-wise labels can be obtained. And we project a single frame point cloud $[x, y, z]$ onto a 2D range-map $[W, H]$ with the label index based on the LiDAR Cartesian to Polar projection formula (as shown in Eq. 1). Where $R = \sqrt{x^2 + y^2 + z^2}$ is the distance of points, $F_v = Fov_{up} + Fov_{down} = 30°$ is the vertical angle, $H_{scale} = 2°$ is the vertical resolution $H_r = Fov_v/H_{scale} + 1 = 16$, $W_r = 1800$ is the Horizontal angular resolution of the LiDAR.

$$\begin{pmatrix} W \\ H \end{pmatrix} = \begin{pmatrix} \frac{1}{2}[1 - \frac{arctan(y,x)}{\pi}]W_r \\ [1 - \frac{arcsin(z/R)+F_{up}}{F_v}]H_r \end{pmatrix} \tag{1}$$

Every time the robot is initially started, or needs to be relocated at intervals, the particles are evenly distributed on the semantic map through the Monte Carlo localization (MCL) based on particle filters. Once particles are scattered anywhere on the map (limit the z-axis height to the sensor installation height), we can generate a semantic range-map from the corresponding particle. Different from the previous work [41] that uses z-axis value as pixel or point distance R, we replaced it with the semantic label index, this helps reduce the variability of range-map distributions. To reduce the complexity, we constrain the robot motion from 6°C of freedom (DoF) $[X, Y, Z, Roll, Pitch, Yaw]$ to three DoF $[X, Y, Yaw]$, considering only motion in the 2D plane of bird's eye view (BEV). Therefore, the robot localization is $L_r = (x, y, yaw)$, and the corresponding observation at L_r is a semantic range-map $SRM_r = (W, H)$.

$$d = \frac{\sum |SRM_r - SRM_p|}{W * H} \tag{2}$$

We compared the current range-map generated from LiDAR scan $SRM_r = (W, H)$ with all the particles' range-map $SRM_{p(i=0,...,n)} = (W, H)$, and calculated their similarities. The robot's current location is inferred from the semantic map with the highest similarity. The observation model can be defined as Eq. 2, the mean of the absolute pixel-wise difference of two images with the same scale $(W * H)$.

4   Experimental Study

4.1   Data Collection and Refinement

Through multiple (different dates) manual control of the robot in the underground parking lot, the random walk method is used to collect data to ensure the diversity of data. Figure 7 compares the different trajectories generated based on Lego-LOAM, the poses may contain drift, and will be corrected in the next operation. Table 2 illustrates more detailed statistical information of the point cloud sequences, and during the collection *seq1* and *seq2* use a limited maximum speed of 1.5 m/s.

On the one hand, the slow speed of the mobile robot leads to the high similarity of continuing frames; on the other hand, considering the computational

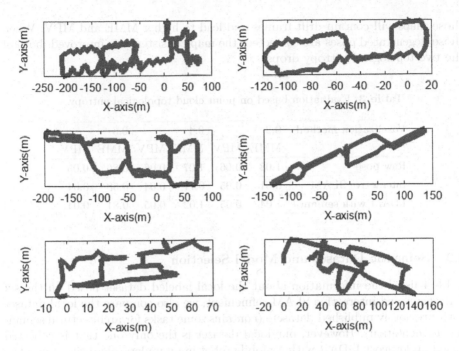

Fig. 7. Six random walks in the underground parking garage during data collection.

Table 2. Statistics of the six sequence trajectories.

Seq #	Frame	Point # (M)	Trajectory (m)	Duration (s)	Avg-speed (m/s)	Max-speed (m/s)
0	7814	318.37	944.31	793.50	1.19	2.37
1	4458	189.48	375.57	726.27	0.34	1.5
2	5471	242.08	652.10	854.24	0.76	1.5
3	5183	238.87	587.29	773.04	0.76	2.11
4	5725	270.13	294.01	863.12	0.57	2.27
5	7571	353.08	585.97	1219.34	1.48	2.27

cost of closed-loop optimization of the interactive SLAM process, the poses with a certain distance ($> 5\,m$) are extracted as candidate key frames by downsampling. Considering human-in-the-loop-based interactive SLAM is mainly optimized based on human subjective observation. Therefore, after optimizing six sets of collected data, an evaluation based on map topology entropy is introduced. In highly structured indoor environments, both Mean Map Entropy (MME) and Mean Plane Variance (MPV) are shown to be highly correlated with the trajectory error of SLAM [42]. Moreover, both the two metrics depend on the total number of points for the final map, the voxelization is first adopted to each map to normalize the map. Table 3 compares the average MME and MPV of the final maps with three scales of voxelization (0.2, 0.4 and 0.6). It can be seen that, when generating a point cloud map with degenerated raw poses, those maps will contain drift frames and lead to higher MME and MPV. When those degenerated poses are corrected, the map consistency is improved, both of the two topological entropy drops.

Table 3. Evaluation based on point cloud topological entropy.

Voxelization method	0.2		0.4		0.6	
	MME	MPV	MME	MPV	MME	MPV
Raw pose	1.08	0.06	1.07	0.06	0.86	0.05
Interactive SLAM	0.81	0.05	0.77	0.04	0.58	0.04
LOAM with semantic	1.04	0.05	1.02	0.05	0.81	0.04

4.2 Semantic Dataset and Model Selection

Table 4 listed the information about the local labeled dataset based on the six collections and interactive SLAM refinement, we also compare the local dataset with previously published datasets (contains some tasks for architectural semantic segmentation). However, our local dataset is the only one that is collected based on low-cost LiDAR with a mobile robot in an underground situation. The biggest challenge of point cloud map construction and data annotation for this kind of scene is the lack of accurate positioning benchmarks, such as GPS or high-end laser trackers that can cooperate. 6261 and 1565 labeled frames are used for model training and testing, respectively, the two subsets are disjoint. Semantic labeling only relies on the downsampled poses ($> 5\,m$), this operation can reduce the similarity of the overall data and improve the learning efficiency. And that is why the final labeled points are less than the total frames of the six sequences in Table 2.

Table 4. Comparison between local and published semantic datasets.

Dataset	Frame	Point Scale (M)	Class #	Sensor	Scenes
HYY(ours)	6261+1565	325.9	8	RS-16	Underground
SemanticKITTI	23201+20351	4549	25	VLP-64E	Street
OakLand3d	17	1.6	5	SICK LMS	Street
Freiburg	77	1.1	4	SICK LMS	Street
Wachtberg	5	0.4	5	VLP-64E	Street
Semantic3D	15/15	4009	8	Terrestrial Laser Scanner	Street
Paris-Lille-3D	3	143	9	VLP-32E	Street

All the models are trained on a GPU desktop with Intel i7-9700 CPU, 16G memory, HDD disk and a single NVIDIA 2080ti GPU. We set the batch = 4, use Adam optimizer with learning rate = 0.0001 in the beginning, and train all models for 80 epochs. Table 5 illustrated the comparison results on the testing set of our local data. The point-wise mean-Intersection over Union (mIoU) is selected to evaluate the model performance. The mIoU is defined according to Eq. 3, where TP_c, FP_c and FN_c correspond to the number of true positive, false positive, and false negative predictions labels for class c compare to the ground truth (GT) of testing set, and $C = 8$ is the total number of classes. However, we ignored the noise or outlier points in Table 5.

$$mIoU = \frac{1}{C} \sum_{c=1}^{C} \frac{TP_c}{TP_c + FP_c + FN_c} \tag{3}$$

Table 5. The semantic segmentation results on test set.

Model	mIoU	Per-Class mIoU							FPS
		Vehicle	Motorcycle	Pedestrian	Road	Column	Wall	Ceiling	
RandlaNet	89.93	96.50	92.67	67.52	93.19	94.42	97.22	87.99	62.50
PolarSeg	94.43	97.78	98.48	81.64	94.36	97.54	98.74	92.45	50.11
Cyclinder3D	95.57	98.50	98.64	82.70	95.86	98.20	99.22	95.87	12.29

It can be seen from the table that the overall mIoU of PolarSeg is slightly lower than that of the Cyclinder3D, but its speed is 50.11 frames per second (FPS). Although RandlaNet achieves the highest FPS at 62.5, however, its mIoU is much lower than the other two models. And Cyclinder3D is too slow which cannot meet the needs of in-vehicle computing units. Taking the mIoU and FPS into consideration, we prefer to choose PolarSeg. Its mIoU is only 1.14 lower than Cyclinder3D, but about 4 times faster. Subsequent semantic localization optimization is based on the point cloud semantic information of vehicles, motorcycles, pedestrians, ground bearing columns, walls and roofs obtained in this step, the category of noise points will be directly eliminated.

4.3 Localization Performance

We first compare our semantic range-map based location (refer as semantic-based) with the original range-map (refer as range-based). Each time we randomly selected one point from the collected sequence (with interactive SLAM refinement) as GT, and adopt the two different localization methods, 10000 particles are used for searching. We repeat this operation 30 times (i.e., 30 poses are used) and calculate the average time and total time as shown in Table 6.

It can be seen that, except when dealing with the seq1 (the trajectory of seq1 is very simple as shown in Fig. 7 column 1-right), our semantic-based method can achieve faster convergence time with 10000 particles MCL, the average time for the six sequences is 10.02 s, involving the semantic guidance reduces 13% calculating time. However, using this algorithm only when the robot is initialized for localization, the improvement is not significant.

Table 6. Comparison of the calculation time.

Seq #	Range-Based		Semantic-Based	
	Average Time (s)	Total Time (s)	Average Time (s)	Total Time (s)
0	11.87	341.29	**9.94**	**253.33**
1	**10.88**	**281.42**	11.39	306.88
2	11.45	304.78	**9.38**	**216.16**
3	11.53	308.82	**9.70**	**247.43**
4	11.36	325.79	**8.77**	**257.69**
5	11.97	274.02	**10.96**	**289.93**
Avg.	11.51	306.02	**10.02**	**261.90**

Considering that the relocation algorithm cannot meet the real-time require-ments, we embed it as a module into the existing SLAM algorithm-LOAM. The algorithm will be used as a back-end optimization module to periodically start (that is, every one minute) to perform a global search and relocation to correct the drift of the robot. We refer to the corrected key frame poses with interac-tive SLAM from previous steps, which means only the poses with the shortest distance to the key frame poses are considered duration evaluation. It is easy to see from Table 3 that even involved with semantic information, the MME of the final point cloud map from LOAM is larger than Interactive SLAM. In the absence of GPS or other precise measurement equipment, it is feasible to use the results of interactive SLAM optimization as GT.

Table 7. Localization and rotation (Yaw) errors between different SLAM back-end optimization.

Seq #	A-LOAM		LOAM w Range-map		LOAM w Semantic Range-map	
	Location (m)	Yaw (deg)	Location (m)	Yaw (deg)	Location (m)	Yaw (deg)
0	1.01	0.16	0.96	0.11	0.84↓	0.07↓
2	0.23	0.32	0.20	0.21	0.16↓	0.08↓
4	1.58	1.18	1.52	0.81	1.19↓	0.50↓

Table 7 illustrates the evaluation results on the three challenge sequences of seq0, seq2 and seq4, their trajectories are more complex as shown in the Fig. 7 left column. The A-LOAM is the baseline algorithm without back-end optimization; LOAM w Range-map uses the range-based strategies and prior distance based point cloud map; LOAM with Semantic Range-map uses the semantic range-map and prior semantic point cloud map for periodic relocation optimization at every one minute period. It can be seen that, with a back-end optimization, both root mean square errors (RMSE) of the localization (x, y) and rotation (yaw) are reduced. In general, the search distance for closed-loop detection is short, and there are few closed loops that can be formed in the trajectory of sequence 04. The estimated position and rotation RMSE of key frames are the largest, and the estimation error can also be significantly reduced by periodic relocation of the back-end. Moreover, with the semantic guidance, LOAM can achieve more remarkable results than the comparison methods.

5 Conclusion and Future Work

In order to improve the autonomous localization and mobility of mobile robots in unstable indoor illumination scenarios, this paper proposes a semantic optimization method based on low-cost LiDAR localization. In order to quickly and efficiently construct LiDAR point cloud data for semantic information acquisition without the aid of GPS or expensive measurement equipment, we introduced human collaboration twice in the entire workflow: 1) the interactive SLAM and 2) semantic data labeling. And the point cloud semantic segmentation model is used to simulate human cognitive ability for real-time point cloud semantic information acquisition. Based on the semantic information, we proposed a novel semantic range-map based MCL to improve the back-end of the A-LOAM. With multiple sequence data collected in a local underground garage, we perform extensive quantitative evaluations and comparative testing on the above workflow. The results show that periodic relocation optimization by introducing semantic information at the back-end can effectively reduce pose drift and overall map degradation. We also plan to introduce the valuable semantic information for the SLAM front-end in the future, improve the understanding of the dynamic environment, and optimize the overall workflow for different senses.

References

1. Luo, Y., Binbin, S., Zheng, X.: Trends and challenges for population and health during population aging-china, 2015–2050. China CDC Weekly 3(28), 593 (2021)
2. Yang, G., et al.: Homecare robotic systems for healthcare 4.0: visions and enabling technologies. IEEE J. Biomed. Health Inform. 24(9), 2535–2549 (2020)
3. Zhang, J., Singh, S.: Loam: lidar odometry and mapping in real-time. In: Robotics: Science and Systems, Berkeley, CA, vol. 2, no. 9, pp. 1–9 (2014)
4. Song, C.K., Uchanski, M., Karl Hedrick, J.: Vehicle speed estimation using accelerometer and wheel speed measurements. Soc. of Automotive Engineers (2002)
5. Barbieri, L., Brambilla, M., Trabattoni, A., Mervic, S., Nicoli, M.: UWB localization in a smart factory: augmentation methods and experimental assessment. IEEE Trans. Instrum. Meas. 70, 1–18 (2021)
6. Wang, L., et al.: Initial assessment of the LEO based navigation signal augmentation system from Luojia-1a satellite. Sensors 18(11), 3919 (2018)
7. Li, Y., He, L., Zhang, X., Zhu, L., Zhang, H., Guan, Y.: Multi-sensor fusion localization of indoor mobile robot. In: 2019 IEEE International Conference on Real-time Computing and Robotics (RCAR), pp. 481–486. IEEE (2019)
8. Campos, C., Elvira, R., Gómez Rodríguez, J.J., Montiel, J.M.M., Tardós, J.D.: Orb-slam3: an accurate open-source library for visual, visual-inertial, and multimap slam. IEEE Trans. Robot. 37(6), 1874–1890 (2021)

9. Shan, T., Englot, B.: Lego-loam: lightweight and ground-optimized lidar odometry and mapping on variable terrain. In 2018 IEEE/RSJ International Conference on Intelligent Robots and Systems (IROS), pp. 4758–4765. IEEE (2018)

10. Cui, J., Niu, J., Ouyang, Z., He, Y., Liu, D.: ACSC: automatic calibration for non-repetitive scanning solid-state lidar and camera systems. arXiv preprint arXiv:2011.08516 (2020)

11. Chen, X., Milioto, A., Palazzolo, E., Giguère, P., Behley, J., Stachniss, C.: Suma++: efficient lidar-based semantic slam. In: 2019 IEEE/RSJ International Conference on Intelligent Robots and Systems (IROS), pp. 4530–4537. IEEE (2019)

12. Koide, K., Miura, J., Yokozuka, M., Oishi, S., Banno, A.: Interactive 3d graph slam for map correction. IEEE Robot. Autom. Lett. **6**(1), 40–47 (2020)

13. Behley, J., et al.: Semantickitti: a dataset for semantic scene understanding of lidar sequences. In: Proceedings of the IEEE International Conference on Computer Vision, pp. 9297–9307 (2019)

14. Zhang, Y., et al.: PolarNet: an improved grid representation for online lidar point clouds semantic segmentation. In: Proceedings of the IEEE/CVF Conference on Computer Vision and Pattern Recognition, pp. 9601–9610 (2020)

15. Zhang, L., Wei, L., Shen, P., Wei, W., Zhu, G., Song, J.: Semantic slam based on object detection and improved octomap. IEEE Access **6**, 75545–75559 (2018)

16. Mur-Artal, R., Tardós, J.D.: Orb-slam2: an open-source slam system for monocular, stereo, and RGB-D cameras. IEEE Trans. Robot. **33**(5), 1255–1262 (2017)

17. Redmon, J., Divvala, S., Girshick, R., Farhadi, A.: You only look once: unified, real-time object detection. In: Proceedings of the IEEE Conference on Computer Vision and Pattern Recognition, pp. 779–788 (2016)

18. Wang, Z., Zhang, Q., Li, J., Zhang, S., Liu, J.: A computationally efficient semantic slam solution for dynamic scenes. Remote Sen. **11**(11), 1363 (2019)

19. Kang, X., Yuan, S.: Robust data association for object-level semantic slam. arXiv preprint arXiv:1909.13493 (2019)

20. Long, X., Zhang, W., Zhao, B.: Pspnet-slam: a semantic slam detect dynamic object by pyramid scene parsing network. IEEE Access (2020)

21. Zhao, H., Shi, J., Qi, X., Wang, X., Jia, J.: Pyramid scene parsing network. In: Proceedings of the IEEE Conference on Computer Vision and Pattern Recognition, pp. 2881–2890 (2017)

22. Zhao, Z., Mao, Y., Ding, Y., Ren, P., Zheng, N.: Visual-based semantic slam with landmarks for large-scale outdoor environment. In: 2019 2nd China Symposium on Cognitive Computing and Hybrid Intelligence (CCHI), pp. 149–154. IEEE (2019)

23. Rosinol, A., Abate, M., Chang, Y., Carlone, L.: Kimera: an open-source library for real-time metric-semantic localization and mapping. In: 2020 IEEE International Conference on Robotics and Automation (ICRA), pp. 1689–1696. IEEE (2020)

24. Fan, Y., et al.: Semantic slam with more accurate point cloud map in dynamic environments. IEEE Access **8**, 112237–112252 (2020)

25. Mahe, H., Marraud, D., Comport, A.I.: Real-time RGB-D semantic keyframe slam based on image segmentation learning from industrial cad models. In: 2019 19th International Conference on Advanced Robotics (ICAR), pp.s 147–154. IEEE (2019)

26. Nicholson, L., Milford, M., Sünderhauf, N.: Quadricslam: constrained dual quadrics from object detections as landmarks in semantic slam. IEEE Robot. Autom. Lett. (RA-L) (2018)

27. Li, R., Wang, S., Dongbing, G.: Ongoing evolution of visual slam from geometry to deep learning: challenges and opportunities. Cogn. Comput. **10**(6), 875–889 (2018)

28. Redmon, J., Farhadi, A.: Yolo9000: better, faster, stronger. In Proceedings of the IEEE Conference on Computer Vision and Pattern Recognition, pp. 7263–7271 (2017)
29. Lehtonen, M., Ostojic, D., Ilic, A., Michahelles, F.: Securing RFID systems by detecting tag cloning. In: Tokuda, H., Beigl, M., Friday, A., Brush, A.J.B., Tobe, Y. (eds.) Pervasive 2009. LNCS, vol. 5538, pp. 291–308. Springer, Heidelberg (2009). https://doi.org/10.1007/978-3-642-01516-8_20
30. He, K., Gkioxari, G., Dollár, P., Girshick, R.: Mask R-CNN. In: Proceedings of the IEEE International Conference on Computer Vision, pp. 2961–2969 (2017)
31. Dong, X., Niu, J., Cui, J., Fu, Z., Ouyang, Z.: Fast segmentation-based object tracking model for autonomous vehicles. In: Qiu, M. (ed.) ICA3PP 2020. LNCS, vol. 12453, pp. 259–273. Springer, Cham (2020). https://doi.org/10.1007/978-3-030-60239-0_18
32. Graeter, J., Wilczynski, A., Lauer, M.: Limo: lidar-monocular visual odometry. In: 2018 IEEE/RSJ International Conference on Intelligent Robots and Systems (IROS), pp. 7872–7879. IEEE (2018)
33. Jian, R., et al.: A semantic segmentation based lidar SLAM system towards dynamic environments. In: Yu, H., Liu, J., Liu, L., Ju, Z., Liu, Y., Zhou, D. (eds.) ICIRA 2019. LNCS (LNAI), vol. 11742, pp. 582–590. Springer, Cham (2019). https://doi.org/10.1007/978-3-030-27535-8_52
34. Zhao, Z., Zhang, W., Jianfeng, G., Yang, J., Huang, K.: Lidar mapping optimization based on lightweight semantic segmentation. IEEE Trans. Intell. Veh. 4(3), 353–362 (2019)
35. Milioto, A., Vizzo, I., Behley, J., Stachniss, C.: Rangenet++: fast and accurate lidar semantic segmentation. In: 2019 IEEE/RSJ International Conference on Intelligent Robots and Systems (IROS), pp. 4213–4220. IEEE (2019)
36. Chen, X.: et al.: Overlapnet: loop closing for lidar-based SLAM. In: Proceedings of the Robotics: Science and Systems (RSS), Freiburg, Germany, pp. 12–16 (2020)
37. Sun, L., Yan, Z., Zaganidis, A., Zhao, C., Duckett, T.: Recurrent-octomap: learning state-based map refinement for long-term semantic mapping with 3-d-lidar data. IEEE Robot. Autom. Lett. 3(4), 3749–3756 (2018)
38. Pan, Y., Gao, B., Mei, J., Geng, S., Li, C., Zhao, H.: Semanticposs: a point cloud dataset with large quantity of dynamic instances. arXiv preprint arXiv:2002.09147 (2020)
39. Hu, Q., et al.: Randla-net: efficient semantic segmentation of large-scale point clouds. In: Proceedings of the IEEE/CVF Conference on Computer Vision and Pattern Recognition, pp. 11108–11117 (2020)
40. Zhu, X., et al.: Cylindrical and asymmetrical 3D convolution networks for lidar segmentation. arXiv preprint arXiv:2011.10033 (2020)
41. Chen, X., Vizzo, I., Läbe, T., Behley, J., Stachniss, C.: Range image-based lidar localization for autonomous vehicles. In: 2021 IEEE International Conference on Robotics and Automation (ICRA), pp. 5802–5808. IEEE (2021)
42. Razlaw, J., Droeschel, D., Holz, D., Behnke, S.: Evaluation of registration methods for sparse 3d laser scans. In: 2015 European Conference on Mobile Robots (ECMR), pp. 1–7. IEEE (2015)

Incorporating Feature Labeling into Crowdsourcing for More Accurate Aggregation Labels

Yili Fang, Zhaoqi Pei, Xinyi Ding, Wentao Xu, and Tao Han(✉)

School of Computer and Information Engineering, Zhejiang Gongshang University,
Hangzhou 310018, China
{fangyl,zhaoqipei,xding,xuwentao6666,hantao}@zjgsu.edu.cn

Abstract. Crowdsourcing is a popular way of collecting crowd wisdom and has been deployed in various senarios. Effective *answer collection* and *answer aggregation* are two important crowdsourcing topics as workers may give incorrect responses. For difficult tasks, workers tend to implicitly use task related information during *answer collection*, and those information could play an important role in aggregating high-quality results. For example, the identification of the size and hair style of one dog in a picture is a simple and necessary prerequisite step for dog breed labeling. However, most existing methods ignore those task related information and fail to achieve high quality data.

In this study, we propose a framework that incorporates the answers of corresponding tasks from workers and their labeling to object features, which we believe are critical task related information for *answer aggregation*. Then, we propose a novel generative probability graph model that can infer the task answers by exploiting label features, as well as worker ability and their responses. We use EM algorithm to estimate model parameters and infer true answers. Experimental results demonstrate that incorporating task related information can greatly improve the accuracy of *answer aggregation*. Compared with state of the art ones that ignore these information, our methods could achieve about 15.9%–36.8% improvement in accuracy.

Keywords: Crowdsourcing · Answer collection · Answer aggregation · Probability graph model

1 Introduction

Crowdsourcing has been successfully applied in solving a large number of practical tasks [4, 20, 21], such as data annotation [25], text translation [34], sentiment analysis [19], etc. It is a valid and inexpensive way for researchers to collect labels from non-expert crowds in open Internet based marketplaces. But the quality of collected data provided by the workers might be very low due to a variety of factors, including their background, skills, and motivation. A commonly used

H. Gao et al. (Eds.): CollaborateCom 2022, LNICST 461, pp. 306–324, 2022.
https://doi.org/10.1007/978-3-031-24386-8_17

method is to collect multiple labels for the same task from different workers, then apply a label aggregation algorithm to infer the true label for each task. In general, crowdsourcing involves *answer collection* and *answer aggregation*. In *answer collection*, due to the unreliability of workers, requesters usually distribute one task redundantly to multiple workers on a crowdsourcing platform, such as *Amazon's Mechanical Turk*[1]. Workers get paid by processing the assigned tasks and submit their responses. In *answer aggregation*, aggregation algorithms are used to deduce high-quality results from redundant noisy answers submitted by workers. In the past few years, researchers have proposed different models to improve the accuracy of aggregation results.

In crowdsourcing, the task related information plays an important role in the answer collection stage and in answer aggregation. In *answer collection*, workers can better complete the task if given these related information. For example, if we want to annotate a picture of an Alaskan Malamute, some workers without relevant knowledge might label it as a Poodle or other dog breeds with large size. In fact, workers often need to use these related information explicitly or not before he/she can give a label. However, existing methods try to obtain high-quality data by assigning tasks to workers with higher abilities [6,7,23], but often ignore some useful task related information, which is important in answer aggregation. We refer to the collection of these task related information as hidden sub-tasks (HSTs) in crowdsourcing. In fact, workers may have implicitly carried out these HSTs when handling one task and they could play an important role in inferring high-quality results. In the task of dog breed classification, the identification of size and hair style of one dog could be thought of as HSTs. In *answer aggregation*, task related information also plays important roles. In the dog labeling example, methods like MV will ignore the fact that *Alaskan Malamute* tends to be large size while *Poodle* tends to be small. But such features could often help exclude some answers thus improve the overall accuracy. Although a lot of aggregation methods have been proposed to improve the quality of the answers provided by workers, they often ask workers to only focus on the final results and ignore task related information (such as the features of an object) [2,24,27,33]. In short, how to collect and harness the task related information to improve the quality of the overall aggregation results is the main focus of the paper.

In this paper, we focus on using feature labels collected from HSTs to improve the overall aggregation results in labeling tasks. In the *answer collection* phase of crowdsouring, we propose a framework to ask workers to explicitly carry out HSTs and record their responses. This framework allows us to collect object's category as well as feature information from workers. For example, we require workers to give their answers not only to dog breed label but also labels for dog features like size, hair style, etc. In the *answer aggregation* phase, we propose a probabilistic model called the Generative model of Labels, Abilities, and Features (GLAF), in which we factorize the conditional probability of the most accurate answer with respect to current object labels, worker abilities, features, and the relationship between object labels and feature labels. In order to represent the effect of feature

---

[1] https://www.mturk.com.

labels to the aggregation results, we use a matrix to represent the relationship between object labels and feature labels. Each element in the matrix represents the probability that one class of objects has a certain feature. The inferred results, workers' abilities and other parameters used in the model are estimated using EM (expectation-maximization) algorithm. Our main contributions are summarized as follows:

- We propose a framework, which allows workers to collect as many feature labels as possible based on the fact that workers are usually better at identifying features than categories.
- We propose a novel generative probability model GLAF, which can infer the answers of tasks by exploiting the relationship between object labels and feature labels.
- We conduct extensive experiments and the results show that incorporating feature labels could significantly improve the results. Compared with other state of the art ones without these information, our model is also superior.

The rest of the paper is organized as follows. Section 2 discusses the related works. Section 3 formalizes the problem studied and outlines our framework for *answer aggregation*. Section 4 introduces the details of our approach. The experimental results are shown in Sect. 5 and we conclude the paper in Sect. 6.

2   Related Work

Since the advent of crowdsourcing [9], it has been successfully applied in artificial intelligence that leverages human intelligence to improve machine performance. It has also been applied in many applications such as entity resolution [31], image annotation [25], audio recognition [10], video annoation [30], etc.

In the *answer collection* phase, obtaining answers for the same task from multiple workers is a simple and direct way to improve the data quality [6,7,23]. Task design and rational assignment of tasks to workers on the crowdsourcing platform are also helpful in collecting high-quality data. At the same time, many works [8,17,22] have proved that collecting more comprehensive information about workers and tasks can help improve the quality of *answer aggregation*. Oyama et al. proposed a framework to collect labels and task related information (such as confidence scores) provided by crowdsourcing workers to improve decision accuracy [22]. Li et al. demonstrated an interactive programming tookit that is a unified solution for answering the crowdsourced top-k queries to control the quality of labels [17]. Hoßfeld et al. developed *two-stage QoE crowdtesting design* which leads to more reliable results [8].

In the phase of *answer aggregation*, not only the true answers of tasks are inferred, but also some other potential useful information. This process is also called truth inference. The agnostic label aggregation algorithms that solely use crowdsourced multiple noisy labels have been extensive researched. These works tried to model the complexities of the crowdsourced labeling from different angles, such as confusion matrices [24,29,36,37],reliability [1,3,13,15,33], intentions [1,14], and difficulties of instances [1,14,32,33], and biases [12,32]of labelers. MV is a simple aggregation method, which takes the value with the highest number of votes as the true label of the task [26]. In addition, Dawid and Skene proposed a classic algorithm DS based on maximum likelihood estimation and EM algorithm. They model the diagnosis results of multiple doctors on the same patient and use a confusion matrix to represent the performance of workers to infer the true label of each task [2]. Inspired by DS, Smyth et al. used a similar method on the Venus image dataset to infer the true value of subjective labels [28]. Raykar et al. proposed a Bayesian method, RY, which adds a specific prior to each category. In this method, crowdsourcing workers have different biases for positive and negative categories and use two parameters to model them [24]. By incorporating worker abilities and object difficulties, Li et al. proposed a family of models to learn the object embeddings from crowdsourced triplet similarity comparisons [16]. A multiple noisy label distribution propagation (MNLDP) method is proposed in [11]. This method at first estimates the multiple noisy label distribution of each instance from its multiple noisy label set. And then it propagates its multiple noisy label distribution to its nearest neighbors. Finally, each instance assimilates a part of the multiple noisy label distributions from its nearest neighbors and at the same time keeps a part of its own original multiple noisy label distribution. All of the above methods [2,16,24,28] only model workers' answers to tasks to infer the true value, while ignoring other task related information such as feature information that may have potential value for inferring the true value of the task. Our research makes full use of feature labels and the relationship between object labels and feature labels.

There are also some existing works that use task related information to help infer the true value. Zhang et al. proposed a cluster-based label aggregation algorithm GTIC [35]. Their method uses a feature vector to represent the task and then use a clustering method to cluster all tasks according to the feature vector of each task. Hang et al. proposed CrowdMKT on the basis of SKT. This model uses knowledge transfer to learn high-level feature vectors of tasks from multiple related data sources and then introduces a probability model to jointly model tasks with high-level features, workers and their annotations [5]. Welinder et al.proposed a method that deals with image formation and annotation process. Each image has different features that are represented in an abstract Euclidean space. Each annotator is modeled as a multidimensional entity with variables representing competence, expertise and bias [32] . PLA (Prediction-based Label Aggregation) is proposed to intelligently aggregate the crowd wisdom and the predicted answers to improve the performance of label aggregation in [18].

Different from these studies, we collect noisy answers and feature labels of the HSTs provided by workers and model worker's abilities and HSTs respectively. After having these data prepared, we focus on incorporating feature labels and its relationship with object labels into *answer aggregation* for more accurate aggregation results.

3   Problem Formulation

In this section, we first define the problem of Turth Inference with feature labels (TIF), then discuss our framework that incorporates feature labeling. The notations used are displayed in Table 1.

Table 1. Table of Notations

Notation	Description
W	Worker set consist of $|W|$ workers
T	Task set consist of $|T|$ tasks
Ω	Category set of a task
$|W|$	Worker numbers
$|T|$	Task numbers
w_j	Anchor worker
t_i	Anchor task
E'	Feature set of a task
E	Feature label space of the task
l_{ij}^z	Category answer of task t_i provided by worker w_j
l_{ij}^e	Feature answer of task t_i provided by worker w_j
$L=\{l_{ij}^z, l_{ij}^e\}$	All set of answers

3.1   Definition of TIF

In our study, we ask workers to give not only answers to tasks but also their labels to different features. We use these noisy data to infer the final results. We call our problem the Truth Inference with feature labels problem (TIF) and define it formally as follows.

Definition 1 (Truth Inference with feature labels (TIF) problem). *Let* $T = \{t_i | i \in I_T\}$ *be the unlabeled task set,* $W = \{w_j | j \in I_W\}$ *be the workers set,* $\Omega = \{c_k | k \in I_\Omega\}$ *be the answer domain set. The problem of TIF is to find a function* $f : \Omega^{|T| \times |W|} \longrightarrow \Omega^{|T|}$, *which generates the most precise answer from all the labels provided by workers for each task.*

Without loss of generality, we consider label aggregation in a classification crowdsourcing task. Let $E' = \{e | e \in I_e\}$ denotes feature labels for a given task. For example, when a worker is working on a task to classify dog breeds, the elements in this set can be traits such as the dog's hair style, body size, etc. Let the vector $E = \{< e_1, e_2, ..., e_m, ..., e_n > | e_m \in \Omega_{e_m}\}$ be the feature label space of the task, and the element in this vector is the specific feature label values of an object. For the dog breeds classification example, the element in this vector can be (long hair, big size). We denote the label set $L = \{L_1, L_2, ..., L_n\}$ where

$L_i \in L$ contains labels that workers give to t_i. Namely, for $\forall t_i \in T$ we get label set $L_i = \{l_{ij}^z, l_{ij}^e | i \in I_T, j \in I_W, e \in I_e\}$ from workers. The problem of TIF is to find a function $f : \Omega^{|T| \times |W|} \times E^{|T| \times |W|} \longrightarrow \Omega^{|T|}$, which generates the most specific label from all the labels provided by workers for each task.

Let $F = \{f | f : \Omega^{|T| \times |W|} \times E^{|T| \times |W|} \longrightarrow \Omega^{|T|}\}$ be the universal set of aggregation algorithms of TIF. Then with the well-defined value function $v : F \longrightarrow \mathbf{R}$ which measures quality of the algorithms, we can formulate the aggregation problem of TIF as to find a function f^*:

$$f^* = \arg\max_{f \in F} v(f). \tag{1}$$

For instance, if there are 100 tasks and 10 workers, one worker has to choose from 4 candidate answers. Each answer has two features and each feature has two possible feature values, then the aggregation algorithm is to find a function with a $100 \times 10 \times 3$ (1 for category, 2 for feature) answer matrix as input and a 100 dimensional answer vector as output.

3.2   Framework of Crowdsourcing with Feature Labeling

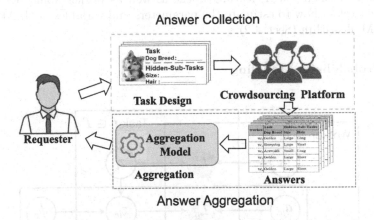

Fig. 1. Framework of crowdsourcing with feature labeling.

To exploit the relationship between object's class and the corresponding feature labels, we propose a novel crowdsourcing framework with feature labeling as shown in Fig. 1. The steps of this workflow are listed as follows.

– **Step 1:** A requester first prepares tasks including the objects that need to be classified and the related information that workers needs to process(such as hair style, size of a dog). Then the requester needs to design the detailed task interface using tools provided by the platform before publishing tasks.

Crowdsourcing platforms like Amazon's Mechanical Turk usually provide flexible tools and APIs that allow requesters to customize the way tasks are presented.

- **Step 2:** Once the requester published the tasks. The platform will assign them to workers based on the requester's requirements and the platform's own policies.
- **Step 3:** For each received task, a worker provides both the answer as well as the feature labels of the corresponding task. One worker will get paid once the platform accepts his/her answers.
- **Step 4:** After collecting all the answers from workers, we run our model with feature labels to infer the aggregated result for each task. Finally, all the aggregated results are returned to the requester.

Using this framework, requesters can easily collect answers to tasks, as well as critical related information that could help improve the aggregation results.

4   GLAF Model

In this section, we introduce a novel probabilistic model that incorporates object label, its relationship with feature labels, as well as worker ability (Sect. 4.1). Then we explain how to estimate the parameters and variables of GLAF model using EM algorithm (Sect. 4.2).

4.1   Probabilistic Modeling

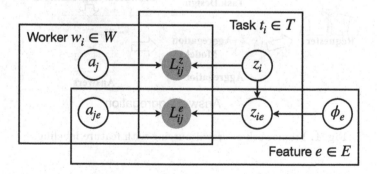

Fig. 2. Probability graph of GLAF model.

Consider a dataset of n tasks, each of which has one of many possible candidate answers. Our goal is to determine the true answer z_i of each task i by querying from workers. The answers depend on several causal factors: (1) the abilities of workers; (2) the relationship between object label and feature labels; and (3) the true answer.

The ability of each worker w_j is modeled by parameter $a = \{a_j, a_{je}\}$. Here $a_j \in (-\infty, +\infty), a_j = +\infty$ means the worker always labels images correctly; $-\infty$ means the worker always labels images incorrectly; $a_j = 0$ means that the worker cannot discriminate the candidate answers. And a_{je} is the same as a_j. The relation between object labels and feature labels is modeled by a parameter matrix $\phi = \{\phi^e | e \in I_E\}$, the value $\phi^e_{k f_{eg}}$ in the matrix represents the probability that the answer k is corresponding with feature label f_{eg}. $\phi^e_{k f_{eg}} = 0$ means that the answer k wouldn't appear together with feature label f_{eg}; $\phi^e_{k f_{eg}} = 1$ means that the answer k would appear with feature label f_{eg} all the time. Let $Z = \{z_i, z_{ie} | i \in I_T, e \in I_E\}$ be the task truth set. Here z_i is the answer truth value of the task t_i and z_{ie} is the truth value of feature e of the task t_i.

The larger a_j is, the more likely one worker could answer the task correctly. So we can present the conditional probability that l^z_{ij} is correct given z_i, a_j with a softmax function as follows:

$$p(l^z_{ij} = z_i | z_i, a_j) = \frac{1}{1 + (K-1)e^{-a_j}}, \tag{2}$$

where K is the number of answers. Note that $p(l^z_{ij} = z_i | z_i, a_j)$ increases with the increase of a_j. When a_j tends to be positive infinity, $p(l^z_{ij} = z_i | z_i, a_j) = 1$ means worker w_j always gives the correct answer. Generally, when ability a_j of worker w_j and category z_i of task t_i are given, we can compute the probability that worker w_j correctly answers category of task t_i by Eq. 2.

The larger a_{je} is, the more likely one worker could answer the task correctly. So the conditional probability that l^e_{ij} is correct given z_i, z_{ie}, a_{je} can be expressed as:

$$p(l^e_{ij} = z_{ie} | z_{ie}, z_i, a_{je}) = \frac{1}{1 + (K_e - 1)e^{-a_{je}}}, \tag{3}$$

where K_e is the number of the alternative of feature e. Again, $p(l^e_{ij} = z_{ie} | z_{ie}, z_i, a_{je})$ increases with the increase of a_{je}. Generally, when ability a_{je} of worker w_j, category z_i of task t_i and feature z_{ie} of task t_i are given, we can compute the probability that worker w_j correctly answers feature e of task t_i by Eq. 3.

We present the relation between object labels and features given ϕ^e, z_i with a number $\phi^e_{k f_{eg}} \in [0, 1]$ as follows:

$$p(z_{ie} = f_{eg} | z_i = c_k, \phi^e) = \phi^e_{k f_{eg}}, \tag{4}$$

If the category z_i of task and the relation matrix ϕ^e between object labels and features are given, we can compute the probability that task t_i has the feature f_{eg} by Eq. 4.

Let $L = \{l^z_{ij}, l^e_{ij} | i \in I_T, j \in I_W, e \in I_E\}$, $\theta = \{a, \phi\}$. We want to find the optimal θ^* that maximizes $P(L|\theta)$. Our objective function is as follows:

$$\theta^* = \arg \max_{\theta} \ln P(L|\theta), \tag{5}$$

where $\ln P(L|\theta)$ is the log likelihood function we want to maximize. In detail, we compute $\ln p(L|\theta)$ as:

$$
\ln p(L|\theta) = \sum_i \ln \left[\sum_k p(z_i|\theta) \prod_j p(l_{ij}^z|z_i, \theta) \right.
$$
$$
\left. \prod_{e,g} p(z_{ie} = f_{eg}|z_i, \theta) \prod_j p(l_{ij}^e|z_i, z_{ie}, \theta) \right]. \tag{6}
$$

We maximize $\ln p(L|\theta)$ to learn the parameters θ and infer the true answers of tasks (Sect. 4.2).

4.2 Inference

We formally introduced the GLAF model as shown in Fig. 2 in Sect. 4.1. In our model, we have l_{ij}^z, l_{ij}^e being the workers answers. The unobserved variables are the true labels z_i, z_{ie}, ability parameters a_j, a_{je} and relation matrix ϕ^e. Our goal is to find the posterior distribution of z_i and select the label z_i with the maximum a posterior estimation as the final answer to task t_i.

For simplicity, the prior distribution of z_i is set to be an uniform discrete distribution over label domain Ω. In addition, we ignore the prior of a_j and a_{je} and the elements in the mapping relationship matrix between object labels and feature labels are initially set as $\frac{1}{K_e}$. Finally, we use EM algorithm to obtain maximum likelihood estimates of the parameters of a_j, a_{je}, ϕ^e.

E Step: Let $l_i = \{l_{ij}^z, l_{ij}^e | j \in I_W, e \in I_E\}$. Then for $\forall i \in I_T$, we compute posterior probability $p(z_i = c_k|L, a, \phi)$ as:

$$
p(z_i = c_k|L, a, \phi)
$$
$$
\propto p(z_i = c_k|a, \phi)p(l_i|z_i = c_k, a, \phi)
$$
$$
\propto p(z_i = c_k|a, \phi) \left[\prod_j p(l_{ij}^z|z_i = c_k, a_j, \phi) \right.
$$
$$
\left. \cdot \prod_e \sum_g p(z_{ie} = f_{eg}|z_i = c_k, \phi^e) \prod_j p(l_{ij}^e|z_i = c_k, a_{je}) \right] \tag{7}
$$

Here we assume features are conditional independent. For $\forall i \in I_T, \forall e \in I_E$, we compute posterior probability
$p(z_{ie}|L, z_i = c_k, a_{je}, \phi^e)$ as:

$$
p(z_{ie} = f_{eg}|L, z_i = c_k, a_{je}, \phi^e)
$$
$$
\propto p(z_{ie} = f_{eg}|z_i = c_k, \phi^e)p(l_i^e|z_{ie} = f_{eg}, z_i = c_k, \phi^e)
$$
$$
\propto p(z_{ie} = f_{eg}|z_i, \phi_e) \prod_j p(l_{ij}^e|z_{ie} = f_{eg}, z_i = c_k, a_{je}) \tag{8}
$$

If answer set L of workers, category z_i of task, ability a_{je} of worker and the relation matrix ϕ^e between object labels and features are given, we can compute the conditional probability distribution of feature e of task t_i by Eq. 8 and its category z_i.

M Step: Let $L = \{l_{ij}^z, l_{ij}^e | i \in I_T, j \in I_W, e \in I_E\}, Z = \{z_i, z_{ie} | i \in I_T, e \in I_E\}$. We compute standard auxiliary function Q:

$$
\begin{aligned}
&Q(a^{old}, \phi^{old}, a, \phi) \\
&= E[\ln p(L, Z | a, \phi)] \\
&= \sum_i E[\ln p(z_i)] + \sum_i E[\ln p(l_i | z_i, a, \phi)] \\
&= Const + \sum_{i,k} \ln p(l_i^z | z_i, a, \phi)\beta_{ik} + \sum_{i,k} \beta_{ik} \sum_e \ln p(l_i^e | z_i, a, \phi) \\
&= Const + \sum_{i,k,j} \ln p(l_{ij}^z | z_i, a, \phi)\beta_{ik} + \sum_{i,k} \beta_{ik} \sum_{e,g} q_{ikeg} \ln p(l_i^e, z_{ie} | z_i, a, \phi) \\
&= Const + \sum_{i,k,j} \ln p(l_{ij}^z | z_i, a, \phi)\beta_{ik} + \sum_{i,k} \beta_{ik} \sum_{e,g} q_{ikeg} \ln p(z_{ie} | z_i, a, \phi) \\
&\quad + \sum_{i,k} \beta_{ik} \sum_{e,g,j} q_{ikeg} \ln p(l_{ij}^e | z_{ie}, z_i, a, \phi),
\end{aligned}
\tag{9}
$$

where

$$
\begin{aligned}
\beta_{ik} &= p(z_i = c_k | L, a^{old}, \phi^{old}), \\
q_{ikeg} &= p(z_{ie} = f_{eg} | L, z_i = c_k, a^{old}, \phi^{old}).
\end{aligned}
$$

We use the old parameters a^{old} and ϕ^{old} to update posterior probability of E step. Then we use results of E step to update new a and ϕ by

$$
(a^*, \phi^*) = \arg\max_{(a, \phi)} Q(a^{old}, \phi^{old}, a, \phi).
\tag{10}
$$

The problem in Eq. 10 is an optimization problem and we use *Lagrange multiplier* method to solve it with the constraint condition $\sum_g q_{ikeg} = 1$. Then we can get the following results:

$$
a_j = \ln(K - 1) - \ln\left(\frac{\sum_i \sum_k \beta_{ik} + K * \alpha}{\sum_i \sum_k \beta_{ik} I(l_{ij}^z, c_k) + \alpha} - 1\right)
\tag{11}
$$

$$
a_{je} = \ln(K_e - 1) - \ln\left(\frac{\sum_i \sum_k \beta_{ik} \sum_g q_{ikeg} + K_e * \alpha}{\sum_i \sum_k \beta_{ik} \sum_g q_{ikeg} I(l_{ij}^e, f_{eg}) + \alpha} - 1\right)
\tag{12}
$$

$$
\phi_{k f_{eg}}^e = \frac{\sum_g \sum_i \beta_{ik} q_{ikeg}}{\sum_g \sum_i \beta_{ik}}
\tag{13}
$$

Algorithm 1: Algorithm 1 EM algorithm for GLAF Model

Input: Label matrix $L = \{l_{ij}^z, l_{ij}^e | i \in I_T, j \in I_W\}$
Output: aggregation labels $Z = \{z_i | i \in I_T\}$
1 **Initialization:**
2 worker j's ability parameter $a_j = 1, a_{je} = 1$
3 **for** $n=0$ to iterations **do**
4   **if** ability errors $<$ tolerance **then**
5   break;
6   **E step:**
7   compute $p(z_i|L, a, \phi)$, $p(z_{ie}|L, z_i, a, \phi)$
8   **M step:**
9   update a, ϕ by $\underset{(a,\phi)}{\mathrm{argmax}}\, E[\ln p(L, Z|a, \phi)]$
10 **return** $z_i = \underset{z_i}{\mathrm{argmax}}\, p(z_i|L, a, \phi)$

---

where $I(\cdot)$ in Eq. 11 and Eq. 12 is an indicator function and we used *additive smoothing* to solve a_j and a_{je} to prevent a_j or a_{je} become infinity. For simplicity, we set the priori $\alpha = 0.1$.

The derivation detail is omitted due to its complexity and numerous formula derivations. We will provide the details and the code upon the publication of this paper. The EM algorithm is summarized in Algorithm 1.

5 Experiments

In this section, we conduct experiments to evaluate our proposed GLAF model. We first describe three simplified versions of our model and the used baselines. Next, we introduce how to generate simulated data and show the impact of parameters and data scale respectively. We describe our implementation of a real crowdsourcing process in AMT, then discuss the results.

5.1 Experiments Setup

We study the effectiveness of our GLAF model through a series of experiments on one synthetic dataset and one real dataset with features labels. The following nine models are used for experimental comparison:

- **MV** directly uses majority votes to integrate annotations without feature labels or modeling of tasks and workers [26].
- **DS** uses one confusion matrix to model the ability of each worker and infers the true answers of tasks using EM algorithm [2].
- **HDS** simplifies the assumption made by DS to consider a confusion matrix with only a single parameter, in which each worker is assumed to have the same accuracy on each class of task, and have the same error probabilities as well [13, 24].

- **FDS** is a simple, yet effective, EM-based algorithm, which can be interpreted as a 'hard' version of DS model that allows much faster convergence while maintaining similar accuracy in aggregation [27].
- **GLAD** is a probabilistic model that simultaneously infers the answer, difficult level of each task, as well as the ability of each worker [33].
- **GLA** uses one parameter to model the ability of each worker and infers the true answers of tasks using EM algorithm, which is the first simplified versions of our method.
- **GLA(f1)** incorporates the feature $f1$ to infer true labels based on the GLA.
- **GLA(f2)** incorporates the feature $f2$ to infer true labels based on the GLA.
- **GLAF** models worker's abilities to label categories and two features ($f1$ and $f2$), and use the relationship between objects and features as parameters to infer truth labels, which is our proposed method in this paper.

The first six methods build models without using feature labels and the relationship between object labels and features. The other three use feature labels and the relationship between object labels and features. For GLAF and its variants, we initially simply let the relationship be uniformly distributed. For the other methods, we set the parameters (if any) following the suggestions of the authors.

5.2   Simulations

Data Preparation. We simulated 100 workers and 1000 tasks. The true answer of each task belongs to the set Z ($Z = \{0, 1, 2, 3\}$) with equal probability. Each task has two features and the value of each feature is 0 or 1. We let the probability of workers answering the task category correctly obey the uniform distribution from $\frac{1}{K}$ to 1 and the probability of workers answering the task feature correctly obey the uniform distribution from $\frac{1}{K_e}$ to 1, where K is the number of categories and K_e is the number of feature e. Then the observed variable l_{ij}^z can be sampled according to Eq. 1 given a worker's ability to label task categories. In the same way, the observed variable l_{ij}^e can be sampled according to Eq. 2 given the ability of a worker to label task features. And the aforementioned mapping relationship between categories and features can be expressed in the probability form of Eq. 3. We ask each task to be answered 10 times. In this way, we obtained 10000×3 labels (1 category and 2 features).

Results. We run each model with different redundancy to compute the consensus annotation and report the accuracy in Fig. 3(a). As expected, the accuracy of all models increase as the redundancy of each task grows. As we can see, our proposed GLAF model that uses both two feature labels achieved the best performance among all models and is also superior to its degenerated versions GLA(f1) and GLA(f2), which use only one feature label. GLA(f1) and GLA(f2) perform better than GLA, which is a commonly used baseline aggregation algorithm without feature labels. DS, HDS, FDS and GLAD come next with regard to accuracy. Among all these models, MV performs the worst, this could due to

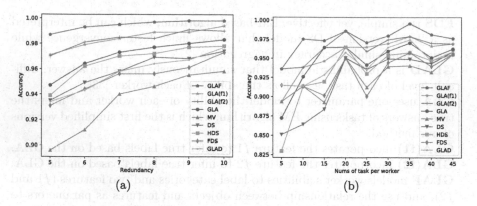

Fig. 3. (a)The accuracies of GLAF model versus other methods for inferring the underlying category labels on simulation data. GLA(s) only uses the features s. (b) The accuracies of GlAF model and other methods vs Numbers of task answered by workers. GLA(s) only uses the features.

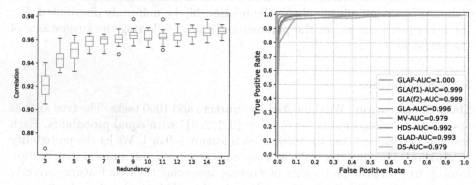

Fig. 4. The ability of GLAF to recover the true a_j parameter on simulation data.

Fig. 5. ROC comparison of GLAF and other models.

the fact that MV directly uses majority vote to integrate annotations without modeling workers ability. Figure 3(b) shows the accuracy when we change the number of tasks performed by worker, again the conclusion is basically the same as in Fig. 3(a), especially when the number of tasks is larger than 30. Overall, the results show that incorporating more features and its relations could significantly improve the model performance.

Correlation. In addition, we change the number of worker from 3 to 15 to see how this impact the learnt parameters. In this simulation, each worker handles 1000 tasks. The truth value of each task belongs to the set Z (Z = 0, 1, 2, 3) with equal probability. The accuracy a_j of each worker was drawn from a uniform distribution. Given these worker abilities, the observed labels l_{ij}^z were sampled according to Eq. 1 using Z. Finally, the EM inference procedure described above was executed to estimate a_j. This procedure was repeated 20 times to smooth out variability between trials. On each trial we computed the correlation between the parameter estimates $\hat{a}_j$ and the true parameter value a_j. The results (averaged over 20 experimental runs) are shown in Fig. 4. As expected, as the number of workers grows, the parameter estimates converge to the true values.

ROC Curves. We performed experiments on simulation dataset to draw roc curves. We can find similar trends as shown in Fig. 3(a). Figure 5 shows the ROC comparisons and AUC values for GLAF model and baseline models. FDS does not output probability distribution data like other methods, so its ROC curve is not shown here. The experimental results demonstrate that our approaches significantly outperform baseline methods without feature data.

5.3   Real-Data

In this section, we first describe the real dataset used and then report the evaluation results of the proposed GLAF model.

Data Preparation. We crawled images of different dogs from *American Kennel Club*[2] and filtered out the images with dead URLs or images with no dogs in it. We finally obtained 820 unambiguous images for experiments.

We used *Amazon Mechanical Turk* and followed the workflow shown in Sect. 3.2. We guarantee the quality of labels by employing high-quality workers in the platform. We gave a brief instruction to guide workers to provide as specific labels as possible. Each task is sent to 20 different workers. For each task, workers were asked to choose the label they gave to the image from a dropdown box and complete two multiple choice questions about the features (hair and size). Hair length includes long hair, short hair and no hair and body sizes include large and small. We collected $820 \times 20 \times 3$ labels (1 category label and 2 feature labels).

After removing the invalid labels, there left 13261 labels annotated by 412 workers and the number of unique labels is 59, which is considerably large compared to other crowdsourcing tagging tasks. For evaluation, we use the groundtruth labels provided by *American Kennel Club*.

Results. The probability distribution of the number of tasks completed per worker is shown in Fig. 6(a). As we can see, most workers completed a limited number of tasks and only a small number of workers had completed more than 100 labeling tasks. Such data sparsity is harmful to aggregation methods with unknown parameters. We count the accuracy of category labels and feature labels given by each worker in the original data set as shown in Fig. 6(b). This agrees

---

[2] https://www.akc.org/.

with our hypothesis that worker is better at labeling obvious features than the entity's category. The two feature labels obtain 180% (hair) and 172% (size) higher accuracy than category on average.

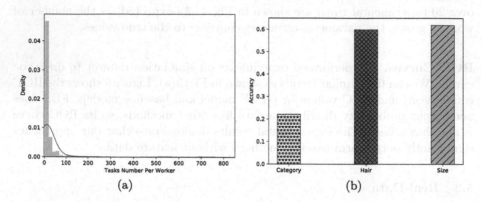

(a)   (b)

Fig. 6. (a)Distribution of the number of tasks answered by workers about original data (b) Accuracies of category and features without any methods processing about original data.

Figure 7(a) shows the accuracy of models when we change workers redundancy level. As expected, more workers brought higher accuracy for all models. GLAF, GLA(f1) and GLA(f1) outperform the GLA, MV, DS, HDS, GLAD and FDS in category labeling. The GLAF model performs the best, which implies that we can improve the quality of category labels via incorporating feature labels into *answer aggregation*. Figure 7(b) shows the accuracy of category labels and features labels obtained from MV, DS, HDS, FDS, GLAD and GLAF. The accuracy of category labels obtained by GLAF is higher than that of MV, DS, HDS, FDS and GLAD. The accuracy of two features labels is lower than category labels in GLAF,FDS and GLAD, and the opposite result is observed in MV, DS and HDS. But it is acceptable for us to improve the quality of category labels at the expense of the quality of feature labels.

ROC Curves. We performed experiments on real dataset to draw roc curves and the results are shown in Fig. 8. FDS does not output probability distribution like other models, so its ROC curve is not shown. We can see that our proposed model significantly outperforms the GLA, GLA(f1), GLA(f2), MV, DS, HDS and GLAD. GLAD and MV follow GLAF and its variants. DS is the worst. The best GLAF improves 20% than the worst DS. And GLAF performs significantly better than GLA(f1) and GLA(f2), which proves our conclusion that features information of tasks is very important for inferring the final result.

Runtime. We further investigate the time consumption of GLAF and compare it with other models. All algorithms are implemented in python. We tested them

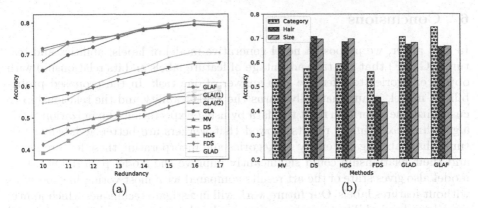

(a)   (b)

Fig. 7. (a)The accuracies of GLAF model and other methods vs Number of workers for the same task on real data. (b) Accuracy of category and features of GLAF model and other methods on real data.

in a workstation with 11th Gen Intel(R) Core(TM) i5-1135G7 @ 2.40 GHz ,eight-core CPU, 16 GB RAM and 64 bit Windows 10 OS. The running time of GLAF includes processing category answers, feature answers and parameters estimation by EM algorithm and MLE time. Figure 9 draws their running time in seconds on real datasets.

The runtime results are as follows:MV(0.02 s), DS(1s), HDS(48s), FDS(18s), GLAD(3215 s)s), GLA(310s), GLA(f1)(522s), GLA(f2)(403s), and GLAF(354s). Figure 9 shows that MV undoubtedly has the minimum time cost while GLAD has the maximum time cost. DS, HDS and FDS has the equal time cost level. GLAF,GLA,GLA(f1) and GLA(f2) have the equal time cost level. And DS, HDS and FDS have less time cost than GLAF and its variants. Our proposed model GLAF has more time cost than DS and its variants, but we have already proved that our proposed model has better performance in accuracy and ROC curves. So we think it is worthwhile to spend about 300 s more for higher accuracy.

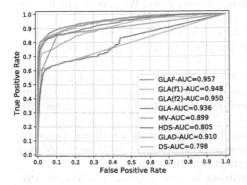

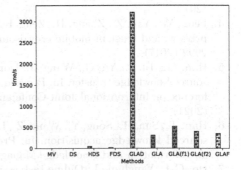

Fig. 8. ROC comparison of GLAF and other models.

Fig. 9. Runtime comparison of GLAF and other models.

6   Conclusions

In this paper, we propose a novel generative model of labels, abilities and features (GLAF) that can take advantage of feature labels and its relationship with object categories to infer the true answer of one task. In the proposed probabilistic model, it automatically learns the worker ability and the relationship to customize the algorithm to fit the data by using Expectation Maximization (EM) algorithm. Experiment results showed that workers are better at labeling features than labeling one entity's categories and incorporating these feature labels and their relationship could significantly improve the model performance. Our model also gives state of the art results compared with most voting-like methods without features labels. Our future work will investigate techniques which jointly model workers' ability to process category labels and features labels, combined with the relationship between feature labels and category labels. We also want to design a form of shared parameters for inference learning to improve model performance.

Acknowledgments. The authors would like to thank anonymous reviewers for their insightful and constructive comments and suggestions that have helped improve the quality of this paper. This research has been supported by the National Nature Foundation of China under grant 61976187 and the Natural Science Foundation of Zhejiang Province under grant (LZ22F020008, LQ22F020002).

References

1. Bi, W., Wang, L., Kwok, J.T., Tu, Z.: Learning to predict from crowdsourced data. In: UAI, vol. 14, pp. 82–91 (2014)
2. Dawid, A.P., Skene, A.M.: Maximum likelihood estimation of observer error-rates using the EM algorithm. J. Roy. Stat. Soc.: Ser. C (Appl. Stat.) **28**(1), 20–28 (1979)
3. Demartini, G., Difallah, D.E., Cudré-Mauroux, P.: ZenCrowd: leveraging probabilistic reasoning and crowdsourcing techniques for large-scale entity linking. In: Proceedings of the 21st International Conference on World Wide Web, pp. 469–478 (2012)
4. Feng, W., Yan, Z., Zhang, H., Zeng, K., Xiao, Y., Hou, Y.T.: A survey on security, privacy, and trust in mobile crowdsourcing. IEEE Internet Things J. **5**(4), 2971–2992 (2017)
5. Han, G., Tu, J., Yu, G., Wang, J., Domeniconi, C.: Crowdsourcing with multiple-source knowledge transfer. In: Proceedings of the Twenty-Ninth International Conference on International Joint Conferences on Artificial Intelligence, pp. 2908–2914 (2021)
6. Han, T., Sun, H., Song, Y., Wang, Z., Liu, X.: Budgeted task scheduling for crowdsourced knowledge acquisition. In: Proceedings of the 2017 ACM on Conference on Information and Knowledge Management, pp. 1059–1068 (2017)
7. Ho, C.J., Vaughan, J.: Online task assignment in crowdsourcing markets. In: Proceedings of the AAAI Conference on Artificial Intelligence, vol. 26, pp. 45–51 (2012)
8. Hoßfeld, T., et al.: Best practices for QoE crowdtesting: QoE assessment with crowdsourcing. IEEE Trans. Multimedia **16**(2), 541–558 (2013)

9. Howe, J.: The rise of crowdsourcing. Wired Mag. **14**(6), 1–4 (2006)
10. Hwang, K., Lee, S.Y.: Environmental audio scene and activity recognition through mobile-based crowdsourcing. IEEE Trans. Consum. Electron. **58**(2), 700–705 (2012)
11. Jiang, L., Zhang, H., Tao, F., Li, C.: Learning from crowds with multiple noisy label distribution propagation. In: IEEE Transactions on Neural Networks and Learning Systems (2021)
12. Kamar, E., Kapoor, A., Horvitz, E.: Identifying and accounting for task-dependent bias in crowdsourcing. In: Third AAAI Conference on Human Computation and Crowdsourcing (2015)
13. Karger, D., Oh, S., Shah, D.: Iterative learning for reliable crowdsourcing systems. In: Advances in Neural Information Processing Systems 24 (2011)
14. Kurve, A., Miller, D.J., Kesidis, G.: Multicategory crowdsourcing accounting for variable task difficulty, worker skill, and worker intention. IEEE Trans. Knowl. Data Eng. **27**(3), 794–809 (2014)
15. Li, H., Yu, B.: Error rate bounds and iterative weighted majority voting for crowdsourcing. arXiv preprint arXiv:1411.4086 (2014)
16. Li, J., Endo, L.R., Kashima, H.: Label aggregation for crowdsourced triplet similarity comparisons. In: Mantoro, T., Lee, M., Ayu, M.A., Wong, K.W., Hidayanto, A.N. (eds.) ICONIP 2021. CCIS, vol. 1517, pp. 176–185. Springer, Cham (2021). https://doi.org/10.1007/978-3-030-92310-5_21
17. Li, Y., Kou, N.M., Wang, H., U, L.H., Gong, Z.: A confidence-aware top-k query processing toolkit on crowdsourcing. Proceed. VLDB Endow. **10**(12), 1909–1912 (2017)
18. Liu, J., Tang, F., Chen, L., Zhu, Y.: Exploiting predicted answer in label aggregation to make better use of the crowd wisdom. Inf. Sci. **574**, 66–83 (2021)
19. Liu, X., Lu, M., Ooi, B.C., Shen, Y., Wu, S., Zhang, M.: CDAS: a crowdsourcing data analytics system. arXiv preprint arXiv:1207.0143 (2012)
20. Ma, Y., Sun, Y., Lei, Y., Qin, N., Lu, J.: A survey of blockchain technology on security, privacy, and trust in crowdsourcing services. World Wide Web **23**(1), 393–419 (2020)
21. Mao, K., Capra, L., Harman, M., Jia, Y.: A survey of the use of crowdsourcing in software engineering. J. Syst. Softw. **126**, 57–84 (2017)
22. Oyama, S., Baba, Y., Sakurai, Y., Kashima, H.: Accurate integration of crowd-sourced labels using workers' self-reported confidence scores. In: Twenty-Third International Joint Conference on Artificial Intelligence (2013)
23. Rahman, H., Roy, S.B., Thirumuruganathan, S., Amer-Yahia, S., Das, G.: Task assignment optimization in collaborative crowdsourcing. In: 2015 IEEE International Conference on Data Mining, pp. 949–954. IEEE (2015)
24. Raykar, V.C., et al.: Learning from crowds. J. Mach. Learn. Res. **11**(4), 1297–1322 (2010)
25. Russell, B.C., Torralba, A., Murphy, K.P., Freeman, W.T.: LabelMe: a database and web-based tool for image annotation. Int. J. Comput. Vision **77**(1–3), 157–173 (2008). https://doi.org/10.1007/s11263-007-0090-8
26. Sheng, V.S., Provost, F., Ipeirotis, P.G.: Get another label? improving data quality and data mining using multiple, noisy labelers. In: Proceedings of the 14th ACM SIGKDD International Conference on Knowledge Discovery and Data Mining, pp. 614–622 (2008)
27. Sinha, V.B., Rao, S., Balasubramanian, V.N.: Fast Dawid-Skene: a fast vote aggregation scheme for sentiment classification. arXiv preprint arXiv:1803.02781 (2018)

28. Smyth, P., Fayyad, U., Burl, M., Perona, P., Baldi, P.: Inferring ground truth from subjective labelling of venus images. In: Advances in Neural Information Processing Systems 7 (1996)
29. Venanzi, M., Guiver, J., Kazai, G., Kohli, P., Shokouhi, M.: Community-based bayesian aggregation models for crowdsourcing. In: Proceedings of the 23rd international conference on World wide web, pp. 155–164 (2014)
30. Vondrick, C., Patterson, D., Ramanan, D.: Efficiently scaling up crowdsourced video annotation. Int. J. Comput. Vision 101(1), 184–204 (2013)
31. Wang, J., Li, G., Kraska, T., Franklin, M.J., Feng, J.: Leveraging transitive relations for crowdsourced joins. In: SIGMOD, pp. 229–240. ACM (2013)
32. Welinder, P., Branson, S., Perona, P., Belongie, S.: The multidimensional wisdom of crowds. In: Advances in Neural Information Processing Systems 23 (2010)
33. Whitehill, J., Wu, T.f., Bergsma, J., Movellan, J., Ruvolo, P.: Whose vote should count more: Optimal integration of labels from labelers of unknown expertise. In: Advances in Neural Information Processing Systems 22, pp. 2035–2043 (2009)
34. Zaidan, O., Callison-Burch, C.: Crowdsourcing translation: Professional quality from non-professionals. In: Proceedings of the 49th Annual Meeting of the Association for Computational Linguistics: Human Language Technologies, pp. 1220–1229 (2011)
35. Zhang, J., Sheng, V.S., Wu, J., Wu, X.: Multi-class ground truth inference in crowdsourcing with clustering. IEEE Trans. Knowl. Data Eng. 28(4), 1080–1085 (2015)
36. Zhang, Y., Chen, X., Zhou, D., Jordan, M.I.: Spectral methods meet EM: a provably optimal algorithm for crowdsourcing. In: Advances in Neural Information Processing Systems 27 (2014)
37. Zhou, D., Basu, S., Mao, Y., Platt, J.: Learning from the wisdom of crowds by minimax entropy. In: Advances in Neural Information Processing Systems 25 (2012)

Cost Performance Driven Multi-request Allocation in D2D Service Provision Systems

Dandan Li[1], Hongyue Wu[1], Shizhan Chen[1(✉)], Lei Dong[1], Zhuofeng Zhao[2], and Zhiyong Feng[1]

[1] College of Intelligence and Computing, Tianjin University, Tianjin, China
{lddan,hongyue.wu,shizhan,2118218002,zyfeng}@tju.edu.cn
[2] Beijing Key Laboratory on Integration and Analysis of Large-Scale Stream Data, North China University of Technology, Beijing, China
edzhao@ncut.edu.cn

Abstract. Device-to-Device (D2D) communication has emerged as a promising technique to cope with the increasing heavy traffic in mobile networks. A critical problem in D2D service is request allocation, which aims to find the best provider for each of the proposed service requests. Most of the existing work focuses on optimizing the communication resource allocation, such as interference management, spectrum allocation, etc. In this paper, we originally address the request allocation problem with the object of maximizing the cost performance of requests. Moreover, we especially consider the impact of multi-service interactions on the service quality in a feasible plan for the provider. To solve this problem, we propose a combinatorial auction-based request allocation model. Furthermore, and develop a pruning-based request allocation algorithm called *RABP* to maximize the overall cost performance of requests. Extensive simulation results demonstrate that *RABP* performs well in improving the cost performance and is conducive to enhancing the load balancing among mobile devices.

Keywords: D2D communication · Request allocation · Cost performance · Combinatorial auction · Multi-service inter-impact

1 Introduction

Over the last few years, the explosive growth of mobile computing applications as well as the ever-improving requirements of users have posed tremendous challenges to current cellular network architecture [1]. According to Ericsson Mobility Report [2], the total mobile network traffic is forecast to exceed 300EB per month by 2026. 5G networks will carry more than half of the world's smartphone traffic. Although edge computing and fog computing have been proposed to share the core network's burden at the edge of the network, in the 5G era, the exponential growth of data traffic in mobile networks has made the spectrum

© ICST Institute for Computer Sciences, Social Informatics and Telecommunications Engineering 2022
Published by Springer Nature Switzerland AG 2022. All Rights Reserved
H. Gao et al. (Eds.): CollaborateCom 2022, LNICST 461, pp. 325–344, 2022.
https://doi.org/10.1007/978-3-031-24386-8_18

resources of the mobile network go short. As a SPECTRUM-AND-ENERGY efficiency technology, device-to-device (D2D) communication has been widely applied in mobile computing. Under a certain level of interference, D2D enables two devices to reuse the spectrum of cellular networks and connects proximity devices directly with each other [3], which brings low translation delay and better quality of service. Thus, D2D is expected to be a key enabling technology supported by the next-generation cellular networks.

According to the Cisco Visual Networking Index projection [4], video services are expected to account for 79% of the total internet traffic by 2022. Thus a representative example of D2D service is video stream service in edge computing. When a video goes viral over the internet, a large number of mobile users make requests for it. This creates immense pressure on the edge. To improve the response speed of the edge, D2D service is utilized to provide higher QoS for demanders, particularly those who are experiencing poor cellular conditions.

Existing surveys on D2D communication largely focus on interference management and power control, such as [5–7]. Another research hotspot is D2D-enabled data traffic offloading. Most of them discuss how to assign tasks to minimize communication delay or energy consumption, such as [8–11]. Part of the research focuses on the D2D content sharing [12–14], aiming to achieve optimal or stable matching between D2D requesters and providers based on the preferences of both sides. Furthermore, some researchers proposed effective incentive mechanisms to guarantee the provider's revenue in the process of data transaction [15–17].

However, two issues have not been addressed in the existing literature. One is that current surveys on D2D mainly focus on the optimization of communication latency or energy while neglecting differences in service quality and price among different providers. However, device performance plays an important role in the D2D service quality. Consider such a scenario, the requester issues a computationally intensive task, as not much data needs to be transferred, the requester would prefer to choose a provider with strong computing power over one with faster communication speed but restricted computing resources if both of them can establish a stable D2D link. Furthermore, the service price is also a vital metric for matching between requesters and providers. The other one is that the impact of multi-service interactions on service quality is not considered when the provider handles many requests at once. As providers are typically resource-constrained mobile users, performing more requests will dramatically increase competition for system resources, thus increasing system load and resulting in service quality degradation. For ease of expression, we name the impact of multi-service interactions on service quality as multi-service inter-impact.

To address the above problems, we originally concentrate on optimizing the quality as well as the price of service on all D2D requests. In detail, we refer to the ratio of service quality to the price of a request as cost performance. We describe multi-service inter-impact in a feasible plan from the existing literature on request scheduling and pricing. To fully express the cost performance of different feasible plans for a provider, we adopt the combinatorial auction based on improved XOR language. We devise a request allocation algorithm $RABP$

to obtain the optimal result. The algorithm consists of two steps, firstly searching for all feasible bid sets, then pruning out the candidate strategies that are concluded not to be the optimal solutions. The simulation results demonstrate that the proposed method significantly outperforms baseline methods. The main contributions of this paper are summarized as follows:

1) Taking into account the multi-service inter-impact, we formulate the request allocation problem and propose a combinatorial auction model based on improved XOR language.
2) We design an algorithm $RABP$ to maximize the overall cost performance of all requests, which can obtain the optimal result.
3) Simulation results demonstrate the proposed algorithm performs better than baseline methods in different scenarios. Additionally, the $RABP$ is conducive to enhancing the load balancing among devices with the increase of the service deployment rate.

The rest of this paper is organized as follows: Sect. 2 reviews the related work. The system model and problem formulation are presented in Sect. 3. The request allocation algorithm is elaborated in Sect. 4. Section 5 and Sect. 6 give the simulation results and conclusions, respectively.

2   Related Work

As one of the key technologies to expand the network capacity, D2D communication has attracted a lot of attention. A number of papers concentrate on the optimization of interference coordination and system throughput. Based on this, different request allocation schemes have been proposed.

Some researchers adopted graph theory to complete the request allocation problem. For example, [3] aimed to maximize the accessed D2D links while minimizing the total power consumption, then modeled the D2D pairing problem as a min-cost max-flow problem and solved it by the Ford-Fulkerson algorithm. [18] studied the problem of maximizing cellular traffic offloading in D2D communication. The author formulated the maximal matching problem in a bipartite graph, proposing a distributed matching algorithm. [19] originally proposed a joint user-relay selection with load balancing schemes, adopting the Kuhn-Munkres algorithm to maximize the overall matching utility.

Some authors addressed stable matching of D2D requesters and providers by using algorithms from matching theory. For example, to encourage data forwarding among cooperative users, [14] modeled the relay nodes selection problem as a stable matching problem and solved it by modified deferred acceptance algorithm. Similarly, [12] proposed a two-sided physical-social-aware provider-demander scheme for matching requesters and providers, and developed a distributed algorithm based on the Dinkelbach iteration and deferred acceptance approach. In [20], the energy-efficient resource allocation between cellular users and D2D users was constructed as a one-to-one matching problem, then the GS algorithm was applied to the energy efficiency optimization scheme.

Many auction models have emerged to solve the incentive problem for D2D providers. [16] designed Rado, a randomized auction mechanism, to provide incentives for users to participate in D2D content sharing. [21] presented a truthful double auction-based model (TAD) to reward the D2D sellers. The auction model that was applied to allocate requests in D2D mainly aimed to improve the spectrum efficiency or control the power consumption. For example, [22] presented an iterative combinatorial auction mechanism to allocate spectrum resources to optimize the system sum rate over the resource sharing of both D2D and cellular modes. [23] proposed a multi-round combinatorial double auction (MCDA) algorithm to optimize the energy efficiency over the resource allocation in D2D.

As most of the research on request allocation aimed to optimize the total utility of communication resources, we focus on the assignment between requests and providers according to the service cost performance. We originally formulate the request allocation problem as an overall cost performance maximization problem and develop an optimal algorithm based on an improved XOR-language combinatorial auction scheme. Beyond that, we take full consideration of the resource constraints of mobile devices.

In cloud computing, some researchers considered the service correlations, which means the service quality and price is not just dependent on itself but also on other services being provided by the cloud. For example, [24] presented a new cooperative coevolutionary approach for dynamic service selection with inter-service correlations. [25] proposed an extended service model which considered the correlation in the service composition process as well as the service matching process. The author designed a reservation algorithm to reserve services with correlations in the matching stage. To systematically model quality correlations and enable efficient queries of quality correlations for service compositions, [26] proposed a novel approach named Q^2C. [27] focused on QoS-aware service composition and took QoS correlations between services into account. Then proposed the service selection method $CASP4NAT$. However, most of them considered the correlations between services by offering discounts to bundle services. This makes sense for large service providers such as the cloud, but not for resource-constrained mobile devices. Furthermore, some research like [27] generates the service correlations at random and only considers correlations between two services. In contrast, we get the impact of multi-service interactions on service quality via the scheduling and pricing model. We consider the degradation in service quality caused by competition for resources by requests in a feasible plan.

3   System Model

3.1   System Architecture

As illustrated in Fig. 1, we consider a **D2D** **S**ervice **P**rovision (**D2DSP**) system which consists of one BS equipped with an edge cloud and multiple mobile devices (MDs). The MDs are divided into two categories: supplying MDs and demanding MDs. The supplying MDs are D2D Providers who send the resource supplying information to BS. The demanding MDs are D2D requesters who send resource demand information (request) to BS. The base station acts as the broker to match the supplying and demanding MDs.

In our paper, the MDs are assumed to have no prior knowledge of others, thus all of them directly send their information to the base station. As shown in Fig. 1, After the BS receives all requests in a period, it broadcasts the requests to the providers who satisfy the following two conditions:

1) **Communication conditions**, which means the provider and requester must be within the D2D communication range of each other, only in this way, can they establish a stable D2D link.
2) **Service conditions**, based on the above, the provider must deploy the service required by the request.

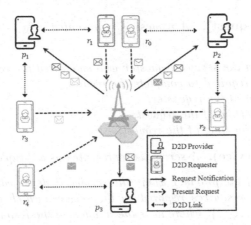

Fig. 1. D2DSP architecture

Figure 1 and Fig. 2 present an example. The distribution of MDs is presented in Fig. 2. Within the 2D area circled by the box, each provider can cover the requests within a dotted ellipse, the rectangle next to the provider represents the service deployed by the provider, the color of the requests illustrates the service required to complete them. So p_1 covers r_1, r_2, r_3 and deploys the services required by them, in this case, p_1 is able to complete r_1, r_2 and r_3. Similarly, p_2 can complete r_0, r_1 and r_2, while p_3 can complete r_1 and r_4. As a result, upon receiving all requests the base station presents r_1 to p_1, p_2, p_3; r_2 to p_1, p_2; r_3 to p_1; r_4 to p_3 and r_0 to p_2, as shown in Fig. 1.

In our paper, a request corresponds to one service, we use the terms request and service interchangeably in the paper. We allocate multiple requests in the chronological order in which they arrive. The definitions of request and service are as follows.

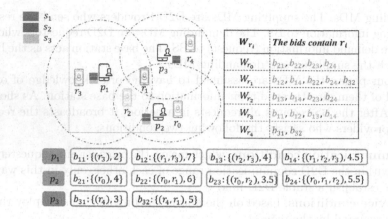

Fig. 2. Auction example

Definition 1 (Request). *A request is represented as a 5-tuple* (d, s, L, t_a, t_e) *, where:*

- *d is the index of the service requester who submitted the request;*
- *s is the service required to complete the request;*
- *L is the location of the requester;*
- t_a *is the arrival time of the request;*
- t_e *is the execution time of the request;*

Definition 2 (Service). *A service is represented as a 3-tuple* $(d, \mathcal{G}, F)$ *, where:*

- *d is the index of the provider where the service is deployed;*
- $\mathcal{G}$ *describes the resources required by the service, which can be denoted as* $\mathcal{G} = \{g_{z_1}, g_{z_2}, \ldots, g_{z_m}\}$, *where m is the number of the resource type,* g_{z_i} *is the amount of the* z_i *kind of resource.*
- *F is the functional description of the service;*

3.2   Scheduling and Pricing Model

As providers receive request information from the base station, they perform scheduling and pricing model to determine the price and quality of service in different feasible plans (or bids). Specifically, we use the scheduling algorithm *RESP* presented in [28] to arrange the requests. Then run the dynamic pricing method in [29] to calculate the service price. The impact of multi-service interactions on service quality will be determined after the two processes. Then the providers can obtain the cost performance of different feasible plans and submit bids to compete for revenue. To elaborate on this, we present the definition of a provider at first.

Definition 3 (Provider). *A provider p is represented as a 5-tuple* $(i, L, \mathcal{S}, \mathcal{A}, \mathcal{V})$, *where:*

- i is the unique index of the provider in our system;
- L is the location of the provider;
- $\mathcal{S} = \{s_1, s_2, \ldots s_n\}$ is the set of services that the provider deployed;
- $\mathcal{A}$ is the function used to describe the available resources of p. Given a time t, the available resources can be denoted as $\mathcal{A}_t = \{a_{z_1,t}, a_{z_2,t}, \ldots, a_{z_m,t}\}$, where z_i is the type of resource, m is the total number of resource types, $a_{z_i,t}$ is the amount of z_i at time t.
- $\mathcal{V} = \{v_{z_1,t}, v_{z_2,t}, \ldots v_{z_m,t}\}$ describes the provider's valuation on its own resources. For example, $v_{z_i,t}$ denotes the price of resource z_i at time t.

The available resources vector $\mathcal{A}$ is the free resources of the provider that can be used to complete requests. The dynamic resource pricing model used by the provider is based on the inventory theory [29–31]. Due to space constraints, we directly give the function between resource price and the available resource amount n and time t, which was derived from Eqs. 9 and 10 in [29]:

$$v_{z_i,t} = \frac{1}{\alpha} \left[\ln \left(1 + \frac{(\frac{k}{e}t)^n \frac{1}{n!}}{\sum_{i=0}^{n-1} (\frac{k}{e}t)^i \frac{1}{i!}} \right) + 1 \right] \tag{1}$$

where n is the available resources of z_i at time t, or called $a_{z_i,t}$. k and α are user-definable constants. According to Eq. (1), the resource price $v_{z_i,t}$ is inversely proportional to the available resource amount $a_{z_i,t}$. The request price can be calculated as a linear summation of the resource type, price and amount, as described in Eq. (2).

$$\rho_r = \rho_s = \sum_{t=r.start}^{r.end} (\mathcal{V}_t \cdot \mathcal{G}_s) \tag{2}$$

where $r.start$ and $r.end$ are the start and end execution time of the request respectively.

Take an example in Fig. 3, the provider can complete request r_1, r_2 and r_3. But the cost performance of r_3 is different in different feasible plans. Specifically, the scheduling algorithm determines the time interval in which the request is to be executed. Meanwhile, the request price is obtained by the resource prices in the time interval. For different feasible plans, the execution order of requests is different and the resource price varies dynamically with the available resource amount. Therefore the service quality may be completely different for a request. Note that we regard the response time as service quality. As the figure shows, the response time of s_3 is 2 s in the first plan, however, it turns 3 s in the second plan and 5 s in the third plan. Moreover, because the third plan consumes more system resources, the resource price at t_1, t_2, t_3, t_4 and t_5 will be higher than it is in the first two plans. Thus the cost performance of the same request in different plans will be quite different, which is the multi-service inter-impact.

3.3 Auction Model

After obtaining the scheduling and pricing information, the provider submits the feasible plans and corresponding cost performance to the base station in the form

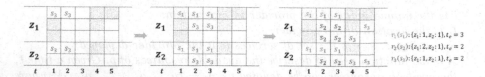

Fig. 3. Scheduling & Pricing example

of bids. In order that each provider can express their will sufficiently, we adopt the combinatorial auction model based on improved XOR bidding language, which means every provider p_i can submit multiple bids $B_i = \{b_{i1}, b_{i2}, \ldots, b_{ik}\}$, and each bid b_{ik} can contain multiple requests. For example in Fig. 2, as the provider p_3 can complete requests r_1 as well as r_4, p_3 presents bids including $b_{31} = \{(r_4), \phi(b_{31})\}$, $b_{32} = \{(r_1, r_4), \phi(b_{32})\}$. In general XOR bidding language, the bidder will presents b_{31}, b_{32} as well as $b_{33} = \{r_1, \phi(b_{33})\}$, but in our scenario, r_4 can only be completed by p_3, so the b_{33} is meaningless and will definitely not appear in the final result as we are aiming to distribute all requests. Thus we call the bidding language as improved XOR bidding language. The definition of a bid is described in Definition 4.

Definition 4 (Bid). *A bid b is represented as a 6-tuple $(i, c, R, P, \mathcal{Q}, \phi)$, where:*

- *i is the index of provider who presents the bid;*
- *c is the number of requests contained in the bid;*
- *$R = \{r_1, r_2, \ldots r_c\}$ is the set of requests in the bid;*
- *$P = \{\rho_{r_1}, \rho_{r_2}, \ldots \rho_{r_c}\}$ is the price set of requests set R;*
- *$\mathcal{Q} = \{q_{r_1}, q_{r_2}, \ldots q_{r_c}\}$ is the service quality set of requests set R;*
- *$\phi(b)$ is the cost performance of b, which can be calculated by:*

$$\phi(b) = \phi(r_1) + \phi(r_2) + \cdots + \phi(r_c) \tag{3}$$

where $\phi(r_i)$ is the cost performance of r_i, which is defined by Eq. (4):

$$\phi(r_i) = q_{r_i}/\rho_{r_i} \tag{4}$$

Because of the multi-service inter-impact on the requests' cost performance, it is a challenging problem to distribute all requests to obtain the best overall cost performance.

3.4 Problem Formulation

After receiving all bids, the base station acts as an auctioneer to dispatch requests aiming to achieve the best overall cost performance. Since in XOR bidding language, a bidder can win at most one bid even if it submits multiple bids, leading to the first constraint for request allocation:

$$\sum_{j=1}^{k} x_{ij} \leq 1, \quad \forall p_i \in P \tag{5}$$

where

$$x_{ij} = \{0, 1\} \tag{6}$$

Among which $x_{ij} = 0$ means the bid b_{ij} is not selected, otherwise b_{ij} is selected. k is the total number of bids submitted by p_i. In addition, a request can only be allocated to one provider, leading to the second constraint:

$$\sum_{b_{ij} \in W_r} x_{ij} \le 1, \quad \forall r \in R \tag{7}$$

W_r is the bid set including request r, Eq. (7) means only one bid can be selected in W_r. Then the overall cost performance maximization problem can now be formulated:

$$Max \quad \sum_{i=1}^{m} \sum_{j=1}^{k} \phi(b_{ij}) \cdot x_{ij}$$

$$s.t. \sum_{j=1}^{k} x_{ij} \le 1, \quad \forall p_i \in P \tag{8}$$

$$\sum_{b_{ij} \in W_r} x_{ij} \le 1, \quad \forall r \in R$$

$$x_{ij} = \{0, 1\}$$

where $\phi(b_{ij})$ is the cost performance of b_{ij}, m is the number of providers. Other mathematical symbols used in this article are presented in Table 1.

Table 1. Mathematical notations.

Symbol	Description
R	Demanding MD set
B	Bids set
P	Supplying MD set
t_{ij}	The jth feasible bid set (candidate strategy) of request r_0 to r_i
T_i	The candidate strategy set of request r_0 to r_i
W_{r_i}	The bid set including request r_i
b_{ik}	The kth bid from the ith provider
l_{R/T_i}	The length of set R or T_i
$R_{t_{ij}/b}$	The requests set of t_{ij} or bid b
$P_{t_{ij}/b}$	The providers set of t_{ij} or bid b
$\phi(t_{ij}/b)$	The cost performance of t_{ij} or bid b

4 The Proposed RABP Algorithm

In this section, we introduce our dispatching algorithm in detail. To better understand the algorithm, we definite the feasible bid set (or called candidate strategy) and candidate strategy set as follows.

Definition 5 (Feasible Bid Set or Candidate Strategy). *A feasible bid set or called candidate strategy t_i can be represented by a 5-tuple $(d, B_{t_i}, R_{t_i}, P_{t_i}, \phi(t_i))$, where:*

- *d is the index of the candidate strategy;*
- *$B_{t_i} = \{b_1, b_2, \dots b_k\}$ is the set of bids in t_i;*
- *$R_{t_i} = \{r_0, r_1, \dots r_k\}$ is the set of requests covering by t_i;*
- *$P_{t_i} = \{p_1, p_2, \dots p_k\}$ is the set of providers of bid in t_i;*
- *$\phi(t_i)$ is the cost performance of t_i, which can be obtained by Eq. (9):*

$$\phi(t_i) = \phi(b_1) + \phi(b_2) + \cdots + \phi(b_k) \tag{9}$$

The feasible bid set or called candidate strategy $t_i = \{b_0, b_1, \dots, b_k\}$ is the bid set that must cover the requests from r_0 to r_i and may cover other requests in R, which we call them *Following Requests*. Feasible means these bids are from different providers and will not overlap a request.

Definition 6 (Candidate Strategy Set). *A candidate strategy set $T_i = \{t_{i1}, t_{i2}, \dots, t_{in}\}$ is the set of candidate strategy t_i that not be pruned.*

Algorithm 1. *RABP* Algorithm

Input: The requests set R, provider set P, bid set B, the bid set of candidates for each request W_r.
Output: Winning bid set $\hat{t}$.
Initialize: $T_0 = \varnothing$, $\hat{t} = \varnothing$, $i = 0$.

1: **for** every $b \in W_{r_0}$ **do**
2:     $t_{new} \leftarrow b$; $R_{t_{new}} \leftarrow R_b$; $P_{t_{new}} \leftarrow P_b$; $\phi(t_{new}) \leftarrow \phi(b)$;
3:     Pruning(t_{new}, T_i);
4: **end for**
5: **for** $i = 1$ *to* l_R **do**
6:     **for** every $t \in T_{i-1}$ **do**
7:         **if** $r_i \in R_t$ **then**
8:             Pruning(t, T_i) ;
9:         **else**
10:             **for** every $b \in W_{r_i}$ **do**
11:                 **if** $P_t \cap P_b = \varnothing$ and $R_t \cap R_b = \varnothing$ **then**
12:                     $t_{new} \leftarrow t \cup b$; $R_{t_{new}} \leftarrow R_t \cup R_b$; $P_{t_{new}} \leftarrow P_t \cup P_b$;
                        $\phi(t_{new}) \leftarrow \phi(t) + \phi(b)$;
13:                     Pruning(t_{new}, T_i);
14:                 **end if**
15:             **end for**
16:         **end if**
17:     **end for**
18: **end for**
19: **return** $\hat{t}$

Upon the base station receives bid set B from all service providers, base station acts as an auctioneer to dispatch requests aiming to maximize the overall cost performance, as depicted in Sect. 3.

To solve the problem optimally, we propose a pruning-based request allocation algorithm $RABP$ as shown in Algorithm 1. The algorithm consists of two steps: enumeration and pruning. To begin, we initialize T_0 with bids in W_{r_0} (lines 1–5) since every bid in W_{r_0} is a feasible bid for r_0, then we call Pruning algorithm to determine whether the candidate strategy t_{new} should be pruned (line 6). The pruning rules will be described later.

Algorithm 2. Pruning Algorithm

Input: The current feasible bid set t_{new} for request r_0 to r_i and all feasible bid sets T_i until now for request r_0 to r_i.

Output: Candidate bid sets T_i.

1: **if** $R_{t_{new}} = R$ **then**
2:    **if** $\phi(t_{new}) > \phi(\hat{t})$ **then**
3:       $\hat{t} \leftarrow t_{new}$;
4:    **end if**
5:    **return**
6: **else**
7:    $j = 0$
8:    **while** $j < l_{T_i}$ **do**
9:       **if** $R_{t_{new}} = R_{t_{ij}}$ **then**
10:          **if** $P_{t_{ij}} \subseteq P_{t_{new}}$ and $\phi(t_{ij}) \geq \phi(t_{new})$ **then**
11:             **return**
12:          **end if**
13:          **if** $P_{t_{new}} \subseteq P_{t_{ij}}$ and $\phi(t_{new}) \geq \phi(t_{ij})$ **then**
14:             remove t_{ij} from T_i
15:          **else**
16:             $j = j + 1$
17:          **end if**
18:       **else**
19:          $j = j + 1$
20:       **end if**
21:    **end while**
22:    add t_{new} to T_i
23:    **return**
24: **end if**

After initializing T_0, we try to find the feasible bid set for r_0 to r_i where $i = 1, 2, \ldots, l_{R_c}$ (lines 7–18). We firstly traverse the candidate strategy t in set T_{i-1}, checking whether t has already covered the request r_i, if so, t is already a feasible bid set for r_0 to r_i, then we call Pruning algorithm to determine whether it should be pruned (lines 9–10). Otherwise, traversing the bid b in W_{r_i} (which is the bid set covering r_i), if the bids in t and the bid b are all from different providers and they will not overlap a request (line 13), then we find a new candidate strategy t_{new} for r_0 to r_i, which is the union of t and b. So we update the request set, provider set and the cost performance of t_{new} (lines 14–17) and running Pruning algorithm to check whether the solution has the possibility of becoming the optimal solution. If not, prune it off.

The pruning rules are presented in Algorithm 2. For the candidate strategy t_{new} for r_0 to r_i, if it contains all requests in R (line 1), we compare the cost performance of t_{new} with $\hat{t}$, if the former is greater, which means t_{new} can obtain a better solution than current optimal solution $\hat{t}$, then we update $\hat{t}$ (lines 2–4) and return. If t_{new} only contains part of the requests in R, compare it to all candidate strategies in the current T_i (lines 7–8), if t_{new} and one of the candidate strategy t_{ij} in T_i have the same requests set (line 9), and the provider set of t_{ij} is the subset of t_{new} and the cost performance of t_{ij} is greater than t_{new}, which means t_{ij} can cover the same requests with less providers while achieving a better cost performance than t_{new}, in this case, t_{new} definitely will not be the optimal solution, the algorithm will not add t_{new} to T_i and return directly (lines 10–11). Otherwise, if the provider set of t_{new} is the subset of t_{ij} and the cost performance of t_{new} is greater than t_{ij}, we remove t_{ij} from T_i since it certainly can not obtain a better solution than t_{new} (lines 12–13). Then add t_{new} to T_i (line 18).

The time complexity of $RABP$ is $O(nhl^2)$, where n denotes the length of R, h denotes the average length of candidate bids W_{r_i} for each request r_i. l denotes the average length of the candidate strategy set (T_i). l has a greater impact on the execution time. It is mainly affected by the bid amount submitted by different providers. Through the pruning operation of algorithm 2, the length of T_i can be effectively reduced, thus lowering the time cost of the algorithm.

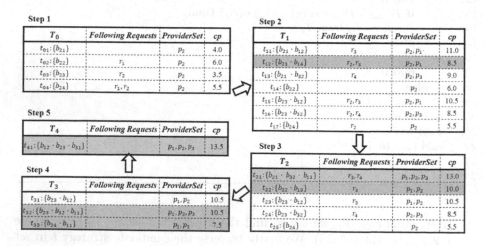

Fig. 4. Example for RABP

Fig. 4 shows the process of using the algorithm to solve the example in Fig. 2. Firstly, we get the T_0 initialized by W_{r_0}, as shown in Step 1. Specially, *Following*

Requests means the requests in t_{ij} except r_0 to r_i. Then we traverse t_{0j} in T_0 to get T_1. For example, t_{01}, we check for whether it contains r_1, as it does not contain, we traverse W_{r_1}, if t_{01} can combine with a bid b in W_{r_1} and does not violate the constraints of the Eq. (8), that is, the intersection of the provider set of b and t_{01} is empty, and the intersection of the request set of the two is empty, such as $t_{01} \cdot b_2$, $t_{01} \cdot b_4$ and $t_{01} \cdot b_{10}$, then we obtain a new solution for r_0 to r_1, t_{11}, t_{12} and t_{13} respectively. If the candidate strategy t_{0j} contains r_1, such as t_{02}, we obtain the new solution directly. Every time we get a new solution for r_1, we run Algorithm 2 to determine whether prune it or not. For example, when we obtain t_{15} after combining t_{03} and b_2, firstly judging whether it contains all requests, if not, we compare it with candidate strategies in current T_1, that is t_{11}, t_{12}, t_{13} and t_{14}, we find t_{15} and t_{12} is in the case of the same request set as well as the provider set, but the overall cost performance realized by t_{15} is greater, thus we remove t_{12} from T_1. Otherwise, if in the same case and the overall cost performance realized by t_{12} is greater than t_{15}, we will not add t_{15} to T_1. For example, in step 4, the new solution t_{33} is in the same case of t_{31}, but the overall cost performance of t_{31} is greater, so we prune t_{33} off. If we find a solution contains all requests, such as t_{21} in Step 3, we compare it with current optimal solution $\hat{t}$, if the overall cost performance of new solution (t_{21}) is better than $\hat{t}$, we update $\hat{t}$, if the new solution is worse than $\hat{t}$, for example t_{32} in Step 4, we prune it off directly. Following this pruning rule, we will get the optimal solution stored in $\hat{t}$ after getting T_5.

5   Simulation

To evaluate the effectiveness of the algorithm proposed in this paper, we carry out two sets of experiments. The first one examines the effectiveness of $RABP$, the second one evaluates the load balancing effect of $RABP$.

We implemented the $RABP$ algorithm in Python. Our experiments were conducted on a Windows machine equipped with an Intel Core i7-9700 processor and 16 GB RAM. As there is no standard experimental platform, we automatically generate the parameters and use them as the experimental data sets.

5.1   Effectiveness Evaluation

In this section, we evaluate the effectiveness of $RABP$. We choose the reciprocal of the response time as the service quality. Each device is equipped with available resources ranging from 5 to 10. Requests are randomly generated with execution time ranging from 3 to 5, the required number of each resource ranging from 2 to 5. The service number is 10. The function of resource price and the available resource of a provider follows Eq. (1). We set $k = 10$ and $\alpha = 1$. Particularly worth mentioning is the location of the providers and requesters, we generate them in a 2D area and ensure that all provider communication ranges cover the entire region, as shown in Fig. 2. Each request can be completed by at least one of the providers covering it. To evaluate the effectiveness of $RABP$, we compare it with the following four methods:

1) Primal-Dual Approximation Algorithm ($PDAA$): The method presented in [32], which adopts a greedy primal-dual algorithm to obtain the approximate solution of problem 8.
2) Auction Efficiency Maximization Algorithm ($AEMA$): The method proposed in [33], which developed a double auction-based scheme to solve the request allocation problem between cloud computing providers and cloud users. We migrate this method to our environment and modify the fitness function to be feasible strategy's (t_i) cost performance.
3) Greedy Algorithm (GA): Greedy by bid density is widely used to solve the winner determination problem in combinatorial auctions [34–36]. Similar to them, our bid density w is calculated as Eq. (10).

$$w_b = \phi(b)/c \tag{10}$$

4) CALP Algorithm ($CALP$): The method presented in [36], was designed to solve the winner determination and payment problem of combinatorial auction.

As analyzed in Sect. 4, the scale of the problem is mainly related to the request number, the provider number, and the service deployment rate (sdr). To examine the impact of these three parameters on the result of our method, we consider three sets of parameters, as shown in Table 2. In each set, one of the three parameters is varied while the others remain fixed. All experiments are repeated 500 times, and we use the average values as the result.

Table 2. Variable settings for effectiveness evaluation.

Set	Request number	Provider number	Service deployment rate
1	8–22	15	0.6
2	15	6–20	0.6
3	15	10	0.1–1.0

To explore the impact of request number on the overall cost performance of requests, we set the parameters according to Set 1 in Table 2. The results, shown in Fig. 5(a), demonstrate that the overall cost performance improves with the increasing number of requests. As the allocated request number increases, the overall cost performance will definitely go up. But from Fig. 5(b), we can see that the average cost performance of requests decreases consistently. This is because when the provider number is fixed, the total available resources of all providers remain the same, as the request number rises, more resources are occupied and the request response time increases, causing the rise in price and the drop in service quality. Therefore, the average cost performance of requests continuously decreases.

Obviously, our algorithm significantly outperforms the other four methods as shown in Fig. 5. The $PDAA$ algorithm can obtain a second good result to

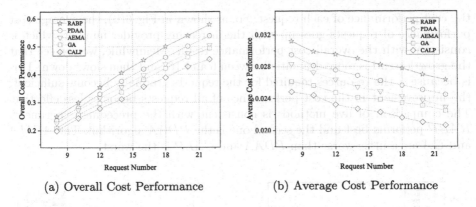

(a) Overall Cost Performance   (b) Average Cost Performance

Fig. 5. Impact of the request number

$RABP$, because it adopts a well-designed primal-dual framework to improve the approximation ratio. The $AEMA$ algorithm employs a double auction model and allocates each request with a greedy selection of the most cost-effective bid, so it cannot get a globally optimal solution. Similarly, the GA algorithm greedily selects bids with the largest bid density. As $AEMA$ and GA not allocate requests from a global perspective, thus the optimality of the results is not guaranteed. $CALP$ uses a linear programming relaxation method to solve the problem, and it can be seen that the approximate ratio is much worse than $PDAA$.

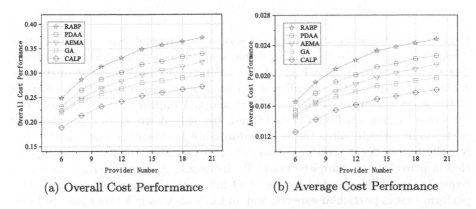

(a) Overall Cost Performance   (b) Average Cost Performance

Fig. 6. Impact of the provider number

Next, we examine the impact of provider number on the result of the overall cost performance. To this end, we set the experimental parameters in accordance with Set 2 in Table 2. The result is shown in Fig. 6. From Fig. 6(a) we can see that the overall cost performance gradually increases as the provider number grows. As more providers will provide more available resources which is conducive to decreasing the response time and request price, thus improving the cost performance of each request. So, as shown in Fig. 6(b), the average cost performance of requests goes up with the increasing provider number, which is consistent with the overall cost performance result. Meanwhile, we can see that the growth trend is more dramatic between 6 and 16, and then slows down. This is because as the resources required for the requests gradually become sufficient, the improvement in the cost performance of all requests becomes less effective. The comparison of five methods is consistent with the preceding experiment: $RABP$ performs best and the second one is the $PDAA$ algorithm. The $AEMA$ and GA are a little worse than $PDAA$ and $CALP$ is the worst.

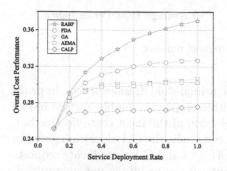
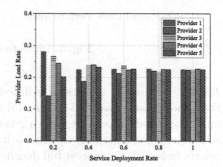

Fig. 7. Impact of the sdr   **Fig. 8.** Load balancing performance with sdr

Finally, we investigate the impact of service deployment rate on the result of overall cost performance. We set the parameters according to Set 3 in Table 2. The results are presented in Fig. 7. From which we can see that our algorithm and $PDAA$ can improve the overall cost performance consistently with the increase of the service deployment rate. $AEMA$ and GA improve the overall cost performance ranging sdr from 0.1 to 0.5 and then slow down. $CALP$ has the worst performance which raises the cost performance between 0.1 and 0.3 and then remains stable. As the service deployment rate increases, the number of requests that a provider can complete gradually increases, thus the average number of requests contained in a bid increases. Other methods greedily select bids that perform best in particular aspects, and on the basis to select other bids. Subjecting to the limitations imposed by already selected bids (constraint limitations in Eq. (8), they can only select among a fraction of the remaining bids, that is, they can only select bids from different providers and which not contain the request covered by selected bids. Thus limiting the optimality of the solution. In contrast, our approach retains all feasible bid sets that are possible to be the optimal solution until the final step. As a result, the superiority of $RABP$ becomes increasingly apparent as the sdr increases.

In summary, whether varying the number of requests, the number of providers, or the service deployment rate, the overall cost performance obtained by *RABP* is significantly better than other methods.

5.2 Load Balancing Performance

In this section, we examine the load balancing performance of *RABP*. To this end, we simulate two scenarios as described below.

Table 3. Variable settings for effectiveness evaluation.

Set	Request number	Provider number	Service deployment rate
1	15	5	0.2–1.0
2	6–20	5	0.6

In the first scenario, we set the parameters according to Set 1 in Table 3 while other parameter settings are the same in the previous section. The result is presented in Fig. 8, which denotes the load balancing effect gradually gets better as the service deployment rate increases. This is because our allocation object is to achieve the best overall cost performance, which means we pursue the lower price as well as request response time. At the same time, a provider equipped with more available resources will bid lower and respond quickly. Thus the probability of winning the bid is greater. Otherwise, the provider with less available resources will bid higher and be less likely to be a winner. So the provider with a lower load rate and more available resources will obtain more requests, promoting load balancing among providers. With the growth of service deployment rate, each request has a greater possibility to be allocated to the provider with sufficient resources, thus improving the load balancing effect.

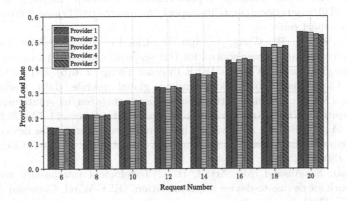

Fig. 9. Load balancing performance with request number

In the second scenario, we set the parameters according to Set 2 in Table 3. We obtain the load rate of providers with the request number continuous increases when the service deployment rate is 0.6. The result is presented in Fig. 9, which demonstrates that the load balancing effect of $RABP$ is excellent when the service deployment rate is 0.6.

6   Conclusion

In this paper, we investigate the request dispatching problem in the D2D environment. We originally focused on the optimization of service cost performance while taking into account the multi-service inter-impact on service quality in a bid. We design a combinatorial auction-based request allocation model, using XOR bid language to motivate providers fully express their matching intention. To solve the request allocation problem optimally, we design the algorithm $RABP$. Extensive simulation results demonstrate that $RABP$ is superior to the $PDAA$, $AEMA$, GA, and $CALP$ in terms of cost performance. Meanwhile, the $RABP$ performs well in load balancing.

As our algorithm is significantly affected by the bid amount, so we will try to design a less complex approach in the future. Furthermore, more complex scenarios with requirements on service quality will be taken into consideration.

Acknowledgement. This work is supported by the National Natural Science Foundation of China grant No. 62102281, and the National Natural Science Key Foundation of China grant No. 62032016 and No. 61832014.

References

1. Jameel, F., Hamid, Z., Jabeen, F., Zeadally, S., Javed, M.A.: A survey of device-to-device communications: Research issues and challenges. IEEE Commun. Surv. Tutor. **20**(3), 2133–2168 (2018)
2. Ericsson: Ericsson mobility report (2021). [Online]. https://www.ericsson.com/49cd40/assets/local/mobility-report/documents/2021/june-2021-ericsson-mobility-report.pdf
3. Zhai, D., Zhang, R., Wang, Y., Sun, H., Cai, L., Ding, Z.: Joint user pairing, mode selection, and power control for D2D-capable cellular networks enhanced by nonorthogonal multiple access. IEEE Internet Things J. **6**(5), 8919–8932 (2019)
4. Cisco: Cisco visual networking index: global mobile data traffic forecast update (2019). [Online]. https://www.cisco.com/c/en/us/solutions/collateral/service-provider/visual-networking-index-vni/white-paper-c11-738429.html
5. Noura, M., Nordin, R.: A survey on interference management for device-to-device (D2D) communication and its challenges in 5G networks. J. Netw. Comput. Appl. **71**(C), 130–150 (2016)
6. Doumiati, S., Assaad, M., Artail, H.A.: Topological interference management framework for device-to-device communication. IEEE Wirel. Commun. Lett. **7**(4), 602–605 (2018)

7. Wang, Q., Wang, W., Jin, S., Zhu, H.B., Zhang, N.T.: Game-theoretic source selection and power control for quality-optimized wireless multimedia device-to-device communications. In: IEEE Global Communications Conference, pp. 4568–4573. IEEE, New York (2014)
8. Tong, M., Wang, X., Wang, Y., Lan, Y.: Computation offloading scheme with D2D for MEC-enabled cellular networks. In: IEEE/CIC International Conference on Communications in China (ICCC Workshops), pp. 111–116 (2020)
9. Tang, J., Tang, H.B., Zhao, N., Cumanan, K., Zhang, S.Q., Zhou, Y.J.: A reinforcement learning approach for D2D-assisted cache-enabled HetNets. In: IEEE Global Communications Conference (2019)
10. He, Y., Ren, J., Yu, G., Cai, Y.: Joint computation offloading and resource allocation in D2D enabled MEC networks. In: IEEE International Conference on Communications (ICC), pp. 1–6 (2019)
11. Jiang, C.L., Cao, T.F., Guan, J.F.: Intelligent task offloading and collaborative computation over D2D communication. China Commun. **18**(3), 251–263 (2021)
12. Wu, D., Zhou, L., Cai, Y.M., Chao, H.C., Qian, Y.: Physical-social-aware D2D content sharing networks: a provider-demander matching game. IEEE Trans. Veh. Technol. **67**(8), 7538–7549 (2018)
13. Song, W., Zhao, Y., Zhuang, W.: Stable device pairing for collaborative data dissemination with device-to-device communications. IEEE Internet Things J. **5**(2), 1251–1264 (2018)
14. Zhao, Y., Song, W., Han, Z.: Social-aware data dissemination via device-to-device communications: fusing social and mobile networks with incentive constraints. IEEE Trans. Serv. Comput. **12**(3), 489–502 (2019)
15. Li, P., Guo, S., Stojmenovic, I.: A truthful double auction for device-to-device communications in cellular networks. IEEE J. Sel. Areas Commun. **34**(1), 71–81 (2016)
16. Zhu, Y., Jiang, J., Li, B., Li, B.: Rado: a randomized auction approach for data offloading via D2D communication. In: Proceedings of the 2015 IEEE 12th International Conference on Mobile Ad Hoc and Sensor Systems, pp. 1–9 (2015)
17. Zhang, Y., Song, L., Saad, W., Dawy, Z., Han, Z.: Contract-based incentive mechanisms for device-to-device communications in cellular networks. IEEE J. Sel. Areas Commun. **33**(10), 2144–2155 (2015)
18. Jiang, J., Zhang, S., Li, B., Li, B.: Maximized cellular traffic offloading via device-to-device content sharing. IEEE J. Sel. Areas Commun. **34**(1), 82–91 (2016)
19. Omran, A., Sboui, L., Rong, B., Rutagemwa, H., Kadoch, M.: Joint relay selection and load balancing using D2D communications for 5G HetNet MEC. In: IEEE International Conference on Communications Workshops (ICC Workshops), pp. 1–5 (2019)
20. Zhou, Z., Ota, K., Dong, M., Xu, C.: Energy-efficient matching for resource allocation in D2D enabled cellular networks. IEEE Trans. Veh. Technol. **66**(6), 5256–5268 (2017)
21. Zhao, Y., Song, W.: Truthful mechanisms for message dissemination via device-to-device communications. IEEE Trans. Veh. Technol. **66**(11), 10:307–10:321 (2017)
22. Xu, C., et al.: Efficiency resource allocation for device-to-device underlay communication systems: a reverse iterative combinatorial auction based approach. IEEE J. Sel. Areas Commun. **31**(9), 348–358 (2013)
23. Xue, J., Ma, Q., Shao, H.: Efficient resource allocation for d2d communication underlaying cellular networks: a multi-round combinatorial double auction. In: Proceedings of the 2018 International Conference on Electronics and Electrical Engineering Technology. EEET 2018, New York, NY, USA, pp. 172–176 (2018)

24. Liang, H., Du, Y.: Dynamic service selection with QoS constraints and inter-service correlations using cooperative coevolution. Futur. Gener. Comput. Syst. **76**, 119–135 (2017)
25. Li, H.-F., Zhao, L., Zhang, B.-H., Li, J.-Q.: Service matching and composition considering correlations among cloud services. In: 2015 IEEE International Conference on Systems, Man, and Cybernetics, pp. 509–514 (2015)
26. Zhang, Y., Cui, G., Deng, S., Chen, F., Wang, Y., He, Q.: Efficient query of quality correlation for service composition. IEEE Trans. Serv. Comput. **14**(3), 695–709 (2021)
27. Deng, S., Wu, H., Hu, D., Zhao, J.L.: Service selection for composition with QoS correlations. IEEE Trans. Serv. Comput. **9**(2), 291–303 (2016)
28. Wu, H., et al.: Revenue-driven service provisioning for resource sharing in mobile cloud computing. In: Maximilien, M., Vallecillo, A., Wang, J., Oriol, M. (eds.) ICSOC 2017. LNCS, vol. 10601, pp. 625–640. Springer, Cham (2017). https://doi.org/10.1007/978-3-319-69035-3_46
29. Gallego, G., van Ryzin, G.: Optimal dynamic pricing of inventories with stochastic demand over finite horizons. Manag. Sci. **40**(8), 999–1020 (1994)
30. Li, Y., Hou, Y.: Joint pricing and inventory replenishment decisions with returns and expediting under reference price effects. Math. Probl. Eng. **2019**, 1–17 (2019)
31. Federgruen, A., Heching, A.: Combined pricing and inventory control under uncertainty. Oper. Res. **47**(3), 454–475 (1999)
32. Le, T.H.T., et al.: Auction mechanism for dynamic bandwidth allocation in multi-tenant edge computing. IEEE Trans. Veh. Technol. **69**(12), 15:162–15:176 (2020)
33. Xu, L., Wang, J., Nallanathan, A., Li, Y.: Resource allocation based on double auction for cloud computing system. In: 18th IEEE International Conference on High Performance Computing and Communications (HPCC), Conference Proceedings, pp. 1538–1543 (2016)
34. Jain, V., Kumar, B.: Auction based cost-efficient resource allocation by utilizing blockchain in fog computing. Trans. Emerg. Telecommun. Technol. e4469 (2022)
35. Zhai, Y., Huang, L., Chen, L., Xiao, N., Geng, Y.: COUSTIC: combinatorial double auction for crowd sensing task assignment in device-to-device clouds. In: Vaidya, J., Li, J. (eds.) ICA3PP 2018. LNCS, vol. 11334, pp. 636–651. Springer, Cham (2018). https://doi.org/10.1007/978-3-030-05051-1_44
36. Parida, S., Pati, B., Nayak, S.C., Panigrahi, C.R.: Offer based auction mechanism for virtual machine allocation in cloud environment. In: Pati, B., Panigrahi, C.R., Buyya, R., Li, K.-C. (eds.) Advanced Computing and Intelligent Engineering. AISC, vol. 1089, pp. 339–351. Springer, Singapore (2020). https://doi.org/10.1007/978-981-15-1483-8_29

Collaborative Mobile Edge Computing Through UPF Selection

Yuanzhe Li[(✉)], Ao Zhou, Xiao Ma, and Shangguang Wang

Beijing University of Posts and Telecommunications, Beijing, China
{buptlyz,aozhou,maxiao18,sgwang}@bupt.edu.cn

Abstract. The distributed deployment and the relatively limited resource of one edge node make it quite challenging to effectively manage resources at the edge. Inappropriate scheduling may result in a quality of service deterioration and brings significant cost. In this paper, we propose a per-user level management mechanism for joint scheduling of user requests and container resources at the edge and study how to minimize average cost as well as satisfy delay constraints. The cost model of the system consists of operating cost, switching cost and delay violation cost. The key idea is to deploy a deep reinforcement learning-based scheduler in the core network to conduct joint network and computation management. To evaluate the performance, we build a test bed namely MiniEdgeCore that contains a full user plane protocol stack and deploy a real-time video inference application on it. A real-world dataset is used as the workload sequence to conduct experiments. The results show that the proposed method can reduce average costs effectively.

Keywords: Mobile edge computing · 5G · Request dispatching · Container management

1 Introduction

With the rapid development of the 5G network and Mobile Edge Computing (MEC), the traditional end-cloud computation is evolving into the end-edge-cloud mechanism. Thanks to this change, end devices are released from heavy computation tasks by offloading tasks to edge nodes. As a result, end devices could be more light and portable, providing more powerful services. This creates several emerging big markets for the next generation of killer applications [33,34]. For example, mobile AR and VR are supposed to create a market of USD 766 billion by 2025, with compound annual revenue growth of 73.3% from 2018 to 2025 [28].

Guaranteeing the Quality of Service (QoS) of computation-intensive and delay-sensitive services in MEC requires dynamic provisioning of computational resources. That is, when the request number per slot increases, the edge node should increase the number of container instances to avoid the long processing delay resulting from requests queuing on the server side. When the request number per slot decreases, the edge node needs to appropriately reduce the number of

© ICST Institute for Computer Sciences, Social Informatics and Telecommunications Engineering 2022
Published by Springer Nature Switzerland AG 2022. All Rights Reserved
H. Gao et al. (Eds.): CollaborateCom 2022, LNICST 461, pp. 345–362, 2022.
https://doi.org/10.1007/978-3-031-24386-8_19

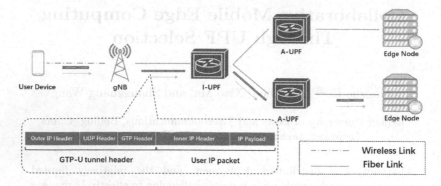

Fig. 1. GTP-U Tunnel

running containers, thereby saving computing resources and improving resource utilization. This is an intuitive method but still far from satisfactory. It has two disadvantages: 1) Starting or terminating instances brings time costs. This process lasts several seconds, during which the service is not available. 2) As each instance serves more than one user, such an adjustment cannot achieve per-user level management. Therefore, changing the number of running container instances is only suitable for coarse granularity and low-frequency management.

In traditional cloud data centers, the per-user level management is achieved by a load balance server. However, owing to the resource limitation of edge nodes, it is very likely that only a few instances are kept for one service. As a result, load balancing within one edge node is not enough. When container instances within one edge node cannot handle all the requests, dispatching user requests among different edge nodes is a practical way [17]. However, how to implement such dispatching is quite challenging. First, traditional load balance in cloud data centers relies on a centralized load balance server, which is not applicable for request dispatching among different edge nodes. Second, using the DNS mechanism in edge systems is not as efficient as it is in cloud computing [16]. As the DNS records are updated periodically according to the Time to Live (TTL) configured by the administrator, the DNS resolving results may remain the same during this time. This means a per-user level dispatching is not applicable and the resolving result may not match the state of the highly dynamic environment. Finally, and most importantly, user request dispatching relies on the selection of User Plane Function (UPF). User packets in the communication network (no matter 4G or 5G) are transferred through GPRS Tunneling Protocol User plane (GTP-U) tunnel, where original IP packets are encapsulated into GTP-U protocol data units (shown in Fig. 1). The original IP address is not used in packet routing within the communication network between gNB and Anchor UPF (A-UPF). Therefore, per-user level management in MEC should rely on the session management and traffic steering provided by the communication network architecture to realize the request dispatching.

Given the above facts, it is clear that achieving a per-user level matching between user requirements and computation resources is essential for MEC to realize its full potential. Thus, we pose a critical question: how to properly dispatch user requests and manage containers at edge nodes in 5G MEC to meet the latency constraints and minimize the total cost. The total cost comes from container operation cost, latency violation cost and container mismatching cost.

Currently, it has become a consensus that resource provision and request dispatching are highly interdependent and should be considered jointly as two levels of QoS guarantee methods [15,24,30]. That is, adjusting computation resource provision to cope with workload change in a long period and dispatching requests of each user to different edge nodes to deal with instantaneous changes. However, prior arts either provide a pure theoretic method based on specific delay models [10,39] or only consider the scheduling of computing resources at the service deployment level [11,24,31,32,36]. In addition, the aforementioned works neglect the key role of the 5G core network in request dispatching. To pave the way for deploying emerging applications such as cloud AR/VR at the edge, this paper focuses on how to achieve joint management of user request dispatching and container instance number scheduling in 5G architecture. The target is to minimize the total operating cost while satisfying the delay constraint.

In this paper, we study how to reduce total operation cost as well as satisfy the low delay requirement. The main contributions are listed as follows:

1) We propose a per-user level user request dispatching and container instance scheduling mechanism. This mechanism takes full consideration of 5G core network architecture and achieves the joint management of network and computation resources.
2) A deep reinforcement learning-based scheduling algorithm is proposed to jointly manage user request dispatching and container instance scheduling. The container switching delay during starting or terminating a container instance is considered so that the proposed method is more practical in real-world scenarios.
3) We build a test bed, namely MiniEdgeCore, to emulate the complicated request dispatching scenarios in MEC. MiniEdgeCore provides a full-stack 5G core network user plane that can dispatch user requests by setting up different GTP-U tunnels. It also has a Docker-based edge node system that works under the guidance of the core network.
4) Extensive experiments are conducted on MiniEdgeCore with a real-world dataset as the workload sequence input. The experiment results show that the proposed method can minimize the average total cost as well as guarantee a low access delay.

2   System Model

2.1   Scenario

As is shown in Fig. 2, we consider a mobile network consisting of base stations, edge nodes and UPFs. The topology of the network is an undirected graph $G =$

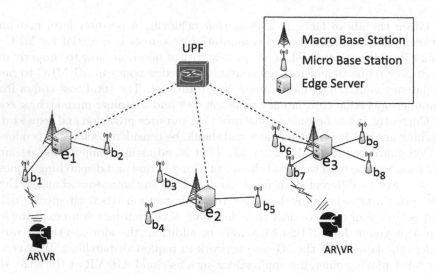

Fig. 2. System topology.

$(B \bigcup E \bigcup U, L)$. Let $B = \{b_1, b_2, \cdots, b_{n_b}\}$ denote the set of base stations, where $n_b(n_b = 1, 2, 3, \dots)$ is the total base stations number. Let $E = \{e_1, e_2, \cdots, e_{n_e}\}$ denote the set of edge nodes, where $n_e(n_e = 1, 2, 3, \dots)$ represents the edge node number. Let $U = \{u_1, u_2, \cdots, u_{n_u}\}$ denote the set of UPFs, where $n_u(n_u = 1, 2, 3, \dots)$ represents the UPF number. L denotes the physical communication links among base stations, edge nodes and UPFs. The operation of the system is described in a set of time slots T, indexed by $t = 1, 2, 3, \dots, T$ with a slot length τ.

At time slot t, there are several user requests. Let R^t denote the set of all requests that exist at time slot t. n_r^t represents the number of user requests in time slot t, i.e., $n_r^t = |R^t|$. r_x^t represents the request of user x at time slot t. If user x is requesting a service at t, $r_x^t \in R^t$. Otherwise, $r_x^t \notin R^t$. Let $\mathcal{B}(r_x^t)$ denote the base station that user i links to. $\mathcal{E}(r_x^t)$ denotes the edge node that is serving r_x^t. $\mathcal{U}(r_x^t)$ denotes the UPFs that is in the connection of r_x^t. As a result, the offloading information of a request is determined by $(\mathcal{B}(r_x^t), \mathcal{E}(r_x^t), \mathcal{U}(r_x^t))$. Each User Equipment (UE) has two types of network connections. The first one is the physical link with the base station. It is determined by user location. Let $\alpha_{xi}^t \in \{0, 1\}$ denote such a physical connection. If $\mathcal{B}(r_x^t) = b_i$, $\alpha_{xi}^t = 1$. Otherwise, $\alpha_{xi}^t = 0$. The other one is the logical link between UE and edge node, which connects the request producer and request consumer. Such a relationship is denoted by $\beta_{xj}^t \in \{0, 1\}$. If $\mathcal{E}(r_x^t) = e_j$, then $\beta_{xj}^t = 1$. Otherwise, $\beta_{xj}^t = 0$.

Generally, a certain number of container instances need to be started to serve these requests in each edge node. Current container platforms support CPU core number limitation for one container [20,23]. In this paper, it is supposed that each container instance works with only one CPU core assigned to it. As a result, the computing resources provided by each edge node at time slot t can be represented by the number of running container instances. Let $m_i^t(m_i^t = 0, 1, 2, \cdots M_i)$ denote the number of running container instances of edge node e_i at time slot t, where M_i represents the maximum number of container instances that can be started at edge node e_i.

In ideal situations, all user requests are dispatched to the nearest edge node to achieve the lowest access delay and best quality of service. However, the nearest edge node is not always the best choice in real world [6,17,35]. Considering computing resources are limited at edge nodes, if the nearest edge node gets overloaded, the total delay may exceed the upper limit as a result of long computation delay. However, the spatial and temporal distribution of user requests is uneven in cities. On the one hand, user number in different regions differs a lot, which makes the request number of different edge nodes at the same time slot vary a lot. On the other hand, user request number changes dynamically at one edge node because of user movement. Therefore, user requests may be routed to other edge nodes to prevent the nearest edge node from getting overloaded.

2.2 Delay

In mobile edge computing, access delay is one of the most important metrics. In most cases, access delay comes from transmission, processing, and backhaul [27]. Transmission delay refers to the delay brought by wireless communication between UE and base stations. Processing delay refers to the time needed for a processor to finish the task and the time consumed by tasks waiting in the queue. Backhaul delay refers to the total time for a packet to wait in the queues of network equipment when it traverses the distance between edge servers and base stations. As request dispatching does not affect the transmission delay of wireless communication, the service delay in this paper involves backhaul delay and processing delay.

Let φ_i and φ_j denote network devices located at the two ends of one link. $d(\varphi_i, \varphi_j)$ denotes the delay between these to devices. Then, the backhaul delay of a user request consists of two parts, i.e., the delay between the base station and UPF as well as the delay between UPF and the edge node. The backhaul delay can be defined as follows:

$$D_N(r_x^t) = d(\mathcal{B}(r_x^t), \mathcal{U}(r_x^t)) + d(\mathcal{U}(r_x^t), \mathcal{E}(r_x^t)), \tag{1}$$

where $D_N(r_x^t)$ denotes the backhaul delay of service request r_x^t.

The computation delay of request r_x^t is defined as the total time it takes from the request's arriving at the edge node to the edge node's sending back the result.

$$D_C(r_x^t) = T_e(r_x^t) - T_s(r_x^t), \tag{2}$$

where $T_s(r_x^t)$ denotes the time edge node receives the request and start to process it. $T_e(r_x^t)$ denotes the time that the process ends.

The total delay consists of communication delay and computation delay. It is given as follows

$$D(r_x^t) = D_N(r_x^t) + D_C(r_x^t).$$ (3)

In real-world scenarios, average delay is not a good indicator of the system because it can be easily affected by extreme values. Besides, pursuing extremely short delays cannot improve the quality of service if delays have already been lower than a specific threshold. As a result, statistical delay guarantee is a more practical way to evaluate the quality of service [19]. We adopt delay ratio as the key metrics to evaluate the network state. To get the delay ratio, the delay of each user request is sampled N_d times in a time slot. Supposing that user x has n_d^t samples satisfying the delay constraint in time slot t, then the delay ratio is defined as follows:

$$\mathcal{R}_x^t = \frac{n_d^t}{N_d}.$$ (4)

2.3   System Cost

For a time period between t_a and t_b ($t_a, t_b \in T$), the total system cost contains three parts, i.e., operating cost, switching cost and delay violation cost. Operating cost refers to the rental cost that tenants are charged according to the number of containers they are using in each time slot. There are many charging systems. Tenants can pay by the year, by month, pay as you use, etc. To simplify the problem, we adopt a charging system of pay by time slot.

$$C_r(t_a, t_b) = p_{run} \sum_{t=t_a}^{t_b} \sum_{i=1}^{n_e} m_i^t,$$ (5)

where $C_r(t_a, t_b)$ denotes the total operating cost, p_{run} represents the cost of one container running for one time slot, m_i^t is the total container number of edge node e_i running in time slot t.

Switching cost comes from operations of starting or terminating a container in an edge node. Changing the number of running containers according to the variation of total workload can prevent operating cost waste but will introduce extra system overhead [4]. Besides, the switching operation cannot take effect immediately because of the startup and termination time of a container. In order to prevent frequent switching operations, switching cost is introduced, which is defined as follows:

$$C_s(t_a, t_b) = p_{switch} \sum_{t=t_a}^{t_b} \sum_{i=1}^{n_e} |m_i^t - m_i^{t-1}|,$$ (6)

where $C_s(t_a, t_b)$ denotes the total switching cost and p_{switch} is the price for one single switching operation.

Delay violation cost results from the potential access delay violation. The violation may come from the long network delay stemming from improper request dispatching. It could also come from the extra computation delay caused by improper resource scheduling. Access delay violation will lead to unacceptable quality of service, and, as a result, the edge operator has to compensate users. Thus, a delay violation cost is introduced.

$$C_{\mathrm{d}}(t_a, t_b) = p_{\mathrm{delay}} \sum_{t=t_a}^{t_b} \sum_{r_x^t \in R^t} \eta_x^t, \tag{7}$$

$$\eta_x^t = \begin{cases} 1, \mathcal{R}_x^t < \mathcal{R}_{\min} \\ 0, otherwise \end{cases}, \tag{8}$$

where $C_{\mathrm{d}}(t_a, t_b)$ denotes the total delay violation cost, p_{delay} is the punishment for one delay violation, $\mathcal{R}_x^t$ is the delay ratio of user x at time slot t, $\mathcal{R}_{\min}$ is the lowest acceptable delay ratio according to service level agreement.

Therefore, the total cost of the system during the period from t_a to t_b can be denoted as follows:

$$C_{\mathrm{total}}(t_a, t_b) = C_{\mathrm{r}}(t_a, t_b) + C_{\mathrm{s}}(t_a, t_b) + C_{\mathrm{d}}(t_a, t_b). \tag{9}$$

Then the average cost per request per slot is defined as follows:

$$C_{\mathrm{req}} = \frac{C_{\mathrm{total}}(t_a, t_b)}{\sum_{t=t_a}^{t_b} n_r^t}. \tag{10}$$

2.4 Problem Formulation

In mobile edge computing, edge service provider changes the number of running containers at different edge nodes to dynamically adjust the computing resource provision to the computing demands of users. Besides, request dispatching is used to route user requests to proper edge nodes in a fine-grained manner to prevent frequent container switching operation and achieve a quick response. It is quite challenging to achieve a joint management of request dispatching and container scheduling with a low cost. This paper studies how to minimize the average cost per request per slot from the perspective of edge service providers.

$$Minimize \ C_{\mathrm{req}}, \tag{11}$$

$$s.t. \ \sum_{i=1}^{n_b} \alpha_{xi}^t = 1, \ \forall 0 \le x \le n_r^t, \tag{12}$$

$$\sum_{j=1}^{n_e} \beta_{xj}^t = 1, \ \forall 0 \le x \le n_r^t, \tag{13}$$

$$m_i^t \le M_i, \tag{14}$$

where Eq. 12 represents that each UE connects to only one base station. Equation 13 guarantees that each user request is responded by only one edge node. Equation 14 represents that the running container number of one edge node cannot exceed the upper limit.

3   Algorithm Design

User requests dispatching and container scheduling in mobile edge computing are typical sequential decision-making problems, which are often modeled
as Markov decision processes [5,29]. This is a challenging problem because it
involves joint management of network and computing resources. In this paper,
Advantage Actor Critic (A2C) algorithm is adopted to solve this problem. First,
we map the problem into Markov decision process. A Markov decision process
$M = (S, A, P, R)$ consists of a finite set of state S, a finite set of actions A,
a state transition probability P and a reward function R. In this problem, the
effect of actions on the system is deterministic, so the key points of this Markov
decision process are the state, action and reward function, which are defined as
follows:

At the beginning of each time slot t, the state of the system is constructed
as the input of the A2C agent, which consists of: 1) The maximum number of
container instances that each edge node can launch, i.e., M_i; 2) The number
of running container instances of each edge node in the current time slot, i.e.,
$M_i - m_i^t$; 3) The dispatching relationship of user requests that are launched in
previous time slots and haven't been terminated; 4) The information on new
user requests that will be launched in this time slot.

Every action $a_t \in A$ in the action set consists of two parts: the information for
container instance management and the information for user request dispatching.
Supposing that there are n_e edge nodes in the system and at most n_q new user
requests in a time slot. Then a_t will be an array with $n_e + n_q$ bits. The first n_e bits
correspond to the container instance operations of each edge node. This paper
assumes that in each time slot, each edge node can only have three container
operations: adding a container, reducing a container, or keeping the number of
containers unchanged. The value of each bit could be 1,0 or -1, respectively. The
last n_q bits correspond to the request dispatching decision and its value refers to
the ID of the target edge node. Since the actual number of user requests in each
time slot satisfies $n_r^t \leq n_q$, the first $n_e + n_r^t$ bits of the entire action array are
valid, and the rest bits are filled with 0 by default. The output of A2C's policy
network is a continuous action array a_t'. The value of each bit of a_t' is limited
between -1.5 and 1.5. Then a_t' is discretized to a_t through an action discreteness
algorithm shown in Algorithm 1.

The reward function is defined as $w^t - c^t$, where $w^t = w_0(n_r^t - \sum_{r_x^t \in R^t} \eta_x^t)$
is the reward brought by requests whose delay ratio meets the requirements. w_0
is the reward for a single request. $c^t = C_{\text{total}}(t - 1, t)$ is the cost of the system
in one time slot.

In 5G architecture, the orchestrator in MEC, acting as an Application Function (AF), can interact with the core network to provide application influence on
traffic routing [1,8]. This mechanism makes it applicable to achieve joint management of 5G network and edge nodes. Therefore, this paper uses a centralized
control method and deploys the A2C agent in the core network to schedule user
requests and edge-side containers jointly.

Algorithm 1. Action Discreteness Algorithm

Input: a'_t
Output: a_t
1: Clamp each bit of a'_t to [-1.5, 1.5]
2: **for** $i = 0$; $i < n_e$; $i + +$ **do**
3:     **if** $a'_t[i] > 0.5$ and $2m_i^t - \sum_{r_x^t \in R^t} \beta_{xi}^t < 2$ **then**
4:         $a_t[i] = 1$
5:     **else if** $2m_i^t - \sum_{r_x^t \in R^t} \beta_{xi}^t \geq 4$ **then**
6:         $a_t[i] = -1$
7:     **else**
8:         $a_t[i] = 0$
9:     **end if**
10: **end for**
11: **for** $i = n_e$; $i < n_e + n_q$; $i + +$ **do**
12:     **if** $i < n_e + n_r^t$ **then**
13:         $a_t[i] = \lfloor n_e(a'_t[i] + 1.5)/3 \rfloor + 1$
14:     **else**
15:         $a_t[i] = 0$
16:     **end if**
17: **end for**
18: **return** a_t.

---

4   Experiment

4.1   5G MEC Experiment Platform

We build a test bed called MiniEdgeCore. The test bed consists of two parts. The first part is a 5G core network system consisting of a simplified control plane and a full-stack user plane. The control plane only implements the necessary functionalities related to traffic steering such as session management and UPF selection. The user plane implements UPF with a full GTP-U protocol stack [2, 3]. GTP-U is widely used in protocol which creates a UDP-based tunnel between gNB and Protocol data unit Session Anchor (PSA) to enable interconnection between UE and external packet data networks such as the Internet and local data network. Generally, there are two roles for UPFs. It can either serve as an Uplink Classifier (UL CL) or as PSA. For the convenience of expression, in the following, we use Intermediate UPF (I-UPF) to refer to the UPF working as ULCL,, and A-UPF to refer to the UPF that serve as PSA.

The second part of the system is edge nodes composed of several servers deployed with Docker [20] system. In each edge node, an AF is implemented based on Docker Python SDK[1], which is in charge of interacting with the core network and starting or terminating a container instance.

To achieve a flexible network architecture, we run network functions in Mininet [21] hosts. Mininet is a Linux-based system that consists of virtual networks, switches and applications running in a real kernel. By leveraging Mininet,

---

[1] https://docs.docker.com/engine/api/.

we can create different net topologies and test realistic network streams in one network node. Besides, the wireless network between UE and gNB is replaced by Ethernet because we were not concerned with the communication status of the wireless terminal. This can help to save the cost of software-defined radio devices and make the system capable of emulating large-number user scenarios.

One network node together with several edge servers composes one cluster that emulates one service area in the city. Multiple clusters linking with each other can emulate complicated request dispatching scenarios in MEC. For one user request, the dispatching is achieved by setting up a GTP-U tunnel. The I-UPF in this tunnel will route request data packets to the target A-UPF, which is connected with an edge node. If the target A-UPF locates in the same cluster, user requests are routed to the local edge node, otherwise, user requests will be processed by edge nodes located in another service area.

4.2   Experiment Setup

The experiment is conducted in the MiniEdgeCore system mentioned above. The application used in the experiment is a live stream real-time action inference. A UE node in MiniEdgeCore pushes a pre-recorded hand motion video to the edge server using an RTSP [25] stream set up by FFMPEG [12]. Then, a processing service based on Mediapipe [14] detects hand locations frame by frame and return hand-knuckle coordinates to the user. In the process of video streaming, the system records the time stamp when a frame is sent, received, and processed so that the backhaul delay and processing delay can be calculated. The system clocks of the servers are synchronized using Network Time Protocol [22].

This experiment is conducted by emulating the user request scenarios in the whole city. We use Edge Computing Dataset[2] as input to provide workload sequence. The dataset records the mobile Internet access log of users in Beijing. Each record in the dataset provides information including phone number (encrypted to protect privacy), location area code and cell identification code of the connected base station, access point name, international mobile device identification code (the first six digits), the start time and end time of network access, upstream and downstream traffic, and gateway information. One example of user request workload sequences is shown in Fig. 3. In this paper, all base stations are divided into six service areas. Each service area is equipped with an edge server. According to the location information of the user's access to the base station, the user's access requests can be mapped to each service area as the input workload of the area.

In this experiment, MiniEdgeCore deploys six service areas, corresponding to the six service areas of the dataset respectively. Each service area has four base stations, and each base station has five UEs. Each UE is in a dormant state by default. MiniEdgeCore activates a different number of dormant UEs in each time slot according to the workload sequence recorded in the dataset. UEs start to upstream video after it is activated. UE requests in one area are offloaded to

---

[2] https://github.com/BuptMecMigration/Edge-Computing-Dataset.

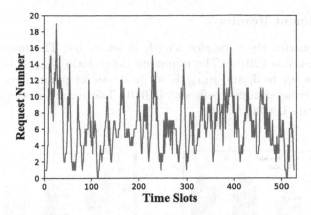

Fig. 3. User request number per time slot.

A-UPFs in different areas by I-UPF. A-UPF is connected to an edge server by binding the physical network card through the Open vSwitch[3]. The edge server is a Lenovo ThinkCenter M910t with a 3.40 GHz Intel Core i7-6700 CPU and a 16G DDR4 memory. Intel Core i7-6700 has four cores. One CPU core is used to run AF which is in charge of communicating with the core network. The remaining three CPU cores are used to run container instances. Each container instance is mapped to one CPU core.

4.3   Benchmark Algorithms

In this section, C_{req} and Average Service Satisfaction Rate are selected as the main metrics. Average Service Satisfaction Rate is defined as the average proportion of users whose request delay ratio meets the requirements. The benchmark algorithms are listed as follows:

1. **Local** All user requests are processed in the edge node within the service area. The edge node will start a new container when the processing delay reaches the upper limit. It terminates a container if instances work in an idle state.
2. **Random** User's service requests are randomly dispatched to different edge nodes. Each edge node adjusts the number of container instances according to its workload. When the upper limit is reached, a new container is started, and the container is terminated when the container is idle.
3. **Greedy** User requests in each time slot are dispatched to the edge node with the most sufficient computing resources in the time slot. Each edge server opens a new container when this server's processing delay reaches the upper limit and closes one container instance when it is idle.

---

[3] https://www.openvswitch.org/.

4.4 Experiment Results

In this experiment, the time slot length is set to 5 s. The maximum service satisfaction delay is 220 ms. The minimum delay ratio $\mathcal{R}_{\min}$ is 0.9. p_{run} is set to 1. p_{switch} is set to 3, and p_{delay} is set to 3. As for parameters used in A2C training, the cross-entropy coefficient is 0.01. The reward discount is 0.9, and the learning rate is 0.001.

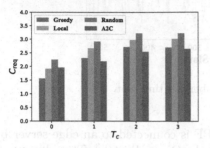 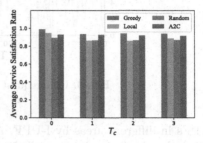

(a) Average cost per request per slot.   (b) Average service satisfaction rate.

Fig. 4. Algorithm performance with different container switching delay.

Figure 4 shows the average cost per request per slot C_{req}(Fig. 4a) and the average service satisfaction rate (Fig. 4b) of each algorithm in the experiment. The horizontal axis T_c in the figure represents container switching delay, that is, the adjustment operation on the number of containers needs to pass T_c time slots to take effect. As shown in the figure, when $T_c = 0$ (container operation takes effect immediately), Greedy achieves the highest service satisfaction rate (98.96%) and the lowest C_{req} (1.56). Local achieves a delay satisfaction rate of 94.68% with a C_{req} of 1.92, and A2C achieves a delay satisfaction rate of 93.03% with a C_{req} of 1.96. The performance of Random is the poorest, and its delay satisfaction rate is less than 90%. However, the performance of A2C begins to stand out when $T_c \neq 0$. As T_c increases from 1 time slot to 3 time slots, A2C maintains the lowest C_{req}, which is on average 4.51% less than Greedy, 14.96% less than Local, and 21.17% less than Random. In terms of average service satisfaction rate, when container switching delay is non-zero, only Greedy and A2C can maintain a service satisfaction rate of above 90%. Both Local and Random are lower than 90%. In the ideal case where the container operation takes effect immediately, Greedy is the optimal strategy. Because the system can immediately adjust the number of running container instances according to the change of workload and dispatch the user's service requests to the edge node with the most abundant computing resources. This can avoid the processing timeout caused by the overload of a single container. However, in real-world scenarios, it takes a certain amount of time for the container instance to start or terminate [4]. In this situation, although Greedy can ensure a high service satisfaction rate, its container operations bring extra costs due to the existence of container

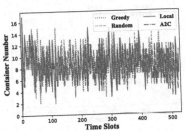 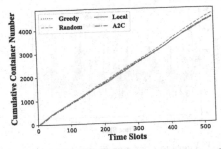

(a) Real-time running container number.   (b) Cumulative running container number.

Fig. 5. Running container number.

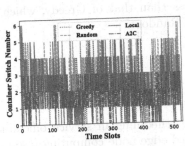 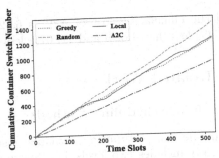

(a) Real-time container switching times.   (b) Cumulative container switching times

Fig. 6. Container switching times

switching delays. A2C has a forward-looking decision-making process through the training of the agent. As a result, the cost of container scheduling is lower.

In order to further explain the reason why A2C achieves the lowest C_{req} in the presence of container switching delay, a complete epoch is analyzed in the case of $T_c = 2$. As shown in Fig. 5, during the whole experiment, the number of running container instances and the number of user requests (see Fig. 3) have a similar fluctuation pattern. Among all algorithms, the real-time running container number of A2C (shown in Fig. 5a) has a smaller fluctuation range than other algorithms. Its cumulative number of containers (shown in Fig. 5b) is basically the same as that of Greedy and Local, and less than that of Random. However, the performance of each algorithm on container switching times is significantly different. As shown in Fig. 6a, the real-time container switching times of A2C are significantly lower than that of other algorithms. The gap of cumulative container switching times (see Fig. 6b) is much more distinct. The cumulative container switching times of A2C are 23.38% less than that of Greedy, 24.06% less than that of Local, and 34.62% less than that of Random. Since A2C has smaller container switching times, the C_{req} of A2C is relatively lower (Fig. 7a),

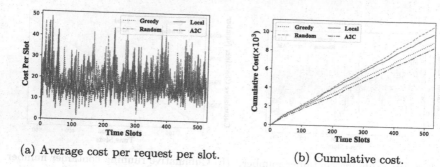

(a) Average cost per request per slot.   (b) Cumulative cost.

Fig. 7. Total cost.

and the cumulative cost of A2C is 6.52% less than that of Greedy, which is 14.74% less than Local and 21. 07% less than Random.

5   Related Work

5.1   Joint Scheduling Methods

In mobile edge computing, dynamic resource scheduling in service offloading generally includes two levels, i.e., coarse-grained edge node computing resource scheduling and fine-grained request dispatching. The former mainly adjusts the provision of computing resources in the edge node dynamically to meet the user requirement in the service area. The latter mainly selects target edge node and chooses transmission path to guarantee that the user side delay meets the QoS requirement.

Existing works mainly focus on the joint optimization of request dispatching at network side and dynamic service placement in the edge node. Ting He et al. [31] study the joint service placement and request scheduling in mobile edge computing with consideration of both sharable resources (storage) and non-shareable resources (communication, computation). They develop a constant-factor approximation algorithm and evaluate performance of the algorithm using simulation. Vajiheh Farhadi et al. [11] try to maximize the expected requests served by edge nodes per slot by optimizing service placement and request scheduling. They leverage trace-driven simulation to evaluate the performance of their algorithm. Konstantinos Poularakis et al. [24] jointly consider storage, communication, computation resource constraints in service placement and request scheduling. Bo Yin et al. [37] introduce the concept of age of information in the study of scheduling in mobile edge computing. They leverage age of information to quantify the information freshness and propose two computationally tractable scheduling policies to minimize age of information. Yiwen Han et al. [15] study distributed request scheduling and dynamic service deployment in edge nodes. They proposed multi-agent reinforcement learning-based algorithm to improve system throughput while reducing system scheduling overhead.

These works are effective but still can be improved. Most of these works study the problem in two time scales, i.e., service deployment at a larger scale and request dispatching at a smaller scale. However, the computing resource management is still coarse-grained. Edge nodes not only have to decide what service to deploy, but also have to schedule how many container instances to run in each time slot. In addition, these works fail to take session management and traffic steering mechanism of 5G core network architecture into consideration.

5.2   Test Beds

Yoohwa Kang et al. [18] implement a test bed system to evaluate their multipath transmission control protocol based on multi-access traffic steering solution. In their test bed, UE get access to the data network through WLAN and 5G gNB. The 5G gNB uses software-defined radio to emulate an LTE gNB. Mingyuan Zang et al. [38] leverage the open source project OpenAirInterface to build an in-lab emulation test bed. They use this test bed to verify mobile edge cache in different network scenarios. Bhaskar Prasad Rimal et al. [26] design a two-level edge computing scheme in a fiber-wireless access network. In order to evaluate the performance of their proposed solution, they implement an experimental test bed with edge applications in optical fiber backhaul networks. Mona Ghassemian et al. share their experience in building a 5G test bed platform in [13]. Their 5G-VINNI project deploys 5G-NR radio as well as virtualized EPC outside to test performance in the 3.6 GHz (first implementation phase) and 5G mmWave (second implementation phase). Multiple use cases are tested including cloud-based gaming, connected care for assisted living, remote robotic control, etc., covering gaming, health and industry. However, such a test bed system is based on Samsung network equipment, which is expensive and may not be suitable for in-lab experiments. Mohammad Kazem Chamran et al. [7] study the independent decision-making of distributed nodes in 5G scenarios by implementing a distributed test bed. Different from traditional centralized decision-making systems, the proposed system consists of Universal Software Radio Peripheral nodes embedded with Raspberry Pi3 B+. That is, test bed nodes can communicate with each other as well as make decisions independently. Ali Esmaeily et al. [9] also leverage OpenAirInterface to implement a test bed for end-to-end network slicing.

The aforementioned systems take advantage of open source projects to implement network emulation. These test beds emulate various network scenarios and can get data close to the real scene. However, limited by the coverage area of software-designed radio, the access limit of total equipment number and the high price of software designed radio devices, these systems lack scalability. Evaluating large-scale research, such as service deployment, mobile edge offloading and user request scheduling, on these systems are difficult.

6 Conclusion

In order to guarantee the QoS of delay-sensitive applications, MEC relies heavily on the dynamic joint management of user request dispatching and edge-side container scheduling. In this paper, we first establish a cost model for service offloading scenarios. Then, we map the joint scheduling problem into a Markov decision process and proposed a reinforcement learning-based algorithm to solve it. Next, instead of conducting simulations leveraging mathematical delay models, we build a test bed called MiniEdgeCore, which provides a full-stack 5G core network user plane and a Docker-based edge node system. MiniEdgeCore implements user request dispatching by setting up GTP-U tunnels to different UPFs. Besides, it uses the interaction process between the core network and the edge nodes to control the starting and terminating of container instances. Finally, experiments are conducted on MiniEdgeCore. A real-time video inference application is deployed on MiniEdgeCore and a real-world dataset is used as workload sequence input. The experiment results show that the proposed method can reduce at least 4.51% of cost.

Acknowledgments. This work was supported in part by the National Key R&D Program of China (No. 2020YFB1805502) and NSFC (U21B2016, 62032003 and 61922017).

References

1. 3GPP: TS 23.501, system architecture for the 5G System. In: Technical Specification (TS) 23.501, 3rd Generation Partnership Project (3GPP). https://www.3gpp.org/ftp/Specs/archive/23_series/23.501/
2. 3GPP: TS 29.060, GPRS Tunneling Protocol (GTP) across the Gn and Gp interface. In: Technical Specification (TS) 29.060, 3rd Generation Partnership Project (3GPP). https://www.3gpp.org/ftp/Specs/archive/29_series/29.060/
3. 3GPP: TS 29.281, General Packet Radio System (GPRS) Tunneling Protocol User Plane (GTPv1-U). In: Technical Specification (TS) 29.281, 3rd Generation Partnership Project (3GPP). https://www.3gpp.org/ftp/Specs/archive/29_series/29.281/
4. Ahmed, A., Mohan, A., Cooperman, G., Pierre, G.: Docker Container Deployment in Distributed Fog Infrastructures with Checkpoint/Restart. In: Proceedings of IEEE International Conference on Mobile Cloud Computing, Services, and Engineering (MobileCloud), pp. 55–62 (2020)
5. Bäuerle, N., Rieder, U.: Markov decision processes. Jahresber. Deutsch. Math.-Verein. **112**(4), 217–243 (2010)
6. Ceselli, A., Premoli, M., Secci, S.: Mobile edge cloud network design optimization. IEEE/ACM Trans. Netw. **25**(3), 1818–1831 (2017)
7. Chamran, M.K., Yau, K.L.A., Noor, R.M.D., Wong, R.: A distributed testbed for 5G scenarios: an experimental study. Sensors **20**(1), 18 (2020)
8. Contreras, L.M., et al.: MEC in 5G networks. Tech. rep., European Telecommunications techreports Institute
9. Esmaeily, A., Kralevska, K., Gligoroski, D.: A cloud-based SDN/NFV testbed for end-to-end network slicing in 4G/5G. In: Proceedings of IEEE Conference on Network Softwarization (NetSoft), pp. 29–35 (2020)

10. Fang, L., Liu, T., Zhu, Y., Yang, Y.: Task offloading and dispatching for MEC with selfish mobile devices and access points. In: Proceedings of IEEE Global Communications Conference (GLOBECOM), pp. 1–6 (2020)

11. Farhadi, V., et al.: Service placement and request scheduling for data-intensive applications in edge clouds. In: Proceedings of IEEE Conference on Computer Communications (INFOCOM), pp. 1279–1287 (2019)

12. FFmpeg: FFmpeg (2022). https://ffmpeg.org/

13. Ghassemian, M., Muschamp, P., Warren, D.: Experience building a 5G testbed platform. arXiv:2008.01628 (2020)

14. Google: Mediapipe (2021). https://google.github.io/mediapipe/

15. Han, Y., Shen, S., Wang, X., Wang, S., Leung, V.C.: Tailored learning-based scheduling for kubernetes-oriented edge-cloud system. In: Proceedings of IEEE Conference on Computer Communications (INFOCOM), pp. 1–10 (2021)

16. Hsu, K.J., Choncholas, J., Bhardwaj, K., Gavrilovska, A.: DNS does not suffice for MEC-CDN. In: Proceedings of ACM Workshop on Hot Topics in Networks (HotNets), pp. 212–218. Association for Computing Machinery, New York, NY, USA (2020)

17. Jia, M., Cao, J., Liang, W.: Optimal cloudlet placement and user to cloudlet allocation in wireless metropolitan area networks. IEEE Trans. Cloud Comput. 5(4), 725–737 (2017)

18. Kang, Y., Kim, C., An, D., Yoon, H.: Multipath transmission control protocol-based multi-access traffic steering solution for 5G multimedia-centric network: design and testbed system implementation. Int. J. Distrib. Sensor Netw. 16(2), 155014772090975 (2020)

19. Li, Q., Wang, S., Yang, F.: QoS driven task offloading with statistical guarantee in mobile edge computing. IEEE Trans. Mob. Comput. 21(1), 278–290 (2020)

20. Merkel, D.: Docker: lightweight linux containers for consistent development and deployment. Linux J. 2014(239), 2 (2014)

21. Mininet: Mininet (2022). http://mininet.org/

22. Network Time Foundation: NTP: the network time protocol (2014). http://www.ntp.org/

23. Podman: Podman (2022). https://podman.io/

24. Poularakis, K., Llorca, J., Tulino, A.M., Taylor, I., Tassiulas, L.: Joint service placement and request routing in multi-cell mobile edge computing networks. In: Proceedings of IEEE Conference on Computer Communications (INFOCOM), pp. 10–18 (2019)

25. Rao, A., Lanphier, R., Schulzrinne, H.: Real Time Streaming Protocol (RTSP). Tech. Rep. 2326 (1998). https://www.rfc-editor.org/info/rfc2326

26. Rimal, B.P., Maier, M., Satyanarayanan, M.: Experimental testbed for edge computing in fiber-wireless broadband access networks. IEEE Commun. Mag. 56(8), 160–167 (2018)

27. Rodrigues, T.G., Suto, K., Nishiyama, H., Kato, N., Temma, K.: Cloudlets activation scheme for scalable mobile edge computing with transmission power control and virtual machine migration. IEEE Trans. Comput. 67(9), 1287–1300 (2018)

28. Siriwardhana, Y., Porambage, P., Liyanage, M., Ylianttila, M.: A survey on mobile augmented reality with 5g mobile edge computing: architectures, applications, and technical aspects. IEEE Commun. Surv. Tutorials 23(2), 1160–1192 (2021)

29. Sutton, R.S., Barto, A.G.: Reinforcement learning: an introduction. In: Adaptive Computation and Machine Learning Series, The MIT Press, Cambridge, Massachusetts, second edition edn (2018)

30. Tan, H., Han, Z., Li, X.Y., Lau, F.C.: Online job dispatching and scheduling in edge-clouds. In: Proceedings of IEEE Conference on Computer Communications (INFOCOM), pp. 1–9. IEEE, Atlanta, GA, USA (2017)
31. He, T., Khamfroush, H., Wang, S., La Porta, T., Stein, S.: It's hard to share: joint service placement and request scheduling in edge clouds with sharable and non-sharable resources. In: Proceedings of International Conference on Distributed Computing Systems (ICDCS), pp. 365–375. IEEE, Vienna (2018)
32. Tong, L., Li, Y., Gao, W.: A hierarchical edge cloud architecture for mobile computing. In: Proceedings of IEEE International Conference on Computer Communications (INFOCOM), pp. 1–9. IEEE, San Francisco, CA, USA (2016)
33. Xu, M., Qian, F., Zhu, M., Huang, F., Pushp, S., Liu, X.: DeepWear: adaptive local offloading for on-wearable deep learning. IEEE Trans. Mob. Comput. **19**(2), 314–330 (2020)
34. Xu, M., Xu, T., Liu, Y., Lin, F.X.: Video analytics with zero-streaming cameras. In: Proceedings of USENIX Annual Technical Conference (ATC), pp. 459–472. USENIX Association (2021)
35. Xu, Z., Liang, W., Xu, W., Jia, M., Guo, S.: Efficient Algorithms for Capacitated Cloudlet Placements. IEEE Trans. Parallel Distrib. Syst. **27**(10), 2866–2880 (2016)
36. Yang, L., Cao, J., Liang, G., Han, X.: Cost aware service placement and load dispatching in mobile cloud systems. IEEE Trans. Comput. **65**(5), 1440–1452 (2016)
37. Yin, B., et al.: Only those requested count: proactive scheduling policies for minimizing effective age-of-information. In: Proceedings of IEEE Conference on Computer Communications (INFOCOM), pp. 109–117 (2019)
38. Zang, M., Zhang, C., Yan, Y.: In-lab testbed for mobile edge caching with multiple users access. In: Proceedings of International Conference on Information and Communication Technology Convergence (ICTC), pp. 450–455 (2019)
39. Zeng, D., Gu, L., Guo, S., Cheng, Z., Yu, S.: Joint optimization of task scheduling and image placement in fog computing supported software-defined embedded system. IEEE Trans. Comput. **65**(12), 3702–3712 (2016)

Deep Reinforcement Learning for Multi-UAV Exploration Under Energy Constraints

Yating Zhou[1], Dianxi Shi[2(✉)], Huanhuan Yang[1], Haomeng Hu[1], Shaowu Yang[1], and Yongjun Zhang[2]

[1] College of Computer, National University of Defense Technology, Changsha 410073, Hunan, China
[2] Artificial Intelligence Research Center (AIRC), National Innovation Institute of Defense Technology (NIIDT), Beijing 100071, China
dxshi@nudt.edu.cn

Abstract. Autonomous exploration is the essential task for various applications of unmanned aerial vehicles (UAVs), but there is currently a lack of available energy-constrained multi-UAV exploration methods. In this paper, we propose the RTN-Explorer, an environment exploration strategy that satisfies the energy constraints. The goal of environment exploration is to expand the scope of exploration as much as possible, while the goal of energy constraints is to make the UAV return to the landing zone before the energy is exhausted, so they are a pair of contradictory goals. To better balance these two goals, we use map centering, and local-global map processing methods to improve the system performance and use the minimum distance penalty function to make the multi-UAV system satisfy the energy constraints. We also use the map generator to generate different environment maps to improve generalization performance. A large number of simulation experiments verify the effectiveness and robustness of our method and show superior performance in benchmark comparison.

Keywords: Multi-UAV exploration · Deep reinforcement learning · Energy constraints

1 Introduction

Autonomous exploration means that the agent, without any prior knowledge, keeps moving in a new environment and constructs a map of the whole environment. It is an essential part of many tasks, such as planetary exploration [1], reconnaissance [2], rescue [3], mowing [4], and cleaning [5]. Compared with single-agent environment exploration, multi-agent environment exploration is more

---

This work was partially supported by the National Natural Science Foundation of China No. 91948303.

H. Gao et al. (Eds.): CollaborateCom 2022, LNICST 461, pp. 363–379, 2022.
https://doi.org/10.1007/978-3-031-24386-8_20

difficult because of cooperation between agents. Despite decades of research, multi-agent environment exploration, as an NP-hard problem [6], remains a complex problem to solve.

Many traditional methods have been proposed in recent years, but these methods rely heavily on experts to manually design heuristic functions for different scenes [7,8]. Research on deep reinforcement learning methods gradually increased [9–16]. However, the current environment exploration strategies based on deep reinforcement learning only focus on exploration efficiency and do not consider energy constraints. Due to the limited battery capacity of UAVs, it is necessary to consider energy constraints for tasks in the real world.

Considering the energy constraints in a real exploration task, the UAV needs to return to the landing zone before the energy is exhausted, which will bring great challenges to the multi-agent exploration task. The first challenge is to design an efficient reward function to ensure that the multi-agent system satisfies the energy constraints. In [17], the energy constraint is considered in the path planning task of a given environment, and a constant penalty is given to the agent when the UAV runs out of energy. But the constant value penalty function is difficult to make the UAV incline to return to the landing area. The second challenge is that meeting the energy constraints and improving the exploration rate are in conflict. Achieving a balance between the two goals requires well-designed solutions. The third challenge is the need to stabilize the performance of multi-UAV exploration systems on different maps.

Based on the above facts, this paper proposes RTN-Explorer, a multi-UAV exploration strategy under energy constraints, while exploring the unknown environment as much as possible while meeting energy constraints. We introduce the minimum distance penalty function. The UAV obtains a penalty proportional to the shortest distance to the landing zone to ensure that the UAV meets the energy constraint. We design a DDQN-based network architecture and introduce map centering, global-local map processing to improve the performance of the multi-UAV exploration system. We also implemented a map generator, which can generate different environment maps for training to improve generalization. We have carried out many experiments and verification to prove the effectiveness of our proposed method. Our contributions are summarized as follows:

1) We introduce energy constraints into exploration tasks based on deep reinforcement learning for the first time. Our minimum distance penalty function effectively improves the return rate to more than 93%, which is 92% higher than the return rate of the constant penalty.
2) We design a DDQN-based network architecture and introduce map centering, global-local map processing to improve the performance of the multi-UAV exploration system. We increase the exploration rate to more than 92.85%.
3) To improve the generalized performance of the multi-UAV system, we design a map generator that can randomly change the position and size of obstacles.

2   Related Work

Autonomous robotic exploration has always been a hot research topic in robotics because of its applications in rescue tasks. Depending on whether deep reinforcement learning techniques are used, existing exploration methods are categorized as 1) classical or 2) deep reinforcement learning.

2.1   Classical Methods for Environment Exploration

Classical methods utilize handcrafted heuristics to allocate goal locations to robots to maximize exploration efficiency [6]. To date, the most common method used for exploring unknown environments is frontier exploration. Zhou et al. [18] introduce a frontier information structure to generate efficient global coverage paths, which completes the exploration tasks with unprecedented efficiency (3–8 times faster) compared to other single robot approaches. But multi-robot exploration is a more effective way to improve the efficiency of exploration. In the multi-robot frontier exploration method [19], each agent makes its own decision to select a target to explore based on the shared frontier. And the multi-robot frontier exploration was improved by ranking the agents to allocate to a particular frontier location based on their distances to the frontier [20]. And Lopez-Perez et al. utilize a distributed multi-robot model to increase robustness [21]. In addition, some works [22–24] improve the practicality of multi-robot exploration by considering inter-robot communication and cooperation.

2.2   DRL Methods for Environment Exploration

Deep reinforcement learning(DRL) methods can enable agents to learn complex exploration strategies through repeated interactions with the environment, thereby improving their decision-making abilities [9]. Many existing DRL approaches only focus on single UAV scenarios. Niroui et al. [10] proposed to combine deep reinforcement learning with frontier exploration. They use deep reinforcement learning to learn exploration strategies and then use traditional navigation methods to complete exploration tasks. Koutras et al. [11] provided a framework for learning exploration/coverage policies that possess strong generalization abilities due to the procedurally generated terrain diversity. However, in the above work, the autonomous exploration strategy is only suitable for single-agent scenarios, which severely limits the efficiency and robustness of the exploration system.

Using multiple agents has several advantages, such as reducing task completion time, improving the fault tolerance of the whole system, and so on. This motivates the need for further research on multi-agent collaborative exploration. In [13], a hierarchical control architecture for networked explorers is proposed. A Voronoi-based exploration algorithm and deep reinforcement learning-based collision avoidance approach are then provided to coordinate the robots efficiently while avoiding sudden obstacles. He et al. [14] proposed a distributed multi-robot exploration algorithm based on deep reinforcement learning (DME-DRL) for structured environments that enables robots to make decisions based on this high-level knowledge. DME-DRL is a distributed algorithm that uses deep neural networks to extract the structural pattern of the environment, and it can work in scenarios with or without communication. Geng et al. [15] presented the attention-based communication neural network (CommAttn) to "learn" the cooperation strategies automatically in the decentralized multi-robot exploration problem. The communication neural network enables the robots to learn cooperation strategies with explicit communication. Moreover, the attention mechanism can precisely calculate whether the communication is necessary for each pair of agents by considering the relevance of each received message, which enables the robots to communicate only with the necessary partners.

2.3 Summary of Limitations

In summary, classical methods utilize hand-crafted heuristics that require domain expert knowledge and extensive manual tuning of utility and cost parameters to achieve expected cooperative behavior [25]. But DRL methods no longer require hand-crafted features/functions. It can learn cooperative policies directly from agent experience. However, existing DRL methods do not take energy constraints into account.

As far as the author knows, the current exploration tasks are mainly used in scenarios such as reconnaissance [2] and rescue [26]. In these scenarios, disregarding the energy constraints is impossible for the UAV because the energy that the UAV can carry is limited. This requires the UAV to return and land before the energy is exhausted. To address these limitations, we introduce RTN-Explorer, the first multi-UAV DRL method that considers energy constraints and UAV return, which uniquely designs input processing, network structure, and energy-constrained rewards. And training in different environments ensures generalization.

3 Problem Formulation

We define the multi-UAV exploration problem as a team of UAVs $I = \{i_1, \ldots i_n\}$ cooperating to explore an unknown environment and generate a global map $\mathcal{G}$. To simplify the problem, we represent the environment as a grid graph $\mathcal{M}$ containing $M \times M$ cells of size c. The set $\mathcal{L}$ represents the start/landing positions, and $\mathcal{L}$ is given by Eq. (1). The lowercase letters l, b, g correspond to their respective environment representation $\mathcal{L}, \mathcal{B}, \mathcal{G}$.

$$\mathcal{L} = \left\{ \left[x_i^l, y_i^l \right]^{\mathrm{T}}, i = 1, \ldots, L, \quad : \left[x_i^l, y_i^l \right]^{\mathrm{T}} \in \mathcal{M} \right\} \tag{1}$$

And the set $\mathcal{B}$ of the positions of the obstacles that the UAVs cannot occupy is given by Eq. (2).

$$\mathcal{B} = \left\{ \left[x_i^b, y_i^b \right]^{\mathrm{T}}, i = 1, \ldots, B, \quad : \left[x_i^b, y_i^b \right]^{\mathrm{T}} \in \mathcal{M} \right\} \tag{2}$$

The global map $\mathcal{G}$ composed of the exploration area is given by Eq. (3).

$$\mathcal{G} = \left\{ \left[x_i^g, y_i^g \right]^{\mathrm{T}}, i = 1, \ldots, G, \quad : \left[x_i^g, y_i^g \right]^{\mathrm{T}} \in \mathcal{M} \right\} \tag{3}$$

3.1   UAV Model

For any UAV $i \in I$, the position of the i-th UAV at time t is defined as $\mathbf{p}_i(t) = [x_i(t), y_i(t), z_i(t)]^{\mathrm{T}} \in \mathbb{R}^3$ with $z_i(t) \in \{0, h\}$. It means that the UAV is either at ground level or in constant altitude h. In addition to the position of the UAV, the state of the i-th UAV includes operating status $\phi_i(t) \in \{0, 1\}$ and battery energy $b_i(t) \in \mathbb{N}$. The action space of each UAV can be defined as Eq. (4).

$$A = \{ \underbrace{\begin{bmatrix} 0 \\ 0 \\ 0 \end{bmatrix}}_{\text{hover}}, \underbrace{\begin{bmatrix} c \\ 0 \\ 0 \end{bmatrix}}_{\text{east}}, \underbrace{\begin{bmatrix} 0 \\ c \\ 0 \end{bmatrix}}_{\text{north}}, \underbrace{\begin{bmatrix} -c \\ 0 \\ 0 \end{bmatrix}}_{\text{west}}, \underbrace{\begin{bmatrix} 0 \\ -c \\ 0 \end{bmatrix}}_{\text{south}}, \underbrace{\begin{bmatrix} 0 \\ 0 \\ -h \end{bmatrix}}_{\text{land}} \} \tag{4}$$

The action of the i-th UAV at time t is $\mathbf{a}_i(t) \in \tilde{A}(\mathbf{p}_i(t))$. $\tilde{A}(\mathbf{p}_i(t))$ is defined by Eq. (5). The UAV can only perform the landing action in the landing zone, otherwise it can only perform the other five actions.

$$\tilde{A}(\mathbf{p}_i(t)) = \begin{cases} A, & \mathbf{p}_i(t) \in \mathcal{L} \\ A \backslash [0, 0, -h]^{\mathrm{T}}, & \text{otherwise} \end{cases} \tag{5}$$

Assume that the UAV can only move one unit distance c in each time slot δ_t. The speed of each UAV is $v_i(t) \in \{0, V\}$, which means that the UAV is either moving at speed $V = c/\delta_t$ or stationary. The position transformation method after the action is executed is shown in Eq. (6). The UAV's position can only be changed when its operating status is active ($\phi_i(t) = 1$).

$$\mathbf{p}_i(t+1) = \begin{cases} \mathbf{p}_i(t) + \mathbf{a}_i(t), & \phi_i(t) = 1 \\ \mathbf{p}_i(t), & \text{otherwise} \end{cases} \tag{6}$$

The transition function of the UAV's operational status is given by Eq. (7). If the UAV is inactive at time t or performs the landing action, it is inactive at time $t + 1$.

$$\phi_i(t+1) = \begin{cases} 0, & \mathbf{a}_i(t) = [0, 0, -h]^{\mathrm{T}} \vee \phi_i(t) = 0 \\ 1, & \text{otherwise} \end{cases} \tag{7}$$

The change of the UAV's remaining energy is represented by Eq. (8). If the state of the i-th UAV at time t is active, then the energy at time $t + 1$ is reduced by one. Otherwise, it remains unchanged.

$$b_i(t+1) = \begin{cases} b_i(t) - 1, & \phi_i(t) = 1 \\ b_i(t), & \text{otherwise} \end{cases} \tag{8}$$

The size of the combined area that all the UAVs can explore at time t is given by Eq. (9), where $D_i(t)$ represents the size of the i-th UAV's exploration area at time t.

$$G(t) = \sum_{i=1}^{I} D_i(t+1) - \sum_{i=1}^{I} D_i(t) \tag{9}$$

3.2 Optimization Problem

The objective of the above problem is to maximize the joint exploration area while satisfying the energy constraint. The maximization problem is given by Eq. (10) optimizing over joint actions $\times_i \mathbf{a}_i(t)$. At the same time, the following five constraints must be satisfied. The first constraint is that each active UAV cannot be in the same position as the other active UAVs to avoid collisions. The second constraint is that the UAV cannot collide with obstacles. The third constraint is that the UAV's residual energy is always greater than or equal to 0. The last two constraints ensure that the UAV is initially in the start/landing zone, active, and at height h.

$$
\begin{aligned}
\max_{\times_i \mathbf{a}_i(t)} & \sum_{t=0}^{T} G(t) \\
\text{s.t. } & \mathbf{p}_i(t) \neq \mathbf{p}_j(t) \vee \phi_j(t) = 0, \ \forall i, j \in I, i \neq j, \forall t \\
& \mathbf{p}_i(t) \notin \mathcal{B}, && \forall i \in \mathcal{I}, \forall t \\
& b_i(t) \geq 0, && \forall i \in \mathcal{I}, \forall t \\
& \mathbf{p}_i(0) \in \mathcal{L} \wedge z_i(0) = h, && \forall i \in \mathcal{I} \\
& \phi_i(0) = 1, && \forall i \in I
\end{aligned}
\tag{10}
$$

3.3 UAV System

Figure 1 is a system-level diagram depicting the sensors and software components of a UAV. The UAV is equipped with a localization module and a scanning camera for exploring the environment. The map processing module generates the current map and feeds it to the reinforcement learning agent. Each UAV is initialized with a fixed movement budget which is its initial energy. The safe controller is responsible for translating the RL agent's proposed action into a safe action, and we will introduce the conversion method in Sect. 4.

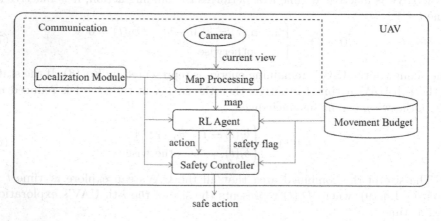

Fig. 1. System-level diagram depicting sensor and software components on the UAV during an multi-UAV exploration task.

4 Deep Reinforcement Learning Framework

In this section, we convert the multi-robot exploration problem under energy constraints into a decentralized partially observable Markov decision process (Dec-POMDP) [27]. The network architecture is shown in Fig. 2. We break down the observations into a map of the start/landing zone, a map of the exploration area, UAV's positions and battery information, and a map of obstacles in the current view. The decomposed views are then subjected to map processing, including map centering and global-local map processing. The global and local maps are fed through convolutional layers with ReLU activation and fully-connected networks to extract features. Then we calculate the next action and reward through the DDQN model trained in Sect. 4.3.

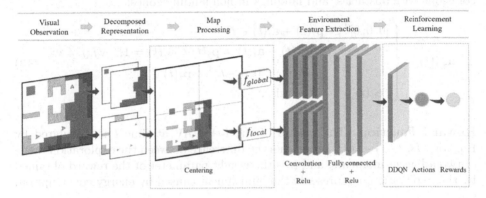

Fig. 2. The architecture of the RTN-Explorer. In decomposed representation, the information of obstacles and the explored area is incrementally increased during the unknown environment exploration.

4.1 Markov Decision Process

The Dec-POMDP is defined through the tuple $(\mathcal{S}, \mathcal{A}_\times, T, R, \Omega_\times, \mathcal{O}, \gamma)$. In the Dec-POMDP, $\mathcal{S}$ represents the state space, $\mathcal{A}_\times$ represents the joint action space and T is the transition probability function. $R : \mathcal{S} \times \mathcal{A} \times \mathcal{S} \mapsto \mathbb{R}$ represents the reward function that maps the current state, action and next state to a real number representing the reward. $\Omega_\times = \Omega^I$ is the joint observation space. $\mathcal{O} : \mathcal{S} \times \mathcal{I} \mapsto \Omega$ represents the observation function that map state and agents to one agent's individual observation. γ is a discount factor, which represents the trade-off between current and future returns.

State Space. The state space of the multi-UAV exploration problem under energy constraints is given by Eq. (11), where the state $s(t) \in \mathcal{S}$ at time t is given by Eq. (12). $\forall i \in \mathcal{I}$, $\mathbf{M} \in \mathbb{B}^{M \times M \times 3}$ is the tensor representation of the set of start/landing zones $\mathcal{L}$, explored area $\mathcal{G}$, and obstacles $\mathcal{B}$. The other elements of the tuple $\mathcal{S}$ represent positions, remaining flying times, and operational status of all agents.

$$S = \underbrace{\mathcal{L}}_{\substack{\text{Landing} \\ \text{Zones}}} \times \underbrace{\mathcal{G}}_{\substack{\text{Explored} \\ \text{Area}}} \times \underbrace{\mathcal{B}}_{\text{Obstacles}} \times \underbrace{\mathbb{R}^{I \times 3}}_{\substack{\text{UAV} \\ \text{Positions}}} \times \underbrace{\mathbb{N}^{I}}_{\substack{\text{Flying} \\ \text{Times}}} \times \underbrace{\mathbb{B}^{I}}_{\substack{\text{Operational} \\ \text{Status}}} \tag{11}$$

$$s(t) = (\mathbf{M}, \{\mathbf{p}_i(t)\}, \{b_i(t)\}, \{\phi_i(t)\}) \tag{12}$$

Safety Controller. Figure 1 shows the architecture of the UAV, which includes the safety controller. As shown in Eq. (13), the safety controller rejects an action with a safety threat and converts the action into a hover action while preserving the safe action. Safety-threatening maneuvers include collisions with other UAVs, collisions with obstacles, and landings in non-landing zones.

$$\mathbf{a}_{s,i}(t) = \begin{cases} [0,0,0]^{\mathrm{T}}, & \mathbf{p}_i(t) + \mathbf{a}_i(t) \in \mathcal{B} \\ & \vee\, \mathbf{p}_i(t) + \mathbf{a}_i(t) = \mathbf{p}_j(t) \wedge \phi_j(t) = 1, \quad \forall j, j \neq i \\ & \vee\, \mathbf{a}_i(t) = [0,0,-h]^{\mathrm{T}} \wedge \mathbf{p}_i(t) \notin \mathcal{L} \\ \mathbf{a}_i(t), & \text{otherwise.} \end{cases} \tag{13}$$

Reward Function. The reward of the i-th UAV at time t is calculated by Eq. (14). $D_i(t+1) - D_i(t)$ represents the difference between the exploration range of two adjacent moments, and α is the weight parameter of the reward obtained by the exploration. ϵ represents the punishment caused by energy consumption.

$$r_i(t) = \alpha \left(D_i(t+1) - D_i(t) \right) + \beta_i(t) + \gamma_i(t) + \epsilon \tag{14}$$

$\beta_i(t)$ is the penalty value when the RL agent's proposed action is rejected by the security controller. β is a hyperparameter.

$$\beta_i(t) = \begin{cases} \beta, & \mathbf{a}_i(t) \neq \mathbf{a}_{i,s}(t) \\ 0, & \text{otherwise} \end{cases} \tag{15}$$

$\gamma_i(t)$ is the penalty for the UAV not landing in the landing zone when the remaining energy is zero. Unlike the method calculated in [17], we do not use a constant as a penalty here but a value proportional to the minimum distance between the UAV and the landing zone. In Eq. (16), $\mathbf{s}$ represents the position vector of the center of the landing zone and λ is a multiplier times the minimum distance. Relative to the constant value penalty, using $\gamma_i(t)$ as the penalty can impose different penalties for landing in a non-landing zone depending on the distance so that the UAV gets less penalty when it is closer to the landing zone.

$$\gamma_i(t) = \begin{cases} \lambda \times dis(\mathbf{p}_i(t), \mathbf{s}), & b_i(t+1) = 0 \wedge \mathbf{p}_i(t+1) = [\cdot, \cdot h]^{\mathrm{T}} \\ 0, & \text{otherwise.} \end{cases} \tag{16}$$

4.2 Map Processing

The map processing methods we introduced include map centering and global-local map processing. Map centering is the transformation of the input map of each UAV into an expanded map with the UAV as the center. It can make the network pay more attention to the information closely related to the current UAV and avoid the influence of invalid details. Localized processing is to crop the centered map and retain the middle part. The localization makes the network pay more attention to the information near the UAV to assist the action decision. Globalized processing is to compress the centered map and extract its features.

Map Centering. For input map $\mathbf{A} \in \mathbb{R}^{M \times M \times n}$, we utilize Eq. (17) for centering to get $\mathbf{B} \in \mathbb{R}^{M_c \times M_c \times n}$, where $M_c = 2M - 1$. $\tilde{\mathbf{p}}$ is the position vector of the current UAV and $\mathbf{x}_{\text{pad}}$ is the fill value of the augmented map.

$$\mathbf{B} = f_{\text{center}} \left(\mathbf{A}, \tilde{\mathbf{p}}, \mathbf{x}_{\text{pad}} \right) \tag{17}$$

The function f_{center} is given by Eq. (18).

$$f_{\text{center}} : \mathbb{R}^{M \times M \times n} \times \mathbb{N}^2 \times \mathbb{R}^n \mapsto \mathbb{R}^{M_c \times M_c \times n} \tag{18}$$

The calculation formula for each element in $\mathbf{B}$ is shown in Eq. (19). It effectively pads map $\mathbf{A}$ with the padding value $\mathbf{x}_{\text{pad}}$.

$$\mathbf{b}_{i,j} = \begin{cases} \mathbf{a}_{i+\tilde{p}_0-M+1,j+\tilde{p}_1-M+1}, & M \leq i + \tilde{p}_0 + 1 < 2M \\ & \wedge M \leq j + \tilde{p}_1 + 1 < 2M \\ \mathbf{x}_{\text{pad}} , & \text{otherwise} \end{cases} \tag{19}$$

Localized Processing. Localized processing transforms $\mathbf{B} \in \mathbb{R}^{M_c \times M_c \times n}$ into $\mathbf{X}$ according to the parameter l.

$$\mathbf{X} = f_{\text{local}} \left(\mathbf{B}, l \right) \tag{20}$$

The function f_{local} is given by Eq. (21).

$$f_{\text{local}} : \mathbb{R}^{M_c \times M_c \times n} \times \mathbb{N} \mapsto \mathbb{R}^{l \times l \times n} \tag{21}$$

Each element in $\mathbf{X}$ is calculated as shown in Eq. (22). $\mathbf{X}$ is obtained by intercepting the middle $l \times l$ part on $\mathbf{B}$.

$$\mathbf{x}_{i,j} = \mathbf{b}_{i+M-\lceil \frac{l}{2} \rceil, j+M-\lceil \frac{l}{2} \rceil} \tag{22}$$

Globalized Processing. Globalized processing transforms $\mathbf{B} \in \mathbb{R}^{M_c \times M_c \times n}$ into $\mathbf{Y}$ according to the parameter g.

$$\mathbf{Y} = f_{\text{global}} \left(\mathbf{B}, g \right) \tag{23}$$

The function f_{glocal} is given by Eq. (24).

$$f_{\text{global}} : \mathbb{R}^{M_c \times M_c \times n} \times \mathbb{N} \mapsto \mathbb{R}^{\left\lfloor \frac{M_C}{g} \right\rfloor \times \left\lfloor \frac{M_C}{g} \right\rfloor \times n} \tag{24}$$

The elements in $\mathbf{Y}$ are defined by Eq. (25). This operation equals an average pooling operation with pooling cell size g.

$$\mathbf{y}_{i,j} = \frac{1}{g^2} \sum_{u=0}^{g-1} \sum_{v=0}^{g-1} \mathbf{b}_{gi+u, gj+v} \tag{25}$$

4.3 Multi-agent Reinforcement Learning

Deep Q-network (DQN) is a Q-learning algorithm based on deep learning, which mainly combines value function approximation and neural network [28]. It adopts the method of target network and experience replay to train the network. Experience replay builds a replay buffer $\mathcal{D}$. New experiences of the agent, represented by quadruples of (s, a, r, s'), are stored in the replay buffer. r represents the reward obtained by performing action a after state s and s' represents the next state. DQN uses a separate target network to estimate the next largest Q value. In order to solve the problem of DQN overestimating the Q value, DDQN improves the target value as:

$$Y^{\text{DDQN}}(s, a, s') = r(s, a) + \gamma Q_{\bar{\theta}} \left(s', \operatorname*{argmax}_{a'} Q_{\theta}(s', a') \right) \tag{26}$$

And its loss function is given by:

$$L^{\text{DDQN}}(\theta) = \mathbb{E}_{s,a,s' \sim \mathcal{D}} \left[\left(Q_{\theta}(s, a) - Y^{\text{DDQN}}(s, a, s') \right)^2 \right] \tag{27}$$

During training, the sampled soft-max policy for exploration of the state and action space is given by Eq. (28). The hyperparameter β is used to balance exploration and exploitation.

$$\pi(a_i \mid s) = \frac{e^{Q_{\theta}(s, a_i)/\beta}}{\sum_{\forall a_j \in \mathcal{A}} e^{Q_{\theta}(s, a_j)/\beta}} \tag{28}$$

The DDQN training process is described in Algorithm 1. Following the initialization of the replay buffer and network parameters, new training begins to reset the state, select a random UAV starting position, and a random mobile budget $b_0 \in \mathcal{B}$ for each UAV. As long as the exploration task is not completed, the event will continue. For each activate UAV i, a new action $a \in \mathcal{A}$ is chosen according to Eq. (28) and the subsequent experience stored in the replay memory buffer $\mathcal{D}$. The main network parameter θ is updated by utilizing the ADAM optimizer to execute gradient steps on data with a small batch of m samples in the replay buffer. Subsequently, updating target network parameter $\bar{\theta}$ and reducing the mobile budget. The exploration task ends when all the UAVs have successfully landed or are at zero power. Then, a new episode begins, unless the maximum number of episodes is N_{max}.

Algorithm 1. DDQN training for exploreation under energy constraints

---

input: maximum training steps N_{max}, initial movement budget range $\mathcal{B}$
output: network parameter θ

1: Initialize D, initialize θ randomly, $\bar{\theta} \leftarrow \theta$
2: **for** $t = 0$ to N_{max} **do**
3:     $\forall i \in \mathcal{I}$, initialize the UAV's state s_i with random starting position and sample initial movement budget b_i uniformly from $\mathcal{B}$
4:     **while** the task is not completed **do**
5:         **for** each UAV $i \in \mathcal{I}$ **do**
6:             **if** the i-th UAV is inactivate **then** continue
7:             Sample a_i according to Eq. (28)
8:             Observe r_i, s_i'
9:             Store (s_i, a_i, r_i, s_i') in $\mathcal{D}$
10:            **for** $j = 1$ to m **do**
11:                Sample (s_j, a_j, r_j, s_j') uniformly from $\mathcal{D}$
12:                $Y_j = \begin{cases} r_j, & \text{if } s_j' \text{ terminal} \\ \text{according to } Eq. (27), & \text{otherwise} \end{cases}$
13:                Compute loss $L_j(\theta)$ according to Eq. (26)
14:            Update θ with gradient loss $\frac{1}{m} \sum_{j=1}^{m} L_j(\theta)$
15:            $\bar{\theta} \leftarrow (1 - \tau)\bar{\theta} + \tau\theta$
16:            $b_i = b_i - 1$

---

5   Experiments

In this section, we evaluate different exploration strategies under different conditions. We conduct simulation experiments on a variety of maps generated by the map generator. The exploration rate and the return rate are the metrics we use to evaluate the agents' performance on different maps and under different scenario instances. We define the exploration rate as the ratio between the amount of explored area and the total area of the ground truth map. The return rate equals the number of UAV successful returns divided by the total number of trials.

5.1   Experiment Setup

The algorithm of DDQN is implemented with TensorFlow [29] and the group of UAVs with a scanning camera. We train the multi-UAV coordinated exploration on a computer with an Intel Xeon W-2235 CPU and an NVIDIA GeForce RTX 3090 GPU. The environment is presented as 32×32 cells space. As shown in Fig. 2, each unit in the environment is assigned to one object: obstacle (grey), the unexplored region (dark grey), the start/landing zone (purple), and UAV (blue). In the training experiment, we assume each UAV can only move one cell within one cell scanning range at a time in the environment. We reinitialize the exploration scene when the UAVs are reaching the maximal steps or completing all the tasks. To demonstrate the robustness of our model, we randomly place the

UAVs in the start/landing zones, generating random environments for the UAVs at each re-initialization. We set the number of UAVs to be a random number in the range of $[2, 6]$, and the energy of the UAVs to be a random number in the range of $[400, 450]$. The key hyperparameters during the training process are listed in Table 1.

Table 1. DDQN hyperparameters

Parameter	Value	Description
$|\theta|$	1,175,302	trainable parameters
$N_{\max}$	3,000,000	maximum training steps
l	17	local map scaling
g	3	global map scaling
$|\mathcal{D}|$	50,000	replay buffer size
m	128	minibatch size
τ	0.005	soft update factor
γ	0.95	discount factor in Eq. (26)
β	0.1	temperature parameter in Eq. (28)
λ	0.2	the minimum distance multiplier in Eq. (16)

5.2   Experiment Results

Comparison of Different Map Processing Methods. To prove the validity of our proposed map processing method, we compared four different map processing methods. Table 2 shows the performances of the exploration systems using four different map processing methods when the number of UAVs ranges from $[2, 6]$. As for the evaluation, Table 2 shows the results from the experiments as averaged over 5000 runs for each different method. We also use different maps generated by the map generator during the test to ensure the reliability of the results.

Increasing the exploration rate and increasing the return rate are conflicting goals. In our experiment, the weight of the exploration reward is greater than the weight of the return failing penalty, so the UAVs will tend to explore the unknown area. This is why no processing method makes the exploration system obtain more than 86% exploration rate and less than 1% return rate. Only using global-local map processing can improve the return rate to a certain extent but reduce a certain exploration rate. Only using map centering can significantly improve the return rate. Combining map centering and global-local map processing, we can get the highest return rate and exploration rate. This is because the local map processing intercepts the central part of the UAV view, strengthens the information around the UAV, and globalizes the centralized view to extract the global features. As the number of UAVs increases, so does the scale of the problem, which leads to a certain reduction in the return rate of UAVs.

Table 2. Performance comparison of different map processing methods.

Map Processing\UAVs		2	3	4	5	6
No processing	Exploration rate	86.25%	90.91%	94.77%	95.18%	96.54%
	Return Rate	0.00%	0.10%	0.22%	0.72%	0.47%
Global-Local	Exploration Rate	83.59%	90.68%	94.22%	95.53%	96.17%
	Return Rate	2.28%	3.66%	3.77%	3.39%	2.75%
Centering	Exploration Rate	87.82%	93.25%	93.68%	93.23%	92.44%
	Return Rate	13.52%	33.55%	64.10%	72.84%	73.87%
Global-Local +Centering	Exploration Rate	**92.85%**	**96.00%**	**97.67%**	**98.40%**	**98.84%**
	Return Rate	**93.10%**	**98.23%**	**97.30%**	**94.16%**	**93.01%**

Comparison of Different Return Strategies. To verify that our return strategy can explore new areas while returning, we compare the exploration rate with the return strategy based on the original path. The strategy of return based on the original path is that when the energy consumption of the UAV reaches half of the initial energy, the UAV returns to the landing zone.

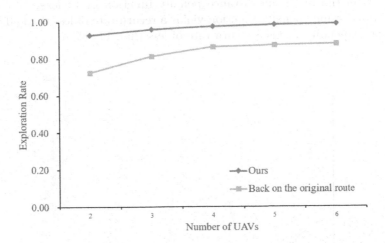

Fig. 3. Comparison of exploration efficiency between RTN-Explorer and the return strategy based on the original path.

As shown in Fig. 3, the abscissa represents the number of robots. We compared the exploration rates of two return strategies with the number of UAVs in [2,6]. It can be seen from Table 1 that our exploration strategy can ensure a high return rate of more than 93%. In terms of exploration rate, our strategy is at least 10.88% higher than the return strategy based on the original route. RTN-Explorer can explore new areas while returning, but the return strategy based on the original path can not explore new areas when returning. So the exploration efficiency of RTN-Explorer is significantly higher than that of returning based on the original path.

Comparison of Different Penalty Functions. As described in Sect. 4, We impose the minimum distance penalty proportional to the shortest distance from the UAV to the landing zone for UAV forced landing in the non-landing zone. Compared with the constant value penalty set in [17], our minimum distance penalty can significantly improve the return rate. Common distances also include European distance and Manhattan distance, which are relatively inexpensive to calculate. So in addition to the constant value penalty, we also compared the performance of the Euclidean distance penalty and the Manhattan distance penalty on the return rate (Fig. 4).

Since there is no correlation between the penalty function of landing in the non-landing area and the exploration rate, we only need to compare the return rate of these four penalty functions in different UAV numbers.

After a lot of experiments, we can get the following conclusion: the minimum distance penalty function we use can effectively improve the return rate. Using the Euclidean distance to the landing zone as the penalty can also obtain a high return rate. But the return rate of the Euclidean distance penalty function is lower than the minimum distance penalty function by at least 7.67%. The Manhattan distance penalty function yields a return rate of less than 60%. And the constant penalty yields a return rate of less than 11.88%.

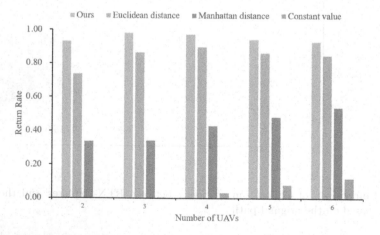

Fig. 4. Comparison of return rate under different penalty functions. The return rate of the method based on the constant value penalty function is 0.00% for two UAVs and 0.41% for three UAVs.

Comparison of Environments with Different Difficulties. At the beginning of each episode, we reinitialize the environment map. We allow the map generator to generate initial environment maps with different complexity according to the difficulty vector. Specifically, the difficulty vector consists of two elements $[d_m, d_t]$.

d_m represents morphological randomness, which can define the shape of obstacles in the environment. d_m controls the area each obstacle may occupy. The bigger the value of d_m, the larger the possible obstacle composite area in the training environment. d_m gets values from $\{1, 2\}$ discrete set.

d_t represents topological randomness, which defines the positions of obstacles on the map. The fundamental positions of the obstacles are equally arranged in a 3 columns - 3 rows format. d_t controls the deviation radius around these base positions. As the value of d_t increases, the topology of obstacles has more unstructured forms. d_t gets values from the $\{1, 2\}$ discrete set.

Higher values in the elements of the difficulty vector correspond to less structured behavior in the obstacles formation. As a result, a trained agent that has been successful in higher-difficulty training setups may have better generalization abilities. It can be seen from Fig. 5 that the environment of different difficulty levels has less impact on exploration rates. In contrast, the return rate is more sensitive to the difficulty of the environment. Nevertheless, when the difficulty vector $lvl = [2, 2]$, the exploration rate can still be maintained at more than 85%, and the return rate can be maintained at more than 70%.

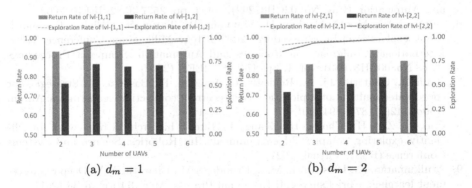

Fig. 5. The sensitivity of the exploration rate and the return rate with respect to the different levels of the difficulty vector.

6 Conclusion

We propose an environment exploration strategy (RTN-Explorer) that satisfies the energy constraints. RTN-Explorer makes the UAV return to the landing zone before the energy is exhausted while ensuring exploration efficiency. Before training, we centralize, globalize, and localize environment map representations to improve performance. To satisfy the energy constraint, we design a penalty function based on the shortest path distance to the landing zone and use the map generator to generate the environment map for training. A large number of simulation experiments show that RTN-Explorer is effective and robust. In order to further improve the stability of the system, we can increase the difficulty dimension in the map generator to increase the randomness of the environment. In future work, we'll expand the UAVs' action space to include altitude and continuous control, which will necessitate a different RL method than Q-learning, as well as adding height information to the agents' observations space.

References

1. Schuster, M.J., et al.: Towards autonomous planetary exploration. J. Intell. Robot. Syst. **93**(3), 461–494 (2019)
2. Hougen, D.F., et al.: A miniature robotic system for reconnaissance and surveillance. In: Proceedings 2000 ICRA. Millennium Conference. IEEE International Conference on Robotics and Automation. Symposia Proceedings (Cat. No. 00CH37065), vol. 1, pp. 501–507. IEEE (2000)
3. Queralta, J.P., et al.: Collaborative multi-robot search and rescue: planning, coordination, perception, and active vision. IEEE Access **8**, 191617–191643 (2020)
4. Huang, Y., Cao, Z., Oh, S., Kattan, E., Hall, E.: Automatic operation for a robot lawn mower. In: Mobile Robots I, vol. 727, pp. 344–354. International Society for Optics and Photonics (1987)
5. Jager, M., Nebel, B.: Dynamic decentralized area partitioning for cooperating cleaning robots. In: Proceedings 2002 IEEE International Conference on Robotics and Automation (Cat. No. 02CH37292), vol. 4, pp. 3577–3582. IEEE (2002)
6. Burgard, W., Moors, M., Fox, D., Simmons, R., Thrun, S.: Collaborative multi-robot exploration. In: Proceedings 2000 ICRA. Millennium Conference. IEEE International Conference on Robotics and Automation. Symposia Proceedings (Cat. No. 00CH37065), vol. 1, pp. 476–481. IEEE (2000)
7. Banfi, J., Quattrini Li, A., Rekleitis, I., Amigoni, F., Basilico, N.: Strategies for coordinated multirobot exploration with recurrent connectivity constraints. Auton. Robot. **42**(4), 875–894 (2018)
8. Cao, C., Zhu, H., Choset, H., Zhang, J.: Tare: a hierarchical framework for efficiently exploring complex 3d environments. In: Robotics: Science and Systems Conference (RSS), Virtual (2021)
9. Arulkumaran, K., Deisenroth, M.P., Brundage, M., Bharath, A.A.: Deep reinforcement learning: a brief survey. IEEE Signal Process. Mag. **34**(6), 26–38 (2017)
10. Niroui, F., Zhang, K., Kashino, Z., Nejat, G.: Deep reinforcement learning robot for search and rescue applications: exploration in unknown cluttered environments. IEEE Robot. Autom. Lett. **4**(2), 610–617 (2019)
11. Koutras, D.I., Kapoutsis, A.C., Amanatiadis, A.A., Kosmatopoulos, E.B.: Marsexplorer: exploration of unknown terrains via deep reinforcement learning and procedurally generated environments. Electronics **10**(22), 2751 (2021)
12. Lee, W.C., Lim, M.C., Choi, H.L.: Extendable navigation network based reinforcement learning for indoor robot exploration. In: 2021 IEEE International Conference on Robotics and Automation (ICRA), pp. 11508–11514. IEEE (2021)
13. Hu, J., Niu, H., Carrasco, J., Lennox, B., Arvin, F.: Voronoi-based multi-robot autonomous exploration in unknown environments via deep reinforcement learning. IEEE Trans. Veh. Technol. **69**(12), 14413–14423 (2020)

14. He, D., Feng, D., Jia, H., Liu, H.: Decentralized exploration of a structured environment based on multi-agent deep reinforcement learning. In: 2020 IEEE 26th International Conference on Parallel and Distributed Systems (ICPADS), pp. 172–179. IEEE (2020)

15. Geng, M., Xu, K., Zhou, X., Ding, B., Wang, H., Zhang, L.: Learning to cooperate via an attention-based communication neural network in decentralized multi-robot exploration. Entropy **21**(3), 294 (2019)

16. Geng, M., Zhou, X., Ding, B., Wang, H., Zhang, L.: Learning to cooperate in decentralized multi-robot exploration of dynamic environments. In: Cheng, L., Leung, A.C.S., Ozawa, S. (eds.) ICONIP 2018. LNCS, vol. 11307, pp. 40–51. Springer, Cham (2018). https://doi.org/10.1007/978-3-030-04239-4_4

17. Theile, M., Bayerlein, H., Nai, R., Gesbert, D., Caccamo, M.: Uav coverage path planning under varying power constraints using deep reinforcement learning. In: 2020 IEEE/RSJ International Conference on Intelligent Robots and Systems (IROS), pp. 1444–1449. IEEE (2020)

18. Zhou, B., Zhang, Y., Chen, X., Shen, S.: Fuel: Fast uav exploration using incremental frontier structure and hierarchical planning. IEEE Robot. Autom. Lett. **6**(2), 779–786 (2021)

19. Yamauchi, B.: Frontier-based exploration using multiple robots. In: Proceedings of the Second International Conference on Autonomous Agents, pp. 47–53 (1998)

20. Bautin, A., Simonin, O., Charpillet, F.: *MinPos*: a novel frontier allocation algorithm for multi-robot exploration. In: Su, C.-Y., Rakheja, S., Liu, H. (eds.) ICIRA 2012. LNCS (LNAI), vol. 7507, pp. 496–508. Springer, Heidelberg (2012). https://doi.org/10.1007/978-3-642-33515-0_49

21. Lopez-Perez, J.J., Hernandez-Belmonte, U.H., Ramirez-Paredes, J.P., Contreras-Cruz, M.A., Ayala-Ramirez, V.: Distributed multirobot exploration based on scene partitioning and frontier selection. Mathematical Problems in Engineering 2018 (2018)

22. Amigoni, F., Banfi, J., Basilico, N.: Multirobot exploration of communication-restricted environments: a survey. IEEE Intell. Syst. **32**(6), 48–57 (2017)

23. Andre, T., Bettstetter, C.: Collaboration in multi-robot exploration: to meet or not to meet? J. Intell. Robot. Syst. **82**(2), 325–337 (2016)

24. Colares, R.G., Chaimowicz, L.: The next frontier: combining information gain and distance cost for decentralized multi-robot exploration. In: Proceedings of the 31st Annual ACM Symposium on Applied Computing, pp. 268–274 (2016)

25. Amato, C., Konidaris, G., Cruz, G., Maynor, C.A., How, J.P., Kaelbling, L.P.: Planning for decentralized control of multiple robots under uncertainty. In: 2015 IEEE International Conference on Robotics and Automation (ICRA), pp. 1241–1248. IEEE (2015)

26. Murphy, R.R.: Human-robot interaction in rescue robotics. IEEE Trans. Syst. Man Cybern. Part C (Applications and Reviews) **34**(2), 138–153 (2004)

27. Oliehoek, F.A., Amato, C.: A concise introduction to decentralized POMDPs. Springer (2016)

28. Mnih, V., et al.: Human-level control through deep reinforcement learning. Nature **518**(7540), 529–533 (2015)

29. Abadi, M., et al.: {TensorFlow}: a system for {Large-Scale} machine learning. In: 12th USENIX Symposium on Operating Systems Design and Implementation (OSDI 16), pp. 265–283 (2016)

Optimization of Large-Scale Knowledge Forward Reasoning Based on OWL 2 DL Ontology

Lingyun Cui[1], Tenglong Ren[1], Xiaowang Zhang[1,2]([✉]), and Zhiyong Feng[1,2]

[1] College of Intelligence and Computing, Tianjin University, Tianjin 300350, China
{cly1213,tenglongren,xiaowangzhang,zyfeng}@tju.edu.cn
[2] Tianjin Key Laboratory of Cognitive Computing and Application, Tianjin, China

Abstract. This paper focuses on the performance of optimized forward reason systems. The main characteristics of forward reasoning are that it is sensitive to the update of data, has a high cost of precomputation closure, and can not be closely related to the characteristics of the specific query. Therefore, it usually makes reason on irrelevant data. Processing this data reduces the performance of the reason system and consumes a lot of memory resources. Backward reasoning can make up for this defect to a certain extent, but its' inherent defect of the high cost of online query rewriting cannot make it efficient in reasoning tasks. We design an efficient reason method, which can effectively combine the advantages of forward reason and backward reason to ensure the completeness of reason as much as possible. It can not only reduce the processing cost caused by data updates and desensitize semantic data to a certain extent but also avoid the high cost caused by query rewriting and greatly reduce the cost of precomputation closure. Finally, we implement the proposed method on a prototype of a forward reason system named SUMA-F and compare it with the current forward reason systems with better performance on various datasets of different sizes. Experiments show that the SUMA-F has high reasoning efficiency, is better than other systems, and has high scalability on large-scale datasets.

Keywords: Forward reasoning · Ontology · RDF data

1 Introduction

The World Wide Web produces a vast amount of data that humans cannot process efficiently and computers cannot understand well. Tim Berners-Lee et al. [1] propose the concept of the Semantic Web, and the development of the Semantic Web makes knowledge expression modes such as knowledge graph and ontology widely used in the research field of query answering. The most critical feature in semantics is the relationship between concept attributes and concepts. Ontology takes the concept of interconnection through attributes as its core and provides a semantic framework for language understanding and generation.

© ICST Institute for Computer Sciences, Social Informatics and Telecommunications Engineering 2022
Published by Springer Nature Switzerland AG 2022. All Rights Reserved
H. Gao et al. (Eds.): CollaborateCom 2022, LNICST 461, pp. 380–399, 2022.
https://doi.org/10.1007/978-3-031-24386-8_21

This plays an important role in the semantic ontology system, which can represent events and objects through various complex semantic combinations, and its grammar is specially designed to express complex lexical meanings so that the ontology can use as few basic concepts as possible to construct descriptions of complex objects and procedures in a composite manner. Chen et al. [7] propose an unsupervised attribute network embedding framework to solve basic and compound relations in attribute networks. It considers the relationship between users and attributes, analyzes all first-order combinations to obtain composite relationships, and outperforms the current state-of-the-art baseline methods. RDFS was proposed because knowledge graphs cannot describe knowledge at the architectural level. RDFS defines inclusion relationships between concepts or roles, domain and value constraints for roles, and implements the classification of individuals. OWL with stronger expressive ability adds cardinality restriction, equivalent individuals, and other knowledge descriptions based on RDFS. In the query answering system, the implicit knowledge contained in the explicit knowledge can be obtained by ontology reasoning, which enriches the original data and returns more abundant results in the query.

There is a lot of research in the field of ontological reasoning, such as [3, 6, 8, 18, 20, 24], which are based on forward materialization. In the process of forward reasoning, the facts in the knowledge base are expanded according to the reason rules to obtain implicit knowledge. The original and newly reasoned data are used as the target data to repeat this reason process continuously. When no new data is generated, the reasoning process end. This whole process is called computing a forward closure. It is worth noting that the process of forward materialization does not change because of the query, and the query operation is simple and efficient. The disadvantage of forward reasoning is also obvious. The data heavily influence it, and it repeats the operation when the data is updated. The forward reason system is inefficient for frequent database updates.

Unlike forward reasoning, backward reasoning is query-driven and matches rules backwards. Backward reasoning is not sensitive to the update of data. It is calculated for specific queries and extends queries according to rules. Backward reasoning is less about data processing and more about searching rules and expanding queries. Ontop [5] is a pure backward reason system based on query rewriting. Although backward reasoning can be well applied in the context of frequent database updates, its operation is relatively complex, and the cost of calculating queries is high. In [19, 22] for backward reasoning, advanced pruning optimization algorithm and dynamic optimization algorithm are proposed to reduce the cost of query computation in backward reasoning.

Because of the inherent defects of forward and backward reasoning, it becomes a challenge to design a method that strikes a balance between forward and backward reasoning, that is, between the high cost of computing a complete closure for all data and the huge cost of complex computations for each query. We propose an efficient forward materialization algorithm, which combines backward reasoning to optimize forward reasoning, reducing the knowledge of precomputation closure and the size of forward matching rules. We propose an efficient query parsing algorithm that maintains a key resource pool (KR-POOL) to hold all the resource entities related to the corresponding query. It can not only do personalized reasoning according to a specific query but also break all the possible knowledge involved in a specific query into the form of one element into the KR-POOL. Compared with the traditional backward chaining algorithm, the algorithm reduces the time complexity of the query rewriting process by simplifying the operation of query processing. We implement all algorithms in the forward reasoning system and ensure completeness of reasoning.

Next, we introduce the three works we have made in this paper and introduce the specific implementation details of these three contributions in later chapters.

- We propose an efficient query parsing algorithm to maintain a key resource pool named KR-POOL, simplifying the complexity of query expansion and other specific query computation.
- We propose a forward reasoning algorithm to reduce the computational closure scale of forward materialization, which can materialize all the data related to the query and dynamically screen the rules to reduce the search scale of rules during reasoning. Optimizing the data and rules effectively reduces the reasoning time, and completeness is guaranteed.
- We implement our method in a forward reason system named SUMA-F and test the effectiveness and scalability of the system on the UOBM [13] dataset with the standard query of the UOBM dataset and achieved good results.

This paper reviews related work in Sect. 2. In Sect. 3, we present a preliminary definition of some of the basics involved in reasoning. We describe the algorithm principle in detail in Sect. 4. In Sect. 5, the architecture diagram of the forward reasoning system SUMA-F is presented. Experimental results are presented in Sect. 6, and conclusions are drawn in Sect. 7.

2   Related Work

With the development of the Semantic Web, related works in ontology reasoning can be divided into forward reasoning, backward reasoning, and hybrid methods based on forward materialization and query rewriting.

Jena [6] and Sesame [3] are relatively early systems that support RDF (Resource Description Framework) data reason, and the reasoning module is only a part of them. They are mainly used for small-scale data reasons on a single machine. Due to the design principle and hardware limitations, their scalability and computational power are poor, and they cannot process large-scale RDF data. Based on forward reason, Pellet's reasoning algorithm, adopted by Pellet [20] performs deductive reasoning on the original dataset offline according to the ontology, expresses the implicit ontology information as new knowledge obtained by explicit reasoning, and expands the original input dataset. In the online stage, query the expanded data set directly. However, the Tableau algorithm adopted by Pellet has high time and space complexity. Pellet is only suitable for processing small and medium-sized data. The main working principle of PAGOdA is to delegate the heavy computational load to the datalog reasoner [14, 16] and only use the hyper-table algorithm [15] when necessary. Sequoia [8] is a consequence-based forward reasoning engine with support for nominals, implementing the calculus of logical $\mathcal{ALCHOIQ}^+$. Ontologies are classified by ontology preprocessing methods. SUMA [17, 18] improves the n-step materialization model, restricts the reasoning to a finite number of steps, and proposes a partial materialization algorithm that can reliably and completely support root conjunctive queries as well as boolean queries with cyclic and fork-shaped structures.

Query rewriting techniques are also used in reason systems such as [5, 9]. Instead of explicitly calculating all the implicit information according to the ontology, Ontop [5] rewrites the query according to the ontology and mapping, and the rewritten query explicitly contains the implicit information in the ontology. Since this query rewriting algorithm is performed online, it has a high time cost. Meanwhile, the mapping used in query rewriting requires human intervention input. In [4], the RDFS entailment rule set is divided into two subsets, and a query rewriting algorithm is proposed for query answering on knowledge graphs without reasoning. The method proposed in [10] can clearly describe the mapping relationship so that the database data can be better interpreted as ontology data.

There are also hybrid methods that combine the forward reason mechanism with the backward reason mechanism. [11] can rewrite the query while still computing the canonical model. [12] mainly filters out false answers using a filtering mechanism. The above approaches all have the disadvantage of being limited to lightweight ontology languages. QueryPie [22] implements a backward reasoning system through the proposed hybrid reasoning approach. The reasoning method computes a part of the forward closure, and the rest of the reasoning part is processed dynamically during the query parsing process. Shi Hui et al. [19] propose a scalable backward chaining-based reasoner, in which the optimization algorithm mentioned in query expansion sorts according to the number of variables contained in the query body clause and then reduces the reason time.

The above are some contributions to the field of ontology reasoning. Some are based on forward reasoning to compute the closure of database data uniformly, and the input query is pattern matched on the data after forward materialization to get the result. Others take the query as the target, extending and rewriting the query in reverse, reasoning about the data in a process contrary to the forward materialization.

Inspired by previous research, our method combines the backward reasoning method to design a forward materialization algorithm so that the forward reasoning system can no longer calculate too many redundant results and reduce redundant computational operations. Perform reverse parsing of the query to parse out the key information in the query, match the rules in the process, and calculate the semantic data containing the necessary explicit information and the semantic data that may reason useful implicit information. The query parsing algorithm for reverse parsing query is designed, and a KR-POOL and reason rule set that are constantly updated with the parsing process is maintained. A rule filtering algorithm is designed, which expands backward according to the query pattern, searches the effective rules recursively, and screens the key rules for the query from a large number of rules in the rule base. Finally, the redundancy of large-scale semantic data is removed to optimize the data scale while ensuring completeness.

3   Preliminaries

We describe some necessary background knowledge in this section, such as RDF graphs, SPARQL queries, Description Logic (DL), and OWL Horst rules.

Definition 1 (RDF Graph). *U, B, and L exist, which are three disjoint infinite sets. U is a Uniform Resource Identifier (URI), B represents a blank node, and L is literals. A finite set of RDF triples (s, p, o) ∈ (U∪B)×U×(U∪B∪L) constitute an RDF graph, where s represents the subject, p represents the predicate, and o represents the object. A triple (s, p, o) is a statement of fact that s and o satisfy relation p or that the corresponding value of s with respect to property p is o.*

Figure 1 shows an RDF statement indicating that Joe knows Jane and an RDF graph consisting of multiple RDF statements.

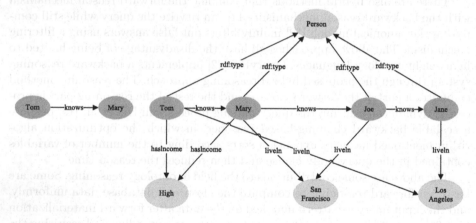

Fig. 1. Figure on the left side of an RDF statement, by multiple RDF statements consisting of RDF Graph on the right.

SPARQL Query. Q is a quadruple of the form (*q-type, m-dataset, pattern, sort-map*). *q-type* represents four query types: SELECT, ASK, CONSTRUCT, DESCRIBE. *m-dataset* specifies the target dataset for pattern matching. *pattern* P searches the input dataset for a specific subgraph and returns the result set of the map. *sort-map* is used to sort the set of mappings produced by pattern matching while returning a specified mapping window.

Description Logic can also be called concept representation language and term logic, which gives formal logic-based semantics. DL consists of concepts, relations, and individuals. Concepts describe the common properties of a set of individuals, interpret concepts as unary predicates of sets of objects, and interpret relations as binary relations between objects. It is characterized by applying a large number of constructors to simple concepts, eventually creating more complex concepts. At the core of description logic is reasoning, that is, the knowledge that is implicitly represented from knowledge explicitly contained in a knowledge base.

The DL knowledge base $\mathcal{K}$ is usually composed of two parts: Tbox ($\mathcal{T}$) and Abox ($\mathcal{A}$). Among them, $\mathcal{T}$ is a set of assertions related to concepts and relations, describing the properties of concepts and relations. $\mathcal{A}$ is a collection of instance assertions that specify attributes of individuals or relationships between individuals. It consists of concept assertion and relation assertion. The most basic description language in DLs is ALC, and other description languages extend based on ALC. The symbols involved and their description are shown in Table 1, and the syntax and semantics of ALC are shown in Table 2 and Table 3.

Table 1. List of notations

Notation	Description
a,b,c,d,e	Individual names
a,b,z	Concept names
C	Concepts
p,s	Role names
r	Roles

DL are the basis for the standard Web ontology languages OWL and OWL 2. OWL provides powerful expressive capabilities, including OWL Lite, OWL DL, and OWL Full, which increase expressive capabilities and computational complexity in turn. The latest version of OWL, OWL 2, is also divided into OWL 2 DL and OWL 2 Full. OWL 2 Full has the strongest expressive power, but it is undecidable. OWL 2 DL adds a few restrictions to the combination of OWL 2 Full and RDFS, preserving decidability. $\mathcal{SROIQ}$ is the underlying

Table 2. Syntax of ALC

Atomic concept	Description
A	Atomic concept
$\bot$	The notion that any explanation is empty
$\top$	The notion that contains any other concept
$\neg A$	Negation
$A \sqcup B$	Take the union of concepts
$A \sqcap B$	Take the intersection of concepts
$\exists R.A$	Existential quantifier restriction
$\forall R.A$	Universal quantifier restriction

Table 3. Semantic of ALC

Atomic concept	Semantic
$\bot$	$\bot^I = \emptyset$
$\top$	$\top^I = \Delta$
$\neg A$	$(\neg A)^I = \Delta / A^I$
$A \sqcup B$	$(A \sqcup B)^I = A^I \cup B^I$
$A \sqcap B$	$(A \sqcap B)^I = A^I \cap B^I$
$\exists R.A$	$(\exists R.A)^I = \left\{ a \in \Delta \mid \exists b \in \Delta \left((a,b) \in R^I \wedge b \in A^I \right) \right\}$
$\forall R.A$	$(\forall R.A)^I = \left\{ a \in \Delta \mid \forall b \in \Delta \left((a,b) \in R^I \rightarrow b \in A^I \right) \right\}$

logic of OWL 2 DL, and this section will focus on the background knowledge of $\mathcal{SROIQ}$.

$\mathcal{SROIQ}$ $\mathcal{K}$ is composed of RBox $\mathcal{R}$, TBox $\mathcal{T}$, and ABox $\mathcal{A}$, the concept of which is defined as $C := \bot \mid \top \mid \neg A \mid \{a\} \mid \geq mR.A \mid \exists R.A$.

A $\mathcal{SROIQ}$ $\mathcal{T}$ contains the concept inclusion axiom $C_1 \sqcap \cdots \sqcap C_n \sqsubseteq C$, the disjoint axiom $Dis(C_1, C_2)$, and the equivalent concept $C_1 \equiv C_2$.

The RBox is a finite set containing the role inclusion axioms or disjoint axioms. Role inclusion axioms are represented as $R_1 \sqsubseteq R_2$ or $R_1 \circ R_2 \sqsubseteq R_3$, and disjoint axioms are represented as $Dis(R_1, R_2)$. Inverse roles and symmetric roles are denoted as Inv(R) and Sym(R), also satisfy Inv(R) = R^- and Inv(R) $\equiv$ R if a role is symmetric. Also, the transitive role is represented as Trans(R), and $R \circ R \sqsubseteq R$ if a role is a transitive role. Fun(R) represents the functional role.

A $\mathcal{SROIQ}$ $\mathcal{A}$ without *unique name assumption* (UNA) includes individual inequality $\neq$ and individual equality $a \doteq b$.

Reason Rules. The rule we use for reason is the combination of the two fragments of OWL Horst and RDFS, shown in Table 6 in the Appendix. Each rule has at least one triple as antecedent, which triggers the outcome of the rule as long as the antecedent of the rule can be satisfied, and there is only one outcome. The OWL Horst fragment [21] is a more complex fragment. Its use is more common and can also be called pD* rule set.

4   Optimize Forward Reasoning with Queries

We describe in this section the implementation details of the proposed algorithms and techniques for optimizing the forward reasoning process. Because forward reasoning is affected by semantic data scale and rules, we optimize forward reasoning by combining terminological triples to filter rules and data optimization for large-scale semantic data driven by given queries. The terminological triple pattern represents those triple schemas that use terms from RDFS or OWL vocabularies as predicates or objects. We propose a query parsing algorithm and design two modules: rule filtering and data optimization.

4.1   Query Parsing Algorithm

We get the relevant SPARQL query before reasoning and then target the query for reverse rule and data filtering. First, we need to parse the query to obtain a collection of multiple query patterns. Second, parse the query patterns according to the query parsing algorithm to get the key information we need in the query and generate the key resource pool KR-POOL for further optimization. KR-POOL contains resource entities that have determined values resolved from the query. We only need to search for variables that meet the conditions based on these resource entities and then generate the solution map. The above process is shown in Algorithm 1.

Algorithm 1. Query Parsing Algorithm

Input: queryPath: the path of query
Output: queryPatternList: a collection of patterns for the query
 1: query.readPath(queryPath)
 2: List⟨String⟩ queryList = query.getQueryList();
 3: queryList.forEach(queryString→{
 4:   BufferedReader br = new BufferedReader(new StringReader(queryString));
 5:   String content = br.readLine();
 6:   Boolean start = false;
 7:   **while** content ≠ '}' **do**
 8:     **if** 'PREFIX' ∈ content **then**
 9:       preReplace = content.split(" ");
10:       preReplaceMap.put(preReplace[1],preReplace[2]);
11:     **end if**
12:     **if** '{' ∈ content **then**
13:       start = true
14:     **end if**
15:     **if** start **then**
16:       QueryModeConvert.convertQueryToModeList(content)→R;
17:     **end if**
18:   **end while**
19: });

Example 1. Table 4 represents a SPARQL query, {p1,p2,p3,p4} is the query pattern set of this query, where pi represents the ith query pattern (i =1,2,3,4). After we get the query pattern set of this query, we perform pattern parsing according to the query pattern set. After parsing, it returns more fine-grained key resource entities than the original query pattern. We put these key resource entities into KR-POOL to form The initial set. KR-POOL is continuously updated in subsequent expansion operations. Figure 2 shows the key resource pool (KR-POOL) generated after parsing, which contains the most direct resources required by the query.

Table 4. An example of SPARQL query

SPARQL Query Q

PREFIX rdf: <http://www.w3.org/1999/02/22-rdf-syntax-ns#>
PREFIX benchmark: <http://semantics.crl.ibm.com/univ-bench-dl.owl#>
SELECT ?x
WHERE {
?x rdf:type Publication . //p1
?x publicationAuthor ?y . //p2
?y rdf:type Faculty . //p3
?y isMemberOf <http://www.Department0.University0.edu> //p4
}

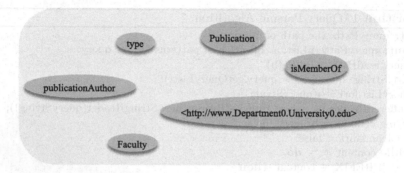

Fig. 2. An example of KR-POOL

4.2 Generate Reason Rule Set

In the process of knowledge reasoning, we first limit the range of resources we need according to the query to some extent, but this is not complete. A lot of implicit knowledge is not represented, and while the scope is defined, some rules are no longer needed because they do not lead to new results. However, reasoning on these rules will undoubtedly cause a waste of time, so we expand the key resource pool and filter the rules simultaneously to form a final reason rule set. The specific implementation details of our algorithm are shown in Algorithm 2.

Example 2. Assume that the knowledge base has two semantic data: *Publication0 type Article* and *Publication1 type Publication*. The existing terminological triplet is *Article SubclassOf Publication*. The KR-POOL obtained by query parsing has two resource entities, *type* and *Publication*. The rules we can match are R1, R2, R5, O13a, O14, and O15. According to the existing conditions, R5 is finally added to the reason rule set. The updated knowledge base is *Publication0 type Article*, *Publication1 type Publication*, and *Publication1 type Publication*.

Algorithm 2. Rule Filtering Algorithm

Input: OWLOntoMap: consists of OWL ontology
        queryPatternList: consists of query patterns for the query
Output: R: extends resource
        FO: filter Owl
1: queryPatternList.Rs→R
2: queryPatternList.Ro→R
3: queryPatternList.Rp→R
4: **while** resource = R.next **do**
5:    **if** resource ∈ OWLOntoMap.keySet() **then**
6:        OWLOntoMap→FO
7:        OWLOntoMap.get(resource)→R
8:    **end if**
9: **end while**

The terminological triples and semantic data in the above examples are simple cases. A real situation, however, is far more complicated than this, so the rules of selection and matching are more complex. Therefore, how to effectively screen and match rules is a key challenge.

We illustrate the process of rule filtering with query pattern p4. Rule filtering is a process in which the query is first decomposed in reverse, then matched with the rules, and the rules that can produce new results are put into the reason rules for the following reason. 1) The resource entities in KR-POOL are matched with the results of rules in the rule table, and the variable values in the antecedents of rules are determined by combining the known terminological triple to obtain a new query pattern after binding. 2) The newly obtained query pattern is taken as the target of the new round. Combined with terminological triple and rule results, the rule antecedents are found by matching recursion. During this process, the matching rules are added to the reason rule set, and the newly added resource entities are added to the KR-POOL until no new matching rules or resource entities are generated. For example, in the dashed line in Fig. 4, *isMemberOf* obtains the new query mode *University0 hasMember ?y* according to the rules O7 and terminological triple *hasMember OWL:inverseOf isMemberOf*, when we continue the recursion with the newly obtained query pattern, we find that the resulting reason rule set and the resource entity are not updated, and we consider the branch terminated. The final reason rule set is O7, R4. Figure 3 shows the updated key resource pool.

4.3 Optimizing Semantic Data

Rule filtering generates a set of reason rules by excluding rules that do not reason the results required by the relevant query. Therefore, in the process of reasoning on large-scale semantic data, it can effectively reduce invalid reasoning and shorten the reasoning time. Furthermore, with the final KR-POOL, our proposed data optimization algorithm can optimize large-scale semantic data in

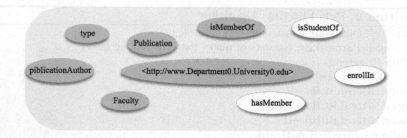

Fig. 3. An example of updated KR-POOL

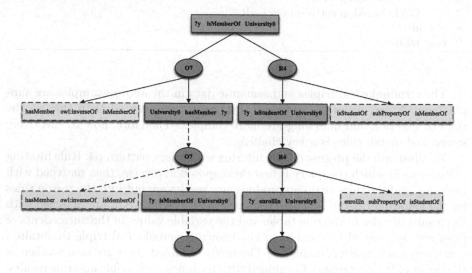

Fig. 4. The process of generating reason rule set

advance, thereby avoiding reason on irrelevant data and further shortening the reason time.

The data filtering process is given in Algorithm 3. According to the key resource entities in the resource pool and large-scale semantic data, efficient matching containing one or more key resource pool entity semantic data are preserved for subsequent forward reasoning. Unmatched data are excluded in advance, which not only reduces materialization time but also greatly optimizes memory.

Example 3. Suppose the following semantic data is waiting for a reason: 1) *ClericalStaff0 isMemberOf University0*, 2) *UndergraduateStudent388 isFriendOf AssociateProfessor6*, 3) *UndergraduateStudent0 enrollIn University0*, 4) *UndergraduateStudent30 hasSameHomeTownWith UndergraduateStudent349*, 5) *FullProfessor1 type Faculty*. The key resource pool is shown in Fig. 3, then data 1),3),5) are filtered out to continue the reasoning, and data 2),4) are eliminated.

Algorithm 3. Data filtering algorithm
Input: D: consists of RDF data
R: consists of resource
Output: AD: consists of RDF data after filter
1: **while** F = D.next **do**
2:   **if** F.RS $\notin$ R and F.RO $\notin$ R and F.RP $\notin$ R **then**
3:     Continue;
4:   **end if**
5:   F$\rightarrow$AD
6: **end while**

5 The System and Implementation of SUMA-F

5.1 Architecture of SUMA-F

We implement three parts of Query Parsing Module, Rule Filter, and Data Filter in the forward reasoning system SUMA-F. The overall system architecture is shown in Fig. 5.

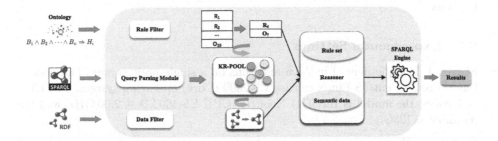

Fig. 5. Frame diagram of SUMA-F

The input of the system is Ontology, RDF data, SPARQL query, and OWL Horst rule, and the output is query result. A total of five modules are Query Parsing module, Rule Filter, Data Filter, Reasoner, and SPARQL Engineer.

Query Parsing Module takes queries as the input, parsing each query into multiple query mode sets, parsing the entities in each query mode in the query mode set, and placing the query mode related entities in the KR-POOL.

The Rule Filter module takes OWL Horst rule as input, matches the query pattern with the rule header according to KR-POOL and query pattern output by the Query Parsing Module, binds unknown variables with the input OWL 2 DL ontology, and continuously expands the query pattern. The matching rules are saved into the reason rule set in the expansion process, and the KR-POOL is updated with the newly added resource entities. This process continues recursively until no new rules are generated in the reason rule set, no new resource entities are added to the KR-POOL, and the recursion stops.

The Data Filter module takes large-scale RDF Data as input and combines the updated KR-POOL to match the three entities of the triple data with the resource entities in the KR-POOL. As long as more than one entity can be matched, the data are regarded as valid data. Otherwise, the data are discarded. After the Data Filter module, the large-scale data screen out some irrelevant data, and the data into the reasoning scale are greatly reduced, while reducing the reasoning scale also has a certain optimization.

The Reasoner module uses the filtered data, and the reason rule set generated by the Rule Filter module as the input for forward reason. The reason data and SPARQL query are used as the input of the SPARQL Engineer to obtain the final result.

6 Experiments

In this section, we implement our algorithm and compare it with other forward reason systems to demonstrate the reason performance and system scalability of SUMA-F. We simulate the dynamic database update scenario and verify that our method can effectively adapt to the frequent data update scenario. By calculating the percentage of irrelevant data reduced, the side reflects the optimization of memory.

6.1 Experimental Settings

SUMA-F is implemented in Java and runs on a single-node server. The node is based on the CentOS Linux release 7.9.2009 (Core) operating system. The CPU is 4 cores, the model is Intel(R) Xeon(R) CPU E5-4603 0 @ 2.00 GHz, and the memory is 128G.

Datasets. We use simulated and real datasets, and experiments are performed on these two datasets. Since UOBM is more expressive than LUBM [23], we chose UOBM as the simulation dataset and tested its 15 standard queries. DBpedia+ with additional tourism axioms on the DBpedia [2] dataset was selected as the real dataset for experimental evaluation of DBpedia+ axioms and 1024 queries against DBpedia+ provided by PAGOdA.

Baselines. We compare SUMA-F with three forward reason systems, SUMA, Pellet, and PAGOdA. SUMA has better performance in forward reasoning. Pellet is an OWL 2 DL reason engine and has reason completeness. PAGOdA shows better performance in scalability, and it is based on RDFox for reason.

Evaluation Criteria. We will design experiments in the following four dimensions: 1) Compare the completeness of reason with the forward reason system. Since the current backward and hybrid reasoning systems usually do not provide explicit instructions for completeness, we compare the completeness of our reasoning method with some complete forward reasoning systems on UOBM and DBpedia+. 2) Test the data expansibility of the system. We test the scalability of our system by recording reason and data loading times for each query on datasets of different sizes. 3) We also verify the effectiveness of data filtering and rule filtering through experiments and manually simulate the reason performance of our system and other forward reason systems when the database is updated. 4) Calculating the percentage of the reduced data in the total data at different data scales reflects the optimization of memory from the side.

6.2   Experimental Results

The Soundness and Completeness Evaluation. We compare reason completeness with SUMA, Pellet, and PAGOdA on UOBM(1), UOBM(100), and DBpedia+, respectively. We can reflect the completeness of reasoning from the side by counting the number of correct answers returned by different queries. Since Pellet cannot return in time the results of queries on both UOBM(100) and DBpedia+ datasets in a limited time, we denote the value as 0. We present the results from the completeness experiments in Table 5. One query on the UOBM dataset failed to return all answers. The number of correct answers that this query should return is 2465, and the number that our method returns is 2404. Despite missing 61 pieces of data, our reason completeness is still 97.5%. And it is speculated that the completeness of the loss is due to the existence of complex roles and relatively complex query patterns, which will continue to be optimized in the future. The number of queries on DBpedia+ that returned the correct answer is 1024, which reaches the completeness of reason.

Table 5. The number of queries with correct results

Dataset	SUMA-F	SUMA	Pellet	PAGOdA
DBpedia+	1024	1024	0	1024
UOBM(1)	14	15	15	15
UOBM(100)	14	15	0	15

The Scalability Test. We test the scalability of UOBM on different data scales. Figure 6(a) shows the trend of data loading time as the data size increases. Figure 6(b) shows the total reason time for 15 standard queries on different data scales.

We test the materialization time according to different queries and compare it with the forward reason system. In Fig. 7, the red line represents the average materialization time, and it can be seen that the materialization time of SUMA-F is less than that of SUMA. For the Q5 query, SUMA-F materializes in 341 ms and returns all correct answers, while SUMA requires 543 ms.

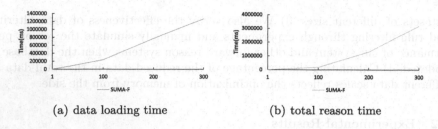

(a) data loading time   (b) total reason time

Fig. 6. Scalability for different data sizes on UOBM

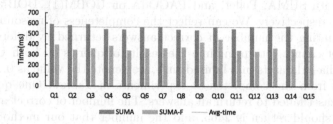

Fig. 7. Experimental results of materialization time

We randomly select six queries with different complexity and compare them with SUMA in terms of data loading time (Fig. 8(a)) and total reason time (Fig. 8(b)) on DBpedia+ dataset. From the results on the experimental graph, it can be seen that for all queries of different complexity, the reason time and data loading time of SUMA-F are much shorter than SUMA. When processing the three queries Q4, Q5, and Q6, due to the small number of answers, SUMA-F greatly reduces the reasoning time through the screening mechanism.

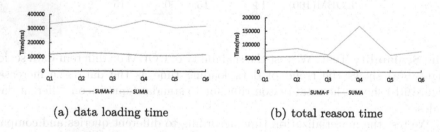

(a) data loading time   (b) total reason time

Fig. 8. Experimental results on DBpedia+

Effectiveness Testing of Data and Rule Filtering. We compare the changes in reason performance of 15 queries before and after data filtering Fig. 9) and rule filtering (Fig. 10) on the UOBM dataset. It can be seen that the data and rule filtering method effectively improves the reason performance and reduces the materialization time. Thus, it is proved that our algorithm is effective for optimizing forward reason.

We manually simulate the update operation of the database, add irrelevant data to the data set to be reasoned in different proportions, and test the change of materialization time between SUMA-F and the traditional forward reason system. Irrelevant data means that for a specific query, no data related to the query answer can be inferred, that is, data that is not helpful for the enrichment of the query answer.

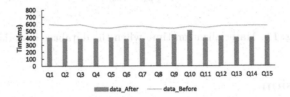

Fig. 9. Results of data filtering methods

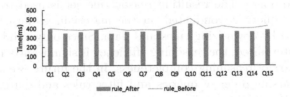

Fig. 10. Results of rule filtering methods

Traditional forward reasoning compute closures indiscriminately for such irrelevant data, while our system avoids reasoning on such data, effectively improving the overall performance. Figure 11 shows the change in materialization time for both systems as the proportion of irrelevant data increases. The value of the abscissa represents the ratio of the amount of added irrelevant data to the original data. It can be seen from the results that SUMA-F fluctuates relatively smoothly with the update of the database. At the same time, SUMA, a traditional forward reason system, shows a large change in materialization time. The updated scale gradually becomes larger, and the upward trend of SUMA's reasoning time becomes more and more obvious. Through the experimental results, we show that SUMA-F reduces the cost of data update to a large extent and realizes it as a forward reasoning system desensitized to data.

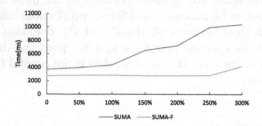

Fig. 11. Materialization time when the database is updated

7   Conclusion

We optimize forward reasoning in this paper with a query-based approach. KR-POOL is generated by parsing queries to filter reason rules and data. An originally large-scale data is refined into data that may produce all the answers required by the query. The resulting reason rule set is used to forward materialize, and the query is conducted on the materialized data set. Memory is effectively saved by downsizing rules and data. Since only valid data and rules are forward materialized, the reasoning efficiency is significantly improved at the expense of a part of reasoning completeness. In the future, we will continue to optimize the parsing order of queries and filter rules and data in a more fine-grained way. OWL 2 DL contains more complex roles, which causes us to lose a part of completeness in the design of the optimization forward reasoning method. We will further study to improve the completeness of reasoning in future work.

Appendix

Table 6. RDFS and OWL Horst rulesets

	Antecedents	Consequent
R1:	p rdfs:domain x, s p o	⇒ s rdf:type x
R2:	p rdfs:range x, s p o	⇒ o rdf:type x
R3:	p rdfs:subPropertyOf q, q rdfs:subPropertyOf r	⇒ p rdfs:subPropertyOf r
R4:	s p o,p rdfs:subPropertyOf q	⇒ s q o
R5:	s rdf:type x, x rdfs:subClassOf y	⇒ s rdf:type y
R6:	x rdfs:subClassOf y, y rdfs:subClassof z	⇒ x rdfs:subClassOf z
O1:	p rdf:type owl:FunctionalProperty, u p v , u p w	⇒ v owl:sameAs w
O2:	p rdf:type owl:InverseFunctionalProperty, v p u, w p u	⇒ v owl:sameAs w
O3:	p rdf:type owl:SymmetricProperty,v p u	⇒ u p v
O4:	p rdf:type owl:TransitiveProperty, u p w, w p v	⇒ u p v
O5:	v owl:sameAs w	⇒ w owl:sameAs v
O6:	v owl:sameAs w, w owl:sameAs u	⇒ v owl:sameAs u
O7a:	p owl:inverseOf q, v p w	⇒ w q v
O7b:	p owl:inverseOf q, v q w	⇒ w p v
O8:	v rdf:type owl:Class, v owl:sameAs w	⇒ v rdfs:subClsaaOf w
O9:	p rdf:type owl:Property, p owl:sameAs q	⇒ p rdfs:subPropertyOf q
O10:	u p v, u owl:sameAs x, v owl:sameAs y	⇒ x p y
O11a:	v owl:equivalentClass w	⇒ v rdfs:subClassOf w
O11b:	v owl:equivalentClass w	⇒ w rdfs:subClassOf v
O11c:	v rdfs:subClassOf w, w rdfs:subClassOf v	⇒ v rdfs:equivalentClass w
O12a:	v owl:equivalentProperty w	⇒ v rdfs:subPropertyOf w
O12b:	v owl:equivalentProperty w	⇒ w rdfs:subPropertyOf v
O12c:	v rdfs:subPropertyOf w, w rdfs:subPropertyOf v	⇒ v rdfs:equivalentProperty w
O13a:	v owl:hasValue w, v owl:onProperty p, u p w	⇒ u rdf:type v
O13b:	v owl:hasValue w, v owl:onProperty p, u rdf:type v	⇒ u p w
O14:	v owl:someValuesFrom w, v owl:onProperty p,u p x, x rdf:type w	⇒ u rdf:type v
O15:	v owl:allValuesFrom u, v owl:onProperty p,w rdf:type v, w p x	⇒ x rdf:type u

References

1. Berners-Lee, T., Hendler, J., Lassila, O.: The semantic web. Sci. Am. **284**(5), 34–43 (2001)
2. Bizer, C., et al.: DBpedia-a crystallization point for the web of data. J. Web Semant. **7**(3), 154–165 (2009)
3. Broekstra, J., Kampman, A., van Harmelen, F.: Sesame: a generic architecture for storing and querying RDF and RDF schema. In: Horrocks, I., Hendler, J. (eds.) ISWC 2002. LNCS, vol. 2342, pp. 54–68. Springer, Heidelberg (2002). https://doi.org/10.1007/3-540-48005-6_7
4. Buron, M.: Efficient reasoning on large-scale heterogeneous data. Ph.D. thesis, Institut Polytechnique de Paris (2020)
5. Calvanese, D., et al.: Ontop: answering SPARQL queries over relational databases. Semant. Web **8**(3), 471–487 (2017)
6. Carroll, J.J., Dickinson, I., Dollin, C., Reynolds, D., Seaborne, A., Wilkinson, K.: Jena: implementing the semantic web recommendations. In: Proceedings of the 13th International World Wide Web Conference on Alternate Track Papers and Posters, pp. 74–83 (2004)

7. Chen, Y., Qian, T., Li, W., Liang, Y.: Exploiting composite relation graph convolution for attributed network embedding. J. Comput. Res. Dev. **57**(8), 1674–1682 (2020)

8. Cucala, D.T., Grau, B.C., Horrocks, I.: Sequoia: a consequence based reasoner for SROIQ. In: Proceedings of the 32nd International Workshop on Description Logics (DL 2019), pp. 1–12 (2019)

9. Eiter, T., Ortiz, M., Simkus, M., Tran, T.K., Xiao, G.: Query rewriting for Horn-Shiq plus rules. In: Proceedings of the 26th AAAI Conference on Artificial Intelligence (AAAI 2012), pp. 22–26 (2012)

10. Gómez, S.A., Fillottrani, P.R.: Materialization of OWL ontologies from relational databases: a practical approach. In: Pesado, P., Arroyo, M. (eds.) CACIC 2019. CCIS, vol. 1184, pp. 285–301. Springer, Cham (2020). https://doi.org/10.1007/978-3-030-48325-8_19

11. Kontchakov, R., Lutz, C., Toman, D., Wolter, F., Zakharyaschev, M.: The combined approach to query answering in DL-Lite. In: Proceedings of the 12th International Conference on the Principles of Knowledge Representation and Reasoning (KR 2010), vol. 10, pp. 247–257 (2010)

12. Lutz, C., Seylan, İ, Toman, D., Wolter, F.: The combined approach to OBDA: taming role hierarchies using filters. In: Alani, H., et al. (eds.) ISWC 2013. LNCS, vol. 8218, pp. 314–330. Springer, Heidelberg (2013). https://doi.org/10.1007/978-3-642-41335-3_20

13. Ma, L., Yang, Y., Qiu, Z., Xie, G., Pan, Y., Liu, S.: Towards a complete OWL ontology benchmark. In: Sure, Y., Domingue, J. (eds.) ESWC 2006. LNCS, vol. 4011, pp. 125–139. Springer, Heidelberg (2006). https://doi.org/10.1007/11762256_12

14. Motik, B., Nenov, Y., Piro, R., Horrocks, I., Olteanu, D.: Parallel materialisation of datalog programs in centralised, main-memory RDF systems. In: Proceedings of the 28th AAAI Conference on Artificial Intelligence, pp. 129–137 (2014)

15. Motik, B., Shearer, R., Horrocks, I.: Hypertableau reasoning for description logics. J. Artif. Intell. Res. **36**, 165–228 (2009)

16. Nenov, Y., Piro, R., Motik, B., Horrocks, I., Wu, Z., Banerjee, J.: RDFox: a highly-scalable RDF store. In: Arenas, M., et al. (eds.) ISWC 2015. LNCS, vol. 9367, pp. 3–20. Springer, Cham (2015). https://doi.org/10.1007/978-3-319-25010-6_1

17. Qin, X., Zhang, X., Yasin, M.Q., Wang, S., Feng, Z., Xiao, G.: SUMA: a partial materialization-based scalable query answering in OWL 2 DL. Data Sci. Eng. **6**(2), 229–245 (2021)

18. Qin, X., Zhang, X., Yasin, M.Q., Wang, S., Feng, Z., Xiao, G.: A partial materialization-based scalable query answering in OWL 2 DL. In: Proceedings of the 25th International Conference on Database Systems for Advanced Applications, pp. 171–187 (2020)

19. Shi, H., Maly, K., Zeil, S.: A scalable backward chaining-based reasoner for a semantic web. Int. J. Adv. Intell. Syst. **7**(1–2), 23–38 (2014)

20. Sirin, E., Parsia, B., Grau, B.C., Kalyanpur, A., Katz, Y.: Pellet: a practical OWL-DL reasoner. J. Web Semant. **5**(2), 51–53 (2007)

21. Ter Horst, H.J.: Completeness, decidability and complexity of entailment for RDF schema and a semantic extension involving the OWL vocabulary. J. Web Semant. **3**(2–3), 79–115 (2005)

22. Urbani, J., van Harmelen, F., Schlobach, S., Bal, H.: QueryPIE: backward reasoning for OWL Horst over very large knowledge bases. In: Aroyo, L., et al. (eds.) ISWC 2011. LNCS, vol. 7031, pp. 730–745. Springer, Heidelberg (2011). https://doi.org/10.1007/978-3-642-25073-6_46

23. Wang, S.-Y., Guo, Y., Qasem, A., Heflin, J.: Rapid benchmarking for semantic web knowledge base systems. In: Gil, Y., Motta, E., Benjamins, V.R., Musen, M.A. (eds.) ISWC 2005. LNCS, vol. 3729, pp. 758–772. Springer, Heidelberg (2005). https://doi.org/10.1007/11574620_54
24. Zhou, Y., Grau, B.C., Nenov, Y., Kaminski, M., Horrocks, I.: PAGOdA: pay-as-you-go ontology query answering using a datalog reasoner. J. Artif. Intell. Res. **54**, 309–367 (2015)

ITAR: A Method for Indoor RFID Trajectory Automatic Recovery

Ziwen Cao[1,2], Siye Wang[1,2,3(✉)], Degang Sun[2], Yanfang Zhang[1], Yue Feng[1,2], and Shang Jiang[1,2]

[1] Institute of Information Engineering, Chinese Academy of Sciences, Beijing, China
{caoziwen,wangsiye,zhangyanfang,fengyue,jiangshang}@iie.ac.cn
[2] School of Cyber Security, University of Chinese Academy of Sciences, Beijing, China
sundegang@iie.ac.cn
[3] School of Computer and Information Technology, Beijing Jiaotong University, Beijing, China

Abstract. With the increasing popularity of Radio Frequency Identification (RFID) technology, indoor applications based on RFID trajectory data analysis are becoming more and more extensive, such as personnel location, tracking, and heat map analysis. The effectiveness of indoor applications relies greatly on high-quality trajectory data. However, due to the constraints of the device and environment, RFID readers will miss reading data in real-world practice, which leads to a large number of indoor trajectories that are incomplete. To enhance trajectory data and support indoor applications more efficiently, many trajectory recovery methods to infer trajectories in free space have been proposed. However, existing methods cannot achieve automated inference and have low accuracy in inferring indoor trajectories. In this paper, we propose an Indoor Trajectory Automatic Recovery framework, ITAR, to recover missing points in indoor trajectories. ITAR adopts a sequence-to-sequence learning architecture to generate complete trajectories. We first construct a directed graph for each trajectory and use a graph neural network to capture complex location transition patterns. Then, we propose a multi-head attention mechanism to capture long-term correlations among trajectory points to improve performance. We conduct extensive experiments on synthetic and real datasets, and the results show that ITAR is superior in performance and robustness.

Keywords: Trajectory recovery · Sequence-to-sequence model · Radio frequency identification · Graph neural network

1 Introduction

Radio Frequency Identification (RFID) technology modernizes indoor object tracking and monitoring systems. This technology relies on two devices: tags (which can emit radio signals encoding identifying information) and readers

H. Gao et al. (Eds.): CollaborateCom 2022, LNICST 461, pp. 400–418, 2022.
https://doi.org/10.1007/978-3-031-24386-8_22

(which detect the signals emitted by tags). Today, most RFID applications use low-cost passive RFID tags, which are preferred for their small size, low price, and low energy requirements. When tags attached to people or objects appear within the reader's detection range, the deployed RFID readers detect these tags and the moving objects to which they are attached. Therefore, RFID technology realizes the identification, location, and tracking of moving objects by attaching tags on different items, such as commodities, equipment, people, etc.

Effective management of indoor RFID tracking data opens new doors for various applications that range from monitoring to analysis of indoor moving objects. This reason for monitoring is that knowing the trajectories of moving assets is helpful in several applications, such as behavior and security analyses. The reasons for such monitoring are manifold, ranging from collecting data to support the behavior analysis over the monitored entities to ensuring security for people and assets. For instance, information on the trajectory followed by monitored people can be used to prevent or look into crimes, and detect dangerous or suspicious situations. Furthermore, information on the trajectory followed by a visitor inside a museum can provide very detailed context-aware information during visiting [13].

However, the unreliability of the raw data captured by the reader is a significant factor hindering the development of such applications. Under normal circumstances, the missing rate of RFID data is between 30%–40% [10]. RFID data missed come from different sources. The read events are often missed due to reader detection capabilities, RFID tag quality, and environmental constraints [4]. Especially in indoor environments where the signal is reflected or blocked by different entities, which leads to readers missing reading tags nearby, that should be detected. Due to the limitation of the acquisition conditions of indoor trajectory data, it is often difficult to obtain a relatively complete record for indoor trajectory. Therefore, it is crucial to reconstruct RFID based indoor trajectories by estimating missing or unobserved locations.

One of the most common solutions to this problem is to impute the missing value by comparing the incomplete trajectories with possible complete trajectories to find the most similar trajectories [12]. Their performance is acceptable when only a small percentage of the locations are missing due to limited movement during a short period. However, their performance degrades significantly in highly sparse scenarios since they fail to model complex mobility regularities effectively. Another line of study is to model the regularity of user transitions among locations to impute missing locations based on the highest transition probability of observed locations [1–3]. However, this strategy is still insufficient. Because the observed RFID trajectory data are not uniform in time, so the transition regularity cannot be inferred for those persistently unobserved locations. None of the above methods can capture the complex sequential dependencies or global data correlations well in indoor environments.

With the popularity of neural networks, deep learning provides a promising computational framework for solving complex trajectory recovery tasks. Many studies have attempted to exploit excellent modeling capacity to better learn effective characteristics from trajectory data. Especially, Recurrent Neural

Networks (RNN) are widely used to model sequential trajectory data [26, 33]. Although these studies have improved the ability to model complex sequential transition patterns to some extent, they only focus on the next step or short-term location prediction. However, a framework that can better simulate movement patterns is needed due to the high uncertainty between two consecutive recordings in indoor trajectories. In addition, traditional methods are often based on the hypothesis that the missing location is known [8, 19], while we usually cannot directly predict the missing trajectory location, which requires that our method should be able to use the global information from the entire trajectory to detect and impute missing trajectories automatically. Therefore, it is difficult to directly apply existing neural network-based trajectory models to indoor space trajectory recovery tasks.

To address the above difficulties, we propose a new Indoor Trajectory Automatic Recovery model named ITAR. Our model achieves automatic imputation of incomplete indoor trajectories by adopting a classical sequence-to-sequence generation framework (i.e., Seq2Seq). In order to effectively capture the complex sequential dependencies between locations in the indoor environment, we adopt a gated graph neural network to encode incomplete trajectories, and adopt a gated recurrent neural network to decode the complete trajectories. Furthermore, to effectively capture the correlation between trajectory points, we employ a multi-head attention mechanism to improve the model performance. With the attention mechanism, our model is able to characterize long-range correlations among trajectory points. In this manner, our model finally enables the automatic imputing of incomplete trajectories and modeling of complex transition patterns. Overall, our main contributions can be summarized as follows:

1. We propose a novel indoor trajectory recovery model for automated RFID trajectory recovery. To the best of our knowledge, this is the first time that deep learning has been applied to the RFID trajectory data imputation research task.
2. We leverage graph neural networks for complex location transition patterns modeling and employ a multi-head attention mechanism for capturing long-range dependencies of indoor trajectory points.
3. We conduct comprehensive experimental studies using both real and synthetic data. Extensive results demonstrate the superiority of the proposed model in terms of effectiveness and robustness.

The rest of this paper is organized as follows. Section 2 presents related work. Section 3 outlines the relevant definitions of the RFID trajectory data. Section 4 describes the trajectory recovery model in detail. Section 5 evaluates the performance of ITAR. Section 6 concludes this paper.

2   Related Work

2.1   RFID Data Imputing

There has been considerable research interest in managing incomplete RFID trajectory data [4, 29]. Due to the detection ability of the reader, the quality of the RFID tag, and the environmental limitations, the phenomenon of missing reading is unavoidable in the process of RFID data collection. Therefore, people have proposed many solutions to impute the RFID trajectory data. Gu et al. [11] first proposed to utilize the grouped trajectory information of monitored objects for RFID data imputation. The trajectory information of monitored objects is implied among massive RFID data. Hu et al. [12] proposed a motion retrospective-based filling algorithm for RFID trajectory data. The algorithm maintains a tracked trajectory event tree based on historical data. Zhao et al. [32] proposed a probabilistic model to clean RFID data for object tracking, which utilizes a Bayesian inference-based algorithm to handle RFID missed reads efficiently. Baba et al. [2,3] proposed a graph model-based RFID data cleaning method, which uses indoor deployment graphs to capture information about the indoor environment and deployed readers and proposes a probabilistic distance perception map to identify false negatives and recover missing information in indoor RFID tracking data. Fazzinga et al. [5,6] proposed a probabilistic framework and a grid-based filtering scheme to clean RFID data. Their solution uses the integrity constraints implied by maps to reduce the inherent uncertainty in trajectory data collected for RFID-monitored objects. Baba et al. [1] proposed a multivariate hidden Markov model (IR-MHMM) to capture and recover the RFID missing data in indoor environments. The method only needs to acquire a small amount of information about the RFID deployment and can learn relevant knowledge from the raw RFID data to impute the indoor trajectory.

2.2   Trajectory Recovery

The traceability of RFID data inspires us to further understand the related research on trajectory recovery [7]. Recovering missing values for trajectories has been an important problem for a long time. Traditional research mainly focuses on mining frequent human movement patterns to recover relevant data. Models such as Markov model [21] and Apriori [17] have been extensively studied. In recent years, deep learning-based models have achieved good performance. Recurrent neural networks (RNNs) and their variants, long short-term memory (LSTM), have been widely used for trajectory data modeling [30]. Existing work can be mainly divided into three categories. The first approach focuses on human mobility recovery using mobility prediction models [8,14]. However, their performance declines in highly sparse scenarios because they only exploit historical information before the missing location and fail to model the spatio-temporal dependencies between the missing location and the locations visited afterward. The second approach is to employ a model-based approach [19,27,28], which captures the multi-level and changing movement patterns of humans. However, these methods are based on the assumption that the historical trajectory of personal movement is known and is not applicable in complex transition scenarios. Recent work in this area treats trajectory recovery problems as time series data recovery problems [16,18]. However, this model fails to capture the complex transition patterns among locations.

Overall, the above methods are not suitable for RFID-based trajectory recovery in indoor scenes. Most of the existing deep learning-based models focus on recovering trajectory data in outdoor GPS-based scenes and ignore trajectory data imputing complex transition patterns in indoor scenes. In contrast, we propose an end-to-end trajectory recovery model based on graph neural networks, which is capable of capturing complex transition patterns and automatically recovering incomplete trajectories.

3 Overview

3.1 Preliminaries

Definition 1: (Trajectory Point). Trajectory points refer to track monitoring points deployed in indoor scenes. RFID reader devices are deployed at each trajectory point. When the RFID reader detects the RFID tag attached to the object, it will record the tag's ID, location, time and other information. Usually, researchers use the triple $<Tagid, Loc, Time>$ to represent the detected object information. Table 1 shows the data records read by the RFID reader device, where $TagID$ is the unique identifier of the tag, representing the detected object. Loc is represented by the number of the reader antenna. Different antennas are distributed at different locations in the room, representing where objects are detected. $Time$ is the timestamp, indicating the time the reader read the tag.

Table 1. RFID trajectory data

Tag ID	Loc	Recording time
1015000A0D3E9368E58F124E	003	2022/7/30 14:20:04
101500A99E4955022988812B	001	2022/7/30 14:23:06
1015002264B2FFBE08B0027A	002	2022/7/30 14:28:12
1015002E496B6C2C93A7794C	001	2022/7/30 14:40:32
1015002E496B6C2C93A7794C	001	2022/7/30 14:42:08
...	...	...

Definition 2: (Road Network). The indoor road network is an undirected graph $G = (V, E)$, where $V = \{v_1, v_2, \ldots, v_K\}$ represents the trajectory points in the indoor scene, $E = \{e_1, e_2, \ldots, e_l\}$ refers to a set of edges that indicate whether the two detection locations are directly reachable in the actual environment. Figure 1 is a monitoring area in an actual system. The topological map above is the road network map from the monitoring area.

Definition 3: (Trajectory). A trajectory T_{id} can be defined as a chronological sequence of locations of a tag ID within a given area, i.e., $T_{id} = \{l_{id}^1, l_{id}^2, \ldots, l_{id}^m\}$, where each l_{id}^i represents a location information in RFID triple $<TagID, Loc, Time>$. Note that if a trajectory point should have been passed but was not observed, the location is named a missing location.

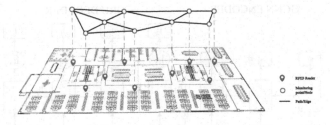

Fig. 1. Indoor road network.

3.2 Problem Definition

Given an incomplete trajectory $T_{id} = \{l_{id}^1, l_{id}^2, \ldots, l_{id}^m\}$ for an arbitrary tag ID, we aim to recover the complete trajectory $\tilde{T}_{id} = \{l_{id}^1, l_{id}^i, l_{id}^j, \ldots, l_{id}^n\}$, where $l_{id}^m = l_{id}^n$. That is to say, for each incomplete trajectory T_{id}, we attempt to infer the missing locations in it automatically with knowing the start and end trajectory points.

4 Methodology

To solve the indoor trajectory recovery problem, we are inspired by the classic Seq2Seq model. The trajectory recovery problem is similar to the machine translation problem, where the incomplete trajectory T_{id} can be treated as the original sentence, and the imputed trajectory $\tilde{T}_{id}$ can be regarded as the translated sentence. Therefore, the Seq2Seq structure can potentially be used to solve the trajectory recovery problem. Our model consists of three main parts. The first part is a sequence-to-sequence (Seq2Seq) neural network model [20], which generates trajectory points incrementally. The second part is a multi-head attention mechanism to capture the correlation between trajectory points. Our attention mechanism considers the dependencies between locations in a global perspective. We use the cross-entropy loss function for model training in the third part.

In this section, we specify ITAR in an asymptotic manner. In Sect. 4.1, we firstly introduce the basic structure of a Seq2Seq-based model for solving the trajectory automatic recovery problem. In Sect. 4.2, we incorporate multi-head attention into Seq2Seq. Then, Sect. 4.3 trains the model by using the cross-entropy loss function. In the following, we elaborate them in details.

4.1 Seq2seq Model

As illustrated in Fig. 2, ITAR is composed of an encoder and a decoder. The encoder learns the spatial dependencies among the trajectory points, while the decoder iteratively predicts the trajectory points using the previous output as the input vector.

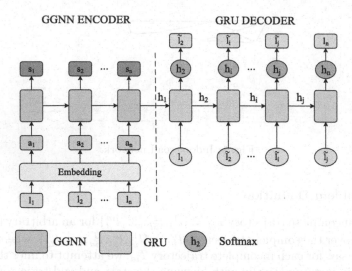

Fig. 2. Structure of ITAR.

Encoder. Previous studies show that gated GNN (ggnn) is able to capture complex transition patterns among nodes, which makes gated GNN suitable for our problem [19]. We process each trajectory separately to capture the complex transition patterns hidden in each trajectory. Specifically, we first construct a directed graph for each trajectory, and then apply gated GNN on each directed graph, which incorporates transition patterns into the encoder.

First, the graph neural network encoder constructs a graph for each incomplete trajectory. Given a trajectory $T_{id} : \{l_1, l_2, \ldots, l_n\}$, we treat each location l_i as a graph node v_i, (l_{i-1}, l_i) is considered as an edge between nodes, where the direction of the edge is from l_{i-1} to l_i. Specifically, let $M_I, M_O \in \mathbb{R}^{d \times d}$ denote the weighted connections of incoming and outgoing edges in the trajectory graph. For example, considering a trajectory $T_{id} : \{l_1, l_2, l_4, l_3, l_2\}$, the corresponding graph and matrix (*i.e*, M_I, M_O) are shown in Fig. 3. We assign a normalized weight to each edge, which is the number of occurrences of the edge divided by the outdegree of that edge's start node. ITAR updates the graph structure by tracking the movement of tags between different locations.

Next, we describe how to embed the trajectory graph into the location vector. We first embed each location $l \in \mathbb{L}$ into an unified low-dimensional latent space s_l, and the location vector $s_l \in \mathbb{R}^d$ denotes a d-dimensional latent space location vector of l. For each location l of the trajectory, a_v extracts contextual information about the neighborhood of location l in the trajectory graph, which can be formalized as:

$$\begin{aligned} \mathbf{a}_v = \text{Concat}\,(&\mathbf{M}_I^v\,([\mathbf{s}_1, \ldots, \mathbf{s}_N]\,\mathbf{W}_I^a + \mathbf{b}_I) \\ &\mathbf{M}_O^v\,([\mathbf{s}_1, \ldots, \mathbf{s}_N]\,\mathbf{W}_O^a + \mathbf{b}_O)) \end{aligned} \tag{1}$$

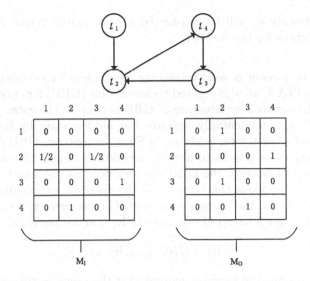

Fig. 3. An example of a trajectory graph structure.

where $\mathbf{W}_I^a, \mathbf{W}_O^a \in \mathbb{R}^{d \times d}$ are variable parameters. $\mathbf{b}_I, \mathbf{b}_O \in \mathbb{R}^d$ are the bias vectors. N is the number of unique locations in the trajectory. $\mathbf{M}_I^v, \mathbf{M}_O^v$ are the incoming and outgoing matrices of the node v in the graph corresponding to the location l.

Finally, due to the spatial dependencies among trajectory points, we employ a gated graph neural network as an encoder to obtain context vectors for incomplete trajectories. The gated graph neural network sequentially updates the hidden state by introducing an update gate $\mathbf{z}_v$ and a reset gate $\mathbf{r}_v$, $\mathbf{z}_v$ and $\mathbf{r}_v$ decide which information to keep and discard, respectively. After that, we construct the candidate state $\tilde{\mathbf{s}}^v$ from the previous state $\mathbf{s}_{v-1}$, the current state $\mathbf{a}_v$ and the reset gate $\mathbf{r}_v$, as described in the Eq. 2. Under the control of the update gate $\mathbf{z}_v$, we combine the previously hidden state $\mathbf{s}_{v-1}$ with the candidate state $\tilde{\mathbf{s}}_v$ to get the final state $\mathbf{s}_v$.

$$\begin{aligned}
\mathbf{z}_v &= \sigma\left(\mathbf{W}_z \mathbf{a}_v + \mathbf{U}_z \mathbf{s}_{v-1}\right) \\
\mathbf{r}_v &= \sigma\left(\mathbf{W}_r \mathbf{a}_v + \mathbf{U}_r \mathbf{s}_{v-1}\right) \\
\tilde{\mathbf{s}}_v &= \tanh\left(\mathbf{W}_h \mathbf{a}_v + \mathbf{U}_h\left(\mathbf{r}_v \odot \mathbf{s}_{v-1}\right)\right) \\
\mathbf{s}_v &= (1 - \mathbf{z}_v) \odot \mathbf{s}_{v-1} + \mathbf{z}_v \odot \tilde{\mathbf{s}}_v
\end{aligned} \tag{2}$$

where $\mathbf{W}_z, \mathbf{W}_r, \mathbf{W}_h \in \mathbb{R}^{d \times 2d}$, $\mathbf{U}_z, \mathbf{U}_r, \mathbf{U}_h \in \mathbb{R}^{d \times d}$ are learnable parameters. σ denotes the sigmoid function and $\odot$ represents element-wise multiplication. $\mathbf{s}_v$ is the final latent location vector with transition-aware after gated graph neural network. To simplify, for getting the context vector of incomplete trajectory, the encoder derives the hidden state $\mathbf{s}_v$ as:

$$\mathbf{s}_v = GGNN(\mathbf{a}_v, \mathbf{s}_{v-1}) \tag{3}$$

where the last state $\mathbf{s}_n$ will be considered as the context vector as well as the initial hidden state for the decoder.

Decoder. The decoder is used to recover incomplete trajectories to complete trajectories. In ITAR, we utilize gated recurrent unit (GRU) for trajectory decoding because the network architecture of GRU is close to the gated graph neural network. GRU also sequentially updates the hidden state by introducing an update gate and a reset gate, as shown in Eq. 2. In contrast, GRU does not need to compute trajectory graphs to obtain embeddings of spatial transition information. At each time step, the GRU decoder decodes the input (the location generated at the previous time step) and the encoded intermediate state into the output location at the current time step. The decoder expresses the hidden state obtained by each round of decoding as $\mathbf{h}_j$ and derives it as:

$$\mathbf{h}_j = GRU(\mathbf{l}_{j-1}, \mathbf{h}_{j-1}) \tag{4}$$

where $\mathbf{l}_{j-1}$ represents the location generated at the previous time step and $\mathbf{h}_{j-1}$ represents the intermediate hidden state. Once we get the hidden state $\mathbf{h}_j$ from the decoder, we use the $softmax$ function to predict the location l_j, where w_l is the $l - th$ column vector from a trainable parameter matrix W_l.

$$\Pr(l \mid \boldsymbol{h}_i) = \frac{\exp\left(\boldsymbol{h}_i^\top \cdot \boldsymbol{w}_l\right)}{\sum_{l' \in \mathcal{L}} \exp\left(\boldsymbol{h}_i^\top \cdot \boldsymbol{w}_{l'}\right)} \tag{5}$$

Furthermore, compared to other seq2seq-based applications applied to trajectory recovery, our task is unique in that the length of the recovered trajectory is unclear. RFID-based indoor trajectories are usually not sampled uniformly in time, making the number of padding points problematic. Fortunately, we usually know the start and end locations of the target trajectory. Therefore, in the training process, we determine whether the location has reached the end location of the target trajectory whenever the current location is predicted. Once the conditions are met, the task of trajectory recovery ends.

4.2 Multi-head Attention

The traditional SeqSeq structure is not ideal for long trajectory imputing. As the trajectory sequence grows, the location information in front of the trajectory sequence will be seriously lost. Even though many papers propose some tricks, such as inputting sentences in reverse order (such as bidirectional LSTM model [31]). However, the improvement in model performance is not apparent. Inspired by the widely used attention mechanism in natural language translation [22], we introduce an attention mechanism into the decoder to model the global correlation of incomplete trajectories. On this basis, we further extend the attention mechanism into a multi-head attention mechanism.

The goal of the attention mechanism is to automatically extract those parts of the incomplete trajectory relevant to the target recovery trajectory and to represent the implicit relationship between the output and the input by generating a context vector $\mathbf{c}$. Multi-head attention utilizes multiple query vectors to compute and select multiple dimensions from the input information in parallel. Each independent attention head focuses on different parts of the input information, and then concentrates to get the final context $\mathbf{c}_j$, which is expressed as:

$$\mathbf{c}_j = \mathbf{c}_j^{(1)} \| \mathbf{c}_j^{(2)} \| \dots \| \mathbf{c}_j^{(H)} \tag{6}$$

Each context vector $\mathbf{c}_j^{(h)}$ is calculated from the weighted sum of all output vectors s from the encoder:

$$\mathbf{c}_j^{(h)} = \sum_{i=1}^{n} \alpha_{j,v}^{(h)} \mathbf{s}_v \tag{7}$$

where $\alpha_{j,v}^{(h)}$ represents the similarity between the query vector (i.e. current hidden state in the decoder) and the key vector (i.e. output from the encoder), which is formulated as:

$$\alpha_{j,v}^{(h)} = \frac{\exp\left(u_{j,v}^{(h)}\right)}{\sum_{v'=1}^{N} \exp\left(u_{j,v'}^{(h)}\right)} \tag{8}$$

$$u_{j,v}^{(h)} = \mathbf{v}^{(h)\top} \cdot \tanh\left(\mathbf{W}_{\mathbf{h}}^{(h)} \mathbf{h}_j + \mathbf{W}_{\mathbf{s}}^{(h)} \mathbf{s}_v\right)$$

where $\mathbf{W}_{\mathbf{h}}^{(h)}, \mathbf{W}_{\mathbf{s}}^{(h)}, v^{(h)}$ are learnable parameters, $\mathbf{h}_j$ denotes the hidden location status from the decoder and $\mathbf{s}_v$ is the output from the encoder.

Therefore, the hidden state $\mathbf{h}_j$ in the decoder is updated to:

$$\mathbf{h}_j = GRU(\mathbf{h}_{j-1}, \mathbf{l}_{j-1}, \mathbf{c}_j) \tag{9}$$

4.3 Model Training

Finally, we elaborate the training process of the end-to-end trained model. We adopt cross-entropy as the loss function:

$$\mathcal{L}(\theta) = - \sum_{(T,\tilde{T})\in\mathcal{D}} \sum_{j=1}^{|\tilde{T}|} \sum_{i=1}^{L} l_i^j \log\left(\tilde{l}_i^j\right) \tag{10}$$

where T is the incomplete trajectory, $\tilde{T}$ is the complete target trajectory, $|\tilde{T}|$ is the length of the $\tilde{T}$ trajectory. L is the set of indoor trajectory points, which represents the category of the output location. l is the ground truth of the target trajectory, and $\tilde{l}_j$ is the predicted location. $\mathcal{D}$ denotes a dataset consisting of incomplete trajectories T and complete trajectories $\tilde{T}$.

During the training process, we apply AdamW stochastic gradient descent to update the parameters θ [15]. First, we construct a suitable training set including incomplete trajectories T and complete trajectories $\tilde{T}$. Then, we initialize the training model parameters θ and randomly shuffle the training set. Finally, we update the ITAR parameter θ using the Eq. 10, where η is the training step size. The Algorithm 1 illustrates the training process of the ITAR model. In addition, our model is implemented in Python and Pytorch. All models are done on Apple computers with M1 chips.

Algorithm 1. ITAR Training.

Input: Trajectories T, $\tilde{T}$, max iteration *epochs*, batch size *batch*
Output: Trained Model θ
Construct training instances T and $\tilde{T}$.
initialize the model parameters θ.
for $i \in \{1, 2, 3, \ldots, epochs\}$ **do**
    Shuffle the training instances D into mini-batches
    for $j \in \{1, 2, 3, \ldots, batch\}$ **do**
        Calculate gradient $\nabla \mathcal{L}(\theta)$ using Eq. 10.
        Update $\theta \leftarrow \theta - \eta \nabla \mathcal{L}(\theta)$.
    end for
end for

---

5   Experiment

In this section, we first introduce the relevant settings of the experiments and then perform a performance comparison and analysis of the experimental results.

5.1   Experimental Setup

Construction of the Evaluation Set. In this experiment, we use two datasets to demonstrate the effectiveness of our proposed algorithm, including a synthetic dataset and an RFID tracking dataset. To facilitate trajectory recovery, we pre-process the raw RFID data. First, we use the redundant filtering algorithm to remove duplicate points and outliers [24], and then use environmental constraints to impute some missing data to form the ground truth trajectory. Finally, we filter out trajectories with lengths less than 7. Table 2 summarizes the final detailed static data for the two RFID trajectory datasets.

- **Synthetic:** We simulate the trajectory of objects in indoor space, record the sampling data of objects at different trajectory points, and synthesize RFID trajectory data accordingly. We use the original trajectory data to represent the ground truth trajectory of the object and form incomplete trajectories by masking different proportions of the data. Since the synthetic data is a trajectory formed by simulation, the model will perform better.

– **RFID Tracking:** We use data from an RFID-based person tracking system as the dataset for this experiment. This dataset was collected at a product expo held in 2018 [9]. The dataset has about 400,000 pieces of data generated by about 10,000 tags over three days.

Table 2. Basic statistics of datasets.

Dataset	Duration	Average Traj length	Loctions	Traj pairs
Synthetic	7 days	11	36	12208
RFID tracking	3 days	14	18	4262

Evaluation Metrics. Our aim is to recover incomplete indoor trajectories. Following previous work [18,25], we mainly adopt three metrics *Accuracy, Recall,* and *Precision* to demonstrate the performance of our model and baseline methods.

Accuracy. *Accuracy* is the primary evaluation metric to judge whether the predicted location is accurate. We use TP to indicate that the predicted location matches the ground truth and FN to indicate that the predicted location does not match. *Accuracy* is formulated as:

$$accuracy = \frac{TP}{TP + FN} \tag{11}$$

Recall. *Recall* is defined as the proportion of correctly classified locations to the length of the target trajectory, which can reflect the recovery trajectory's integrity. The *recall* calculation is shown in Eq. 12, where ∩ represents the longest common subsequence of the recovered trajectory T_R and the ground truth T_G, and ‖ represents the length of the trajectory.

$$recall = \frac{|T_R \cap T_G|}{|T_G|} \tag{12}$$

Precision. *Precision* refers to the ratio of the number of correctly classified locations to the length of the recovered trajectory generated by the model, which can reflect the quality of the recovered trajectory. We use *Precision* to evaluate the performance by comparing the recovered trajectory T_R with the ground truth T_G. The formula of *precision* is:

$$precision = \frac{|T_R \cap T_G|}{|T_R|} \tag{13}$$

Task Setting. For each of the two datasets, we split the dataset into training, validation, and test sets with a split ratio of 7:2:1. Since the preprocessed trajectory data is complete, we generate incomplete trajectories by randomly masking the complete trajectories. The inherent data missing rate of data collected by RFID equipment is 30% [10], coupled with other factors such as environmental interference, so the missing rate in actual scenarios will be higher. We evaluate the robustness of our ITAR by masking different rates of trajectory points. The masking location indicates that the trajectory point is missing. We choose the missing rate mr as 30%, 50%, 70% respectively. A higher mr indicates that the number of missing points in the incomplete trajectory is larger, and the difficulty of trajectory recovery is greater. We generate incomplete trajectories for prediction and use the complete trajectories as the ground truth for evaluation. We repeat the above procedure three times for reliable evaluation and report the average results for both datasets.

Baselines. We compare the proposed ITAR with several representative baselines. Among them, the first is the latest RFID-based indoor trajectory data imputation algorithm. The last three are state-of-the-art deep learning-based trajectory imputation models which can extract more complex features.

- IR-MHMM [1]: This is the latest research in the field of RFID trajectory recovery, which uses a Multi-variate Hidden Markov Model (IR-MHMM) to capture and recover the missing data of RFID-based trajectory in indoor environments.
- PeriodicMove [19]: This is a latest model-based trajectory recovery method. It exploits gated graph neural networks to mine user movement preferences and utilizes various attention mechanisms to model regularity and periodic patterns of user movements. We adapt to the current task by reserving the fill location.
- DHTR [23]: The method designs a subseq2seq model with a Kalman filter to recover trajectories in free space. We mainly refer to the bidirectional LSTM in the main part of the method for experimental comparison.
- MTrajRec [18]: This is the state-of-the-art method in the field of trajectory recovery, which models the forward sequential mobility transition through a gated neural network and will enhance the performance of trajectory recovery with an attention mechanism. In order to adapt to our task, we only refer to the sequence numbers of the recovered trajectories without considering the specific coordinates of the recovered trajectories.

5.2   Result and Analysis

Overall Performance. We compare ITAR with other baseline models in terms of *Accuracy*, *Precision*, and *Precision*. Table 3 gives the trajectory recovery performance of different methods with different missing rates. We can have the following observations.

Table 3. Overall performance comparison in terms of *Accuracy*, *Recall* and *Precision*. The best result for each evaluation metric is in bold. A larger missing rate indicates a larger number of missing points in incomplete trajectories.

Dataset	Methods	30%			50%			70%		
		Accuracy	Recall	Precision	Accuracy	Recall	Precision	Accuracy	Recall	Precision
Synthetic	IR-MHMM	0.5213	0.6212	0.6614	0.4253	0.5023	0.5528	0.3438	0.4249	0.4423
	PeriodicMove	0.8648	0.8839	0.8839	0.7413	0.8014	0.8014	0.6013	0.7333	0.7333
	DHTR	0.8270	0.8687	0.8747	0.7205	0.7930	0.8036	0.5912	0.7058	0.7299
	MTrajRec	0.8811	0.9108	0.9175	0.7338	0.8008	0.8112	0.6035	0.7193	0.7416
	ITAR	**0.9252**	**0.9467**	**0.9498**	**0.8067**	**0.8681**	**0.8807**	**0.6895**	**0.7936**	**0.8168**
Tracking	IR-MHMM	0.3827	0.4623	0.4766	0.3024	0.3635	0.3865	0.2283	0.3398	0.3245
	PeriodicMove	0.6413	0.7812	0.7812	0.5097	0.6690	0.6690	0.4142	0.5849	0.5849
	DHTR	0.6542	0.7270	0.7968	0.5147	0.6229	0.6683	0.3647	0.5272	0.6361
	MTrajRec	0.6608	0.7523	0.8143	0.5278	0.6308	0.6712	0.3809	0.5533	0.6364
	ITAR	**0.7311**	**0.8243**	**0.8874**	**0.5995**	**0.6904**	**0.7303**	**0.4402**	**0.6043**	**0.6874**

1. Traditional Hidden Markov-based approaches perform the worst among all evaluation metrics on both datasets. Although the method attempts to find the transition patterns of tags, its performance is still unacceptable, especially with a high missing rate, as it fails to capture complex transition patterns between locations.
2. In recent years, RNN-based deep learning methods have outperformed traditional methods, and state-of-the-art deep learning methods, including DHTR and MTrajRec, have achieved satisfactory performance because they can model simple translation patterns between locations. Although DHTR uses bidirectional LSTM for encoding, in our application, its actual effect is no better than that of MTrajRec with unidirectional GRU. One possible reason is that the missing trajectory points in our scene are irregular. As a result, the before and after dependencies between locations are not obvious. Furthermore, our ITAR achieves further performance gains over state-of-the-art deep learning methods, as ITAR can capture complex location transition patterns.
3. ITAR outperforms all baselines on all evaluation metrics on both datasets. These vast improvements show that our proposed ITAR can well simulate position transition patterns to recover trajectories. When the missing rate is 50%, *Accuracy*, *Recall*, and *Precision* of ITAR outperform the best baseline MTrajRec by 9.9%, 8.4%, and 8.4% on the Synthetic dataset, respectively. *Accuracy*, *Recall*, and *Precision* outperform the best baseline MTrajRec by 7.1%, 9.4%, and 8.8% on the RFID tracking dataset, which proves the effectiveness of our ITAR in indoor trajectory recovery. The fundamental reason for this progress is that, on the one hand, we utilize GGNN to model complex transition patterns, and on the other hand, we employ a multi-head attention mechanism to capture correlations between locations.

Robustness Analysis. We evaluate the robustness of ITAR by varying the proportion of missing trajectory points. An increase in the missing rate means an increase in the number of missing points, leading to increased uncertainty between any two consecutive points. We increased the percentage of missing trajectory points in trajectories from 30% to 70%, and the results are shown in Table 3. We can find that as the missing rate increases, the performance of ITAR and other baselines on all evaluation metrics decreases. However, the higher the missing rate, the more pronounced the performance improvement of ITAR. Specifically, when the missing rate is 70%, ITAR still maintains a good recovery effect and is better than the best baselines on average of 14.91%, 9.78%, and 9.08% in terms of *Accuracy*, *Recall*, and *Precision*. This validates the robustness of our model in capturing complex transition patterns between locations and demonstrates its robust ability to reconstruct individual indoor trajectories.

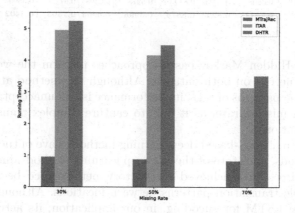

Fig. 4. Running efficiency.

Running Efficiency. To evaluate the efficiency of ITAR, we compared the algorithm's running time with DHTR and MTrajRec models, which also employ the seq2seq architecture for easy comparison. As shown in Fig. 4, we find that the running time of ITAR and other baseline models decreases as the missing rate increases because ITAR utilizes an automatic inference model. As the missing rate increases, the accuracy of the model decreases, and thus the system's run time decreases slightly. In addition, due to the multi-head attention mechanism adopted by ITAR, its running speed is slightly slower than that of the MTrajRec algorithm, but the accuracy rate is much higher. Therefore, this difference can be ignored.

Importance of the Attention Mechanism. In this section, we remove the attention mechanism from ITAR to test its contribution, as shown in Table 4. Results for ITAR-noAttn were significantly lower compared to ITAR. We enumerate the average performance change in ITAR on the two datasets after removing the attention mechanism with a missing rate of 50%. Among them, *Accuracy* decreased by 32.83%, *Recall* decreased by 25.79%, and *Precision* decreased by

24.55%, which shows that the attention mechanism occupies a critical position in our model. One possible reason is that the attention mechanism can effectively enforce the spatial constraints on missing locations and establish dependencies between locations.

Table 4. Importance of the attention mechanism.

Method	Accuracy	Recall	Precision
ITAR	0.7031	0.7793	0.8055
ITAR-noatten	0.4723	0.5783	0.6077
Reduced performance	**32.83%**	**25.79%**	**24.55%**

Parameter Tuning. Apart from evaluating the components of our proposed model MTrajRec, there are two important parameters to tune in our model.

Hidden size d. We refer to previous studies [19] to observe performance changes by adjusting the hidden size d in the range of {16, 32, 64, 128, 256, 512}. From the results presented in Fig. 5, it can be seen that as the hidden size increases, the performance gradually improves, and when it is larger than a certain value, the performance begins to decrease slightly. On the one hand, it shows that a moderate d can better represent the hidden information between locations, which is enough to capture the transition patterns. On the other hand, using redundant dimensions increases model complexity and forces the model to overfit to training, which may reduce the generalization ability of our model on the test set. We find that when the hidden layer size is 128, ITAR can achieve a trade-off between model efficiency and accuracy. Therefore, the default hidden layer size of ITAR is 128.

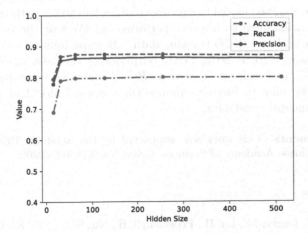

Fig. 5. Impart of hidden size d.

Head number H. We adjust the head number H in the range of $\{1, 2, 3, 4, 5, 8\}$, and Fig. 6 shows the performance change. We can see that in most cases, the number of attention heads does not show a clear trend in the performance change, which means that the effect of attention head number is not significant. Considering that more heads leads to stronger model expressiveness and more computational cost, we finally fixed the number of heads to 4 in order to make a compromise between performance and efficiency.

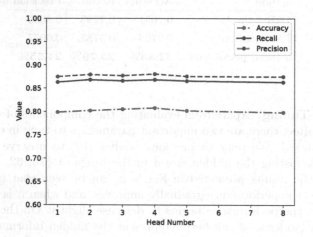

Fig. 6. Impart of head number H.

6   Conclusion

In this paper, we propose a novel end-to-end deep learning model ITAR for automatic trajectory recovery in indoor spaces. We introduce a graph neural network in the Seq2Seq model to capture complex transition patterns and employ an attention mechanism to improve performance. We test the proposed model with synthetic and real RFID tracking data. The experimental results show that when the missing rate is 50%, ITAR outperforms the best baseline by 8.5%, 8.9% and 8.6% in terms of *Accuracy*, *Recall* and *Precision* respectively. In future work, we plan to further enhance the proposed model by incorporating more environmental constraints.

Acknowledgments. This work was supported by the Strategic Priority Research Program of Chinese Academy of Sciences, Grant No. XDC02040300.

References

1. Baba, A.I., Jaeger, M., Lu, H., Pedersen, T.B., Ku, W.S., Xie, X.: Learning-based cleansing for indoor RFID data. In: Proceedings of the 2016 International Conference on Management of Data, pp. 925–936 (2016)

2. Baba, A.I., Lu, H., Pedersen, T.B., Xie, X.: Handling false negatives in indoor RFID data. In: 2014 IEEE 15th International Conference on Mobile Data Management, vol. 1, pp. 117–126. IEEE (2014)
3. Baba, A.I., Lu, H., Xie, X., Pedersen, T.B.: Spatiotemporal data cleansing for indoor RFID tracking data. In: 2013 IEEE 14th International Conference on Mobile Data Management, vol. 1, pp. 187–196. IEEE (2013)
4. Derakhshan, R., Orlowska, M.E., Li, X.: RFID data management: challenges and opportunities. In: 2007 IEEE International Conference on RFID, pp. 175–182. IEEE (2007)
5. Fazzinga, B., Flesca, S., Furfaro, F., Parisi, F.: Cleaning trajectory data of RFID-monitored objects through conditioning under integrity constraints. In: EDBT, pp. 379–390 (2014)
6. Fazzinga, B., Flesca, S., Furfaro, F., Parisi, F.: Offline cleaning of RFID trajectory data. In: Proceedings of the 26th International Conference on Scientific and Statistical Database Management, pp. 1–12 (2014)
7. Fazzinga, B., Flesca, S., Furfaro, F., Parisi, F.: Interpreting RFID tracking data for simultaneously moving objects: an offline sampling-based approach. Expert Syst. Appl. **152**, 113368 (2020)
8. Feng, J., et al.: DeepMove: predicting human mobility with attentional recurrent networks. In: Proceedings of the 2018 World Wide Web Conference, pp. 1459–1468 (2018)
9. Feng, Y., Huang, W., Wang, S., Zhang, Y., Jiang, S.: Detection of RFID cloning attacks: a spatiotemporal trajectory data stream-based practical approach. Comput. Netw. **189**, 107922 (2021)
10. Floerkemeier, C., Lampe, M.: Issues with RFID usage in ubiquitous computing applications. In: Ferscha, A., Mattern, F. (eds.) Pervasive 2004. LNCS, vol. 3001, pp. 188–193. Springer, Heidelberg (2004). https://doi.org/10.1007/978-3-540-24646-6_13
11. Gu, Yu., Yu, G., Chen, Y., Ooi, B.C.: Efficient RFID data imputation by analyzing the correlations of monitored objects. In: Zhou, X., Yokota, H., Deng, K., Liu, Q. (eds.) DASFAA 2009. LNCS, vol. 5463, pp. 186–200. Springer, Heidelberg (2009). https://doi.org/10.1007/978-3-642-00887-0_15
12. Hu, K.F., Li, L., Lu, Z.P.: AgCleaning: a track data filling algorithm based on movement recency for RFID track data. In: Applied Mechanics and Materials, vol. 490, pp. 1330–1337. Trans Tech Publ (2014)
13. Huang, W., Zhang, Y., Feng, Y.: ACD: an adaptable approach for RFID cloning attack detection. Sensors **20**(8), 2378 (2020)
14. Liu, Q., Wu, S., Wang, L., Tan, T.: Predicting the next location: a recurrent model with spatial and temporal contexts. In: Thirtieth AAAI Conference on Artificial Intelligence (2016)
15. Loshchilov, I., Hutter, F.: Fixing weight decay regularization in Adam (2017)
16. Luo, Y., Cai, X., Zhang, Y., Xu, J., et al.: Multivariate time series imputation with generative adversarial networks. In: Advances in Neural Information Processing Systems, vol. 31 (2018)
17. Morzy, M.: Prediction of moving object location based on frequent trajectories. In: Levi, A., Savaş, E., Yenigün, H., Balcısoy, S., Saygın, Y. (eds.) ISCIS 2006. LNCS, vol. 4263, pp. 583–592. Springer, Heidelberg (2006). https://doi.org/10.1007/11902140_62
18. Ren, H., et al.: Mtrajrec: map-constrained trajectory recovery via seq2seq multi-task learning. In: Proceedings of the 27th ACM SIGKDD Conference on Knowledge Discovery and Data Mining, pp. 1410–1419 (2021)

19. Sun, H., Yang, C., Deng, L., Zhou, F., Huang, F., Zheng, K.: Periodicmove: shift-aware human mobility recovery with graph neural network. In: Proceedings of the 30th ACM International Conference on Information and Knowledge Management, pp. 1734–1743 (2021)

20. Sutskever, I., Vinyals, O., Le, Q.V.: Sequence to sequence learning with neural networks. In: Advances in Neural Information Processing Systems, vol. 27 (2014)

21. Tong, C., Chen, H., Xuan, Q., Yang, X.: A framework for bus trajectory extraction and missing data recovery for data sampled from the internet. Sensors **17**(2), 342 (2017)

22. Vaswani, A., et al.: Attention is all you need. In: Proceedings of the 31st International Conference on Neural Information Processing Systems. NIPS 2017, pp. 6000–6010. Curran Associates Inc., Red Hook (2017)

23. Wang, J., Wu, N., Lu, X., Zhao, W.X., Feng, K.: Deep trajectory recovery with fine-grained calibration using Kalman filter. IEEE Trans. Knowl. Data Eng. **33**(3), 921–934 (2019)

24. Wang, S., Cao, Z., Zhang, Y., Huang, W., Jiang, J.: A temporal and spatial data redundancy processing algorithm for RFID surveillance data. Wirel. Commun. Mob. Comput. **2020** (2020)

25. Wheeb, A.H.: Performance analysis of VOIP in wireless networks. Int. J. Comput. Netw. Wirel. Commun. (IJCNWC) **7**(4), 1–5 (2017)

26. Wu, H., Chen, Z., Sun, W., Zheng, B., Wang, W.: Modeling trajectories with recurrent neural networks. In: IJCAI (2017)

27. Xi, D., Zhuang, F., Liu, Y., Gu, J., Xiong, H., He, Q.: Modelling of bi-directional spatio-temporal dependence and users' dynamic preferences for missing poi check-in identification. In: Proceedings of the AAAI Conference on Artificial Intelligence, vol. 33, pp. 5458–5465 (2019)

28. Xia, T., et al.: AttnMove: history enhanced trajectory recovery via attentional network. In: Proceedings of the AAAI Conference on Artificial Intelligence, vol. 35, pp. 4494–4502 (2021)

29. Xie, L., Yin, Y., Vasilakos, A.V., Lu, S.: Managing RFID data: challenges, opportunities and solutions. IEEE Commun. Surv. Tutor. **16**(3), 1294–1311 (2014)

30. Yang, C., Sun, M., Zhao, W.X., Liu, Z., Chang, E.Y.: A neural network approach to jointly modeling social networks and mobile trajectories. ACM Trans. Inf. Syst. (TOIS) **35**(4), 1–28 (2017)

31. Zhao, J., Xu, J., Zhou, R., Zhao, P., Zhu, F.: On prediction of user destination by sub-trajectory understanding: a deep learning based approach. In: the 27th ACM International Conference (2018)

32. Zhao, Z., Ng, W.: A model-based approach for RFID data stream cleansing. In: Proceedings of the 21st ACM International Conference on Information and Knowledge Management, pp. 862–871 (2012)

33. Zheng, S., Yue, Y., Hobbs, J.: Generating long-term trajectories using deep hierarchical networks. In: Advances in Neural Information Processing Systems, vol. 29 (2016)

A Longitudinal Measurement and Analysis of Pink, a Hybrid P2P IoT Botnet

Binglai Wang[1,2], Yafei Sang[1(✉)], Yongzheng Zhang[3], Shuhao Li[1], Ruihai Ge[1], and Yong Ding[1]

[1] Institute of Information Engineering, Chinese Academy of Sciences, Beijing, China
{wangbinglai,sangyafei,lishuhao,geruihai}@iie.ac.cn
[2] School of Cyber Security, University of Chinese Academy of Sciences, Beijing, China
[3] China Assets Cybersecurity Technology CO., LTD., Beijing, China
zhangyz@cacts.cn

Abstract. With the ubiquitous deployment of Internet of Things (IoT) devices in many fields, more and more IoT botnets have taken a variety of penetration methods to infect vulnerable IoT devices. Nowadays, a substantial Peer-to-Peer (P2P) IoT botnet named Pink has infected over 1.6 million IoT devices since January 2020, and its impact once exceeded other notorious IoT botnets, such as Mirai, Hajime, Mozi, and so on. Pink is the first IoT botnet using a hybrid topology with centralized and decentralized network architectures. Its two distinct features can be summarized as follows. (i) Different from the conventional P2P IoT botnet based on the public Distributed Hash Table (DHT) service, Pink introduces a novel mechanism called B-segment to build a P2P network, which makes it challenging to track the entire botnet. (ii) Pink is the first IoT botnet to leverage third-party services to propagate configuration files, thereby increasing its resilience. In this paper, we propose an active detection method to measure and understand the development and changes of the Pink botnet continuously. Through daily and continuous measuring of the Pink botnet since January 2022, we firstly provide a comprehensive view of its inapparent network, including bot sizes, global geographic distribution, daily activity, configuration analysis, and Pink botnet countermeasures. We believe that our measurement result is infinitely close to the boundary of the Pink network. Through this study, we reveal that deeper penetration attacks are occurring in the IoT field, and there is an urgent need to improve the security protection of IoT devices. Meanwhile, we hope that this study can promote future research on IoT botnets.

Keywords: Botnet · P2P · C&C · IoT · Pink · Network

1 Introduction

A survey reported by IoT-Analytics reveals that 30.9 billion Internet of Things (IoT) devices are expected to be in extensive use worldwide by 2025 [12,14].

© ICST Institute for Computer Sciences, Social Informatics and Telecommunications Engineering 2022
Published by Springer Nature Switzerland AG 2022. All Rights Reserved
H. Gao et al. (Eds.): CollaborateCom 2022, LNICST 461, pp. 419–436, 2022.
https://doi.org/10.1007/978-3-031-24386-8_23

Unfortunately, these devices with severe flaws are prone to be infected by various IoT botnets, which fundamentally change the internet threat landscape. Although the various attacks and vulnerabilities launched by IoT botnets have been in-depth analyses [4,7,13], there remains much to understand about how the underlying ecosystem work of infected IoT devices. For example: How are the compromised IoT devices geographically distributed? How large can a global IoT botnet grow daily? How does an IoT botnet maintain software updates rapidly and thoroughly? To answer these questions and more, we present an in-depth measurement and analysis of a prevalent IoT botnet, Pink, in this paper.

Pink provides three novel characteristics, which are essential forward-looking significance for studying P2P IoT botnets. (1) Pink is the first IoT botnet with a hybrid topology with centralized and decentralized architectures to distribute attack instructions. The architecture can present high fault tolerance, which can remedy a single point of failure in a central C&C network and distribute configuration files in real-time. (2) Pink is the first P2P IoT botnet to apply an anti-track mechanism. Pink customized P2P communication and mixed it into Network Time Protocol (NTP) service. Then, the messages sent to the other bots are difficult to be detected through network features. (3) Different from Hajime [8] and Mozi [2], Pink is the first P2P IoT botnet built with the B-segment mechanism instead of using the public Distributed Hash Table (DHT) service. The advantage of the B-segment mechanism is two-fold: (i) deeper concealment making up for the defect that the DHT-based mechanism is easy to be tracked; (ii) more flexible network management by probing the alive Pink bot in Class B IPs. We present the details of the B-segment mechanism in Sect. 2. Therefore, the measurement and analysis of the Pink is instructive for understanding and governance of P2P IoT botnets. With this work, our contributions can be summarized as follows:

- **To the best of our knowledge, we are the first to elaborate a comprehensive study of the large-scale Pink IoT botnet.** We investigate the properties of Pink, *e.g.*, network scale, geographical distribution, bot lifetime, communication patterns, and so on.

- **We propose an active measurement method, which can not only track Pink bots but also can be extended to other similar P2P IoT botnets.** The key novelty of this approach lies in two points: (i) It infiltrates the entire Pink botnet by actively sending customized message packets conforming to known Pink bots, and (ii) It passively waits for active interaction from more unknown zombie bots because they can sense the existence of our probe nodes through other Pink bots. Compared with the public-DHT-crawler-based method (adopted to measure Hajime and Mozi), our solution can reduce unnecessary costs and apply to other IoT botnets using P2P DHT communication.

- **We offer two fundamental insights on Pink botnet from our measurement study.** (i) By analyzing the network behavior of prevalent Pink binary samples, we find that P2P communication dominates in distributing config files; we believe that other P2P IoT botnets will adopt the P2P network construction method based on the B-segment mechanism in the future. (ii) From the perspective of geographical distribution, 99% of Pink bots are located in China and show a B-segment distribution with a long lifetime, suggesting that the attack target of the Pink controller is well-defined and widely distributed in China.

2   Preliminaries

Pink is a hybrid architecture botnet with P2P and central C&C communication patterns. This architecture enhances its robustness and facilitates the attacker's control of the entire botnet. In this section, we introduce Pink composition and operation that are most relevant to our study.

2.1   Pink Composition

Through our tracking and analysis, we divided the Pink botnet into five parts: Botmaster, Third-party, P2P, Central Command and Control (Central C&C), and Pink bot. The structure of the Pink botnet is shown in Fig. 1. Different from conventional IoT botnets like Hajime or Mozi that only use the DHT method to complete configuration distribution tasks, Pink botnet has adopted three communication patterns, including third-party, P2P communication, and central C&C, to improve the robustness of the entire botnet. The attacker can operate the three patterns through Botmater to send the configuration files to Pink bots. Each component plays a different role in the botnet. We provide the details in this section.

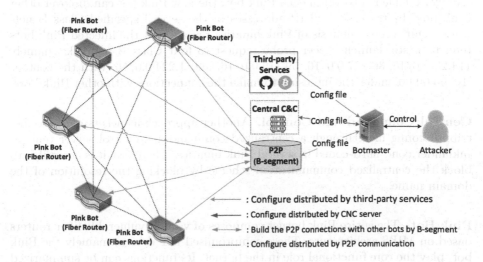

Fig. 1. The structure of Pink botnet.

Botmaster. Pink botnet presents a command relay role, namely botmaster, to send commands to other bots. When the attacker needs a botnet to perform specific actions, it only needs to send a configuration file to the Botmaster. Then, to ensure the correct distribution of the configuration file in the botnet, Botmaster has utilized three communication patterns, including third-party services, P2P, and central C&C, to deliver the configuration file. After receiving the configuration file, the Pink bot will execute the commands defined in the new configuration file and distribute this file to its neighbor Pink bots.

Third-Party Services. Pink botnet leverages another scheme to deliver configuration files. The attacker uses the third-party services Github [10] and BTC [16] to propagate the config file. First, Pink bots can leverage the transaction records in a specific BTC wallet to obtain the topic tags related to the GitHub project. Second, Pink bots will go through the issues of these projects and look for a hidden Git project. This scheme has a robust anti-strike capability. The reason is that the specified BTC wallet must be blocked to disrupt the GitHub-based distribution logic of Pink.

B-segment. Pink botnet provides a unique mechanism that enables new Pink bots to rapidly discover other existing Pink bots and make a connection. Its principle is that the IPv4 address space of many vulnerable IoT devices is distributed in the same Class B network, whose first 16 bits are the network part of the address. Therefore, a considerable number of Pink bots accumulate after infection, resulting in their IP addresses showing the characteristics of specified Class B distribution. Then, with the help of the fixed P2P communication port (Network Time Protocol) in each Pink bot, the new Pink bot can discover other Pink bots by traversing all IP addresses in the several specified Class B networks. Our reverse analysis of Pink binaries reveals that the infected Pink bots tend to firstly launch a peer probe request to four Class B networks, namely 114.25.0.0/16, 36.227.0.0/16, 59.115.0.0/16, and 1.224.0.0/16, with the content '1C 00 00 00' under the intension to make the connections with other Pink bots.

Central Command and Control. Another approach attackers use is to distribute config files through a centralized command-and-control server (cnc.pi-nklander.com) hard-coded in several Pink binaries. Therefore, it is accessible to block the centralized communication scheme by blocking the resolution of the domain name.

Pink Bot. The entire Pink botnet composes of various vulnerable fiber routers based on MIPS architecture. These compromised IoT devices, namely the Pink bot, play the core functional role in the botnet. Its functions can be summarized as follows: (1) As a vital component of the P2P network, it leverages the B-segment mechanism to discover other Pink bots and maintains a neighbor list to disseminate command configuration files issued by the Botmaster hierarchically.

(2) As an executor of a network attack, the Pink bot will follow the instructions to respond to the target with specified attacks like DoS, HTTP message injection, etc. (3) Distinct from the conventional IoT botnet, the Pink bot can flash the original firmware of the fiber router to achieve long-term persistence.

2.2   Pink Operation

Although Pink bot has updated several versions since the first discovery, its overall function and operation mechanism have not been changed significantly. In this section, we conduct a reverse analysis of a sample captured in November 2021 to illustrate the working mechanism of the Pink botnet. We split its behavior chain into three stages: infection, initialization, and maintenance.

Infection. Unlike the propagation method of worm-like IoT botnet Mirai [11], the Pink botnet adopts a novel infection method, namely centralized target scanning. During the infection phase, the Pink botnet controller will look for new targets to infect. First, it will utilize the B-segment mechanism to enumerate all IP addresses and scan the potential new target for specific vulnerabilities. The operation is because many identical IoT devices are distributed in the same Class-B IP and have the same vulnerabilities to exploitation by the attacker. The apparent feature can help the botnet controller quickly discover potential vulnerable IoT devices. Once the potential new target with vulnerabilities is located, the controller will plant the new malicious sample on the new target. In this way, Pink's botnet proliferates and continues to expand. For instance, the attacker leverages the vulnerability originating from misconfiguration in a TCP-17998 control service to gain control of the relevant various fiber routers.

Initialization. The initialization stage aims to join the entire Pink botnet and synchronize the latest configuration file. Pink is an IoT botnet with hybrid network topology, including central C&C and P2P. Therefore, when a Pink sample is planted on a vulnerable IoT device, it will attempt to discover other bots in the P2P network and communicate with the central C&C server in its first execution. Firstly, The Pink bot binds port number 123, commonly used by the NTP service, to communicate with other bots. Subsequently, it can launch various customized probe requests to many IP addresses enumerated from four B-segment addresses ("114.25.0.0/16", "36.227.0.0/16", "59.115.0.–0/16", "1.224.0.0/16") until discovering other active Pink bots and initialize a Pink bot neighborhood table. Simultaneously, through static reverse analysis of Pink samples, we find that the new Pink bot will send a request to the specified central C&C server to acquire the configuration file in the initial stage.

Maintenance. When the attacker needs the botnet to perform specific actions, it only needs to send a customized configuration file with the latest instruction information to any Pink bot through the P2P network or central C&C server.

Table 1. Description of the specified fields in a config file.

Field	Description
verify	Timestamp when the command is issued
cncip/port	Specified IP and port of the latest centralized server
dlc/dl	Pink binary download URL and its Hash check value
sd0/sdp0	Specified DNS server address to resolve a DNS query
srvk	Public key content (base64 encoding) of centralized server
pxy	Specified proxy option

Table 1 presents the required fields in the configuration file. After completing the initialization phase task, the Pink bot needs to maintain communication with other bots to update the neighbor bots table and continuously obtain the new configuration files to take corresponding actions.

2.3   Comparison of IoT Botnets

Table 2. Comparison of IoT botnets

Botnet	Start	Detection[a]	C&C	Protocol	Size	Persistence[b]	Attack[c]
Mirai	2016	E	Centralized	IRC	>100k	W	>1
Bashlite	2014	E	Centralized	IRC	>50k	W	>1
Hajime	2016	M	Decentralized	DHT	>1000k	M	1
Mozi	2019	M	Decentralized	DHT	>1000k	M	2
Pink	2019	C	Hybrid	NTP	>1500k	S	4

[a] Detection indicates the difficulty of distinguish the C&C traffic of different IoT botnet from the abnormal traffic. (E:Easy, M:Moderate, C:Challenging)
[b] Persistence represents the survivability of a Pink bot in a infected IoT device. (W:Weak, M:Medium, S:Strong)
[c] Attacks describe the attack modules in the sample.

In recent years, more and more vulnerable IoT devices have been compromised by various IoT botnets to take network attacks. Table 2 compares Pink and other IoT botnets from seven aspects. Compared with the four widely spread existing IoT botnets, the Pink botnet has a more significant size, more sophisticated C&C channel, more attack modules, more robust scalability, and more complete countermeasures with vendors. The details can be summarized as follows: (1) Although Pink emerged later than other IoT botnets, the number of IoT devices infected by Pink is much higher than other IoT botnets, exceeding 1.5 million. (2) Pink is the first IoT botnet with centralized and decentralized C&C channels. This hybrid network topology can not only make up for the defect of a single point of failure but also have the characteristics of real-time command distribution. (3) From the life cycle perspective, the lifetime of a Pink bot is much longer than that of other IoT botnet nodes; the analysis of Pink binaries reveals that it may be related to the ability that the Pink bot can flash the original firmware of IoT devices and bind UDP 123 port to trick some users into treating them as a standard NTP service to enhance concealment; (4) From the defense perspective, the Pink bot presents multiple countermeasures to security researchers' mitigation solutions; for instance, the attacker issues the commands to shut down the service through a centralized C&C server, making the vendor unable to patch the compromised IoT devices.

3   Measurement Method

In this section, we propose an active scanning method to infiltrate and measure the entire Pink botnet.

3.1   Active Scanning Method

In bot-scale detection of Pink botnet, we conducted a similar breadth-first search based on the B-segment mechanism, aiming to obtain unknown Pink bots in hierarchical order. Based on the principles and characteristics of the Pink, we figured out that the new Pink bot can join the Pink botnet through the built-in eight startup B-segment addresses, as shown in Table 3.

Table 3. Eight startup B-segment IP addresses hard-coded in the Pink samples

B-segment address	Ports	B-segment address	Ports
114.25.0.0/16	123	61.230.0.0/16	123
36.227.0.0/16	123	110.16.0.0/16	123
59.115.0.0/16	123	118.41.0.0/16	123
1.224.0.0/16	123	211.205.0.0/16	123

The execution flow of our active scanning method is composed of the following three stages. First, we need to initialize a probing table with the above B-segment addresses to enumerate all potential IP addresses to be scanned. After that, our detection bots will construct a customized UDP packet with the payload '1C 00 00 00' and send them to the targets above. Since the sent packets follow the Pink communication pattern, the IP addresses of our detection bots will be added to the Pink bot's P2P communication table and even propagated to other Pink bots. Consequently, there is a certain probability that our probe bots can acquire access packets from other unknown bots in the Pink. To increase the likelihood, we need to send customized packets to as many Pink bots as possible above. At this point, we are unsure whether the access to our detection bots is from the real Pink bots. Then, our detection bots will attempt to parse the received data according to the principle of processing messages by Pink bots. If the target bot returns a config file, it is a real Pink bot, and our detection bots can add the resolved B-segment addresses to the probing table in Step (1) for further processing. If the target bot returns a Network Time Protocol (NTP) packet, it suggests the message is from a standard NTP server.

Algorithm 1. Pink Bot Recognition through Received Messages

Input: *Received_message*: Bytes sent to our measurement program;
Output: *Pink_bot_tag*: The tag represents whether the message's source; *Config_file*:
Parse the config file from the received message;

1: **if** $NTP(Received\_message) == True$ **then**
2:    // The source sending the messages is a NTP server.
3:    Pink_bot_tag=False;
4:    return;
5: **end if**
6: **if** $Received\_message.Payload ==' 0000001D'$ **then**
7:    // The source sending the messages is a Pink bot without C&C server.
8:    Pink_bot_tag=True;
9:    return;
10: **end if**
11: **if** $Is\_Pink(Received\_message) == True$ **then**
12:    // extract the config file if the received message belongs to Pink
13:    Config_file=Pink_decrypt(Received_message);
14:    Pink_bot_tag=True;
15: **end if**

We utilize Algorithm 1 to present how to identify the packets related to the Pink bots from the response packets, including NTP and Pink communication packets, respectively. Initially, the first step is to determine the messages of NTP servers through the timestamp feature (line 1). From the reverse analysis of several Pink binary samples, we know that a Pink bot's response message depends on whether it has obtained the C&C server info when receiving a customized UDP packet with content '1C 00 00 00'. If the target bot does not have C&C information, it will respond with '1D 00 00 00'. When the target bot has already gotten the C&C information, it replies with the signature of the C&C data and the corresponding config file. Therefore, we use two branches to deal with the response message from a Pink bot. One is to process the message with payload '1D 00 00 00', which indicates that the Pink sender bot doesn't have any C&C server info (line 6). The other is to extract the config file from the received message and parse the latest instruction info.

3.2 Method Evaluation

According to the key metrics for botnet structures [6], we define two evaluation metrics, namely effectiveness ratio and bots' daily increment, to discuss the rationality of the active scanning method. The former metric is used to verify the effectiveness of the active scanning method, and the latter is applied to present that our approach can adapt to the change in Pink botnet's scale.

Effectiveness. We distinguish the real Pink bot through the feature of whether the communication payload contains a config file. If the received content includes a config file, it can be considered that the bot sending this message is a real Pink bot. We introduce a critical metric *effectiveness ratio*, which depicts the

Fig. 2. Effectiveness ratio.

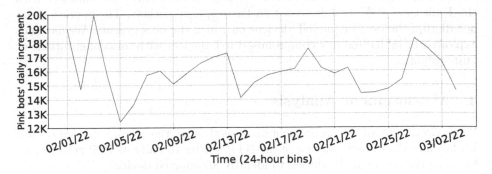

Fig. 3. New Pink bots.

proportion of real captured Pink bots to all collected nodes per day. It is denoted as V_i and can be calculated as follow:

$$V_i = \frac{\Psi(i)}{\Pi(i)} \tag{1}$$

The number i specifies a date, such as 2022-02-14. In the equation, $\Pi(i)$ describes the total number of captured bots perday and $\Psi(i)$ represents the number of real bots filtered per day from $\Pi(i)$. Based on the raw packet data collected by the active scanning method, we calculate the metric V_i from Feb 22, 2022, to Mar 9, 2022, as shown in Fig. 2. Obviously, all days' effectiveness ratio exceeds 0.998, suggesting that our method can collect Pink bots effectively. It should be noted that the tiny gap from 100% represents the proportion of collected standard NTP service, and this phenomenon cannot affect measurement results.

Bot's Daily Increment. Figure 3 shows the number of new Pink bots captured daily by the active scanning method. We cannot guarantee 100% coverage of all Pink bots because some pink bots are on the periphery or even isolated. However, We reckon that the following reasons account for why the detected bots occupy most of the Pink network. First, the number of B-segment addresses to which the Pink bots belong tends to be stable, with almost no new additions. Secondly, the number of new Pink bots added each day is relatively stable with no significant fluctuation.

The prototype system of our active scanning method is deployed in twenty Virtual Private Servers (VPS), and we report measurements from January 31, 2022, to April 13, 2022. Throughout our active measurement results, we collected 1,542,558 unique IP addresses, most of which are located in regions like China and South Korea. We present a detailed analysis of the Pink botnet's measurement in Sect. 4.

3.3 Ethical Considerations

In the scope of our study, the active scanning method only communicates with the Pink bots' P2P module to obtain the response packets. The operations do not disrupt the bots or the IoT devices on which the bots execute. We have not exploited or infiltrated any compromised IoT devices with misconfigurations or vulnerabilities.

4 Measurement Analysis

We perform a detailed measurement analysis through the acquired bot info about Pink. Since Pink makes full use of the NTP service to build its P2P network, we leverage the detected IP address to identify an infected device.

4.1 One-Day Monitoring

Figure 4 presents the number of online and new bots we capture in each 5-minute interval over a day (02/28/22). The reason why we choose this date is that our scanning system acquires the highest number of online bots and scanning results remain relatively stable all day.

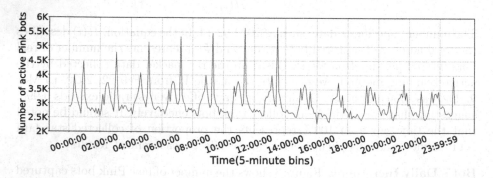

Fig. 4. The number of online Pink bots.

Figure 4 shows that the number of distinct bots presents a periodic cycle state and is maintained at about 2500 to 5000 every 5 min. We attribute this

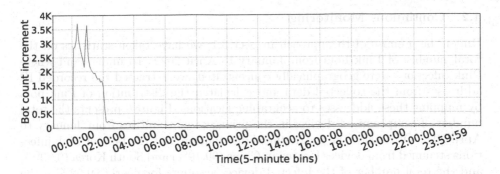

Fig. 5. The number of new Pink bots.

phenomenon to the fact that our prototype system needs to scan the Pink bots table cyclically to determine whether the bot is online. It takes about an hour to complete a full scan. And each small wave peak in Fig. 4 is that our scanning method obtains new reachable bots (unknown Pink bots). Figure 5 presents the change in the number of new Pink bots acquired every 5 min. It reveals that the new Pink bots count during the first period increases rapidly, and when the increment reaches the peak, it drops quickly. Subsequently, the detected increment has gradually stabilized between 50 and 100. If we regard Pink networks as a graph, the area we acquire within two hours may only be the densest and the most accessible part. As for the Pink bots on the periphery or temporarily isolated, we need to continuously scan the obtained Pink bots to collect the message from the remaining unknown Pink bots as much as possible. The smooth increment in the latter phase of Fig. 5 reveals the number of hard-to-scan bots in the Pink.

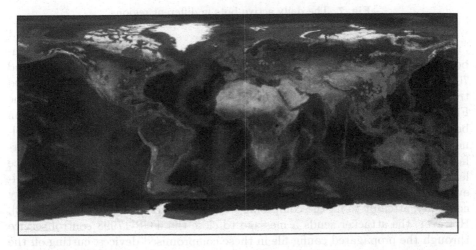

Fig. 6. The geographical distribution of infected devices.

4.2 Continuous Monitoring

Under the premise of th approach in Sect. 3.1, we have taken statistics on the total number of Pink bots from January to April 2022. To understand where Pink infections were geographically concentrated, we extracted the recorded IP addresses from the collected data and calculated the distribution of Pink bots by mapping these addresses to geographic locations. Figure 6 presents the total number of compromised devices in the primary two countries from January to April 2022. Obviously, the geographical distribution that the bulk of Pink infections stemmed from devices located in China (99.10%) and South Korea (0.89%), and the total number of the infected devices accounts for nearly 99.99% in the above two countries. The remaining infection devices in the other countries do not even exceed 0.01%, far less than the number of compromised devices in China and South Korea. Compared with most bots infected by Mozi botnet are diverse and widely distributed worldwide, the primary target devices of Pink infection are fiber routers distributed in China. It suggests that the author of Pink botnet was concerned about potential avenues in China when it was designed.

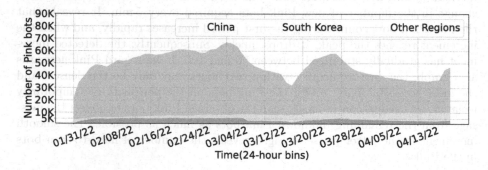

Fig. 7. The daily active bots in different regions.

Figure 7 shows the number of active Pink bots in different regions. The number of active Pink bots collected per day in China is around stable 30K and 70K. It is worth noting that Fig. 7 shows a slow recovery after a clear downward trend in the number of active Pink bots around mid-March 2022. We combine Fig. 5 to track Pink and attribute this phenomenon to the fierce competition between attackers and security researchers for compromised devices. The vulnerability under attack originated from a TCP-17998 control service, an interface for vendors to operate the machines. Since misconfiguration of the service leads to open access in the public network, the attacker gains control of the relevant fiber routers. Then, device vendors, with the assistance of a cybersecurity company, attempt to fix the compromised devices through the above service [3]. However, the attacker sends a message to close the TCP-17998 control service through the propagated config file in these compromised devices, cutting off the vendor's control over the devices. Finally, the only option left for the vendor is to physically access the fiber router, disassemble the debugging interface or replace the unit. And the number of active Pink bots detected in our two figures reflects the intensity of the war during the period.

4.3 Bot Analysis

Birth and Death. We conduct an in-depth tracking and statistical analysis of Pink in Sect. 4.1 and Sect. 4.2. Figure 8 presents the number of births and deaths about Pink bots per day from 3 February 2022 to 2 March 2022. The births imply the new Pink bots are obtained every day, and deaths mean that known Pink bots are not active now (the infected devices have been repaired by vendors or have been offline due to network reasons). We can find that the number of Pink bots generated accounts for a quarter of the total detected online bots per day in the botnet, with the number of extinguished Pink bots gradually increasing. It suggests that the entire Pink botnet is in a significant dynamic change. During the measurement period, the number of Pink's births just started to present a downward trend and remained stable, while the number of deaths offered a growth trend. The reason is that vendors and the cybersecurity community have been working on methods to govern the Pink botnet. With the efforts of various vendors, we firmly believe that the number of Pink's deaths will increase significantly, and Pinks' births will gradually decrease.

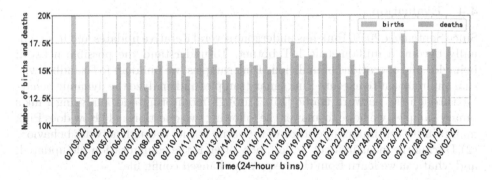

Fig. 8. The number of birth and death bots in Pink botnet for a day.

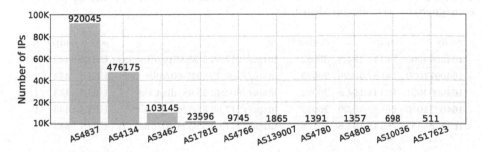

Fig. 9. Top ten ASes ranked based on the number of Pink bot infected IP addresses.

Bot ASes Distribution. These observations stemmed from 1,542,558 distinct IP addresses located across 15 Autonomous Systems (ASes) spanning several regions between January 2022 and April 2022. As already mentioned, we utilize MaxMind's[1] GeoLite database to explore the geographic distribution of collected Pink IP addresses and find that 99% of them are located in China. It suggests that China is the region most affected by this botnet. During the initial execution of a new Pink bot, it constantly scans various IP addresses from B-segment. It then attempts to establish connections with other compromised bots in the Pink P2P botnet. As shown in Fig. 9, we map millions of compromised devices' IPs to their corresponding Autonomous Systems (ASes). It reveals that 99% of the infected IPs in our collected data only reside in the top three ASes, mainly in China. Evidently, the remaining 1% of Pink bots are spread sporadically over random Ases spanning 15 regions. In conclusion, we can conclude the two interesting findings about the Pink botnet. (1) The whole Pink botnet is primarily composed of a single type of fiber router located in China, suggesting that the attacker has a perfect understanding of the exploit and distribution of these embedded devices. (2) The IP addresses of the compromised devices exhibit an aggregated B-segment distribution feature, allowing attackers to build an advanced P2P IoT botnet through enumerating and probing various IP addresses in the B-segment table.

4.4   Evaluation

Since September 2019, Pink has undergone several iterative updates and has gradually become a million-scale IoT botnet. To understand the possible network behavior and operations of malicious Pink samples, we build an IoT sandbox virtual environment to execute Pink binary samples and analyze the dynamic behavior through the network traffic [15]. Through monitoring and analyzing Pink's binary samples, we hope to answer the following two questions: (1) How does Pink maintain the continuous operation of the entire botnet through network behavior? (2) During the measurement period, how often is the configuration file updated, and what can we learn from the frequently changed config file?

Table 4. Several key fields in the common captured config file (URL1–https://gitee. com/ghy8/bh/raw/master/dlist.txt)

verify	cncip1	cncport1	dl	sd0	sdp0	pxy
1646064005	78.141.194.8	35662	http://217.69.5.95:8010/dlist.txt	URL1	443	1
1640971039	140.82.40.29	26022	http://209.250.247.60/dlist.txt	URL1	443	1
1646064001	78.141.194.8	26022	http://80.240.25.98/dlist.txt	URL1	443	1
1640971040	140.82.40.29	26022	http://217.69.5.95/dlist.txt	URL1	443	1
1648784552	78.141.194.8	35778	http://217.69.5.95:8010/dlist.txt	URL1	443	1

---

[1] MaxMind: http://www.maxmind.com/en/home.

Communication Traffic and Network Behavior. We leverage IoTPoT to execute several prevalent Pink binaries and collect these samples' communication data [15]. As described in Sect. 2.1, Pink employs three communication modes to propagate the config file in the botnet. Table 5 presents the proportion of communication protocol packets in a Pink sample. From the Table, we can learn that more than 85% of the communication behavior belongs to UDP protocol, and only less than 15% is TCP protocol. The reason is that the Pink botnet primarily constructs a P2P botnet through a customized UDP protocol (78.96%) to maintain communication among millions of bots. From the traffic analysis results, we figured out that Pink bots were attempting to send customized UDP packets to many enumerated IPs from B-segment addresses and waiting for the responses. Since there must be a small number of Pink bots addresses in the B-segment, traversing the IPs makes it bound to find several of them. Then the bot can discover other active Pink bots and join the entire botnet. TCP-based P2P and C&C communication are the other primary methods of acquiring config files. It is worth noting that the TCP connections (5.69%) among Pink bots depend on whether the P2P connections based on UDP protocol have been established, indicating that UDP-based P2P connections dominate the entire botnet communication. As for the centralized C&C communication, we can find that the server address that the Pink sample communicated with has become invalid, suggesting that updating config files through a centralized server is unreliable. In summary, the above three network behavior of Pink bots is to acquire config files from other Pink bots or centralized server.

Table 5. Distribution of Pink Communication Protocol. (UDP, User Datagram Protocol; TCP, Transmission Control Protocol; C&C, Command and Control Private Protocol;)

Protocol	Packets	Proportion
P2P-UDP	43141	78.96%
P2P-TCP	3109	5.69%
DNS	3494	6.4%
C&C	4891	8.95%

Configuration Analysis. The config file dominates the update of binary samples and the delivery of commands in the entire Pink botnet. Therefore, the analysis of config file updates is critical to understanding the function of the entire Pink botnet. As described in Sect. 2.1, we know that several fields (cncip1, cncporta, dl, and sd0) are required during the propagation of the configuration file in the Pink botnet. Table 4 presents several key fields in the prevalent config file collected during the measurement period. The dl field provided a specified download URL of the sample update, and we only captured three changes during the measurement period. It is worth noting that the download address of this field is prone to invalidation. We can speculate that the main reason is that the download server may have been countered by security researchers or shut down by attackers.

5 Related Work

Over the last decade, attacks from IoT botnets and their variants gradually became the primary threat to IoT devices [18]. This phenomenon attracted lots of attention from the security community, focusing on the measurement, analysis, mitigation, and disruption of IoT botnets [20]. In 2017, Antonakakis et al. leveraged a diverse set of vantage points, including network telescope probes, Internet-wide banner scans, IoT honeypots, command and control (C&C) milkers, DNS traces, and logs provided by attack victims, to conduct a broad study of the Mirai botnet [4]. It was the first formal step to studying and understanding IoT botnet comprehensively. However, these measurement methods had limited effect on understanding and analyzing decentralized P2P IoT botnets.

Other closely related IoT botnets to Pink were the widely studied Hajime [7, 9] and Mozi [1,2,19]. Both used an existing Kademlia-based DHT to distribute C&C information, and similar active DHT measurements were performed to track the above P2P IoT botnets. According to Hajime's DHT design, Herwig et al. provided over a year of retrospective measurement analysis of Hajime, including its size, its C&C infrastructure, its evolution, and the compromised IoT devices [8]. Tengfei et al. also measured the quick spread of the Mozi botnet through a similar breadth-first search based on the topological structure of the DHT network [19]. Obviously, the detection method of the two studies above was effective for measuring P2P IoT botnets based on the DHT OVERNET network but was not suitable for the non-DHT P2P IoT botnet like Pink; we extend it in several key ways.

First, Pink represents a step in the evolution of the P2P IoT botnet in that it leverages the B-segment mechanism (described in Sect. 2.1) instead of the traditional DHT method to build its sophisticated P2P C&C infrastructure. To obtain the infrastructure, we leverage Pink's P2P design to infiltrate the entire botnet and attract messages from other unknown Pink bots. Second, Pink often updates the payloads and incorporates new attack vectors. Using the collected data, we analyze Mozi bots' geographical dispersion and explore the impact of payload updates on the botnet size, location, and composition. Finally, intending to mitigate the attacks from Pink, we summarize its network and distribution features to speculate the possible reasons why the Pink botnet has been active since 2020.

The most immediately related prior works were the studies of the Pink botnet performed by 360 Netlab [3], NSFOCUS [17], and Cyware [5] in the wake of the Pink discovery. The previous studies primarily involved short-term P2P network measurements and reverse engineering of botnet payloads. By comparison, we achieve more prolonged and more comprehensive studies of Pink, allowing us to observe the distribution of bots, the lifetime of various bots, and the impact of payload updates on the botnet.

6   Conclusion

The Pink botnet was first discovered and analyzed by 360 Netlab in January 2020 and has been developed for nearly two years [3]. During this period, we have witnessed its peak development and compromised over 1.6 million devices, most of which are located in China. Pink adopts a novel P2P network establishment mechanism, which needs to brute force the IP addresses in several specified Class B IP addresses. Compared with the previous mechanism based on the public DHT service, it can accelerate the establishment of a P2P network and make it challenging to track the entire Pink botnet, enhancing the hidden ability. Throughout the in-depth analysis of the communication protocol of Pink bots, we propose an active scanning method to simulate some nodes that can communicate with Pink bots to attract responses from other unknown Pink bots. By continuously monitoring the online bots and obtaining more unknown bots, we conduct a comprehensive analysis of Pink's emergency and growth, geographical distribution, the composition of communication data, and the commands in the configuration file. We hope these findings can serve as an alarm for vendors and security researchers to improve the patching of vulnerable IoT devices.

Acknowledgment. We thank the anonymous reviewers for their insightful comments. This work is supported by The National Key Research and Development Program of China (No. 2019YFB1005201, No. 2019YFB1005203 and No. 2019YFB1005205).

References

1. Alex, T., Hui, W., Genshen, Y.: Mozi is dead and the poison remains (2021). https://blog.netlab.360.com/the_death_of_mozi_cn/
2. Turing, A., Wang, H.: Mozi, another botnet using DHT (2019). https://blog.netlab.360.com/mozi-another-botnet-using-dht/
3. Turing, A., Wang, H.: Pink, a botnet that competed with the vendor to control the massive infected devices (2021). https://blog.netlab.360.com/pink-en/
4. Antonakakis, M., et al.: Understanding the MIRAI botnet. In: 26th USENIX security symposium (USENIX Security 2017) (2017)
5. Cyware: Experts disclose pink botnet amidst multiple DDoS alerts (2021). https://cyware.com/news/experts-disclose-pink-botnet-amidst-multiple-ddos-alerts-662e d0c4
6. Dagon, D., Gu, G., Lee, C.P., Lee, W.: A taxonomy of botnet structures. In: Twenty-Third Annual Computer Security Applications Conference (ACSAC 2007), pp. 325–339. IEEE (2007)
7. Edwards, S., Profetis, I.: Hajime: analysis of a decentralized internet worm for IoT devices. In: Rapidity Networks, Security Research Group, Technical report (2016)
8. Herwig, S., Harvey, K., Hughey, G., Roberts, R., Levin, D.: Measurement and analysis of Hajime, a peer-to-peer IoT botnet. In: Network and Distributed System Security (NDSS) Symposium (2019)
9. Van Der wiel, J., Vicente Diaz, Y.N.: Hajime, the mysterious evolving botnet (2017). https://securelist.com/hajime-the-mysterious-evolving-botnet/78160/

10. Kalliamvakou, E., Gousios, G., Blincoe, K., Singer, L., German, D.M., Damian, D.: The promises and perils of mining github. In: Proceedings of the 11th Working Conference on Mining Software Repositories, pp. 92–101 (2014)
11. Kambourakis, G., Kolias, C., Stavrou, A.: The MIRAI botnet and the IoT zombie armies. In: IEEE Military Communications Conference (MILCOM) (2017)
12. Lueth, K.L.: State of the IoT 2020: 12 billion IoT connections, surpassing non-IoT for the first time (2020). https://iot-analytics.com/state-of-the-iot-2020-12-billion-iot-connections-surpassing-non-iot-for-the-first-time/
13. Marzano, A., et al.: The evolution of bashlite and Mirai IoT botnets. In: 2018 IEEE Symposium on Computers and Communications (ISCC), pp. 00813–00818. IEEE (2018)
14. Meulen, R.v.d.: Gartner says 8.4 billion connected "things" will be in use in 2017 up 31 percent from 2016. In: Gartner. Letzte Aktualisierung (2017)
15. Pa, Y.M.P., Suzuki, S., Yoshioka, K., Matsumoto, T., Kasama, T., Rossow, C.: IoTpot: a novel honeypot for revealing current IoT threats. J. Inf. Process. 24(3), 522–533 (2016)
16. Sidhu, J.: SysCoin: a peer-to-peer electronic cash system with blockchain-based services for e-business. In: 2017 26th International Conference on Computer Communication and Networks (ICCCN), pp. 1–6. IEEE (2017)
17. Team, C.: Experts disclose pink botnet amidst multiple DDoS alerts (2021). https://cyberintelmag.com/malware-viruses/pink-botnet-malware-infected-more-than-1-6-million-devices-according-to-researchers/
18. Trendmicro: IoT botnet (2016). https://www.trendmicro.com/vinfo/us/security/definition/iot-botnet
19. Tu, T.F., Qin, J.W., Zhang, H., Chen, M., Xu, T., Huang, Y.: A comprehensive study of mozi botnet. Int. J. Intell. Syst. (2022)
20. Vu, S.N.T., Stege, M., El-Habr, P.I., Bang, J., Dragoni, N.: A survey on botnets: incentives, evolution, detection and current trends. Future Internet (2021)

VT-GAT: A Novel VPN Encrypted Traffic Classification Model Based on Graph Attention Neural Network

Hongbo Xu[1,2], Shuhao Li[1,2], Zhenyu Cheng[1(✉)], Rui Qin[1], Jiang Xie[1,2], and Peishuai Sun[1,2]

[1] Institute of Information Engineering, Chinese Academy of Sciences, Beijing 100093, China
{xuhongbo,lishuhao,chengzhenyu,qinrui,xiejiang,sunpeishuai}@iie.ac.cn
[2] School of Cyber Security, University of Chinese Academy of Sciences, Beijing 100049, China

Abstract. Virtual Private Network (VPN) technology is now widely used in various scenarios such as telecommuting. The importance of VPN traffic identification for network security and management has increased significantly with the development of proxy technology. Unlike other tasks such as application classification, VPN traffic has only one flow problem. In addition, the development of encryption technology brings new challenges to VPN traffic identification.

This paper proposes VT-GAT, a VPN traffic graph classification model based on Graph Attention Networks (GAT), to solve the above problems. Compared with existing VPN encrypted traffic classification techniques, VT-GAT solves the problem that previous techniques ignore the graph connectivity information contained in traffic. VT-GAT first constructs traffic behavior graphs by characterizing raw traffic data at packet and flow levels. Then it combines graph neural networks and attention mechanisms to extract behavioral features in the traffic graph data automatically. Extensive experimental results on the Datacon21 dataset show that VT-GAT can achieve over 99% in all classification metrics. Compared to existing machine learning and deep learning methods, VT-GAT improves F1-Score by about 3.02%–63.55%. In addition, VT-GAT maintains good robustness when the number of classification categories varies. These results demonstrate the usefulness of VT-GAT in the VPN traffic classification.

Keywords: Traffic classification · VPN · Encrypted traffic · Graph attention networks · Graph classification

1 Introduction

Virtual private network (VPN), a type of encrypted communication technology, is now commonly used in various scenarios such as identity concealment, censorship avoidance, and telecommuting. Therefore, it is often used by criminals

H. Gao et al. (Eds.): CollaborateCom 2022, LNICST 461, pp. 437–456, 2022.
https://doi.org/10.1007/978-3-031-24386-8_24

to engage in pornography, network intrusion, data theft, and other illegal activities. Achieving accurate VPN traffic classification is essential to preventing and tracking cybercrime incidents.

In the early days, Deep Packet Inspection (DPI) method could obtain high accuracy by examining packets. However, with the popularity of encryption technology, traffic content becomes unresolvable, which leads to DPI methods becoming unusable. Soon after, the concept of flow is proposed. Packets with the same quintuple information (source IP, source port, destination IP, destination port, and IP protocol) are defined as a flow. Most of the existing encrypted traffic classification techniques cut the traffic at packet or flow level [1] and then use machine learning algorithms or deep learning algorithms to automatically learn the extracted traffic features, which can often achieve good results. However, when users use VPN applications for identity obfuscation, the number of flows extracted from the traffic will drop dramatically. As shown in Fig. 1, the server-side IP address and port of the packet sent by the user are replaced by the VPN application. Therefore, VPN traffic cannot be split into multiple flows by server IP address and port. This phenomenon is known as the only one flow problem [2]. Only one flow problem can significantly reduce the extractable traffic features, thus severely affecting the performance of existing traffic classification techniques.

Finding practical and robust features is a feasible way to solve the single-flow problem. We note that previous works mainly focused on the spatio-temporal features of traffic. Moreover, the graph connectivity behavioral features implied by the traffic are generally ignored. Using only traditional deep learning methods does not extract the connection behavior features of the flows quickly and effectively from the existing features. Therefore, In this paper, we propose VT-GAT, a graph neural network model that fuses graph behavior features and spatio-temporal traffic features to address the above problems. Firstly, we extract traditional spatio-temporal traffic features and traffic behavior graph features from the original traffic. We then use graph attention networks (GAT) [3] to learn the combined features automatically. Compared with existing techniques, VT-GAT enriches the traffic features by introducing traffic behavior graph information. We conduct extensive comparison experiments between our model and other models on the Datacon21 dataset to demonstrate the effectiveness of VT-GAT.

The contributions of this paper are summarized as follows.

1) We present a method for extracting traffic behavior graphs from VPN encrypted traffic. It can transform the traffic classification problem into a graph classification problem. Through experimental validation, this method can effectively improve the model's classification accuracy.
2) We propose the VT-GAT model based on graph attention networks. As far as we know, this is the first model that uses graph neural networks to achieve VPN traffic classification. VT-GAT integrates spatio-temporal features of traffic and graph behavioral features to achieve classification, which makes up for the shortcomings of existing techniques. Furthermore, VT-GAT enhances

the robustness of the model by aggregating the features of neighboring nodes based on the graph attention mechanism.

3) We present a traffic graph dataset[1] suitable for VPN encrypted traffic classification. Moreover, we implement a prototype system based on the VT-GAT model and conduct experiments on the recently released dataset Datacon21. The experimental results show that VT-GAT achieves the best performance in all evaluation metrics (Accuracy, Recall, Precision, and F1-Score) compared to existing machine learning and deep learning methods.

The rest of the paper is organized as follows. Section 2 presents background and summarises related work on traffic classification. Section 3 describes the construction process of VT-GAT in detail. Section 4 describes the experimental setup and analyzes the experimental results. After a brief discussion in Sect. 5, Sect. 6 concludes the paper.

2   Background and Related Work

2.1   The only One Flow Problem Challenge

As shown in Fig. 1, the VPN application takes over the user's traffic data in the VPN proxy environment. In the traffic captured at the gateway, the destination address of the traffic packets sent by the user is the VPN proxy server instead of the actual destination address. At the VPN proxy server, the actual address of the packet is decrypted. And these traffic packets are then sent by the proxy server to the actual destination address. The VPN proxy is a middleman between the user and the target server. The destination address of all traffic packets sent by the user is the VPN proxy server. This phenomenon is the only one flow problem [2]. As shown in Fig. 2, only one flow problem causes the traffic data captured at the gateway to form a star-shaped network. Flow-based traffic classification methods are severely impacted due to the reduction of classifiable flows. Only one flow problem brings a great challenge to VPN traffic classification.

2.2   Related Work

Network traffic classification techniques have been extensively studied [4]. Based on the chronological order of technology development, we classify the related work on traffic classification into the following three categories.

Methods Based on Rules. Rules-based traffic identification methods focus on identifying traffic by matching feature fields. One of the most commonly used methods is DPI. This method is widely used in traffic classification tasks such as application identification and intrusion detection. The core principle of DPI

---

[1] The dataset can be found at https://anonymous.4open.science/r/VPN_Traffic_Grap h_Dataset-EDA0. Researchers who use the dataset should indicate the source of data by citing this paper.

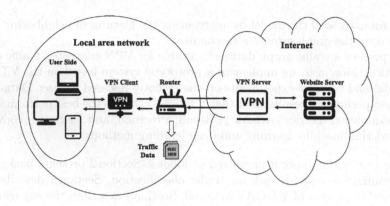

Fig. 1. The only one flow problem challenge

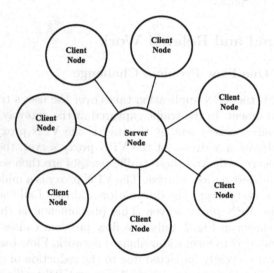

Fig. 2. Star communication network

is to use pattern matching to locate traffic. It does this by searching for specific strings or regular expressions in the content of traffic packets, which relies on the unencrypted transmission of traffic data [5].

In [6], the authors first develop a system called nDPI for protocol classification using packet headers and payloads. This system supports the detection of more than 170 protocols. In [7], the authors propose a pattern language similar to regular expressions to summarize the rules of packet sequences, which is then integrated into the DPI system to enhance its identification capability.

Methods Based on Machine Learning. With the popularity of encryption technology, DPI techniques are no longer suitable for encrypting traffic because they match packet contents based on payload. The popularity of CDN technology has also drastically reduced the accuracy of IP-based and port-based methods. In addition, DPI techniques require constant manual updating of rules to adapt to traffic changes. To solve the above problems, machine learning methods are commonly applied to encrypted traffic classification. After feature extraction and selection, machine learning algorithms can often achieve good classification results.

In [8], the authors convert the number of occurrences of flow-level features (e.g., TCP stream length, SSL/TLS handshake information type, etc.) into frequency distributions. The frequency distribution data extracted from the encrypted traffic is then used to identify applications by incorporating the Random Forest. In [9], by re-labeling the data misjudged by the model through reinforcement learning, the authors improve the classification accuracy of App-Scanner [10]. In [11], the authors propose a more robust feature called the sliding window JS divergence feature. They then use machine learning algorithms (SVM, Random Forest, Bayesian) to learn traditional and newly discovered traffic classification features. In [12], the authors propose a semi-supervised clustering technique FlowPrint. The main principle of Flowprint is to classify network flows based on the correlation of temporal features between flow destinations.

Methods Based on Deep Learning. Machine learning methods can address the shortcomings of rules-based methods and enable the detection of encrypted traffic. However, machine learning methods often rely on expert experience to filter traffic features, and feature selection needs to be updated according to different data. Deep learning has gradually become a research hotspot favored by scholars with its powerful automatic feature extraction capability [13]. Many scholars use deep learning for automatic traffic feature extraction to solve the above problem.

In [14], the authors extract the header bytes of network traffic packets and achieve the accurate real-time traffic classification through a self-attentive mechanism, thus optimizing the feature extraction steps. In [15], the authors combine convolutional auto-encoding (CAE) and convolutional neural network (CNN) to classify encrypted traffic. In [1], the authors apply LSTM and CNN to learn traffic's temporal and spatial features by combining packet-level and flow-level features, respectively. Chen et al. [2] propose a novel method called AI-FlowDet. It leverages the CNN model to find behavior change points in traffic data.

Deep learning methods have achieved good results in some tasks such as application classification, intrusion detection, etc. Unfortunately, the above work lacks a targeted design for VPN traffic. There is still much room for improvement in classification effectiveness for VPN traffic due to the only one flow problem.

In summary, with the development of encryption technology and the existence of only one flow problem, existing techniques cannot meet the VPN encrypted traffic classification requirements. We note that existing techniques focus only on the traffic's spatio-temporal features while ignoring the traffic's graph interaction behavior features. Moreover, extracting graph interaction behavior features can help improve the classification performance of VPN traffic. Therefore, we propose VT-GAT, a VPN encrypted traffic classification method that combines spatio-temporal features of traffic and graph interaction behavior features.

3   Methodology

In this section, we introduce the construction method of VT-GAT. First, we introduce the method of constructing traffic behavior graphs from the original traffic. Then we briefly describe the basic principles of graph neural networks and graph attention networks. Finally, we show the overall structure of VT-GAT.

3.1   Traffic Behavior Graph Construction

Extraction of Node Features. Flow is one of the commonly used concepts in traffic classification. It comprises a sequence of packets with the same IP quintet characteristics (source IP, source port, destination IP, destination port, and protocol). The interval between consecutive packets in a flow is less than a fixed threshold, e.g., 10s. We obtain the node features of the traffic graph at the flow level. First, we use a combination of IP addresses and application ports to identify nodes uniquely. Then, we use CICFlowMeter [16,17] to extract flow level features. For each network flow, the source and destination addresses are determined based on the transmission direction of its first packet. After removing irrelevant information such as IP addresses and ports, we retain seventy-seven-dimensional features, which can be classified into the following four categories.

- Aggregate features: These features are the overall features of traffic obtained in network flows, including total duration, the total number of packets, total packet length, etc.
- Time features: These features mainly contain original and statistical features associated with time, including the average time between packets sent, the total time between packets sent, etc.
- Statistical features: These features are obtained from statistics based on packet size (excluding aggregation features), including the number of upstream packets per second, packet length mean value, packet length standard deviation, etc.
- Content features: These features are the features of packet content fields, including the number of FIN packets, the number of SYN packets, the number of ACK packets, etc.

The details of the extracted features are shown in Table 1. The flow ID identifies these features. Specifically, for a particular node p, its node features are equal to the average of all the associated flow features. We perform Min-Max normalization on the node features to accelerate the model training convergence. After normalization, all data are converted to float type data in the range 0–1.

Table 1. Flow-level features

Index	Name	Attributes	Direction	Category
1	Flow duration	–	All	Aggregated features
2–3	Total Packet	–	Fwd, Bwd	Aggregated features
4–5	Total Length of Packet	–	Fwd, Bwd	Aggregated features
6–7	Header Length	–	Fwd, Bwd	Aggregated features
8	Down/Up Ratio	–	All	Aggregated features
9	Average Packet Size	–	All	Aggregated features
10–11	Init Win bytes	–	Fwd, Bwd	Aggregated features
12–13	PSH Flags	–	Fwd, Bwd	Content features
14–15	URG Flags	–	Fwd, Bwd	Content features
16–23	Flag Count	FIN, SYN, RST, PSH, ACK, URG, CWR, ECE	All	Content features
24	Protocol	–	All v	Content features
25–28	Flow IAT	Max, Min, Mean, Std	Fwd, Bwd, All	Temporal features
29–38	IAT	Max, Min, Mean, Std, Sum	Fwd, Bwd, All	Temporal features
39–42	Active	Max, Min, Mean, Std	All	Temporal features
43–46	Idle	Max, Min, Mean, Std	All	Temporal features
47–54	Packet Length	Max, Min, Mean, Std	Fwd, Bwd, All	Statistical features
55	Flow Bytes/s	–	All	Statistical features
56	Flow Packets/s	–	All	Statistical features
57–58	Packets/s	–	Fwd,Bwd	Statistical features
59–63	Packet Length	Max,Min, Mean, Std, Variance	All	Statistical features
64–65	Segment Size	Avg	Fwd, Bwd	Statistical features
66–67	Bytes/Bulk	Avg	Fwd, Bwd	Statistical features
68–69	Packet/Bulk	Avg	Fwd, Bwd	Statistical features
70–71	Bulk Rate	Avg	Fwd, Bwd	Statistical features
72–73	Subflow Packets	–	Fwd, Bwd	Statistical features
74–75	Subflow Bytes	–	Fwd, Bwd	Statistical features
76	Act Data Pkts	-	Fwd	Statistical features
77	Seg Size	Min	Fwd	Statistical features

Edge Construction Method. To extract graph structure features more comprehensively, we use a sliding window approach to sample the graph data. Within each traffic sliding window, we count the number of packet connections between any two nodes. Next, an edge is constructed between the nodes with more than one connection. VT-GAT automatically learns the weights between different nodes through the attention mechanism. Thus the weights of all edges are set to be equal. The combined edge data and node data are the corresponding traffic graph data. We input all node features and edge data into the graph neural network (GNN) [18] to reduce the reliance on expert knowledge. The complex feature selection process can be omitted by the graph neural network's powerful automatic feature selection capability. As shown in Algorithm 1, after generating the sliding traffic windows, all the sliding traffic windows are processed to generate traffic graphs sequentially. Each window corresponds to the generation of a traffic graph sample.

Algorithm 1: The construction of the traffic behavior graph

Input: A sequence of traffic packets P, A sequence of node features F
Output: The corresponding sequence of traffic behaviour graphs
$\qquad G = (g_1, \ldots, g_n)$
Set the sliding time window T_s and the sliding interval M_s, then generate a list
of sliding time window intervals $T = [(L_1, R_1), \ldots, (L_n, R_n)]$ using P ;

for $i = 1$ *to* n **do**
$\quad$ Filter the eligible sequences $O = (O_1, \ldots, O_m)$ from the time window
$\quad$ $(L_i, R_i) \in T$;
$\quad$ Initialize the dictionary of edge weights D ;
$\quad$ Initialize the set of edges E and the set of nodes V ;
$\quad$ **for** $j = 1$ *to* m **do**
$\quad\quad$ Get the IP and Port information of O_j to form the source address
$\quad\quad$ identification IPS_1 and the destination address identification IPS_2;
$\quad\quad$ **if** $IPS_1 \notin V$ **then**
$\quad\quad\quad$ | Add a vertex with IPS_1 to V;
$\quad\quad$ **end**
$\quad\quad$ **if** $IPS_2 \notin V$ **then**
$\quad\quad\quad$ | Add a vertex with IPS_2 to V;
$\quad\quad$ **end**
$\quad\quad$ **if** $(IPS_1, IPS_2) \in D$ **then**
$\quad\quad\quad$ | $D(IPS_1, IPS_2) = D(IPS_1, IPS_2) + 1$
$\quad\quad$ **else**
$\quad\quad\quad$ | $D(IPS_1, IPS_2) = 1$
$\quad\quad$ **end**
$\quad$ **end**

$\quad$ **for** $(d_l, d_r) \in D$ **do**
$\quad\quad$ | $E.append((d_l, d_r))$ /* Add an edge between d_l and d_r to E $\qquad$ */
$\quad$ **end**
$\quad$ **for** $v \in V_i$, $f \in F$ **do**
$\quad\quad$ update $v = (v, f)$ /* Aggregate the feature f of node v by
$\quad\quad\quad$ identification $\qquad$ */
$\quad$ **end**
$\quad$ $G.append((E, V))$
end

3.2   GAT Model Construction

Graph Neural Networks and Graph Classification Tasks. Graph neural networks are a series of machine learning techniques for analyzing graph data. Due to the mighty expressive power of GNN, the research of graph neural networks has gradually become a hotspot in recent years [19]. The graph convolutional neural network (GCN) [20] is the most classical graph neural network, which generates embeddings representation of nodes by aggregating features of neighbors. GAT [3] is an improved version of the GCN. It extends the basic features of nodes through the attention mechanism.

This paper transforms the traffic classification problem into a graph classification problem by traffic behavior graph construction. The graph classification task is defined as follows. We define a set of labeled graph datasets as $H = (G, L)$, where G is a list of graphs and L is a list of graph labels. The graph classification task aims to learn a mapping function ϕ on the dataset H for predicting the unlabeled graph sample labels.

Graph Attention Mechanism. GAT adds the attention mechanism to GCN. During the aggregation process of the GCN, the feature weights of all adjacent nodes are equal. In contrast, GAT uses the weighted representations of neighbor nodes to update nodes. The calculation process of the attention score is shown in Fig. 3. For a graph G with n nodes, the initial features of n nodes can be expressed as $\mathbf{H} = \{\mathbf{h}_1, \mathbf{h}_2, \cdots, \mathbf{h}_n\}$, $\mathbf{h}_i \in \mathbb{R}^F$, $i = 1, 2, \cdots, n$. F is the initial feature dimension of each node. For the central node i, first, through a shared weight matrix W of $F * F'$, the feature transformation of node i and its neighbor j is performed, and F' is the new node feature dimension. Then we calculate the attention scores of nodes i and j and obtain the final attention coefficient through the softmax function. This process can be expressed as follows.

$$\mathbf{z}_i = W\mathbf{h}_i \tag{1}$$

$$e_{ij} = \text{LeakeyReLU}\left(\mathbf{a}^T\left(\mathbf{z}_i \| \mathbf{z}_j\right)\right) \tag{2}$$

$$\alpha_{ij} = \text{softmax}_j\left(e_{ij}\right) = \frac{\exp\left(e_{ij}\right)}{\sum_{k \in \mathcal{N}_i} \exp\left(e_{ik}\right)} \tag{3}$$

In Eq. 2, $\|$ represents the vector splicing operation, and $\mathbf{a}$ represents the attention vector, which is used to convert the vector into a scalar value. $(\cdot)^T$ represents the vector transpose operation, e_{ij} represents the attention score. In Eq. 3, α_{ij} represents the attention coefficient. $\mathcal{N}_i$ represents all first-order neighbors of node i and includes i itself. The representation of the central node can be updated with the weighted sum of neighbor features, as shown in Eq. 4.

$$\mathbf{h}_i' = \sigma\left(\sum_{j \in \mathcal{N}_i} \alpha_{ij}\mathbf{z}_j\right) \tag{4}$$

In Eq. 4, σ is the nonlinear activation function, and $\mathbf{z}_j$ is the vector representation of node j after feature transformation.

Besides, GAT uses the multi-head attention mechanism to learn node features of different dimensions. Figure 4 describes the process of using attention heads $K = 3$. Lines of different styles represent different dimensions of graph attention calculations. Finally, GAT combines the results of K times to obtain the final vector representation of this node $\mathbf{h}_i''$. The formula of the multi-head attention mechanism is as follows.

$$\mathbf{h}_i'' = \|_{k=1}^K \sigma \left(\sum_{j \in \mathcal{N}_i} \alpha_{ij}^k \mathbf{z}_j^k \right) \tag{5}$$

GAT adaptively learns the weights of different neighbor nodes from different dimensions, which enhances the expressive ability of the graph neural network.

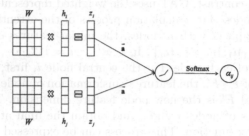

Fig. 3. Attention score calculation

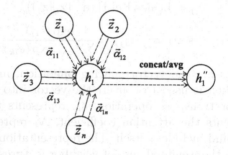

Fig. 4. Multi-head attention mechanism

Architecture of VT-GAT Model. As shown in Fig. 5, we obtained the optimal model structure after parameter optimization. The first two layers of the VT-GAT are two consistent-shaped graph attention convolution layers. Both layers have sixty-four hidden layer cells, eight attention heads, and Relu activation functions. Moreover, they are separated by a dropout layer with a dropout rate of 0.5. After two graph attention convolution layers is a global average pooling layer. Finally, there is a linear layer of size 100. The activation function of the output node is the LogSoftmax function. LogSoftmax function can speed up the convergence, improve data stability and prevent data overflow.

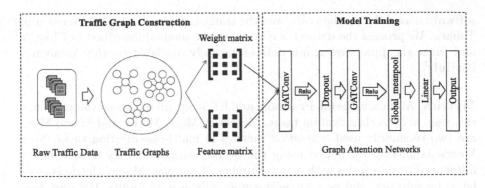

Fig. 5. Architecture of VT-GAT for VPN encrypted traffic classification

A complete VPN traffic classification process is as follows.

Step1: Input a PCAP file containing raw traffic. This file contains multiple packet-level traffic. Then we slice and dice the raw traffic into streams according to quintuple information (source IP, source port, destination IP, destination port, and IP protocol).

Step2: Select all packet and flow level data within a specific sliding time window to build the traffic behavior graphs.

Step3: Input the data into the VT-GAT model for training and predicting.

Step4: VT-GAT outputs a label to the traffic behavior graph composed of flows within each time window. This label represents the type of VPN application for the multiclassification task and whether the flow is VPN application traffic for the binary classification task.

4   Experiment Setup and Implementation

In this section, we design five VPN encrypted traffic classification experiments to demonstrate the applicability and efficiency of VT-GAT. We compare VT-GAT with other models and explore its robustness.

4.1   Experimental Setup

Dataset. The current dataset commonly used in VPN traffic classification is mainly ISCX VPN-nonVPN Dataset 2016 [17], but this dataset is too obsolete. Due to the continuous updates of technologies such as encryption technology and CDN technology in recent years, the traffic data in the ISCX VPN-nonVPN Dataset 2016 significantly differs from the current traffic characteristics. Therefore, we additionally choose the Datacon21 dataset. Datacon21 dataset [21] is released in 2021 in the DataCon2021 Big Data Security Analytics Competition. It consists of a total of one hundred categories and 218,168 flow samples. The traffic of this dataset is generated by automatically visiting the list of websites in the windows platform using the selenium library. The same encrypted proxy software is used during the visits, and the traffic is captured simultaneously using Tshark. We process the dataset according to the method described in Chap. 3.1 and make the processed graph dataset publicly available on the Anonymous GitHub[2].

Metrics. Accuracy, Recall, Precision, and F1-Score are common evaluation metrics used in data classification tasks. Moreover, Micro Metric and Macro Metric are two commonly used evaluation metrics in multi-classification tasks. Micro Metric is directly calculated using the overall sample, and its results may be influenced by categories with a high number of samples. Macro Metric is calculated by category, and rare categories may influence its results. Because Accuracy is equal to each micro-metric (Micro-F1, Micro-Recall, Micro-Precision) in a multi-classification task, we choose the Macro method for Recall, Precision, and F1-Score in this paper. Assuming that there are n categories of samples $0, 1, 2, \cdots, N$ in the dataset, we need to calculate Precision and Recall for each category and then average them to obtain Macro-Precision and Macro-Recall. We then calculate the F1-Score for each category and average them to obtain the Macro-F1. Equations 6, 7, 8, 9 and 10 are the calculation method of Macro Metric for Accuracy, Precision, Recall, and F1-Score, respectively.

– Accuracy :

$$Accuracy = \frac{TP + TN}{TP + FP + FN + TN} \tag{6}$$

– Precision :

$$Precision_i = \frac{TP_i}{TP_i + FP_i}, Precision = \frac{1}{n} \times \sum_{i=1}^{n} Precision_i \tag{7}$$

– Recall:

$$Recall_i = \frac{TP_i}{TP_i + FN_i}, Recall = \frac{1}{n} \times \sum_{i=1}^{n} Recall_i \tag{8}$$

– F1-Score:

$$F1\text{-}Score_i = 2 \times \frac{Precision_i \times Recall_i}{Precision_i + Recall_i}, \quad i = 0, 1, 2, \cdots, N \tag{9}$$

$$F1\text{-}Score = \frac{1}{n} \times \sum_{i=1}^{N} F1\text{-}Score_i \tag{10}$$

In Eqs. 6, 7, and 8, TP refers to the number of samples whose actual and predicted results are both positive. TN refers to the number of samples whose actual and predicted values are negative. FP refers to the number of samples that are predicted to be positive but whose actual value is negative. FN represents the number of samples in which the actual value is positive, but the predicted value is negative.

---

[2] https://anonymous.4open.science/r/VPN_Traffic_Graph_Dataset-EDA0.

Experimental Settings. VT-GAT is implemented in Python 3.8 based on PyTorch Geometric[3]. Other comparison models are implemented by Keras and sklearn. The experiments are carried out on a Ubuntu server with Intel(R) Xeon(R) Silver 4110 8-core processor @ 2.10 GHz, 128 GB of RAM, and three NVIDIA TITAN XPs GPUs, each having 12 GB of memory.

Baseline Models. To fully evaluate the performance of VT-GAT, we select six classical machine learning methods (SVM, KNN, NaiveBayes, Decision Tree, Random Forest, Logistic Regression) and three deep learning methods (DNN, CNN, LSTM) [22] for comparison. Although these machine learning models were proposed relatively early, these models have been fully verified in traffic classification tasks [1,23], and are currently widely used baseline models in traffic classification. Due to the specificity of graph classification methods, we concatenate all flows of a single graph sample into one flow sample in the dataset of the compared models. This setup ensures that the number of classification samples for the other methods and VT-GAT is identical, thus ensuring fairness in the comparison experiments. Besides, we also choose the recently proposed CLD-Net model [22] for comparative experiments with our model.

Hyperparameter Settings. In this experiment, the training and test sets are randomly divided in a ratio of 8:2. The sample sizes of the training and test sets are 174,534 and 43,634, respectively. We train our model and deep learning models using a maximum of 500 training epochs and an Adam optimizer with a learning rate of 10^{-4}. The activation function for all models is Relu. The DNN model consists of three fully connected layers of size 1024, each followed by a BatchNormalization layer. Finally, there is a fully connected layer of size 100. The LSTM model starts with an LSTM layer of size 256, followed by three fully connected layers of size 128, 64, and 100. The CNN model consists of two 1D convolutional layers of size (32, 7). There are two MaxPooling layers after the convolutional layer. Finally, there is a fully connected layer of size 100. The sliding window size is 300 s, and the sliding interval is 100 s. In order to ensure a fair comparison, all methods are parameterized to the best effect.

4.2 Analysis of Results

Comparison with Classical Machine Learning Algorithms. In this section, we compare the VT-GAT model with six classical machine learning algorithms.

In Table 2, we show the performance comparison results between VT-GAT and other algorithms. The results show that VT-GAT outperforms the other algorithms in all metrics. Due to the abnormal effect of SVM and NaiveBayes algorithms, it is evident that these two algorithms are not suitable for VPN traffic classification. So we do not include these two algorithms in comparison with

---

[3] https://github.com/pyg-team/pytorch_geometric.

Table 2. Performance comparison of VT-GAT and machine learning algorithms

Model	Accuracy	Precision	Recall	F1-Score
SVM	0.0443	0.1394	0.0468	0.0219
KNN	0.4357	0.4274	0.3620	0.3613
NaiveBayes	0.0855	0.1504	0.0691	0.0343
Decision Tree	0.9675	0.9478	0.9426	0.9448
Random Forest	0.9817	0.9747	0.9611	0.9666
Logistic Regression	0.7253	0.6634	0.6420	0.6506
VT-GAT	**0.9986**	**0.9977**	**0.9961**	**0.9968**

VT-GAT. Compared to the worst-performing algorithm (KNN), VT-GAT improved the different classification metrics by 56.29%–63.55%. Even compared to the best performing algorithm (Random Forest), VT-GAT improved all metrics by 1.69%–3.5%. These results indicate that the construction of traffic graphs can significantly help in VPN traffic classification. It is also clear from the results that tree-based models generally perform better than other machine learning models. This result is because flow-level traffic data is essentially tabular data. The tree-based models generally performed better in the task of classifying tabular data. The experimental results in this section also follow the findings of Shwartz-Ziv et al. [24]. It can be seen from the results that some algorithms (KNN, SVM, Naive-Bayes) perform very poorly. This result is due to the encrypted properties of VPN traffic and the only one flow problem that loses many effective features that can be used for classification. These algorithms cannot find practical features among the existing features that support their classification. These reasons lead to severe overfitting of these algorithms, resulting in poor classification results.

Comparison with Deep Learning Algorithms. In this section, we compare the VT-GAT with deep learning algorithms (DNN, CNN, LSTM), and the results are shown in Table 3.

Table 3. Performance comparison of VT-GAT and deep learning algorithms

Model	Accuracy	Precision	Recall	F1-Score
DNN	0.9380	0.9203	0.9109	0.9149
CNN	0.8490	0.8162	0.8055	0.8070
LSTM	0.8649	0.8292	0.8097	0.8147
VT-GAT	**0.9986**	**0.9977**	**0.9961**	**0.9968**

As can be seen from the results, VT-GAT improves by 6.06%–19.06% in all metrics compared to other deep learning algorithms. Deep learning algorithms use only the spatio-temporal features of the traffic. However, VT-GAT combines graph behavioral features with spatio-temporal features. By comparison, we demonstrate the effectiveness of VT-GAT in introducing behavioral features of traffic graphs. Among the various deep learning algorithms, the DNN is more effective than the others because flow-level traffic features are closer to tabular data. There are partial spatio-temporal correlations between the different feature attributes, which can be learned by the time-series-based LSTM and the spatial-based CNN. These correlations, however, are not very close. Therefore, the performance of DNN that is more suitable for learning tabular data is the best. In addition, Random Forest outperforms all deep learning algorithms. This result is in line with the No Free Lunch Theorem [25]. We can conclude that the tree model (Random Forest, Decision tree) is the most suitable flow-based method for VPN traffic classification. However, among all types of VPN traffic classification methods, VT-GAT is the most superior method. It can be seen from the comparison of different indicators that the F1-Score of the DNN model decreases more than the accuracy. This is because the F1-Score is determined by the recall and precision, and its influencing factors are more than the accuracy, which leads to the instability of the DNN model. Decision trees and Random Forests have similar magnitudes of change. And VT-GAT has the smallest changes in different indicators, which also shows that VT-GAT is more robust than other baseline models.

Performance with Different Number of Categories. The number of websites and applications is exploding with Internet technology's development. To verify the robustness of the VT-GAT, we design experiments with different numbers of categories (10, 30, 50, 80, and 100, respectively). This experiment compares the best-performing deep learning algorithm (DNN) and the two best-performing machine learning algorithms (Random Forest and Decision Tree). We randomly select a fixed number of categories for the experiments, and the results are shown in Fig. 6 and Fig. 7.

Experimental results show that most models perform well when the number of categories is small. As the number of categories gradually increases, the performance of Random Forest, Decision Tree, and DNN show a significant decrease by more than 1.5%. This phenomenon is expected as the increase in categories increases the similarity between samples, thus making the classification task more difficult. In contrast, the classification performance of VT-GAT remains almost unchanged. The overall variation of our model is less than 0.5% and remains at a high level, demonstrating the better robustness of VT-GAT. Furthermore, VT-GAT has the potential to be applied to real-world classification tasks for massive VPN traffic categories.

Performance Comparison of VT-GAT and CLD-Net. In order to further verify the application effect of VT-GAT in practical scenarios, we selected the recently proposed CLD-Net model [22] to verify it on the ISCX VPN-nonVPN Dataset 2016 [17]. The selected task is a binary classification task, that is, to

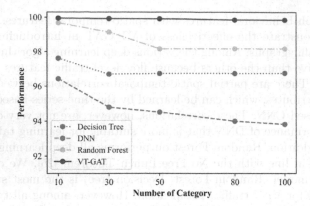

Fig. 6. Accuracy with different number of categories

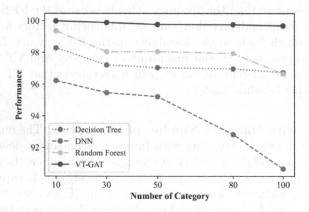

Fig. 7. F1-Score with different number of categories

determine whether a given network flow is traffic generated by a VPN application. The experimental results are shown in Fig. 8.

The experimental results show that the VT-GAT model is 1.38%–2.79% better than the CLD-Net model (Accuracy: 2.79%, Precision: 1.38%, Recall: 2.11%, F1-Score: 2.01%). It can be seen from the above results that the VT-GAT model has good applicability in both the VPN traffic identification task and the VPN application identification task. By relying on the solid identification ability of VT-GAT, it helps to help trace the type of VPN application that hackers use during the intrusion process, which is of great significance in identifying the attacker's identity.

Assessment of Execution Time. In order to better evaluate the performance of the model, we conduct a time performance comparison experiment. Since the training part of the supervised model can be performed in advance, we do not compare the model training time. In addition, most of the time cost of

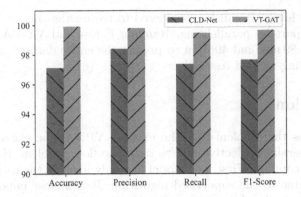

Fig. 8. Comparison of CLD-Net and VT-GAT

the model inference process is in the data feature preprocessing part, and the actual inference time (excluding the preprocessing process) of all methods can be completed within 30 s. The total inference time for flow-based methods is similar. Therefore, we only select the graph-based model VT-GAT for comparison with the flow-based model Random Forest. The experimental results are shown in Fig. 9.

Results show that VT-GAT can complete the prediction of thousand-level flow data within 3 min. The statistics show that the inference time consumption of VT-GAT in all orders of magnitude is about 3.4–7.4 times that of the Random Forest. Since VT-GAT needs to construct the traffic graph data, it has more time overhead than flow-based methods. Although the classification accuracy of Random Forest is not as good as that of VT-GAT, it runs very efficiently. As the size of the data increases, the time overhead for the feature extraction part also

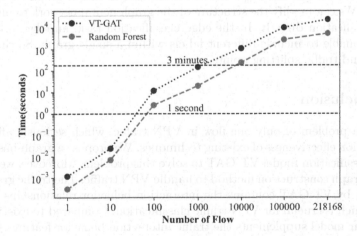

Fig. 9. Inference time comparison of different algorithms

reaches hourly levels. It can be considered to reduce the time cost of the data preprocessing part by parallelizing. Random Forest and VT-GAT have taken approximately 89 min and 406 min to predict the entire dataset (about 3.7 GB, including training set and test set).

5   Discussion

VT-GAT solves the problem that the existing VPN traffic classification techniques are generally ineffective due to only one flow problem. However, there are some shortcomings. First, our model can only identify the categories in the training data due to the supervised algorithm. It is almost impossible to collect the traffic of all websites or applications in a realistic environment. Some semi-supervised methods (e.g., FlowPrint [12]) can identify unknown categories, although their accuracy cannot match that of VT-GAT.

Secondly, during data collection, only one category of traffic is collected at the same time. In the real world, there may be multiple types of traffic generated at the same time. In the graph classification, the same graph may contain traffic data generated by different applications. To alleviate this problem, we use sliding windows to find the splitting points of traffic between different categories. However, the performance of VT-GAT may be degraded when there are no obvious traffic splitting points.

Our model will be further enhanced to address the above problem in future work. Graph contrast learning [18] is a self-supervised learning algorithm for graph data, which can solve the problem of graph data with missing labels or complex labeling. By introducing graph contrast learning, we can solve the problem that VT-GAT cannot identify unseen categories. In addition, during the traffic interaction, a flow is intuitively seen as an edge connecting two nodes. VT-GAT transforms edge features to node features while building the graph and then transforms the edge classification problem into a graph classification problem. We can modify the structure of the graph neural network to implement edge classification directly. In the edge classification task, an edge has a label. It is reasonable to include different labels within a single graph. So there is no need to find traffic splitting points.

6   Conclusion

There is a problem of only one flow in VPN traffic, which seriously affects the classification effectiveness of existing techniques. We propose a graph-based VPN traffic classification model VT-GAT to solve this problem. Moreover, we develop a traffic graph construction method to handle VPN traffic. The traffic graph data generated by VT-GAT contains the interaction behavior relationships between nodes, which is crucial for VPN traffic classification. Compared to existing techniques, our model supplements the traffic interaction behavior features based on the original spatio-temporal features and automatically learns the traffic graph differences among different categories via GAT. In addition, we release a traffic graph dataset that is useful for classifying VPN traffic. The results of comparative experiments on the Datacon21 dataset show that VT-GAT significantly improves all metrics compared to existing machine learning and deep learning methods (Accuracy: 1.69%–56.29%, Precision: 2.3%–57.03%, Recall: 3.5%–63.41% and F1-Score: 3.02%–63.55%). These results illustrate the great potential of GNN-based traffic classification methods for the VPN traffic classification.

In future work, we plan to use self-supervised learning methods to enhance our model.

Acknowledgements. We thank the anonymous reviewers for their insightful comments. This work was supported in part by the National Key Research and Development Program of China under Grant No. 2019YFB1005205.

References

1. Xie, J., Li, S., Yun, X., Zhang, Y., Chang, P.: HSTF-model: an http-based trojan detection model via the hierarchical spatio-temporal features of traffics. Comput. Secur. **96**, 101923 (2020)
2. Chen, H.Y., Lin, T.N.: The challenge of only one flow problem for traffic classification in identity obfuscation environments. IEEE Access **9**, 84110–84121 (2021)
3. Veličković, P., Cucurull, G., Casanova, A., Romero, A., Lio, P., Bengio, Y.: Graph attention networks. arXiv preprint arXiv:1710.10903 (2017)
4. Papadogiannaki, E., Ioannidis, S.: A survey on encrypted network traffic analysis applications, techniques, and countermeasures. ACM Comput. Surv. (CSUR) **54**(6), 1–35 (2021)
5. Finsterbusch, M., Richter, C., Rocha, E., Muller, J.A., Hanssgen, K.: A survey of payload-based traffic classification approaches. IEEE Commun. Surv. Tutor. **16**(2), 1135–1156 (2013)
6. Deri, L., Martinelli, M., Bujlow, T., Cardigliano, A.: NDPI: open-source high-speed deep packet inspection. In: 2014 International Wireless Communications and Mobile Computing Conference (IWCMC), pp. 617–622. IEEE (2014)
7. Papadogiannaki, E., Halevidis, C., Akritidis, P., Koromilas, L.: OTTer: a scalable high-resolution encrypted traffic identification engine. In: Bailey, M., Holz, T., Stamatogiannakis, M., Ioannidis, S. (eds.) RAID 2018. LNCS, vol. 11050, pp. 315–334. Springer, Cham (2018). https://doi.org/10.1007/978-3-030-00470-5_15
8. Ren, Q., Yang, C., Ma, J.: App identification based on encrypted multi-smartphone sources traffic fingerprints. Comput. Netw. **201**, 108590 (2021)
9. Taylor, V.F., Spolaor, R., Conti, M., Martinovic, I.: Robust smartphone app identification via encrypted network traffic analysis. IEEE Trans. Inf. Forensics Secur. **13**(1), 63–78 (2017)
10. Taylor, V.F., Spolaor, R., Conti, M., Martinovic, I.: AppScanner: automatic fingerprinting of smartphone apps from encrypted network traffic. In: 2016 IEEE European Symposium on Security and Privacy (EuroS&P), pp. 439–454. IEEE (2016)
11. Wang, S., Yang, C., Guo, G., Chen, M., Ma, J.: SSAPPIDENTIFY: a robust system identifies application over shadowsocks's traffic. Comput. Netw. **203**, 108659 (2022)
12. van Ede, T., et al.: Flowprint: semi-supervised mobile-app fingerprinting on encrypted network traffic. In: Network and Distributed System Security Symposium (NDSS), vol. 27 (2020)

13. Rezaei, S., Liu, X.: Deep learning for encrypted traffic classification: an overview. IEEE Commun. Mag. **57**(5), 76–81 (2019)
14. Xie, G., Li, Q., Jiang, Y.: Self-attentive deep learning method for online traffic classification and its interpretability. Comput. Netw. **196**, 108267 (2021)
15. Guo, L., Wu, Q., Liu, S., Duan, M., Li, H., Sun, J.: Deep learning-based real-time VPN encrypted traffic identification methods. J. Real-Time Image Proc. **17**(1), 103–114 (2020)
16. Lashkari, A.H., Draper-Gil, G., Mamun, M.S.I., Ghorbani, A.A.: Characterization of tor traffic using time based features. In: ICISSp, pp. 253–262 (2017)
17. Draper-Gil, G., Lashkari, A.H., Mamun, M.S.I., Ghorbani, A.A.: Characterization of encrypted and VPN traffic using time-related. In: Proceedings of the 2nd International Conference on Information Systems Security and Privacy (ICISSP), pp. 407–414 (2016)
18. Zeng, J., Xie, P.: Contrastive self-supervised learning for graph classification. In: Proceedings of the AAAI Conference on Artificial Intelligence, vol. 35, pp. 10824–10832 (2021)
19. Xu, K., Hu, W., Leskovec, J., Jegelka, S.: How powerful are graph neural networks? arXiv preprint arXiv:1810.00826 (2018)
20. Kipf, T.N., Welling, M.: Semi-supervised classification with graph convolutional networks. arXiv preprint arXiv:1609.02907 (2016)
21. DataCon-Community: Datacon open dataset - datacon2021 - encrypted proxy traffic dataset track open dataset, 24 December 2021. [Online; Accessed 14 June 2022]
22. Hu, X., Gu, C., Wei, F.: CLD-net: a network combining CNN and LSTM for internet encrypted traffic classification. In: Security and Communication Networks 2021 (2021)
23. Lotfollahi, M., Jafari Siavoshani, M., Shirali Hossein Zade, R., Saberian, M.: Deep packet: a novel approach for encrypted traffic classification using deep learning. Soft Comput. **24**(3), 1999–2012 (2020)
24. Shwartz-Ziv, R., Armon, A.: Tabular data: deep learning is not all you need. Inf. Fusion **81**, 84–90 (2022)
25. Wolpert, D.H., Macready, W.G.: No free lunch theorems for optimization. IEEE Trans. Evol. Comput. **1**(1), 67–82 (1997)

Images Processing and Recognition

Landmark Detection Based on Human Activity Recognition for Automatic Floor Plan Construction

Zhao Huang[1] (iD), Stefan Poslad[1], Qingquan Li[2], Jianping Li[3], and Chi Chen[3](✉)

[1] School of Electronic Engineering and Computer Science, Queen Mary University of London, London E1 4NS, UK
{zhao.huang,stefan.poslad}@qmul.ac.uk

[2] School of Architecture and Urban Planning, Shenzhen University, Shenzhen 58000, China
liqq@szu.edu.cn

[3] State Key Laboratory of Information Engineering in Surveying, Mapping and Remote Sensing, Wuhan University, Wuhan 430072, China
{lijianping,chichen}@whu.edu.cn

Abstract. Landmark detection technology has a wide range of applications in people's lives, including map correcting, localization and navigation, etc. Besides, landmarks are also utilized to label different areas for automatic floor plan construction. Currently, vision-based landmark detection methods have some limitations, such as light, camera shaking, and privacy-invasive. In addition, deep learning-based methods increase the time consumption of marking labels due to the huge requirement for data. Targeting the above challenges, our work first proposes a landmark detection approach based on Human Activity Recognition (HAR) for automatic floor plan construction, which introduces a self-attention model to recognize various landmarks by walker's daily activities due to their strong correlation. First, the accelerometer and gyroscope sensor data are extracted and eliminated by a Gaussian filter and are divided into the same length segments by slide window. Next, it is input into the self-attention network to train a human activity recognition model. Finally, the corresponding relationship between human activities and landmarks is created to detect landmarks through the trained HAR model. Empirical results on two publicly available USC-HAD and OPPORTUNITY datasets show our proposed approach can recognize landmarks effectively.

Keywords: Landmark detection · Automatic floor plan construction · Human activity recognition · Sensors · Self-attention

1 Introduction

Recently, localization is the technique to determine the position of an object or a person [1]. An indoor localization system is a system that attempts to find the accurate position of the object inside a building, mall, etc. The popularity of mobile computing [2–6] stimulates extensive research on the localization of persons or assets. In the present era

H. Gao et al. (Eds.): CollaborateCom 2022, LNICST 461, pp. 459–477, 2022.
https://doi.org/10.1007/978-3-031-24386-8_25

of mobile devices, location information is crucial in a wide range of applications such as manufacturing, healthcare, etc. In order to meet the user's needs, the location information of persons or assets is required which can be provided by the indoor localization system, which tries to identify the position of moving devices with the help of some fixed nodes and some mobile computing devices [7]. However, floor plan construction is an important stage to achieve accurate indoor localization.

Currently, there are numerous approaches to automatic floor plan construction that have been proposed [8–10], because floor plan construction is an important stage to achieve accurate indoor localization. Most maps lack labels for different spaces, they just construct the outline of buildings [11]. However, it is necessary to name some special places, such as where is a bedroom, where is a stair, where is the door of the kitchen, etc. Thus, labeling these spaces using landmarks becomes a good choice. Landmarks that are frequently used include some special structures of buildings or roads, some symbolic objects, etc. In an indoor environment, daily landmarks include doors, stairs, beds, chairs, etc., which often cause humans to perform some special actions, such as walking upstairs or downstairs, opening or closing a door, and sleeping, as shown in Fig. 1.

Fig. 1. Landmarks in our daily life

A great deal of landmark detection methods has been published [12–15] due to their importance in marking areas for automatic floor plan construction and assisting in the construction of sparse maps. These landmark detection approaches can be divided into two categories: signal-based [16–18] and vision-based [19–21]. Vision-based are using computer vision technology to detect special objects as landmarks, but the limitation of these approaches includes two aspects, on one hand, the estimation accuracy is significantly affected by light and camera shaking. Meanwhile, the vision-based methods have a common privacy-invasive issue that are people concerned about. On the other hand, the data-driven landmark detection method based on deep learning algorithms [22, 23] is more popular due to its automatic feature extraction capabilities rather than mandate domain knowledge to craft shallow heuristic features, but deep learning methods require massive training data, which means people have to spend a lot of time labeling a large amount of data for training a reliable model, as a result, it dramatically increases the workload of manually signing labels. Compared to vision-based methods, signal-based such as radar, lidar, wifi, etc. have the multipath effect issue, and the performance changes with surroundings, which causes an unstable system. Meanwhile, deployment is more complex than mobile sensors. For example, in [16], scattering information from the polarimetric radar is used to detect point-shaped landmarks, which don't consider line-shaped landmarks, meanwhile, the scattering information is unstable and easily changes with surroundings. In [21], drogue's landmark detection is developed for autonomous aerial refueling of unmanned aerial vehicles, but the jitter of the camera or drogue in the air and the change of light will have a great impact to measure the position. But mobile and wearable sensors, particularly tiny sensors not only avoid being disturbed by the shape and surroundings of landmarks but also overcome the limitation of light and shaking of the camera.

Nevertheless, landmark detection approaches based on mobile or wearable sensors avoid the huge workload of labeling, because the label is just recorded when collecting data rather than marking objects from pictures one by one. Meanwhile, it also does not need to extract features from pictures to detect landmarks. Motivated by the above reasons, we introduce a unified and novel landmark detection method for automatic floor plan construction based on human activity recognition (HAR) using the self-attention network, where HAR is firstly adopted to detect the landmark in an indoor environment owing to the close relationship between human daily activities and landmarks. The reason why we choose a self-attention network is that it not only gets the global and local connection synchronously within one step but also will not be limited by the sequence length for the capture of long-term dependence like the RNN network. Meanwhile, the results of each step do not depend on the previous step and can be made into a parallel mode. Compared with CNN and RNN, the parameters are fewer and the complexity of the model is lower. Compared to the other landmark detection methods, our approaches not only avoid the negative impact of light and camera shaking but also solve the privacy-invasive problem. Meanwhile, the workload of labeling data decreases significantly for experiment operators due to the convenience of only recording the labels when collecting sensor data of different activities. The process of our approach is as follows, firstly, the timestep records, accelerometer, gyroscope, and IMU data are input into a sensor modality attention to calculate the attention score, and then, these attention scores are utilized to infer the relative weights of each time-step in the sequence and transform the presentation of each time-step. Following that, global temporal attention is used to rank the importance when predicting the categories of human behaviors. What's more, the human activity model based on self-attention is trained. Finally, the trained HAR model is utilized to recognize human daily activities, which means the landmarks also are detected according to the corresponding relationship between human activities and landmarks, so the name of labels in the floor plan can be obtained. The main novelties of this paper include 1) firstly proposing to build the corresponding relationship between waypoints and human daily activities for the automatic landmark detection task, which is different from vision-based methods in this domain, this approach is a scheme with fewer privacy issues for detecting landmarks automatically through human behaviors rather than using images. 2) developing a novel landmark detection based on human activity recognition for automatic floor plan construction. Currently, the state-of-the-art vision-based landmark detection approaches have common issues: camera shaking and light changing. For signal-based methods, the surroundings changes will cause landmark estimation error, which is unstable. But our proposed method overcomes the limitation of vision-based and signal-based methods and enhanced the robustness. 3) automatically labeling areas, such as where is the bedroom, kitchen, etc.

The rest of the paper is organized as follows. The related work is covered in Sect. 2. Section 3 will present the proposed methodology, including the framework, sensor modality attention, self-attention block, global temporal attention, and landmark detection. Finally, in Sect. 4, the performance of the proposed approach will be shown, and the following is the conclusion and future work.

2 Related Work

With the development of automatic floor plan construction technologies, more and more landmark detection methods are being used to assist in labeling different areas in a floor plan using these recognized landmarks. Typical landmark detection can be divided into three categories: image-based and signal-based. The image-based methods extract features from a set of pictures near the landmarks, while the signal-based is to receives the flection signals as the features to identify landmarks.

The majority of landmark detection is based on images, with machine learning or deep learning algorithms extracting features. For instance, Rous et al. [20] developed a natural landmark detection model based on a priori knowledge of the shape and functionality of searched structures, which combines region based as well as edge-based elements to detect indoor landmarks, especially for these have clear line structures and large homogenous color surfaces. But the model is unstable due to the lighting fluctuations. Zheng et al. [22] designed an efficient and robust landmark detection model using 3D deep learning in volumetric data, which greatly improves the detection speed and generalization capability, however, it is still more time-consuming than the current methods due to the double training process. Han et al. [24] proposed a multi-resolution regression-guided landmark detection frame to recover Haar-like appearance features from CT pictures and locate human organs, this framework overcame the problem of inaccurate matching due to the distant and changed corresponding structures. Unfortunately, the performance is poor for identifying larger organs. Likewise, A large-scale anatomical landmarks detection approach is presented by Zhang et al. [25], compared to other methods, this algorithm greatly reduces the requirement for training data, however, the fixed patch size used caused the high difference between various landmarks. Jheng et al. [26] demonstrated a convolutional neural network (CNN)-based algorithm (GUTAID) for landmark detection, which achieved and further characterize polyps for optical diagnosis. But the experimental images are not enough, and some images are not high-definition images. On the whole, the common limitations of these landmark detection approaches are the high requirement for light and heavy workload of data labeling.

Zhang, Z. et al. [27]. Designed an optimal facial landmark detection model based on Deep Convolutional Network (TCDCN), which successfully uses the back-propagation algorithm to enhance the generalization, unfortunately, the number of tasks is limited. Liu et al. [28] confuse millimeter-wave radar and camera to improve the performance of target recognition and the environmental awareness capabilities of the autonomous vehicle under severe weather conditions but the efficiency will face the challenge of one-way sensor failure. Wang et al. [29] introduce the fine-grained channel state information (CSI) from off-the-shelf WiFi to detect users' baggage, this scheme is low-cost and eligible for deployment, but the performance is easily disturbed by bag material. Beltrán et al. [30] first design an efficient LiDAR-based 3D object detection for driving environments by using a state-of-art CNN framework, which is suitable for on-board operation, however, the number of channels is limited, which causes the loss of some discriminative features and lower the performance of this method. Zhou et al. [11] introduce an Activity Landmarkbased Indoor Mapping system via Crowdsourcing (ALIMC), which constructs the landmark-based indoor map without any prior knowledge by connecting human activity patterns with the landmarks, but all these activities can not be recognized by a common model and the accuracies of the traditional detection algorithms are not better than deep learning methods. Zhou et al. [31] develop a fast, fine-grained, and low-cost floor plan construction system using sound signals suitable for heterogeneous microphones on commodity smartphones, which achieves good performance, unfortunately, the sound signals are easy to be distributed by noise from surroundings, which causes the bad robustness.

Many publications focus on human activity recognition [32, 33], including wearable sensor-based HAR and vision-based HAR. Varshney et al. [34] introduced the multiple CNN streams to recognize human activities from video by fusing spatial and temporal information, where the average and convolution fusion methods are discussed. Although this method outperforms other approaches, the model does not support multiple input modalities. Liu et al. [35] proposed a compound deep neural network including two sub-networks to generate optical flow images and extract the spatial-temporal information from RGB images respectively, and the spatial-temporal information is integrated to recognize human activities. Although this method achieves a good result, the complexity of network the remains to be improved. A human activity behavior based on stacked sparse autoencoder, and the history of binary motion image is shown by Gnouma et al. [36], which simplified the complexity of silhouette extraction, the limitation of this method is only some special behaviors can be identified. Snoun et al. [37] recognized activities using fine-tuning pre-trained CNNs via human skeletons from the frames, although it almost achieved good accuracy, the performance heavily relies on the result of pose estimation. Murad et al. [38] develop a HAR framework based on deep recurrent neural networks (DRNNs), which can process the variable-length sequences from the input layer, however, the data used is small scale and the generalization is poor. The embedding-based inception neural network and recurrent neural network landmark detection are developed by Xu et al. [39] to classify actions with multi-dimensional features, achieving high accuracy and good generalization, but the kernel size of the model remains optimized. A pattern-based HAR model is proposed by Zhang et al. [40], which established a correlation between signal variation from diffraction sensors and human actions so as to match them. Similar to Zhang, Yan et al. [41] designed a WiAct to recognize activities through the correlations between body movement and the changes of Channel State Information (CSI) signals changes due to various human activities. However, the two approaches are disturbed heavily by noise and the signal is easy to be sheltered. Bashar et al. [42] produced a time-frequency-based human activities recognition model using activity-driven hand-crafted features, which achieve comparable accuracy and reduce the computation time, but the production of hand-crafted features is time-consuming.

3   Methodology

This section describes the details of our landmark detection approach, the aim of this method is to train a landmark detection model based on human activity pattern recognition by introducing a self-attention mechanism without any recurrent architectures. The method includes four parts: sensor modality attention, self-attention block, global temporal attention, and landmark detection, the detailed specification is shown in the below subsequent sections.

3.1   The Framework of Our Proposed Method

The framework of the proposed approach is illustrated in Fig. 2, the accelerometer and gyroscope data are denoised through a Gaussian filter and then the sensor modality attention is utilized to calculate the weight of the two sensor's data according to their attention score respectively. Following this, the weighted sensor data are transferred into a fixed-size vector over single time steps through a 1-D convolution. Afterward, the values of the two math functions: sine and cosine, are added to the fixed vectors for encoding the position information of the samples in the sequence. Except for that, the feature presentation is scaled through the sqrt function and input into the self-attention block model.

In the self-attention block, the dot product is applied to obtain the new feature presentation of each time step and this new presentation is the input of the global temporal attention layer, and this layer generates the final feature presentation through learning parameters to set varying attention across the temporal dimension [43], Finally, the final feature presentation is utilized by the fully connected and soft-max layers.

3.2   Sensor Modality Attention

The aim of the sensor modality attention mechanism is to obtain the various contribution from the different modalities of sensors and then reduce the impact of lower contribution sensor data, taking sitting as an example, the data from these sensors placed on people's legs contain lower information, so the sensor modality attention mechanism is used to reduce the related weights. It means the sensor modality attention can capture the dependencies through learning such relationships using 2-D convolution across time-step and sensor values [43].

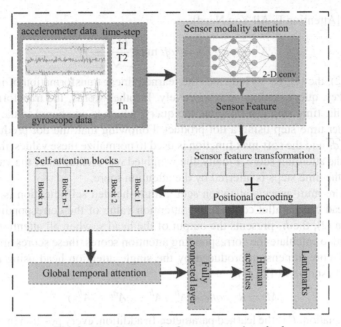

Fig. 2. The framework of our proposed method.

Firstly, the sensor data is converted to single-channel data, and then k convolutional filters are introduced to reshape the single-channel data into k channels data. Following this, the k channel data are converted back to one-channel data using a single convolution. To generate different attention scores for the various modality of sensors, the sensor-wise soft-max function is applied, the definition of this sensor-wise is as follows:

$$S_k^{(t_i)} = \frac{\exp(q_k^{t_i})}{\sum_k \exp(q_k^{t_i})}$$

(1)

In this equation, k is the label of sensors. Thus, the weight of the input can be calculated by this equation. Besides, the sensor modality attention also provides feature maps to show the interpretation of this model.

3.3 Self-attention Block

Self-attention layer is the core layer, which consists of self-attention blocks and each block also contains one multi-headed self-attention and one position-wise feed-forward layer [Saif Mahmud]. There are two main functions for this self-attention, one is to infer the relative weights of each time step in the sequence according to the similarity between this time step and all other time steps, and the other is that the feature presentation of each time step is transformed through building the relationship between the weights and the importance of information from other time-steps. Equation (2) show the process of calculation [Attention Is All You Need].

$$A^{h_s}(Q, K, V) = soft\max(\frac{Q \cdot K^T}{\sqrt{d_k}})V \tag{2}$$

In Eq. (2), the (Q, K, V) indicates the learned linear transformation of input, Q, K, and V are key, query, and value respectively. In other words, the transformed vector of one specific time step can integrate the query, which is compared to the key vector at every other time step using a dot product. Following that, the dot product value is scaled by $\sqrt{d_k}$ and the soft-max function is used to normalize these values, the output of softmax is the attention score. Finally, the weighted representation of the value vectors for each of the time steps is inferred by the attention score.

To capture muti-aspects attention score, multi-headed self-attention is developed, and each head can parallel compute the attention value of the corresponding aspects. As shown in (2), the h_s presents the output of the head s, when all attention heads are concatenated to calculate the corresponding attention scores, these scores are converted back to the score dimension produced by the single attention head using the learned parameter. As shown in Eq. (3).

$$M = R \cdot concat(A^{h_1}, A^{h_2}, ...A^{h_{n-1}}, A^{h_n}) \tag{3}$$

In this equation, R is the learned parameter. In addition, every position in one block is corresponding to the position-wise feed-forward layer independently, which means the weights of the same block are consistent, but it is different across the blocks. Meanwhile, both sub-layers include one normalization layer and one residual connection.

3.4 Global Temporal Attention

TO rank the importance when predicting the categories of human behaviors, the attention score of each time-step output from the self-attention blocks and learned related parameters are input into the global temporal attention model. Firstly, the function C_s is built for capturing the temporal context when calculating the attention score, as shown in Eq. (4).

$$C^{(t_i)} = \tanh(R \cdot S^{(t_i)} + P) \tag{4}$$

In Eq. (4), R and P are the learned parameters generated from self-attention blocks.

$$\psi^{(t_i)} = \frac{\exp((C^{(t_i)})^T \cdot C_s)}{\sum_t \exp(C^{(t_i)} \cdot C_s)} \tag{5}$$

As for the ranking, which is calculated by Eq. (5) and utilized to produce a weighted average of the representations of all the time steps in an activity window [], meanwhile, it is input into the feed-forward layers as a feature vector to classify human behaviors.

$$N_i = \sum_t \psi^{(t_i)} S^{(t_i)} \tag{6}$$

Finally, the weights of all time steps are used to calculate the weighted summation by Eq. (6), which also forms a feature vector. To improve the efficiency of training, the dropout layer is added to the self-attention blocks and the fully connected layer, which is also used after positional encoding.

3.5 Landmark Detection

Compared to image-based and appearance-based landmark detection technology, our approach estimates landmarks through human activity recognition based on a self-attention mechanism, the advantage of our method is that it is not affected by the light and appearance of objects. However, how constructing the relationship between human behaviors and landmarks is a key stage. As we know, the area of human activities and landmarks are the same place when people take activities, which indicates human actions and landmarks are interchangeable. Thus, the correlation between human behaviors and landmarks of our work is constructed and shown in Table 1. 12 kinds of human daily activities, containing: walking upstairs and downstairs, up and down elevators, sitting and sleeping, opening and closing doors, opening and closing fridges, and opening and closing dishwashers, are correlated with 6 common landmarks: stair, elevator, chair, bed (bedroom), door, fridge, and dishwasher (kitchen).

From Table 1, it is obvious that different human activities have corresponding landmarks. So, these landmarks are recognized easily when the related human behaviors are classified accurately through the self-attention mechanism.

Table 1. The correlation between human behaviors and landmarks.

Behavior	Landmark	Behavior	Landmark
Up/downstairs	Stair	Open/close a door	Door
Up/down elevators	Elevator	Open/close fridges	Fridge
Sitting	Chair	Open/close dishwashers	Dishwasher (kitchen)
Sleeping	Bed (bedroom)	\	\

To estimate the performance of different algorithms for landmark detection, this paper introduces the macro average F1-score (MAF1-score) as the metric, as shown in Eq. (7).

$$MAF1\_score = \frac{1}{|N|} \sum_{j=1}^{N} \frac{2 * P_j * \mathrm{Re}_j}{P_j + \mathrm{Re}_j} \qquad (7)$$

In this equation, N is the class quantity of human activities, j is the label of each class, P_j and Re_j indicates the precision and recall of the j class.

4 Experiment Results

To verify the efficiency of this landmark detection algorithm based on human activity recognition, the two publicly available USC-HAD and OPPORTUNITY datasets are chosen to carry out experiments, because various daily activities data is included in both datasets, and the hardware of this experiment is a computer with an intel i7-9750H CPU, and the working frequency of this CPU is 2.6G Hz.

4.1 Dataset and Preprocessing

4.1.1 Dataset Description

1) USC-HAD Dataset: The USC human activity (USC-HAD) dataset [44] collected a triaxial accelerometer and gyroscope data using the MotionNode sensing platform, which contains 12 general human activities, and invites 14 participants to install the MotionNode sensors on their front right hip to collect data. Meanwhile, the sampling frequency is set to 100 Hz, and everyone repeats each activity five times, the parameters include: the activity's name, subject number, etc. are recorded by a nearby observer. The human daily activities include walking downstairs/upstairs, turning left/right going along with a circle, sitting, etc.

2) OPPORTUNITY Dataset: The OPPORTUNITY dataset [45] is a public dataset, which is published on the UCI Machine Learning repository and records both static/periodic and sporadic activities from wearable, objects, and ambient sensors in daily living. This dataset records 4 subjects performing 16 types of activities, and each person undertakes one ADL session and one drill session five times, and the drill run consists of 20 repetitions activities. The difference between the ADL session and the drill run session is that the ADL collects a series of human morning activities, which is continuous, and the drill run records some repetitive activities, including opening/closing a door, opening/closing a fridge, sleeping, etc. The frequency sampling of the Drill run is 32 Hz.

4.1.2 Data Preprocess

1) USC-HAD Dataset Preprocessing

In this dataset, there are six types of human daily activities: sitting and sleeping, walking upstairs and downstairs, up-elevators, and down-elevators, which are chosen to perform our experiments. These activities are corresponding to four common landmarks in our daily life: chairs, beds, stairs, and elevators. To accurately estimate the four landmarks through the six actions, Firstly, the raw data of the six activities from the accelerometer and gyroscope are extracted and input into a gaussian filter for reducing the noise produced from collecting data. Then, these filtered data are divided into many segments by the fixed windows with 50% overlapping, the window size is 32. Finally, the Leave-One-User-Out (LOOCV) strategy is adopted to split the data of 14 users into 14 different groups respectively.

Figure 3 shows the signal changes of the accelerometer and gyroscope when users perform taking up-elevator and down-elevator, walking upstairs and downstairs, as can be seen from these pictures, the accelerometer and gyroscope signals have a strong periodicity totally. Compared to (a) and (b), the pictures from (c) and (d) show more regular changes. In Fig. 3 (a) and (b), the value of the z-axis decreases or increases obviously because taking the up-elevator and down-elevator only causes the acceleration changes in the vertical direction, but (c) and (d) are different due to producing acceleration changes in three directions, which indicates that up-elevator and down-elevator are harder to recognize than walking upstairs and downstairs.

2) OPPORTUNITY Dataset Preprocess

    The six kinds of activities from the OPPORTUNITY dataset: opening and closing a door, opening and closing a fridge, and opening and closing a dishwasher are introduced to identify three types of landmarks. The reason why we choose the six activities is that the three corresponding landmarks with the six actions are an indispensable part of our life, which exist in our office, home, supermarket, etc. Firstly, an interpolation algorithm with the "movmedian" method is utilized to fill in the missing data due to the incomplete collected data from IMUs, where the window size is set to 10. Then, the Gaussian filter is adapted to relieve the negative impact of noise and the size of the window is designed to be 20. Followed by this, a fixed window with 50% overlapping divides these signals into the 32 points segments in a row. Finally, the accelerometer and gyroscope data of five Activities of Daily Living (ADLs) and the Drill from Subject 1, the Drill data and the data range from ADL1 to ADL3 of subjects 2 and 3, are extracted from the public dataset for training data, and the rest data from subject2 and subject3 are abstracted for testing the efficiency of the trained model [46].

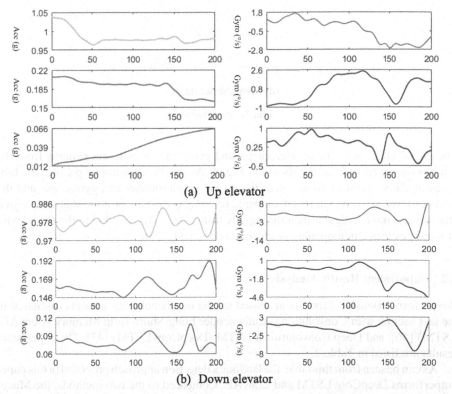

Fig. 3. Accelerometer and Gyroscope signal changes of different activity patterns, (a)–(d) present different activities using different color curves, X-axis presents the number of sampling points, Y-axis presents sensor value. (a) up elevator. (b) down elevator. (c) walk upstairs. (d) walk downstairs.

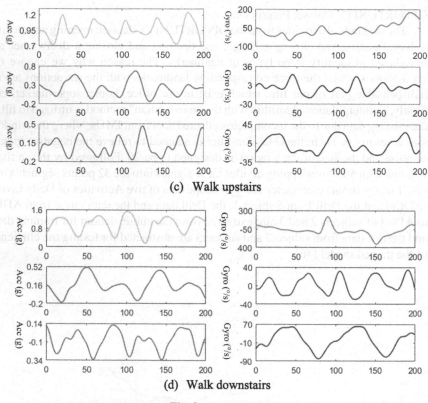

(c) Walk upstairs

(d) Walk downstairs

Fig. 3. (*continued*)

The signal changes of the accelerometer and gyroscope to different patterns from the sensors on the right wrist are shown in Fig. 4. As can be seen in this picture, the four types of daily activities are not sensitive to the accelerometer and gyroscope, and the value of three axes change less. Compared to walking upstairs or downstairs, the signal changes are more irregular than the signals from other activities due to the complexity of hand gestures when opening or closing a door, fridge, etc.

4.2 Experiment Result Analysis

We perform extensive experiments based on the two benchmark datasets discussed in the last section with Convolutional Autoencoder Long Short-Term Memory (ConvAE-LSTM) [46], and Deep Convolutional LSTM (DeepConvLSTM) [47]. The experiment results are listed in Table 2.

As can be seen from this table, the landmark detection approach proposed in this paper outperforms DeepConvLSTM and ConvAE. Compared to the two methods, the Macro F1-score of our method improves from 0.69 (DeepConvLSTM) and 0.76 (ConvAE) to 0.84 respectively for the USC-HAD dataset and increases by 0.08 (DeepConvLSTM) and 0.05 (ConvAE-LSTM) for OPPORTUNITY dataset.

Figure 5 presents the classification details of different human activities from the USC-HAD dataset when the self-attention model is used. As shown in the figure, the four landmarks can be recognized totally through the corresponding human activities. However, sleeping and upstairs have the highest f1-score (more than 0.94), while downstairs has the lowest F1-score (0.61) with the greatest misclassification (0.26). To measure the performance of this landmark detection algorithm, the average F1-score of the corresponding activities from the same landmark is applied to present the f1-score of this landmark. Thus, based on the correlation between human behaviors and landmarks (Table 1), we can conclude that the bed (bedroom) has the highest recognition efficiency, while the elevator and stairs have lower F1 scores, which means the bedroom is easy to label automatically when constructing the floor plan.

The classification of human daily activities from the OPPORTUNITY dataset is shown in Fig. 6. It can be seen from these pictures, Opening the door1 and the fridge outperform other activities, and the F1-score is up to 0.985 and 0.9 respectively, but closing the dishwasher has the highest misclassification (up to 0.4). The average F1 scores of doors1, doors2, fridge, and dishwasher are 0.91, 0.66, 0.79, and 0.69, separately.

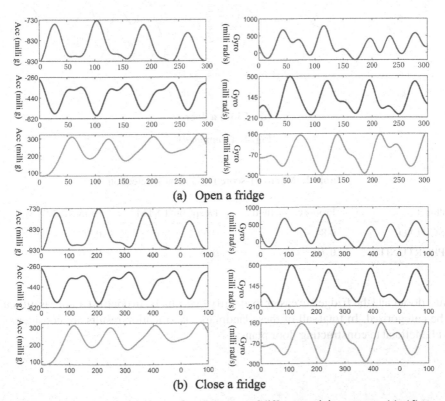

(a) Open a fridge

(b) Close a fridge

Fig. 4. Accelerometer and Gyroscope signal changes of different activity patterns, (a)–(d) present different activities using various color curves, X-axis presents the number of sampling points, Y-axis presents sensor value. (a) open a fridge. (b) close a fridge. (c) open a door. (d) close a door.

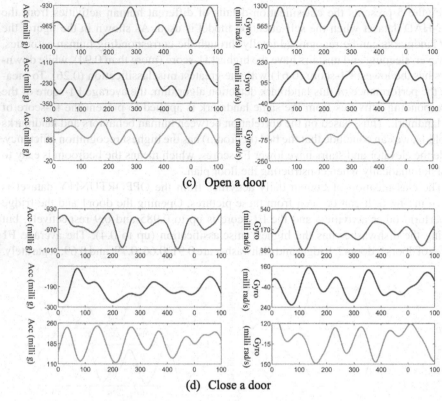

(c) Open a door

(d) Close a door

Fig. 4. (*continued*)

Table 2. Macro F1-score for landmark detection

Dataset	Proposed method	DeepConvLSTM	ConvAE-LSTM
USC-HAD	0.84	0.69	0.76
OPPORTUNITY	0.76	0.68	0.71

Thus, door1 and the fridge are easier to identify than others, in contrast, door2 is difficult to be categorized. In total, all of these landmark classification results are considerable and beneficial to constructing floor plans.

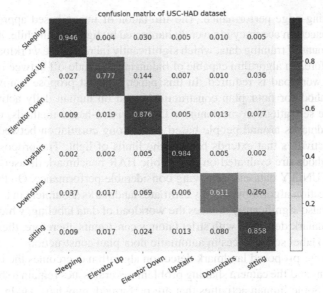

Fig. 5. The confusion matrix of the USC-HAD dataset.

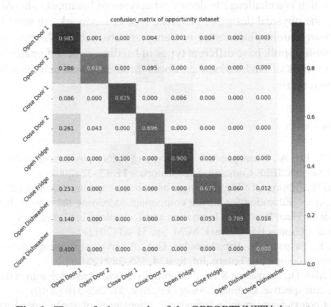

Fig. 6. The confusion matrix of the OPPORTUNITY dataset.

5   Conclusion and Future Work

Landmark detection technology is growing in popularity due to its widespread use in localization and mapping research, and image-based landmark detection methods have achieved cutting-edge performance. The limitation of image-based approaches, however, is that detection accuracy is severely hampered by light. Meanwhile, it necessitates a massive amount of training data, which significantly increases the workload of labeling labels. Therefore, an algorithm capable of balancing the trade-off between performance and labeling workload is required. In this paper, we first propose a novel landmark detection method for floor plan construction based on human daily activity recognition using the self-attention mechanism. Unlike vision-based methods, our approach estimates landmarks around people based on a strong correlation between landmarks and human activities that extends beyond the limits of light. The proposed landmark detection methods are evaluated on two public HAR benchmark datasets: USC-HAD and OPPORTUNITY datasets, achieving considerable performance. On the whole, the landmark detection algorithm not only estimates landmarks accurately in low-light environments but also significantly reduces the workload of data labeling, which is advantageous for landmark detection with strict latency constraints, therefore, these landmarks can be used to label some places in automatic floor plan construction.

Although our proposed landmark detection algorithm overcomes the constraints of light conditions and the camera shaking problem, several issues remain to be considered in the future. Some human activities that are performed, may have landmarks that can be ad hoc. For example, to improve the estimation efficiency, not all landmarks need to be detected, which is a challenge to decide what types of landmarks should be detected. What's more, the physical design of the same type of landmark can vary. For example, the doors of many public places, such as transport hubs, school libraries, supermarkets, etc., may be push or pull, have different types of handles, or be automatic, so estimating these different types of landmarks, e.g., doors through human activities become more challenging in real life.

References

1. Yanying, G., Lo, A., Niemegeers, I.: A survey of indoor positioning systems for wireless personal networks. IEEE Commun. Surv. Tutorials **11**, 13–32 (2009)
2. Forman, G.H., Zahorjan, J.: The challenges of mobile computing. Computer **27**, 38–47 (1994)
3. Barry, B., et al.: Educating for mobile computing: addressing the new challenges. In: Proceedings of the Final Reports on Innovation and Technology in Computer Science Education 2012 Working Groups Haifa, Israel: ACM, pp. 51–63 (2012)
4. Kakousis, K., Paspallis, N., Papadopoulos, G.A.: A survey of software adaptation in mobile and ubiquitous computing. Enterp. Inf. Syst. **4**, 355–389 (2010)
5. Ladd, D., Alan, D., Avimanyu, S., et al.: Trends in mobile computing with in the is discipline: a ten-year retrospective. Commun. Assoc. Inf. Syst. **27**, 285–316 (2010)
6. Gay, G.: Context-aware mobile computing: affordances of space, social awareness, and social influence. Synthesis Lectures on Human-Centered Informatics. Morgan and Claypool Publishers, San Rafael. vol. 2, pp. 1–62 (2009)
7. Sana.: A survey of indoor localization techniques. IOSR J. Electr. Electron. Eng. (IOSR-JEEE). **6**, 69–76 (2013)
8. Alzantot, M.: Youssef, M.: Crowdinside: automatic construction of indoor floorplans. In: Proceedings of the 20th International Conference on Advances in Geographic Information Systems, New York, United States, pp. 99–108 (2012)

9. X. Zhang, Y. Jin, et al. CIMLoc: A crowdsourcing indoor digital map construction system for localization. In 2014 IEEE Ninth International Conference on Intelligent Sensors, Sensor Networks and Information Processing (ISSNIP), Singapore, pp. 1–6, IEEE (2014)

10. Elhamshary, M., Alzantot, M., Youssef, M.: JustWalk: a crowdsourcing approach for the automatic construction of indoor floorplans. IEEE Trans. Mob. Comput. **18**(10), 2358–2371 (2018)

11. Zhou, B., Li, Q., Mao, Q., Tu, W., et al.: ALIMC: activity landmark-based indoor mapping via crowdsourcing. IEEE Trans. Intell. Transp. Syst. **16**(5), 2774–2785 (2015)

12. Amarasinghe, D., Mann, G.K., Gosine, R.G.: Landmark detection and localization for mobile robot applications: a multisensor approach. Robotica **28**(5), 663–673 (2010)

13. Alansary, A., Oktay, O., et al.: Evaluating reinforcement learning agents for anatomical landmark detection. Med. Image Anal. **53**, 156–164 (2019)

14. Nilwong, S., Hossain, D., et al.: Deep learning-based landmark detection for mobile robot outdoor localization. Machines **7**(2), 25 (2019)

15. Wang, Z., Vandersteen, C., Raffaelli, C., Guevara, N., Patou, F., Delingette, H.: One-shot learning for landmarks detection. In: Engelhardt, S., et al. (eds.) Deep Generative Models, and Data Augmentation, Labelling, and Imperfections. Lecture Notes in Computer Science, vol. 13003, pp. 163–172. Springer, Cham (2021). https://doi.org/10.1007/978-3-030-88210-5_15

16. Weishaupt, F., Will, P.S., et al.: Robust point-shaped landmark detection using polarimetric radar. In: 2021 IEEE Intelligent Vehicles Symposium (IV), pp. 859–865, IEEE (2021)

17. Narayana, K., Goulette, F., Steux, B.: Planar landmark detection using a specific arrangement of LIDAR scanners. In: IEEE/ION Position, Location and Navigation Symposium, pp. 1057–1069, IEEE, May 2010

18. Ravankar, A., Hoshino, Y., Kobayashi, Y.: Robust landmark detection in vineyards using laser range sensor. In: The Proceedings of JSME annual Conference on Robotics and Mechatronics (Robomec), pp. 1A1-E03 (2019)

19. Sun, S., Yin, Y., et al.: D. Robust landmark detection and position measurement based on monocular vision for autonomous aerial refueling of UAVs. IEEE Trans. Cybern. **49**(12), 4167–4179 (2018)

20. Rous, M., Lupschen, H., et al.: Vision-based indoor scene analysis for natural landmark detection. In: Proceedings of the 2005 IEEE International conference on Robotics and Automation, Barcelona, Spain, pp. 4642–4647 (2005)

21. Sun, S., Yin, Y., Wang, X., Xu, D.: Robust landmark detection and position measurement based on monocular vision for autonomous aerial refueling of UAVs. IEEE Trans. Cybern. **49**(12), 4167–4179 (2018)

22. Zheng, Y., Liu, D., Georgescu, B., Nguyen, H., Comaniciu, D.: 3D deep learning for efficient and robust landmark detection in volumetric data. In: Navab, N., Hornegger, J., Wells, W.M., Frangi, A.F. (eds.) Medical Image Computing and Computer-Assisted Intervention – MICCAI 2015. Lecture Notes in Computer Science, vol. 9349, pp. 565–572. Springer, Cham (2015). https://doi.org/10.1007/978-3-319-24553-9_69

23. Schwendicke, F., et al.: Deep learning for cephalometric landmark detection: systematic review and meta-analysis. Clin. Oral Invest. **25**(7), 4299–4309 (2021). https://doi.org/10.1007/s00784-021-03990-w

24. Han, D., Gao, Y., Wu, G., Yap, P.-T., Shen, D.: Robust anatomical landmark detection for MR brain image registration. In: Golland, P., Hata, N., Barillot, C., Hornegger, J., Howe, R. (eds.) Medical Image Computing and Computer-Assisted Intervention – MICCAI 2014. Lecture Notes in Computer Science, vol. 8673, pp. 186–193. Springer, Cham (2014). https://doi.org/10.1007/978-3-319-10404-1_24

25. Zhang, J., Liu, M., Shen, D.: Detecting anatomical landmarks from limited medical imaging data using two-stage task-oriented deep neural networks. IEEE Trans. Image Process. **26**(10), 4753–4764 (2017)
26. Jheng, Y.-C., et al.: A novel machine learning-based algorithm to identify and classify lesions and anatomical landmarks in colonoscopy images. Surg. Endosc. **36**(1), 640–650 (2021). https://doi.org/10.1007/s00464-021-08331-2
27. Zhang, Z., Luo, P., et al.: Facial landmark detection by deep multi-task learning. In: European Conference on Computer Vision, Part II, Zurich, Switzerland, pp. 94–108, 6–12 Sep 2014
28. Liu, Z., et al.: Robust target recognition and tracking of self-driving cars with radar and camera information fusion under severe weather conditions. IEEE Trans. Intell. Transp. Syst. **23**(7) 6640–653 (2021)
29. Wang, C., Liu, J., Chen, Y., et al.: Towards in-baggage suspicious object detection using commodity wifi. In: 2018 IEEE Conference on Communications and Network Security (CNS), pp. 1–9. IEEE, May 2018
30. Beltrán, J., Guindel, C., Moreno, F.M., et al.: BirdNet: a 3D object detection framework from lidar information. In: 2018 21st International Conference on Intelligent Transportation Systems (ITSC), pp. 3517–3523. IEEE, November 2018
31. Zhou, B., Elbadry, M., Gao, R., Ye, F.: Towards scalable indoor map construction and refinement using acoustics on smartphones. IEEE Trans. Mob. Comput. **19**(1), 217–230 (2019)
32. Dubois, A., François, C.: Human activities recognition with RGB-Depth camera using HMM. In: 2013 35th Annual International Conference of the IEEE Engineering in Medicine and Biology Society (EMBC). IEEE, Osaka, Japan, 3–7 Jul 2013
33. Wang, K., He, J., Zhang, L.: Attention-based convolutional neural network for weakly labeled human activities' recognition with wearable sensors. IEEE Sens. J. **19**(17), 7598–7604 (2019)
34. Varshney, N., Bakariya, B.: Deep convolutional neural model for human activities recognition in a sequence of video by combining multiple CNN streams. Multimedia Tools Appl. **81**, 1–13 (2021). https://doi.org/10.1007/s11042-021-11220-4
35. Liu, Z., Han, Y., Chen, Z., Fang, Y., Qian, H., Zhou, J.: Human activities recognition from videos based on compound deep neural network. In: Liu, Qi., Liu, X., Shen, T., Qiu, X. (eds.) The 10th International Conference on Computer Engineering and Networks. Advances in Intelligent Systems and Computing, vol. 1274, pp. 314–326. Springer, Singapore (2021). https://doi.org/10.1007/978-981-15-8462-6_37
36. Gnouma, M., Ladjailia, A., Ejbali, R., Zaied, M.: Stacked sparse autoencoder and history of binary motion image for human activity recognition. Multimedia Tools Appl. **78**(2), 2157–2179 (2018). https://doi.org/10.1007/s11042-018-6273-1
37. Snoun, A., Jlidi, N., Bouchrika, T., Jemai, O., Zaied, M.: Towards a deep human activity recognition approach based on video to image transformation with skeleton data. Multimedia Tools Appl. **80**(19), 29675–29698 (2021). https://doi.org/10.1007/s11042-021-11188-1
38. Murad, A., Pyun, J.Y.: Deep recurrent neural networks for human activity recognition. Sensors **17**(11), 2556 (2017)
39. Xu, C., et al.: InnoHAR: a deep neural network for complex human activity recognition. IEEE Access **7**, 9893–9902 (2019)
40. Zhang, F., et al.: Towards a diffraction-based sensing approach on human activity recognition. In: Proceedings of the ACM on Interactive, Mobile, Wearable and Ubiquitous Technologies **3**(1), 1–25 (2019)
41. Yan, H., et al.: WiAct: a passive WiFi-based human activity recognition system. IEEE Sens. J. **20**(1), 296–305 (2019)
42. Bashar, S.K., Abdullah, A.F., Ki, H.C.: Smartphone based human activity recognition with feature selection and dense neural network. In: 42nd Annual International Conference of the

IEEE Engineering in Medicine and Biology Society (EMBC), Montreal, Canada, pp. 20–24 (2020)

43. Mahmud, S., Tonmoy, M.: et al.: Human activity recognition from wearable sensor data using self-attention. arXiv preprint arXiv:2003.09018. (2020)

44. Zhang, M., Sawchuk, A.A.: USC-HAD: a daily activity dataset for ubiquitous activity recognition using wearable sensors. In: Proceedings of the 2012 ACM Conference on Ubiquitous Computing, Pittsburgh, USA, pp. 1036–1043 (2012)

45. Roggen. D., Calatroni, A., et al:. Collecting complex activity datasets in highly rich networked sensor environments. In: 2010 Seventh International Conference on Networked Sensing Systems (INSS), Kassel, Germany, pp. 233–240, IEEE (2010)

46. Thakur, D., Biswas, S., Ho., et al.: ConvAE-LSTM: convolutional Autoencoder Long Short-Term Memory Network for Smartphone-Based Human Activity Recognition. IEEE Access **10**, 4137–4156 (2022)

47. Lim, X.Y., Gan, K.B., et al.: Deep ConvLSTM network with dataset resampling for upper body activity recognition using minimal number of IMU sensors. Appl. Sci. **11**(8), 3543 (2021)

Facial Action Unit Detection by Exploring the Weak Relationships Between AU Labels

Mengke Tian[1,2], Hengliang Zhu[3]($\boxtimes$), Yong Wang[2], Yimao Cai[1], Feng Liu[4],
Pengrong Lin[2], Yingzhuo Huang[2], and Xiaochen Xie[2]

[1] School of Integrated Circuits, Peking University, Beijing 100871, China
mtianaa@connect.ust.hk
[2] Beijing Microelectronics Technology Institute, Beijing 100076, China
[3] Fujian University of Technology, Fuzhou 350118, China
hengliang_zhu@fjut.edu.cn
[4] Ericsson Communications Co. Ltd., Beijing 100102, China

Abstract. In recent years, facial action unit (AU) detection attracts more and more attentions and great progress has been made. However, few approaches solve AU detection problem by applying the emotion information, and the specific influence of emotion categories to AU detection is not investigated. In this paper, we firstly explore the relationship between emotion categories and AU labels, and study the influence of emotion for AU detection. With emotion weak labels, we propose a simple yet efficient deep network that uses limited emotion labels to constraint the AU detection. The proposed network contains two architectures: a main net and an assistant net. The main net can learn semantic relation between AUs, especially the AUs related to emotions. Moreover, we design a dual pooling module embedded into the main net to further promote the results. Extensive experiments on two datasets show that the AU detection can obtain benefits with the weak labels of AUs. The proposed method has a significant improvement on baseline and achieves state-of-the-art performance compared with other methods. Furthermore, because only the main net is used for testing, our model is very fast and achieves over 278 fps.

Keywords: Action Unit(AU) detection · Emotion · Semantic relation

1 Introduction

Facial action unit detection plays an important role in various facial related tasks, such as expression analysis, interactive games, affective computing and behavioral science. Facial action unit is coded by the Facial Action Coding System (FACS) [1] and this system captures the slight different instant changes on facial appearance. Each AU depicts the movement of individual facial muscle, and some specific AUs can show high-level semantic expression when they are

H. Gao et al. (Eds.): CollaborateCom 2022, LNICST 461, pp. 478–495, 2022.
https://doi.org/10.1007/978-3-031-24386-8_26

co-occurrence. Action unit detection is a multi-label classification problem and lots of excellent works [2–4] solve this task by learning multiple AUs together. However, we observe that the different AU has different occurrence rate. It is difficult to train multi-label images by using the data with unbalanced distribution. On the other hand, the relation between all AUs is weak, but only specific AUs contain strong correlations, such as AU6 and AU12 define the happiness emotion. So both emotion categories and AUs can be used to represent facial behaviors. Though some researchers [3,5] applied the strategies of region enhancement for AU detection, the relations between emotion and AUs are ignored.

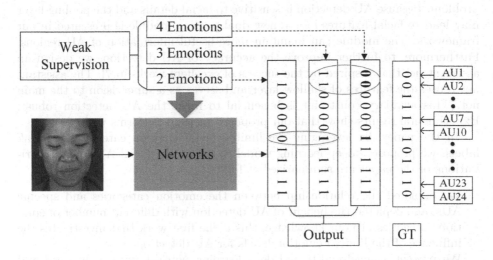

Fig. 1. Illustration of using different weak relationships. With more fine-grained emotion categories, more AUs are precisely detected. For example, AUs in red circles regions are corrected. (Color figure online)

In order to solve the above problems, the relations between emotion and AU labels are considered in this paper. Human beings have seven basic emotions (i.e., happiness, sadness, surprise, fear, anger, disgust and contempt) and each emotion is consisted of different AUs. From the Table 1, some specific AUs come from the same emotion and have a strong relationship between them. These co-occurrence AUs describe facial semantic information. Therefore, we explore the relations between emotion category and specific AUs to improve the performance of AU detection. However, the public AU databases have limited AU labels, for example, BP4D database provides only 12 AU labels, but there have 28 main facial AU codes. In other words, some emotions can not be identified due to the lacking of the AU labels. To alleviate this issue, we treat emotion categories as weak labels and propose a simple partition of emotion categories for AU dataset. We design three groups, including 2, 3 and 4 emotion categories. Take 4 emotion categories as example, three emotions can be ensured by using the provided AU labels and other uncertain emotions are classified as one category. With emotion-level supervision, we propose a light-weighted architecture for AU detection. As shown in Fig. 1, with the weak relationships of limited emotion categories, the AU detection can obtain benefits. We can see that more fine-grained emotion categories, the results are better.

As mentioned above, the emotion categories can provide rich context among AUs. So how to efficiently use emotion categories to supervise facial AU multi-label learning is challenging. Deep learning based methods achieve superior performance and extract more discriminative features, especially in recognition tasks. In this paper, we proposed a efficient AU detection method to solve this problem. Because AU detection is sensitive to facial details and the pooling layer may lead to facial features loss, a new dual pooling module is presented in our framework. The module can maintain more useful information of AU regions. Furthermore, to further improve the accuracy of AU detection, we design an assistant net that inspired by the success of excellent works [6,7]. The assistant net reuses the features of shallow layer and serves as a supervision to the main net. This auxiliary constraint is beneficial to make the AU detection robust. Experimental results show that our proposed method performs well.

In the paper, by leveraging the limited facial emotion categories as weak labels, we propose a deep learning model to detect the facial AUs. The contributions of the paper are summarized as follows:

- We explored the relationship between the emotion categories and specific AUs, and depicted the benefit of AU detection with different number of emotion categories. To our knowledge, this is the first work that investigates the influence of the limited emotion labels for AU detection.
- We present a novel end-to-end deep learning network with high speed and accuracy, which consists of a main net and an assistant net. Moreover, a new dual pooling module is embedded in the network to preserve the more useful facial details.
- Experimental analysis shows the effectiveness of the proposed components in the whole network and demonstrates superiority over the state-of-the-art approaches.

Table 1. Emotion-related facial action units.

Emotion	Action Units
Happiness	6 + 12
Sadness	1 + 4 + 15
Surprise	1 + 2 + 5 + 26
Fear	1 + 2 + 4 + 5 + 20 + 26
Anger	4 + 5 + 7 + 23
Disgust	9 + 15 + 16
Contempt	12 + 14

2   Related Work

Automated AU detection has a noticeable improvement in recent years. Researchers extract different features from a face image to represent the desired semantic information. According to the difference of features, these methods are classified into conventional methods and deep learning methods.

2.1   Conventional Methods

In conventional approaches, various handcraft features are applied to represent a face and classical classifiers are used to learn the models. Some researchers extract features from the whole face image and some researchers extract features from regions around facial landmarks. Valstar et al. [8] applied Gabor wavelet features extracted around facial landmarks and learned the representation by Adaboost framework, and the final labels are classified by using SVM. Some works [9–11] also applied handcraft features extracted around facial landmarks. Jiang et al. [2] applied histograms of Local Phase Quantization (LPQ) to extract the discriminative features for AU detection. Zhao et al. [12] proposed a joint learning method that detecting the patch and AUs label simultaneously. By fusing the geometry information and multiple orientation Gabor features, Fabian et al. [13] achieved fast and accurate AUs detection performance. The patch is around the facial landmarks and SIFT features are extracted. Song et al. [14] addressed this topic by analyzing co-occurrence and the sparsity of action units. Wu et al. [4] proposed a new constraint to jointly learning the AU labels and facial landmarks localization. Girard et al. [15] exploited a regression framework to estimate the intensity of action unit regions and addressed this problem by employing linear partial least squares. In summary, these conventional methods made efforts by applying discriminative features and robust classifiers.

2.2   Deep Learning Methods

Due to the strong ability of learning discriminative features, deep learning is one of the most hot topics in the last few years, and CNNs have been used in almost all the computer version tasks. Inspired by the locally connected layer [16], Zhao et al. [5] proposed a region-based CNN method to capture structural information in different facial regions. In this method, a new region layer is proposed to divide the image into small patches and each patch is learned individually. In the last convolutional layer, these patches are combined into one image. EAC [3] proposed two novel nets to make the neural network to pay more attention to AUs interest regions to improve the accuracy. Corneanu et al. [17] learned the AU detection in two stages and these two stages are patch learning and structure learning. Han et al. [18] proposed an Optimized Filter Size (OFS) for AU detection. In this model, the filter size is alterable. That is to say when the model is learning AU labels, filters weights and sizes could be learned at the same time. Hao et al. [19] proposed a three-layer hybrid Bayesian network and expression information was used to assist the AU recognition. Shao et al. [20,21] use facial landmarks to extract the meaningful local features for AU detection, but there network is very complex. Zhang et al. [22] proposed a method that leveraging prior probabilities of expression-independent and expression-dependent AU to learn the multiple AU classifiers. Hao et al. [19] captured the global relationships among AUs and expressions For BP4D, they used 4612 apex frames as samples in the experiment. Zhang et al. [22] proposed prior probabilities on AUs, including expression-independent and expression-dependent AU probabilities. They utilized 391 apex frames and 8 AUs on BP4D, while we use 12 AUs and total 146577 frames.

Different with the above two methods, we design the coarse emotion labels based on the AU labels and use emotion to supervise AU detection. Shao et al. [23] used the attention mechanism to capture the AU-related local features and pixel-level relations for AUs. Li et al. [24] utilized the self-supervised representation learning method to to encode the movements of AUs and head motions. Due to the lack of accurate annotations, Shao et al. [25] proposed an end-to-end unconstrained facial AU detection to deal with the situations with the unconstrained variability in facial appearances.

3   The Proposed Method

In Sect. 3.1, we introduce the generation of emotion categories and the weak relationships of AUs for AU detection. Then, the structure of the whole network is described in Sect. 3.2, as shown in Fig. 2. In Sect. 3.3, we design a dual pooling module and demonstrate its effectiveness.

3.1   Weak Relationships of AUs

AU detection is affected with various factors, such as pose, illumination, facial appearance and pedestrians identity. So how to improve the performance of facial

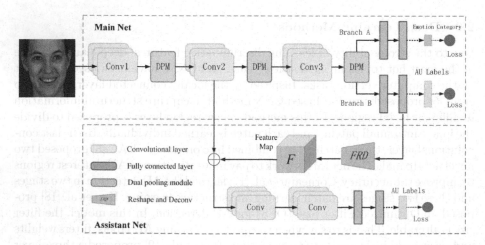

Fig. 2. The architecture of our AU detection model (best viewed in color). (Color figure online)

AU detection is a challenging problem. In order to improve the performance of AU detection, some researches focus on the facial region by applying the facial landmarks information. For example, [3,20,26] used facial landmarks to help the facial AU detection. However, these methods learn features that are sensitive to local regions without considering the global information of the face. We observe that facial emotions are produced by the change of muscle group, and can represent the global facial semantic features. Different group of AUs occurrence can generate different emotions. Their are some works [19,22] used expression information to assist AU detection. These works ignored the situation that how to use the image without emotion labels. In contrast, we regard the face without emotion label as hybrid emotion category.

Table 2. The 4 coarse emotion categories in the BP4D and DISFA datasets.

BP4D	Happiness	Sadness	Contempt	Hybrid
AUs	6 + 12	1 + 4 + 15	12 + 14	others
DISFA	Happiness	Sadness	Surprise	Hybrid
AUs	6 + 12	1 + 4 + 15	1 + 2 + 5 + 6	others

Without giving the ground truth labels on emotions, it is really hard to infer a definite label by only looking at the combination of AUs. We found that the facial emotion has close relations with AUs [27]. Emotion categories are easily defined as a unique set of AUs (see Table 1). For example, sadness contains AU1, AU4 and AU15. When these specific AUs co-occurrence, the face appears corresponding emotion and the semantic information of the face is involved. So we leverage the emotion categories to learn facial semantic features to provide a constraint for the AUs recognition. Because the labels of emotion are not provided in the BP4D and DISFA databases, the emotion categories are defined by using the combination of specific AUs. Based on the FACS, we design three groups of emotion category, including 2, 3 and 4 emotion categories. The detail partitions of 2 and 3 coarse emotion categories are described in Sect. 4.4. Here, we talk about the 4 coarse emotion categories, as shown in Table 2. It includes 3 emotions that can be identified and one hybrid emotion that can not be identified. These 4 coarse labels of emotion are used as weak relationships for the AU detection. Thus, our model can deal with the face images that emotions are uncertain.

Given the AU detection training dataset $S = (I^{(n)}, Y^{(n)}), n = 1, 2, ..., N$ with N training images, where I denotes an face image with ground-truth labels Y. Then we defined a vector $Y = [y_1, y_2, ..., y_C]$, y_i is a binary variable of each AU. We set $y_i = 1$ if the $i - th$ AU is occurrence in an image I, and $y_i = 0$ otherwise. C is the number of AU labels in the dataset S. Let the symbol $\mathbf{W}$ as the parameters of the network, $\widehat{Y} = [\widehat{y}_1, \widehat{y}_2, ..., \widehat{y}_C]$ denotes the detected results of AU labels.

For emotion supervision, we use a softmax layer to predict the probability of emotion. The loss of emotion recognition (branch A) is obtained by

$$\mathcal{L}_e(\mathbf{W}, \theta_e) = \varphi_{softmax}(I; \mathbf{W}, \theta_e) \tag{1}$$

where θ_e denotes the classifier parameter for the emotion recognition. The AU detection can be regarded as a multi-label binary classification problem, and we use the multi-label sigmoid cross-entropy loss for AU detection [5]. The loss of AU detection (branch B) is defined as follows.

$$\mathcal{L}_m(\mathbf{W}, \theta_m) = -\frac{1}{N} \sum_{n=1}^{N} \sum_{i=1}^{C} \xi(y_i) log P(\widehat{y_i}^{(n)} | I; \mathbf{W}, \theta_m)$$
$$+ (1 - \xi(y_i)) log P(\widehat{y_i}^{(n)} | I; \mathbf{W}, \theta_m). \tag{2}$$

where $\xi(\cdot)$ is a sign function, and it returns 1 when the $i - th$ AU is occurrence, otherwise returns 0. θ_m is the classifier parameter for the AU detection in the main net. $P(\widehat{y_i} | I; \mathbf{W}, \theta_m)$ denotes the confidence score of the $i - th$ AU detection. Note that, our method does not use external data and domain adaption technologies. We believe that this weak relationships method can also be used in other visual tasks with limited labels.

3.2   Overview of Framework

As shown in Fig. 2, the architecture of our AU detection model consists of three components: the main net, the dual pooling module and the assistant net. The main net is a task for AU detection and the assistant net applies weak relationships of AUs to provide a constraint to the AU branch.

Main Net for AU Detection. Our main net is very simple and contains three convolutional layers. Because the surroundings of AU are regional and subtle, the texture changes of these facial regions could influence the accuracy of different AU detection. We observe that when the multiple continual convolution layers are used, the details of facial information will be lost in the final output (the feature map). In order to hold sufficient facial information from its previous layer, we only use three convolutional layers in the main net, as illustrated in Fig. 2. The parameters of three convolutional layers are shared between the emotion classification and AU detection. The features collected from the shared convolutional layers across different semantic levels. At the end of the main net, we use two fully connected layers (FCL) to model the spatial correlations of the entire image. This designing is simple and efficient for features extraction.

The input image is a 200×200 RGB image, then it is sent to a convolutional layer (Conv1) with 96 filters, kernel size 11×11 and stride 4. The non-linear transformation (ReLU) is also used after each convolutional layer, and the outputs of Conv1 are size of 48×48 feature maps. For simplicity, the parameters of Conv1 are denoted as $96 \times 48 \times 48, 11 \times 11, 4$. The parameters of the main

Table 3. The parameter settings of the main net.

No	Layer	Parameters
0	Input	$200 \times 200 \times 3$
1	Conv1	$96 \times 48 \times 48, 11 \times 11, 4$
2	DPM	$96 \times 24 \times 24$
3	Conv2	$256 \times 24 \times 24, 5 \times 5, 2$
4	DPM	$256 \times 12 \times 12$
5	Conv3	$384 \times 12 \times 12, 3 \times 3, 1$
6	DPM	$384 \times 6 \times 6$

net can be found in Table 3. The Conv1 layer generates 96 feature maps, which are passed into a dual pooling layer (DPM, the blue box in Fig. 2). The DPM outputs 96 feature maps with size 24×24, and more details will be provided in Sect. 3.3. In the main net, we use three convolutional layers and three DPMs to avoid losing too much facial features. Finally, two branches behind the last DPM with each two fully connected layers to capture the global spatial information across the input image. Branch A is used for emotion classification, and branch B is used for AU detection. For each branch, the output of fully connected layers is a 4096 feature vector, which can extract the discriminative features.

Assistant Net with Feature Fusing. Previous works [28–30] indicate that the high-level semantic features help the category recognition of image, and the low-level visual features contribute to preserve detailed structures.

Motivated by the skip connections [31], we combine the deep layer and shallow layer to improve AU detection. We propose an assistant net to improve the ability of feature extraction in our model. The assistant net structure mainly contains two convolutional layers with kernel size 3 and stride 1, and two FCLs with size 4096. The FRD block in the assistant net contains a feature reshaper and deconvolution structure (the gray trapezoid in Fig. 2). The FRD reshapes the feature vector of FCL into $64 \times 8 \times 8$ feature maps. Then, the feature maps are up-sampled to the same size with the outputs of Conv2 layer. The Conv2 layer and feature map are combined to feed into the following convoltuional layer. The integrated feature maps F can be defined as

$$Comb = Concat(conv2, F), \tag{3}$$

where $Concat$ is the cross-channel concatenation operator. By this way, the whole network can learn rich structure information to improve the feature representations around the AU regions. Experimental results show that the assistant net can promote the accuracy of AU detection.

The Total Loss. Our proposed deep model has three loss layers, as shown in Fig. 2 (the purple circle). The loss $L_a(\mathbf{W}, \theta_a)$ in the assistant net is similar to the main net, where θ_a is the classifier parameter for the AU detection in the assistant net.

The total loss for AU detection can be written by

$$\mathcal{L}_{final}(\mathbf{W}, \theta) = \alpha_1 \mathcal{L}_m(\mathbf{W}, \theta_m) + \alpha_2 \mathcal{L}_a(\mathbf{W}, \theta_a)$$
$$+ \alpha_3 \mathcal{L}_e(\mathbf{W}, \theta_e). \tag{4}$$

where α_i is the loss weight to balance the loss of each task. In our experiment, we set $\alpha_i = 1, i = 1, 2, 3$. To solve above the loss function, we utilize the stochastic gradient descent (SGD) algorithm to get the optimal values.

3.3　Dual Pooling Module

Facial action units detection is sensitive to details of the face, in order to extract more useful features, we design a dual pooling module that can retain more detail features. The size of output feature map after convolutional layer is much smaller than the input, for example, the size of the image changed from 200×200 to 48×48 via the Conv1 layer. Therefore, lots of facial features lost in this process.

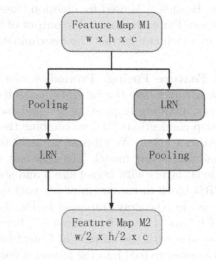

Fig. 3. The architecture of the dual pooling module. The DPM contains two components, and each one takes feature maps with $w \times h \times c$ resolutions as input. Then pooling and response normalization operators down-sample the feature maps to the same spatial size. Finally, the concatenation and ReLU non-linearity layer are used to output the integrated feature maps.

In order to transfer more facial details to the following convolutional layer, we embed the DPM into the main net to improve the performance of AU detection, the structure of DPM is displayed in Fig. 3. The module consists of two complementary and symmetric components. Each component contains one 3×3

pooling layer with stride 2 and one Local Response Normalization (LRN) layer with local size 5. Given the input feature maps $\mathbf{F}(\mathbf{I})$ with size $t = [w \times h \times c]$, the size of output feature maps is $r = [w/2 \times h/2 \times c]$. Thus, the integrated feature maps are generated by

$$Comb = Concat(P_l(\mathbf{F}(\mathbf{I}); \Omega_l), P_r(\mathbf{F}(\mathbf{I}); \Omega_r)) \tag{5}$$

where $P_i(\mathbf{F}(\mathbf{I}); \Omega_i)$ denotes left or right components operator with parameters Ω_i, $i \in \{l, r\}$. The function $P_i(\cdot; \cdot)$ helps to down-sample and normalize the input high-resolution feature maps.

By applying the DPM, more facial features can be retained to boost the performance in AU detection. As illustrated in Fig. 4, without the DPM, the feature maps lost much information (the middle column). When using the DPM, more facial information are preserved (the third column). Experimental results show that the proposed DPM conspicuously improves the accuracy of AU detection by 0.8% on BP4D dataset, as list in Table 8. We think that the DPM module can be applied into other detail-sensitive visual tasks.

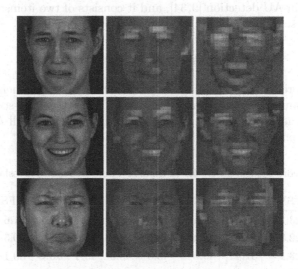

Fig. 4. Visualization of feature maps with or without DPM, the middle column without DPM and the third column is using DPM.

4   Experiments and Results

4.1   Settings

Datasets: The public databases used in this paper are BP4D [32] and DISFA [33]. The AU databases are difficult to obtain due to huge manual labeling work is needed. Here we give a brief review of these two AU databases.

BP4D: There are 41 participants and each participant is involved in 8 sessions that capture both 2D and 3D videos. More than 140000 frames can be obtained from these 328 videos, and 49 facial landmarks are provided to crop the face from the original images. For fair comparison, 12 AUs are evaluated and 3-fold cross validation are conducted like DRML [5] and EAC [3].

DISFA: This dataset contains 27 participants including 12 women and 15 men, each of participant has 4845 frames. Facial landmarks and AU intensities are provided. The AU intensities are from 0 to 5 and we use the images with intensities equal or over 2 like DRML [5]. There are more than 100000 images and we use 58000+ images. Similar to EAC [3], we use the pre-trained model from BP4D and fine-tuning on this database. The 3-fold cross validation is conducted and 8 AUs are evaluated.

Evaluation Metrics: Two metrics: the F_β-score and the average accuracy (%) are used to measure the performance of AU detection. We compute the performance with accuracy (%) following the previous work [3]. F_β-score metric is widely used in AU detection [9,34], and it consists of two items: precision and recall. The F_β-score of each AU label is given by

$$F_\beta = \frac{(1 + \beta^2) \times precision_i \times recall_i}{\beta^2 \times precision_i + recall_i} \tag{6}$$

Following the previous works [3,5], we set $\beta = 1$ in our experiment where recall and precision are treated as equally relevant. Then we get F1-score evaluation for all AUs. In addition, we compute the average results over all AU labels. For simplicity, we omit % in all the results in our experiments.

Table 4. F1-score results on BP4D database. The best results are shown in **bold**.

AU	LSVM	JPML	DRML	CPM	EAC	ROI	DSIN	OFS	Ours
1	23.2	32.6	36.4	43.4	39.0	36.2	**51.7**	41.6	45.6
2	22.8	25.6	**41.8**	40.7	35.2	31.6	40.4	30.5	**41.8**
4	23.1	37.4	43.0	43.3	48.6	43.4	**56.0**	39.1	54.6
6	27.2	42.3	55.0	59.2	76.1	77.1	76.1	74.5	**78.5**
7	47.1	50.5	67.0	61.3	72.9	**73.7**	73.5	62.8	73.4
10	77.2	72.2	66.3	62.1	81.9	**85.0**	79.9	74.3	82.0
12	63.7	74.1	65.8	68.5	86.2	87.0	85.4	81.2	**87.7**
14	64.3	**65.7**	54.1	52.5	58.8	62.6	62.7	55.5	62.2
15	18.4	38.1	33.2	36.7	37.5	**45.7**	37.3	32.6	38.9
17	33.0	40.0	48.0	54.3	59.1	58.0	**62.9**	56.8	61.7
23	19.4	30.4	31.7	39.5	35.9	38.3	38.8	41.3	**43.6**
24	20.7	42.3	31.0	37.8	35.8	37.4	41.6	–	**47.3**
AVG	35.3	45.9	48.3	50.0	55.9	56.4	58.9	53.7	**59.8**

Implementation Details: To train a deep learning model, we need larger numbers of face images. Similar to DRML's experiment settings [5], we choose BP4D to train our model. We first split the dataset into 3 folds, and each time two folds are used for training and the third fold for testing. A post-processing is used in our method. We use 3 emotions which can be ensured to judge the corresponding AU labels. This process can give 0.1% improvement on final results. In our network, all the weights of loss function are set to 1 without optimization. If the weights are optimized, the results can be further improved. We found that the distribution of AUs in the database was unbalance, and some AUs were much more than others. However, we did not do any data balancing operation for the training, but directly trained on the original data. Our network could still achieve good results in the case of unbalance distribution of data samples.

For each face image, we crop and scale the original image into a $200 \times 200 \times 3$ image. In order to enhance the diversity of training data, horizontally flipping is used. We train our model with an open source deep learning framework Caffe [35], and directly feed the input images into the network. The proposed network is trained on an Intel Core computer with an i7-6850K CPU and a single GeForce GTX 1080Ti GPU. In our experiments, the base learning rate is initialized with 0.0001, which is reduced after every 10000 iterations. We set the total number of iterations to 40000. The momentum is 0.9 and weight decay of 0.0005 is used.

Running Time: For training stage, it takes us about 2 h to train the deep model. Because the output of branch B is the final result of AUs detection, the structures of network that irrelevant to this output can be pruned in testing stage, such as branch A and the assistant net. Thus, the speed of AU detection is very fast. In testing, our network takes 0.0036s (278 FPS) to process an image (average 200×200).

4.2 Comparison with State-of-the-Art Methods

We compare our method with state-of-the-art methods in this Section, the compared approaches including LSVM [36], JPML [12], APL [37], DRML [5], CPM [38], EAC-Net [3], ROI [39], DSIN [17] and OFS [18]. LSVM [36], JPML [12] and APL [37] are conventional methods and other methods are deep learning-based methods.

Tables 4 and 5 show the F1-score and accuracy results of 12 AUs on BP4D database. We can see that our algorithm outperforms all other methods on this challenging database in term of average results. For some AUs, the performance is significantly improved. DSIN [17] and OFS [18] are the most recent works which utilized the CNN models and our method also give better results compared with them. OFS [18] only reports the average F1-score result of 11 AUs and average accuracy is 72.2%. DSIN [17] does not provide the accuracy results. Therefore, we do not show the AU accuracy result of DSIN [17]. In our method, some AUs are not as good as others, the reason may be is the unbalance of AUs distribution.

Table 5. Accuracy results on BP4D database. The best results are shown in **bold**.

AU	LSVM	JPML	DRML	EAC	Ours
1	20.7	40.7	55.7	68.9	**72.8**
2	17.7	42.1	54.5	73.9	**76.3**
4	22.9	46.2	58.8	78.1	**78.8**
6	20.3	40.0	56.6	78.5	**79.3**
7	44.8	50.0	61.0	69.0	**70.1**
10	73.4	75.2	53.6	77.6	**77.9**
12	55.3	60.5	60.8	84.6	**85.9**
14	46.8	53.6	57.0	60.6	**63.5**
15	18.3	50.1	56.2	78.1	**79.2**
17	36.4	42.5	50.0	70.6	**72.7**
23	19.2	51.9	53.9	81.0	**81.4**
24	11.7	53.2	53.9	82.4	**84.0**
AVG	32.2	50.5	56.0	75.2	**76.8**

Table 6. F1-score results on DISFA database.

AU	APL	DRML	EAC	DSIN	Ours
1	11.4	17.3	41.5	**42.4**	39.1
2	12.0	17.7	26.4	39.0	**65.2**
4	30.1	37.4	66.4	**68.4**	67.9
6	12.4	29.0	**50.7**	28.6	40.8
9	10.1	10.7	**80.5**	46.8	46.4
12	65.9	37.7	**89.3**	70.8	73.2
25	21.4	38.5	88.9	**90.4**	89.8
26	26.9	20.1	15.6	**42.2**	37.2
AVG	23.8	26.7	48.5	53.6	**57.4**

Tables 6 and 7 show the F1-score and accuracy results of 8 AUs on DISFA database. On this database, our method is the best in term of average results. For the average F1-score, the result of our method is increased by 7% compared with DSIN. For the average accuracy, our result is 85%, better than EAC-Net [3] (80%). In addition, OFS [18] uses 10 AUs to train and conducts 9 folds cross-validation on DISFA database, the F1-score is 55.3% and accuracy is 85.0%. From the Table 7, we also see that the results of some AUs (i.e., AU1, AU2, AU6, AU25 and AU26) are greatly improved when applying our method.

Table 7. Accuracy results on DISFA database.

AU	APL	DRML	EAC	Ours
1	32.7	53.3	85.6	**90.5**
2	27.8	53.2	84.9	**94.5**
4	37.9	60.0	**79.1**	76.8
6	13.6	54.9	69.1	**79.4**
9	64.4	51.5	88.1	**91.1**
12	94.2	54.6	**90.0**	84.1
25	50.4	45.6	80.5	**88.1**
26	47.1	45.3	64.8	**75.5**
AVG	46.0	52.3	80.6	**85.0**

4.3   Ablation Study

In this paper, we propose three components to improve the performance of AU detection and each component shows a benefit to the whole process. In order to show the affect of each component for AU detection, we conduct our experiments on BP4D database. Notably, we follow the three subsets partition of DRML [5]. The subset {1,2} are used for training and the subset {3} is used for testing. For simple notation, we define as follows: the main net without DPM and branch A is used as baseline (BL), the main net without DPM as MT-net, the main net as M-net, the whole network as Final-net. Table 8 shows the results of our experiments. From the table, we can see that each component gives an improvement to the results. For example, when using emotion categories, the result of MT-net increases 1.6 point compared with BL. When both the emotion categories and DPM are used, the accuracy of M-net is 58.4, achieving 0.8 point improvement over the MT-net. The assistant net rises about 1.3 point based on M-net, reaching 59.7% of accuracy. Therefore, both emotion supervision, DPM module and assistant net have significant contributions to the whole framework.

4.4   Analysis and Future Work

In this paper, we propose a post-processing that uses results of emotion to ensure the labels of related AUs. Though this step gives little improvement, it is useful and we will integrate it into the network to make the whole procedure full automation. The accuracy of emotion classification are 84.6% and 77.7% for DISFA and BP4D databases respectively. The accuracy result of BP4D is not good, due to the unbalance of emotion category. Over half of the images on BP4D database are hybrid emotion category, and images of other three emotion categories are less. That is to say, only limited part of data are benefited from branch A in the main net. We will use other methods to further divide the images belonging to the hybrid emotion category.

Table 8. F1-score results with different components in our model.

AU	BL	MT-net	M-net	Final-net
1	41.8	49.7	45.8	50.3
2	33.9	31.1	40.9	42.7
4	55.8	55.4	56.5	51.3
6	79.6	78.8	80.3	79.9
7	66.4	68.1	69.5	66.1
10	86.9	86.4	85.4	85.9
12	89.1	87.7	88.8	87.9
14	59.9	62.3	58.5	63.9
15	32.0	37.5	37.2	32.7
17	56.8	59.7	60.0	63.0
23	32.6	34.6	37.4	47.5
24	36.6	40.0	40.0	45.3
AVG	56.0	57.6	58.4	59.7

5 Conclusion

In this paper, we defined the label of emotions by using the combination of specific AUs. Then, a light-weighted deep network was proposed to apply the weak relationships to constraint AU detection. Specifically, we observed that with more emotion categories, the performance of AU detection was better. We also designed an assistant net and proposed a dual pooling module to be embedded in the main net. The DPM can protect the detailed facial structure and the assistant net can further improve the main net to capture semantic information. Experimental results show that our method is effectiveness for AU detection. Moreover, the proposed network is very simple and runs in real time, so our model can be applied for facial related tasks in mobile applications.

References

1. Ekman, P., Rosenberg, E.L.: What the face reveals: basic and applied studies of spontaneous expression using the facial action coding system (facs), 2nd ed. (2005)
2. Jiang, B., Martínez, B., Valstar, M.F., Pantic, M.: Decision level fusion of domain specific regions for facial action recognition. In: 22nd International Conference on Pattern Recognition, ICPR 2014, Stockholm, Sweden, 24–28 Aug 2014, pp. 1776–1781 (2014)
3. Li, W., Abtahi, F., Zhu, Z., Yin, L.: EAC-net: Deep nets with enhancing and cropping for facial action unit detection. IEEE Trans. Pattern Anal. Mach. Intell. **40**(11), 2583–2596 (2018)
4. Wu, Y., Ji, Q.: Constrained joint cascade regression framework for simultaneous facial action unit recognition and facial landmark detection. In: 2016 IEEE Conference on Computer Vision and Pattern Recognition, CVPR 2016, Las Vegas, NV, USA, 27–30 June 2016, pp. 3400–3408 (2016)

5. Zhao, K., Chu, W.-S., Zhang, H.: Deep region and multi-label learning for facial action unit detection. In: 2016 IEEE Conference on Computer Vision and Pattern Recognition, CVPR 2016, Las Vegas, NV, USA, 27–30 June 2016, pp. 3391–3399 (2016)

6. He, K., Zhang, X., Ren, S., Sun, J.: Deep residual learning for image recognition. In: 2016 IEEE Conference on Computer Vision and Pattern Recognition, CVPR 2016, Las Vegas, NV, USA, 27–30 June 2016, pp. 770–778 (2016)

7. Huang, G., Liu, Z., van der Maaten, L., Weinberger, K.Q.: Densely connected convolutional networks. In: 2017 IEEE Conference on Computer Vision and Pattern Recognition, CVPR 2017, Honolulu, HI, USA, 21–26 July 2017, pp. 2261–2269 (2017)

8. Valstar, M.F., Pantic, M.: Fully automatic facial action unit detection and temporal analysis. In: IEEE Conference on Computer Vision and Pattern Recognition, CVPR Workshops 2006, New York, NY, USA, 17–22 June 2006, p. 149 (2006)

9. Eleftheriadis, S., Rudovic, O., Pantic, M.: Multi-conditional latent variable model for joint facial action unit detection. In: 2015 IEEE International Conference on Computer Vision, ICCV 2015, Santiago, Chile, 7–13 Dec 2015, pp. 3792–3800 (2015)

10. Koelstra, S., Pantic, M., Patras, I.: A dynamic texture-based approach to recognition of facial actions and their temporal models. IEEE Trans. Pattern Anal. Mach. Intell. **32**(11), 1940–1954 (2010)

11. Wang, Z., Li, Y., Wang, S., Ji, Q.: Capturing global semantic relationships for facial action unit recognition. In: IEEE International Conference on Computer Vision, ICCV 2013, Sydney, Australia, 1–8 Dec 2013, pp. 3304–3311 (2013)

12. Zhao, K., Chu, W.-S., De la Torre, F., Cohn, J.F., Zhang, H.: Joint patch and multi-label learning for facial action unit detection. In: IEEE Conference on Computer Vision and Pattern Recognition, CVPR 2015, Boston, MA, USA, 7–12 June 2015, pp. 2207–2216 (2015)

13. Benitez-Quiroz, C.F., Srinivasan, R., Martínez, A.M.: Emotionet: an accurate, real-time algorithm for the automatic annotation of a million facial expressions in the wild. In: 2016 IEEE Conference on Computer Vision and Pattern Recognition, CVPR 2016, Las Vegas, NV, USA, 27–30 June 2016, pp. 5562–5570 (2016)

14. Song, Y., McDuff, D., Vasisht, D., Kapoor, A.: Exploiting sparsity and co-occurrence structure for action unit recognition. In: 11th IEEE International Conference and Workshops on Automatic Face and Gesture Recognition, FG 2015, Ljubljana, Slovenia, 4–8 May 2015, pp. 1–8 (2015)

15. Gehrig, T., Al-Halah, Z., Ekenel, H.K., Stiefelhagen, R.: Action unit intensity estimation using hierarchical partial least squares. In: 11th IEEE International Conference and Workshops on Automatic Face and Gesture Recognition, FG 2015, Ljubljana, Slovenia, 4–8 May 2015, pp. 1–6 (2015)

16. Taigman, Y., Yang, M., Ranzato, M., Wolf, L.: DeepFace: closing the gap to human-level performance in face verification. In: 2014 IEEE Conference on Computer Vision and Pattern Recognition, CVPR 2014, Columbus, OH, USA, 23–28 June 2014, pp. 1701–1708 (2014)

17. Corneanu, C., Madadi, M., Escalera, S.: Deep Structure Inference Network for Facial Action Unit Recognition. In: Ferrari, V., Hebert, M., Sminchisescu, C., Weiss, Y. (eds.) ECCV 2018. LNCS, vol. 11216, pp. 309–324. Springer, Cham (2018). https://doi.org/10.1007/978-3-030-01258-8_19

18. Han, S., Meng, Z., O'Reilly, J., Cai, J., Wang, X., Tong, Y.: Optimizing filter size in convolutional neural networks for facial action unit recognition. CoRR, vol. abs/1707.08630 (2017)

19. Hao, L., Wang, S., Peng, G., Ji, Q.: Facial action unit recognition augmented by their dependencies. In: 13th IEEE International Conference on Automatic Face & Gesture Recognition, FG 2018, Xi'an, China, 15–19 May 2018, pp. 187–194 (2018)

20. Shao, Z., Liu, Z., Cai, J., Ma, L.: Deep Adaptive Attention for Joint Facial Action Unit Detection and Face Alignment. In: Ferrari, V., Hebert, M., Sminchisescu, C., Weiss, Y. (eds.) ECCV 2018. LNCS, vol. 11217, pp. 725–740. Springer, Cham (2018). https://doi.org/10.1007/978-3-030-01261-8_43

21. Shao, Z., Liu, Z., Cai, J., Ma, L.: Jaâ-net: joint facial action unit detection and face alignment via adaptive attention. Int. J. Comput. Vis. **129**, 1–20 (2021)

22. Zhang, Y., Dong, W., Hu, B.-G., Ji, Q.: Classifier learning with prior probabilities for facial action unit recognition. In: 2018 IEEE Conference on Computer Vision and Pattern Recognition, CVPR 2018, Salt Lake City, UT, USA, 18–22 June 2018, pp. 5108–5116 (2018)

23. Shao, Z., Liu, Z., Cai, J., Wu, Y., Ma, L.: Facial action unit detection using attention and relation learning. In: IEEE Transactions on Affective Computing, vol. PP, p. 1 (2019)

24. Li, Y., Zeng, J., Shan, S., Chen, X.: Self-supervised representation learning from videos for facial action unit detection. In: Conference on Computer Vision and Pattern Recognition (CVPR), pp. 10924–10933 (2019)

25. Shao, Z., Cai, J., Cham, T.-J., Lu, X., Ma, L.: Unconstrained facial action unit detection via latent feature domain. In: IEEE Transactions on Affective Computing, vol. PP, p. 1 (2021)

26. Devries, T., Biswaranjan, K., Taylor, G.W.: Multi-task learning of facial landmarks and expression. In: Canadian Conference on Computer and Robot Vision, CRV 2014, Montreal, QC, Canada, 6–9 May 2014, pp. 98–103 (2014)

27. Martinez, A.M.: Computational models of face perception. Curr. Dir. Psychol. Sci. **26**(3), 263 (2017)

28. Bau, D., Zhou, B., Khosla, A., Oliva, A., Torralba, A.: Network dissection: quantifying interpretability of deep visual representations. In: 2017 IEEE Conference on Computer Vision and Pattern Recognition, CVPR 2017, Honolulu, HI, USA, 21–26 July 2017, pp. 3319–3327 (2017)

29. Zeiler, M.D., Fergus, R.: Visualizing and understanding convolutional networks. In: Fleet, D., Pajdla, T., Schiele, B., Tuytelaars, T. (eds.) Computer Vision–ECCV 2014. ECCV 2014. LNCS, vol. 8689, pp. 818–833 Springer, Cham (2014). https://doi.org/10.1007/978-3-319-10590-1_53

30. Mahendran, A., Vedaldi, A.: Understanding deep image representations by inverting them. In: IEEE Conference on Computer Vision and Pattern Recognition, CVPR 2015, Boston, MA, USA, 7–12 June 2015, pp. 5188–5196 (2015)

31. Shelhamer, E., Long, J., Darrell, T.: Fully convolutional networks for semantic segmentation. IEEE Trans. Pattern Anal. Mach. Intell. **39**(4), 640–651 (2017)

32. Zhang, X., et al.: A high-resolution spontaneous 3D dynamic facial expression database. In: IEEE International Conference and Workshops on Automatic Face and Gesture Recognition, pp. 1–6 (2013)

33. Mavadati, S.M., Mahoor, M.H., Bartlett, K., Trinh, P., Cohn, J.F.: DISFA: a spontaneous facial action intensity database. In: IEEE Transactions on Affective Computing, vol. 4, no. 2, pp. 151–160 (2013)

34. Valstar, M.F., Pantic, M.: Fully automatic facial action unit detection and temporal analysis. In: IEEE Conference on Computer Vision and Pattern Recognition, CVPR Workshops 2006, New York, NY, USA, 17–22 June 2006, p. 149 (2006)

35. Jia, Y., et al.: Caffe: convolutional architecture for fast feature embedding. In: ACM MM, pp. 675–678 (2014)

36. Fan, R.-E., Chang, K.-W., Hsieh, C.-J., Wang, X.-R., Lin, C.-J.: LIBLINEAR: a library for large linear classification. J. Mach. Learn. Res. **9**, 1871–1874 (2008)
37. Zhong, L., Liu, Q., Yang, P., Huang, J., Metaxas, D.N.: Learning multiscale active facial patches for expression analysis. IEEE Trans. Cybernetics **45**(8), 1499–1510 (2015)
38. Zeng, J., Chu, W.-S., De la Torre, F., Cohn, J.F., Xiong, Z.: Confidence preserving machine for facial action unit detection. In: 2015 IEEE International Conference on Computer Vision, ICCV 2015, Santiago, Chile, 7–13 Dec 2015, pp. 3622–3630 (2015)
39. Li, W., Abtahi, F., Zhu, Z.: Action unit detection with region adaptation, multi-labeling learning and optimal temporal fusing. In: 2017 IEEE Conference on Computer Vision and Pattern Recognition, CVPR 2017, Honolulu, HI, USA, 21–26 July 2017, pp. 6766–6775 (2017)

An Improved Dual-Subnet Lane Line Detection Model with a Channel Attention Mechanism for Complex Environments

Zhong-qin Bi[1], Kai-an Deng[1(✉)], Wei Zhong[2], and Mei-jing Shan[3]

[1] School of Computer Science and Technology, Shanghai University of Electric Power,
Shanghai, People's Republic of China
20208007@mail.shiep.edu.cn
[2] No. 34 Research Institute, CECT, Guilin, Guangxi, People's Republic of China
[3] Institute of Information Science and Technology, East China University of Political Science
and Law, Shanghai, People's Republic of China

Abstract. Recently, many lane line detection methods have been proposed in the field of unmanned driving, and these methods have obtained good results in common conditions, such as sunny and cloudy conditions. However, these methods generally perform poorly in poor visibility conditions, such as foggy and rainy conditions. To effectively solve the problem of lane line detection in a foggy environment, this paper proposes a dual-subnet model that combines a defogging model and a lane line detection model based on stacked hourglass model blocks. To strengthen the features of important channels and weaken the features of nonimportant channels, a channel attention mechanism is introduced into the dual-subnet model. The network uses dilated convolution (DC) to reduce the network complexity and adds a residual block to the defogging subnet to improve the defogging effect and ensure detection accuracy. By loading the pretrained weights of the fog-removing subnets into the dual-subnet model, the visibility is enhanced and the detection accuracy is improved in the foggy environment. In terms of datasets, since there is currently no public dataset of lane lines in foggy environments, this paper uses a standard optical model to synthesize fog and adds a new class of foggy lane line data to TuSimple and CULane. Our model achieves good performance on the new datasets.

Keywords: Complex environment · Lane detection · Defogging · Channel attention mechanism

1 Introduction

Self-driving technology imitates human driving by making decisions and performing intelligent operations, such as gear shifting, collision avoidance, object detection, and lane departure warnings, by the car system [1]. These accurate decisions and operations made by artificial intelligence will greatly reduce the burden of human drivers and can

© ICST Institute for Computer Sciences, Social Informatics and Telecommunications Engineering 2022
Published by Springer Nature Switzerland AG 2022. All Rights Reserved
H. Gao et al. (Eds.): CollaborateCom 2022, LNICST 461, pp. 496–515, 2022.
https://doi.org/10.1007/978-3-031-24386-8_27

effectively prevent traffic accidents caused by human error. Unmanned driving technology integrates key technologies from many frontier disciplines [2, 3]. Lane line detection technology is one of the important technologies for realizing unmanned driving, and it plays an important role in autonomous navigation systems and lane departure assist systems [2, 4, 5]. The information input sensors for lane line detection generally include cameras, lidar, and global positioning systems (GPS) [6]. However, among the sensors for lane line detection, lidar has high accuracy and is not easily affected by weather; it is expensive, and GPS positioning technology is not accurate and cannot meet real-time requirements. The processing algorithm is relatively mature, and camera sensors are the main sensors for lane line detection at present. Therefore, choosing to process images and videos with cameras as sensors is more common in the current lane line detection task.

A lane line is an important traffic safety feature that has the functions of distinguishing road areas, specifying driving directions, and providing guidance information for pedestrians [7]. In the actual driving environment, the general lane line detection algorithm is sufficient because highways are in good condition and the lane markings are clear; on foggy and rainy days with bad weather conditions, the detection algorithm is often affected by light and rain. It can fail in complex urban road conditions, the lane lines can be blocked due to the shuffle of vehicles and pedestrians, the lane markings can be incomplete and faded, the shadows of trees beside the roads in the country can distort lane lines, and lane lines might not be visible on urban roads and in tunnels where the light changes rapidly. In clear conditions, for roads with obvious ups and downs, lane line detection is inaccurate [8]. The above mentioned road conditions are all problems faced in the current lane line detection task and can be divided into the following four aspects: poor road light, changes in the strong and weak light in the environment; incomplete and damaged lane markings; other objects on the road blocking the lane lines; and changes in the road slope.

The lane line detection algorithm needs to meet the requirements of detection accuracy. Although detection technology based on deep learning has achieved satisfactory results, the general lane line detection method in some harsh environments still has poor detection results. The main challenge for a generic approach, especially in foggy environments (one of the most common weather phenomena in driving scenarios), is that they often fail to detect lane lines. This is because the specific spectrum between the captured object and the camera is absorbed and scattered by very small suspended water droplets, ice crystals, dust, and other particles, reducing the effectiveness of feature extraction from these images for lane line detection [9]. To improve the performance of object detection in foggy environments, previous works often regard enhancing the visibility of foggy images as a preprocessing step. Image dehazing is beneficial not only for human visual perception of image quality but also for many systems that must operate under different weather conditions, such as intelligent vehicles, traffic monitoring systems, and outdoor object recognition systems. However, a model that combines dehazing and detection methods will have increased complexity and increased parameter numbers due to the additional dehazing task, which will eventually lead to a decrease in detection speed. In addition, training a convolutional neural network (CNN)-based detection network requires a large quantity of data. Since there is no public lane line dataset containing images in a foggy environment, many lane line detection models cannot fully learn the lane line features in foggy environments, resulting in inaccurate results.

In this paper, we propose a new dual-subnet lane detection model to solve the problem of lane detection in foggy environments. In summary, the main contributions of this paper are as follows.

- To reduce the complexity of the dual-subnet model and reduce the number of model parameters as much as possible, we choose the lightweight AOD-Net [10] as the defogging subnet.
- To improve the dehazing effect, the subnetwork combines the channel attention mechanism to focus on extracting the features of important channels and fuses the hazy image of the input model as a residual block into three connection layers.
- In the detection subnetwork, we use a stacked hourglass network model. We introduce a channel attention mechanism into the downsampling layer of the original model to extract more features about lane lines, and dilated convolution (DC) is used to reduce the network complexity to ensure detection accuracy.
- We use the standard optical model to synthesize fog to add a new class of foggy lane lines to TuSimple and CULane. We conduct a comprehensive experiment on the new datasets to comparatively evaluate and demonstrate the effectiveness of the proposed model.

The remainder of this paper is organized as follows. Section 2 describes the related works, Sect. 3 introduces the relevant preliminary knowledge used in this paper, Sect. 3 describes the proposed method, Sect. 4 presents the experimental results and Sect. 5 describes the conclusion of this paper.

2 Related Work

In the past two decades, research on lane line detection technology has achieved good results. At present, the main methods are divided into traditional methods and methods based on deep neural networks, and another category is the combination of traditional image processing and deep learning.

2.1 Traditional Methods

Traditional methods detect lane lines by manually designing detection operators according to the characteristic morphology of lane lines and rely on feature-based [11] and model-based [12] detection methods.

Feature-based detection methods use the colour and greyscale features of a road image [13] and combine the Hough transform [14] to realize lane line detection, in which the detected element is generally a straight lane line. In addition, algorithms, such as the particle filter [15], Kalman filter [16, 17], Sobel filter [18], Canny filter [19], and finite impulse response (FIR) filter [20], are commonly used in lane line detection methods. This method can adapt to the change in road shape and has a fast processing speed, but when the road environment is complex, postprocessing is needed, which reduces the real-time performance; when lane lines are incomplete or occluded, the detection performance of the algorithm decreases [21].

The model-based detection algorithm usually constructs a lane line curve model and regards a lane line as a straight-line model, a higher-order curve model, and so on. The principle of this method is to fit the geometric model structure of the lane line by the least square method, random sampling agreement (RANSAC) algorithm, Hough transform [8], or another method according to the geometric structure characteristics of the lane line and obtain the model parameters to create a lane line detection method. The advantage of this detection algorithm is that it can reduce the impact of missing lane lines and has better environmental adaptability; the disadvantage is that if the detected road environment is inconsistent with the present model, the detection effect will be reduced.

2.2 Methods Based on Deep Neural Networks

For the lane line detection task, the process of using deep learning technology for detection is as follows: first, establish a marked lane line dataset, then train the lane line detection network on the dataset, and finally, use the trained network for the actual lane line detection task. Since the CNN AlexNet [22] won the 2012 ImageNet Large-scale Visual Recognition Challenge (ILSVRC), CNNs have been widely used in image classification, object classification, etc., due to their sparse connections and translation invariance. Excellent results have been achieved in the fields of tracking, target detection, semantic segmentation, etc., and these results have brought new ideas to research on lane line detection. Early CNN-based methods (e.g., [23, 24]) extract lane line features through convolution operations. Lane detection methods can be divided into semantic segmentation methods, row classification methods and other methods.

Segmentation-Based Methods. This method extracts the feature data of the image, carries out the image binarization semantic segmentation, divides each pixel into the lane or the background, and filters and connects the pixels of the lane line. Finally, it is decoded into a group of lane lines on the segmentation feature map by postprocessing. For example, GCN [25] and SCNN [26] do not need to manually combine different traditional image processing techniques according to specific scenes and can directly extract accurate images from input images in more complex scenes. In SCNN, the author proposes an effective scheme specifically designed for a slender structure; however, the method is slower (7.5 fps) due to larger backbones. In addition, GAN-based methods (such as EL-GAN [27]), attention maps [28], and knowledge distillation [29] (such as SAD [30]) provide new ideas for lane detection. A self-attention distillation (SAD) module is proposed to aggregate contextual information. This module uses a lighter backbone but has high efficiency and real-time performance.

Row-Wise Classification Methods. The row-by-row classification method is a simple method for lane detection based on input image meshes. For each row, the model predicts the cell most likely to contain partial lane markings. It also requires a postprocessing step to build the lane set. This method was first introduced in E2E-LMD [31] and achieved good results. In [32], by using this method, the model loses some accuracy, but the number of computations is small, and the detection speed is fast (up to 300 fps or more). Moreover, the global receptive field can also deal with complex scenes well.

Other Methods. PolyLaneNet [33] proposed a model based on deep polynomial regression. In this approach, the model outputs a polynomial for each lane. Although it is fast, this method is highly biased towards straight lanes compared with curve lanes due to the imbalance of the lane detection dataset. In [34], lane lines are modelled by the curve description function, and lane lines are described by predicting the third-order Bezier curve based on the Bessel curve description (curve description can be realized by a small number of control points).

3   Proposed Method

In this section, a new dual-subnet model, which combines the defogging model with the lane line detection model, is introduced. The model achieves this goal through two subtasks: visibility enhancement after defogging and lane line detection. The basic structure of the dual-subnet model is shown in Fig. 1. The entire model structure is divided into two main modules, and the lane detection subnet module is divided into a resizing module and a prediction module.

- Defog subnet module: The defog module is composed of a CNN. The defog subnet module estimates the parameters required for defogging based on the input foggy image and then uses this parameter value as the input adaptive parameter to estimate the clear image after defogging. In other words, the clean image tensor after defogging is obtained to achieve the effect of feature enhancement (visibility of lane line feature).
- Resizing module: The resizing module consists of three convolutional layers, which resize the output of $256 \times 128 \times 32$ obtained from the defog subnet to $64 \times 32 \times 128$.
- Prediction module: The prediction module consists of three stacked hourglass modules. The output branch predicts confidence, offset, and embedding features. Three output branches are applied at the ends of each hourglass block. The loss function can be calculated from the outputs of each hourglass block.

3.1   Defogging Subnet Module

The original AOD-Net model consists of a K estimation module and a clean image generation module. According to formulas (1)–(4) in [10], the K estimation module mainly estimates $K(x)$ from the input $I(x)$, and the clean image generation module uses $K(x)$ as its input adaptation parameter to estimate $J(x)$, that is, to obtain the final clean image. The K estimation module utilizes 5 convolutional layers, and the 1st to 5th convolutional layers use convolution kernels of size 1*1, 3*3, 5*5, 7*7 and 3*3, respectively, through 3 layers. The connection layer fuses filters of different sizes to form multiscale features. As shown in Fig. 2, to make the K(x) module extract more

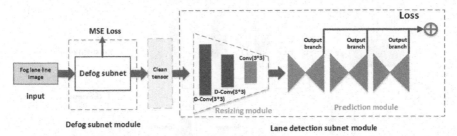

Fig. 1. Dual-subnet model: First, the foggy lane line image was processed through the defog subnet to obtain the clean feature map tensor with the same size as the input, which was resized to a 64 × 32 × 128 feature map by resizing the network, and then the adjusted feature map was input to the prediction network for lane line detection.

accurate fog features and effectively improve the dehazing effect, we introduce the channel attention mechanism SE block into the defogging subnet. The channel attention mechanism introduced by us can greatly improve the network performance, although it will increase the computational consumption by a small amount. Moreover, the AOD-Net model is a lightweight network, so it can improve the subnet haze removal effect under the condition of ensuring the model prediction time. The input original image is added to the connection layer of the network as a residual block, and finally, the feature tensor of the clean image is obtained and input into the detection subnet. Table 1 shows the network details of the dehazing subnet.

In the specific detection process, the foggy RGB lane line image of size $512 \times 256 \times 3$ is converted into three matrices of size 512×256 as the input of the dual-subnet model, where the numbers in the matrix represent the pixels in the image. In the defogging subnet, the $512 \times 256 \times 3$ matrix is input into "conv1" with a convolution kernel size of 1×1, and the result of "conv1" is input into "SeLayer1" (channel attention layer 1). Then, we input the result of "SeLayer1" to "conv2" with a convolution kernel size of 3×3 and then input the result of "conv2" to "SeLayer2". The "concat1" concatenates features from the "SeLayer1","SeLayer2" and input image. The result of "concat1" is used as the input of "conv3", and then the calculation continues. Similarly, "concat2" concatenates those from "SeLayer2", "SeLayer3" and the input image; "concat3" concatenates those from "SeLayer1", "SeLayer2", "SeLayer3", "SeLayer4" and the input image. After 5 convolutional layers, the clean tensor generation module finally retains the dehazed lane line feature map (clean tensor) with a size of $512 \times 256 \times 3$ as the input of the lane line detection module.

3.2 Resizing Module

As shown in Fig. 1, the resizing network is contained in the detection module behind the fogging subnet. To save memory and prediction time, the network is adjusted to reduce the size of the input image tensor. To make the output denser, it is suitable for instance segmentation tasks, and we increase the receptive field without reducing the resolution. We transform the first and second layers of the original resizing network into dilated

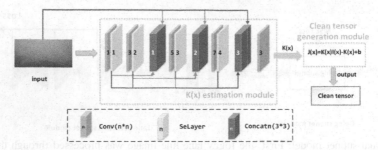

Fig. 2. Improved AOD-Net

Table 1. Details of the defogging subnet

Layer	Size/Stride	Output size
Input data		512*265*3
Conv1	1/1	512*265*3
SeLayer1		512*265*3
Conv2	3/1	512*265*3
SeLayer2		512*265*3
Concat1		512*265*9
Conv3	5/1	512*265*3
SeLayer3		512*265*3
Concat2		512*265*9
Conv4	7/1	512*265*3
SeLayer4		512*265*3
Concat3		512*265*15
Conv5 (K)	3/1	512*265*3

convolution operations with dilated rates of 3 and 2, respectively. Table 2 shows the details of tuning the network component layer.

Before detection, the lane line feature maps of size $512 \times 256 \times 3$ obtained by the defogging subnet are input into the resizing network. In the first layer of the resizing network, 32 convolution kernels with a size of 3×3 and dilated rate of 3 are used, and feature maps with a size of $256 \times 128 \times 32$ are obtained through the convolution of the first layer. In the second layer, 64 convolution kernels with a size of 3×3 and dilated rate of 2 are used, and feature maps of $128 \times 64 \times 64$ are obtained through the second layer convolution. In the third layer, 128 standard convolution kernels with a size of 3 $\times$ 3 are used, and feature maps of $128 \times 64 \times 64$ are obtained through the third layer convolution. Finally, $128 \times 64 \times 32$ feature maps were input into the stacked hourglass network.

Table 2. Details of resizing the network

Layer	Size/Stride/Padding	Dilation	Output size
Input data			512*265*3
Conv + PReLU + BN	3/2/2	3	256*128*32
Conv + PReLU + BN	3/2/1	2	128*64*64
Conv + PReLU + BN	3/2/1		64*32*128

3.3 Prediction Module

The PINet [35] lane line detection model uses a deep learning model inspired by stacked hourglass networks to predict some key points on a lane line. The model transforms the clustering problem of predicting key points into an instance segmentation problem to generate points on the lanes and discriminate the predicted points into individual instances. The network for extracting lane line features and making detections in this model consists of four stacked hourglass networks, so the network size can be adjusted according to the computing power of the target system (cutting several hourglass modules) without changing the network structure or performing extra training. The original PINet model is finished by stacking 4 hourglass blocks, with three output branches applied at the end of each hourglass block. They are the prediction confidence, offset, and embedding features, respectively. The loss function can be calculated based on the output of each hourglass block.

This stacked network model can transfer information to deeper layers, thus improving detection accuracy. Therefore, with knowledge distillation, we can expect better performance in cropped networks. However, with the increase in the number of stacked hourglass models, the number of parameters of the whole detection model also increases, and the detection speed is reduced. To balance high detection accuracy and high detection speed, our model stacks three hourglass blocks. The basic structure of the hourglass model is shown in Fig. 3. Some jump connections transfer information of different scales to deeper layers, and each colour block is a bottleneck module. These bottleneck modules are shown in Fig. 4. There are three types of bottlenecks: the same bottleneck, the down bottleneck, and the up bottleneck. The same bottleneck produces output of the same size as the input. The first layer of the "down bottleneck" is replaced by a dilated convolutional layer with a filter size of 3, a stride of 2, a padding of 2, and a dilated rate of 2. Add a channel attention mechanism after each "down bottleneck". Table 3 shows the detailed information about the detection subnet.

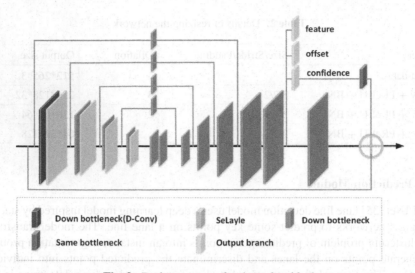

feature

offset

confidence

Down bottleneck(D-Conv)   SeLayle   Down bottleneck

Same bottleneck   Output branch

Fig. 3. Basic structure of an hourglass block

During detection, 128 feature map tensors with a size of 64×32 output from the resizing network are input to the stacked hourglass model. First, the feature map tensor with a size of $4 \times 2 \times 128$ is obtained through four downsampling layers, and then the feature map with a size of $64 \times 32 \times 128$ is restored after four upsampling layers. Each output branch has three convolution layers and generates a 64×32 grid. Confidence values about the key point existence, offset, and embedding feature of each cell in the output grid are predicted by the output branches. The channel of each output branch is different (confidence: 1, offset: 2, embedding: 4), and the corresponding loss function is applied according to the goal of each output branch.

Table 3. Lane line detection subnet details

	Layer	Size/Stride	Output size
	Input data		64*32*128
Encoder	Bottleneck (down)		32*16*128
	SeLayer1		32*16*128
	Bottleneck (down)		16*8*128
	SeLayer2		16*8*128
	Bottleneck (down)		8*4*128
	SeLayer3		8*4*128
	Bottleneck (down)		4*2*128
	SeLayer4		4*2*128

(*continued*)

Table 3. (*continued*)

	Layer	Size/Stride	Output size
(Distillation layer)	Bottleneck		4*2*128
	Bottleneck		4*2*128
	Bottleneck		4*2*128
	Bottleneck		4*2*128
Decoder	Bottleneck (up)		8*4*128
	Bottleneck (up)		16*8*128
	Bottleneck (up)		32*16*128
	Bottleneck (up)		64*32*128
Output branch	Conv + PReLU + BN	3/1	64*32*64
	Conv + PReLU + BN	3/1	64*32*32
	Conv	1/1	64*32*C

3.4 Loss Function

The training of the entire network relies on the dehazing loss and detection loss. A simple mean squared error (MSE) loss function is used in the defog subnet model. The detection loss is the sum of the output losses of each hourglass block, and the output branch of each hourglass network block includes four loss functions. As shown in Table 3, three loss functions are applied separately to each cell of the output grid. Specifically, the output branch generates 64 grids, and each cell in the output grid consists of 7 channels of predicted values, including confidence values (1 channel), offset values (2 channels), and embedded feature values (4 channels). The confidence value determines whether the keypoint of the traffic line exists. The offset value locates the exaction location of

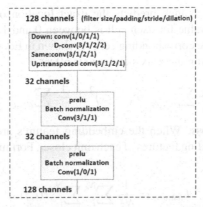

Fig. 4. Bottleneck details. The three kinds of bottlenecks have different first layers according to their purposes.

the keypoint predicted by the confidence value and utilizes the embedding feature to distinguish the key point as a single instance. The distillation loss function for extracting teacher network knowledge is adapted to the distillation layer of each encoder.

Dehazing Loss. MSE is the average value of the square of the difference between the predicted value and the true value calculated element by element. The calculation formula is shown in formula (1), where n is the total number of sample sets, $\hat{y}$ is the predicted value of the ith sample, and y is the true value of the ith sample.

$$Loss(\hat{y}, y) = \frac{1}{n} \sum (\hat{y}_i - y_i)^2 \tag{1}$$

Confidence Loss. The confidence output branch predicts the confidence value for each cell. The confidence value is close to 1 if there is a key point in the cell and 0 otherwise. The output of the confidence branch has 1 channel and is fed into the next hourglass module. As shown in Eq. (2), the confidence loss consists of two parts, the presence loss and the absence loss. The presence loss is used for cells containing key points, and the absence loss is used to reduce the confidence value of each background cell. No loss is computed in cells with predicted confidence values above 0.01.

$$L_{exist} = \frac{1}{N_e} \sum_{c_C \in G_e} (c_c^* - c_c)^2,$$

$$L_{non-exist} = \frac{1}{N_n} \sum_{c_C \in G_e} (c_c^* - c_c)^2 + 0.00001 * \sum_{c_c \in G_n} c_c^2 \tag{2}$$

$$c_c > 0.01$$

where N_e represents the number of cells containing key points, N_n represents the number of cells that do not contain any key points, G_e represents a set of cells containing keypoints, G_n represents a set of cells containing points, and c_c represents the confidence level of the predicted value. For each cell in the output branch, c_c^* represents the true value.

Offset Loss. The offset branch predicts the exact location of the keypoint for each output cell. The output value for each cell is between 0 and 1, and the value indicates the position relative to the corresponding cell. As shown in Eq. (3), the offset branch has two channels for predicting the x-axis and y-axis offset.

$$L_{offset} = \frac{1}{N_e} \sum_{C_x \in G_e} (c_x^* - c_x)^2 + \frac{1}{N_e} \sum_{C_y \in G_e} (c_y^* - c_y)^2 \tag{3}$$

Embedding Feature Loss. When the embedding features are the same, the training branch makes the embedding features of each unit closer. Formula (4) is the loss function of the feature branch:

$$L_{feature} = \frac{1}{N_e^2} \sum_i^{N_e} \sum_j^{N_e} l(i, j),$$

$$l(i, j) = \begin{cases} \|F_i - F_j\|_2, I_{ij} = 1 \\ \max(0, K - \|F_i - F_j\|_2), I_{ij} = 0 \end{cases} \tag{4}$$

where F_i represents the predictive embedding feature of cell i, I_{ij} represents whether cell I and cell j are the same instances and K is a constant such that K > 0. If $I_{ij} = 1$, the cells are the same instance, and if $I_{ij} = 0$, the cells are different instances.

Distillation Loss. The more stacked hourglass modules there are, the better detection performance is, so the deep hourglass module can be the teacher network. After using the distillation learning method, the short network that is lighter than the teacher network will show better performance. The distillation loss is shown in Eq. (5).

$$L_{distillation} = \sum_m^M D(F(A_M) - F(A_m)),$$

$$F(A_M) = S(G(A_m)), S : spatial softmax,$$

$$G(A_m) = \sum_{i=1}^C |A_{mi}|^2, G : R^{C \times H \times W} \to R^{H \times W}, \tag{5}$$

where D represents the sum of squares and A_m represents the distillation layer output of the mth hourglass module. M represents the number of hourglass modules, and A_{mi} represents the ith channel of A_m. Similar to the summation and exponential sum operations, the absolute value (|·|) operations are calculated elementwise.

The total detection loss is the weighted sum of the above four loss terms, and the total loss is shown in Eq. (6).

$$L_{total} = \gamma_e L_{exist} + \gamma_n L_{non-exist} + \gamma_o L_{offset} + \gamma_f L_{feature} + \gamma_d L_{distillation} \tag{6}$$

γ_o is set to 0.2, γ_f to 0.5, and γ_d to 0.1. Both γ_e and γ_n are set to 1, with γ_e varying from 1.0 to 2.5 during the last 40 training periods.

4 Experiments

In this section, we first introduce the dataset details and the information for adding foggy lane lines to TuSimple [36] and CULane [26]. Second, we describe the evaluation indexes of the two datasets, the experimental environment and the implementation details. Finally, we show our experimental results and make some comparisons and analyses of the results.

4.1 Dataset

Most of the images in TuSimple were taken on sunny days with good lighting conditions and are often used for lane detection on structured roads. CULane is a large and challenging dataset that provides many challenging road detection scenarios. In this paper, a new class of foggy lane scenario types is added to TuSimple and CULanet by using the fog synthesizing method of the atmospheric scattering model, and the fogged dataset is used to train and verify our model. To simulate the influence of different degrees of fog, the key parameter brightness A ranges from 0.68 to 0.69, and the fog concentration parameter Beta ranges from 0.11 to 0.12. The original image is shown in Fig. 5 below, and the image after fogging by the above method is shown in Fig. 6. Table 4 shows a detailed data comparison of the two datasets before and after the fogging operation. Table 5 shows the comparison of the test set of the CULane dataset before and after the fogging operation.

Fig. 5. The original image   **Fig. 6.** Image after fogging

Table 4. Comparison of the datasets and the fogged datasets

Category	TuSimple	Fogged TuSimple	CULane	Fogged CULane
Frames	6,408	7,637	133,235	140,544
Train	3,268	4,036	88,880	96,864
Validation	358	358	9,675	9,675
Test	2,782	3,601	34,680	43,680
Resolution	1280 × 720	1280 × 720	1640 × 590	1640 × 590
Scenarios	1	2	9	10

4.2 Evaluation Indicators

Because different lane datasets have different collection devices and collection methods, as well as different lane line labelling methods, different indicators are generally used to evaluate the accuracy and speed of detection. This paper adopts the official TuSimple and CULane evaluation criteria.

(a) TuSimple

The main evaluation indexes of this dataset are accuracy, false positives and false negatives. The specific expressions are shown in (7), (8) and (9). Table 6 shows the meaning of each symbol.

$$Accuracy = \frac{\sum_{clip} C_{clip}}{\sum_{clip} S_{clip}} \tag{7}$$

Table 5. Comparison of the test sets of CULane and fogged CULane

Category	CULane	Fogged CULane
Normal	9,610	9,610
Crowded	8,115	8,115
Night	7,040	7,040
No line	4,058	4,058
Shadow	936	936
Arrow	900	900
Dazzle light	486	486
Curve	415	415
Crossroad	3,120	3,120
Fog	0	9,000

$$FalsePositive = \frac{F_{pred}}{N_{pred}} \qquad (8)$$

$$FalseNegative = \frac{M_{pred}}{N_{gt}} \qquad (9)$$

Table 6. The meaning of each symbol

Variable	Definition
C_{clip}	Number of correct points detected
S_{clip}	Number of true points
N_t	Number of lanes
F_{pred}	Number of lanes with errors detected
M_{pred}	Number of missed lanes
N_{gt}	Number of lanes with actual labels
N_{pred}	Actual number of lanes

(b) CULane

The CULane contains images of various road types, such as sheltered, crowded, urban, and nighttime roads. We followed the official evaluation criteria [B] to evaluate the CULane. According to [B], assuming that the width of each traffic line is 30 pixels, the intersection-over-union (IoU) ratio between the prediction of the evaluation model and the ground truth is calculated. Predictions above a certain threshold are considered truly positive. Assuming that the threshold is set strictly at 0.5, the final score of the F1-measure is taken as the final evaluation indicator. The definition of the F1-measure is shown in (10).

$$F1_{measure} = \frac{2 * Precision * Recall}{Precision + Recall} \tag{10}$$

$$Precision = \frac{TP}{TP + FP} \tag{11}$$

$$Recall = \frac{TP}{TP + FN} \tag{12}$$

TP denotes a true positive; that is, the prediction is true, and the reality is also true. FP denotes a false positive; that is, the prediction is true, but the reality is false. FN denotes a false negative; that is, the prediction is false, but the reality is true.

4.3   Experimental Environment and Implementation Detail

The experiments in this paper are performed in an Ubuntu16.04 operating system. The hardware configuration used in the experiment is as follows: CPU: Intel Core i9-10900K; GPU: NVIDIA RTX 3080. The programming language used is Python 3.7, and the deep learning development framework is PyTorch 1.8.

In the process of model training, the defogging subnetwork is first trained separately, then the weight of the defogging subnetwork is loaded and the partial network is frozen, and finally, the whole dual network is trained.

In the training process of the defogging subnet, the indoor NYU2 Depth Database processed by the atmospheric scattering model to synthesize fog in [10] is used, and the Gaussian random variable is used to initialize the weights. Using ReLU neurons, momentum and decay parameters are set to 0.9 and 0.0001, batch_size is set to 8, learning rate is set to 0.001, and training iteration period is set to 10. Then, when training the whole dual-subnet model, the weights trained by the defogging subnet are loaded into the dual-subnet model as pretrained weights, and this part of the defogging subnet is frozen. Then, the whole dual-subnet model is trained with fogged TuSimple and CULane. In the whole training process of the dual-subnet model, the confidence threshold was set to 0.36, the learning rate was set to 0.00001, the batch_size was set to 6, and the training iteration period was set to 1000. The distance threshold used to distinguish each instance is 0.08.

4.4   Experimental Results and Analysis

Fogged TuSimple.   This paper requires exact X-axis and Y-axis values to test our dual-subnet model on the fogged TuSimple. The nH values in Tables 7 and 8 indicate that the network consists of n hourglass modules. Detailed evaluation results are shown in Table 7, and Fig. 7 shows the results on the images in the test set of the fogged TuSimple dataset. Table 7 summarizes the performance of our method, PINet(1H~4H), PolyLaneNet and SCNN(ResNet18, ResNet34, ResNet101) on the test set of fogged TuSimple. The first-

and second-best results are highlighted in red and blue, respectively, in Table 7. It can be seen from the results that the detection accuracy of the dual-subnet model with only three hourglass blocks is higher than that of the PINet model with four hourglass blocks. Therefore, the dual-subnet model achieves a good improvement in detection accuracy with the benefits of using a lighter model and calculating fewer parameters. By comparing the following detection algorithms, our method achieves better detection accuracy on the test set of foggy datasets, which also demonstrates the effectiveness of our defog subnet.

The last two columns of Table 7 show the number of frames set and parameters on the RTX 3080 GPU based on the number of hourglass modules. When only one hourglass block is used, the network detection speed is approximately 32 frames per second. When using four hourglass blocks, the dual-subnet model can run at 17 frames per second. Clipping a corresponding number of hourglass blocks can evaluate shorter networks without retraining. As the number of hourglass blocks increases, the dual-subnet model has higher performance and slower detection speed. The confidence thresholds are 0.35 (4H), 0.32 (3H), 0.30 (2H) and 0.52 (1H).By comparison, PolyLaneNet can output polynomials representing lane markers in images and obtain lane estimation values without post-processing, which can reach 115 FPS with fewer parameters. Although our method has a small number of parameters, it still needs to be defogged, so the detection speed is slow.

Table 7. Evaluation results on fogged TuSimple.

Method	Acc	FP	FN	fps	parameter(M)
PINet (1H)	89.42%	0.182	0.090	40	1.08
PINet (2H)	90.38%	0.168	0.084	35	2.08
PINet (3H)	91.75%	0.156	0.072	30	3.07
PINet (4H)	92.50%	0.150	0.080	25	4.06
PolyLaneNet[33]	91.16%	0.120	0.094	115	4.05
SCNN(ResNet18)[26]	90.67%	0.131	0.095	21	12.66
SCNN(ResNet34)[26]	91.14%	0.123	0.090	22	22.78
SCNN(ResNet101)[26]	91.82%	0.110	0.081	14	44.21
Ours (1H)	90.87%	0.171	0.092	32	1.20
Ours (2H)	91.01%	0.159	0.089	27	2.20
Ours (3H)	92.53%	0.147	0.072	22	3.19
Ours (4H)	92.54%	0.103	0.086	17	4.18

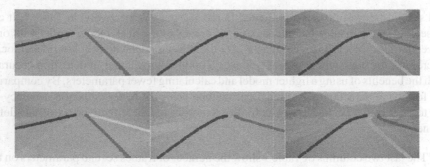

Fig. 7. Results on fogged TuSimple. The first row is the ground truth; the second row is the predicted results of the dual-subnet model.

Fogged CULane. Table 8 summarizes the performance of our method, PINet(1H~4H) and SCNN(ResNet18, ResNet34, ResNet101) on the test set of fogged CULane. The first- and second-best results are highlighted in red and blue, respectively, in Table 8. The following conclusions can be drawn from the experimental results in this paper. First, the detection accuracy of the dual-subnet model in a foggy environment is much higher than that of the original PINet model, and the detection effect in the dazzle light environment is also significantly improved. This is because our defog subnet has good de-fogging and de-noise effect in the fog and dazzling light environment, which makes the characteristics of the lane line more obvious. Second, in normal, no lane line, strong light and foggy environments, the dual-subnet model with three stacked hourglass blocks has higher detection accuracy than the original PINet model with four stacked hourglass blocks; that is, it realizes higher detection accuracy with a lighter model. However, the lane line detection subnets in the dual-subnet model in this paper are based on the key point estimation method, and local occlusion or unclear traffic lines will have a negative impact on performance. Therefore, the dual-subnet model performs poorly in crowded, arrow and curved environments. Finally, the dual-subnet model obtains a high F1 value on fogged CULane.

Figure 8 intuitively shows the detection effect of our dual-subnet model on the images in the test set of the fogged CULane dataset. Although the detection effect of our method is improved in the fogged environment, the detection effect of most methods is not good enough because vehicles block part of the lane lines in the figure.

Table 8. Evaluation results on fogged CULane.

Category	Normal	Crowed	Night	No Line	Shadow	Arrow	Dazzle Light	Curve	Crossroad(fp)	Fog
Proportion	22%	18.68%	16.12%	9.29%	2.14%	2.06%	1.11%	0.95%	7.14%	20.6%
PINet (1H)	82.17	61.22	48.97	36.60	59.01	75.31	56.10	57.41	1930	51.06
PINet (2H)	86.50	65.73	55.67	40.18	63.22	81.12	59.03	60.24	1892	52.97
PINet (3H)	87.47	66.45	55.89	40.30	64.67	80.55	59.45	60.01	1701	58.90
PINet (4H)	87.61	66.42	55.98	40.58	64.69	80.60	59.69	60.08	1622	59.81
SCNN(Res18)	88.03	65.39	56.10	39.69	62.15	78.18	58.50	58.21	1828	57.38
SCNN(Res34)	89.36	65.69	57.21	39.91	63.30	79.84	59.12	58.52	2178	58.69
SCNN(Res101)	90.01	66.41	58.09	40.20	65.01	81.76	60.22	60.21	1744	59.80
Ours (1H)	83.30	60.41	48.01	36.39	58.33	71.85	57.64	57.57	1869	56.21
Ours (2H)	87.21	64.51	54.29	40.12	62.76	76.23	59.20	60.78	1794	57.14
Ours (3H)	88.01	65. 49	54.33	40.61	63.01	79.89	60.39	60.03	1622	63.01
Ours (4H)	88.03	65.76	54.77	40.70	63.85	78.97	61.03	60.15	1540	64.53

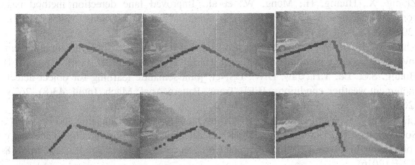

Fig. 8. Results on fogged CULane. The first row is the ground truth; the second row is the predicted results of the dual-subnet model.

5 Conclusion

In this paper, we propose a new dual-subnet model for lane detection in a foggy environment. The dual-subnet model combined with the defogging subnet module and the lane line detection module used the lightweight defogging subnet to improve the visual conditions in a foggy environment to improve the lane line detection accuracy. Our dual-subnet model achieves high accuracy and a low false positive rate and guarantees the safety of autonomous vehicles because the model rarely predicts the incorrect lane lines. Especially for detection in foggy environments, our dual-subnet model can improve the detection accuracy while ensuring fewer model parameters. However, in terms of detection speed, to realize visual enhancement, a preprocessing defogging process is added to our model, so the performance in terms of detection efficiency needs to be improved. In addition, in terms of datasets, a class of foggy lane line scenes was added to TuSimple and CULane by using a standard optical model, and these new datasets will be convenient for follow-up studies on lane line detection in foggy environments.

References

1. Narote, S.P., Bhujbal, P.N., Narote, A.S., Dhane, D.M.: A review of recent advances in lane detection and departure warning system. Pattern Recognit. **73**, 216–234 (2018)
2. Lv, C., Cao, D.P., Zhao, Y.F., et al.: Analysis of autopilot disengagements occurring during autonomous vehicle testing. IEEE/CAA J. Automatica Sinica **5**(1), 58–68 (2018). https://doi.org/10.1109/JAS.2017.7510745
3. Pei, S., Wang, S., Zhang, H., et al.: Methods for monitoring and controlling multi-rotor micro-UAVs position and orientation based on LabVIEW. Int. J. Precis. Agric. Aviat. **1**(1), 51–58 (2018)
4. Narote, S.P., Bhujbal, P.N., Narote, A.S., et al.: A review of recent advances in lane detection and departure warning system. Pattern Recogn **73**, 216–134 (2018). https://doi.org/10.1016/j.patcog.2017.08.014
5. Zhao, Z., Zhou, L., Zhu, Q.: Preview distance adaptive optimization for the path tracking control of unmanned vehicle. J. Mech. Eng. **54**(24), 166–173 (2018). (in Chinese)
6. Hillel, A.B., Lerner, R., Levi, D., et al.: Recent progress in road and lane detection: a survey. Mach. Vis. Appl. **25**(3), 727–745 (2014)
7. Zhang, X., Huang, H., Meng, W., et al.: Improved lane detection method based on convolutional neural network using self-attention distillation. Sens. Mater. **32**(12), 4505 (2020)
8. Chao, W., Huan, W., Chunxia, Z., et al.: Lane detection based on gradient-enhancing and inverse perspective mapping validation. J. Harbin Eng. Univ. **35**(9), 1156–1163 (2014)
9. Huang, S.C., Le, T.H., Jaw, D.W.: DSNet: joint semantic learning for object detection in inclement weather conditions. IEEE Trans. Pattern Anal. Mach. Intell. **43**(8), 2623–2633 (2020)
10. Li, B., Peng, X., Wang, Z., et al.: An All-in-One Network for Dehazing and Beyond (2017)
11. Somawirata, I.K., Utaminingrum, F.: Road detection based on the color space and cluster connecting. In: 2016 IEEE International Conference on Signal Image Process, pp. 118–122. IEEE (2016)
12. Qi, N., Yang, X., Li, C., Lu, R., He, C., Cao, L.: Unstructured road detection via combining the model-based and feature-based methods. IET Intell. Transp. Syst. **13**, 1533–1544 (2019)
13. Tapia-Espinoza, R., Torres-Torriti, M.: A comparison of gradient versus color and texture analysis for lane detection and tracking. In: 2009 6th Latin American Robotics Symposium, LARS 2009, pp. 1–6 (2009). https://doi.org/10.1109/LARS.2009.5418326
14. Küçükmanisa, A., Tarım, G., Urhan, O.: Real-time illumination and shadow invariant lane detection on mobile platform. J. Real-Time Image Proc. **16**(5), 1781–1794 (2017). https://doi.org/10.1007/s11554-017-0687-2
15. Wang, Y., Dahnoun, N., Achim, A.: A novel system for robust lane detection and tracking. Signal Process. **92**, 319–334 (2012). https://doi.org/10.1016/j.sigpro.2011.07.019
16. Aly, M.: Real time detection of lane markers in urban streets. In: IEEE Intelligent Vehicles Symposium Proceedings, pp. 7–12 (2008). https://doi.org/10.1109/IVS.2008.4621152
17. Mammeri, A., Boukerche, A., Lu, G.: Lane detection and tracking system based on the MSER algorithm, Hough transform and kalman filter. In: MSWiM 2014 - Proceedings of 17th ACM International Conference on Modeling, Analysis and Simulation of Wireless and Mobile Systems, pp. 259–266 (2014). https://doi.org/10.1145/2641798.2641807
18. Mu, C., Ma, X.: Lane detection based on object segmentation and piecewise fitting. TELKOMNIKA Indones J. Electr. Eng. **12**(5), 3491–3500 (2014)
19. Wu, P.-C., Chang, C.-Y., Lin, C.H.: Lane-mark extraction for automobiles under complex conditions. Pattern Recognit. **47**(8), 2756–2767 (2014)

20. Aung, T., Zaw, M.H.: Video based lane departure warning system using hough transform. In: International Conference on Advances in Engineering and Technology, pp. 29–30 (2014)
21. Marzougui, M., Alasiry, A., Kortli, Y., Baili, J.: A lane tracking method based on progressive probabilistic hough transform. IEEE Access **8**, 84893–84905 (2020). https://doi.org/10.1109/ACCESS.2020.2991930
22. Krizhevsky, I.S., Hinton, G.E.: Imagenet classification with deep convolutional neural networks. In: Advances in Neural Information Processing Systems, pp. 1097–1105 (2012)
23. Kim, J., Lee, M.: Robust lane detection based on convolutional neural network and random sample consensus. In: Loo, C.K., Yap, K.S., Wong, K.W., Teoh, A., Huang, K. (eds.) ICONIP 2014. LNCS, vol. 8834, pp. 454–461. Springer, Cham (2014). https://doi.org/10.1007/978-3-319-12637-1_57
24. Gurghian, T.K., Bailur, S.V., Carey, K.J., Murali, V.N.: Deeplanes: end-to-end lane position estimation using deep neural networksa. In: Proceedings of the IEEE Conference on Computer Vision and Pattern Recognition Workshops, pp. 38–45 (2016)
25. Zhang, W., Mahale, T.: End to end video segmentation for driving: lane detection for autonomous car, arXiv:1812.05914 (2018)
26. Pan, X., Shi, J., Luo, P., Wang, X., Tang, X.: Spatial as deep: spatial CNN for traffic scene understanding. In: Thirty-Second AAAI Conference on Artificial Intelligence (2018)
27. Ghafoorian, M., et al.: EL-GAN: Embedding Loss Driven Generative Adversarial Networks for Lane Detection (2019)
28. Zagoruyko, S., Komodakis, N.: Paying more attention to attention: improving the performance of convolutional neural networks via attention transfer, arXiv:1612.03928 (2016)
29. Hinton, G., Vinyals, O., Dean, J.: Distilling the knowledge in a neural network, arXiv preprint arXiv:1503.02531 (2015)
30. Hou, Y., Ma, Z., Liu, C., Loy, C.C.: Learning lightweight lane detection CNNs by self-attention distillation. In: Proceedings of the IEEE International Conference on Computer Vision, pp. 1013–1021 (2019)
31. Yoo, S., Lee, H., Myeong, H., et al.: End-to-end lane marker detection via row-wise classification. In: 2020 IEEE/CVF Conference on Computer Vision and Pattern Recognition Workshops (CVPRW). IEEE (2020)
32. Qin, Z., Wang, H., Li, X.: Ultra fast structure-aware deep lane detection. In: Vedaldi, A., Bischof, H., Brox, T., Frahm, J.-M. (eds.) ECCV 2020. LNCS, vol. 12369, pp. 276–291. Springer, Cham (2020). https://doi.org/10.1007/978-3-030-58586-0_17
33. Tabelini, L., Berriel, R., Paixao, T.M., Badue, C., De Souza, A.F., Oliveira-Santos, T.: PolyLaneNet: lane estimation via deep polynomial regression. In: ICPR (2020)
34. Feng, Z., Guo, S., Tan, X., et al.: Rethinking efficient lane detection via curve modelling. In: Proceedings of the IEEE/CVF Conference on Computer Vision and Pattern Recognition, pp. 17062–17070 (2022)
35. Ko, Y., Lee, Y., Azam, S., et al.: Key Points Estimation and Point Instance Segmentation Approach for Lane Detection (2020)
36. The tusimple lane challenge. http://benchmark.tusimple.ai/

Facial Expression Recognition Based on Deep Spatio-Temporal Attention Network

Shuqin Li[1,2], Xiangwei Zheng[1,2(⊠)], Xia Zhang[3], Xuanchi Chen[1,2], and Wei Li[4(⊠)]

[1] School of Information Science and Engineering,
Shandong Normal University, Jinan, China
xwzhengcn@163.com
[2] Shandong Provincial Key Laboratory for Distributed Computer Software
Novel Technology, Jinan, China
[3] Internet Diagnosis and Treatment Center, Taian City Central Hospital,
Taian, China
[4] Shandong Normal University Library, Shandong Normal University, Jinan, China
157953429@qq.com

Abstract. Facial expression recognition is extremely critical in the process of human-computer interaction. Existing facial expression recognition tends to focus on a single feature of the face and does not take full advantage of the integrated spatio-temporal features of facial expression images. Therefore, this paper proposes a facial expression recognition based on a deep spatio-temporal attention network (STANER) to capture the spatio-temporal features of facial expressions when they change subtly. A facial expression recognition with an attention module based on spatial global features (SGAER) is created firstly, where the addition of the attention module is able to quantify the importance of each part of the expression feature map and thus extract the spatial global appearance features at the time of subtle expression changes from a single frame expression image. Then, facial expression recognition with C-LSTM based on temporal local features (TLER) is built to process image sequences of facial regions linked to expression creation and extract dynamic local temporal information about expressions. Experiments are carried out on CK+ and Oulu-CASIA datasets. The results showed that STANER can achieve better performance with the accuracy rates of 98.23% and 89.52% on the two mainstream datasets, respectively.

Keywords: Facial expression recognition · Spatio-temporal features · Deep attention network

1 Introduction

With the rapid development and application of human-computer interaction [3] in various fields (e.g., healthcare [11], smart home [14]), facial expression recognition (FER) has gained more and more attention due to its important role

H. Gao et al. (Eds.): CollaborateCom 2022, LNICST 461, pp. 516–532, 2022.
https://doi.org/10.1007/978-3-031-24386-8_28

in human-computer interaction. Ekman *et al.* [5] in the 1970s defined human facial expressions into six categories: anger, contempt, sadness, fear, happy and surprise. With the study of facial expressions, contempt was added as a basic expression by Matsumoto [25], so that emotions are now commonly classified into seven basic categories.

In some circumstances, changes in facial expressions appear to be very minor in the facial region and a fundamental difficulty in FER is capturing the features of minor changes in expression images. Although the process of facial expression production is very complex, it was found that it is mainly assessed by the main regions of the face (e.g., eyes, nose, mouth, etc.) after early studies [1,7,24]. Therefore, it is more helpful for FER to emphasize the detection of dynamic temporal change features of expressions from consecutive frames of important regions of the face.

According to the feature representation, FER is now classified into two categories: static image-based methods and dynamic sequence-based methods [18]. Static image-based methods [21,28,32] extract spatial appearance features well, but they ignore the dynamic temporal information generated during facial expression changes. On the contrary, dynamic sequence-based methods [13,39,40] extract dynamic temporal information well, but they overlook the change in the spatial appearance of the image. Hence, it is a difficult task to extract and apply the spatio-temporal features of facial expression images in FER activities.

In this paper, a facial expression recognition based on a deep spatio-temporal attention network (STANER) is developed to learn both subtle expression change features and dynamic change features of key facial regions. The first branch is FER with attention module based on spatial global features (SGAER), which is intended to leverage those subtle expression change features that are normally missed because certain tiny changes in expressions are difficult to capture. The second branch is FER with C-LSTM based on temporal local features (TLER), which is proposed to acquire dynamic local temporal features in consecutive expression frames. Based on a sequence of key facial regions that generate facial expressions, i.e., eyes, nose and mouth. These local consecutive frames are fed into the C-LSTM block to obtain high-level temporal features after extracting the shallow features, capturing the dynamic information of the local facial regions.

The contributions of this work are summarized as follows:

(1) A STANER is proposed to capture the spatio-temporal features of facial expression images to improve the robustness of facial expression recognition. The superiority of STANER has been demonstrated by extensive experiments on the mainstream datasets CK+ [23] and Oulu-CASIA [38].

(2) A SGAER branch is designed to solve the problem that when the magnitude of facial muscle changes is small and subtle facial expression change features are difficult to capture. The module optimizes the utilization of spatial features by using the attention created to track the subtle features of expression changes.

(3) A TLER branch is established to learn dynamic fine-grained temporal features of key local regions of the face. TLER detects spatio-temporal informa-

tion of local sequences using C-LSTM blocks constructed by convolutional neural networks (CNN) [17] and long short-term memory neural networks (LSTM) [10].

The rest of this paper is structured as follows. The survey of FER is discussed in Sect. 2. In Sect. 3, STANER method is described. In Sect. 4, the experimental analysis and their results are discussed to prove the efficiency of proposed method. Finally, the conclusion of the paper is presented in Sect. 5.

2   Related Works

2.1   Facial Expression Recognition

FER research has been conducted by traditional methods [21,39] and deep learning methods [13,28]. Traditional methods, including Local Binary Patterns (LBP) [32], Scale-invariant Feature Transform (SIFT) [22], Histogram of Oriented Gradients (HOG) [8], are adopted to extract facial expression image features, which are then fed into a classifier (e.g., Support Vector Machine SVM [2]) for the classification task. Pan et al. [29] proposed to bridge the gap between visual features and emotions by using both the use of CNNs and HOG to obtain more comprehensive VFER features and SVM for expression recognition. This method had good performance and outperformed the current level of conventional techniques. However, when the information becomes more complex, the representational capacity of hand-crafted features diminishes and classic approach models are unable to adequately fit large-scale complicated data. It was not until the introduction of deep learning [9], its subsequent rapid development in various fields and the great success of deep neural networks in many pattern recognition tasks based on large data and complex scenes that more and more researchers started to conduct experiments with deep learning-based facial expression recognition [18].

In recent years, CNNs have been increasingly popular in FER tasks. Kim et al. [15] combined multiple deep CNNs for training and won the FER international competition EmotoW2015. Liu et al. [20] used several CNNs with different structures for FER with good results. In addition, recurrent neural networks (RNNs) have also been employed in FER because they are better at predicting dynamic temporal aspects of arbitrary length sequences [4,6]. Researchers have discovered that LSTMs [10] are better at solving gradient disappearance and gradient explosion during training and they are commonly used to learn temporal features in FER. Zhang et al. [36] proposed a PHRNN-MSCNN, which consists of a partially hierarchy-based bidirectional RNN and CNN. In order to extract spatial appearance aspects and temporal order features of facial expression images, Liang et al. [19] suggested a network framework combining CNN and BiLSTM. Along with the development of FER, attention was introduced to FER because of its ability to better capture local regions. In FER, the attention focuses more on regional details of facial expression changes and filters out redundant information irrelevant to expression generation. Zhang et al. [37] proposed ECA-Resent for FER, using effective channel attention (ECA) to amplify the weight of effective information and suppress the weight of invalid information. Sun et al. [33] combined feature attention weights of graphs and CNN to improve the accuracy of FER. Minaee et al. [26] used a deep learning method based on an attentional convolutional network that can focus on the regions most relevant to expressions, resulting in improved FER. Pei et al. [31] proposed an end-to-end spatially indexed attention model (SIAM) to extract valid potential appearance representations from CNN feature maps, which were then fed into the temporal attention layer constructed by LSTM to model temporal dynamics. Finally, the output feature vectors were weighted and averaged to improve the efficiency.

2.2 Extraction of Spatio-Temporal Features

FER methods can be classified into static image-based methods and dynamic sequence-based methods according to the feature representation [18]. In the static image-based methods, Zhao et al. [40] created a peak-piloted deep network (PPDN) to learn the association between peak expression images and non-peak expression images and capture their spatial appearance features. Yang et al. [34] designed a DeRL that can create neutral face images by training a face born on any input and learning the deposits (or residues) that remain in the middle of the generative model for FER. In the dynamic sequence-based methods, Liu et al. [21] proposed a facial expression recognition framework 3DCNN-DAP, which combined 3DCNN with deformable convolution to localize facial change regions and used a part-based representation for FER. Jung et al. [13] proposed DTAGN to capture temporal information of facial expression and automatically extract useful features from the raw data.

Both static image-based methods and dynamic sequence-based methods consider only one-sided facial expression features. To extract more efficient expression features and apply them to FER, more and more studies turn to the spatio-temporal properties of images for FER. Yu et al. [35] learned the spatio-temporal feature representation of facial expressions simultaneously by a DCPN network. Liang et al. [19] proposed to use CNN combined with BiLSTM to extract spatial features of each frame and dynamic temporal features of consecutive frames. Ryo Miyoshi et al. [27] proposed an enhanced convolutional long short-term memory (ConvLSTM) algorithm that could automatically recognize facial expressions in videos, which mainly used jump connections in spatio-temporal orientation and time gates to suppress gradient disappearance. Pan et al. [30] proposed a mainstream framework to fuse both spatial and temporal information to be utilized. The framework mainly consisted of CNN and LSTM. Jeong et al. [12] proposed a deep joint spatio-temporal feature recognition method for facial expressions. Firstly, the spatio-temporal features of facial expression images were extracted by 3DCNN. Then the whole facial signs are analyzed by using geometric network, and finally 23 facial sign points are selected to represent the dynamic muscle movements of the whole face. Zhu et al. [41] proposed a cascaded attentional facial expression recognition network with a pyramid structure and considering local spatial features, multi-scale-stereoscopic spatial context feature and temporal features to locate the changing features on dynamically changing regions (e.g., eyes, nose and mouth) as accurately as possible.

3   The Proposed Method

3.1   Overview

STANER is shown in Fig. 1. SGAER and TLER are the two key components of the approach. To begin, the facial key regions are cut from the input facial image sequence and input to TLER to extract high level temporal information. Then, the peak frame is chosen and fed into SGAER to learn spatial appearance features with an emphasis on subtle expression change features. At the end of the model, the recognition results from the two branches of the parallel structure are fused using decision-level fusion techniques, enabling the model to synthetically capture the spatio-temporal characteristics of subtle expression changes as they occur. The key branches of the proposed method are detailed in the following.

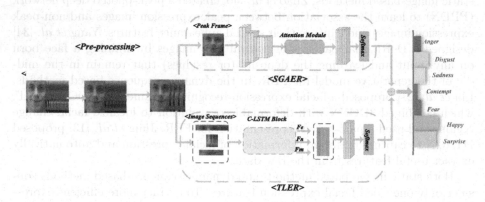

Fig. 1. Overview of the proposed method.

3.2   FER with Attention Module Based on Spatial Global Features

Subtle changes in distinct face regions that are linked together to make an expression are frequently used to create expressions. Capturing the intricacies of expressions is critical at FER. Therefore, SGAER is constructed to learn the nuances of expressions, in addition to quantifying the correlation of each position in the expression feature map and understanding the nuances of facial regions caused by expressions. The structure of the method is shown in Fig. 2.

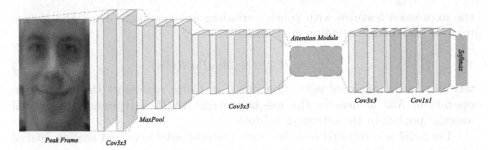

Fig. 2. Network structure of SGAER.

SGAER is composed of the front-end convolutional, the attention module and the end convolutional layer. The front-end convolution is made up of the first 10 layers of VGG-16. The structure of the constructed attention module is shown in Fig. 3. Shallow spatial appearance features are extracted from selected single-frame images through the front-end convolution, which is passed through the attention module to produce feature maps with attention. The processed feature maps are then transferred to the end convolution layer to obtain fine-grained appearance features. The attention is weighted in the range [0,1] using the *Sigmoid* function in the last layer of the attention module.

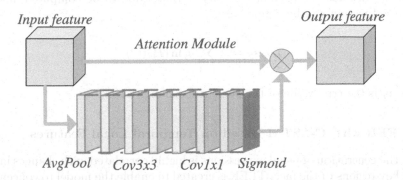

Fig. 3. Attention Module.The 3×3 convolutional kernel increases the received domain of feature information and acquires more spatial contextual information. The 1×1 convolutional kernel integrates multi-channel information into a single channel.

SGAER is designed in the following way. Firstly, the selected peak frame Ip is fed into the front-end convolution of SGAER to pick up the shallow spatial global features U of the expression image. Then, the spatial features at different locations after transmitting U to the attention module are given different weights and the main regional features generated by facial expressions are enhanced and the expression features with subtle variations are amplified. Thus, the feature map M containing attention is formed.

$$M = \sigma \{Conv[w; AvgPool(U)]\} \tag{1}$$

where σ is the *Sigmoid* activation function; *Conv* represents the convolution operation; And w denotes the weight matrix; *AvgPool* represents the global average pooling in the attention module.

Then, M is computed together with the originally obtained shallow spatial global features U to obtain the final feature map F.

$$F = (1 + M) \otimes U \tag{2}$$

where $\otimes$ denotes multiplication between elements.

F is sent to the end convolutional layer to extract the spatial appearance features F_G. And finally, F_G is input to the *SoftMax* layer for final expression classification to generate expression classification result $P_G(C)$, where C is the number of facial expressions classification categories; x denotes the input vector of the *SoftMax* function and $P_G(C)$ is defined as:

$$P_G(C) = S(x)_C = \frac{e^{x_C}}{\sum_i^c e^{x_i}} \tag{3}$$

where x_i denotes the computed output value of the ith category in the output vector, x_c denotes the current category output value to be computed, and the final loss function can be defined as:

$$Loss_S = -\sum_{i=1}^{C} y_i \ln (P_G(C)) \tag{4}$$

where y_i is the true value of the current facial expression.

3.3   FER with C-LSTM Based on Temporal Local Features

Since the generation of facial expressions is highly correlated with changes in only a few key regions of the face, TLER is created to enable the model to concentrate on learning the dynamic temporal changes in the facial regions associated with expression generation in consecutive frames. Figure 4 depicts the structure of TLER.

The TLER consists of a C-LSTM block and an end convolution. The shallow spatial features of the local sequences are extracted by the first few convolutional layers of the C-LSTM block, they are reconstructed into vectors and then passed through the LSTM to obtain the dynamic change information of the local sequences. Finally, the high-level semantic information of the expression features is learned by the end convolution. LSTM is proved to recover the temporal features of the expression sequence, and it is composed of an input gate, an output gate and a forget gate. Among them, the input gate determines which values the

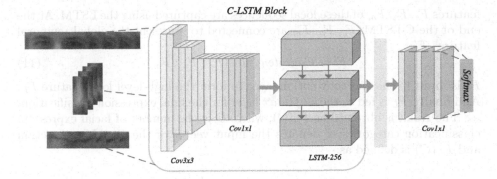

Fig. 4. Network structure of TLER.

unit will update; the output gate determines which values will be finally output and the forget gate defines which information the unit will discard. Where forget gate is defined as f_t:

$$f_t = \sigma \left(W_f x_t + W_f h_{t-1} + b_f \right) \tag{5}$$

input gate is defined as i_t:

$$i_t = \sigma \left(W_i x_t + W_i h_{t-1} + b_i \right) \tag{6}$$

$$g_t = \tanh \left(W_g x_t + W_g h_{t-1} + b_g \right) \tag{7}$$

$$c_t = f_t \otimes c_{t-1} + i_t \otimes g_t \tag{8}$$

output gate is defined as o_t:

$$o_t = \sigma \left(W_o x_t + W_o h_{t-1} + b_o \right) \tag{9}$$

$$h_t = o_t \otimes \tanh \left(c_t \right) \tag{10}$$

where h_{t-1} is the LSTM hidden layer output at moment $t-1$; x_t is the input vector. And c_t is the current update cell. g_t is the current alternative update cell, which contains all the update information of the current time node. W and b denote the weight matrix and bias value, respectively. σ is *Sigmoid* activation function and *tanh* is the hyperbolic tangent activation function; $\otimes$ denotes multiplication between elements.

The input to TLER is the extracted consecutive frames I_e, I_n, I_m of the three key facial regions of eyes, nose and mouth associated with the generated facial expressions. The processed local region image sequences are fed into the constructed C-LSTM block. Region-based low-level features are first generated by the CNN of the C-LSTM block and then the fine-grained dynamic temporal features F_e, F_n, F_m of these local sequences are captured using the LSTM. At the end of the C-LSTM, F_e, F_n, F_m are connected to represent the global temporal features F':

$$F' = Concatenation\,(F_e : F_n : F_m) \tag{11}$$

F' is input to the end convolution layer to form the high-level local feature F_L. And finally, F_L is fed to the $Softmax$ layer for the final expression classification.

The result is obtained as $P_L(C)$, where C is the number of facial expression classification categories; x denotes the input vector of the $SoftMax$ function and $P_L(C)$ is defined as:

$$P_L(C) = S(x)_C = \frac{e^{x_C}}{\sum_i^c e^{x_i}} \tag{12}$$

where x_i denotes the computed output value of the ith category in the output vector; x_c denotes the current category output value to be computed.

The final loss function can be defined as:

$$Loss_T = -\sum_{i=1}^{C} y_i \ln\,(P_L(C)) \tag{13}$$

where y_i is the true value of the current facial expression.

Researchers have found that combining multiple networks for FER can yield more diverse information to ensure complementarity of features, often resulting in better recognition than individual networks. In the process of expression change, the overall spatial appearance features and local dynamic change features are equally important. In order to make the constructed model take into account the local dynamic change features while utilizing the spatial appearance change of expressions and without emphasizing or ignoring one feature, a simple average decision fusion method is used in the paper to fuse the expression classification results of SGAER and TLER, which is calculated as follows.

$$O(C) = argmax\,(\alpha P_G(C) + (1 - \alpha)P_L(C)) \tag{14}$$

where α is 0.5. O represents the final output category of facial expression.

The loss function $Loss$ of the whole network is:

$$Loss = Loss_G + Loss_T \tag{15}$$

in which, $Loss_G$ and $Loss_T$ represent the final loss functions of SGAER and TLER, separately.

3.4 Algorithmic Description

The algorithm of STANER is described as follows:

Algorithm 1: STANER for FER

Require: Dataset D;
Output : Facial expression category: O

1 **for** *images in dataset D* **do**
2   face cropping, grayscale processing and data augmentation obtain
        dataset D^*
3 **end**
4 **for** *images in dataset D^** **do**
5   Selecting peak frame: I_p and partial Sequences: I_e, I_n, I_m
6 **end**
7 **for** $I_p \in D^*$ **do**
8     $P_G(C) \leftarrow$ SGAER (I_p);
9     $Calculate \rightarrow Loss_G = -\sum_{i=1}^{C} y_i \ln(P_G(C))$
10 **end**
11 **for** $I_e, I_n, I_m \in D^*$ **do**
12     $P_L(C) \leftarrow$ TLER (I_e, I_n, I_m);
13     $Calculate \rightarrow Loss_L = -\sum_{i=1}^{C} y_i \ln(P_L(C))$
14 **end**
15 **for** $P_G(C), P_L(C)$ **do**
16     $Calculate: O(C) = \mathrm{argmax}(\alpha P_G(C) + (1-\alpha) P_L(C))$
17 **end**
18 $Calculate: Loss = Loss_T + Loss_G$
19 Output:O

---

4 Experiments

This section first describes the datasets and data preprocessing, followed by the implementation details of the proposed method and finally the experimental results and analysis.

4.1 Datasets

Two facial expression datasets named CK+ [23] and Oulu-CASIA [38] are used to evaluate this model.

The extended Cohn-Kanada database (CK+) [23] is made up of 593 sequences from 123 distinct people. Anger (An), disgust (Di), fear (Fe), happy (Ha), sadness (Sa) and surprise (Su) are the six basic emotion categories in this dataset. In addition, there is a unique term known as "contempt." Only 327 sequences out of 118 patients were tagged with seven expressions and they all started with a neutral expression and finished with a peak expression. The training and test sets are built using 10-fold cross-validation.

Oulu-CASIA [38] is more complex than CK+ and contains 480 image sequences recorded by 80 individuals under normal lighting conditions, with six basic emotion categories. Each of the six expressions has a sequence, each starting with a neutral expression and ending with a peak expression. The dataset is processed using the same 10-fold cross-validation.

Due to the fact that the experimental dataset is acquired from a real environment, all images in the CK+ and Oulu-CASIA datasets are first cropped and grayscale processed in order to prevent the effect of other expression-independent noise such as jewelry, lighting and color on the FER [18]. Then, the processed dataset is horizontally flipped to enhance the data to avoid the overfitting problem caused by the limited number of training samples. Finally, the peak frame of the facial expression image sequence is selected as the input of SGAER in the new dataset that had been processed. The 68 facial marker points of the face are identified using the Dlib [16], the eyes, nose and mouth regions are extracted. The consecutive frames of the local region are used as the input of TLER.

4.2   Evaluation Metrics and Implementation Details

The recognition accuracy Acc of expression classification is used to evaluate the model's overall classification capabilities. which is defined as:

$$Acc = \frac{TP + TN}{TP + TN + FP + FN} \tag{16}$$

where FP represents false positive, FN represents false negative, TP represents true positive, TN represents true negative.

The parameter selection for the experiment is as follows:

The number of training networks is set to 150 epochs, and the training batch size is set to 64. The initial learning rate is 10^{-4}. The first 100 epochs remain the same and the learning rate is set to 10^{-5} after 100 epochs.

4.3   Ablation Experiments

Table 1 illustrates the Acc of ablation experiments on CK+ and Oulu-CASIA datasets. The result of C1 is to extract low-level features of the face from a single frame image using the first ten layers of VGG-16 and then input these features into the end convolutional layer to learn advanced feature information for FER. C2 is a FER that extracts spatio-temporal features of local facial sequences using only TLER. C3 is a FER that uses only SGAER. C4 is the fusion model of C1 and C2. STANER is the method proposed in this work, which utilizes both static-based and dynamic-based methods to capture the spatio-temporal features of the face for FER.

The experimental results of C1, C2 and C4 indicate that using only static image-based methods and dynamic sequence-based methods does not lead to good FER performance because they tend to consider only one-sided expression features. The fusion models of static image-based methods and dynamic

Table 1. *ACC* of ablation experiments on CK+ and Oulu-CASIA

Methods	CK+	Oulu-CASIA
C1	91.64%	79.40%
C2	92.70%	80.23%
C3	94.52%	82.66%
C4	96.19%	86.50%
STANER(Our method)	98.23%	89.52%

sequence-based methods can obtain complete cues of face expression changes and capture spatio-temporal features. The application of attention increases the performance of FER in both the static image-based methods and the fusion model, as seen by the comparison of C1, C3, C4 and STANER recognition results. This demonstrates that FER benefits from focusing on subtle expression change features, and that using attention not only allows the model to better explore the spatial appearance features of the original image, but also allows the model to capture more fine-grained high-level semantic features, greatly improving the model's proactivity.

4.4 Confusion Matrix

To measure the specific manifestation of STANER on each expression category, the confusion matrices of STANER on CK+ and Oulu-CASIA datasets are shown in Fig. 5(a) and (b). Figure 5(a) demonstrates that STANER is more accurate in recognizing disgust, fear, happy on CK+ and does well with contempt, which is not easily distinguished. Figure 5(b) illustrates that STANER not only has the highest recognition rate for surprise and happy on Oulu-CASIA, but also discriminates fear and anger, two frequently confused expression categories.

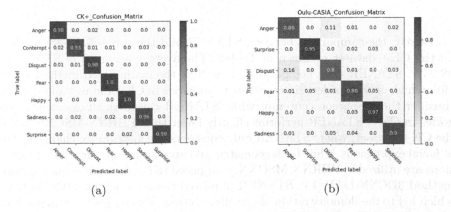

Fig. 5. The confusion matrix. (a) The confusion matrix on CK+. (b) The confusion matrix on Oulu-CASIA.

4.5   Comparisons with Existing Methods

Tables 2 and 3 show the performance comparison of STANER with existing mainstream methods on CK+ and Oulu-CASIA, respectively. It can be seen that STANER exhibits better properties than most methods.

Table 2. Comparison of FER *Acc* on CK+ Dataset

Methods	Experiment Setting	ACC(%)
3DCNN-DAP [21]	10 folds	92.40%
ECA-ResNet [37]	10 folds	94.58%
DTAGN [13]	10 folds	97.25%
PPDN [40]	10 folds	99.30%
DeRL [34]	10 folds	97.30%
PHRNN-MSCNN [36]	10 folds	98.50%
Our method	10 folds	98.23%

Table 3. Comparison of FER *Acc* on Oulu-CASIA Dataset

Methods	Experiment setting	ACC(%)
ResNeXt-50 + pyramid + cascaded attention block + GRU [41]	10 folds	89.29%
DTAGN [13]	10 folds	81.46%
PPDN [40]	10 folds	84.59%
DeRL [34]	10 folds	88.00%
DCPN [35]	10 folds	86.23%
PHRNN-MSCNN [36]	10 folds	86.25%
Our method	10 folds	89.52%

Firstly, the comparison between STANER and the state-of-the-art methods on the CK+ dataset is shown in Table 2. The average accuracy of STANER is 98.23%. STANER does not perform as well as the static-based method PPDN [40], which only considers six expression categories in CK+ dataset and does not consider the expression contempt while STANER considers all expression categories in CK+. STANER performs slightly lower than PHRNN-MSCNN [36] on the CK+ dataset, where STANER only considers the appearance change feature of facial expressions, while both geometric and appearance information of expressions are utilized in PHRNN-MSCNN. Compared to the dynamic sequence-based method 3DCNN-DAP [13], STANER improved the accuracy by 4.03% in CK+, which led to the demonstration of the effectiveness of using spatial-temporal features in the FER task. STANER also improved in CK+ compared to the static image-based method using attention, ECA-Resnet [37], because it did not focus only on single-sided facial expression features, but also considered information about the temporal variation of expressions.

Then, the comparison of STANER with other methods on the Oulu-CASIA dataset is shown in Table 3. The average accuracy of STANER is 89.52%. The accuracy of STANER is improved by 4.93% compared to that of PPDN [40] using a static image-based method. STANER is compared with the approach that exploits the spatio-temporal information of facial expression images. Compared with the DTAGN [13], STANER's recognition accuracy on Oulu-CASIA dataset is improved by 8.06%. STANER improves the recognition performance by 3.29% over the DCPN designed by Yu et al. [35] on Oulu-CASIA. It improved 3.27% over the PHRNN-MSCNN model proposed by Zhang et al. [36].STANER outperforms the Oulu-CASIA dataset compared to a cascaded attentional facial expression recognition network with a pyramidal structure that simultaneously considers local spatial features,multi-scale-stereoscopic spatial context feature and temporal features, as presented by Zhu et al. [41].

5 Conclusion and Future Work

In this study, STANER is designed to improve the performance of facial expression recognition when facial expressions change subtly. STANER can not only make full use of the spatio-temporal change information of incoming expressions, but also localize key parts of the face by attention to better utilize the features generated when facial expressions change subtly.

Specifically, SGAER is firstly constructed in order to learn the spatial appearance information of facial expressions when they change, and the attention module in SGAER can more precisely localize specific regions with significant dynamic changes. Secondly, TLER is constructed to extract temporal features from key local facial parts. For the input expression image sequences, the main parts related to facial expression changes (i.e., image sequences of eyes, nose, and mouth) are cropped, and temporal features are extracted using C-LSTM. Finally, SGAR and TLER are further fused using an average decision level strategy to obtain different expressions for recognition. Through extensive experiments, the excellent recognition properties of STANER on CK+ and Oulu-CASIA are demonstrated.

To apply STANER to more complex, realistic and natural environments, future work will include: (1) training and validating the model in complex natural environment datasets to further improve the accuracy and robustness of the model; (2) using a more accurate attention mechanism to capture changes in the appearance of key parts of the face during the spatial feature extraction stage; (3) using the model to design a real-time facial expression recognition system to improve the human-computer interaction capability of the model; and (4) improving the model network structure to reduce computation and save resource consumption.

Acknowledgements. This work is supported by Shandong Provincial Project of Graduate Education Quality Improvement (No. SDYJG21104, No. SDYJG19171, No. SDYY18058), the OMO Course Group "Advanced Computer Networks" of Shandong Normal University, the Teaching Team Project of Shandong Normal University, Teaching Research Project of Shandong Normal University (2018Z29), Provincial Research Project of Education and Teaching (No.2020JXY012), the Natural Science Foundation of Shandong Province (No. ZR2020LZH008, ZR2021MF118, ZR2019MF071).

References

1. Chen, L., Zhou, M., Su, W., Wu, M., She, J., Hirota, K.: Softmax regression based deep sparse autoencoder network for facial emotion recognition in human-robot interaction. Inf. Sci. **428**, 49–61 (2018)
2. Cortes, C., Vapnik, V.: Support-vector networks. Machine learning **20**(3), 273–297 (1995)
3. Deng, J., Pang, G., Zhang, Z., Pang, Z., Yang, H., Yang, G.: cGAN based facial expression recognition for human-robot interaction. IEEE Access **7**, 9848–9859 (2019)
4. Donahue, J., et al.: Long-term recurrent convolutional networks for visual recognition and description. In: Proceedings of the IEEE Conference on Computer Vision and Pattern Recognition, pp. 2625–2634 (2015)
5. Ekman, P., Friesen, W.V.: Constants across cultures in the face and emotion. J. Pers. Soc. Psychol. **17**(2), 124-129 (1971)
6. Graves, A., Mohamed, A.R., Hinton, G.: Speech recognition with deep recurrent neural networks. In: 2013 IEEE International Conference on Acoustics, Speech and Signal Processing, pp. 6645–6649. IEEE (2013)
7. Happy, S., Routray, A.: Automatic facial expression recognition using features of salient facial patches. IEEE Trans. Affect. Comput. **6**(1), 1–12 (2014)
8. Happy, S., Routray, A.: Robust facial expression classification using shape and appearance features. In: 2015 Eighth International Conference on Advances in Pattern Recognition (ICAPR), pp. 1–5. IEEE (2015)
9. Hinton, G.E., Osindero, S., Teh, Y.W.: A fast learning algorithm for deep belief nets. Neural Comput. **18**(7), 1527–1554 (2006)
10. Hochreiter, S., Schmidhuber, J.: Long short-term memory. Neural Comput. **9**(8), 1735–1780 (1997)
11. Ilyas, C.M.A., Haque, M.A., Rehm, M., Nasrollahi, K., Moeslund, T.B.: Facial expression recognition for traumatic brain injured patients. In: International Conference on Computer Vision Theory and Applications, pp. 522–530. SCITEPRESS Digital Library (2018)
12. Jeong, D., Kim, B.G., Dong, S.Y.: Deep joint spatiotemporal network (DJSTN) for efficient facial expression recognition. Sensors **20**(7), 1936 (2020)
13. Jung, H., Lee, S., Yim, J., Park, S., Kim, J.: Joint fine-tuning in deep neural networks for facial expression recognition. In: Proceedings of the IEEE International Conference on Computer Vision, pp. 2983–2991 (2015)
14. Khowaja, S.A., Dahri, K., Kumbhar, M.A., Soomro, A.M.: Facial expression recognition using two-tier classification and its application to smart home automation system. In: 2015 International Conference on Emerging Technologies (ICET), pp. 1–6. IEEE (2015)

15. Kim, B.K., Lee, H., Roh, J., Lee, S.Y.: Hierarchical committee of deep CNNs with exponentially-weighted decision fusion for static facial expression recognition. In: Proceedings of the 2015 ACM on International Conference on Multimodal Interaction, pp. 427–434 (2015)
16. King, D.E.: Dlib-ml: a machine learning toolkit. J. Mach. Learn. Res. **10**, 1755–1758 (2009)
17. LeCun, Y., Bengio, Y., Hinton, G.: Deep learning. Nature **521**(7553), 436–444 (2015)
18. Li, S., Deng, W.: Deep facial expression recognition: a survey. In: IEEE Transactions on Affective Computing (2020)
19. Liang, D., Liang, H., Yu, Z., Zhang, Y.: Deep convolutional BiLSTM fusion network for facial expression recognition. Vis. Comput. **36**(3), 499–508 (2020)
20. Liu, K., Zhang, M., Pan, Z.: Facial expression recognition with CNN ensemble. In: 2016 International Conference on Cyberworlds (CW), pp. 163–166. IEEE (2016)
21. Liu, P., Han, S., Meng, Z., Tong, Y.: Facial expression recognition via a boosted deep belief network. In: Proceedings of the IEEE Conference on Computer Vision and Pattern Recognition, pp. 1805–1812 (2014)
22. Liu, Y., Wang, J., Li, P.: A feature point tracking method based on the combination of SIFT algorithm and KLT matching algorithm. J. Astronautics **32**(7), 1618–1625 (2011)
23. Lucey, P., Cohn, J.F., Kanade, T., Saragih, J., Ambadar, Z., Matthews, I.: The extended Cohn-Kanade dataset (CK+): a complete dataset for action unit and emotion-specified expression. In: 2010 IEEE Computer Society Conference on Computer Vision and Pattern Recognition-workshops, pp. 94–101. IEEE (2010)
24. Majumder, A., Behera, L., Subramanian, V.K.: Automatic facial expression recognition system using deep network-based data fusion. IEEE Trans. Cybern. **48**(1), 103–114 (2016)
25. Matsumoto, D.: More evidence for the universality of a contempt expression. Motiv. Emot. **16**(4), 363–368 (1992)
26. Minaee, S., Minaei, M., Abdolrashidi, A.: Deep-emotion: facial expression recognition using attentional convolutional network. Sensors **21**(9), 3046 (2021)
27. Miyoshi, R., Nagata, N., Hashimoto, M.: Enhanced convolutional LSTM with spatial and temporal skip connections and temporal gates for facial expression recognition from video. Neural Comput. Appl. **33**(13), 7381–7392 (2021)
28. Mollahosseini, A., Chan, D., Mahoor, M.H.: Going deeper in facial expression recognition using deep neural networks. In: 2016 IEEE Winter Conference on Applications of Computer Vision (WACV), pp. 1–10. IEEE (2016)
29. Pan, X.: Fusing hog and convolutional neural network spatial-temporal features for video-based facial expression recognition. IET Image Proc. **14**(1), 176–182 (2020)
30. Pan, X., Ying, G., Chen, G., Li, H., Li, W.: A deep spatial and temporal aggregation framework for video-based facial expression recognition. IEEE Access **7**, 48807–48815 (2019)
31. Pei, W., Dibeklioğlu, H., Baltrušaitis, T., Tax, D.M.: Attended end-to-end architecture for age estimation from facial expression videos. IEEE Trans. Image Process. **29**, 1972–1984 (2019)
32. Shan, C., Gong, S., McOwan, P.W.: Facial expression recognition based on local binary patterns: a comprehensive study. Image Vis. Comput. **27**(6), 803–816 (2009)
33. Sun, W., Zhao, H., Jin, Z.: A visual attention based ROI detection method for facial expression recognition. Neurocomputing **296**, 12–22 (2018)

34. Yang, H., Ciftci, U., Yin, L.: Facial expression recognition by de-expression residue learning. In: Proceedings of the IEEE Conference on Computer Vision and Pattern Recognition, pp. 2168–2177 (2018)
35. Yu, Z., Liu, Q., Liu, G.: Deeper cascaded peak-piloted network for weak expression recognition. Vis. Comput. **34**(12), 1691–1699 (2018)
36. Zhang, K., Huang, Y., Du, Y., Wang, L.: Facial expression recognition based on deep evolutional spatial-temporal networks. IEEE Trans. Image Process. **26**(9), 4193–4203 (2017)
37. Zhang, P., Liu, Y., Hao, Y., Liu, J.: Deep facial expression recognition algorithm combining channel attention. In: 2021 4th International Conference on Artificial Intelligence and Pattern Recognition, pp. 260–265 (2021)
38. Zhao, G., Huang, X., Taini, M., Li, S.Z., PietikäInen, M.: Facial expression recognition from near-infrared videos. Image Vis. Comput. **29**(9), 607–619 (2011)
39. Zhao, G., Pietikainen, M.: Dynamic texture recognition using local binary patterns with an application to facial expressions. IEEE Trans. Pattern Anal. Mach. Intell. **29**(6), 915–928 (2007)
40. Zhao, X., et al.: Peak-piloted deep network for facial expression recognition. In: Leibe, B., Matas, J., Sebe, N., Welling, M. (eds.) ECCV 2016. LNCS, vol. 9906, pp. 425–442. Springer, Cham (2016). https://doi.org/10.1007/978-3-319-46475-6_27
41. Zhu, X., He, Z., Zhao, L., Dai, Z., Yang, Q.: A cascade attention based facial expression recognition network by fusing multi-scale spatio-temporal features. Sensors **22**(4), 1350 (2022)

Author Index

Printed in the United States
by Baker & Taylor Publisher Services

Printed in the United States
by Baker & Taylor Publisher Services